SECTION *of* **LITIGATION**

AMERICAN BAR ASSOCIATION

D1131882

ELECTRONIC EVIDENCE

LAW AND PRACTICE

Second Edition

PAUL R. RICE

**Defending Liberty
Pursuing Justice**

Cover design by ABA Publishing

12 11 10 09 08   5 4 3 2 1

Cataloging-in-Publication data is on file with the Library of Congress
ISBN: 1-60442-084-7
          978-1-60442-084-5

Electronic evidence: law and practice / Rice, Paul R.

Contents

Foreword ix

Acknowledgments xiii

Dedication xv

Introduction xvii

CHAPTER 1   **Discovery of Electronic Evidence** 1
  I.   The Evolution of E-discovery 3
  II.   The Rules of E-discovery 11
     A. Electronically Stored Information Is Discoverable 12
     B. Parties Must Give Early Attention to E-discovery 16
       1. Initial Disclosures 17
       2. Conference of the Parties 21
       3. Discovery Planning Conference 23
     C. Two Tiers of Discoverable Information—Data That Is Not
       Reasonably Accessible 28
       1. Approaches to Cost Allocation 37
       2. Another Approach to Cost Allocation 46
       3. Sampling as a Factor in Cost Allocation 46
       4. Cost Allocation in Practice 47
     D. Privilege and the Discovery of Electronically Stored
       Information 49
     E. Written Discovery 53
       1. Testing and Sampling 53
       2. Form of Production 53
       3. Rule 33(d)—Interrogatories 56
       4. Subpoenas 56
     F. Sanctions and the Spoliation "Safe Harbor" 57
  III. The Practical Side of E-discovery 59
     A. Counsel Must Acquire a Working Understanding of
       Potentially Relevant ESI 59
       1. Build an E-discovery Team 61

2. Understand and Improve Information Technology
Architecture 62
3. Develop a Preservation Process .63
4. Developing a Retention Plan 73
5. Issuing Instructions to Custodians to Preserve Potentially
Relevant Records 75
6. Design and Implement E-discovery Guidelines 76
7. Identify a Preferred Vendor Network 76
8. Consider Acquiring or Licensing Appropriate Tools 77

CHAPTER 2   **Spoliation** **79**
I.   Overview 80
II.   The Basics 86
A. When Does the Duty to Preserve Arise? 89
B. Does the Client's Obligation to Preserve Create Duties for
Legal Counsel? 101
C. What Must Be Retained and Preserved? 106
1. Privileged Materials 116
2. Duration of the Duty to Preserve 118
D. Prejudice to Discovering Party 120
III.   Is Bad Faith Required? 133
IV.   Consequences of Spoliation 153
A. Spoliation Is an Implied Admission by Conduct 168
B. Logical Inference Instructions 172
C. The Strange Spoliation Presumption 172
D. Authority for Penalizing Destruction 176
V.   Burden of Persuasion 179
VI.   Choice of Law Question 180
VII.   Proving the Claim of Spoliation—You're Not Bound By the
Rules of Evidence 180
VIII. Evidence of Spoliation—Evidence of One's Conduct to Prove
the Truth of Its Implied Message—Is It Hearsay? 181
IX.   Spoliation and the Attorney-Client Privilege 182
X.   Standard of Appellate Review 183
XI.   Computers and the Internet Expand Every Possibility 183
A. Do Not Delete Records or Destroy Equipment 186
B. Save the Hard Drives 188
C. Don't Forget Personal Digital Assistants and Jump Drives . . .188
D. Informal Encouragement to Others to Preserve Data 189

CHAPTER 3   **Confidentiality and the Attorney-Client Privilege** .**191**
I.   The Attorney-Client Privilege and Its Elements 193
A. History of the Confidentiality Requirement 195
B. Evolution of the Confidentiality Requirement 198

1. Ever-Expanding Circle 198
2. Ignoring Confidentiality 201
   a. Stolen documents 201
   b. Judicially compelled disclosures 203
   c. The unauthorized agent exception 206
   d. Inadvertent disclosures—the "oops" rule 207
   e. Disclosures under protective orders or with
      reservations 210
3. Confidentiality Must Be Maintained and Documented—
   The Increasing Problem of Outside Agents Functioning
   as Employees 215
C. E-mail—An Extension of Existing Services and
   Technology 221
   1. From Face-to-Face Communications to Letters 221
   2. From Letters to Telephones 221
   3. From Telephones to Computers 222
D. Employees' Personal Expectation of Confidentiality in E-mail
   Communications 224
E. Data Behind Electronic Evidence—Metadata 234
F. Electronic Presentations 236
G. Measures to Preserve Confidentiality? 239
H. Asserting Attorney-Client Privilege for E-mails: The Practical
   Details, a Growing Concern 243
   1. Expanding the Role of In-House Counsel—Jeopardizing
      the Applicability of the Privilege 244
   2. Complicating the Distinction Between Communications
      and Information 248
   3. How Is the Document Described in a Privilege Log? 252
   4. Are Operating Assumptions About the Purpose of
      Communications Appropriate Based on the Individuals
      to Whom They Have Been Disseminated? 258
      a. When business and legal communications can be
         separated 261
      b. When business and legal advice are inextricably
         intertwined 264
I. Spoliation and the Crime/Fraud Exception to the Attorney-
   Client Privilege 289
J. Work Product Immunity Vis-à-Vis E-evidence 291

Chapter 4   **Best Evidence/Original Writing Rule 297**
I. The Basics 298
II. E-Evidence and the Original Writing Rule 303
III. The Added Complexity of Summaries of Voluminous Materials ...307
A. The Hearsay Dimensions of Summaries 308

1. Non-hearsay Argument 309
2. Residual Exception Solution 310
B. Insurmountable Hearsay Problems Created by Summaries of
Voluminous Materials from the Internet 311
C. The Evidentiary Status of Summaries under the Voluminous
Writings Exception to the Original Writing Rule 312

CHAPTER 5   **Presumptions** **315**
I.   The Basics 317
II.   Common Law Presumptions That Can Be Relevant to
Authenticating E-commerce and E-mail 323
A. Receipt of Mailed Letters 323
B. Authority to Transact Business 325
C. Authority to Use an Instrumentality .325
D. Responsibility for Damage or Loss .326
III. Authentication of E-commerce—Problems with Presumptions
under the Federal Rules of Evidence 326

CHAPTER 6   **Authentication** **333**
I.   The Basics 335
II.   Methods of Authentication 339
A. Self-identification 348
1. Self-identification by the *Sender*: Establishing That a
Letter Was Actually Written by the Person Named as
Author 348
2. Self-identification by the *Recipient*: Establishing That a
Message Was Received by the Fact That It Was Sent to
That Individual's Address and He Responded to It 350
B. Content 352
C. Extrinsic Circumstances 354
III. Authenticating Digital Photographs 357
A. The Key Is the Chain of Custody 360
B. Desirable Enhancement Versus Unacceptable Manipulation . . .362
C. Authenticate the Computer Program Too 367
D. The Internet Complication 367
E. A Spoliation Problem 368
IV.   Authentication of Web Page Postings from the Internet 369
A. Relaxation of Authentication Requirements 374
B. Self-authentication and the Internet .376
1. Public Document Under Seal 381
2. Business Solicitations and Postings 382
3. Government Postings 384
4. Newspapers and Periodicals 385
5. Limits of Self-authentication 385

C. Authenticating with Technology 386
  1. Data Trails 386
  2. Electronic Signatures 387
  3. Public Key Infrastructure 390
  4. Biometric Authentication 391
V. Authentication of Computer Animations, Models, and
  Simulations 391
VI. Authentication of Authenticating Technology 393
VII. Other Issues Relating to Authentication of E-evidence 395
A. Chain of Custody 395
B. Expanded Pretrial Discovery May Justify a Lesser
  Foundation 399
C. Admissibility and Weight: Two Bites at the Same Apple 400
D. A Reality Check 400

CHAPTER 7   Hearsay 401
I. The Basics 403
A. Two Truths of Hearsay 404
II. Hearsay Admissible Through Exceptions 409
A. Multiple Levels of Hearsay 410
B. Writings Are Like Another Person Speaking, Repeating the
  Out-of-Court Declarations of the Author 412
III. Why Is It Relevant? 414
IV. Mechanically Produced Statements Are Not Hearsay 415
V. Evidence from the Internet 417
A. Nonhearsay from the Internet 417
B. Hearsay from the Internet 421
C. Admissible Hearsay under Applicable Exceptions 422
VI. A Reality Check on Hearsay 430
A. The Internet as Part of Business or Government Records 430
B. Web Pages Are Not Business Records of the Internet
  Service Provider (ISP) 433
C. Government Records and Reports 433
VII. Constitutional Dimensions of Hearsay 435
A. The Accused's Right of Confrontation 436
  1. Two-Prong *Ohio v. Roberts* Test 438
  2. The "Testimonial" Standard of *Crawford v. Washington* ..439
  3. Why "Testimonial"? 441
  4. Does the "Testimonial" Label Give an Absolute Right? ...443
B. Due Process 446
  1. Due Process Before *Crawford* 446
    a. Excluding hearsay offered by an accused 446
    b. Excluding hearsay offered by the government 447
  2. Due Process After *Crawford* 448
C. Constitutional Wild Card 449

CHAPTER 8   **Science and Technology** **463**
   I.   Judicial Screening Under the Common Law 464
       A. The Advent of the *Frye* "General Acceptance" Test 465
       B. Expanding the Scope of *Frye* 466
   II.   Judicial Screening Under the Federal Rules of Evidence 467
       A. Out of the *Frye*ing Pan, Into the Fire? 468
       B. The Logic of *Daubert* 468
   III.   Consequences for E-science and E-technology 472

CHAPTER 9   **Judicial Notice** **477**
   I.   The Basics 478
   II.   Judicial Notice Under the Federal Rules of Evidence 479
       A. Things *Not* Addressed in Rule 201 481
       B. Distinguishing Judicial Notice of Adjudicative Facts/Jury
          Notice of Facts/Judicial Notice of Legislative Facts 481
   III.   Judicial Notice and E-commerce 483
   IV.   Evidence from Web Pages: A Practical Assessment 484

CHAPTER 10   **Future's Challenge** **491**

Index **495**

Foreword

I recall, years ago, putting myself through law school by programming computers. We had no concept, then, of the Internet, which was far away in the future. We didn't use e-mail, obviously. Later, as a lawyer, I recall interrogatories and document requests that filled whole rooms or even warehouses with paper, but at least we knew what to do with them. The simplicity of those days is long gone. I had my first serious e-discovery experience about five years ago, and for all of the lawyers, it was as though we had all landed on a different planet.

The Federal Rules had not yet come into being, to create the great divide in e-discoverability, with items that can be easily retrieved becoming discoverable under the usual standards, while difficult-to-retrieve evidence is not usually discoverable unless it meets a balancing test that compares the difficulty of retrieval against the need for the evidence. We were not accustomed, as paper lawyers, to anything quite resembling this dichotomy. Consequently, we fought at length over whether given data had "really" been deleted and whether it was retrievable—somehow retrievable, in ways that electronics experts knew, using techniques that were like magic to us. And the rules still beg some of the same questions. How do we determine the difficulty of retrieval? How do we prove it? How do we determine the need for evidence that, after all, is not available and that therefore is unknown, making it difficult to determine the need for it? The answer, of course, is that we rely upon various kinds of data processing experts much more than in the past. These experts become not just sources of information, but guides to guesses about whole categories of information we can get or must retrieve.

Back in the old days, we were only dimly aware of the issue of spoliation. Under today's rules, upon the filing of a lawsuit, or sometimes even upon the arising of a potential controversy, the parties immediately and automatically become bound to carry out various duties of preservation. But back then, we wondered about that. "Do we need to tell our people to keep all this stuff?" We were familiar, from the past, with the idea of court orders that required us to preserve evidence, but we had encountered a new world, one that possibly required us to be proactive without a court order. We struggled to project what the litigation might be about, but we did not know, back then, to instruct our clients, firmly, to set aside their usual data destruction policies and act so that we preserved what was relevant. Today, the penalty for failing to do so may be that the jury will receive an instruction that becomes a virtual directed verdict against our client, saying that missing e-documents can be treated as supporting the opposing party. This is an area, too, where some of the major questions are still unanswered, where lawyers have to guess, and where development and redevelopment are constant.

Then, there was the problem of privileges and immunities—a problem that was no less strange. We kept finding privileged and unprivileged documents intertwined in ways that probably would not have happened with paper documents. Separating business advice from legal advice, for example, required more effort than we were used to. And inevitably, there were instances of inadvertent disclosure, more frequently than in the past, as well as of situations in which the legal advice was so intertwined with the discoverable information that one could not be disclosed without the other. All of these issues have undergone fundamental changes, with more changes—and then, still more—to come.

We were clueless about the issue of proof by e-evidence. In principle, I think we thought that this was an easy issue; we would just treat electronically generated documents the same way we would treat paper ones. But the evanescence and mutability of electronic documents changes the picture. Take the original writing (or best evidence) rule, for example. It might seem reasonable to say that a series of electronic impulses makes a document, and the resulting printout is an "original." But is it really? Documents of this kind can be altered in ways that do not leave a trace. In fact, this is one of the attractions of the electronic medium: the ability of a writer to turn out reams of documents based on a template, with each one differing slightly from the next. In such an unstable world, it dawned on us that we would have to develop a new explanation of the original writings rule. Then there was the even more difficult issue of authentication. What did it take to put the series of electronic clicks that made up a received e-mail properly into evidence? The same instability of the medium made it more difficult to pin down rules for establishing the authenticity of e-documents. We finally figured out that we might be able to use a "custodian" of the electronic system as our primary witness, but we would need a team of systems engineers standing by just in case. I know that lawyers still find themselves in the same doubtful position, sometimes, but with more confusing law to contend with.

I t gradually dawned on us that the function of experts would change in major respects when we handled e-evidence. We might have needed our systems engineers to explain to the jury the limits of available information, or even to interpret some of it. These tasks were different in character from the testimony required of the usual expert.

Fortunately, we settled the case, probably in part because both sides faced such difficult questions in figuring out what we could discover and prove. And although there is more law in this area now than before, the open questions are still there. And the answers, though they keep changing, can be better understood, thanks to the advice given by Paul Rice in this volume.

—**David Crump**
John B. Neibel Professor of Law
University of Houston

Acknowledgments

In the preparation of this book, I have been blessed with the assistance of a number of individuals who must be acknowledged and thanked. The research underlying this work was both broad and extensive. Initially, Benjamin Saul took the laboring oar as my Dean's Fellow in his senior year of legal studies. Ben's work was later complemented by the superb research skills of his successors, David Kerwin, Jordan Rubinstein, Peter White, Gregory Lambert, Robert Tannenbaum, and Davis Sluis. The edits by Wayne Holcombe in the first edition were nothing less than superb. David Sluis edited the second edition and his work was equally valuable.

Because my expertise is evidence law, and the book deals with computer science, I found it necessary to seek contributions from others with greater experience in those areas. In the first edition, David Kerwin, who has been involved in the computer industry both before and after law school, authored with me the chapter on electronic discovery. In the first edition, the discovery chapter dealt only with where electronic evidence might be found. David's contributions were the foundation upon which the expanded discovery chapter in the second edition was built. The current discovery chapter, authored by Gilbert Keteltas and John Rosenthal, partners in the Howry firm in Washington, D.C., is significantly different in that it now addresses discovery of that electronic evidence under the new revisions to the Federal Rules of Civil Procedure. It reflects their broad experience with electronic evidence both before and after the new rules.

While teaching at the Washington College of Law for the past 35 years I have been generously supported by that institution and its current dean, Claudio Grossman. Without the special grants, research assistance, release time and special teaching opportunities afforded me, this project would not have been possible.

Dedication

Jane Bird Rice
Partner of more than 40 years and still best friend

Introduction

Although estimates vary, it is widely agreed that electronic commerce (e-commerce) over networks, such as the Internet, is experiencing explosive growth. Electronic evidence arising from this commerce (e-evidence) can take many forms. Data files, Internet postings, and e-mails are perhaps the most common. E-evidence can also come in the form of so-called "background" information. Background information refers to such things as audit trails, access control data, and other non-printed information. E-evidence can also take the form of residual data, that is, data that remains on hard drives after being deleted or in printer and fax memories. The unique problems posed by e-evidence have received little attention in the Federal Rules of Evidence. Rather, the admissibility of all of these forms of e-evidence is determined by the same evidentiary standards that apply to all other forms of evidence. As a consequence, lawyers and judges must resort to common law principles to devise solutions. It is hoped that this book will assist in that effort.

In order to ensure that electronic records comply with the recordkeeping requirement of federal law, and that established rules of evidence are applied to the use of certain electronic records at trial, Congress has enacted 15 U.S.C. § 7001 (2001).[1] Section 7001 establishes a general validity of electronic signatures, records, and contracts used in national and international commerce—although no party is *required* to use an electronic form, a party cannot *invalidate* a legal instrument or transaction solely because it was formed, signed, or recorded electronically.[2] With electronic records receiving the same treat-

---

1. *See* Appendix I.
2. Subsection (a) establishes the general validity of electronic records, signatures, and contracts, although under subsection (b), no party is *required* to agree to the use of such records. Under subsection (c)(1), a consumer disclosure required in writing can be in electronic form if (A) the consumer knowingly consents to its use, and under subsection (B) if, prior to consenting, the consumer is provided with a "clear and conspicuous statement" that the information could be provided in paper

ment as other forms of evidence under the Federal Rules of Evidence, this book will explore the range of evidentiary problems encountered in e-commerce transactions and electronic communications, from discovery to trial, and their solutions.

I. DISCOVERY OF ELECTRONIC EVIDENCE

Before e-evidence can be offered in a judicial proceeding, it first must be discovered. While discovery tools and techniques under the Federal Rules of Civil Procedure are virtually the same for all types of evidence, the electronic format has created a vast range of places where relevant evidence can potentially be found.[3] However, it also has compounded the problems in the production of that evidence and the assertion of privilege claims. Understanding this range of potential sources and problems is important for both the discovering and the producing parties because they have primary responsibility for structuring the discovery undertaking and resolving disputes about production format and preservation responsibilities.

Under the Federal Rules of Civil Procedure, the producing party is responsible for retrieving relevant records and information demanded by the discovering party that are within the producing party's "possession, custody or control."[4] Therefore, to avoid running afoul of the rules against destroying relevant evidence—spoliation—everyone must know what should be preserved when notice is given of its potential relevance in either pending or anticipated litigation.[5] Similarly, if one engages in a regular document retention and/or destruction practice, one needs to know where to retrieve the information to be retained or destroyed and how that can best be accomplished. E-evidence adds a

---

form. Subsection (C) requires that the consumer be made aware, prior to consenting, of the hardware and software requirements used for access to and retention of such records. Under subsections (d) and (e), if a statute or regulation requires retention of contracts or records, then that requirement is met if done electronically, conditioned on the requirements that the records "accurately reflect" the information they contain, that the information remains accessible to those who are entitled under rule of law, and that those records can be "accurately reproduced" for later reference by the parties entitled. 15 U.S.C. § 7001 (2001).

   3. *See* Chapter One, "Discovery," *infra*.

   4. Rule 26(a)(1)(A)(ii) of the Federal Rules of Civil Procedure.

   5. *See* Chapter Two, "Spoliation," *infra*.

new wrinkle to document-purging practices because documents created or stored on computer hard drives are more difficult to purge. When they are erased, they are only deleted from the active portion of the drive. They still exist on the hard drive in their original form until the spaces where they are stored are used again to store another document. But even then, shadows of the original document still exist and can be retrieved until each space has been written over or reused up to three times. The fact that e-evidence is often "hard to kill" could have implications for the discovery process when the producing party has destroyed all of the apparently available copies.

The party demanding disclosure must know how broadly to word discovery demands to ensure that the responding party will search all reasonably available sources. Understanding the many and varied sources of e-evidence may also give clues about other sources when information has become unavailable from the most obvious source. In addition, knowledge of these many sources will help ensure the preservation of existing data if the demanding party notifies the respondent of the imminent discovery request, the potential relevance of the documents, and the various forms and sources in which they may exist. Notification, actual or constructive, creates a duty on the respondent's part to preserve the evidence, and failure to do so can give rise to a cause of action in some jurisdictions and result in adverse inferences or other appropriate sanctions.[6]

The Internet diminishes the security of much electronic information and, thus, its degree of perceived confidentiality. When attorneys and clients communicate via the Internet (e.g., through e-mail services), the mode of communication jeopardizes the concept of confidentiality upon which the attorney-client privilege is premised. While the use of such insecure means of communication could be seen as negating the objective reasonableness of any expectation of confidentiality (and, therefore, as a waiver of the privilege protection), such decisions are highly unlikely because of changing attitudes toward the element of confidentiality.[7] The use of e-mail, therefore, will not make fewer communications subject to the protection of the attorney-client privilege merely as a result of the nature of the format. In fact, because the e-mail format has geometrically increased the number of

---

6. *Id.*
7. *See* Chapter Three, "Attorney-Client Privilege," *infra.*

communications created, due to the ease of circulation, the number of attorney-client privilege claims has increased geometrically as well.

II. USING THE ELECTRONIC EVIDENCE AT TRIAL

Litigation involving electronic evidence will involve the same evidentiary issues as litigation in other contexts. A foundation is a prerequisite to the introduction of any evidence. Witnesses, other than experts,[8] must be identified and shown to possess personal knowledge of the facts they will be asked to relate.[9] Tangible items, identified by exhibit numbers, must be authenticated by one or more sponsoring witnesses, who must identify the items and explain how they relate to the cause of action. Sponsoring witnesses are excused only when the item in question is self-authenticating.[10]

The authentication of e-evidence taken from the Internet poses particular problems because of the unique opportunities for fraud in the electronic format. For example, headers to e-mails can be manipulated and databases can be altered both from within and without a company. Accordingly, there is a heightened burden for establishing the authenticity of what is presented in court. For unexplained reasons, however, some courts apparently have abandoned the rigors of the common law and have shifted the burden to the opponent challenging authenticity—in effect, presuming authenticity and reliability despite the enhanced risks, unless specific problems are identified by the opponent.

When the statements of third parties are offered to prove the truth of the stories told in those statements, the statements constitute hearsay[11] and are excluded unless a recognized hearsay exception applies.[12] Such statements are hearsay regardless of whether they are repeated in the testimony of a witness or are offered through documents.[13] The Internet makes a vast array of statements available to the world. These statements may or may not be based on the personal knowledge of the

---

8. *See* FED. R. EVID. 703

9. *See* FED. R. EVID. 602.

10. *See* FED. R. EVID. 902 and Chapter Six, "Authentication," *infra*.

11. *See* FED. R. EVID. 801, 802 and Chapter Seven, "Hearsay," *infra*.

12. *See* FED. R. EVID. 803, 804, 807.

13. *See* Chapter Seven, "Hearsay," *infra*.

author. As a consequence, hearsay, and multiple levels of it, are a frequent problem. The vastness of the data also increases the need to create summaries to allow for the convenient use of the materials in the courtroom. The range of authentication and hearsay issues involved in the use of such summaries in lieu of the original writings is explored.

Whenever the content of a written instrument is being proven, the Best Evidence or Original Writing Rule requires that the original be offered in court.[14] This rule poses no serious problems for the admissibility of evidence taken from the Internet because all printouts from a computer screen are considered "originals," and in their absence, mechanically produced copies or "duplicates" are admissible as if they were originals. The laxity of what is considered an "original" from a computer database may create the same problems of fraud and inaccuracy that the Best Evidence Rule was designed to avoid. If this materializes, the concerns addressed by the Best Evidence Rule will reappear in the form of arguments to the judge and jury concerning the weight that the jury should ascribe to the disputed evidence.

Throughout this text there are citations to cases in both federal and state courts in which existing evidence rules have been applied to e-evidence. Many of those cases are discussed in the text. In the absence of case authority, an analysis is offered of how the principles of the common law and the Federal Rules of Evidence might bear on each question. In these instances, discussions of policy are a necessary part of the analysis.

I have identified judicial applications of evidence rules to e-evidence that appear to conflict with common law principles and practices, and attempted to give the reader some perspective on the significance of such conflicts. Occasionally, alternative rationales are offered for the holdings of various courts, in order to give readers a better understanding of the implicit logic that may be driving those courts' decisions.

---

14. *See* Chapter Four, "Best Evidence—Original Writing Rule," *infra*.

Discovery of Electronic Evidence

1

Gil Keteltas and John Rosenthal*

I.   The Evolution of E-discovery   3

II. The Rules of E-discovery   11

   A. Electronically Stored Information Is Discoverable   12

   B. Parties Must Give Early Attention to E-discovery   16

      1. Initial Disclosures   17

      2. Conference of the Parties   21

      3. Discovery Planning Conference   23

   C. Two Tiers of Discoverable Information—Data That Is Not Reasonably Accessible   28

      1. Approaches to Cost Allocation   37

      2. Another Approach to Cost Allocation   46

      3. Sampling as a Factor in Cost Allocation   46

      4. Cost Allocation in Practice   47

   D. Privilege and the Discovery of Electronically Stored Information   49

---

* Gil Keteltas and John Rosenthal are partners in Howrey LLP's Global Litigation Group, and are based in Washington, D.C. Their practice includes complex litigation. They also chair the firm's electronic discovery practice and represent clients in active litigation involving electronic discovery, and in the development of corporate electronic discovery programs. This chapter also incorporates material from the last edition's chapter of the same name, authored by David Kerwin.

1

E. Written Discovery   53

1. Testing and Sampling   53

2. Form of Production   53

3. Rule 33(d)—Interrogatories   56

4. Subpoenas   56

F. Sanctions and the Spoliation "Safe Harbor"   57

III. The Practical Side of E-discovery   59

A. Counsel Must Acquire a Working Understanding of Potentially Relevant ESI   59

1. Build an E-discovery Team   61

2. Understand and Improve Information Technology Architecture   62

3. Develop a Preservation Process   63

4. Developing a Retention Plan   73

5. Issuing Instructions to Custodians to Preserve Potentially Relevant Records   75

6. Design and Implement E-discovery Guidelines   76

7. Identify a Preferred Vendor Network   77

8.   Consider Acquiring or Licensing Appropriate Tools   77

E-discovery: Although this shorthand reference to the discovery of electronic evidence does not appear in the most recent edition of *Black's Law Dictionary*,[1] it is now ubiquitous in the world of litigation. Invitations to e-discovery seminars put on by lawyers, judges, and vendors of e-discovery services and software now regularly clutter most lawyers' paper and electronic mailboxes. And while *Black's Law Dictionary* does not mention e-discovery, more than three million pages on the Internet do, along with legal publications, treatises, articles and blogs, teeming with advice on the discovery of electronic evidence.

What a difference a few years make. Not long ago, discovery mainly involved the collection of paper by lawyers and paralegals armed with cardboard boxes, sticky notes, and copy machines. The electronic scanning and coding of paper documents or the occasional

---

1. BLACK'S LAW DICTIONARY (8th ed. 2003).

production of information on a computer disk[2] set the standard for technologically advanced discovery practices. Electronic discovery was on the radar screens of a limited group of lawyers and an even more limited group of judges.

In a formal sense, all that changed on December 1, 2006, with the enactment of amended Federal Rules of Civil Procedure relating to the discovery of "electronically stored information" or "ESI." While the rules were altered, in many respects they simply make clear that the basic principles applicable to paper discovery also apply to ESI. But applying the principles of paper to the computerized storage of information is a task with complexities that will continue to evolve as the technologies for generating, storing, and retrieving electronic information evolve.

This chapter provides a basic understanding of the world of e-discovery, explains the recent changes to the rules of e-discovery, and provides practical advice on how to handle e-discovery questions in a cost-efficient and defensible manner.

I. THE EVOLUTION OF E-DISCOVERY

E-discovery involves the preservation, collection, processing, and production of electronically stored information. This may sound simple, but it involves new and growing complexities. The simple reality is that over 90 percent of information generated by litigants today is electronic, and one-third of that electronic information will never be reduced to paper form at any time.[3] Today, the evidence in most cases is electronic.[4] But herein lies the problem or, for some, the opportu-

---

2. Storch v. IPCO Safety Prods. Co., No. Civ. A. 96-7592 1997 WL 401589, at *2 (E.D. Pa. July 16, 1997) ("in this age of high-technology—it is not unreasonable for the defendant to produce the information on computer disk for the plaintiff").

3. In re Bristol-Myers Squibb Sec. Litig., 205 F.R.D. 437, 440 n.2 (D.N.J. 2002); *see also Best Practices Recommendations & Principles for Addressing Electronic Document Production,* in THE SEDONA PRINCIPLES: SECOND EDITION (hereafter THE SEDONA PRINCIPLES), p. 1 (June 2007) ("more than ninety percent of all information is created and stored in an electronic format").

4. Bills v. Kennecott Corp., 108 F.R.D. 459, 462 (D. Utah 1985) ("In the last fifteen years, computerized record keeping has rapidly replaced the less accurate manual systems, and it is no wonder that computer-stored information has become involved in every type of litigation."); Anti-Monopoly, Inc. v. Hasbro, Inc., No. 94 Civ. 2120 (LMM) (AJP), 1995 WL 649934 (S.D.N.Y. Nov. 3, 1995) (same).

nity: discovery of ESI is complex and costly. That complexity and cost is rooted in the inherent differences between paper and electronically stored information.[5] In *Byers v. Illinois*, which predated the Federal Rules amendments by almost four years, the court explained these differences in the context of e-mail, just one of many forms of ESI:

> Chief among these differences is the sheer volume of electronic information. E-mails have replaced other forms of communication besides just paper-based communication. Many informal messages that were previously relayed by telephone or at the water cooler are now sent via e-mail. Additionally, computers have the ability to capture several copies (or drafts) of the same e-mail, thus multiplying the volume of documents. All of these e-mails must be scanned for both relevance and privilege. Also, unlike most paper-based discovery, archived e-mails typically lack a coherent filing system. Moreover, dated archival systems commonly store information on magnetic tapes which have become obsolete. Thus, parties incur additional costs in translating the data from the tape into useable form.[6]

ESI is easy to create, store, and copy. Years ago, the number of copies of a document was limited by the per-page copying cost and the limited physical space—usually measured in filing cabinets or drawers—in which information could be stored. While some organizations might outgrow their on-site storage space and send documents offsite, offsite storage of hard-copy documents has a real and easily measurable cost. In recognition of this cost, and the fact that much of this archived paper-based information was stale with no current business purpose, many corporations implemented records management pro-

---

5. *See* Thompson v. HUD, 219 F.R.D. 93, 97 (D. Md. 2003) (discussing differences between electronic and paper-based records); Byers v. Ill. State Police, No. 99 C 8105, 2002 U.S. Dist. LEXIS 9861, at *32 (N.D. Ill. June 3, 2002) ("the Court is not persuaded by the plaintiffs' attempt to equate traditional paper-based discovery with the discovery of e-mail files"); *see also* THE SEDONA PRINCIPLES, p. v ("Simply put, the way in which information is created, stored and managed in electronic environments is inherently different from the paper world. For example, the simple act of typing a letter on a computer involves multiple (and ever-changing) hidden steps, databases, tags, codes, loops, and algorithms that have no paper analogue.").

6. Byers, *id.*

grams, providing for the disposal of obsolete records—meaning records without a current business purpose that the corporation is not required by law to retain.

The story is different with ESI. Electronic documents can be created, copied and forwarded in seconds. Storage today is readily available and relatively inexpensive. The average personal computer is sold with 80 gigabytes of storage (enough to hold millions of pages of paper).[7] As a result, the volume of electronically stored information is dramatically larger than the volume of paper traditionally stored.[8] And while some records management tasks can be automated in the electronic world (for example, e-mail can be automatically deleted after a certain number of days, presuming there is no requirement to retain it), other electronic documents may simply sit on a computer hard drive—out of sight and out of mind—until that drive no longer exists.

Computing systems were often designed and built for redundancy. As a result, ESI is not easily deleted or discarded. Those systems often replicate or back up data, either within the computer's own computing system or within a backup system. Moreover, it may be possible to locate and recover ESI that the average user believes has been deleted. For example, a computer hard drive stores information on mirrored platters in bits and bytes.[9] Those bits and bytes are indexed in

---

7. Estimating "pages" per gigabyte is more an art than a science. One expert commentator noted that most equivalency estimates—which often appear to be stated with great certainty—have "all the credibility of an Elvis sighting." C. Ball, *Expert Explodes Page Equivalency Myth*, L. TECH. NEWS (Aug. 8, 2007). The number of pages per gigabyte will vary significantly based on the types of files at issue.

8. Rowe Entm't, Inc. v. William Morris Agency, Inc., 205 F.R.D. 421, 429 (D.N.Y. 2002) (Given low costs of storage, "[i]nformation is retained not because it is expected to be used, but because there is no compelling reason to discard it."); Byers, 2002 U.S. Dist. LEXIS 9861, at *32-*33 (commenting on "the sheer volume of electronic information"); *see also* FED. R. CIV. P. 34 Advisory Committee Notes (2006) ("the growth in electronically stored information and in the variety of systems for creating and storing such information has been dramatic").

9. "A Byte is the basic measurement of most computer data and consists of 8 bits. Computer storage capacity is generally measured in bytes. Although characters are stored in bytes, a few bytes are of little use for storing a large amount of data. Therefore, storage is measured in larger increments of bytes. *See* Kilobyte, Megabyte, Gigabyte, Terabyte, Petabyte, Exabyte, Zettabyte and Yottabyte (listed here in order of increasing volume)." THE SEDONA CONFERENCE GLOSSARY: E-DISCOVERY & DIGITAL INFORMATION MANAGEMENT, SECOND EDITION, p. 7 (December 2007).

"file allocation tables" that track where files are stored on a platter. When a user hits delete, the delete command merely indicates that the area on the platter where that information is currently stored can be overwritten with new information. Until overwritten, the information, in whole or in part, can be recovered. In fact, even when a hard drive is corrupt and thought to be unusable, "the data may be retrievable with forensics."[10]

Apart from its greater volume, ESI generally is not stored in one central repository within a corporation, but rather in what is commonly called an "unstructured" computing environment composed of thousands of personal computers and hundreds of servers (storage devices containing information or software applications shared by multiple users).[11] Contrary to popular (and sometimes judicial) belief, these systems are not centrally indexed and, as a result, it is not easy to search across them to locate relevant ESI. Once relevant ESI is located, moving it from one location to another without the use of a forensic tool can potentially change or alter the ESI. All of this makes it extremely difficult to identify, preserve, collect, and produce ESI within the confines of most corporate environments.

Another key difference between ESI and paper is that ESI has multiple layers. In addition to the basic visual layer that is seen on the computer screen, ESI typically has other layers of information often referred to as "metadata." There are generally two types of metadata. The first is often referred to as "system metadata"—fields of information that travel with the document, such as "author," "recipient," "date created," and "file path." The second is "application metadata"—information within the document, such as tracked changes in a word-processing document,

---

10. *Id.* at p. 21. Forensics is the "scientific examination and analysis of data held on, or retrieved from, ESI in such a way that the information can be used as evidence in a court of law." *Id.* at p. 23. The creation of a forensic copy of ESI typically involves making "an exact copy of an entire physical storage media (hard drive, CD-ROM, DVD-ROM, tape, etc.), including all active and residual data and unallocated or slack space on the media." *Id.* The making of forensic images requires skill and expertise, not just in the creation of the image, but also in recording the detail necessary to demonstrate—sometimes years down the road—authenticity and chain of custody.

11. THE SEDONA CONFERENCE GLOSSARY, p. 47.

or pivot tables[12] and formulas within a spreadsheet.[13]

Unlike its paper counterpart, ESI can be manipulated and searched. The format in which it is collected and produced can therefore be a significant factor in litigation, depending upon the nature of the case. For example, where electronically stored information is produced in a static format—that is, an image of the document as it would look on the computer screen without the associated metadata—those images would not be searchable as produced. Some have used this process to "dump" large amounts of electronic images on an opponent, which usually then requires the party to examine the production page by page at considerable expense.[14] In contrast, information produced with its related metadata can be more easily loaded into a litigation review database and searched and categorized in multiple different ways— according to either the metadata or the text within the body of the document.

Electronic documents also are different in how they are produced and managed for litigation. Lawyers are used to dealing in paper or static images that are fixed with production numbers (or "bates" stamps) and confidentiality designations. This is not quite so easy to accomplish with a native electronic document (an electronic file that contains the information you would see when printing the document along with hidden but accessible information about its "associated file structure").[15] The management and protection of native documents once they are produced—including, for example, protection from alteration by another party—can be a significant challenge in litigation.

On the other hand, it *may* be more cost-efficient to collect, process, and load native documents in a document review system for the purpose of analyzing those documents for responsiveness, privilege,

---

12. A pivot table is a tool to summarize and simplify data in a database.

13. *See, e.g.,* Williams v. Sprint/United Mgmt. Co., 230 F.R.D. 640, 646 (D. Kan. 2005) (metadata is "information about a particular data set which describes how, when, and by whom it was collected, created, accessed, or modified and how it is formatted") (quoting THE SEDONA GUIDELINES: BEST PRACTICE GUIDELINES AND COMMENTARY FOR MANAGING INFORMATION & RECORDS IN THE ELECTRONIC AGE, Appx. F); D'Onofrio v. SFX Sports Group, Inc., 247 F.R.D. 43, 46 (D. D.C. 2008) (same).

14. It is this concern that led the Federal Rules Committee to encourage the parties to agree on form of production and, absent agreement, to produce "information in a form or forms in which it is *ordinarily maintained* or in a form or forms that are *reasonably usable.*" FED. R. CIV. P. 34(b).

15. THE SEDONA CONFERENCE GLOSSARY, p. 35.

and categorization in their native form. Courts and litigants are currently struggling with the appropriate production format—even under the Amended Rules—and it is likely to be some time before technology advances to the point that there will be a clear winner in terms of imaged versus native production format in the context of the discovery of ESI.

At the end of the day, the complexity and cost of e-discovery, if not conducted correctly and reasonably, could drive the cost of litigation above and beyond the potential financial exposure of the litigation. One judge aptly summarized what is at stake given the intersection of discovery demands and the vast capabilities of information technology: "Courts now face the challenge of overseeing discovery at a time when potential access to electronically stored information is virtually limitless, and when the costs and burdens associated with full discovery could be more outcome-determinative, as a practical matter, than the facts and substantive law."[16]

Since the 1970 amendments to the Federal Rules of Civil Procedure, in which Rule 34(a) was modified to expressly allow discovery of "data compilations," parties have been required to respond to request for the production of ESI.[17] A number of state courts wrestled

---

16. Cache La Poudre Feeds, LLC v. Land O'Lakes Farmland Feed, LLC, 244 F.R.D. 614, 620 (D. Colo. 2007).

17. FED. R. CIV. P. 34(a) advisory committee's note (2006). FED. R. CIV. P. 34(a)(1) (2005) (amended 2006) ("Any party may serve on any other party a request to produce documents (including data compilations from which information can be obtained, translated, if necessary, by the respondent through detection devices into reasonably usable form)"); *see also* FED. R. CIV. P. 34 Advisory Committee Notes (2005) (amended 2006) (Rule 34 "applies to electronic data compilations from which information can be obtained only with the use of detection devices"); Crown Life Ins. Co. v. Craig, 995 F.2d 1376 (7th Cir. 1993) (Rule 34 makes computer data discoverable); Antioch Co. v. Scrapbook Borders, Inc., 210 F.R.D. 645, 652 (D. Minn. 2002) ("that deleted information, on the Defendants' computer equipment, may well be both relevant and discoverable"); MHC Inv. Co. v. Racom Corp., 209 F.R.D. 431 (S.D. Iowa 2002) (mentioning, without comment, the general discoverability of e-mail); Collette v. St. Luke's Roosevelt Hosp., No. 99 CIV. 4864 GEL, 2002 WL 31159103 (S.D.N.Y. Sept. 26, 2002) (passing without comment on the general discoverability of e-mail); Rowe Entm't, 205 F.R.D. at 428 (finding that "[e]lectronic documents are no less subject to disclosure than paper records" and that "Rules 26(b) and 34 of the [FRCP] instruct that computer stored information is discoverable under the same rules that pertain to tangible, written materials"); McPeek v. Ashcroft, 202 F.R.D. 31, 31 (D. D.C. 2001) (ordering that during discov-

with questions of the discovery of electronic information,[18] with some adopting specific rules laying the groundwork for such discovery.[19] In fact, it has been black-letter law in the federal system for well over a decade that parties are required to produce electronic documents.[20]

But in reality, most litigants, their counsel, and the courts essentially pretended that electronic documents did not exist. Only in rare instances did parties demand, or judges require, the discovery and production of electronically stored information. Even then, the parties produced the ESI either in paper by printing it out or in a non-searchable static image format.

Over the last decade parties began to dip their toes in the e-discovery ocean, but only on a very limited basis, seeking mainly electronic mail while ignoring the wide array of other types of ESI, from MS Office documents to databases. The judicial approach to e-discovery was not uniform, but instead was a patchwork of decisions largely

---

ery "the producing party has an obligation to search available electronic systems for information demanded"); Simon Prop. Group L.P. v. mySimon, Inc., 194 F.R.D. 639, 640 (S.D. Ind. 2000) (holding that "computer records, including records that have been 'deleted', are documents discoverable under Fed. R. Civ. P. 34"); Santiago v. Miles, 121 F.R.D. 636, 640 (W.D.N.Y. 1998) (a "request for raw information in computer banks is proper and the information is obtainable under the discovery rules").

18. *See, e.g.,* Dodge, Warren & Peters Ins. Servs., Inc. v. Riley, 130 Cal. Rptr. 2d 385, 391 (Cal. Ct. App. 2003) (confirming discoverability of information on computer and computer storage media); Unnamed Physician v. Bd. of Trustees of St. Agnes Med. Ctr., 113 Cal. Rptr. 2d 309 (Cal. Ct. App. 2001) (ordering, for purposes of a physician review hearing, that the hospital allow the physician access to all documents relating to the hospital's computer system, excepting those of a proprietary nature); Linnen v. A.H. Robins Co., No. 97-2307, 1999 WL 462015 (Mass. Super. Ct. June 16, 1999) (commenting that a discovery request for electronic documents is no different "in principal, from a request for documents contained in any office file cabinet").

19. *See, e.g.,* Ill. Supreme Court Rules 201(b)(1) (revised June 1, 1995) (confirming that "documents" include "communications and all retrievable information in computer storage"); TEX. R. CIV. P. 196.4 (procedure for "discovery of data or information that exists in electronic or magnetic form"); Delaware Default Standard for Discovery of Electronic Documents (subsequently revised March 2, 2007); Supreme Court of Miss., No. 89-R-99001-SCT, Court Order 13 (May 29, 2003) (amending Rule 26 of the MISS. R. CIV. P. to provide for the "discovery of data or information that exists in electronic or magnetic form").

20. *See* Anti-Monopoly, Inc. 1995 WL 649934, at *2 ("[T]oday it is black-letter law that computerized data is discoverable if relevant").

applying then-current discovery rules to technologies and processes that did not exist when the rules were first crafted.

In or around 2004, however, there was a dramatic shift in the focus on e-discovery. Organizations such as The Sedona Conference attempted to set out best practices regarding the discovery of ESI.[21] Several high-profile pre-amendment decisions also dramatically advanced the legal framework surrounding the discovery of ESI. Most notably, jurists like Shira Scheindlin in *Zubulake v. UBS Warburg LLC*[22] and John Facciola in *McPeek v. Ashcroft*[23] attempted to set forth the legal framework to address the discovery of ESI. Perhaps what attracted the most attention were high-profile sanction cases that raised the stakes for parties that failed to appropriately preserve, collect, and/or produce ESI.[24]

The process for amending the Federal Rules to more comprehensively address ESI began shortly after the 2001 Amendments to the Federal Rules took effect. In August 2004, the Advisory Committee on the Federal Rules of Civil Procedure met and published for public comment a set of draft amendments to the Federal Rules specifically addressing electronic information. The committee held three public

---

21. In spring of 2002, The Sedona Conference Working Group Series assembled a group of lawyers, consultants, academics, and jurists to identify best practices in e-discovery. In 2004, the Working Group first published *The Sedona Principles: Best Practices Recommendations and Principles for Addressing Electronic Document Production*, which became the definitive pre-rule amendment to the Federal Rules of Civil Procedure. Many of the principles set forth therein became the basis of some of the concepts that found their way into the Federal Rules. All Sedona Conference publications are *available at* www.thesedonaconference.org.

22. *See, e.g.,* Zubulake v. UBS Warburg LLC (Zubulake V), 229 F.R.D. 422 (S.D. N.Y. 2004) (jury awarded former employee $29 million in a discrimination suit following an adverse jury instruction directing jurors to presume that certain e-mails that were not preserved or produced would be detrimental to the defendant's case).

23. McPeek v. Ashcroft, 212 F.R.D. 33, 36 (D. D.C. 2003).

24. *See* United States v. Philip Morris USA, Inc., 327 F. Supp. 2d 21 (D. D.C. 2004) (imposing $2.75 million as sanction for failure to preserve, and deletion of, ESI; also barred Philip Morris from calling certain witnesses); Coleman (Parent) Holdings, Inc. v. Morgan Stanley & Co., No. CA 03-5045 AI, 2005 Extra LEXIS 94 (Fla. Cir. Ct. Mar. 23, 2005) (court issued adverse influence instruction based on destruction of e-mail, ultimately leading to $1.58 billion judgment), *rev'd on other grounds,* No. 4D05-2606 (Fla. Dist. Ct. App. Mar. 23, 2007).

hearings and heard oral testimony from dozens of witnesses. Over 180 written comments were submitted. As a result of the hearings and public comments, the committee made a variety of revisions to the proposed rules.

Ultimately, the revised proposed rules were forwarded to the Standing Committee on Rules of Practice and Procedure in May of 2005, and in September 2005 the Judicial Conference of the United States recommended that the U.S. Supreme Court adopt amendments to the Federal Rules of Civil Procedure without any substantive changes. In April 2006, the U.S. Supreme Court adopted the proposals, again, without any substantive changes. The amended Federal Rules became effective on December 1, 2006.

II. THE RULES OF E-DISCOVERY

Rather than simply confirm that ESI falls within the scope of Fed. R. Civ. P. 34(a), the Federal Rules Advisory Committee set forth in the rules a framework for how ESI should be preserved, collected, and produced. Significantly, the comments to the rules went beyond the normal practice of merely outlining any changes. The comments are extensive and substantive, expanding upon the meaning and scope of the rules, and are recommended, if not required, reading for both new and seasoned e-discovery practitioners.

Many states have followed the lead of the Federal Rules Committee and adopted identical or similar provisions.[25] The National Con-

---

25. *See, e.g.*, ARIZ. R. CIV. P. 16, 26, 26.1, 33, 34, 37, and 45 (amended Jan. 1, 2008) (rules govern the preservation, disclosure, and discovery of electronically stored information); Ind. Rules of Trial Procedure 26, 34, 37 (Jan. 1, 2008) (largely mirroring Federal Rules amendments); LA. CODE CIV. P. Arts. 1424, 1460, 1461, and 1462 (June 25, 2007) (allowing discovery of electronically stored information); MINN. R. CIV. P. 16, 26, 33, 34, 37, 45 (July 1, 2007); MONT. R. CIV. P. 16, 26, 33, 34, 37, 45 (Feb. 28, 2007); N.H. Super. Ct. Rule 62 (March 1, 2007) (provision (c)(4) requires the parties to meet, confer, and try to reach agreement on the "scope of discovery, including particularly with respect to information stored electronically or in any other medium," with particular attention to accessibility, cost, form of production, and preservation); N.J. Rules Governing Civil Practice in the Superior Court, Tax Court and Surrogate's Court, Rules 1:9, 4:5B, 4:10, 4:17, 4:18, 4:23 (Sept. 1, 2006) (governing discovery of "electronically stored information"); N.Y. Uniform Civil Rules of the Supreme and County Courts, § 202.70, Commercial Div. of the Sup. Ct., Rule 8(b) (Jan. 17, 2006) (requiring counsel to "confer with regard to anticipated electronic discovery issues" enumerated in the rule); Local

ference of Commissioners on Uniform State Laws (NCCUSL) adopted Uniform Rules Relating to the Discovery of Electronically Stored Information in 2007. As the NCCUSL explained:

> [T]he Drafting Committee decided not to reinvent the wheel. It was the Drafting Committee's judgment that the significant issues relating to the discovery of information in electronic form had been vetted during the Federal Rules amendment process. Accordingly, this draft mirrors the spirit and direction of the recently adopted amendments to the Federal Rules of Civil Procedure. The Drafting Committee has freely adopted, often verbatim, language from both the Federal Rules and comments that it deemed valuable. The rules are modified, where necessary, to accommodate the varying state procedures and are presented in a form that permits their adoption as a discrete set of rules applicable to discovery of electronically stored information.[26]

The federal amendments themselves primarily cover six areas that are relevant to the discovery of ESI: (1) the discoverability of ESI; (2) the need for early attention to electronic discovery; (3) the presumption that ESI that is "not reasonably accessible" need not be produced in the first instance; (4) questions of privilege tied to the unique nature of ESI; (5) forms of production and interrogatories; and (6) sanctions.

A. Electronically Stored Information Is Discoverable

The amendments to Rule 34(a) were intended to "confirm that discovery of electronically stored information stands on equal footing with discovery of paper documents."[27] Rule 34 expressly allows parties to request "electronically stored information"—an elastic phrase that will

---

Rules of N.C. Bus. Ct., Rules 17.1 and 18.6 (procedures for the preservation and discovery of electronic documents); Utah R. Civ. P. 26, 33, 34, 37, 45 (Nov. 1, 2007).

26. NCCUSL, Uniform Rules Relating to the Discovery of Electronically Stored Information (Chicago 2007) p. 2; *see also* Conference of Chief Judges, Guidelines for State Trial Courts Regarding Discovery of Electronically-Stored Information (Williamsburg, Va., National Center for State Courts, 2006).

27. Fed. R. Civ. P. 34(a) advisory committee's note.

allow litigants and courts to adapt to the evolution of information creation and management technologies.[28] The rules purposely do not define "electronically stored information," instead noting that the phrase is intended to "cover all current types of computer-based information" and be "flexible enough to encompass future changes and developments."[29]

In some cases, it is simple to identify electronically stored information. The classic forms that are the most likely to be sought or produced in litigation include e-mail, documents created using office software applications (e.g., WordPerfect, Word, Excel, Powerpoint, etc.), and images (like PDFs, digital photographs, etc.). However, the post-amendment case law interpreting the phrase "electronically stored information" also involves less obvious and arguably more fleeting forms of information, including data temporarily stored by computers for minutes or even seconds.[30]

In *Columbia Pictures v. Bunnell*, for example, the court considered what it described as a question of first impression: "Is the information held in a computer's Random Access Memory [RAM] 'electronically stored information' under Federal Rule of Civil Procedure 34?" RAM is computer hardware that retains information for a short time to speed the efficiency of certain computer operations (e.g., actions that are frequently executed).[31] The *Columbia Pictures* plaintiffs alleged that defendants' Web site facilitated piracy by allowing Internet users to find, watch, and distribute copyrighted movies and television shows.[32]

---

28. FED. R. CIV. P. 34(a).

29. FED. R. CIV. P. 34(a) advisory committee's note ("The wide variety of computer systems currently in use, and the rapidity of technological change, counsel against a limiting or precise definition of electronically stored information.").

30. *See* Columbia Pictures Indus. v. Bunnell, No. CV 06-1093 FMC (JCx), 2007 U.S. Dist. LEXIS 46364 (C.D. Cal. May 29, 2007), *review denied*, 245 F.R.D. 443 (C.D. Cal. 2007) (concluding that information written to Random Access Memory (RAM)—a temporary storage medium used to increase a computer's efficiency—is electronically stored information); Healthcare Advocates, Inc. v. Harding, No. 05-3524, 2007 U.S. Dist. LEXIS 52544 (E.D. Pa. July 20, 2007) (court implicitly concluded that information temporarily stored in cache files was discoverable, but refused to sanction firm for inadvertent loss from automatic computer processes).

31. SEDONA CONFERENCE GLOSSARY, p. 43.

32. Columbia Pictures, 245 F.R.D. at 445.

Plaintiffs sought discovery of server log data that would expose the identity of those who used the Web site as well as the copyrighted materials they accessed. But the information was stored in a computer's RAM and was typically retained for anywhere from a few seconds to a few hours. The case drew a lot of interest, and many amici encouraged the court to conclude that information held in RAM was too ephemeral to be considered electronically *stored* information and could be captured, if at all, only at great expense. The court rejected this argument:

> Defendants and *amici* seek to engraft on the definition of "stored" an additional requirement, that the information be not just stored, but stored "for later retrieval." They argue that "electronically stored information" cannot include information held in RAM because the period of storage, which may be as much as six hours, is too temporary. The Court finds this interpretation of "stored" unsupported by the text of the Rule, the accompanying commentary of its drafters, or Ninth Circuit precedent involving RAM. The Court holds that data stored in RAM, however temporarily, is electronically stored information subject to discovery under the circumstances of the instant case.[33]

The broad potential sweep of the phrase "electronically stored information" can be overwhelming for a company preparing an electronic discovery response plan. The initial step of inventorying types and sources of ESI may begin simply enough (computers, servers, etc.). But the list can quickly grow. What about chat logs that record instant-message exchanges, voicemail stored electronically, or digital copy machines that scan an original into memory and print from that memory? A thoughtful lawyer, sitting with a knowledgeable IT employee, will be able to identify scores of potential sources and types of ESI in no time. Then comes the next question—what should be done with that list?

A number of amici in the *Columbia Pictures* case expressed a similar concern, arguing that recognition of RAM as electronically stored information would impose a unwieldy burden on corporate records

---

33. *Id.* at 446.

managers. The court's discussion of those concerns is instructive, especially for those who stay up at night worrying about all the possible places electronic information might be stored. In short, the court explained that its finding that RAM constituted electronically stored information was only the start of an inquiry that would also consider relevance, burden, and alternatives:

> In response to *amici*'s concerns over the potentially devastating impact of this decision on the record-keeping obligations of businesses and individuals, the Court notes that this decision does not impose an additional burden on any Web site operator or party outside of this case. *It simply requires that the defendants in this case, as part of this litigation, after the issuance of a court order, and following a careful evaluation of the burden to these defendants of preserving and producing the specific information requested in light of its relevance and the lack of other available means to obtain it,* begin preserving and subsequently produce a particular subset of the data in RAM under Defendants' control.[34]

Companies should develop consistent, repeatable e-discovery response protocols that can be adjusted to fit the facts of the case. It is not feasible to ensure that every possibly relevant piece of electronically stored information is preserved when a lawsuit is filed.[35] But it is possible—based on the facts and nature of a case—to promptly make good-faith, informed decisions about the preservation of potentially relevant data, and to identify potential problem spots so they can be addressed with opposing counsel and, if necessary, the court.

At bottom then, the reference to electronically stored information by the Federal Rules Committee and the many states that have adopted similar or identical provisions effectively means that e-discovery is now anticipated in all cases. At the federal level, it is mandated regardless of whether the opposing party specifically requests that electronic

---

34. *Id.* at 448 (emphasis added).

35. Zubulake v. UBS Warburg (Zubulake IV), 220 F.R.D. 212, 217 (S.D.N.Y. 2003) ("Must a corporation, upon recognizing the threat of litigation, preserve every shred of paper, every e-mail or electronic document, and every backup tape? The answer is clearly, 'no.' Such a rule would cripple large corporations.").

information be produced. In other words, the days of lawyers and clients burying their heads in the sand and pretending that electronic records are not relevant and need not be preserved or produced in litigation are over.

B. Parties Must Give Early Attention to E-discovery

E-discovery is complex, expensive, and potentially unpredictable. The amendment to the Federal Rules sought to address these issues by requiring parties to focus on e-discovery early in the process, with the aim of coming to basic agreements on the scope and conduct of e-discovery as well as those areas that are off-limits.

The most dramatic impact of the new rules is that they demand an early substantive focus by the parties and the court on discovery in general, and electronic discovery in particular. Rules 16(b), 26(a), 26(f), and Form 35 are specifically designed to force early identification and communication of electronic discovery issues, whether they relate to the preservation, collection, review, or production of ESI. These changes are intended to minimize the later emergence of more significant and, by then, possibly intractable ESI problems. In combination, these rules tell the parties that they must, at the outset of litigation, discuss many topics relating to the discovery of ESI. The rules also require litigants to report the substance of their discussions to the court, and make clear that any problems identified in the parties' early discussions should be addressed expeditiously.

Although there has been little more than a year's experience under the rules, the case law suggests that courts are taking those requirements seriously. In *Hill v. Eddie Bauer*, a class action alleging unfair labor and business practices under California law, the court admonished the parties and, particularly, the plaintiffs, for submitting a joint stipulation on discovery that "does not address the recent amendments to the Federal Rules of Civil Procedure pertaining to electronic discovery."[36] And in *Crutcher v. Fidelity National Insurance Co.*, the court

---

36. Hill v. Eddie Bauer, 242 F.R.D. 556, 565 n.10 (C.D. Cal. 2007).

37. Crutcher v. Fid. Nat'l Ins. Co., No. 06-5273, 2007 U.S. Dist. LEXIS 8208, at *7-*8 (E.D. La. Feb. 5, 2007).

38. *See infra*, Section II.F, "Sanctions and the Spoliation 'Safe Harbor.'"

39. Fed. R. Civ. P. 26(a) (emphasis added).

found a subpoena invalid and denied a motion to compel because the plaintiffs did not comply with the requirement to develop a proposed discovery plan addressing, among other things, issues relating to the disclosure and discovery of electronically stored information.[37] Moreover, as discussed below, the accuracy of initial disclosures and related actions concerning electronically stored information can be critical factors in sanctions decisions.[38]

1. Initial Disclosures

Federal Rule of Civil Procedure Rule 26(a) requires parties to include in their initial disclosures "a copy—or a description by category and location—of, all documents, *electronically stored information*, and tangible things that the disclosing party has in its possession, custody, or control and may use to support its claims or defenses, unless solely for impeachment."[39] How this provision will be enforced remains to be seen and is likely to vary by court. In some jurisdictions, and during initial implementation under the rules, disclosures are likely to be superficial, disclosing little more than the fact that the party in question has "computers" and "ESI on various systems." But some courts are requiring more detailed descriptions of the party's IT architecture, including numbers and types of computers, servers, applications, and databases.[40]

Disclosures must be based on an accurate understanding of a party's information technology (IT) architecture and the relevant categories and locations of information that may be used to support claims or defenses in a particular case. Given the potential complexity of this task, many corporations have not waited for litigation to inventory and map out their IT assets and architecture. Lawyers must have a working understanding of their client's sources and locations of electronic discovery. As Judge Shira Scheindlin explained in the landmark *Zubulake* case:

> [C]ounsel must become fully familiar with her client's document retention policies, as well as the client's data retention architecture. This will invariably involve speaking with information technology personnel, who can explain system-wide

---

40. *See, e.g.*, In re Electronically Stored Information, Suggested Protocol for Discovery of Electronically Stored Information ¶ 5 (D. Md.).

backup procedures and the actual (as opposed to theoretical) implementation of the firm's recycling policy. It will also involve communicating with the "key players" in the litigation, in order to understand how they stored information.[41]

The importance of accurate disclosures cannot be emphasized enough. When a disclosure is made, an attorney must certify that it is "complete and correct as of the time it is made."[42] Where a certification, without justification, is not complete and accurate, the court, "upon motion or on its own, *must impose* an appropriate sanction on the signer, the party on whose behalf the signer was acting, or both. The sanction may include an order to pay the reasonable expenses, including attorney's fees, caused by the violation."[43] Recently, courts have not hesitated to impose sanctions under this provision for counsel's failure to reasonably investigate the facts before certifying disclosures.[44]

Given the risks of inconsistency from case to case, clients should develop checklists for the identification and disclosure of ESI, identi-

---

41. Zubulake V, 229 F.R.D. at 432. Judge Scheindlin went on to explain: "To the extent that it may not be feasible for counsel to speak with every key player, given the size of a company or the scope of the lawsuit, counsel must be more creative. It may be possible to run a system-wide keyword search; counsel could then preserve a copy of each 'hit.' Although this sounds burdensome, it need not be. Counsel does not have to review these documents, only see that they are retained." *Id; see also* In re Seroquel Prods. Liab. Litig., 244 F.R.D. 650, 663 (M.D. Fla. 2007) ("AZ and its counsel had a responsibility at the outset of the litigation to 'take affirmative steps to monitor compliance so that all sources of discoverable information are identified and searched.'") (citation omitted).

42. Fed. R. Civ. P. 26(g)(1)(A).

43. Fed. R. Civ. P. 26(g)(3) (emphasis added).

44. *See* R&R Sails Inc. v. Ins. Co. of Pa., 2008 WL 2232640 (S.D. Cal. Apr. 18, 2008) (sanctioning client and its outside counsel based in part on failure to make an adequate inquiry under Rule 26(g)); Qualcomm Inc. v. Broadcom Corp., No. 05cv1958-B (BLM), 2008 U.S. Dist. LEXIS 911 (S.D. Cal. Jan. 7, 2008) (sanctioning multiple attorneys for inaccurate certifications under 26(g), among other grounds; some attorneys were also referred to the bar for consideration of disciplinary measures); *id.* at *56-*57, *81 ($5,000 in sanction plus costs related to the failure); Wingnut Films, Ltd. v. Katja Motion Pictures Corp., No. CV 05-1516 RSWL (SHx), 2007 U.S. Dist. LEXIS 72953 (C.D. Cal. Sept. 18, 2007) (required the offending party to pay for the costs of a vendor to search agreed-upon sources of ESI, and invited additional briefing on whether the party should pay a sanction of $125,000); E*Trade Secs. LLC v. Deutsche Bank AG, 230 F.R.D. 582, 593-95 (D. Minn. 2005),

fying both potential sources and types of ESI that might be relevant to a case (even if not all sources and types are relevant to a particular case). These templates can and should be shared with outside counsel, and updated as necessary. Indeed, it is important for outside counsel to be aware of a client's e-discovery capabilities and limitations. Otherwise, counsel might seek in one case what its client is not willing or able to produce in another. Or counsel, without a reasonable understanding of its clients' types and sources of ESI, or processes for managing ESI, may make commitments that its client simply cannot meet.

Third, disclosures can provide a preview of an opponent's substantive case. The kind of meaningful discussion about electronic discovery anticipated by the rules will often involve discussions about the claims and defenses at issue in the litigation and related discovery topics and key personnel.

Fourth, the initial disclosures should give an initial glimpse of your opponent's readiness to engage in electronic discovery, and may also raise red flags in terms of preservation of electronic records. Where your opponent's disclosures are vague or inadequate, consider following up initially by letter. Continuing vague or inadequate disclosures can be addressed through a 30(b)(6) deposition of a person or persons with knowledge of the following topics (as appropriate):

- The organization's computer systems and configurations
- The operating systems and software used by the organization
- IT policies and practices (ranging from policies covering employee use of corporate IT to computer maintenance)
- Preservation of electronic records relevant to the matter
    - Written records management policies
    - Pre-litigation retention/destruction practices (including automated data deletion practices)
    - Steps taken to identify, preserve and collect potentially relevant data
    - Technology used (or available) for preservation, search, and collection
    - Human input limiting the scope of preservation (e.g., the use of key word searching or data sampling to define the scope of material preserved)
    - Timing
    - Notice to document custodians and follow-up

- Identification and collection of potentially relevant data
- Data backups and archives (including schedule, procedures, format, retention times, archive purposes, identification of universe of existing backups, and past data recovery and restoration activities)
- Claims that relevant ESI is not reasonably accessible
- Personnel responsible for the functions listed above

While some attorneys seek some or all of this information through interrogatories, the Rule 26 disclosure and planning process—which requires discussion and disclosure of these topics—will often make interrogatories unnecessary. And where the Rule 26 process is insufficient, the party seeking information will have a strategic edge in the more candid arena of a deposition, where the deponent(s) must respond without the filter of a lawyer reviewing interrogatory responses.

Note, however, that invasive discovery on the adequacy of your opponent's electronic preservation or production efforts—for example, having your experts or a third party examine your opponent's hard drives—is likely to be permitted only where there is evidence that your opponent's actions are deficient.[45] Absent evidence of deficiencies, courts have been disinclined to allow significant discovery into an opponent's information systems.[46]

---

45. *See, e.g.*, Playboy Enters., Inc. v. Welles, 60 F. Supp. 2d 1050, 1051 (S.D. Cal. 1999) (defendant's "custom and practice" of deleting e-mail throughout the litigation, including responsive e-mail, justified testing and sampling or defendant's hard drive); Simon Prop. Group, 194 F.R.D. at 640 (plaintiff was permitted to attempt to recover deleted computer files from the computers of four people given "troubling discrepancies with respect to defendant's document production").

46. *See, e.g.*, Williams v. Mass. Mut. Life Ins. Co., 226 F.R.D. 144, 146 (D. Mass. 2005) ("Before permitting such an intrusion into an opposing party's information system—particularly where, as here, that party has undertaken its own search and forensic analysis and has sworn to its accuracy—the inquiring party must present at least some reliable information that the opposing party's representations are misleading or substantively inaccurate.") (citations omitted); Scotts Co. v. Liberty Mut. Ins., No. 2:06-CV-899, 2007 U.S. Dist. LEXIS 43005, at *5 (S.D. Ohio June 12, 2007) (court refused to allow extensive forensic search of defendant's sources of ESI based on "mere suspicion" that information was withheld, stating, "Plaintiff is no more entitled to access to defendant's electronic information storage systems than to defendant's warehouses storing paper documents.").

2. Conference of the Parties

Perhaps the most significant changes to the Federal Rules are those associated with the Rule 26(f) Conference, which require the parties to develop a proposed discovery plan indicating, among other things, (i) "any issues about disclosure or discovery of electronically stored information, including the form or forms in which it should be produced," and (ii) "any issues about claims of privilege or of protection as trial-preparation material, including—if the parties agree on a procedure to assert such claims after production—whether to ask the court to include their agreement in an order."[47] While privilege issues present burdens in both the paper and electronic worlds, the Advisory Committee noted that privilege burdens "often become more acute" with large volumes of ESI.[48]

The changes to Rule 26(f) should transform the initial meet and confer process from a meaningless pro forma meeting in which little or nothing is achieved to a substantive meeting whose results will directly affect the litigation. First, defendants (particularly large corporations) now have something to gain from the pretrial conference by clearly defining the scope of the preservation and discovery of ESI and, thus, the associated risks and costs. For example, the conference can now be used to limit the time period, the systems, and the number of people whose information must be preserved and/or searched. Second, the discovery conference is a means to frame the issues for the Rule 16 conference. It is important to set out a reasonable position in the face of an unreasonable requesting party so the Rule 16 conference can be used to obtain some limitations on the scope and amount of the ESI to be discovered.

While some courts already had, and enforced, robust Rule 26(f) practices before the rules amendments, for many lawyers accustomed to "drive-by" 26(f) conferences that result in non-substantive scheduling orders and discovery plans, the recent amendments should mean a big change. The 26(f) conference is now more likely to be a major event, early in the life of a case, where the parties must be prepared for a substantive discussion about likely discovery topics. As with disclosure of ESI, the Rule 26(f) conference requires substantial preparation. The Advisory Committee noted that "[i]n appropriate cases identifica-

---

47. FED. R. CIV. P. 26(f).
48. FED. R. CIV. P. 26(f) Advisory Committee Notes.

tion of, and early discovery from, individuals with special knowledge of a party's computer system may be helpful" to this process.[49]

Where ESI is complex—as will often be the case—a client and lawyer may rely on a liaison from within (or even outside) the company to assist with disclosures and interaction with an opponent.[50] In *Crown Park Corp.*, plaintiff filed an ex parte motion for an order requiring defendants to preserve electronically stored information. The magistrate declined to issue such an order, but required the parties to meet and confer regarding the preservation of electronic documents. In addition, the magistrate required that the "meet and confer discussions . . . be attended by an electronic document consultant retained by" each party, and that the respective consultants "have sufficient knowledge of" each party's electronic documents to facilitate good-faith efforts "to resolve all issues regarding the production of electronic documents without court action."[51]

The court in *Seroquel Products Liability Litigation* approached this issue with the benefit of hindsight, but in the unfortunate context of a sanctions motion in multi-district product liability litigation. There, the magistrate admonished the defendant for not cooperatively involving technical experts early in the process, stating:

> [M]any of the technical problems identified . . . likely could have been resolved far sooner and far less expensively had AZ cooperated by fostering consultation between the technical staffs responsible for production. Instead, AZ shielded its third-party technical contractor from all contact with Plaintiffs. This approach is antithetical to the Sedona Principles and is not an indicium of good faith.[52]

---

49. *Id.*

50. *See, e.g.,* THE SEDONA PRINCIPLES, SECOND EDITION, p. 20 ("Often, neither counsel nor the court will have sufficient technical knowledge to understand the systems at issue. In preparing for court conferences or meet-and-confer conferences, counsel should consult with their clients' information technology departments and vendors regarding the technical issues involved in data preservation."); *see also* In re Seroquel Prods. Liab. Litig., 244 F.R.D. at 662; Crown Park Corp. v. Dominican Sisters of Mary Mother of the Eucharist, No. 06-10621, 2006 U.S. Dist. LEXIS 19739 (E.D. Mich. Apr. 14, 2006).

51. Crown Park Corp., 2006 U.S. Dist. LEXIS 19739, at *3-*4.

52. In re Seroquel Prods. Liab. Litig., 244 F.R.D. at 662.

The Committee Notes to Rule 26(f) explain that "[t]he particular issues regarding electronically stored information that deserve attention during the discovery planning stage depend on the specifics of the given case."[53] Some examples of the types of potential issues contemplated by the committee include:

(1) the topics of ESI for which discovery will be sought;

(2) "the time period for which discovery will be sought";

(3) "sources of such information within a party's control that should be searched for electronically stored information";

(4) "whether the information is reasonably accessible to the party that has it";

(5) the "burden or cost of retrieving and reviewing the information";

(6) the "form or forms in which electronically stored information might be produced";

(7) "whether [metadata] should be produced";

(8) "Any issues regarding preservation of discoverable information."

(9) "whether the parties can facilitate discovery by agreeing on procedures for asserting claims of privilege or protection after production"; and

(10) "the balance between the competing needs to preserve relevant evidence and to continue routine operations critical to ongoing activities."[54]

3. Discovery Planning Conference

Rule 16(b) provides that the court's scheduling order may include "[provisions] for disclosure or discovery of electronically stored information" and "any agreements the parties reach for asserting claims of privilege or of protection as trial-preparation material after [production]."[55] The rules envision that the 26(f) conference of the parties will precede and, indeed, inform the 16(b) discovery planning conference. While Rule 16(b) notes that the court may adopt the parties' agreement, if any, for protection against privilege waiver, the rules do not require that litigants reach such an agreement, and do not allow the

---

53. FED. R. CIV. P. 26(f) advisory committee's note.

54. *Id.* (2006).

55. FED. R. CIV. P. 16(b)(6).

court to adopt such a provision absent agreement of the parties.[56] While discovery conferences were held in various degrees by judges prior to the rules amendments, the complexities of e-discovery, and the potential loss of information where key questions of preservation and production are not addressed at the outset, create incentives for lawyers and the court that simply did not exist in the world of paper.

The amendment to Rule 16 is designed to "alert the court to the possible need to address the handling of discovery of electronically stored information early in the litigation," recognizing that "the court's involvement early in the litigation will help avoid difficulties that might otherwise arise."[57] Importantly, the inclusion of electronic discovery as a topic for the Rule 16 conference means that, in most cases, parties can no longer ignore the issue of ESI unless and until asked about it. The significant risks of providing incorrect or incomplete information at the onset of litigation, as well as the significant opportunities to limit the scope of preservation and discovery of ESI, require preparation and focus as soon as, if not well before, litigation is filed.

Courts generally expect counsel to "become knowledgeable about their clients' information management systems and their operation, including how information is stored and retrieved."[58] As an example of the heightened level of familiarity expected by some courts, consider the following excerpt from the Suggested Protocol for Discovery of ESI adopted by the U.S. District Court for the District of Maryland. First, the court notes that, "[i]nsofar as it relates to ESI, prior planning and preparation is essential for a Conference of Parties pursuant to Fed. R. Civ. P. 16, 26(f), and this Protocol."[59] The Protocol goes on to state that court's expectation that counsel:

Become reasonably familiar with their respective clients' current and relevant past ESI, if any, or alternatively, identify a person who can participate in the Fed. R. Civ. P. 26(f) Conference of Parties *and who is familiar with at least the following*:

---

56. Fed. R. Civ. P. 16(b)(6) advisory committee's note (2006) ("The rule does not provide the court with authority to enter such a case-management or other order without party agreement, or limit the court's authority to act on motion.").

57. *Id.*

58. Initial Order Regarding Planning and Scheduling, U.S. Dist. Ch., Thomson for the Dist. of Kan. (rev. 12/1/06).

59. In re *Electronically Stored Information*, Suggested Protocol for Discovery of Electronically Stored Information, ¶ 5 (D. Md.).

(1) E-mail systems; blogs; instant messaging; Short Message Service (SMI) systems; word-processing systems; spreadsheet and database systems; system history files, cache files, and cookies; graphics, animation, or document presentation systems; calendar systems; voicemail systems, including specifically whether such systems include ESI; data files; program files; Internet systems; and intranet systems. This Protocol may include information concerning the specific version of software programs and may include information stored on electronic bulletin boards, regardless of whether they are maintained by the party, authorized by the party, or officially sponsored by the party, provided, however, this Protocol extends to the information only to the extent such information is in the possession, custody, or control of such party. To the extent reasonably possible, this includes the database program used over the relevant time, its database dictionary, and the manner in which such program records transactional history in respect to deleted records.

(2) Storage systems, including whether ESI is stored on servers, individual hard drives, home computers, "laptop" or "notebook" computers, personal digital assistants, pagers, mobile telephones, or removable/portable storage devices, such as CD-ROMs; DVDs; floppy disks; zip drives; tape drives; external hard drives; flash, thumb or "key" drives; or external service providers.

(3) Backup and archival systems, including those that are on-site, off-site, or maintained using one or more third-party vendors. This Protocol may include a reasonable inquiry into the backup routine, application, and process and location of storage media, and requires inquiry into whether ESI is reasonably accessible without undue burden or cost; whether it is compressed, encrypted, and the type of device on which it is recorded (e.g., whether it uses sequential or random access); and whether software that is capable of rendering it into usable form without undue expense is within the client's possession, custody, or control.

(4) Obsolete or "legacy" systems containing ESI and the extent, if any, to which such ESI was copied or transferred to new or replacement systems.

(5) Current and historical Web site information, including any potentially relevant or discoverable statements contained on that

(or those) site(s), as well as systems to back up, archive, store, or retain superseded, deleted, or removed Web pages, and policies regarding allowing third parties' sites to archive client Web site data.

(6)   Event data records automatically created by the operation, usage, or polling of software or hardware (such as recorded by a motor vehicle's GPS or other internal computer prior to an occurrence), if any and if applicable, in automobiles, trucks, aircraft, vessels, or other vehicles or equipment.

(7)   Communication systems, if any and if applicable, such as ESI records of radio transmissions, telephones, personal digital assistants, or GPS systems.

(8)   ESI erasure, modification, or recovery mechanisms, such as meta-data scrubbers or programs that repeatedly overwrite portions of storage media in order to preclude data recovery, and policies regarding the use of such processes and software, as well as recovery programs that can defeat scrubbing, thereby recovering deleted but inadvertently produced ESI, which in some cases may even include privileged information.

(9)   Policies regarding records management, including the retention or destruction of ESI prior to the client receiving knowledge that a claim is reasonably anticipated.

(10)   "Litigation hold" policies that are instituted when a claim is reasonably anticipated, including all such policies that have been instituted and the date on which they were instituted.

(11)   The identity of custodians of key ESI, including "key persons" and related staff members, and the information technology or information systems personnel, vendors, or subcontractors who are best able to describe the client's information technology system.

(12)   The identity of vendors or subcontractors who store ESI for, or provide services or applications to, the client or a key person; the nature, amount, and a description of the ESI stored by those vendors or subcontractors; contractual or other agreements that permit the client to impose a "litigation hold" on such ESI; whether or not such a "litigation hold" has been placed; and, if not, why not.[60]

---

60. *Id.* ¶ 6 (emphasis added).

This list of topics is daunting, even for experienced e-discovery practitioners. But only a portion of these topics is likely to be relevant in any given case, and relevance and burden should be considered in applying these protocols. For example, the details of meta-data scrubbers will not be important where meta-data is unlikely to be at issue. The Maryland protocols acknowledge as much, noting that the anticipated "level of familiarity is conditioned upon the nature of the pleadings, the circumstances of the case, and the factors contained in Fed. R. Civ. P. 26(b)(2)(C)" (discussed below).[61]

As a practical matter, many federal judges will incorporate provisions relating to the discovery of ESI into the Rule 16 case management order. As a result, the parties will be expected to meet in advance of the Rule 16 conference to discuss and reach an agreement on the scope of preservation and discovery, as well as the actual process for discovery of ESI in a particular case. In addition, the Rule 16 conference can be used as a vehicle to try to limit the scope of the discovery of ESI in the case of an overly aggressive requesting party.

Our experience to date is that a party who is prepared for a Rule 16 conference is likely to achieve what he or she wants from the conference. Preparation is also critical to enable a party to participate in the Rule 16 conference in good faith, and to avoid creating greater risk down the road (by, for example, providing inaccurate information about the nature, extent, or preservation of ESI). Both counsel and client must be aware that Rule 16(f)(1) permits a court to issue "any just orders" where a party or its counsel "is substantially unprepared to participate—or does not participate in good faith—in the conference."[62] And Rule 16(f) appears to leave the court little leeway in deciding *whether* to impose a sanction once noncompliance with Rule 16 is found. Under Rule 16(f)(2), "the court *must* order the party, its attorney, or both to pay the reasonable expenses—including attorney's fees—incurred because of any noncompliance with this rule, unless the noncompliance was substantially justified or other circumstances make an award of expenses unjust."[63] While we have not seen cases applying this provision to failures in the electronic discovery process, we suspect that e-discovery-related sanctions based on this language are on the horizon.

---

61. *Id.*
62. Fed. R. Civ. P. 16(f)(1).
63. Fed. R. Civ. P. 16(f)(2) (emphasis added).

C. Two Tiers of Discoverable Information—Data That Is Not Reasonably Accessible

Amended Rule 26(b)(2)(B) creates a two-tier approach to the discoverability of ESI. Tier I should not be surprising. A party must provide discovery of relevant, reasonably accessible ESI. Tier I recognizes that "[e]lectronic storage systems often make it easier to locate and retrieve information," and that these efficiencies should be "taken into account in determining reasonably the scope of discovery."[64]

But there is also a second tier—ESI that "can be accessed only with substantial burden and costs."[65] Recognizing that it could be unreasonable to impose these burdens and costs on a responding party in particular litigation, Rule 26(b)(2)(B) states that "[a] party need not provide discovery of electronically stored information from sources that the party identifies as not reasonably accessible because of undue burden or cost."[66] The burden is then on the responding party to "identify, by category or type" the source of the inaccessible information and provide "enough detail to enable the requesting party to evaluate the burdens and costs of providing the discovery and the likelihood of finding responsive information on the identified sources."[67] The committee did not elaborate upon the types of information that are "not reasonably accessible." As a result, it will take some time for the lower courts to set out a workable framework for identifying what types of data are "not reasonably accessible."

This rule applies to production, not preservation. A party may have the obligation to preserve relevant data that is "not reasonably accessible" even though it may not ultimately have an obligation to produce that information.[68] The two-tiered approach envisions that sources of potentially relevant ESI that are not considered by a party to be reasonably accessible will be preserved long enough to allow the parties and the court to consider and address the discoverability of that information. Moreover, to facilitate a resolution of reasonable accessibility questions, a party must "identify, by category or type, the sources

---

64. FED. R. CIV. P. 26(b)(2)(B) advisory committee's note.
65. *Id.*
66. FED. R. CIV. P. 26(b)(2)(B).
67. FED. R. CIV. P. 26(b)(2) advisory committee's note.
68. *See* Chapter Two, "Spoliation."

containing potentially responsive information that it is neither searching or producing."[69]

These disclosures must be sufficient to allow the "requesting party to evaluate the burdens and costs of providing the discovery and the likelihood of finding responsive information on the identified sources."[70] Where an attorney decides not to preserve information—a decision that potentially risks sanctions—there must be a reasoned basis for that decision that can be articulated, perhaps years later. In close cases, an attorney is advised to seek agreement of the other side, to move for a court order approving (in advance) the decision not to preserve, or to simply preserve the information pending a determination concerning whether it must be searched and produced.[71] A requesting party may obtain discovery on the accessibility of information, which could include depositions of knowledgeable witnesses, inspection of the purportedly inaccessible information or systems, or sampling of the information claimed to be inaccessible.

A number of factors will influence the determination of whether data is treated as "not reasonably accessible."

First, is the information routinely used by the party claiming inaccessibility? If so, a claim that the material is not reasonably accessible will not be credible. When opposing a claim of inaccessibility, consider limited discovery on your opponent's claims. For example, you may ask: (1) how many times the information was accessed in the past year; (2) who is able to access the information; (3) for what purposes is the information accessed; and (4) whether any special tools are required to access the information. The goal is to piece together a simple story—the information is easily accessible when your opponent wants to retrieve it for everyday purposes. It is only "not reasonably accessible," you would hope to convince the court, when disclosure is requested in litigation.

Second, is the information retained for disaster recovery purposes only? Courts and the Rules Committee have used this as an example of information that may not be reasonably accessible.[72] One reason

---

69. *Id.*

70. *Id.*

71. *See* Chapter Two, "Spoliation."

72. Fed. R. Civ. P. 26(b)(2) advisory committee's note; *see also* The Sedona Principles: Best Practices Recommendations & Principles for Addressing Electronic Document Production (Second Edition), p. 18 ("Examples of such sources may include,

for this view is that, in some backup systems, what you might consider to be a record or document is not found in a single place. Instead, information may be fragmented and disorganized, spread over multiple locations. The cost of piecing such information together can be high. Still, claims that information is retained for disaster recovery can be probed in discovery as well. How often is the information accessed? Are there ever occasions when the information is accessed other than a disaster? When and how often? And finally, what constitutes a disaster? (Is it simply whenever the CEO deletes something and wants to recover it?)

Third, is the information maintained in an obsolete or legacy format? Computer technologies change. Software changes. And the hardware and media (e.g., tapes) used to store and read information change. As a result, information will sometimes be stored on media that simply cannot be read by a party using that party's existing software or hardware. Recovery of such information by an outside vendor can be quite expensive. And, of course, because the information cannot be read in the first place, it can be difficult even to decide that it is likely to contain relevant information.

Even if the responding party shows that the information is not reasonably accessible, the court may nonetheless order discovery if the requesting party shows good cause. Factors considered in determining whether or not good cause exists to order discovery of the inaccessible information include:

- the specificity of the discovery request;
- the quantity of information available from other and more easily accessed sources;
- the failure to produce relevant information that seems likely to have existed but is no longer available on more easily accessed sources;
- the likelihood of finding relevant, responsive information that cannot be obtained from other, more easily accessed sources;

according to the Advisory Committee, backup tapes that are intended for disaster recovery purposes and are not indexed, organized, or susceptible to electronic searching; legacy data that remains from obsolete systems and is unintelligible on the successor systems; and data that was 'deleted' but remains in fragmented form, requiring a modern version of forensics to restore and retrieve."); *see also* McPeek, 202 F.R.D. at 33-34; Rowe Entm't, 205 F.R.D. at 429.

- predictions as to the importance and usefulness of the further information;
- the importance of the issues at stake in the litigation; and
- the parties' resources.[73]

If the requesting party shows good cause for the production of inaccessible data, the court may specify conditions for discovery, including requiring the requesting party to pay part or all of the producing party's costs of obtaining information from sources that are not reasonably accessible.

The expanding scope and increasing costs of electronic discovery[74] have accentuated the issue of cost-sharing. In the past, the resolution of the question of who should bear the financial burden associated with discovery has been consistent: the producing party.[75]

---

73. These factors are discussed below in the context of the cases that apply to them.

74. The costs associated with electronic discovery are high because companies typically store huge numbers of electronic documents, and the retrieval of such documents is rarely routine. Costs must be incurred creating special programs to translate backup tapes, retrieving deleted files, or re-creating "legacy" formats. Such costs are increased when this special programming requires the use of special equipment or programming experts. *See* Peter Brown, *Discovery and Use of Electronic Evidence*, 391 PLI/Pat 391, 398 (2003). The following are examples of costs that have been incurred: Murphy Oil USA, Inc. v. Fluor Daniel, Inc., No. Civ. A 99-3564, 2002 WL 246439 (E.D. La. Feb. 19, 2002), $6.2 million to restore and print e-mail from 93 backup tapes; Rowe Entm't, 205 F.R.D. 421 ($9,750,000 to restore 200 backup tapes, $75,000 plus $247,000 for retrieval and review of e-mail messages, $395,000 to restore and $120,000 to review 523 backup tapes, $403,000 to restore 47 backup tapes and retrieve e-mail from 126 desktop PCs); In re Bristol Myers Squibb, 205 F.R.D. 437 ($432,000 to scan 3,086,000 pages). *See generally* Kenneth J. Withers, Electronic Discovery, National Workshop for U.S. Magistrate Judges, June 12, 2002.

75. *See* In re Brand Name Prescription Drugs Antitrust Litig., Nos. 94 C897, MDL 997, 1995 WL 360526, at *2 (N.D. Ill. June 15, 1995) (finding that guidelines applicable to discovering paper documents are applicable to allocating costs associated with discovering electronic documentation; unless expense or burden is "undue," party producing data will bear costs of production); Bills, 108 F.R.D. at 463 (noting that costs could be shifted when they amounted to undue burden on responding party, court refused to "set forth an ironclad formula into which the facts of this or another case can be placed for determination of what 'undue' means under Rule 34. Such a formula would be judicially imprudent and wholly impractical in view of the diverse nature of the claims, discovery requests and parties before the Court in a variety of cases and situations. The question must be resolved

Recently, however, judicial attitudes appear to be changing.[76]

Before the recent surge in electronic discovery, this burden was seldom oppressive, because the party in possession of the documents could simply give the requesting party access to the files and the requesting party would then bear the costs of staffing to review the files.[77] Present-day production of electronic documents is not nearly this simple, and the costs borne by the party in possession of the docu-

---

on a case-by-case basis. . . . However, certain propositions will be applicable in virtually all cases, namely, that information stored in computers should be as freely discoverable as information not stored in computers, so parties requesting discovery should not be prejudiced thereby; and the party responding is usually in the best and most economical position to call up its own computer stored data." Court denied motion to shift discovery costs because "(1) the amount of money involved is not excessive or inordinate; (2) the relative expense and burden in obtaining the data would be substantially greater to the requesting party as compared with the responding party; (3) the amount of money required to obtain the data as set forth by the defendant would be a substantial burden to plaintiffs; (4) the responding party is benefited in its case to some degree by producing the data in question."); *cf.* Oppenheimer Fund, Inc. v. Sanders, 437 U.S. 340, 358 (1978) (mentioning that the presumption with regard to discovery requests is that "the responding party must bear the expense of complying with discovery requests, but he may invoke the "court's discretion under Rule 26(c) to grant orders protecting him from 'undue burden or expense'").

76. This changing attitude was reflected in the recent opinion in *AAB Joint Venture v. United States*, 75 Fed. Cl. 432, 443 (2007), where the court noted: "To permit a party 'to reap the business benefits of such technology and simultaneously use that technology as a shield in litigation would lead to incongruous and unfair results.'" Linnen v. A.H. Robins Co., 1995 WL 462015, at *6. Under the discovery rules, "the presumption is that the responding party must bear the expense of complying with discovery. . . . In assessing whether cost-shifting to the requesting party is appropriate, court have employed the marginal utility test . . . or have looked to various factors [delineated in the leading cases discussed in this text]. Following either approach, the Court must attempt to balance the likelihood that restored documents will prove relevant to the instant litigation with whether the cost of restoration places an undue burden on Defendant."

77. *See* Peter Brown, *Discovery and Use of Electronic Evidence*, 391 PLI/Pat 391, 398. This assumes, of course, that the files did not contain privileged materials. If they did, such disclosures could waive privilege claims absent a protective order and agreement of the parties. *See infra* section II.D, Privilege and the Discovery of Electronically Stored Information. *See also* section III, Confidentiality and the Attorney Client Privilege.

ments are far greater.[78]

The case law on burden and cost allocation reflects a debate that began before the rules amendments and is continuing under the amended rules. Underlying this debate is a tension between holding a company responsible for the technology it chooses (and its use of that technology) and recognizing that some information management—in particular, management for disaster recovery purposes—is not designed with ready accessibility in mind. Some courts have justified placing the increased burden of producing difficult-to-access data upon the producing party by reasoning that companies consciously choose their information technologies and, as a result, should not be able to use the costs of employing these technologies "as a shield in litigation."[79] On the other hand, courts have recognized that some technologies—especially backup technologies—are simply not intended for everyday business use, and thus are not designed for easy accessibility.[80]

---

78. Because most intra-corporate communications are now on e-mail, the increased volume also has increased the number of privilege claims that must be made to protect the confidentiality of those communications. *See* Chapter Three, "Privileges," *infra*.

79. In re Brand Name Prescription Drugs Antitrust Litig., 1995 WL 360526, at *2 ("if a party chooses an electronic storage method, the necessity for a retrieval program or method is an ordinary and foreseeable risk"); Stout v. Wolff Shoe Co., No. 3:04-cv-23231-JFA, 2007 U.S. Dist. LEXIS 24833 (D.S.C. Mar. 31, 2007) ("translating information obtained from a computer database into a reasonably understandable form is a necessary and foreseeable burden on the responding party"); Linnen, 1999 Mass. Super. LEXIS 240, at *17-*18 (The significant costs of retrieving information from backup tapes "is one of the risks taken on by companies which have made the decision to avail themselves of the computer technology now available to the business world."); Daewoo Elecs. Co. v. United States, 650 F. Supp. 1003, 1006 (Ct. Int'l Trade 1986) ("The normal and reasonable translation of electronic data into a form usable by the discovering party should be the ordinary and foreseeable burden of a respondent in the absence of a showing of extraordinary hardship. The government has made no such showing.").

80. McPeek, 202 F.R.D. at 33-34 (noting that backup tapes are principally deployed to protect against destruction of data if the network crashes, not to catalogue information for business purposes, so to require a responding party to pay for the full expense of backup tape restoration may be unreasonable); *Rowe Entm't*, 205 F.R.D. at 429 (court noted that the principle that a party should reasonably foresee and, therefore, bear all the costs of searching and retrieving its electronic records, even if "unassailable in the context of paper records . . . does not translate well into the realm of electronic data.").

This will be an area to watch as the technologies of archiving and disaster recovery evolve. Hardware and software developers are paying attention to developments under the electronic discovery rules and the pressure points those rules create for companies and their IT and records management staff. As hardware and software change, the currently inaccessible (or the "difficult to access"), may become accessible. As a result, cost-shifting precedent of the past may not be a reliable guide to how courts will rule in the future.[81]

It is now increasingly difficult for any business of any size to succeed without using some form of digital technology. But digital technology also increases the potential costs of discovery—often to levels that are difficult to bear (and that may exceed the value of the case). As a result, the fairness of the presumption under which courts have operated—that the responding party must bear the costs of responding to discovery[82]— is increasingly being questioned. Of course, courts have always had the power to require the sharing of costs through a balancing of interests based on the unique circumstances of each case and the parties involved.[83]

If the nature of the discovery and the client's circumstances create special needs, you can argue for cost shifting as a condition for discovery under Rule 26(b)(2)(B). In addition, under Rule 26(c), courts

---

81. *See, e.g.,* C. BALL, WHAT JUDGES SHOULD KNOW ABOUT DISCOVERY FROM BACK-UP TAPES (2007) ("newer backup tape technologies build in some indexing features"); L. Buckley, *2008 Trends: Data Protection, Archiving and Disaster Recovery Challenges for the SMB*, COMPUTER TECH. REV. (2008) (citing "bewildering number of point solutions and possible combinations for data protection and archiving," including "deduplication, sophisticated archiving, e-mail archiving").

82. Oppenheimer, 437 U.S. at 358 ("Under [the discovery] rules, the presumption is that the responding party must bear the expense of complying with discovery requests.").

83. Sattar v. Motorola, Inc., 138 F.3d 1164 (7th Cir. 1998) (if on-site discovery option failed, then costs of copying tapes would be shared equally among parties); Zonaras v. General Motors Corp., No. C-3-94-161, 1996 WL 1671236 (S.D. Ohio Oct. 17, 1996) (while benefits from requested discovery were significant, evidence might prove to be inadmissible; accordingly, court ordered that costs of producing backup materials relating to test crashes with dummies would be shared equally); Williams v. Du Pont, 119 F.R.D. 648 (W.D. Ky. 1987) (while responding party generally absorbed costs of production, discovering party had to pay additional costs when it sought production in particular format for its own convenience).

have the power to grant protective orders to avoid "undue burden or expense."[84]

Judges have used this power to limit the costs of discovery that a producing party must bear. However, what constitutes an "undue burden or expense" has not been clearly defined by the Advisory Committee on the Federal Rules of Civil Procedure or the courts.[85]

Courts determine undue expense or burden on a case-by-case ba-

---

84. FED R. CIV. P. 26(c) provides:

Rule 26. General Provisions Governing Discovery; Duty of Disclosure

. . . .

(c) Protective Orders. Upon motion by a party or by the person from whom discovery is sought, accompanied by a certification that the movant has in good faith conferred or attempted to confer with other affected parties in an effort to resolve the dispute without court action, and for good cause shown, the court in which the action is pending or, alternatively, on matters relating to a deposition, the court in the district where the deposition is to be taken may make an order which justice requires to protect a party or person from annoyance, embarrassment, oppression, or undue burden or expense, including one or more of the following:

(1) that the disclosure or discovery not be had;
(2) that the disclosure or discovery may be had only on specified terms and conditions, including a designation of the time or place;
(3) that the discovery may be had only by a method of discovery other than that selected by the party seeking discovery;
(4) that certain matters not be inquired into, or that the scope of the disclosure or discovery be limited to certain matters;
(5) that discovery be conducted with no one present except persons designated by the court;
(6) that a deposition, after being sealed, be opened only by order of the court;
(7) that trade secret or other confidential research, development, or commercial information not be revealed or be revealed only in a designated way; and
(8) that the parties simultaneously file specified documents or information enclosed in sealed envelopes to be opened as directed by the court. If the motion for a protective order is denied in whole or in part, the court may, on such terms and conditions as are just, order that any party or other person provide or permit discovery. The provisions of Rule 37(a)(4) apply to the award of expenses incurred in relation to the motion.

85. Bills, 108 F.R.D. at 463.

sis, taking into account the following factors: (1) whether the costs involved are "excessive or inordinate"; (2) whether "the relative expense and burden in obtaining the data would be substantially greater to the requesting party as compared with the responding party"; (3) whether the costs incurred by the producing party would be a substantial burden on the requesting party; and (4) whether and to what extent the responding party's case would benefit from the production.[86] These fact-bound standards, however, provide little concrete guidance.

Additionally, discovery can be used as "a weapon capable of imposing large and unjustifiable costs on one's adversary."[87] This was acknowledged in *In re American Home Assurance Co.,*[88] where the Texas Court of Appeals concluded that Texas's equivalent to Rule 26(c) (i.e., Tex. R. Civ. P. 192.6(b)) should be used to prevent this from happening. In applying Rule 192.6(b), the court evaluated whether "the burden or expense of the proposed discovery outweighs its likely benefit, taking into account the needs of the case, the amount in controversy, the parties' resources, the importance of the issues at stake in the litigation, and the importance of the proposed discovery in resolving the issues."[89] The court went on to say that a party seeking a protective order that would shift costs has the burden of producing evidence that supports its claim. When dealing with electronic discovery, such proof, insofar as expenses are concerned, may largely concern the potential need to hire experts to re-create files and/or entire hard drives. Similarly, the court in *Anti-Monopoly, Inc. v. Hasbro*[90] found that the costs associated with developing a computer program to retrieve requested data from the producing party's computer system should be shifted to the requesting party. Although such outcomes have been rare, as costs increase and electronic discovery becomes even more common in litigation, the possibilities for shifting costs have increased.

Under Rules 26(b)(2) and 26(c) of the Federal Rules of Civil Procedure, the options available to courts to distribute the burdens of pretrial discovery are limited "only [by] the court's own imagination

---

86. *Id.* at 464

87. *Id.* (quoting Frank H. Easterbrook, *Discovery as Abuse*, 69 B.U. L. REV. 365 (1989)).

88. 88 S.W.3d 370, 373 (Tex. App. 2002).

89. *Id.* at 374.

90. No. 94 Civ. 2120 (LMM) (AJP), 1996 WL 22976, at *2 (S.D.N.Y. Jan. 23, 1996).

and the quality and quantity of the factual information provided by the parties to be used by the court in evaluating the Rule 26(b)(2) factors."[91] For example:

> The court can . . . shift the cost, in whole or part, of burdensome and expensive Rule 34 discovery to the requesting party; it can limit the number of hours required by the producing party to search for electronic records; or it can restrict the sources that must be checked. It can delay production of electronic records in response to Rule 34 request until after the deposition of information and technology personnel for the producing party, who can testify in detail as to the systems in place, as well as the storage and retention of electronic records, enabling more focused and less costly discovery. A court also can require the parties to identify experts to assist in structuring a search for existing and deleted electronic data and retain such an expert on behalf of the court.[92]

To obtain such judicial restructuring of discovery and reallocation of costs, it is essential that a party must make more than *ipse dixit* assertions about overbroad, burdensome, and prohibitively expensive discovery demands. Parties must make *particularized showings* to the court through affidavits, deposition excerpts, or other evidentiary submissions.

1. Approaches to Cost Allocation

Even before the Federal Rules were amended, many courts had established standards for cost allocation. One early attempt used as a guide by other courts[93] was outlined in *Rowe Entertainment, Inc. v. William Morris Agency, Inc.*[94] In *Rowe*, the court used an eight-factor balanc-

---

91. Thompson, 219 F.R.D. at 99.

92. *Id.*

93. Other cases employing the Rowe factors, or some modification thereof, are Zubulake v. UBS Warburg LLC, No. 02 Civ. 1243 (SAS), 2003 U.S. Dist. LEXIS 7939 (S.D. N.Y. May 13, 2003); Byers, 2002 U.S. Dist. LEXIS 9861; and Murphy Oil USA, Inc., 2002 WL 246439.

94. 205 F.R.D. at 430-32. In *Rowe*, the plaintiffs were minority concert promoters who claim that they had been prevented from entering the market for promoting events with white bands through the discriminatory and anticompetitive actions of the defendants. In pursuing their action, the plaintiffs requested broad production

ing test to determine who would pay for the production of requested documents. These factors included: (1) the specificity of the discovery request; (2) likelihood of a successful search;[95] (3) availability from other sources; (4) the purposes for which the electronic documents were retained; (5) benefit to the parties; (6) total costs; (7) the ability and incentive to control costs; and (8) the parties' resources. The court went on to explain how each of these factors should be considered:

- *Specificity of discovery request:* The less specific the request, the more appropriate it is to shift the expense to the requesting party.
- *Likelihood of a successful search:* The more likely it is that the requested documents will contain relevant information, the fairer it is to place the expense upon the producing party.
- *Availability from other sources:* If equivalent information has already been made available or if such information is available through a less expensive source, then shifting the expense to the requesting party is appropriate.
- *Purpose of retention:* If the party in possession of the data currently uses the requested information for business purposes, it should expect to bear the costs of producing such information when involved in litigation. If that party has maintained the information for archival/emergency purposes or has simply neglected to discard it, it should not be saddled with the production costs.
- *Benefit to the parties:* If the responding party benefits from the search in question, shifting costs is less appropriate. Such benefit may come from accessing useful information for the current litigation or the development of a program that is applicable in the responding party's everyday business.
- *Total costs:* What constitutes an amount high enough to war-

---

of electronically stored data, including e-mails, backup tapes and hard drives. The production was predicted to be costly. Rowe, 205 F.R.D. at 423.

95. The court in McPeek v. Ashcroft, 202 F.R.D. at 34, referred to this factor as the concept of marginal utility. "The more likely it is that the backup tape contains information that is relevant to a claim or defense, the fairer it is that the [responding party] search at its own expense. The less likely it is, the more unjust it would be to make [that party] search at its own expense. The difference is 'at the margin.'"

rant cost shifting is a decision for the court. In most cases involving restoration or re-creation of electronic systems, it is safe to assume that the amount involved will be high enough to validate cost shifting.[96]

- *Ability and incentive to control costs:* When dealing with incremental discovery, the expense should be placed on the party who controls how expansive the discovery will be.
- *Parties' resources:* It is appropriate to consider the financial backgrounds of each party to determine if one cannot bear even modest expenses. In such a case, cost shifting may be appropriate.

If the producing party wishes to conduct a review of materials before production to ensure that no privileged documents are given to the requesting party, *Rowe* held that the costs associated with such a review shall be borne by the producing party.[97] As with non-electronic documents, a court cannot compel the production of a privileged electronic document unless the privilege has been waived or an exception to the privilege is present.[98] Accordingly, even if the court orders cost shifting, the producing party may still bear the substantial expense of reviewing the documents prior to production.

While acknowledging that the *Rowe* factors have become the "gold standard" for deciding requests to reallocate electronic evidence production costs, Judge Scheindlin in *Zubulake v. UBS Warburg LLC*[99] took issue with a number of the *Rowe* factors. Characterizing them as incomplete and biased in favor of cost shifting because equal weight is given to all factors, Judge Scheindlin delineated what she described as a more neutral standard that maintains the presumption that responding parties generally will pay the costs of production. Her new standard modified some of the *Rowe* factors and eliminated others.

---

96. In Rowe, it was estimated that producing the requested files would costs between $200,000 and $300,000, amounts deemed substantial by both parties. 205 F.R.D. at 431. The *Rowe* court cited Oppenheimer, 437 U.S. at 361-62, as a guidepost for determining what is substantial. In Oppenheimer, the Supreme Court stated that "a threshold expense of $16,000 . . . hardly can be viewed as an insubstantial burden."

97. 205 F.R.D. at 432 ("[I]f any defendant elects to conduct a full privilege review of its e-mails prior to production, it shall do so at its own expense.").

98. *Id.* (citing In re Dow Corning Corp., 261 F.3d 280, 284 (2d Cir. 2001)).

99. 217 F.R.D. 309, 322-23 (S.D.N.Y. 2003) (Zubulake I).

Factors Added by *Zubulake* to the *Rowe* Test

1. Because Rule 26 requires consideration of the "amount in controversy, the parties' resources, the importance of the issues at stake in the litigation, and the importance of the proposed discovery in resolving the issues," Judge Scheindlin added the amount in controversy and the importance of the issues at stake in the litigation as relevant factors. She concluded that adding these factors would counterbalance the factor of total cost, which typically weighs heavily in favor of cost shifting. When total cost of production is small compared to "the amount in controversy," the total cost may not tip the balance in favor of cost shifting.

2. Rather than considering "the resources available to each party," the court concluded that the focus should be on "the total costs of production as compared to the resources available to each party."

3. Because some cases have the potential for broad public impact, "the importance of the issues at stake in the litigation" is occasionally a critical consideration. The *Zubulake* court advocated permitting broad discovery in cases involving "toxic tort class actions, environmental actions, so-called 'impact' or social reform litigation, cases involving criminal conduct, or cases implicating important legal or constitutional questions."

Factors Eliminated from the *Rowe* Test

1. "The specificity of the discovery request." Acknowledging that specificity is a critical factor in balancing the necessary discovery against the need to control unnecessary costs, the court concluded that this already is part of the second and sixth *Rowe* factors. The court, therefore, concluded that the first factor should be "the extent to which the request is specifically tailored to discovery relevant information."

2. "[T]he purposes for which the responding party maintains the requested data." In the court's opinion, this factor is typically unimportant. "Whether the data is kept for a business purpose or for disaster recovery does not affect its accessibility, which is the practical basis for calculating the cost of production. Although a business purpose will often coincide with accessibility—data that is inaccessible is unlikely to be used or needed in the ordinary course of business—the concepts are not cote-

rminous. . . . As long as the data is accessible, it must be produced."

Building on the *Rowe* foundation, Judge Scheindlin crafted a new seven-factor test for assessing requests for cost shifting for the production of data from inaccessible sources:

1. The extent to which the request is specifically tailored to discover relevant information;
2. The availability of such information from other sources;
3. The total cost of production, compared to the amount in controversy;
4. The total cost of production, compared to the resources available to each party;
5. The relative ability of each party to control costs and its incentive to do so;
6. The importance of the issues at stake in the litigation; and
7. The relative benefits to the parties of obtaining the information.

These modifications of the *Rowe* factors not only clarified the "gold standard," they polished it by ranking the factors in order of descending importance.[100]

---

100. Judge Scheindlin explains:

> Weighting the factors in descending order of importance may . . . avoid a mechanistic application of the test. The first two factors—comprising the marginal utility test—are the most important. These factors include: (1) The extent to which the request is specifically tailored to discover relevant information and (2) the availability of such information from other sources.
>
> The second group of factors addresses cost issues: "How expensive will this production be?" and, "Who can handle that expense?" These factors include: (3) the total cost of production compared to the amount in controversy, (4) the total cost of production compared to the resources available to each party, and (5) the relative ability of each party to control costs and its incentive to do so. The third "group"—(6) the importance of the litigation itself—stands alone, and as noted earlier will only rarely come into play. But where it does, this factor has the potential to predominate over the others. Collectively, the first three groups correspond to the three explicit considerations of Rule 26(b)(2)(iii). Finally the last factor—(7) the relative benefits of production as between the requesting and producing parties—is the least important because it is

When *Zubulake*[101] applied the revised standards to the circumstances of the case, the court granted the request for some measure of cost shifting. Applying factors (1) and (2), the court concluded that the request for e-mail communications was tailored to the most potentially relevant e-mail, which might constitute the only evidentiary means of proving discrimination. Accordingly, this factor tipped against cost shifting.

Applying factors (3), (4) and (5), the court weighed cost estimates in the range of $166,000 against the (albeit wildly different) estimates of what was at stake in the action—from $1.5 million to $19 million. It was clear, however, that this was not a small or frivolous case. While the responding party "should not be required to pay for the restoration of inaccessible data if the cost of that restoration was significantly disproportionate to the value of the case," the court concluded that the cost of restoration was not significantly disproportionate to the projected value of the *Zubulake* claim. This factor, therefore, weighed against cost shifting. Other factors pointed in opposing directions. Thus, even though the plaintiff had been unemployed for two years, she was financially secure. Nevertheless, the company's resources dwarfed the plaintiff's, and the plaintiff's counsel was fronting huge expenses because of the potential value of the recovery. The court concluded that because the costs of restoration were not within the control of either party, this factor ultimately was neutral.

Applying factor (6), the court concluded that discrimination cases are common, and this one did not present any unique issues. Consequently, the judge concluded that this should not be a factor in the cost-shifting calculation.

On factor (7), the court concluded that the discovery clearly favored the plaintiff, who might have proven her case through the e-mails produced. At the same time, the defendant might have produced information that could form the basis for a motion for summary judgment. Nevertheless, this factor weighed in favor of cost shifting. Finally the judge concluded:

> fair to presume that the response to a discovery request generally benefits the requesting party. But in the unusual case where production will also provide a tangible or strategic benefit to the responding party, that fact may weight *against* shifting costs.

Zubulake I, 217 F.R.D. at 323 (footnote omitted).

101. 216 F.R.D. 280 (S.D.N.Y. 2003).

Factors one through four tip against cost-shifting (although factor two only slightly so). Factors five and six are neutral, and factor seven favors cost-shifting. As noted in my earlier opinion in this case, however, a list of factors is not merely a matter of counting and adding; it is only a guide. Because some of the factors cut against cost shifting, but only *slightly so*—in particular, the possibility that the continued production will produce valuable new information—some cost-shifting is appropriate in this case, although UBS should pay the majority of the costs. There is plainly relevant evidence that is only available on UBS's backup tapes. At the same time, Zubulake has not been able to show that there is indispensable evidence on those backup tapes (although the fact that Chapin apparently deleted certain e-mails indicates that such evidence may exist).

The next question is how much of the cost should be shifted. It is beyond cavil that the precise allocation is a matter of judgment and fairness rather than a mathematical consequence of the seven factors discussed above. Nonetheless, the analysis of those factors does inform the exercise of discretion. Because the seven-factor test requires that UBS pay the lion's share, the percentage assigned to Zubulake must be less than fifty percent. A share that is too costly may chill the rights of litigants to pursue meritorious claims. However, because the success of this search is somewhat speculative, any cost that fairly can be assigned to Zubulake is appropriate and ensures that UBS's expenses will not be unduly burdensome. A 25 percent assignment to Zubulake meets these goals.[102]

Judge Scheindlin had acknowledged in a previous decision in the same action that "[c]ourts must remember that cost-shifting may effectively end discovery, especially when private parties are engaged in litigation with large corporations. As large companies increasingly move to entirely paper-free environments, the frequent use of cost-shifting will have the effect of crippling discovery in discrimination and retaliation cases. This will both undermine the 'strong public policy favoring resolving disputes on their merits,' and may ultimately deter the filing of potentially meritorious claims."[103]

---

102. Zubulake, 216 F.R.D. at 289 (citations and footnotes omitted).
103. Zubulake I, 217 F.R.D. at 317-18 (citation omitted).

Subsequently, applying the same standards in *Xpedior Creditor Trust v. Credit Suisse First Boston (USA), Inc.*,[104] Judge Scheindlin concluded that the requested cost shifting was inappropriate. She analyzed the *Zubulake* factors as follows: (1) and (2) The tailored request focused on the most likely sources of information and the fact that the records were available only on a decommissioned system, thereby requiring the restoration of the records weighed against cost shifting. (3) The cost of production, although not small ($400,000), was relatively insignificant in comparison to the $7 billion allegedly at stake. This factor weighed against cost shifting. (4) The party seeking the discovery was bankrupt and the producing party had net revenues of $5.7 billion in the previous year. This did not favor cost shifting. (5) Parties were working together to control costs. This factor was neutral. (6) The litigation did not raise public policy issues that might affect cost shifting because it involved a contract dispute between sophisticated commercial entities. (7) The producing party was required to produce the same documents in related litigation; thus both the demanding and the producing parties benefited by the production costs being incurred. Consequently, this was a neutral factor. In balance, Judge Scheindlin concluded that the producing party must bear its own cost of production.

Applying the *Zubulake* seven-part test in *Quinby v. WestLB AG*,[105] the court, as in *Zubulake,* made clear that a party could not create its own financial burden by converting materials it should have foreseen would be discoverable into inaccessible formats, and then expect the discovering party to assume any portion of those additional costs. If, however, the changing of formats was innocent, perhaps performed as a routine matter for e-mails of employees when they leave the company, cost shifting would be considered. In *Quinby,* e-mails of departed employees were deleted and, therefore, available only from backup tapes. As in *Zubulake*, the court also found in favor of cost shifting for a limited class of materials and allocated 30% of those costs to the plaintiff, rather than the 25% shift announced in *Zubulake*.

Given the discretionary and fact-specific nature of cost shifting, as evidenced in these cases, there is no precise formula. As the *Quinby* court weighed the seven *Zubulake* factors, the court's conclusions were:

---

104. No. 02 Civ. 9149 (SAS), 2003 WL 22283835, at *5-*6 (S.D. N.Y. Oct. 2, 2003).

105. 2006 WL 2597900 (S.D. N.Y. Sept. 5, 2006).

(1) the marginal relevance of the documents to the claim of the plaintiff weighed in favor of cost sharing; (2) although there were no other sources for the evidence—a fact that normally weighs against cost shifting—the marginal relevance of the information still favored cost sharing; (3) the high amount in controversy and the substantial benefit that the plaintiff stood to gain weighed in favor of cost shifting; (4) the resources available to each party to absorb the costs of production weighed marginally against cost shifting because the bank was such a profitable enterprise; (5) the fact that the plaintiff insisted on broad discovery that increased the costs of production through an outside vendor (who was more expensive than necessary) marginally weighed in favor of cost sharing; (6) the claim being asserted by the plaintiff, while important, was not unique, thereby making this factor neutral; and (7) the fact that the plaintiff had much more to gain from the discovery undertaking than the defendant (a fact that would seem to always be true) prompted the court to conclude that it weighed in favor of cost shifting. In the end, both the decisions to shift costs and the percentages that each party may be required to bear are highly fact-dependent, relying heavily on the discretion of the trial judge and her perception of fairness.[106]

Where costs are reallocated, at the very minimum, courts should require the parties to keep detailed records of the costs associated with electronic production tasks to be used in final cost allocations.[107]

---

106. *See, e.g.,* Ameriwood Indus., Inc. v. Liberman, No. 4:06CV524-DJS, 2006 WL 3825291 (E.D. Mo. Dec. 27, 2006) (court allowed mirroring of hard drives and shifted costs to requesting party because: (1) the requestor did not object, and (2) the responding party did not mirror drives in the normal course of business); Analog Devices, Inc. v. Michalski, No. 01 CVS 10614, 2006 WL 3287382, at *6 (N.C. Super. Ct. Nov. 1, 2006) ("The uncertainty of the cost combined with the potential probative value of the discovery is too great to deny Defendants' motion. On the other hand, the potential cost of production combined with the great uncertainty as to the contents of the requested documents is too great to require Plaintiff to bear the full burden of production on its own. Neither party's ability to pursue its litigation goals will be impacted by cost-sharing. The Court can retain the ability to assess the costs fully to one side or the other at the end of the case."); Balboa Threadworks, Inc. v. Stucky, No. 05-1157-JTM-DWB, 2006 WL 763668 (D. Kan. Mar. 24, 2006) (court ordered mirroring of defendant's sources of ESI at requesting party's expense and ordered the parties to meet and confer regarding protection of privilege).

107. Black & Veatch Int'l Co. v. Foster Wheeler Energy Corp., 211 F.R.D. 641, 642 (D. Kan. 2002).

2. Another Approach to Cost Allocation

There is an interesting alternative to the balancing test employed by federal courts in the allocation of the ever-increasing costs of discovery. New York law reverses the presumption about who bears those costs. The discovering party typically bears all costs.[108] Although this rule was developed in the world of paper, it has been extended to the world of electronically stored information.[109] This reversal of burden forces restraint on the discovering party and serves as a check on the use of discovery as an adversarial weapon. Courts need only decide whether the material is discoverable. The only cost reallocation performed by New York courts relates to the prevention of parties from incurring unreasonable expenses in complying with discovery demands.[110]

3. Sampling as a Factor in Cost Allocation

The application of the standards in *Rowe* or *Zubulake* should be based on concrete factual information rather than assumptions about what relevant information may be found in which places and at what costs. In many cases such estimates will be exaggerated. Sampling of data— for example, by restoring and searching only a small portion of the data—can be a tool to develop better estimates of both the cost of production and the likelihood that restoration and searching will yield unique and responsive information. Such sampling can facilitate informed decisions about cost reallocation. This will provide evidence about the type of documents that can be retrieved from certain backup tapes, over what span of time, and at what cost.[111]

---

108. Schroeder v. Centro Pariso Tropical, 233 A.D.2d 314 (N.Y. App. Div. 1996); Rubin v. Alamo Rent-a-Car, 190 A.D.2d 661 (N.Y. App. Div. 1993); Lipco Elec. Corp. v. ASG Consulting Corp., 798 N.Y.S.2d 345 (N.Y. 2004).

109. Lipco Elec. Corp., *id.*

110. N.Y. C.P.L.R. 3103(a) gives courts the authority to issue protective orders to prevent parties from incurring unreasonable expenses in complying with discovery demands.

111. AAB Joint Venture, 75 Fed. Cl. at 443-44 ("The Court finds that a reasonable solution is for Defendant to restore a portion of the back-up tapes from time periods specified by Plaintiff. . . . A phased approach will allow the Court to engage in a more meaningful benefit-burden analysis before determining whether to require cost-shifting or cost-sharing. After Defendant restores a portion of the back-up tapes and identifies responsive documents contained therein, Plaintiff will then

At first glance, it might appear that the requesting party would typically be the party advocating sampling. But in practice, we see parties opposing potentially onerous demands for information that is difficult and expensive to access proposing a phased approach to resolving the question of whether information should be restored and searched. The first phase will often be sampling.

4. Cost Allocation in Practice

As discussed above, the law in this area is mixed. Some courts weigh various factors and limit discovery from sources that are difficult to access. Others—sometimes in stark language—hold corporations responsible for technology they choose and the implication of that choice

---

have the opportunity to review responsive material to determine if it contains relevant evidence and if additional restoration of back-up tapes is warranted. The Court believes that restoration of one-fourth of the total back-up tapes should be adequate to determine whether the tapes are likely to possess relevant evidence. Defendant shall bear the cost of restoration of the initial sample of back-up tapes and screening the sample to identify responsive documents.") (citations and footnote omitted); Hagemeyer N. Am., Inc. v. Gateway Data Scis. Corp., 222 F.R.D. 594, 602 (E.D. Wis. 2004) (Gateway was required to restore a sample of backup tapes, after which the parties were required to make additional submissions addressing whether the burden or expense of satisfying the entire request is proportionate to the likely benefit. Then the court would be able to address in a more informed way Gateway's search of all backup tapes.); Zubulake I, 217 F.R.D. at 324 ("Requiring the responding party to restore and produce responsive documents from a small sample of backup tapes will inform the cost-shifting analysis . . . . When based on actual sample, the marginal utility test will not be an exercise in speculation—there will be tangible evidence of what the backup tapes may have to offer. There will also be tangible evidence of the time and cost required to restore the backup tapes, which in turn will inform the second group of cost-shifting factors. Thus by requiring a sample restoration of backup tapes, the entire cost-shifting analysis can be grounded in fact rather than guesswork."); McPeek, 202 F.R.D. at 34-35 ("Given the complicated questions presented [and] the clash of policies . . . I have decided to take small steps and perform, as it were, a test run. Accordingly, I will order DOJ to perform a backup restoration of the e-mails attributable to Diegelman's computer during the period of July 1, 1998 to July 1, 1999. . . . The DOJ will have to carefully document the time and money spent in doing the search. It will then have to search in the restored e-mails for any document responsive to any of plaintiff's requests for production of documents. Upon the completion of this search, the DOJ will then file a comprehensive, sworn certification of the time and money spent and the results of the search. Once it does, I will permit the parties an opportunity to argue why the results and the expense do or do not justify any further search.").

in terms of the ease with which data can be accessed. Thus, the determination of what is "not reasonably accessible" is a judgment call based upon the degree of relevance of the ESI to the litigation, as compared to the cost to produce that data.

At the end of the day, "inaccessible" (in the average case) is likely to be construed as backup tapes that are used for disaster recovery (not archival purposes) and fragmented[112] and deleted data contained on a hard drive. With computer records, all computerized electronic documents in active files will be treated like hard-copy documents retained in accessible file cabinets. Such documents must be produced at the expense of the responding party. Cost reallocation, because of undue expense and burden, arises in the electronic context only when documents are stored off-line in an inaccessible format that requires the data to be restored, defragmented, or reconstructed in order to be usable. In the vast majority of enterprises, this will be in the form of backup tapes or erased, fragmented, or damaged data on current and replaced hard drives.[113] Moreover, reasonable accessibility is likely to be a dynamic concept. As technology evolves and is adapted and applied to the world of electronic discovery, this innovation could render the reasonably inaccessible accessible.

As a practical matter, a proponent of an inaccessibility claim is best served by an early agreement on inaccessibility that is memorialized in writing and endorsed by the court. Such an agreement may be

---

112. SEDONA CONFERENCE GLOSSARY, p. 23 ("In the course of normal computer operations when files are saved, deleted or moved, the files or parts thereof may be broken into pieces, or fragmented, and scattered in various locations on the computer's hard drive or other storage medium, such as removable discs.").

113. In Zubulake I, 217 F.R.D. 309, Judge Scheindlin compared and contrasted undue expense and burden in the world of paper documents. "In the world of paper documents, for example, a document is accessible if it is readily available in a useable format and reasonably indexed. Examples of inaccessible paper documents could include (a) documents in storage in a difficult to reach place; (b) documents converted to microfiche and not easily readable; or (c) documents kept haphazardly, with no indexing system, in quantities that make page-by-page searches impractical. But in the world of electronic data, thanks to search engines, any data that is retained in a machine-readable format is typically accessible." *Id.* at 318. She then explores the range of storage media that will determine whether electronic data is accessible. The subsequent allocation of costs based on this analysis is reported at Zubulake v. UBS Warburg LLC, 216 F.R.D. 280 (S.D.N.Y. 2003).

easier to come by when both parties face a potential burden in accessing ESI. The parties might adopt a simple statement like:

> The parties agree that electronically stored information that is not reasonably accessible under the Federal Rules of Civil Procedure, including, without limitation, information stored for purposes of disaster recovery (e.g., backup tapes), is not subject to preservation, search or production.

Such an agreement is also more likely where the proponent of an inaccessibility claim can show that the information is likely to be duplicative of reasonably accessible sources; that the cost of sampling is expected to be high; and that the source is unlikely to yield information of significance to the case. This showing may require interviews with, and discovery from, knowledgeable personnel.

D. Privilege and the Discovery of Electronically Stored Information

E-discovery increases the amount of information to review before production, and so the risk of inadvertently producing privileged information and/or work product also increases when e-discovery is involved.[114] Apart from the burdens of privilege review, the nature of certain electronic information—for example, a string of e-mails in which sections of the string contain information labeled as privileged—raises challenging questions as to how privilege claims should be asserted.

Amended Rule 26(b)(5)(B) provides procedures for dealing with the inadvertent production of privileged information. Under the amended rule, if a party asserts a claim of privilege after inadvertently producing privileged materials, the receiving party must: (i) "promptly return, sequester, or destroy" the material and any copies of the material; (ii) refrain from using or disclosing the information until the privilege claim is resolved; and (iii) "take reasonable steps" to retrieve any material disclosed to third parties.

While this rule provides procedures for handling inadvertently produced privileged material, it does not provide guidance for determining whether or not producing the material waives the privilege. In fact, the Committee Notes expressly state, "Rule 26(b)(5)(B) does not

---

114. *See* Chapter 3, "Confidentiality and the Attorney-Client Privilege."

address whether the privilege or protection that is asserted after production was waived by the production."[115] In December 2007, a Senate bill was introduced to amend the Federal Rules of Evidence "to address the waiver of the attorney-client privilege and the work product doctrine."[116] The legislation would implement Evidence Rule 502, proposed by the Judicial Conference of the United States and transmitted to Congress.[117] As this chapter went to press, the bill was approved by the Senate Judiciary Committee without amendment. Barring an unexpected hurdle, it should become law in December 2008.

In proposing the rule embodied in the pending bill, the Rules Advisory Committee noted that the current waiver law created significant legal expense, and sometimes "extravagant" privilege claims, where lawyers feared possible privilege waiver.[118] The proposed rule would impose five protections against waiver of privilege or work product:

(1)   Rule 502(a) would limit the scope of a waiver in a federal proceeding only to the information disclosed. A broader waiver of privilege as to related, undisclosed communications would only be found for intentional waivers whose fairness requires consideration of the disclosed and undisclosed material together.[119]

(2)   Where a disclosure "in a federal proceeding or to a federal office or agency . . . is inadvertent," the holder of the claimed privilege or work product protection "took reasonable steps to prevent disclosure," and the holder also acted promptly to rectify the error, "the disclosure does not operate as a waiver in a

---

115. FED. R. CIV. P. 26(b)(5)(b) advisory committee's note.

116. S. 2450, 110th Cong. (2007).

117. Unlike other amendments to procedural rules, rules that create, abolish or modify evidentiary privileges "shall have no force or effect unless approved by Act of Congress." *See* 28 U.S.C. § 2074(b). The time line for consideration of this bill is not known.

118. *See* Letter from Comm. on Rules of Practice and Procedure of the Judicial Conf. of the U.S. to the Senate Judiciary Comm. (Sept. 26, 2007), p.3 (hereafter Letter from Comm. on Rules of Practice and Proc.).

119. FED. R. EVID. 502(a) (proposed). The Rules Committee explained that a subject matter waiver under Rule 502(a) "is reserved for those unusual situations in which fairness requires a further disclosure of related, protected information, in order to prevent a selective and misleading presentation of evidence to the disadvantage of the adversary." *Id.* advisory committee's note.

federal [or state] proceeding."[120] In language particularly relevant to review and production of ESI, the committee explained that "a party that uses advanced analytical software applications and linguistic tools in screening for privilege and work product may be found to have taken 'reasonable steps' to prevent inadvertent disclosure."[121]

(3) Proposed Rule 502(c) addresses uncertainty concerning the interaction between federal and state courts in cases of privilege waiver. Where privileged or protected information is disclosed at the federal level, "state courts must honor Rule 502 in subsequent state proceedings."[122] And admissibility of disclosures in state proceeding in "a subsequent federal proceeding is determined by the law that is most protective against waiver."[123]

(4) Proposed Rule 502(d) recognizes that a federal court "order that the privilege or protection is not waived by disclosure connected with the litigation pending before the court" is binding in other federal or state proceedings.[124] This is intended to ensure that privilege order will be effective.

(5) Proposed Rule 502(e) recognizes that the parties to litigation can enter agreements concerning the effect of disclosure of privileged or protected information, but those agreements are only effective if incorporated into a court order.[125] This reflects existing case law.[126]

Some states are considering or implementing similar provisions. For example, the Arkansas Supreme Court recently approved changes to its Civil Procedure Rule 26(b)(5) and Rule 502(e) of the Arkansas Rules of Evidence to address the risk of inadvertent waiver of privilege. Rule 26(b)(5) provides for a presumption of inadvertence if the

---

120. Fed. R. Evid. 502(b) (proposed).

121. Fed. R. Evid. 502(b) (proposed) advisory committee's note. These tools, however, require specialized technical and scientific knowledge to be defensible. Victor Stanley, Inc. v. Creative Pipe, Inc., 2008 WL 2221841, at *5 (D. Md. May 29, 2008).

122. Letter from Comm. on Rules of Practice and Proc., p. 4.

123. *Id; see also* Fed. R. Evid. 502(c) (proposed).

124. Fed. R. Evid. 502(d) (proposed).

125. Fed. R. Evid. 502(e).

126. *See* Chapter 3, "Confidentiality and the Attorney-Client Privilege."

producing party notifies its opponent within 14 days of discovering the inadvertent production.[127] And Evidence Rule 502(e) provides that inadvertent disclosure "does not operate as a waiver if the disclosing party follows the procedure specified in Rule 26(b)(5) of the Arkansas Rules of Civil Procedure and, in the event of a challenge by a receiving party, the circuit court finds in accordance with Rule 26(b)(5)(D) that there was no waiver."[128]

The Arkansas explanation for these changes shows that courts at the state level are as concerned as their federal counterparts about the risk of inadvertent disclosure in an electronic world. The Supreme Court of Arkansas said:

> Lawyers do their best to avoid mistakes, but they sometimes happen. Discovery has always posed the risk of the inadvertent production of privileged or protected material. The advent of electronic discovery has only increased the risk of inadvertent disclosures. This amendment addresses this risk by creating a procedure to evaluate and address inadvertent disclosures, including disputed ones.[129]

We expect that rules will soon be implemented at the federal and state levels concerning inadvertent production and privilege waiver. Practitioners in this area are advised to make certain they are aware of the most recent developments in the jurisdictions in which they practice.

There is another side to the privilege discussion. Given the larger volumes of information produced in an electronic world, the number of privilege claims has also grown exponentially. While this issue is not unique to the eletronic world, ESI creates new levels of complexity. For example, how should privilege claims be resolved where only part of an e-mail string appears to be privileged? What about a privileged e-mail that contains an attachment? Should the attachment be treated as privileged? A number of courts are beginning to wrestle with these ESI-driven questions.[130]

---

127. Ark. R. Civ. P. 26(b)(5) (2008).

128. Ark. R. Evid. 502(e) (2008).

129. Ark. R. Civ. P. 26, Reporter's Notes (2007 Amendments).

130. *See* Chapter III, "Confidentiality and the Attorney-Client Privilege"; *see also, e.g.,* In re Vioxx Prods. Liab. Litig., 501 F. Supp. 2d 789 (E.D. La. 2007) (discussing these questions in the context of 30,000 documents—representing 500,000 pages—claimed as privileged); Muro v. Target Corp., No. 04 C 6267,

E. Written Discovery

Amended Rules 33(d), 34(b), and 45 address the process and procedures for requesting, and responding to requests for, production of
ESI, interrogatories, and subpoenas.

1. Testing and Sampling

Amended Rule 34(a) clarifies that a party may request an opportunity
to "test" or "sample" ESI, as opposed to merely inspecting or copying
such information. Testing or sampling provides the requesting party
with direct access to the responding party's electronic information systems, raising issues of burden, intrusiveness, confidentiality, and privilege.[131] However, as with any other form of discovery, such issues can
be addressed under the Federal Rules that limit the scope of discovery,
such as Rules 26(b)(2) and 26(c). In addition, the Committee Notes
warn, "[c]ourts should guard against undue intrusiveness resulting from
inspecting or testing such systems."[132] Nonetheless, we anticipate that
testing and sampling will be used with greater frequency in response
to claims that certain ESI is "not reasonably accessible," or that its
production would be unduly burdensome.

2. Form of Production

Rule 34(b) provides procedures for requesting and responding to requests for ESI. A request may "specify the form or forms in which
electronically stored information is to be produced." However, the responding party may object to the requested form. If the responding
party objects to the requested form (or if the request does not specify
the form), the responding party must state the form or forms that it
intends to use. However, the responding party must produce the infor-

---

2007 WL 3254463 (N.D. Ill. Nov. 2, 2007) (a lawyer's privileged communication
forwarding other nonprivileged e-mails can be treated as privileged in its entirety); In re Universal Serv. Fund Tel. Billing Practices Litig., 232 F.R.D. 669 (D.
Kan. 2005) (claims of privilege must be individually made over each e-mail in a
string); United States v. Chevron Texaco, 241 F. Supp. 2d 1065 (N.D. Cal. 2002)
(finding that Chevron could not claim entire string as privileged, but also could
not separate string into separate parts because the communications were not
independent).
   131. *See* Discussion of Sampling, II.C.3.
   132. FED. R. CIV. P. 34(a) advisory committee's note.

mation in the form in which it is "ordinarily maintained" or in a "reasonably usable" form. In other words, like other forms of discovery, the production of ESI is subject to "requirements to protect against deliberate or inadvertent production in ways that raise unnecessary obstacles for the requesting party."[133] Finally, under Amended Rule 34(b), a party need not produce the same ESI in more than one form.

The rule was designed to set out a process for agreeing (or disagreeing) on the production format of ESI. The committee recognized that addressing these issues prior to the actual production could save the parties significant amounts of time and money. The Committee Notes explain, "A party that responds to a discovery request by simply producing electronically stored information in a form of its choice, without identifying that form in advance of the production . . . runs a risk that the requesting party can show that the produced form is not reasonably usable and that it is entitled to production of some or all of the information in an additional form."[134]

This rule raises a very hot issue—the production of data as TIFF/PDF images versus native production. A native document is the document as it sits on the computer system with its associated metadata. In the past, responding parties have generally resisted producing documents in native format for several technical reasons: (i) production numbers cannot be affixed on each page; (ii) confidentiality designations cannot be affixed per page; and (iii) information cannot be redacted. More significantly, native documents are searchable and contain hidden and embedded data that is not available in a TIFF/PDF version of the same document, and there are concerns that a native document could be altered after production.

In hearings on the then-proposed Amended Federal Rules, the Advisory Committee struggled with the format issue. It initially provided that ESI should be produced as "ordinarily maintained," meaning native. There was a great deal of pushback during the hearings due to the technical limitations in producing native documents (for example, difficulties in numbering or redacting native data). For this reason, the committee added the language in a "reasonably usable form," but it did not define that phrase. The only guidance that the committee provided is that "the option to produce in a reasonably usable form does

---

133. FED. R. CIV. P. 34(b) advisory committee's note.
134. *Id.*

not mean that a responding party is free to convert electronically stored information from the form in which it is ordinarily maintained to a different form that makes it more difficult or burdensome for the requesting party to use the information efficiently in the litigation."[135] There was discussion during the hearings that it is not reasonable to take a record that is searchable in its native form and then produce a non-searchable TIFF/PDF image without any metadata. The Committee Notes reflect this discussion by noting, "If the responding party ordinarily maintains the information . . . in a way that makes it searchable by electronic means, the information should not be produced in a form that removes or significantly degrades this feature."[136]

As a result, it is likely that some federal courts will not permit (as they have in the past) a producing party to produce only a non-searchable TIFF/PDF version of ESI. In that case, at least some metadata, and possibly an extracted text-searchable version of the document, may have to be produced. In addition, courts are likely to require that at least some ESI be produced in native form because of the inability to read or manipulate the data in a TIFF/PDF format, even one that is searchable.

Another question tied up in the native versus non-native production debate is whether metadata—or the hidden text, code, and other information associated with a file—must be produced. The production of metadata can impose additional costs (in terms of both the form of production and review). And in many cases, metadata will simply have no relevance to the substantive claims and defenses.[137] As one court observed, based on the Sedona Principles and comments to Rule 34, "emerging standards of electronic discovery appear to articulate a general presumption against the production of metadata, but provide a clear caveat when the producing party is aware or should be reasonably aware that particular metadata is relevant to the dispute."[138]

---

135. *Id.*

136. *Id.*

137. Wyeth v. Impax Labs., Inc., No. 06-222-JJF, 2006 U.S. Dist. LEXIS 79761, at *2 (D. Del. Oct. 26, 2006) ("[m]ost metadata is of limited evidentiary value, and reviewing it can waste litigation resources"); Ky. Speedway, LLC v. NASCAR, Inc., No. 05-138-WOB, 2006 U.S. Dist. LEXIS 92028 (E.D. Ky. Dec. 18, 2006) ("In most cases and for most documents, metadata does not provide relevant information."); *see also* Chapter Two, "Spoliation."

138. *Williams*, 230 F.R.D. at 652.

Of course, there may in fact be instances where metadata *is* relevant to the substance of the case or to authenticating a document. In those circumstances, the requesting party should be prepared to explain its need for metadata. Moreover, the question of whether metadata is subject to production is different than whether it is subject to preservation. The Sedona Working Group observed that "the failure to preserve and produce metadata may deprive the producing party of the opportunity later to contest the authenticity of the document if the metadata is material to that determination."[139]

Format of production will be a significant issue under Amended Rule 34. It is important for litigants to stake out a position as to how they will request and produce ESI. Consistency on this issue is paramount. For example, it will be difficult to argue in one case that a TIFF/PDF production is appropriate because of the difficulty of managing a native production from a litigation perspective, while at the same time producing ESI in native form in another case. In addition, it will be difficult to resist production in a certain format in one case if you are demanding production in that format in another. The responding party is likely to discover the inconsistency in your production format approach and exploit that inconsistency with the court to obtain its preferred production format.

3. Rule 33(d)—Interrogatories

Rule 33(d) provides that a responding party may identify ESI from which an interrogatory answer may be derived in lieu of answering the interrogatory. But before making such a response, the responding party should understand that the other side may use that response as an opportunity to seek direct access to electronic information systems (for example, databases). Thus, there may be a strategic advantage to simply responding to an interrogatory rather than identifying ESI as responsive.

4. Subpoenas

Rule 45 applies the rules and procedures discussed above to the rules and procedures governing subpoenas. Specifically, the amendments to Rule 45 (i) recognize that ESI can be sought by subpoena; (ii) allow for testing and sampling of subpoenaed ESI; (iii) apply to subpoenas the procedures set forth in Rule 34(b) for specifying and objecting to

---

139. SEDONA PRINCIPLES, SECOND EDITION, p. 61.

the form of production of ESI and the procedures set forth in 26(b)(5) for assertion of privilege after production; and (iv) protect the responding party from undue burden or expense and from producing ESI that is "not reasonably accessible."

F. Sanctions and the Spoliation "Safe Harbor"

E-discovery presents unique preservation issues because electronic systems routinely alter and delete data, thereby creating a risk that relevant information will be inadvertently destroyed. Recognizing this unique aspect of electronic evidence, Rule 37(f) was intended to carve out a "safe harbor" for electronic information that is lost as a result of the routine operation of an electronic system, provided that the operation of the system was in good faith. Specifically, Rule 37(f) provides: "Absent exceptional circumstances, a court may not impose sanctions under these rules on a party for failing to provide [ESI] lost as a result of the routine, good-faith operation of an electronic information system."[140]

Factors considered in assessing a party's good-faith operation of its electronic system include:

- whether or not the party took steps to comply with any court order or agreement between the parties concerning preservation of electronic information;
- whether or not the party suspended or modified the routine operation of the electronic system to ensure the preservation of relevant information; and
- for information that is not reasonably accessible, whether the information is likely to be discoverable and not available from reasonably accessible sources.[141]

What this amended rule means and to what extent it will provide producing parties any protection remains to be seen. It will take several years of judicial consideration before a producing party can rely upon Rule 37 as a defense to the destruction of ESI. We do know that Rule 37 applies only to sanctions that are imposed under the Federal Rules and will not provide any protection from sanctions imposed by a court based upon its inherent powers.

---

140. *See* Chapter Two, "Spoliation."
141. Fed. R. Civ. P. 37(f) advisory committee's note.

It is also clear that good faith will be the key to any protection available under Rule 37. In that regard, commentators and the Committee Notes make clear that "good faith" includes taking into consideration the need to implement an appropriate legal hold where appropriate. Thus, the Committee Notes state, "Good faith in the routine operation of an information system may involve a party's intervention to modify or suspend certain features of that routine operation to prevent the loss of information."[142] The Committee Notes later explain that such an intervention or modification is often called a "litigation hold."[143] However, it is not clear what the "routine" operation of an electronic system is. The Sedona Working Group described some types of information that may be lost in routine operation and could fall within the protections of this "safe harbor":

> Computer systems manage data dynamically, meaning that the data is constantly being cached, rewritten, moved and copied. For example, a word-processing program will usually save a backup copy of an open document into a temporary file every few minutes, overwriting the previous backup copy. In this context, imposing an absolute requirement to preserve all information would require shutting down computer systems and making copies of data on each fixed disk drive, as well as other media that are normally used by the system. Costs of litigation would routinely approach or exceed the amount in controversy.[144]

Until the judiciary has the opportunity to develop the meaning of Rule 37's safe harbor, litigants should not count it as a protection from the imposition of sanctions relating to e-discovery. In addition, the risk of sanctions underscores the importance of trying to reach enforceable agreements, memorialized in court orders, concerning the scope of preservation. Resolving these questions early in the case can minimize later claims that the scope of preservation is inadequate. Take, for example, the introductory language of an order in the *Genetically Modified Rice* litigation—a multi-district litigation of significant scope:

---

142. *Id.*
143. *Id.*
144. THE SEDONA PRINCIPLES, SECOND EDITION, pp. 34-35.

The Parties recognize that they must take steps to preserve documents and other materials relevant to the claims and defenses asserted in this Action. The Parties recognize that the law with respect to preservation efforts is not fully developed and also recognize that such preservation efforts can become unduly burdensome and unreasonably costly unless those efforts (a) are targeted to those documents reasonably likely to be relevant or lead to the discovery of relevant evidence related to the issues in this matter; and (b) take account of the unique preservation issues presented by electronically stored information. The Parties agree that these Guidelines define the scope of their preservation obligations for the purposes of this litigation.[145]

In negotiating such an agreement, a party could seek to limit preservation and/or production obligations by:

- Defining the time period of relevant discovery and limiting obligations accordingly;
- Limiting discovery to key individuals, discussed and agreed upon by the parties (and, if appropriate, expressly excluding individuals or categories of individuals from preservation or discovery obligations);
- Agreeing to key words to be used in searches that will generate the universe of documents subject to preservation and discovery; and
- Attempting to limit the number of archives that must be searched when there are multiple archives that likely contain duplicative information.

III. THE PRACTICAL SIDE OF E-DISCOVERY

A. Counsel Must Acquire a Working Understanding of Potentially Relevant ESI

As you begin your journey into the brave new world of e-discovery, heed the sage observation of Yogi Berra: "If you don't know where

---

145. Agreed Order Regarding Preservation of Communications, Documents, Electronic Data, and Other Tangible Items, In re Genetically Modified Rice Litig., No. 4:06 MD-1811-CDP (June 5, 2007).

you're going, you're going to be lost when you get there." To apply the rules of electronic discovery, counsel must acquire a basic understanding of the ESI potentially at issue in a case and how that information can be preserved, collected, and produced. Electronic discovery is not something that is turned on and off as litigation demands it. Newly filed litigation now demands immediate attention to a host of potentially complex technological questions. Without advance preparation, it may not be possible for a defendant—or, for that matter, a plaintiff who has not thought through sources and types of relevant ESI in advance of filing—to answer those questions in the short time from case filing to initial disclosures under Rule 26. For example, the failure to promptly address uncertainty about the scope and duty of a party's obligation to preserve ESI isn't just a matter of procrastination. Instead, the lack of a prompt focus on this question risks the loss of information, which will be difficult to characterize as inadvertent and could result in significant spoliation sanctions down the road.[146]

Many corporations are developing comprehensive electronic discovery response programs. Some such programs are treated as a legal function and may simply involve protocols for handling the preservation and collection of ESI once litigation is filed. Other programs may integrate electronic discovery practice with the corporate records management function. And many corporations are also turning to established and emerging technologies (or law firms or vendors skilled in the use and application of such technologies) that address one or more aspects of the electronic discovery process (e.g., preservation, search, retrieval, processing, review, and production).[147]

Companies that actively prepare for electronic discovery will have strategic advantages over their less-prepared opponents and will ultimately reduce the cost and risk associated with e-discovery. Indeed, where a party lacks a reasonable policy or plan to secure relevant ESI once litigation is filed, it will be much more difficult to defend breakdowns in preservation efforts that occur in litigation. The key is developing a reasonable, defensible, and consistent e-discovery response program. The existence of such a program will:

---

146. *See* Chapter Two, "Spoliation."

147. Each year, Socha Consulting conducts a survey of the market leaders in both e-discovery services and software. These annual surveys are a good starting point to identify the software and service vendors in a rapidly changing market. *See* http://www.sochaconsulting.com/.

- provide a corporation with protection if relevant ESI is inadvertently destroyed or withheld from production;
- reduce the costs associated with e-discovery; and
- ensure consistency in e-discovery across a corporation's cases.

In the early stages of developing an e-discovery response program, it is likely that an organization or its counsel will identify holes in the process, or procedures that create risk for the organization but may be difficult to address quickly. Apart from identifying things that need to be fixed, a comprehensive review of an organization's readiness for electronic discovery may suggest actions that should be taken in the early stages of litigation to provide protection to the company.

The level of sophistication of outside counsel will vary widely, with some knowing relatively little about e-discovery and others knowing a great deal. Accordingly, it is important that clients alert their outside counsel to their internal practices and expectations concerning e-discovery. And outside counsel must ensure that clients' key personnel are involved in discovery responses concerning ESI. While it is unreasonable for clients to expect all of their litigation counsel to be at the cutting edge of e-discovery, clients should and do expect their counsel to (1) have a working understanding of the rules of electronic discovery, and (2) know enough to realize when additional expertise is required.

In building an effective e-discovery response program, an organization should consider the following steps.

1. Build an E-discovery Team

A successful e-discovery response program requires an appropriate team with clear delineation of roles. The typical team should include members from (i) the legal department, (ii) information technology, and (iii) records management. The size of the team will depend on the size of the organization and the amount of litigation the company normally faces. The team's size and its resources also depend upon how much of the e-discovery process (preservation, collection, processing, review, and production) a corporation wants to handle internally and how much it wants to outsource.

2. Understand and Improve Information Technology Architecture

Architecture, in the IT environment, "refers to the hardware, software or combination of hardware and software comprising a computer system or network."[148] Given the need for early attention to e-discovery, the e-discovery team must understand the company's information technology architecture. This will allow the company to design and implement an appropriate e-discovery response program that can address each element of its architecture during the e-discovery process, including the following systems: (i) e-mail, (ii) unstructured data storage (e.g., NT servers),[149] (iii) document management systems, (iv) Web environment, (v) databases, and (vi) applications. In addition, the team must understand any IT or records management policies that apply to technology uses or to sources of ESI.

Litigants and clients—whether seeking or responding to discovery requests or making initial determinations about what to preserve—should inventory potential types and sources of ESI. At the corporate level, this inventory may be part of a broader review and update of records management programs to address the management of ESI from its creation to its ultimate retirement.[150] In compiling this inventory, or in preparing to request or respond to requests for ESI, the practitioner should understand that ESI includes more than electronic records that resemble traditional documents when printed (like word-processing

---

148. SEDONA CONFERENCE GLOSSARY, p. 3.

149. Unstructured Data "[r]efers to masses of data which either do not have a data structure or have a data structure not easily readable by machine. Examples of unstructured data may include audio, video and unstructured text such as the body of an e-mail or word-processing document. Data with some form of structure may also be referred to as unstructured if the structure is not helpful for the processing task at hand." SEDONA CONFERENCE GLOSSARY, p. 52.

150. The reality is that corporations almost universally save far too much ESI that has almost no (or very little) business value. Legal record retention requirements are limited. The Supreme Court's decision in *Arthur Andersen v. United States,* 544 U.S. 696 (2005), confirmed that records may be retired pursuant to a reasonable records management program. To reduce the risks associated with e-discovery, it is important to take reasonable and legitimate steps to reduce your inventories of ESI through updating and modernizing your records management program. Any records retention program would, of course, have to include procedures to stop the retirement of relevant records if and when legal hold obligations attached (e.g., when litigation is reasonably anticipated).

documents and printed e-mail). Types of ESI include electronic mail, word-processing files, electronic calendars, databases, voice mail, spreadsheets, chat logs, media files—in other words, anything created, stored, or accessed using a computer. But ESI also includes data about the data—that is, metadata—which can describe "how, when, and by whom ESI was collected, created, accessed, modified, and how it is formatted."[151] Potential sources of ESI include network servers (central computers containing information or software shared by multiple users),[152] intranets and extranets (secure, Internet-style networks used to convey information either within or outside an organization), desktop and laptop computers, personal digital assistants (like Blackberries, Palm Pilots or Treos), wireless communication devices, and external storage media (zip drives, thumb drives, hard drives, etc.).

This list of potential types and sources of ESI is merely illustrative. Many types and sources may not be relevant in a particular case. But, early in any litigation, parties should identify and preserve those sources of information that may contain information related to the claims or defenses at issue. Where questions about preservation may be controversial, a party should have a frank discussion with its opponents and try to reach agreement on what will (and will not) be preserved. Where agreement is not possible, early involvement of the court may be necessary. The rules anticipate that unresolved issues will be identified to the court prior to, and addressed during, the Rule 16 conference.[153]

3. Develop a Preservation Process

Most of the cases to date in which e-discovery problems have resulted

---

151. THE SEDONA CONFERENCE GLOSSARY: E-DISCOVERY & DIGITAL INFORMATION MANAGEMENT, SECOND EDITION, p. 33 (December 2007).

152. *Id.* at p. 47 (December 2007).

153. Numerous courts—in local rules and standing orders — require the parties to identify unresolved issues, or potential issues, that they expect will arise in connection with the preservation or discovery of electronically stored information. *See, e.g.,* Local Rule 26.1 (E.D. and W.D. Ark.) (outline for Rule 26(f) report must discuss "problems which the parties anticipate may arise in connection with electronic or computer-based discovery" and any "protective orders which should be entered"); Local Civil Rule 16.1 (D. Alaska) (covering amendments through Dec. 1, 2006) (must specify matters about which the parties could not reach agreement; the court's Scheduling and Planning Conference Report template requires the parties to report how "[d]isclosure or discovery of electronically stored information should be handled").

in significant sanctions involve the producing party's failure to preserve ESI.[154] With the discoverability of electronically stored information now firmly established, counsel must take steps to identify and preserve potentially relevant ESI. Federal Rule 26(f), in fact, requires the parties to address the issue of preservation in the context of the meet-and-confer process. This is the first time that the term "preservation" appears in Federal Rules. To fully understand this obligation in the context of preparing for electronic discovery, we need to set forth the basic legal framework and then the practical considerations of preserving ESI.[155]

(a) Legal Framework of Preservation

A duty to preserve records arises only when the party possessing the evidence has "notice" of the records' relevance in the litigation.[156] A party is on notice to preserve records when it receives a formal discovery request calling for the production or identification of the records.[157] In addition, a party is on notice to preserve relevant records upon the filing of a complaint. The most often cited standard regard-

---

154. *See* Chapter Two, "Spoliation"; *see also* Qualcomm Inc. v. Broadcom Corp., No. 05cv1958-B (BLM), 2008 U.S. Dist. LEXIS 911 (S.D. Cal. Jan. 7, 2008); Wingnut Films, Ltd., 2007 U.S. Dist. LEXIS 72953; Morgan Stanley & Co. v. Coleman (Parent) Holdings, Inc., 955 So. 2d 1124 (Fla. Dist. Ct. App. 2007), *review denied,* No. SC07-1251, 2007 WL 4336316 (Fla. Dec. 12, 2007); Zubulake IV, 220 F.R.D. at 216; Philip Morris, 327 F. Supp. 2d 21.

155. This section provides an introduction to the preservation issues that are discussed comprehensively in the next chapter, "Spoliation."

156. *See* Nation-Wide Check Corp. v. Forest Hills Distribs., Inc., 692 F.2d 214, 218 (1st Cir. 1982) (there is an evidentiary rationale for an adverse inference where a "party who has notice that a document is relevant to litigation . . . proceeds to destroy the document"); Zubulake IV, 220 F.R.D. at 216 ("The obligation to preserve evidence arises when the party has notice that the evidence is relevant to litigation or when a party should have known that the evidence may be relevant to future litigation.") (internal quotation marks omitted); United States ex rel. Koch v. Koch Indus., Inc., 197 F.R.D. 463, 482 (N.D. Okla. 1998) (a litigant must "preserve evidence that it knows or should know is relevant to imminent or ongoing litigation"); Turner v. Hudson Transit Lines, Inc., 142 F.R.D. 68, 72-73 (S.D. N.Y. 1991) (party has a duty to preserve evidence when it "has notice of its relevance" to actual or imminent litigation); *see also* ABA Litigation Section, Civil Discovery Standard 10 (The Preservation of Documents. When a lawyer who has been retained to handle a matter learns that litigation is probable or has been commenced, the lawyer should inform the client of its duty to preserve potentially relevant documents and of the possible consequences of failing to do so.).

ing the duty to preserve records upon the filing of a complaint is set forth in *Wm. T. Thompson Co. v. General Nutrition Corp.:*

> While a litigant is under no duty to keep or retain every document in its possession once a complaint is filed, it is under a duty to preserve what it knows, or reasonably should know, is relevant in the action, is reasonably calculated to lead to the discovery of admissible evidence, is reasonably likely to be requested during discovery, and/or is the subject of a pending discovery request.[158]

A difficult question arises as to whether and when a duty to preserve documents arises prior to the filing of a complaint. Under certain circumstances, a litigant has a pre-litigation obligation to preserve relevant records.[159] Unfortunately, there is no bright-line rule or standard for when that duty arises. Various federal and state courts have issued ad hoc opinions on this issue. The central theme of each opinion is that a duty to preserve documents arises when a potential party has "reasonable notice" of both the "contemplation" or "anticipation" of litigation and the existence of potentially relevant documents.[160] Stated another way, a duty arises to preserve records in the context of an "anticipated" or "contemplated" legal matter when there is a concrete and identifiable threat of specific litigation.[161]

---

157. Turner, 142 F.R.D. at 72-73 ("Of course, a party is on notice once it has received a discovery request.").

158. 593 F. Supp. 1443, 1455 (C.D. Cal. 1984).

159. Kronisch v. United States, 150 F.3d 112, 126 (2d Cir. 1998); Bomar Instrument Corp. v. Texas Instruments, Inc., 25 Fed. R. Serv. 2d (Callaghan) 423 (N.D. Ind. 1977) ("some duty must be imposed in [pre-litigation] lest the fact-finding process in our courts be reduced to a mockery").

160. *See* Silvestri v. Gen. Motors Corp., 271 F.3d 583, 591 (4th Cir. 2001); *see also* Fujitsu Ltd. v. Fed. Express Corp., 247 F.3d 423, 436 (2d Cir. 2001); *Kronish*, 150 F.3d at 126 (obligation to preserve can arise "when a party should have known that the evidence may be relevant to future litigation"); Cache La Poudre Feeds, 244 F.R.D. at 620 ("To ensure that the expansive discovery permitted by Rule 26(b)(1) does not become a futile exercise, putative litigants have a duty to preserve documents that may be relevant to pending or imminent litigation."); Capellupo v. FMC Corp., 126 F.R.D. 545, 551 (D. Minn. 1989) (preservation duty arises "when a party is on notice that documents in its possession are relevant to existing or future litigation").

161. *See also* ABA Civil Discovery Standard 10—Comment:

Generally, the existence of such notice will be a fact-specific inquiry. As examples, courts have been willing to find that a party is on notice where it had previously participated in a similar lawsuit involving substantially the same subject matter and issues.[162] Courts have also found a party is on notice to preserve documents where it is specifically threatened with litigation.[163] Notably, a number of courts have held that the threat of litigation must be explicit. For example, letters that suggested negotiated resolution or business settlement of a potential dispute, without specifically threatening litigation, have been held insufficient to trigger a preservation obligation.[164]

Ultimately, the determination of whether or not there is an obligation to preserve potentially relevant records is predicated upon good faith and reasonableness, given the circumstances and available information. The following factors should be considered in making this determination:

> The point at which the duty to preserve materials arises is not the same in all cases. Although the language of Fed. R. Civ. P. 37 and similar state rules suggests that sanctions may be levied only when the document destruction conflicts with a court order (issued in the course of the case), this limitation has not been widely followed. The more common rule is that the duty is triggered when a party becomes aware that litigation has commenced, and arises even earlier where the party has notice that litigation is likely to take place. For the duty to attach before a suit has been filed, however, the litigation must be probable, not merely possible. (Citations omitted.)

162. Telectron, Inc. v. Overhead Door Corp., 116 F.R.D. 107 (S.D. Fla. 1987); Struthers Patent Corp. v. The Nestle Co., 558 F. Supp. 747 (D.N.J. 1981).

163. *See, e.g.*, Capellupo, 126 F.R.D. at 547 (employee had threatened class-action suit to manager, who directed a memo to the general counsel expressing concern of the filing of a class action); *but see* Wal-Mart Stores, Inc. v. Johnson, 106 S.W.3d 718 (Tex. 2003) (holding that, despite an investigation of customer injured by reindeer statues falling from shelf, Wal-Mart did not reasonably anticipate litigation, as customer indicated no serious injuries upon leaving the store).

164. *See, e.g.*, Cache La Poudre Feeds, 244 F.R.D. at 623 (letter that "hinted at the possibility of a non-litigious resolution," and "did not threaten litigation and did not demand that Land O'Lakes preserve potentially relevant materials" did not trigger preservation obligation); *see also* Ind. Mills & Mfg., Inc. v. Dorel Indus., Inc., No. 1:04cv01102-LJM-WTL, 2006 U.S. Dist. LEXIS 45637 (S.D. Ind. Aug. 12, 2006) (letter claimed infringement but did not threaten litigation, instead suggesting a possible resolution); Claude P. Bambuger Int'l, Inc. v. Rohm & Haas Co., No. 96-1041 (WGB) 1997 U.S. Dist. LEXIS 22770 (D. N.J. Aug. 12, 1997) (pre-complaint letter proposed resolution of dispute without threatening litigation).

- type of claimant (e.g., employee, attorney, anonymous);
- nature and specificity of the claim;
- business relationship between the company and the claimant;
- whether the threat is direct, implied or inferred;
- whether the claimant is known to be aggressive or litigious;
- whether a party who could assert a claim is aware of the claim or not;
- likelihood that data relating to a claim will be lost or destroyed; and
- whether the company is involved in other similar claims.[165]

Some parties provide a potential litigation opponent a preservation notice, which may be sent before or after litigation is filed, to trigger or confirm an obligation to preserve potentially relevant information. Such notices may simply be intended to trigger preservation obligations and prevent the recipient from claiming it had no basis to conclude that litigation was reasonably anticipated before a complaint was filed. Others are more expansive and seek to define the scope of document preservation obligations.

Just to be clear, a preservation letter is not necessary to trigger an opponent's duty to preserve, which independently exists when litigation is reasonably anticipated.[166] But a demand for preservation is particularly advisable where the claims involve recent actions or there is a likelihood that relevant electronically stored information will be lost if it is not preserved prior to the filing of litigation. In *Cache La Poudre Feeds*, the court noted that a demand letter sent two years before litigation commenced, and which did not threaten litigation or demand preservation, was insufficient to trigger a duty to preserve ESI. The court explained, "Given the dynamic nature of electronically stored information, prudent counsel would be wise to ensure that a demand letter sent to a putative party also addresses any contemporaneous preservation obligations."[167]

---

165. *See* Sedona Conference Draft Commentary on Legal Holds (April 2007).

166. Cache La Poudre Feeds, 244 F.R.D. at 623 ("The common-law obligation to preserve relevant material is not necessarily dependent upon the tender of a preservation letter.") (internal quotation marks omitted); Thompson v. HUD, 219 F.R.D. 93, 100 (D. Md. 2003) (preservation request not necessarily given "the independent obligation of an adverse party to preserve such information").

167. Cache La Poudre Feeds, 244 F.R.D. at 623.

Such letters are, of course, often helpful with opposing parties, but they may also be critical to the preservation of evidence by parties not named in the complaint. You should send a prompt notice to all third parties who possess information that may be relevant to your litigation. With such notification, you can establish a clear point in time when their obligation to preserve potentially relevant information arose. A potential plaintiff should consider sending notification letters to unnamed parties even before litigation has actually begun so that preservation may begin at the earliest possible time, before any potentially relevant information has been innocently destroyed.[168]

How detailed or lengthy should a preservation letter be? In general, a simple letter is sufficient if it alerts the recipient to the nature of the case and claims and directs the recipient to preserve paper records and electronically stored information (with, perhaps, a non-exclusive list of potential sources of such information). Consider the following sample:

Sample Preservation Letter

We represent [insert name of party] in connection with [pending/anticipated litigation] involving [*describe claims in detail, including time frame, parties, transactions, and other issues to which evidence may be relevant*].

This matter is likely to involve discovery of paper and electronically stored information in your possession, custody or control. Please take immediate steps to preserve all information that relates to the claims described above including, without limitation, [*corporation's name's*] computer system, removable media, any existing backup data, and any other relevant electronic data existing in any format. The electronically stored information subject to this request includes, but is not limited to, electronic mail, any electronic communications, any word-processing documents (e.g., Word, Word Perfect, etc.), any database spreadsheets (e.g., Excel, etc.), any databases (e.g., Access, SQL, etc.), electronic calendars, electronic planners, telephone logs, network logs, and network mainte-

---

168. As explained in Chapter Two, "Spoliation," *infra*, the duty to preserve arises when it becomes apparent that evidence possessed by a company may be relevant to an existing dispute.

> nance logs. [*This list should be tailored as appropriate to a given case.*] Electronically stored information preserved in accordance with this letter should be kept as it is maintained in the ordinary course of business.
>
> I would like to arrange a time in the near future to discuss discovery and discovery of electronically stored information in this case. In the meantime, I know that you will undertake to ensure that the above information is appropriately preserved pending the service of our formal discovery demand. If any portion of this letter, or any term used in it, is unclear, vague, or might be clarified in any way, please contact [*identify contact person with contact information*] for further direction.

Preservation letters are often more involved than this, either because of the nature of the case or because the sender is attempting to impose onerous obligations on the recipient. For example, preservation letters could discuss a need to preserve in specific formats (e.g., native) or a need to preserve metadata or backup tapes (if so, preferably targeted to backup tapes likely to hold data relevant to the case that is not available from other sources). A preservation letter could, in cases involving a recently or soon-to-be-terminated employee, demand preservation of the employee's computer.

If you are making a preservation request, keep the following in mind:

- Your requests may be directed back at you. So think twice before demanding that your opponent do things you are unwilling or unable to do.
- Your request should be targeted. A blunderbuss preservation request that appears designed to impose e-discovery costs that are disproportionate (either to the facts of the case or to the relief requested) is likely to be treated by a court as unreasonable (and could trigger a motion for protection).
- Technical terms—to the extent they are not obvious—should be defined.

If you are the recipient of a preservation letter, how should you respond? In many cases, the letter will set forth obligations that go beyond your legal preservation obligations or are otherwise overly burdensome. In such cases, you should promptly respond, object to taking requested actions that exceed your legal obligations, identify actions that you believe are unduly burdensome, and offer to meet and confer to discuss these problems. In some cases, it may be necessary to seek protection from the court, either through the Rule 16 conference or by separate motion.

It may also be that you receive a preservation demand from an erstwhile opponent—or, possibly, a party seeking a quick settlement of questionable claims—that is heavy on burden but spare on detail. You could use the demand as an opportunity to request additional information about the claims or defenses or your opponent's views as to the likely topics for discovery, or the key words that could be used to search for and define the universe of responsive documents.[169]

Finally, we have seen clients receive onerous preservation demands before any litigation is filed which contain little or no detail about the anticipated claims (let alone sufficient detail to allow the client to make good-faith decisions about what should be preserved). If you are the recipient of such a letter, your prompt response should: (1) state that the sender has not supplied sufficient information to make good-faith decisions about whether, and what, information should be preserved; (2) object that the demand is overly burdensome and seeks to impose obligations beyond those required by law (citing specific examples); and (3) clearly indicate where you do not intend to preserve information as specified in the letter.

(b) *The Work Product Tension*

A party must suspend its normal document retention policy and implement a litigation hold to ensure the preservation of relevant documents if the party reasonably anticipates litigation.[170] As a result, the duty to preserve evidence—to implement a hold—could arise prior to litigation where the parties have received sufficient notification, formal or otherwise, that litigation is reasonably foreseeable.[171] Thorny

---

169. If you settle on the use of key words to identify and define the universe of responsive documents, that agreement should be memorialized in writing and endorsed by the court in a case management order specifying the agreed limitation on preservation obligations.

170. *See, e.g.,* Thompson, 219 F.R.D. at 100.

171. Silvestri, 271 F.3d at 591; *see also* Scott v. IBM Corp., 196 F.R.D. 233, 249 (D.N.J. 2000) ("While a litigant is under no duty [to] keep or retain every document in its possession, even in advance of litigation it is under a duty to preserve what it

questions involving the duty to preserve can arise for parties who routinely label internal documents or communications "Attorney Work Product," which only applies to documents "prepared in anticipation of litigation" and typically allows discovery of such materials only upon a showing of substantial need.[172]

As the courts look to objective evidence and the actions of the parties in determining whether there was an anticipation of litigation for application of the work product doctrine, so do the courts look to evidence and actions suggesting an anticipation of litigation in determining the timing of the parties' litigation hold obligations.[173]

Although the phrase "anticipation of litigation" is common to the standards for applying the work product doctrine and determining the timing of a party's litigation hold obligations, only a few cases have made the connection.[174] In *Rambus, Inc. v. Infineon Technologies AG,* the defendant moved to compel the plaintiff to produce documents pertaining to its document retention policy.[175] Although the plaintiff

---

knows, or reasonably should know, will likely be requested in reasonably foreseeable litigation.").

172. FED. R. CIV. P. 26(b)(3).

173. Scott, 196 F.R.D. at 249.

174. Rambus, Inc. v. Infineon Techs. AG, 220 F.R.D. 264, 280-81 (E.D. Va. 2004); AAB Joint Venture, 75 Fed. Cl. at 445 (In analyzing whether actions constituted work product or simply regular business activities, the court started by looking at the date when "[d]efendant could reasonably have anticipated litigation and was, therefore, obligated to preserve documents for discovery purposes. It would be incongruous for the Court to find that Defendant had a duty to preserve documents for discovery because of impending litigation, yet could not assert the work product doctrine to protect documents prepared in anticipation of that litigation."); Samsung Elecs. Co. v. Rambus Inc., 439 F. Supp. 2d 524, 567 (E.D. Va. 2006) ("The Court has not relied here on the fact that Rambus labeled a number of the relevant business documents as work product in determining that Rambus anticipated litigation with DRAM manufacturers when it destroyed relevant documents, but it is nonetheless a permissible inference."). *But see* Hynix Semiconductor Inc. v. Rambus, Inc., No. C-00-20905 RMW, 2006 U.S. Dist. LEXIS 30690, at *66-*67 (N.D. Cal. Jan. 4, 2006) ("The fact that Rambus has previously claimed work product protection for some documents dated prior to late 1999 does not dictate a finding that Rambus was anticipating litigation at the time the documents were created. A reference to 'work product' on a privilege log does not support the conclusion that litigation was anticipated because the log was prepared by California lawyers. California law differs from federal law in that it protects a lawyer's work product prepared 'in a nonlitigation capacity.' Thus, 'the protection afforded by the privi-

claimed the documents were subject to both the attorney-client privilege and the attorney work product doctrine, the defendant argued that there was "ample evidence . . . to support a finding that [the plaintiff] implemented a document destruction program in order to destroy documents that might have proved unfavorable in litigation . . . and did so at a time when it anticipated patent litigation. . . ."[176]

While analyzing the objective facts to determine the timing of the plaintiff's litigation hold obligation, the *Rambus* court suggested a link between work product designations and the litigation hold timing. The court began its examination by analyzing the timing and circumstances surrounding the plaintiff's implementation of its document retention program.[177] The court then observed that the timing of the plaintiff's work product claims (as described in its privilege log) suggested that the plaintiff anticipated litigation while it simultaneously developed and implemented its document retention program:

> [S]ubstantive entries on [the plaintiff's] privilege log are relevant to this topic. For instance, entry number 315 on [the plaintiff's] privilege log documents an entry reflecting [ ] legal advice pertaining to the legal strategy for enforcement of [the plaintiff's] patents. [The plaintiff] has claimed both the attorney-client and work product privileges for this document. The work product privilege, however, by definition does not apply unless the document was created in "anticipation of litigation." Notably, the document reflected at entry number 315 was created in March 1998, the same time frame in which [the plaintiff] was developing its document retention program. Thus, if, as [the plaintiff] claims, the document truly was created in an-

---

lege [under California law] is not limited to writings created by a lawyer in anticipation of a lawsuit. It applies as well to writings prepared by an attorney while acting in a nonlitigation capacity.'") (citation omitted).

175. 220 F.R.D. at 280-81.

176. *Id.* at 280. The defendant argued that the crime/fraud exception to the attorney-client privilege and the work product doctrine (*i.e.,* "otherwise privileged communications or work product made for, or in furtherance of, the purpose of committing a crime or fraud will not be privileged or protected"), *id.,* applied to "pierce" the plaintiff's privilege claims. The Rambus, Inc. court ultimately found that the crime/fraud exception applied to materials or communications created to plan or implement spoliation. *Id.* at 283.

177. *Id.* at 285-88.

ticipation of litigation, that fact would also tend to support a finding of spoliation.[178]

The *Rambus* court's subsequent grant of defendant's motion to compel ultimately relied on the results of an in camera review rather than plaintiff's work product designations.[179]

The primary risk is that a party receiving a privilege log might identify work product claims made years before litigation was filed and use it as a reason to make an issue of the timing of legal hold. This is an area where the law will continue to develop. For example, a work product claim might relate to anticipation of *different* litigation than the case requiring document preservation. Still, it is worth understanding and considering that a court could equate "anticipation of litigation" in the contexts of work product and the trigger for a litigation hold. In the worst-case scenario, this could lead to sanctions, including a possible spoliation inference instruction. Parties can reduce this risk by carefully distinguishing between work product and privilege claims. Privileged attorney-client communications do not require anticipation of litigation.[180] Where a communication is privileged, a work product claim may create additional risk without much in the way of additional protection.

4. Developing a Retention Plan

Many companies today are not equipped to satisfy their obligations to

---

178. *Id.* at 287 n.31 (citation omitted).

179. Rambus, Inc. v. Infineon Techs. AG, 222 F.R.D. 280, 296-99 (E.D. Va. 2004).

180. In many cases, the work product designation is routinely applied to communications between attorney and client, usually along with a claim that materials are also privileged attorney-client communications. But attorney-client privilege and the work product doctrine serve different purposes:

> While the attorney-client privilege "is intended to encourage clients to be forthcoming and candid with their attorneys so that the attorney is sufficiently well-informed to provide sound legal advice," the work-product doctrine "is intended to preserve a zone of privacy in which a lawyer can prepare and develop legal theories and strategy 'with an eye toward litigation,' free from unnecessary intrusion from his adversaries." "At its core, the work-product doctrine shelters the mental processes of the attorney, providing a privileged area within which he can analyze and prepare his client's case."

preserve electronically stored information. The easiest way to reduce the risk of sanctions is to design, implement, and enforce a preservation plan to ensure the appropriate preservation of records in the context of actual, or reasonably anticipated, litigation. Such a plan should be put in place without waiting for litigation. But at a minimum, once litigation is filed, a comprehensive document preservation plan must be put in place.[181] Since most litigation is unique, the plan will have to be adapted to the facts of the particular case, taking into account that the ideal preservation plan will:

- Identify the relevant records and the likely sources of those records, including the "key players" or "custodians" in the organization who may have knowledge concerning the facts, claims or defenses.
- Identify data that is "not reasonably accessible" and whether that data will be preserved in the first instance.
- Identify facts relating to burden to the extent you determine it is not possible or practical to preserve certain data.
- Determine reasonable methods of document preservation.
- Map out the preservation process and the parties responsible for implementing the process.
- Provide for the dissemination and tracking of a substantive preservation notice that: (i) summarizes the key issues in the case; (ii) informs the recipient of the duty to preserve both

---

181. *See, e.g.,* Danis v. USN Commc'ns, Inc., 53 Fed. R. Serv. 3d (Callaghan) 828 (N.D. Ill. 2000) ("Given notice and understanding of the obligations to preserve all discoverable hard copy and electronic data, one would expect that USN's next step would have been to implement a comprehensive written document preservation plan with specific criteria for finding and securing . . . relevant evidence for the litigation."). In re Triton Energy Ltd., No. 5:98CV256, 2002 U.S. Dist. LEXIS 4326, at *18-*19 (E.D. Tex. Mar. 7, 2002) (even though defendant "preserved and produced" a "large quantity of documents" relating to implement a document preservation plan resulted in a failure to preserve and produce responsive documents held by outside officers and directors); In re Kmart Corp., 371 B.R. 823, 855 (Bankr. N.D. Ill. 2007) (Court criticized "dilating and disjointed disclosure and production efforts" and required a "systematic search of all documents on" two shared corporate drives, each containing millions of files); In re Prudential Ins. Co. of Am. Sales Practices Litig., 169 F.R.D. 598, 615 (D.N.J. 1997) ("When the Sept. 15, 1995 Court Order to preserve documents was entered, it became the obligation of senior management to initiate a comprehensive document preservation plan and distribute it to all employees").

paper and electronic records that relate to those issues; and (iii) provides clear instructions concerning how the recipient can comply with the preservation obligation (either herself or by contacting a designated individual).

- Provide for prompt human follow-up with key players to ensure compliance with preservation obligations.
- Provide for periodic updating of preservation notices.
- Set forth procedures for lifting the preservation notice when circumstances no longer require preservation.

5. Issuing Instructions to Custodians to Preserve Potentially Relevant Records

The obligation to retain discoverable materials is an affirmative one; it requires that the agency or corporate officers having notice of discovery obligations communicate those obligations to employees in possession of discoverable materials.[182] Accordingly, outside counsel and in-house counsel must take reasonable steps to advise potential custodians of the obligations to preserve potentially relevant records. Today, this is most often done with a notice or "legal hold order" direct to specific custodians.[183] While there are no precise legal requirements as to the specific contents that must be contained in a legal hold order, we believe a reasonable notice will (i) identify the general nature of the litigation; (ii) set forth the obligation to preserve potentially relevant records; (iii) provide a general a description of those records to be preserved; and (iv) furnish the name of a contact person within to answer any questions regarding the legal hold order.

Once a legal hold *notice* is issued, we suggest that the "key players" receiving the notice be contacted to answer any questions they may have regarding the notice.[184] Key players are those people likely to be central to the issues in the litigation or likely to be in possession, custody or control of the key documents in the litigation.

---

182. National Ass'n of Radiation Survivors v. Turnage, 115 F.R.D. 543, 557-58 (N.D. Cal. 1987).

183. Zubulake IV, 220 F.R.D. at 218 ("Once a party reasonably anticipates litigation, it must suspend its routine document retention/destruction policy and put in place a 'litigation hold'").

184. *See* Zubulake V, 229 F.R.D. 422.

The failure to put such a program in place can result in much more costly and invasive procedures designed to recover data that was not preserved in the first instance.[185] Such failures could also result in monetary or other sanctions that may affect the outcome of litigation (e.g., an adverse inference that deleted information would be harmful to the deleting party).[186]

6. Design and Implement E-discovery Guidelines

Process and consistency are paramount in dealing with e-discovery. The best way to ensure a defensible and cost-efficient process that can be applied across all of a company's cases is to have a set of written guidelines that address each step in the ESI process, including:

- A checklist of items to be addressed in the Rule 26(f) conference, like preservation issues, discovery cutoff dates, and scope
  of ESI at issue, including backup tapes and databases.
- Model language to be used for Rule 26 disclosures, document
  requests/responses, and interrogatories/answers.
- Collection protocols, including (i) a collection plan meeting,
  (ii) a process for conducting manual versus automated collec-
  tions, (iii) training the collection staff, and (iv) a template for
  conducting interviews with document custodians.
- Production protocols that outline the standard format in which
  the corporation will produce ESI, including (i) whether and
  which metadata will be produced, (ii) under what circumstances
  native documents will be produced, and (iii) how ESI will be
  labeled, including production numbers and confidentiality
  designations.
- A plan for reviewing electronic data should include (i) establishing a coding or annotation protocol, (ii) training for the

---

185. *See, e.g.,* In re Triton Energy Ltd., 2002 U.S. Dist. LEXIS 4326, at *19-*20 (Given concerns about document preservation once litigation was filed, the court appointed a special master and a "forensic computer specialist to retrieve infor-mation from Triton's computer storage systems (including servers and hard drives) and those of all other former officers and directors. . . . The computer specialist will conduct non-destructive testing of these systems to determine what docu-ments and e-mails, if any, have been deleted.").

186. *See* Chapter Two, "Spoliation."

reviewers, (iii) procedures for handling privileged information, trade secrets, and redactions; and (iv) a system for quality control.

7. Identify a Preferred Vendor Network

E-discovery vendors may be necessary to assist in collecting, processing, hosting, review, and production. Not all vendors are created equal.
Quality, performance, and cost vary widely among vendors. Corporations should identify and forge relationships with key vendors that are
retained in the e-discovery process. Contracts should be negotiated
with key vendors. Outside counsel should be required to use preferred
vendors to ensure that their client is obtaining the lowest prices with a
dependable vendor. But note that a vendor's performance must be
monitored. One recent example shows that even well-known law firms
using well-known vendors can experience significant and costly breakdowns in the process.[187] Given the relative newness and complexity
of this area, such breakdowns are not only possible, but probable.

8. Consider Acquiring or Licensing Appropriate Tools

A wide variety of tools are available to assist corporations in the e-
discovery process, from archivers to assist in preservation to automated search and retrieval technologies, to litigation support tools for
managing and reviewing the production. These tools are expensive,
and their performances vary widely. Careful consideration should be
given to whether these tools should be licensed or acquired to assist in
controlling the costs associated with e-discovery.

---

187. *See, e.g.,* Anthony Lin, *Sullivan & Cromwell Suit Against Vendor High-
lights Problems With E-discovery*, N.Y. L. J. (Jan. 7, 2008).

Spoliation

2

I.   Overview 80

II.   The Basics 86

       A. When Does the Duty to Preserve Arise? 89

       B. Does the Client's Obligation to Preserve
          Create Duties for Legal Counsel? 101

       C. What Must Be Retained and Preserved? 106

          1. Privileged Materials 116

          2. Duration of the Duty to Preserve 118

       D. Prejudice to Discovering Party 120

III.   Is Bad Faith Required? 133

IV.   Consequences of Spoliation 153

       A. Spoliation Is an Implied Admission by
          Conduct 168

       B. Logical Inference Instructions 172

       C. The Strange Spoliation Presumption 172

       D. Authority for Penalizing Destruction 176

V.   Burden of Persuasion 179

VI.   Choice of Law Question 180

VII.   Proving the Claim of Spoliation—You're Not
       Bound By the Rules of Evidence 180

VIII. Evidence of Spoliation—Evidence of One's Conduct to
Prove the Truth of Its Implied Message—Is It
Hearsay? 181

IX.   Spoliation and the Attorney-Client Privilege 182

X.   Standard of Appellate Review 183

XI.   Computers and the Internet Expand Every Possibility 183

A. Do Not Delete Records or Destroy Equipment 186

B. Save the Hard Drives 188

C. Don't Forget Personal Digital Assistants and Jump
Drives 188

D. Informal Encouragement to Others to Preserve
Data 189

I.   OVERVIEW

Spoliation is an act of obstruction that jeopardizes the search for truth. It
includes a number of activities ranging from destruction to subterfuge,
making false statements, fabricating evidence, hiding assets, attempting
to influence jurors improperly, bribing witnesses, and destroying or altering relevant evidence.[1] The concept of penalties for spoliation originated
in the common law doctrine *"contra spoliatorem omnia praesumuntur,"*

---

1. *See, e.g.,* Monsanto Co. v. Ralph, 382 F.3d 1374, 1378 (Fed. Cir. 2004)
(infringer gave perjured statements and destroyed evidence); Hanke v. Cal. Auto
Dealer's Exchange, Inc., 2004 WL 1435944, at *5 (Cal. App. June 28, 2004) (jury
instruction on willful destruction of evidence supported by fact that videotape of
event was reused in violation of company policy when litigation could reasonably have been anticipated); Am. Multi-Cinema, Inc. v. Walker, 2004 WL 2340691,
at *3 (Ga. App. Oct. 19, 2004) (not spoliation for second report to be filed when
there is "no evidence that the first draft was destroyed or altered"); Lipschitz v.
Stein, 781 N.Y.S.2d 773, 777 (N.Y. Sup. Ct. App. Div. 2004) (patient log was
altered); Bronson v. Umphries, 138 S.W.3d 844, 854 (Tenn. Ct. App. 2003) ("The
doctrine of spoliation of evidence permits a court to draw a negative against a
party that has intentionally, and for improper purpose, destroyed, mutilated, lost,
altered, or concealed evidence.").

which means "all things are presumed against the destroyer."[2] Spoliators should not benefit from their wrongdoing.

While the concerns underlying the doctrine of spoliation are the same whether they involve conventional documentary evidence or computer-generated evidence, courts and commentators recognize that computers are distinctive, given "the routine alteration and deletion of information that attends ordinary use."[3] And while paper-based spoliation principles and case law may be instructive on many of the issues arising with electronically stored information (ESI), the reader is advised to consider recent changes to federal and state procedural rules that govern sanctions for the destruction of ESI,[4] along with a developing body of case law focused on unique questions of spoliation that arise in the electronic environment (discussed more fully below).

The act of destroying evidence can be an implied admission by conduct that the actor's legal position is so weak that he cannot succeed without eliminating evidence.[5] The injured party should be permitted to prove this and argue it to the jury as a logical inference from the destruction, regardless of what sanctions the court elects to impose.[6] In addition to the

---

2. Armory v. Delamirie, 93 Eng. Rep. 664 (K.B. 1722). In Armory, an individual took a ring that he found to a jeweler for appraisal. The jeweler later returned the ring without the gem that it originally contained. At the subsequent trial for the lost jewel, the judge instructed the jury to "presume the strongest" against the jeweler "and make the value of the best jewels the measure of . . . damages." As a result, significant damages were awarded. For a more thorough examination of the history of courts' responses to the destruction of evidence, *see* J. GORELICK, S. MARZEN & L. SOLUM, DESTRUCTION OF EVIDENCE §§ 1.2-1.5 (Wiley 1989).

3. FED. R. CIV. P. 37, Advisory Committee Notes.

4. *See, e.g.,* FED. R. CIV. P. 37(f), which provides that "[a]bsent exceptional circumstances, a court may not impose sanctions under these rules on a party for failing to provide electronically stored information lost as a result of the routine, good-faith operation of an electronic information system."

5. State v. Hartsfield, 2004 WL 1336238, at *4 (Iowa June 16, 2004) ("This inference is based on the rationale that a party's destruction of evidence is 'an admission by conduct of the weakness [of that party's] case.'").

6. United States v. Bolzer, 367 F.3d 1032, 1037 (8th Cir. 2004) (Even in a criminal case it is not inappropriate for government to argue permissible inferences that can be drawn from evidence produced. In light of his subsequent confession, the government certainly could argue the inference that he wiped down the weapon in an effort to conceal his guilt.); Parkinson v. Guidant Corp., 315 F. Supp. 2d 760, 762 (W.D. Pa. 2004) ("[E]vidence that one party destroyed evidence relevant to the

evidentiary value of acts of spoliation, the court can impose sanctions for those destructive acts.

If the court is asked to intercede and finds spoliation, it can impose a number of sanctions. First, if the act is seen as one of discovery abuse, the presiding judge can impose penalties under Federal Rule of Civil Procedure (Fed. R. Civ. P.) 37 (ranging from imposing costs to entering summary judgment for the aggrieved party).[7] Second, independent of the discovery process, the court has inherent powers to protect the integrity of the judicial process and to ensure fairness. This inherent power permits the court to sanction spoliation that occurs prior to court orders or to discovery.[8] Pursuant to this authority, courts have: recognized a logical inference about which the jury is instructed; recognized a formal presumption that the evidence would have been negative to the destroying party; excluded evidence offered by the spoliator; and imposed a variety of monetary sanctions.[9] Because the power of courts to impose spoliation sanctions on non-parties is limited,[10] some states have recognized a cause of action against those individuals.[11]

---

dispute being litigated is admissible and such evidence permits a spoliation inference that the destroyed evidence would have been unfavorable to the position of the offending party."); Scott v. IBM Corp., 196 F.R.D. 233, 248 (D. N.J. 2000) (Although sanctions were denied because the destruction was the result of negligence rather than willfulness, the court noted that a negative inference is still appropriate.); United States ex rel. Koch v. Koch Indus., Inc., 197 F.R.D. 463, 486 (N.D. Okla. 1998) (Court explained that party whose evidence was destroyed is "not precluded from informing the jury as to which relevant computer tapes were destroyed and the impact that the destruction has had" on his case.).

7. FED. R. CIV. P. 37(b) (giving court broad discretion to impose delineated sanctions or any other sanction it deems just); Metropolitan Opera Ass'n., Inc. v. Local 100, 212 F.R.D. 178 (S.D.N.Y. 2003) (Court found liability on part of defendant and imposed plaintiff's attorney's fees as sanction.).

8. Trial courts have the inherent power to sanction parties for the destruction of evidence as well as the improper obtaining of evidence. Gumbel v. Pitkin, 124 U.S. 131 (1988) (court has the inherent authority to sanction a party who attempts to introduce improperly obtained evidence); Fayemi v. Hambrecht & Quist, Inc., 174 F.R.D. 319 (S.D.N.Y. 1997).

9. See Austin v. City and County of Denver, 2006 U.S. Dist. LEXIS 47451 (D. Colo. July 13, 2006) (discussing when monetary sanctions are appropriate).

10. McGuire v. Sigma Coatings, Inc., 48 F.3d 902, 907 (5th Cir. 1995) (sanctioning of third party was reversed because court lacked personal jurisdiction).

11. See note 205, infra and accompanying text (listing those states in which spoliation gives rise to an independent tort action).

This inherent power to sanction for conduct that impedes the fair resolution of disputes has led one court to endorse an adverse inference when e-mail communications have not been destroyed, but their production has been inexcusably delayed until the beginning of trial, thereby denying the demanding party a fair opportunity to use them in trial preparation.[12]

If the destruction of relevant electronic databases is feared, a court can issue an injunction[13] and order the potentially offending party to allow a court-appointed expert to copy the data, recover deleted files, and perform searches under guidelines that protect both the discovering and producing parties. Under the express provisions of Fed. R. Civ. P. 16(b)(5) and the court's inherent case management powers, it may also issue an order to preserve evidence.[14]

---

12. Residential Funding Corp. v. DeGeorge Fin. Corp., 306 F.3d 99, 106-07 (2d Cir. 2002). *See* Costello v. City of Brigatine, 2001 U.S. Dist. LEXIS 8687 at *76-77 (D. N.J. 2001) ("When the contents of a document are relevant to an issue in the case, the spoliation inference is nothing more than the common-sense observation that a party who hides relevant evidence until the eve of trial did so out of a well-founded fear that the contents would harm him."). To justify this inference, the party seeking the instruction must show "(1) that the party having control over the evidence had an obligation to timely produce it; (2) that the party that failed to timely produce the evidence had a 'culpable state of mind'; and (3) that the missing evidence is 'relevant' to the party's claim or defense such that a reasonable trier of fact could find that it would support that claim or defense." *See* Brewer v. Quaker State Oil Refining Corp., 72 F.3d 326, 334 (3d Cir. 1995) ("No favorable inference arises when the circumstances indicate that the document or article in question has been lost or accidentally destroyed, or where the failure to produce it is otherwise properly accounted for."); Parkinson v. Guidant Corp., 315 F. Supp. 2d 760, 763 (W.D. Pa. 2004) ("For a spoliation inference to arise, it is essential both that the evidence in question be within the party's control and that there has been an actual suppression or withholding of the evidence.").

13. Injunctions will only be issued when there is an imminent threat that evidence will be lost or destroyed. A claimed threat, "unaccompanied by any showing of reasonable grounds for believing that the evidence in question is imperilled, is insufficient." Matos v. Clinton School Dist., 367 F.3d 68, 74 (1st Cir. 2004) ("Absent something that indicates a need for immediate relief, a plaintiff's request for a preliminary injunction ordinarily ought to be rejected.").

14. For a discussion of when courts should grant preservation orders, *see* Treppel v. Biovail Corp., 233 F.R.D. 363, 370-71 (S.D.N.Y. 2006) (because preservation orders are burdensome and expensive, they should not be issued in the absence of a clear demonstrated need); Capricorn Power Co., Inc. v. Siemens Westinghouse Power Corp., 220 F.R.D. 429, 433-34 (W.D. Pa. 2004) ("While remaining consistent with the Federal Rules of Civil Procedure, but still addressing the need to perform

There is disagreement about the standard that must be met by the party seeking a preservation order, although some guidance appears in the recent amendments to the Federal Rules of Civil Procedure and the Advisory Committee Notes accompanying those amendments. Some courts require that the standard for obtaining an injunction must be met.[15] This standard requires that the movant show "irreparable injury and . . . either (a) a likelihood of success on the merits or (b) sufficiently serious questions going to the merits and a balance of hardships tipping decidedly in the movant's favor.[16] Other courts apply a balancing test that focuses on the irreparable nature of the injury that may result without the order and the burdens it will place on the party ordered to preserve.[17] Both tests are,

---

the judicial duty to oversee and decide discovery disputes, this Court believes that a balancing test which considers the following three factors should be used when deciding a motion to preserve documents, things and land: 1) the level of concern the court has for the continuing existence and maintenance of the integrity of the evidence in question in the absence of an order directing preservation of the evidence; 2) any irreparable harm likely to result to the party seeking the preservation of evidence absent an order directing preservation; and 3) the capability of an individual, entity, or party to maintain the evidence sought to be preserved, not only as to the evidence's original form, condition or contents, but also the physical, spacial and financial burdens created by ordering evidence preservation."); Pueblo of Laguna v. United States, Fed. Cl. 133, 137-38 (2004) (Because this power is to be exercised with restraint, it is required "that the one seeking a preservation order demonstrate that it is necessary and not unduly burdensome. . . . To meet the first prong of this test, the proponent ordinarily must show that absent a court order, there is significant risk that relevant evidence will be lost or destroyed—a burden often met by demonstrating that the opposing party has lost or destroyed evidence in the past or has inadequate retention procedures in place. . . . More than that, the proponent must show that the particular steps to be adopted will be effective, but not overbroad—the court will neither lightly exercise its inherent power to protect evidence nor indulge in an exercise of futility."); African-American Slave Descendants' Litig., 2003 WL 24085346, at *1-2 (N.D. Ill. July 14, 2003).

15. *See, e.g.,* Madden v. Wyeth, 2003 WL 21443404, at *1 (N.D. Tex. April 16, 2003) and Pepsi-Cola Bottling Co. of Olean v. Cargill, Inc., 1995 WL 783610, at *3-4 (D. Minn. Oct. 20, 1995).

16. Green Party of N.Y. State v. N.Y. State Bd. of Elections, 389 F.3d 411, 418 (2d Cir. 2004).

17. Capricorn Power Co. v. Seimens Westinghouse Power Corp., 220 F.R.D. 429, 433 (W.D. Pa. 2004) (Under this test the court considers "1) the level of concern that the court has for the continuing existence and maintenance of the integrity of the evidence in question in the absence of an order directing preserva-

however, inadequate at the pretrial stage, because they require an assessment of evidence that has not yet been revealed in the context of a case that has not yet been fully developed.

For information generated, stored, and managed using computers, preservation of relevant evidence can be difficult and costly. It requires balancing "between the competing needs to preserve relevant evidence and to continue routine operations critical to ongoing activities."[18] Failure to strike an appropriate balance by, for example, issuing a blanket preservation order requiring a party to cease or alter all routine computer operations "could paralyze the party's activities."[19] Based on these unique aspects of the systems that create and manage electronically stored information, the Federal Rules of Civil Procedure and many state equivalents require the parties "to discuss any issues relating to preserving discoverable information" and to develop a proposed discovery plan incorporating, among other things, the parties' views and proposals on "any issues relating to disclosure of discovery of electronically stored information."[20]

It is clearly preferred that the parties work out preservation issues based on a meaningful and candid discussion of possible preservation problems. Preparation for such a discussion, which must occur early in litigation, will take time. If the parties cannot agree, either can then seek a preservation order from the court. But "[t]he requirement that the parties discuss preservation does not imply that court should routinely enter preservation orders. A preservation order entered over objection should be narrowly tailored. Ex parte preservation orders should issue only in exceptional circumstances."[21]

This chapter first explores the elements of spoliation and how courts have responded differently to the requirements of intent and bad faith. Because of the ancient nature of this doctrine and the relatively new state of electronic evidence, the body of case law relied upon will be predominantly non-electronic. The principles established, however, are equally

---

tion of the evidence; 2) any irreparable harm likely to result to the party seeking the preservation of evidence absent an order directing preservation; and 3) the capability of an individual, entity, or party to maintain the evidence sought to be preserved, not only as the evidence's original form, condition, or contents, but also the physical, spatial and financial burden created by ordering evidence preservation.").

18. FED. R. CIV. P. 26(f), Advisory Committee Notes.
19. *Id.*
20. *Id.*
21. *Id.*

applicable to the computer age and cases involving electronic evidence. The last part of the chapter will explore unique concerns with electronic evidence.

II. THE BASICS

The doctrine of spoliation requires that a party (1) have destroyed evidence[22] (2) knowing that it is relevant to issues in (3) pending or reasonably foreseeable litigation.[23] In the absence of pending or reasonably foreseeable litigation, a party's good-faith discarding of evidence pursuant to a normal practice is not sanctionable and, in fact, may be a good

---

22. Mere speculation that evidence might have existed and been destroyed will not suffice. Otero v. Wood, 316 F. Supp. 2d 612, 619-20 (S.D. Ohio 2004) ("Plaintiff has not established that the evidence that was allegedly destroyed ever actually existed. . . . Plaintiff urges this Court to build further inferences—that this video would have provided the 'smoking gun' to prove her case, that someone realized how harmful the video would be, and that someone somehow destroyed the tape. . . . Plaintiff's speculations do not suffice to warrant an inference or a presumption in her favor."). Similarly, when a party fails to collect potentially useful evidence, it is seen as the same as destroying evidence that is already extant. In United States v. Martinez-Martinez, 369 F.3d 1076, 1087 (9th Cir. 2004), for example, the defendant claimed that the government was guilty of spoliation because it did not test his bodily fluids when he was arrested. Rejecting this claim, the court held that "[a]bsent such a test, there was no existing evidence for the authorities to destroy."

23. *See, e.g.,* Super. Fed. Bank v. Mackey, 129 S.W.3d 324, 340 (Ark Ct. App. 2003), where appellees questioned appellant "about the whereabouts of the 1999 approved contractors list, personnel evaluations of Tom Wetzel, and loan committee minutes that would have referenced the initial land-acquisition loan. Although there was testimony that these items should have existed, none could be found and no credible explanation was given for their absence." As a consequence, the court gave the following instruction to the jury:

> If you find that a party intentionally destroyed, lost or suppressed documents in this case with the knowledge that their contents may be material to a pending claim, you may draw the inference that the content of the documents would be unfavorable to that party's defense. When I use the term "material" I mean evidence that could be a substantial factor in evaluating the merit of the claim in this case.

The appellate court held that this instruction on a negative inference against the spoliator was appropriate.

practice if handled correctly.[24] Courts have split over whether the act of destruction must be (A) intentional or (B) in bad faith (that is, for the purpose of suppressing harmful information), or may be premised on negligence.[25] Courts premising spoliation sanctions on the negligent destruction of evidence believe that culpability is on a continuum and those responsible for an adverse party not being able to prove his case should not be permitted to benefit from their culpable behavior even if it may have been unintentional. As explained in *Wiedmann v. Bradford Group, Inc.*,[26] "'The destruction of relevant evidence . . . has a pernicious effect on the truth-finding function of our courts.' . . . The doctrine of spoliation allows a court to impose sanctions and remedies for the destruction of evidence in civil litigation, 'based on the premise that a party who has negligently or intentionally lost or destroyed evidence known to be relevant for an upcoming legal proceeding should be held accountable for any unfair prejudice that results.'"[27] In most jurisdictions, however, the doctrine of spoliation refers to the *intentional* destruction of evidence

---

24. *See, e.g.,* Conderman v. Rochester Gas & Elec. Corp., 262 A.D.2d 1068, 1070, 693 N.Y.S.2d 787 (4th Dept. 1999). The regular destruction of data is a wise practice because it reduces the costs of (1) preservation, as well as (2) searching, (3) retrieving, and (4) claiming privilege on materials from that preserved database in future litigation. However, as discussed elsewhere in this text, organizations with such destruction policies must take immediate action to ensure that destruction under those policies cease when litigation is reasonably anticipated in which information scheduled for destruction may be relevant. This is done through what has been dubbed "hold" notices.

25. Residential Funding Corp. v. DeGeorge Fin. Corp., 306 F.3d 99, 109 (2d Cir. 2002); Zubulake v. UBS Warburg LLC, 220 F.R.D. 422, 431 (S.D.N.Y. 2004) ("In this circuit, a 'culpable state of mind' . . . includes ordinary negligence.").

26. 444 Mass. 698, 705, 831 N.E.2d 304, 310 (2005).

27. *See* Vesta Fire Ins. Co. v. Milam & Co. Constr., 901 So. 2d 84, 97 (Ala. 2004); Porter v. Irvin's Interstate Brick & Block Co., 691 N.E.2d 1363, 1365 (Ind. Ct. App. 1998); Cecil County Dept. of Social Servs. v. Russell, 861 A.2d 92, 106 (Md. Ct. Spec. App. 2004); Ward v. Consol. Rail Corp., 693 N.W.2d 366, 370-71 (Mich. 2005); Foust v. McFarland, 698 N.W.2d 24, 31 (Minn. Ct. App. 2005); Bass-Davis v. Davis, 117 P.3d 207, 210-11 (Nev. 2005); Segura v. K-Mart Corp., 62 P.3d 283, 286 (N.M. 2002); Mead v. Papa Razzi Rest., 840 A.2d 1103, 1108 (R.I. 2004); Wolfe v. Virginia, 580 S.E.2d 467, 475 (Va. Ct. App. 2003).

relevant to a case.[28] The requirements in the majority of jurisdictions for the spoliation sanction of an adverse inference instruction were delineated by the court in *State v. Hartsfields*:[29]

> (1) evidence exists, (2) it is in the possession or under the control of [a party], (3) it would have been admissible at trial, and (4) the [party] intentionally destroyed the evidence.

When these elements have been established, an adverse inference instruction or other sanction may be appropriate.[30] Issues surrounding each of these elements are discussed below.

---

28. Beers v. Bayliner Marine Corp., 236 Conn. 769, 777, 675 A.2d 829, 832 (1996) ("the spoliation must have been intentional" for the adverse inference to be drawn); Desselle v. Jefferson Parish Hosp. Dist. No. 2, 2004 WL 2291445, at *8 (La. App. Oct. 12, 2004) ("The theory of 'spoliation of evidence' refers to an intentional destruction of evidence for purpose of depriving opposing parties of its use. . . . Allegations of negligent conduct are insufficient.'"); Ward v. Consol. Rail Corp., 472 Mich. 77, 84, 693 N.W.2d 366, 371 (2005) ("It is well settled that missing evidence gives rise to an adverse presumption only when the complaining party can establish 'intentional conduct indicating fraud and a desire to destroy [evidence] and thereby suppress the truth.'"); Murray v. Dev. Servs. of Sullivan County, Inc., 149 N.H. 264, 271, 818 A.2d 302, 309 (2003) ("We construe its argument to be based upon the general rule that an adverse inference— that the missing evidence would have been unfavorable—can be drawn only when the evidence was destroyed deliberately with a fraudulent intent."); Beverly v. Wal-Mart Stores, Inc., 2000 Okla. Civ. App. 45, 3 P.3d 163 (Okla Civ. App. 1999) ("[T]he presumption arises only in cases of 'willful destruction [or] suppression.'"); Cresthaven Nursing Residence v. Freeman, 134 S.W.3d 214, 225 (Tex. Ct. App. 2003). The logic of requiring an intentional destruction before spoliation sanctions are imposed was explained in State v. Hartsfield, 681 N.W.2d 626, 630 (Iowa 2004): "[W]hen evidence is intentionally destroyed, 'the fact finder may draw the inference that the evidence destroyed was unfavorable to the party responsible for its spoliation.' [State v. Langlet, 283 N.W.2d 330, 333 (Iowa 1979)] This inference is based on the rationale that a party's destruction of evidence is 'an admission by conduct of the weakness [of that party's] case.' *Id.* Accordingly, 'the spoliation inference is not appropriate when the destruction is not intentional.' *Id.*"

29. 681 N.W.2d 626, 631 (Iowa 2004).

30. In Byrnie v. Town of Cromwell, 243 F.3d 93, 107-12 (2d Cir. 2001), the court found that an adverse inference instruction was appropriate when (1) the party had control over the evidence, (2) an obligation to preserve it, (3) destroyed it (4) with a "culpable state of mind," and (5) the destroyed evidence was "relevant" to the party's claim or defense in that a reasonable trier of fact could find that it supported that claim or defense.

A.   *When Does the Duty to Preserve Arise?*

Unless otherwise required by law,[31] no individual or entity is obliged to preserve records.[32] A duty to preserve relevant evidence, however, arises at that point when a reasonable person has been put on notice, by whatever means,[33] or otherwise should have known[34] that litigation is immin-

---

31. For example, there may be a preexisting requirement to preserve employment records, Byrnie v. Town of Cromwell, 243 F.3d 93, 107-12 (2d Cir. 2001); medical records, Keene v. Brigham & Women's Hospital, Inc., 439 Mass. 223, 235, 786 N.E.2d 824, 833 (2003); and payroll records, Wiedmann v. Bradford Group, Inc., 444 Mass. 698, 707, 831 N.E.2d 304, 310 (2005).

32. It is unreasonable to expect retention of everything (because of cost and inconvenience). A duty cannot be found without identifiable litigation because its issues are the only measures of logical relevance.

33. Beck v. Haik, 377 F.3d 624, 632 (6th Cir. 2004) (An audio dispatch tape was destroyed because a Freedom of Information Act request was not filed with the appropriate office. The duty to preserve existed independent of the formal request because an oral request had been made and communicated to the proper office.); Silvestri v. General Motors Corp., 271 F.3d 583, 591 (4th Cir. 2001) ("The duty to preserve material evidence arises not only during litigation but also extends to that period before the litigation when a party reasonably should know that the evidence may be relevant to anticipated litigation."); Kronisch v. United States, 150 F.3d 112, 126 (2d Cir. 1998) ("The obligation to preserve evidence arises when the party has notice that the evidence is relevant to litigation—most commonly when suit has already been filed, providing the party responsible for the destruction with express notice, but also on occasion in other circumstances, as, for example, when a party should have known that the evidence may be relevant to future litigation."); Fakhro v. Mayo Clinic Rochester, 2004 WL 909740, at 3 (D. Minn. Mar. 31, 2004) (Mayo Clinic not required to preserve 20 feet of electrocardiogram's "rhythm strips" printed out during procedure because they disclosed nothing abnormal about heart rhythms following procedure and this was confirmed by other available evidence); Computer Assoc. Int'l, Inc. v. Am. Fundware, Inc., 133 F.R.D. 166, 169 (D. Colo. 1990) (Pre-litigation correspondence gave actual notice and created a duty to preserve.) The court held:

> All reasonable inferences lead inexorably to the conclusion that [the defendant] must have been aware that [plaintiff's] source code would be the subject of a discovery request long before it stopped destroying older versions, and I so find. It is inconceivable that after the [pre-litigation] meeting, [defendant] did not realize that the software in its possession would be sought during discovery. Certainly commencement of the action settled any doubts. Thereafter the request for production, followed by the motion to compel, provided repeated, insistent reminders of the duty to preserve this irreplaceable evidence. Yet the

ent and that the evidence may be relevant to that litigation.[35] One must be

destruction proceeded. . . . Even assuming that maintenance of only a single, updated version of the source code was, in other circumstances, a bona fide business practice, any destruction of versions of the code [three weeks after the service of the complaint] could not be excused as a bona fide business practice.

Baxley v. Hakiel Indus. Inc., 280 Ga. App. 94, 95, 633 S.E.2d 360 (Ga. App. 2006) (no duty to preserve videotape that was destroyed long before suit was brought).

34. Fujitsu Ltd. v. Fed. Express Corp., 247 F.3d 423, 436 (2d Cir. 2001).

35. Mastercard Int'l, Inc. v. Moulton, 2004 WL 1393992, at *4 (S.D.N.Y. June 22, 2004) ("The e-mails in question were received by defendants during the period following the filing of plaintiff's lawsuit. Moreover, a large number of them presumably arrived after defendants' lawyer had reminded defendant Kevin Moulton of his obligation to preserve evidence and after plaintiff had served a document request that called for the production of such e-mails. In these circumstances, defendants plainly had an obligation to preserve the e-mails in question, since they were relevant to the pending litigation and had been requested by plaintiff."); In re Holocaust Victim Assets Litig., 319 F. Supp. 2d 301, 320 (E.D. N.Y. 2004) (Swiss banks engaged in "systematic" destruction of relevant documents once those documents were 10 years old, even though they were relevant to legitimate claims that were being made and that, if substantiated through documentation, would expose the banks to liability. The fact that the destruction was a regular practice and did not violate Swiss law was irrelevant to the court's finding of spoliation.); Barsoum v. NYC Hous. Auth., 202 F.R.D. 396, 400 (S.D.N.Y. 2001) ("This obligation is triggered not only when a party has been put on notice by a discovery demand explicitly requesting the evidence, but also when a party has been served with a complaint or anticipates litigation."); Shaffer v. RWP Group, Inc., 169 F.R.D. 19, 24 (E.D. N.Y. 1996) ("A condition precedent to this Court's imposition of sanctions is whether RWP knew or should have known that the destroyed evidence was relevant to pending, imminent or reasonably foreseeable litigation."); Turner v. Hudson Transit Lines, Inc., 142 F.R.D. 68, 72-73 (S.D.N.Y. 1991) (It is not necessary that a formal document request have been made. "[T]he complaint itself may alert a party that certain information is relevant and likely to be sought in discovery." "[N]o duty to preserve arises unless the party possessing the evidence has notice of its relevance."); Wm T. Thomason Co. v. General Nutrition Corp., 593 F. Supp. 1443, 1445 (C.D. Cal. 1984) ("Sanctions may be imposed on a litigant who is on notice that documents and information in its possession are relevant to litigation, or potential litigation, or are reasonably calculated to lead to the discovery of admissible evidence, and destroys such documents and information. While a litigant is under no duty to keep or retain every document in its possession once a complaint is filed, it is under a duty to preserve what it knows, or reasonably should know, is relevant in the action, is reasonably calculated to lead to the discovery of admissible evidence, is reasonably

particularly conscious of this duty when anticipating bringing legal actions. Timing those actions in coordination with document destruction

---

likely to be required during discovery and/or is the subject of a pending discovery request."); Linnen v. A.H. Robins Co., Inc., 1999 WL 462015, at *9-10 (Mass. Sup. Ct. June 16, 1999) (company failed to discontinue recycling of backup tapes after order to preserve materials was issued by the court); Murray v. Dev. Servs. of Sullivan County, Inc., 149 N.H. 264, 271, 818 A.2d 302, 309 (2003) ("The timing of the document destruction is not dispositive on the issue of intent, however, and an adverse inference can be drawn even when the evidence is destroyed prior to a claim being made."); Serrano v. Rajamani, 2004 WL 938480, at *1 (N.Y. Sup. Ct. App. Div. April 20, 2004) ("[T]he loss or destruction of those materials did not constitute spoliation of evidence because defendant did not know that the materials might be needed for future litigation."); Lawrence Ins. Group, Inc. v. KPMG Peat Marwick, 773 N.Y.S.2d 164, 167 (N.Y. Sup. Ct. App. Div. 2004) ("Here, on the one hand, defendant's employee affirmed that, unless ordered held, work papers are routinely destroyed after six years. Plaintiff asserts that the large and sudden reversal involving a $35 million deficit, without any obvious business reason for its occurrence, should have, along with some evidence of in-house communication concerning this topic, the obvious unhappiness of the client and the existence of similar lawsuits, prompted defendant to put a hold on these papers and not destroy them."); DiDomenico v. C & S Aeromatik Supplies, Inc., 252 A.D.2d 41, 41-42 (N.Y. A.D. 1998) (fact that evidence destroyed prior to commencement of action and being requested by adverse party is not a cognizable excuse for destruction); Reingold v. Wet'N Wild Nevada, Inc., 113 Nev. 967, 944 P.2d 800, 971 (1997) ("Wet 'N Wild claimed that all records are destroyed at the end of each season. This policy means that the accident records are destroyed even before the statute of limitations has run on any potential litigation for that season. It appears that this records destruction policy was deliberately designed to prevent production of records in any subsequent litigation. Deliberate destruction of records before the statute of limitations has run on the incidents described in those records amounts to suppression of evidence. If Wet 'N Wild chooses such a records destruction policy, it must accept the adverse inferences of the policy."); Fire Ins. Exch. v. Zenith Radio Corp., 103 Nev. 648, 747 P.2d 911 (1987) ("[E]ven where an action has not been commenced and there is only a potential for litigation, the litigant is under a duty to preserve evidence which it knows or reasonably should know is relevant to the action." After having their expert witness examine a television set that was determined to be the source of a residential fire, the company allowed the television set to be destroyed, knowing that there would be a subrogation claim.); Martinez v. Abbott Labs., 2004 WL 1944403, at *7 (Tex. App. Aug. 31, 2004) (no duty arose to isolate pump or download information because there was no reason for the nurse to suspect that the PCA pump was malfunctioning or was misprogrammed).

practices to strategically improve a litigation position is particularly reprehensible.[36] This duty is present even if the company will not be joined as

---

36. Samsung Electronics Co., Ltd. v. Rambus Inc., 439 F. Supp. 2d 524, 535-36 (E.D. Va. 2006) ("[P]re-filing destruction of evidence can preclude any potential defendant from a full and fair opportunity to conduct discovery crucial to the defense of a patent infringement claim. To allow a party, which was anticipating litigation, to avoid sanctions under [35 U.S.C.] § 285 because it had the foresight to commit the spoliation of evidence before filing its infringement claim would be utterly irrational and would defeat the very purpose for which the judicial system condemns spoliation of evidence. . . . Thus, the Court finds that where a patentee has destroyed evidence before the filing of an infringement claim, but at the time when the patentee anticipated, or reasonably should have anticipated, litigation, that spoliation constitutes misconduct during the litigation . . . . It is difficult to imagine conduct that is more worthy of being considered litigation misconduct or more worthy of sanction than spoliation of evidence in anticipation of litigation because that conduct frustrates, sometimes completely, the search for truth. And, it creates extra expense in the judicial process in the effort to uncover that which has been destroyed. The rule urged by Rambus—that the sanction of an attorney's fees award cannot be imposed if the spoliation precedes anticipated litigation—would rightly hold the judicial system up to scorn and ridicule. . . . It is nonsensical to assert that the fees incurred by Rambus' litigation targets in dealing with those issues cannot be awarded (if they are otherwise awardable) merely because Rambus destroyed the evidence before it engaged in litigation. Nothing in [prior case law] suggests that the Federal Circuit has countenanced such a result. Thus, it is not appropriate to employ the standard for a finding of sham litigation where the ground asserted for the exception case finding is pre-filing spoliation in anticipation of litigation."). Such conduct will not only result in spoliation sanctions, but also will destroy the attorney-client privilege protection under the crime/fraud exception. Rambus, Inc. v. Infineo Tech. AG, 222 F.R.D. 280, 298 (E.D. Va. 2004) ("Document retention programs, lawfully implemented, are certainly permissible. But, even lawful programs must be suspended or adjusted when litigation is reasonably anticipated and the in-place program runs the risk of destroying potentially relevant materials. As the record now stands, Rambus' conduct here defies that precept in that Rambus actually started a program because it anticipated that it would soon begin litigation. The fact that the litigation commencement date was deferred by Rambus does not alter that fact. Instead, it permits the inference that Rambus deliberately destroyed documents while it improved (in its view) its litigation posture and while it refined its litigation strategy and slightly altered its litigation targets. Research has disclosed no precedent for finding that such conduct is legitimate or that document destruction under those circumstances can be clothed with propriety merely by calling it a 'document retention program.'").

a party in the litigation.[37] The duty also arises despite the fact that destruction may be sanctioned by statute, and therefore is not illegal.[38] This does not mean that a document retention or destruction policy and actual or anticipated litigation cannot coexist. "[A] company can modify its policy to preserve documents reasonably thought relevant to the actual or anticipated litigation. To accomplish that, however, the company must inform its officers and employees of the actual or anticipated litigation, and identify for them the kinds of documents that are thought to be relevant to it."[39]

It is not always clear when courts will conclude that litigation was reasonably imminent or what evidence they will hold was relevant. There is notice of litigation, of course, with the service of the complaint.[40] Notice that litigation is imminent can also be provided in a court order to preserve evidence and informal discovery requests. However, a party may be put on notice much earlier by more informal and indirect means.

For example, in *Computer Assoc. Int'l, Inc. v. American Fundware, Inc.,*[41] the court held that the defendant was on notice after pre-litigation meetings that failed to resolve a dispute over a software licensing agreement. The court found it "inconceivable" that the meetings did not put the defendant American Fundware on notice that the basis of the dispute, the computer source code, would be the subject of litigation and sought dur-

---

37. Non-parties will usually be fined as a discovery sanction. If the company is a party to the litigation, the range of potential penalties for spoliation is greater. For example, judgment can be entered against the party, or evidentiary inferences and presumptions can be used at the trial. Regardless of the company's involvement in the litigation, if spoliation occurs in a state jurisdiction that recognizes a separate cause of action, the potential consequences will be the same.

38. In re Holocaust Victim Assets Litig., 319 F. Supp. 2d 301 (E.D. N.Y. June 1, 2004) (Swiss law permitted banks to destroy records that were 10 years old. Even though victims of Nazi persecution and their heirs were seeking access to those records, they were systematically destroyed to hide those assets and conceal their inappropriate transfer to the Deutsche Bank. It was held that the Claims Resolution Tribunal appropriately employed presumptions relating to claims to certain closed accounts.).

39. Samsung Electronics Co. v. Rambus Inc., 439 F. Supp. 2d 524, 565 (E.D. Va. 2006) (The court also noted that the company with the destruction policy could also collect the relevant documents and segregate them to accomplish the same goal.).

40. Capellupo v. FMC Corp., 126 F.R.D. 545 (D. Minn. 1989).

41. 133 F.R.D. 166, 168 (D. Colo. 1990).

ing discovery. In contrast, simply because a few individuals within a company may have mentioned that a fellow worker may sue does not necessarily mean that the company was on notice of potential litigation. In *Zubulake v. UBS Warburg*,[42] for example, correspondence between two employees indicated that they contemplated the possibility that a fellow employee might sue. The Court noted that this would not "generally impose a firm-wide duty to preserve." The Court went on to conclude that when communications are circulated among various levels of supervisors and co-workers in which threats of a lawsuit are considered, the relevant people have contemplated litigation and the duty to preserve arises. In *Renda Marine, Inc. v. United States*,[43] the court concluded that litigation was reasonably anticipated after a heated dispute about differing site conditions, when a "cure notice" was issued to the plaintiff with a threat to terminate for default delays. "Notice of a claim 'does not refer to any particular statistical probability that litigation will occur; rather, it simply means that litigation is more than merely an abstract possibility or unwarranted fear. The underlying inquiry is whether it was reasonable for the investigating party to anticipate litigation and prepare accordingly.'"[44] It also does not require a court order to preserve, even though an adversary could have obtained such an order during the pendency of a case.[45]

Administrative proceedings that precede litigation also can serve as notice to preserve evidence. In *McGuire v. Acufex Microsurgical Inc.*,[46] the defendant-employer was held to be on notice once the plaintiff filed a sexual harassment charges at the Massachusetts Commission Against Discrimination. Because these administrative hearings were an administrative prerequisite to federal discrimination litigation, the court held that the parties incurred an obligation to preserve evidence under the Federal Rules of Civil Procedure.

Litigation does not have to be certain to be considered "imminent" or "reasonably foreseeable." In *Scott v. IBM Corp.*,[47] the court found that company managers were put on notice of litigation because of the sensi-

---

42. 220 F.R.D. 212, 217 (S.D.N.Y. 2003).

43. 58 Fed. Cl. 57, 62 (2003).

44. Rowe v. Albertsons, Inc., 2004 WL 2252064, at *2 (10th Cir. Oct. 7, 2004) (citing National Tank Co. v. Brotherton, 851 S.W.2d 193, 204 (Tex. 1993)).

45. Thompson v. H.U.D., 219 F.R.D. 93, 100 (D. Md. 2003).

46. 175 F.R.D. 149 (D. Mass. 1997).

47. 196 F.R.D. 233, 249 (D. N.J. 2000).

tive nature of a particular layoff. The court held that "while litigation was not guaranteed, it could be viewed as reasonably foreseeable," because the employee had made prior claims of racial discrimination.

Even a communication from an outsider raising issues of corporate misconduct may be enough to put a company on notice that documents relating to that conduct should be preserved.[48] Litigation also has been found to be foreseeable when the party has been faced with similar law-suits in the past,[49] or when it has sent its own investigators to gather information on an accident or event.[50]

It is often advisable, therefore, for a party to disseminate broadly, and as quickly as possible, information about a developing dispute, with details of the issues and evidence that could be relevant.[51] This advice applies with particular force in the context of litigation involving e-evidence because it can be so easily and quickly purged.[52]

If a party fears destruction of databases, a court can issue an injunction and order the potentially offending party to allow a court-appointed expert to copy the data, recover deleted files, and perform searches under guidelines that protect both sides. The court in *Dodge,*

---

48. *See, e.g.,* Computer Assoc., 133 F.R.D. at 169 (holding that pre-litigation communications between the parties was enough to put the document destroyers on notice both that litigation was foreseeable and that the documents related to central issue to be litigated).

49. *See, e.g.,* Lee v. Boyle-Midway Household Prods., 792 F. Supp. 1001 (W.D. Pa. 1992) (granting summary judgment to a defendant for plaintiff's spoliation of evidence prior to commencement of product liability claim).

50. *See, e.g.,* Capitol Chevrolet v. Smedly, 614 So. 2d 439 (Ala. 1993) (holding it was reasonably foreseeable that an insurance company might sue after it sent its own expert to inspect and photograph accident scene).

51. The obligation to preserve evidence arises prior to the filing of a complaint where an individual is on notice that litigation is likely to be commenced. *See* Capellupo v. FMC Corp., 126 F.R.D. 545, 550-51, n.14 (D. Minn. 1989); Shimanovsky v. General Motors Corp., 181 Ill. 2d 112, 692 N.E.2d 286 (1998) ("Thus, the appellate court has determined that a potential litigant owes a duty to take reasonable measures to preserve the integrity of relevant and material evidence. This duty is based on the court's concern that, were it unable to sanction a party for the presuit destruction of evidence, a potential litigant could circumvent discovery rules or escape liability simply by destroying the proof prior to the filing of a complaint."). For a sample letter of notification of anticipated litigation, *see* Chapter One, "Discovery," *supra.*

52. *See* section XI, Computers and the Internet Expand Every Possibility, *infra.*

Warren & Peters Insurance Services v. Riley[53] found this remedy particularly appropriate after the plaintiff's showing of irreparable harm if the data were lost. The court noted that the imposition on the defendant was minimal: the files were copied in the defendant's presence and after working hours, so as not to interfere with business; the information obtained would be available only through agreement between the parties, or a court order; and finally, Dodge, the requesting party, bore the initial cost, subject to reallocation by the court.

If a company routinely destroys records pursuant to an established document retention policy, litigation must be either filed or imminent[54] before the court will consider spoliation sanctions. Even then, courts usually require a complaining party to demonstrate either bad faith or gross negligence.[55] Many jurisdictions follow the "reasonably foreseeable" stan-

53. 130 Cal. Rptr. 2d 385, 391 (Cal. App. Dist. Ct. 2003).

54. Lewy v. Remington Arms Co., 836 F.2d 1104, 1112 (8th Cir. 1988) ("[E]ven if the court finds the policy to be reasonable given the nature of the documents subject to the policy, the court may find that under the particular circumstances certain documents should have been retained notwithstanding the policy."); Scott v. IBM Corp., 196 F.R.D. 233, 249 (D. N.J. 2000) (Because company managers were on notice of sensitive nature of particular layoff because prior claims of racial discrimination had been made by the employee, the court held that "while litigation was not guaranteed, it could be viewed as reasonably foreseeable."); Willard v. Caterpillar, 40 Cal. App. 4th 892, 48 Cal. Rptr. 2d 607, 620-21 (Cal. App. 1995) (finding that manufacturer was not required to preserve documents for decades in the absence of reasonably foreseeable litigation, simply because of the possibility that some documents might be relevant to future litigation); Laport v. Lake Mich. Mtg., 252 Ill. App. 3d 221, 228 (Ill. Ct. App. 1991) (sanctions not appropriate where destruction was pursuant to established company policy and before lawsuit was filed).

55. *See, e.g.,* Coates v. EEOC, 756 F.2d 524 (7th Cir. 1985) (because employee destroyed records after being erroneously told that they were not needed in a pending class action, an adverse inference was not justified because of the absence of bad faith); Vick v. Texas Employment Comm'n, 514 F.2d 734 (5th Cir. 1975) (destruction of employment records pursuant to routine practice, even after commencement of action, did not warrant an adverse inference because bad faith was not apparent); Southeast Mental Health Ctr., Inc. v. Pac. Ins. Co., Inc., 439 F. Supp. 2d 831, 840 (W.D. Tenn. 2006) ("The inference is rebuttable and 'arises only when the spoliation occurs in circumstances indicating fraud and a desire to suppress the truth. It does not arise when the destruction was a matter of routine with no fraudulent intent.'"); Arnez v. Duane Reade, Inc., 824 N.Y.S.2d 767 (Sup. Ct. 2006) ("[S]anctions would be inappropriate here since the videotape was recycled in the normal course of defendant's business prior to notice of this litigation . . . [and] there has been no showing that its failure was willful, contumacious or in bad

dard, requiring litigation to be "likely."[56]

If a document is destroyed despite the existence of a company policy to retain it, is a spoliation instruction appropriate without a further demonstration that a duty to preserve existed? In *Albertson's, Inc. v. Arriaga*,[57] the court held that a duty must be established and concluded that no such duty had been shown. A dissenting judge persuasively argued that since the missing videotape was of a shoplifting in which the defendant was charged with being the lookout, the duty to preserve arose when the individuals were arrested on the shoplifting charge. At that point the store reasonably knew that the evidence was relevant to a pending charge.

Once notice of impending litigation is given, notified parties have an obligation to (1) develop policies for document or data preservation that may be inconsistent with established destruction practices, including putting a hold on all regular document destruction policies,[58] (2) disseminate those new policies to the employees who need to know, and (3) confirm that the policies are being followed.[59] Because notice of impending litiga-

---

faith."); McLean v. Bourget's Bike Works, Inc., 2005 WL 2493479, at *4 (Tenn. Ct. App. Oct. 7, 2005) ("The doctrine of spoliation of evidence permits a court to draw a negative inference against a party who has intentionally, and for an improper purpose, destroyed, mutilated, lost, altered, or concealed evidence.").

56. Capellupo v. FMC Corp., 126 F.R.D. 545, 550-51 (D. Minn. 1989).

57. 2004 WL 2045389 (Tex. App. Sept. 15, 2004).

58. Zubulake v. UBS Warburg, LLC, 220 F.R.D. 212, 218 (S.D.N.Y. 2003). *See* Convolve, Inc. v. Compaq Computer Corp., 223 F.R.D. 162, 176 (S.D.N.Y. 2004).

59. Creative Science Sys., Inc. v. Forex Capital Markets, 2006 WL 870973, at *5-6 (N.D. Cal. April 4, 2006) (obligation to communicate notice of litigation and need to preserve relevant evidence); Danis v. USN Commc'ns, Inc., 2000 WL 1694325, at *14 (N.D. Ill. Oct. 23, 2000) (After issuing broad directive that all documents were to be preserved, "Mr. Elliott personally took no affirmative steps to ensure that the directive was followed. Mr. Elliott did not direct that USN implement a written, comprehensive document preservation policy, either in general or with specific reference to the lawsuit; he did not instruct that any e-mail or other written communication be sent to staff to ensure that they were aware of the lawsuit and the need to preserve documents; and he did not meet with the department heads after this staff meeting to follow up to see what they had done to implement the document preservation directive."); Nat'l Ass'n of Radiation Survivors v. Turnage, 115 F.R.D. 543, 557-58 (N.D. Cal. 1987) ("It is no defense to suggest, as the defendant attempts, that particular employees were not on notice. To hold otherwise would permit an agency, corporate officer, or legal department to shield itself from discovery obligations by keeping its employees ignorant. The obligation to retain

tion is usually given to legal counsel first, "the obligation to preserve evidence runs first to counsel, who then has a duty to advise and explain to the client its obligations to retain pertinent documents that may be relevant to the litigation.[60]

Danis v. USN Communications, Inc.[61] illustrates the kinds of actions a court may require a party to take. At the defendant's board meeting, officers and managers discussed the need for a document preservation program. The USN staff, in fact, issued a broad directive containing a "substantial warning" "not to throw out anything." Despite the warning, the court found that USN was negligent, since many employees destroyed relevant documents because they were unaware of the preservation policy. The attorney in charge of implementing the program delegated the responsibility to a subordinate with little or no experience in document preservation. Both had failed to draft and implement a comprehensive written policy about the lawsuit and the kinds of documents that were to be preserved, failed to send e-mails to the staff to ensure that they were made aware of the lawsuit, and failed to follow up personally to see that employees complied with the directive. USN argued that because the individual employees responsible for document destruction were unaware of the preservation directive, USN should not be held responsible. The court ruled that this was no defense.

Under similar facts, the court in *National Ass'n of Radiation Survivors v. Turnage*[62] reasoned that ignorance on the part of employees could not be recognized as a defense because it would "permit an agency, corporate officer, or legal department to shield itself from discovery obligations by keeping its employees ignorant."

As *Danis* and *Radiation Survivors* point out, a party must take steps to ensure compliance with a document preservation program. Sending notices by e-mail may be inadequate if some of the relevant employees or agents do not have access to that service, do not regularly read their e-

---

discoverable materials is an affirmative one; it requires that the agency or corporate officers having notice of discovery obligations communicate those obligations to employees in possession of discoverable materials.").

60. Telecom Int'l Am., Ltd. v. AT&T, 189 F.R.D. 76, 81 (S.D.N.Y. 1999); Kansas-Nebraska Natural Gas Co. v. Marathon Oil Co., 109 F.R.D. 12, 18, (D. Neb. 1983).

61. 2000 WL 1694325, at *28 (N.D. Ill. Oct. 23, 2000).

62. 115 F.R.D. 543, 557-58 (N.D. Cal. 1987).

mail, or are accustomed to receiving hard copies of important notifications.[63] In the face of litigation, document preservation is not a passive obligation.[64] A company cannot shield itself from responsibility because of its employees' actions. "The obligation to preserve documents that are potentially discoverable materials is an affirmative one that rests squarely on the shoulders of senior corporate officers."[65]

This obligation to preserve documents cannot be satisfied by relying on the belief that someone else will retain them.[66] "The document retention policies . . . do not trump the Federal Rules of Civil Procedure or requests by opposing counsel, even if the requests primarily are informal."[67] Further, a party cannot hide behind the fact that the destruction pursuant to a retention policy was conducted by an outside agent assisting the party in preparing for trial. For example, in *Trigon Insurance Co. v. United States*,[68] a litigation consultant, AGE, was assisting the government in arranging for expert testimony. Pursuant to a document retention policy, e-mails were destroyed that should have been preserved and produced to the opposing party because they were relevant to the bases of the experts' testimony. The agent's conduct resulted in a finding that the government had willfully and intentionally destroyed the evidence.

Nor can the United States scapegoat AGE's document retention policy. AGE held itself out to have expertise in litigation consulting. AGE is the

---

63. In re Prudential Ins. Co. of Am. Sales Practices Litig., 169 F.R.D. 598, 604 (D. N.J. 1997).

64. Larson v. Bank One Corp., 2005 WL 4652509, at *11 (N.D. Ill. Aug. 18, 2005).

65. In re Prudential Ins. Co. of Am. Sales Practices Litig., 169 F.R.D. 598, 617 (D. N.J. 1997).

66. Struthers Patent Corp. v. Nestle Co., 558 F. Supp. 747, 765 (D. N.J. 1981) ("[I]t is immaterial that Hudson Transit may have believed that the original records would be available from the new bus owner. In fact this assumption proved unwarranted, since efforts to obtain the records from the new owner have failed. Nor was it a reasonable assumption: according to the government regulations that Hudson Transit itself cites, the new owner would only have been required to preserve the records for a year after the sale in 1987. In any event, a party's discovery obligations are not satisfied by relying on non-parties to preserve documents.").

67. Trigon Ins. Co. v. United States, 204 F.R.D. 277, 289 (E.D. Va. 2001).

68. 204 F.R.D. at 289 (court declined to exclude testimony because enough deleted e-mails had been retrieved by forensic experts to permit reasonable cross-examination, but court gave negative inference instruction to jury).

agent of the United States in arranging for the expert testimony to be given in this action on behalf of the United States. As such, AGE is charged with knowing that materials reviewed by a testifying expert must be preserved and eventually produced to the opposing party. . . . AGE's execution of a document retention policy that is at odds with the rules governing the conduct of litigation does not protect the United States from a finding of intentional destruction.[69]

A duty to preserve may arise even if an individual or entity does not have possession of the property in question.[70] As long as one once exercised control or had the opportunity to exercise control after the need to preserve was apparent, a failure to take appropriate measures to preserve may be actionable. For example, in *Dardeen v. Kuehling*,[71] State Farm had a contractual relationship with its insured, Alice Kuehling. Kuehling called State Farm the same day the plaintiff fell on the sidewalk and asked whether or not she could remove some bricks so no one else would get hurt. Ronald Couch, a State Farm agent, replied that it would be okay for the plaintiff to remove the bricks. Even though the measures were appropriate in the circumstances, Couch did not recommend that Keuhling take pictures or videotape the sidewalk, nor did he offer to send an investigator to do so prior to the removal of the bricks[72] in order to preserve evidence necessary to prove the underlying suit. The court held that State Farm violated a duty to the injured party.

---

69. *Id.*

70. Perez-Velasco v. Suzuki Motor Co. Ltd., 266 F. Supp. 2d 266, 268 (D. P.R. 2003) ("If a party cannot fulfill this duty to preserve because he does not own or control the evidence, he still has an obligation to give the opposing party notice of access to the evidence or of the possible destruction of evidence if the party anticipates litigation involving that evidence."); China Ocean Shipping Co. v. Simone Metals Inc., 1999 WL 966443 (N.D. Ill. Sept. 30, 1999) (A railroad car involved in a derailment was stored on a lot owned by a third party. The railroad company made no effort to see that the car was preserved for reasonably anticipated litigation purposes. The company in possession of the car gave no notice to the railroad company that it intended to destroy the car. The court found both the railroad company and the possessor of the car guilty of spoliation.); Creazzo v. Medtronic, Inc., 2006 Pa. Super 152, 903 A.2d 24 (Pa. Super. Ct. 2006) ("The fact that the actual loss occurred while the device was in the custody of a third party does not ameliorate that responsibility, given the Creazzos' knowledge of their own pending claim and the nature of their claim as one based on a manufacturing defect.").

71. 801 N.E.2d 960 (Ill App. 5th Dist. 2003).

72. *Id.* at 964.

Parties can be held responsible for destructive acts of third parties who act as their agents. In *Bouve & Mohr, LLC v. Banks*,[73] for example, an off-duty police officer served as a security guard for an apartment complex owner who was being sued by a rape victim. After a reported rape, the tenant was taken to a Rape Crisis Center for examination, and evidence was collected in a rape kit. The security guard used his status as a police officer to obtain custody of the rape kit evidence and was responsible for its destruction, despite the fact that the tenant had requested that it be preserved. The sole reason for the police officer/guard taking custody of this evidence was to facilitate the property owner in the civil suit that was pending. The criminal investigation, which the officer also controlled, had been precipitously closed prior to that time. Therefore, there was no police purpose being served by his actions. "An agency relationship exists where one person, expressly or by implication, authorizes another to act for him or subsequently ratifies the acts of another in his behalf. An agency relationship may be proven by circumstantial evidence of the conduct of the parties. In this case, the record contains circumstantial evidence that Gray, [the officer/guard], acted as B&M's agent in destroying or compromising the rape kit. . . . [Therefore,] sanctions were warranted against B&M for its agent's spoliation of evidence."

B. Does the Client's Obligation to Preserve Create Duties for Legal Counsel?

What obligation does this duty to preserve create for legal counsel? Is counsel's duty fulfilled by notifying the client of its duty, which includes the obligation to notify all relevant actors in the company? In the recent decision in *Zubulake v. UBS Warburg* (hereafter *Zubulake V*),[74] counsel did considerably more than this,[75] but the court concluded that all neces-

---

73. 274 Ga. App. 758, 762-63, 618 S.E.2d 650, 654-55 (2005).

74. 229 F.R.D. 422 (S.D.N.Y. 2004).

75. UBS's in-house counsel "issued a litigation hold in August 2001 and repeated that instruction several times from September 2001 through September 2002. Outside counsel also spoke with some (but not all) of the key players in August 2001." The hold order was circulated to many (but not all) of the key players in the litigation, and this was repeated twice. Outside counsel notified the company that this hold order applied to backup tapes as soon as backup tapes became an issue in the case. Outside counsel communicated directly with many of the key players and impressed upon them the preservation obligation. Counsel also instructed employees to produce copies of their active computer files relating to Zubulake.

sary steps had not been taken to fulfill counsel's duty under Fed. R. Civ. P. 26(e) to produce and supplement information responsive to the opposing party's discovery requests. The court outlined the continuing efforts that must be made to ensure that relevant documents are properly preserved and produced.[76]

Prefacing this delineation of counsel's duty, the court noted that the continuing duty under Rule 26 to supplement disclosures "strongly suggests that parties also have a duty to make sure that discoverable information is not lost," and counsel has a duty to take efforts to ensure that the client is both aware of and making reasonable efforts to meet that obligation. The court identified three steps that should generally be taken by legal counsel:

First, counsel must issue a "litigation hold" at the outset of litigation or whenever litigation is reasonably anticipated. The litigation hold should be periodically reissued so that new employees are aware of it, and so that it is fresh in the minds of all employees.

---

76. FED. R. CIV. P. 26(e) provides:

> **(e) Supplementation of Disclosures and Responses.** A party who has made a disclosure under subdivision (a) or responded to a request for discovery with a disclosure or response is under a duty to supplement or correct the disclosure or response to include information thereafter acquired if ordered by the court or in the following circumstances:
>
> **(1)** A party is under a duty to supplement at appropriate intervals its disclosures under subdivision (a) if the party learns that in some material respect the information disclosed is incomplete or incorrect and if the additional or corrective information has not otherwise been made known to the other parties during the discovery process or in writing. With respect to testimony of an expert from whom a report is required under subdivision (1)(2)(B), the duty extends both to information contained in the report and to information provided through a deposition of the expert, and any additions or other changes to this information shall be disclosed by the time the party's disclosures under Rule 26(a)(3) are due.
>
> **(2)** A party is under a duty seasonably to amend a prior response to an interrogatory, request for production, or request for admission if the party learns that the response is in some material respect incomplete or incorrect and if the additional or corrective information has not otherwise been made known to the other parties during the discovery process or in writing.

Second, counsel should communicate directly with the "key players" in the litigation, i.e., the people identified in a party's initial disclosures and any subsequent supplementation thereto. Because these "key players" are the "employees likely to have relevant information," it is particularly important that the preservation duty be communicated clearly to them. As with the litigation hold, the key players should be periodically reminded that the preservation duty is still in place.

Finally, counsel should instruct all employees to produce electronic copies of their relevant active files. Counsel must also make sure that all backup media that the party is required to retain is identified and stored in a safe place. In cases involving a small number of relevant backup tapes, counsel might be advised to take physical possession of backup tapes. In other cases, it might make sense for relevant backup tapes to be segregated and placed in storage. Regardless of what arrangement counsel chooses to employ, the point is to separate relevant backup tapes from others. One of the primary reasons that electronic data is lost is ineffective communication with information technology personnel. By taking possession of or otherwise safeguarding all potentially relevant backup tapes, counsel eliminates the possibility that such tapes will be inadvertently recycled.[77]

Are the steps outlined by Judge Scheindlin directives that counsel must follow or simply suggestions that could ensure that the cli*ent fulfills its production responsibilities? Because preserving and producing requested evidence is ultimately the client's duty, is it appropriate to impose such explicit responsibilities on counsel? If counsel has made reasonable efforts to apprise the client of its production and preservation obligations, why should more be required? If, as was true in *Zubulake*, the culprits were corporate employees who were willfully destroying relevant evidence that they knew should be produced, should this problem be addressed by imposing greater responsibilities on lawyers to ride herd over the production process (thereby increasing the costs for all litigants in all cases), or should more severe sanctions have been levied against the wrongdoers?[78] Does Judge Scheindlin intend to sanction coun-

---

77. Zubulake, 229 F.R.D. at 433-34.

78. In Zubulake V, the court imposed two sanctions. First, it directed that the additional discovery costs created by this willful conduct be borne by UBS. Second, it ordered that a negative inference instruction be given at trial. If more severe sanctions had been imposed, like striking the defendant's answer or entering partial summary judgment, might this not have been a far greater deterrence to future acts of spoliation than the supervision that legal counsel has now been directed to undertake?

sel for failing to fulfill this responsibility?[79] Answers are not clear.

Since a lawyer is an agent of his client, the reality of this decision is that the client must take certain measures to protect itself against spoliation sanctions, and counsel is in the best position to instruct the client on the scope and breadth of that responsibility.[80] Whether the client or the lawyer assumes the responsibility for taking the delineated steps to ensure the preservation of all potentially material evidence is irrelevant. What is important is that the steps be taken, because without reasonable efforts like those outlined by Judge Scheindlin, severe consequences can be befall both the attorney and the client.[81]

---

79. Under FED. R. CIV. P. 11(b)(2) the court may impose a sanction that is "sufficient to deter repetition of such conduct or comparable conduct by others similarly situated." This could include the forfeiture of fees in the representation of the client who engaged in spoliation because of improper supervision.

80. *See* Telecom Int'l Am. Ltd. v. AT&T Corp., 189 F.R.D. 76, 81 (S.D.N.Y. 1999) ("Once on notice, the obligation to preserve evidence runs first to counsel, who then has a duty to advise and explain to the client its obligations to retain pertinent documents that may be relevant to the litigation."). *But see* the Advisory Committee Note to FED. R. CIV. P. 26(e), which was cited and relied upon in Zubulake V, where it is noted that "the lawyer under a continuing burden must periodically recheck all interrogatories and canvass all new information."

81. *See* Metropolitan Opera Ass'n., Inc. v. Local 100, Hotel Employees & Restaurant Employees Int'l Union, 212 F.R.D. 178, 222 (S.D.N.Y. 2003) (default judgment was ordered as a discovery sanction because "counsel (1) never gave adequate instructions to their clients about the clients' overall discovery obligations, what constitutes a 'document' or what was specifically called for by the Met's document request; (2) knew the Union to have no document retention or filing systems and yet never implemented a systematic procedure for document production or for retention of documents, including electronic documents; (3) delegated document production to a layperson who did not even understand himself (and was not instructed by counsel) that a document included a draft or other non-identical copy, a computer file and an e-mail; (4) never went back to the layperson designated to assure that he had 'establish[ed] a coherent and effective system to faithfully and effectively respond to discovery requests'; and (5) in the face of the Met's persistent questioning and showings that the production was faulty and incomplete, ridiculed the inquiries, failed to take any action to remedy the situation or supplement the demonstrably false responses, failed to ask important witnesses for documents until the night before their depositions and, instead, made repeated, baseless representations that all documents had been produced.").

The responsibilities of outside counsel for the actions of the client were again illustrated in *Qualcomm Inc. v. Broadcom Corp.*,[82] where the client had not adequately responded to discovery demands, and there were red flags regarding the abuse that Qualcomm's lawyers saw or should have seen and tried to correct. Ignoring these warning signals, the lawyers made no efforts to see that more appropriate searches were conducted, and they made representations to the court that were either knowingly false or inadequately verified. As a consequence, the client was fined over $8.5 million, and most of its lawyers were reported to the California State Bar for additional sanctioning.

The lesson of *Qualcomm* is that lawyers, by signing, and thereby certifying, pleadings and discovery responses, and making factual representations to the court about the client's compliance with discovery obligations (including preservation of discoverable materials), cannot passively accept whatever the client tells them. The lessons from both *Zubulake* and *Qualcomm* are that lawyers must be more active in the entire discovery process, which requires attention to evolving needs that are exposed by the developing evidence and unfolding events. The full dimensions of this new digital age responsibility are, of course, undefined. What actions are reasonable, and therefore necessary, will turn on the facts of each case. Perhaps counsel's responsibilities in the production process will be inherently greater than his or her involvement in the many and varied ways in which clients can intentionally or unintentionally destroy relevant data. Regardless, in the future, lawyers should be overly cautious on the spoliation, as well as the production, aspects of discovery because professional reputations and livelihoods are potentially at stake. Unfortunately, this will accelerate the increasing costs of litigation for all parties—both the good and the bad, the informed and uninformed.

In fulfilling both the client's and the attorney's obligation to employ good faith in identifying and preserving relevant evidence, and preparing for the initial discovery conference with opposing counsel (Fed. R.Civ. P. 26), the first step is to place a hold on the destruction of all potentially relevant information and to communicate this preservation obligation to all employees through means that are likely to be read or heard. After placing this hold on destruction of documents relating to identified issues, the next step is identifying specific people and sources. This is done through interviews with employees. In those interviews, counsel should:

---

82. 2008 U.S. Dist. LEXIS 911 (S.D. Cal. Jan. 7, 2008).

(1) attempt to ascertain
    (a) who has what,
    (b) in what locations, and
    (c) in what formats;
(2) reemphasize each individual's legal obligation to preserve the relevant and specifically identified data possessed;
(3) ask that the obligation to preserve be communicated to others as quickly as possible; and
(4) request that outside sources of data be made available to counsel for examination.

C.   What Must Be Retained and Preserved?

The simple answer is all potentially relevant evidence. This includes any evidence that could be helpful in proving or disproving a claim or defense. "Relevant evidence" is defined in Fed. R. Evid. 401 as "evidence having any tendency to make the existence of any fact that is of consequence to the determination of the action more probable or less probable than it would be without the evidence." As one court has explained:

> While a litigant is under no duty to keep or retain every document in its possession once a complaint is filed, it is under a duty to preserve what it knows, or reasonably should know, is relevant in the action, is reasonably calculated to lead to the discovery of admissible evidence, is reasonably likely to be requested during discovery, and/or is the subject of a pending discovery request.[83] This includes hard copies of written communications, active computer

---

83. Jeanblanc v. Oliver T. Carr Co., 1992 WL 189434, at *2 (D. D.C. 1992) (quoting Wm. T. Thompson Co. v. General Nutrition Corp., Inc., 593 F. Supp. 1443, 1447 (C.D. Cal. 1984)); Glotzbach v. Froman, 827 N.E.2d 105, 110 (Ind. Ct. App. 2005) ("Midwest and Drew had a 'special relationship' to support the recognition of a duty to preserve evidence from the explosion. Not only was Midwest Drew's employer at the time of the explosion, Midwest knew the pump and related items were needed for the IOSHA investigation and had specifically been instructed by an IOSHA officer not to dispose of them. Darling witnessed the explosion and knew that Drew had been gravely injured while working for Midwest. Midwest knew and reasonably should have known that Drew might likely have a claim against the manufacturer of the pump involved in the explosion. A mere seven days after the explosion, and after having been instructed by an IOSHA official to preserve the evidence, Darling instead disposed of all the equipment and debris, as well as Drew's clothing and wallet.").

files,[84] hard drives, back-up tapes,[85] codes (both passwords and computer codes),[86] and e-mail records.[87]

Backup tapes have created preservation problems. They are expensive and, because of that expense, used primarily for purposes of disaster recovery. Therefore, they are periodically reused, and the previously backed-up data is lost. Most courts that have addressed this issue have held that if the backup tapes are inaccessible and the documents on them are otherwise available on the active drives of company computers, preservation is unnecessary.[88] This view, however, is not universal.[89] If, however, the documents are not otherwise available,

---

84. Febres Morales v. Challenger Caribbean Corp., 8 F. Supp. 2d 126 (D. P.R. 1998); Gates Rubber Co. v. Bando Chem. Indus., Ltd., 167 F.R.D. 90 (D. Colo. 1996).

85. Zubulake v. UBS Warburg, 220 F.R.D. 212, 218 (S.D.N.Y. 2003) (holding that backup tapes should not be destroyed unless it is certain that same information is available from other sources); United States v. Koch Indus., Inc., 197 F.R.D. 463, 486 (N.D. Okla. 1998) ("Plaintiffs have failed to carry their burden of proof to establish by a preponderance of the evidence that KII destroyed the computer files intentionally or with bad faith. Therefore, no 'adverse inference' jury instruction should arise from KII's destruction of the computer tapes." In this case, the court refused to permit party who destroyed tapes to offer any evidence generated from destroyed tapes.); Synanon Church v. United States, 579 F. Supp. 967 (D. D.C. 1984).

86. Cabinetware Inc. v. Sullivan, 1991 WL 327959, 22 U.S. P.Q.2d 1686 (E.D. Cal. 1991); Computer Assoc. Int'l, Inc. v. Am. Fundware, Inc., 133 F.R.D. 166 (D. Colo. 1990).

87. Mosaid Tech. Inc. v. Samsung Elecs. Co., 348 F. Supp. 2d 332 (D. N.J. 2004) (Samsung failed to put a "litigation hold" on all technical e-mails relevant to the litigation and was sanctioned with an inference instruction and costs); Procter & Gamble Co. v. Haugen, 179 F.R.D. 622 (D. Utah 1998); Linnen v. A.H. Robins Co., Inc., 1999 WL 462015 (Mass. Sup. Ct. June 16, 1999).

88. "As a general rule, . . . a party need not preserve all backup tapes even when it reasonably anticipates litigation." Zubulake v. UBS Warburg LLC, 220 F.R.D. 212 (S.D.N.Y. 2003). This conclusion was followed in Oxford House, Inc. v. City of Topeka, 2007 U.S. Dist. LEXIS 31731 (D. Kan. April 27, 2007); Cache La Poudre Feeds, LLC v. Land O'Lakes, Inc., 244 F.R.D. 614 (D. Colo. 2007); Columbia Pictures Indus. v. Bunnell, 2007 U.S. Dist. LEXIS 46364 , *55 (C.D. Cal. May 29, 2007); E*Trade Sec. LLC v. Deutsche Bank AG, 230 F.R.D. 582, 592 (D. Minn. 2005).

89. In AAB Joint Venture v. United States, 75 Fed. Cl. 432, 2007 U.S. Claims LEXIS 56, *26 (Ct. Cl. Feb. 28, 2007), the court held that "the scope of the duty to preserve extends to electronic documents, such as e-mails and back-up tapes."

preservation is essential and a litigation hold must include the backup tapes.[90]

An even more difficult problem involves the drives on computers that temporarily store documents that are currently being used and then erase them when the computer is turned off. This temporary memory is called RAM (Random Access Memory). Its purpose is to make the documents more quickly accessible during use. In rare instances, these temporary drives have proven to be important in litigation, and courts have had to confront the question of whether the parties who failed to preserve the information on those drives should be sanctioned for permitting relevant evidence to be destroyed.[91] While the courts imposed an obligation to commence preserving information on those drives when this issue surfaced, neither party was sanctioned because the duty to preserve was not previously known, no specific requests to preserve had been made by the demanding party, and no court orders were violated. It is not clear that courts will be so forgiving in the future, now that the issue has been aired. If the preservation of RAM is important to litigation, it is not only important for the producing party to anticipate that, it is incumbent on the discovering party to specifically mention it in notices of potential litigation and discovery demands. At the very latest, this is an issue that parties need to discuss in their initial discovery conference mandated by the recent revisions to Rule 26(f) of the Federal Rules of Civil Procedure.

Because the definition of relevant evidence remains so broad, parties should err on the side of preservation—particularly when information is stored on a computer, where preservation is relatively cheap and

---

90. In the Zubulake opinion, Judge Scheindlin, after generally excusing the preservation of backup tapes, acknowledged that "[i]f a company can identify where particular employee documents are stored on backup tapes, then the tapes storing the documents of 'key players' to the existing or threatened litigation should be preserved if the information contained on those tapes is not otherwise available." Zubulake, 220 F.R.D. at 218.

91. Columbia Pictures Indus. v. Bunnell, 2007 U.S. Dist. LEXIS 46364 (C.D. Cal. May 29, 2007); Healthcare Advocates, Inc. v. Harding, 497 F. Supp. 2d 627 (E.D. Pa. 2007). While each court acknowledged the need to preserve the RAM in the unique factual circumstances of those cases, neither imposed sanctions because the parties could not reasonably have known of their responsibility vis-a-vis the temporary drives, and thus acted in good faith.

convenient.[92] While preservation may be cheap, enormous costs can result from the preserved data, because what is retained for discovery purposes in one case may be sought by litigants in a future case. Information that might be outside the scope of what would be preserved for the litigation at hand in order to avoid spoliation sanctions could be sought simply because it is available. Does a client have the obligation to continue to preserve what has been preserved from the past simply because it may be relevant in the subsequent litigation? Searching sources of such data (e.g., backup tapes) can be onerous and expensive. Nevertheless, the answer is clearly yes. Since the evidence exists, is reasonably believed to be relevant, and can continue to be preserved with minimal additional costs, it cannot be destroyed simply because production from the database might prove to be onerous. The reason why the documents exist is irrelevant to the spoliation issue. If, however, the resulting production effort creates unfair burdens for the producing party because, for example, of the volume of privilege issues, or the key word search is prohibitively time-consuming and costly, such difficulties might warrant a reallocation of costs associated with the production of marginally relevant evidence. If, however, production reveals important information, reallocation of costs is unlikely. Simply because a party is big, prosperous, and has enormous amounts of relevant information does not warrant the party being relieved of its production burdens. Arguing that such a party should receive special concessions may be perceived as being a bit like the criminal defendant, convicted of killing his parents, pleading for mercy because he is an orphan.

Normal document destruction should continue only after potential litigants have *explicitly* acquiesced.[93] In the litigation, this could appro-

---

92. Serrano v. Rajamani, 6 A.D.3d 1191 (N.Y. App. Div. 2004) demonstrates the type of evidence that might be discarded without consequence. The plaintiff sought journal articles and medical texts that the defendant reviewed or relied upon in treating plaintiff. The court held that the unavailability of those materials was excusable because the "defendant did not know that the materials might be needed for future litigation."

93. *See, e.g.,* Crabtree v. Nat'l Steel Corp., 261 F.3d 715, 721 (7th Cir. 2001) ("Granite City Steel destroyed the RIF documents only after maintaining them for two years (one year longer than required under company policy) and only after giving notice to the IDHR that it was doing so. Additionally, most of the RIF documents were not relevant to Crabtree's case because his lawsuit did not challenge the RIF, and those that were relevant—Crabtree's own RIF evaluations—were preserved and produced.").

priately be addressed in the early discussions that Rule 26(f) requires parties have on the scope of electronic evidence discovery.[94] During such conferences, parties are expected to have candid discussions on such things as the sources of relevant information, the scope of preservation to be undertaken, key players in the process, and search terms that will be used on particular databases.

If litigants require preservation of normally discarded hard copies (paper), the demanding party should pay for any special storage or retrieval expenses. Normal retrieval expenses for communications remaining on a non-litigant's hard drive (whether active or replaced) are not typical expenses to which litigants are expected to contribute. Normal document production by both litigants and third parties (regardless of how the parties have chosen to maintain them) is considered an expense that must be borne by the members of society.[95] The defendant in *Linnen v. A.H. Robins Co.*[96] tried to argue that restoring and reproducing communications from backup tapes constituted an undue burden and expense, but the court disagreed. "To permit a corporation . . . to reap the benefits of such technology and simultaneously use that technology as a shield in litigation would lead to incongruous and unfair results."[97] Of course, in special circumstances parties may seek judicially ordered compensation through a protective order after the action is filed.[98] If the producing party de-

---

94. Rule 26(f) of the FEDERAL RULES OF CIVIL PROCEDURE provides, in part:

    (1) Conference Timing. . . . [T]he parties must confer as soon as practicable—and in any event at least 21 days before a scheduling conference is to be held or a scheduling order is due under Rule 16(b).

    (2) Conference Content; Parties' Responsibilities. In conferring, the parties must . . . discuss any issues about preserving discoverable information; and develop a proposed discovery plan.

95. Linnen, 1999 WL 462015, at *1 ("[T]his is one of the risks taken on by companies which have made the decision to avail themselves of the computer technology now available to the business world. To permit a corporation such as A.H. Robins to reap the business benefits of such technology and simultaneously use that technology as a shield in litigation would lead to . . . unfair results.").

96. 1999 WL 462015 (Mass Sup. Ct. 1999).

97. *Id.* at *6.

98. Rule 26 of the FEDERAL RULES OF CIVIL PROCEDURE provides in part:

V. Depositions and Discovery

Rule 26

GENERAL PROVISIONS GOVERNING DISCOVERY; DUTY OF DISCLOSURE

. . . .

stroyed relevant evidence responsive to a discovery demand, the expenses involved in re-creating that evidence from backup tapes and other original sources should be borne by the producing/destroying party as a penalty for its act of spoliation.[99]

The types of evidence that parties have had to retain, like the standard of logical relevance itself, are quite fact-specific. Some scholars have argued that originals can be destroyed when electronic or photographic copies have been made because such copies are classified as "duplicates" under Fed. R. Evid. 1001(4) and made admissible as if they were the originals under Fed. R. Evid. 1003. This suggests that the practice of destroying originals could continue after litigation has commenced without creating spoliation problems.[100] But even though all computer printouts are considered originals for best evidence purposes,[101] it would be unwise to destroy hard copies that existed when litigation is reasonably anticipated because those copies might contain handwritten notes and interlineations that would not appear in subsequent copies produced by the computer. Because these notations by employees could be considered vicarious admissions of the employer,[102] destroying the hard copies would destroy potentially important evidence the would not exist elsewhere. This explains why so many copies of the same documents must be produced in the discovery process when found in sepa-

---

(c) **Protective Orders.** Upon motion by a party or by the person from whom discovery is sought, accompanied by a certification that the movant has in good faith conferred or attempted to confer with other affected parties in an effort to resolve the dispute without court action, and for good cause shown, the court in which the action is pending or alternatively, on matters relating to a deposition, the court in the district where the deposition is to be taken may make any order which justice requires to protect a party or person from annoyance, embarrassment, oppression, or undue burden or expense
. . . .

99. United States ex rel. Koch v. Koch Indus., Inc., 197 F.R.D. 488, 490-91 (N.D. Okla. 1999). *See* Spoliation, Chapter 2, *infra.*

100. J. Kinsler & A. MacIver, *Demystifying Spoliation of Evidence,* 34 Tort & Ins. L. J. 761, 779-82 (1999) ("Because the Federal Rules of Evidence generally treat electronic and photographic reproductions as originals and because there is no federal law requiring companies to retain hard copies of records, there would seem to be no reason for companies to retain originals once the records have been reproduced.").

101. *See* Chapter Four, "Best Evidence—Original Writing Rule," *infra.*

102. *See,* Chapter Seven, "Hearsay," *infra.*

rate files. The only safe practice is to retain all copies of all documents that exist at the time a duty to preserve arises.

Wiginton v. Ellis[103] illustrates the expected scope of document retention. The plaintiff filed a class action alleging sexual harassment. The complaint identified 10 individuals and four offices. Immediately after the action was filed, the plaintiff's attorney sent a letter to the defendant's counsel requesting that certain documents not be destroyed.[104] When the defendant, CBRE, instructed its employees to retain documents, it instructed them to "comply with the CBRE record retention policy and to not destroy any records of any type that 'pertain to Amy Wiginton.'"[105] Despite this notice and instruction, CBRE continued its normal document destruction policies and "did not in-

---

103. 2003 WL 22439865 (N.D. Ill. Oct. 27, 2003).

104. First, the letter asked CBRE to "not destroy, conceal or alter any paper or electronic files and other data generated by and/or stored in CBRE's computers and storage media . . . or any other electronic data, such as voice mail that relates in any way to the subject matter of this litigation, or any information which is likely to lead to the discovery of admissible evidence . . . This issue is especially important here because CBRE controls virtually all of the documents that will be at issue." *Id.* at *2. The letter also described electronic data and storage media that would be subject to a discovery request and instructed CBRE:

> to preserve all e-mails, both sent and received, whether internally or externally; all word-processed files, including drafts and revisions; all spreadsheets, including drafts and revisions; all databases; all presentation data or slide shows produced by presentation software . . . all Internet and Web-browser-generated history files, caches and 'cookies' files generated at the work station of each employee and/or agent in CBRE's employ and on any and all backup storage media. . . . Further, you are to preserve any log or logs of network use by employees or otherwise . . . and to preserve all copies of your backup tapes and the software necessary to reconstruct the data on those tapes, so that there can be made a complete, bit-by-bit 'mirror' evidentiary image copy of the storage media of each and every personal computer (and/or workstation) and network server in CBRE's control and custody, as well as image copies of all hard drives retained and not longer in service, but in use at any time from July 1, 1990 to the present.

Id. at *1. Plaintiff's attorney also requested that CBRE forward a copy of this letter to all persons with custodial responsibility for any of the items referenced in the letter.

105. *Id.* at *2.

form its director of network services that any electronic information should be retained, and never informed its employees about the need to retain any documents that might be relevant to the lawsuit, as opposed to any documents dealing specifically with Amy Wiginton." Backup tapes were also destroyed, and former employees' hard drives, including that of Wiginton's former supervisor, were not saved, despite the fact that the court had issued a preservation order.[106]

The judge concluded that CBRE could not reasonably claim it was not required to maintain the following data:

1. Electronic data such as e-mails or Internet use records.
2. The documents other than those specifically related to Amy Wiginton (materials relating to the alleged harassers and the offices in which they worked).

The judge concluded that the document retention letter "lacked the appropriate scope."

While not all e-mails had to be preserved, those that dealt with sexually explicit material should have been. The court rejected the claim that searching for such materials would be too costly and time-consuming. To the contrary, the e-mail system had spam filters, and among the non-spam e-mails, searches could be conducted for sexually explicit words. Similarly, searches could be made for sexually explicit images. "The fact that such searches might not have turned up all sexually explicit e-mails does not excuse CBRE from looking for *any* e-mails."

---

106. *Id.* Similar abuses occurred in Wachtel v. Guardian Life Ins. Co., 2006 WL 1320031 (D. N.J. May 12, 2006) (deliberately failing to preserve and diligently search for and produce all responsive documents from all places they knew they were retained, not informing legal counsel or the court of the company's discretionary employee destruction policy for e-mails older than 30 days, not advising either legal counsel or the court that the company removed 90-day-old e-mails to backup tapes, making it impossible for employees to fully respond to subpoenas; leaving critical information out of affidavits to mislead the judge; and using legal counsel to delay discovery by misinforming counsel who, in turn, made erroneous representations to the court).

Such preservation orders are only binding on a party over whom the court has personal jurisdiction. *See* In re Ski Train Fire in Kaprun, Austria, on Nov. 11, 2000, 2003 WL 22909153 (S.D.N.Y. Dec. 9, 2003).

A comparable failure of document retention policy was discussed in *Larson v. BankOne Corp.*[107] While BankOne appeared to have no comprehensive document retention policy during the relevant time period, the policy that it claimed existed was flawed in a number of ways. First, it was labeled "proposed." Second, it provided no specific guidance regarding the litigation in question. Third, the policies were not properly disseminated to BankOne employees because there was no general dissemination in writing to all employees, and no steps were taken to ensure that employees read and understood the electronic version of the policy. Finally, no steps were taken to ensure that the policies were being followed.

Parties should be careful and broadly construe what might be relevant to the anticipated litigation. "A party cannot destroy documents based solely on its own version of the proper scope" of its document retention responsibilities.[108] A narrow scope should be adopted only with judicial approval.

Documents that are created during the pendency of a case should not be treated any differently than documents created prior to the initiation of the lawsuit. If documents are relevant to an action, the time when they were created should not affect the duty to preserve them. Special circumstances, however, may exist that would justify modifying the duty to preserve if the evidence in question was costly to retain, dangerous, part of an established protocol of destructive and beneficial testing, or unnecessary in light of other available evidence.[109] In such circumstances, it would be wise for the party contemplating destruction to notify the interested parties and seek judicial approval in order to avoid subsequent repercussions.

The electronic age has vastly expanded the scope of what must be preserved. Not only are new document formats available (e.g., e-mails, computer-generated documents, and the hardware on which those documents are created and stored), there is a vast amount of somewhat hidden information stored within documents about the data that is evident on the face of the documents. This is called "metadata," or "data about data." It is information describing the history, tracking, and management of an electronic communication. The simplest example of this would be a word-

---

107. Larson v. BankOne Corp., 2005 WL 4652509, *37-39 (N.D. Ill. Aug. 18, 2005).

108. *Id.* at *36; Dieirsen v. Walker, 2003 WL 21317276 at *5 (N.D. Ill. June 6, 2003).

109. *See, e.g.,* In re St. Jude Med., Inc. Silzone Heart Valve Prod. Liability Litig., 2002 WL 341019 (D. Minn. Mar. 1, 2002).

processing document that has been distributed electronically. If the metadata has not been deleted through a "scrubbing" process, the recipient can uncover deleted past versions of the text or data by pressing the undo function key. Metadata, however, includes a much broader range of things, such as the author's name or initials; a company or organization name; identification of the computer, network server, or hard disk where documents are saved; names of previous document authors; document revisions and previous versions; hidden text or cells; template information; other file properties and summary information; embedded objects; and personal comments.

In documents like spreadsheets and data tables, this metadata may be crucial to understanding what has been produced. The metadata provides information about how the visible data was created and organized. For this reason, when documents are produced by a business, they may have to be provided in the form in which they are maintained (with the metadata intact), unless the parties reach a different agreement in the initial discovery-planning conference required by Fed. R. Civ. P. 26(f). This is a discovery question that turns on whether the obligation to produce electronic documents in the form in which they are regularly maintained means in their native format as an active file.[110]

---

110. *See, e.g.,* Mich. First Credit Union v. Cumis Ins. Soc'y, Inc., 2007 WL 4098213 (E.D. Mich. Nov. 16, 2007) (refusing to require production of metadata because the documents were also kept in paper form, and producing metadata would be too expensive relative to the value of what it would provide); Celerity v. Ultra Clean Holding, Inc., 476 F. Supp. 2d 1159 (N.D. 2007) (Production of metadata required for an opinion of noninfringement to which multiple revisions had been made. "Celerity's counsel read to the Court a portion of a billing record from UCT which included notation about multiple revisions of the opinion. However, UCT produced only the final version, not any of the earlier drafts. UCT explained that the author overwrote the older drafts in the process of writing the final version. Celerity expressed interest in receiving the metadata which would reflect these earlier drafts. To the extent this exists it shall be produced."); Ky. Speedway v. Nat'l Ass'n. of Stock Car Auto Racing, Inc., 2006 U.S. Dist. LEXIS 92028 (E.D. Ky. Dec. 18, 2006) ("I respectfully disagree with [the] conclusion that a producing party 'should produce the electronic documents with their metadata intact, unless that party timely objects . . . , the parties agree that the metadata should not be produced, or the producing party requests a protective order.'" The court refused to order the production of metadata because it would have been overly burdensome and no particularized need had been demonstrated by the demanding party.); Wyeth v. Impax Labs., 245 F.R.D. 169 (D. Del. 2006) (Production of documents in Tagged Image File Format (TIFF), rather than in their native form, was found acceptable because

It is critical that metadata be discussed at the discovery-planning conference and an agreement be reached regarding its permissible destruction. If there is no agreement regarding metadata, its production could multiply costs when the documents in which the metadata is attached are found not to be privileged, because the underlying metadata of each document would have to be uncovered, deciphered, and screened for those portions that are potentially privileged. Because of the cost, inconvenience, and absence of relevance of most of this information, some courts "articulate a general presumption against the production of metadata" unless the requesting party demonstrates a particularized need for the native format.[111]

It is important to understand that even if there is an agreement with the adverse party about the production of metadata and its production is excused, that is only half of the issue. If the metadata contains potentially relevant evidence but the producing party is excused from producing it because of disproportionate costs and insufficiently demonstrated need, the party possessing it should nonetheless continue preserving the metadata unless destruction is either agreed to or otherwise sanctioned by the court.[112]

To avoid such problems, metadata should regularly be destroyed. Software programs are available that reliably remove metadata. This "scrubbing" of documents, however, can only be done without spoliation sanctions if it is done as a matter of course in the daily maintenance of the documents, and the documents have not become relevant to reasonably anticipated litigation.

1.   Privileged Materials

The spoliation doctrine is designed to punish, and thereby deter, the destruction of evidence that might have assisted the opposing party in proving its claims. If the materials destroyed were privileged and therefore not available to the opposing side in the first instance, the doctrine does not

---

there had been no prior agreement on how production should be made, no showing of particularized need for the metadata, and production would have been too burdensome); Williams v. Sprint/United Mgmt. Co., 230 F.R.D. 640, 651 (D. Kan. 2005) ("Emerging standards of electronic discovery appear to articulate a general presumption against the production of metadata.") .

111. Wyeth v. Impax Labs., Inc., 248 F.R.D. 169, 171 (D. Del. 2006); Williams v. Sprint/United Mgmt. Co., 230 F.R.D. 640, 651 (D. Kan. 2005).

112. *See* text at note 95, *supra.*

apply.[113] Of course, if the privilege is subsequently waived, the destruction is actionable.[114] Because the issues of waiver and exceptions to the privilege will not have been raised and resolved by a court before material is disposed of, the destruction of materials that one believes to be privileged could turn out to be incorrect, and later construed as an intentional act of spoliation.[115]

The scope of resulting waiver can be potentially broad.[116] Therefore, a party should take care to preserve all potentially relevant documents, regardless of what is believed about its privileged status. This is particularly true when a client raises the defense of reliance on advice of counsel, as the defendant did in *Mosel Vitelic Corp. v. Micron Tech., Inc.*[117] At meetings where attorneys discussed a patent opinion, the defendant passed out a draft patent opinion letter, on which the other attorneys would add notes. He later incorporated those notes into a master copy of the opinion letter stored on his computer, but he failed to save the older versions. He also threw out the marked versions from the meetings. The court found intentional spoliation had occurred in two ways: first, when he discarded the notes, and second, when he erased the previous versions from his computer.

---

113. Bloom v. Lewis, 97 N.M. 435, 437-38, 640 P.2d 935, 937-38 (Ct. App. 1980). The privilege in this particular instance was the work product immunity, and the discovering party did not demonstrate a compelling need to override the protection.

114. Fuller v. Preston State Bk., 667 S.W.2d 214, 220 (Tex. App. 1983) (indicating that evidence about destruction of bank minutes should have been admitted because bank waived its privilege claim for those minutes by producing another document that opened general subject matter for exploration).

115. *See, e.g.,* Mosel Vitelic Corp. v. Micron Tech., Inc., 162 F. Supp. 2d 307 (D. Del. 2000). The client was found to have waived the attorney-client privilege by relying on the advice of counsel in a patent infringement action. The scope of this waiver was found to extend to communications within its attorney's files even if they had not been sent to the client. Therefore, the attorney's destruction of notes and drafts was found to be an act of spoliation. The court sanctioned an instruction about the negative inference that may drawn by the jury and awarded attorney's fees to the injured party.

116. Usually, the scope of waiver will be defined by the subject matter of the disclosed communication, modified upward or downward by the standard of fairness, considering such factors as timing, context, unfair advantage, and the like. *See* PAUL R. RICE, ATTORNEY-CLIENT PRIVILEGE IN THE UNITED STATES, §§ 9:78, et seq. (West Group, 2d ed. 1999).

117. 162 F. Supp. 2d 307, 310 (D. Del. 2000).

2.   Duration of the Duty to Preserve

"The scope of the duty to preserve evidence is not boundless. A potential spoliator need do only what is reasonable."[118] The duration of the duty to preserve depends on a number of factors relating to the circumstances of the preservation. These can include (1) the nature of the items or conditions (automobile, swimming pool, gate or documents), (2) the inconvenience and expense involved in preservation, (3) the need to make repairs or changes, (4) the importance of the condition or instrumentality to the litigation, and (5) whether a reasonable opportunity has been given to interested parties to examine and test the items or conditions.

In *Townes v. Cove Haven, Inc.*,[119] for example, the plaintiff claimed that her husband had drowned in a swimming pool due to the negligent operation of the pool by the defendant. The defendant preserved the pool for two years after the accident, which afforded the plaintiff a reasonable opportunity to avail herself of the evidence. The court excused the defendant's eventual remodeling of the pool because the plaintiff "knew exactly where the pool was located; she had over one year from the date of the complaint to request inspection of the pool."[120] Concluding that the defendant acted reasonably by preserving the condition as long as it did, the court noted that "the doctrine of spoliation does not require them to retain on their property indefinitely what Plaintiff alleges to be a negligent condition."

Similarly, in *Sterbenz v. Attina,*[121] the court declined to sanction the defendant for destroying an automobile three months after the defendant notified plaintiff's counsel of its location, informing him that the vehicle was collecting storage charges and should be removed as soon as possible. The lawyer failed to contact the auto body shop and did not even retain an expert to examine the vehicle for more than four months. The car was subsequently sold and became unavailable. The court explained that "any detriment suffered by plaintiff was thus the product of her counsel's dilatory and unprofessional handling of the case, and not by any tortious conduct on defendants' part." By contrast, in *In re*

---

118. Kolanovic v. Gida, 17 F. Supp. 2d 595, 602 (D. N.J. 1999).
119. 2003 WL 22861921, *1 (S.D.N.Y. Dec 2, 2003).
120. *Id.* at *4.
121. 205 F. Supp. 2d 65, 73 (E.D. N.Y. 2002).
122. 121 F. Supp. 2d 404, 420 (D. Del. 2000).

Wechsler,[122] spoliation sanctions were imposed for the destruction of a vessel after storage for only two weeks, even though another party had already agreed to pay for the vessel's continued storage.

In *Crabtree v. National Steel Corp.*,[123] the defendant destroyed the RIF documents after maintaining them for two years (one year longer than required under company policy). This was excused, however, because it was done only after giving notice to the opposing party that it was planning the destruction, the documents were not very important to the litigation, and those that were important were otherwise preserved.

In criminal litigation, the government's obligation to preserve relevant evidence may not extend beyond the exhaustion of the defendant's direct appeals.[124] Because of the frequency of collateral attacks on convictions through extraordinary writs such as habeas corpus, and the constantly improving scientific tests that can be conducted on evidence to establish the innocence of convicted individuals, it may be prudent for the government to retain material evidence for a longer period of time. There is no existing precedent, however, requiring that this be done.

If items that must be preserved are documents on the hard drive of a computer, there is little reason to discard the hard drive, even if the hard drive needs to be replaced to give the computer greater memory capacity, and even if the entire computer needs to be replaced to take advantage of technological improvements.[125] There would seldom be an excuse for not removing the hard drive and storing it in a secure environment for as long as the documents it contains are relevant to anticipated litigation. Both the expense and inconvenience are slight. Of course, if an agreement can be reached with the opposing party on an alternative method of preserving documents from an old hard drive, or the court otherwise approves other methods of preservation because relevant information would not be sacrificed by the transfer, economics and convenience might reasonably dictate the use of more convenient technologies that are easier and cheaper to scan for documents responsive to discovery demands.

---

123. 261 F.3d 715, 721 (7th Cir. 2001).

124. People v. Barnwell, 6 A.D.3d 1147 (N.Y. App. Div. 2004).

125. For departing employees whose hard drives contain relevant documents that must be preserved, it may occasionally be easier and less expensive, and could avoid inadvertent destruction of those documents, if the hard drives from their computers are simply replaced and those old drives stored for safekeeping.

The operating rule of thumb should be that, if a duty to preserve has attached, a party and its counsel should continue to preserve relevant evidence until a compelling reason to change or destroy arises, and then only after adequate notice has been given to the opposing party of (1) the availability of the evidence for examination and (2) the planned destruction. If the obligation to preserve has not clearly ended, an agreement with the opposing counsel or a court order is preferable. However, acquiescence through silence, by the opposing party's failure to object, should establish good faith and reasonableness on the client's part when there are compelling reasons for the destruction, and thereby protect that destruction from spoliation sanctions.

D.   Prejudice to Discovering Party

The act of document destruction by itself will not justify imposing sanctions on the culpable party. There must be circumstantial evidence that supports the facts to be inferred from the missing materials. There must be some basis from which "the trier of fact [can] determine in what respect it would have been detrimental."[126] Otherwise, jurors may be encouraged to read too much or too little into the absence of the evidence.[127] The facts reasonably inferred from the destroyed materials must not be reliably provable through some other means. If there is no harm, there is no foul. When the evidence in the destroyed documents is otherwise available, there is no harm, and therefore, no sanctionable conduct.[128]

---

126. Turner v. Hudson Transit Lines, 142 F.R.D. 68, 76 (S.D.N.Y. 1991).

127. INA Aviation Corp. v. Untied States, 468 F. Supp. 695, 700 (E.D. N.Y. 1979).

128. Matsuura v. E.I. du Pont de Nemours & Co., 330 F. Supp. 2d 1101, 1127 (D. Haw. 2004) ("All of the Plaintiffs base their spoliation claims on the destruction of plants from the alleged Costa Rica Field test. Because all of the Plaintiffs allege that evidence other than those plants proved the harmful effects of Benlate, the destruction of the plants did not result in their inability to prove the Underlying Cases. The Matsuura Plaintiffs' spoliation claims fail as a matter of law."); Corporate Interiors, Inc. v. Pappas, 2004 WL 750507 (N.Y. Sup. April 7, 2004).

While the demonstration of prejudice can be seen as an element of a spoliation claim,[129] the Second Circuit has held that where destruction is deliberate, "sanctions will normally follow, irrespective of the perpetrator's motivation, unless the [responsible party] can bear the heavy burden of demonstrating that no prejudice resulted to the [party seeking discovery]."[130] Similarly, Ohio appears to shift the burden on the issue of prejudice to the party who altered or destroyed the evidence. The wrongdoer must "prove that the other side was not preju-

---

129. *See* Crandall v. City & County of Denver, 2006 WL 2683754, at *2 (D. Colo. Sept. 19, 2006) ("It appears to this Court that whenever a sanction has been levied in the reported cases, the moving party has established some element of harm—that the documents destroyed were relevant to the issues in the lawsuit, or, stated another way, that the moving party has suffered prejudice because of the destruction of evidence. Mere existence of a document [in this case e-mail] destruction policy within a corporate entity, coupled with a failure to put a comprehensive 'hold' on that policy once the corporate entity becomes aware of litigation, does not suffice to justify a sanction absent some proof that, in fact, it is potentially relevant evidence that has been spoiled or destroyed. . . . Plaintiff, in essence, proposes that the Court create a presumption in favor of spoliation whenever a moving party can prove that records that might have contained relevant evidence have been destroyed. The Court understands the logic of this argument but does not find any support in case law. . . . Only the bad faith loss or destruction of evidence will support the kind of adverse inference that Plaintiffs seek, *i.e.*, that the supposedly deleted e-mails would *in fact* have been unfavorable to Defendant."); Consol. Aluminum Corp. v. Alcoa, Inc., 244 F.R.D. 335, 2006 WL 2583308, at *8 (M.D. La. July 19, 2006) ("[S]ome extrinsic evidence of the content of the emails is necessary for the trier of fact to be able to determine in what respect and to what extent the emails would have been detrimental."); Frey v. Gainey Transp. Servs., Inc., 2006 WL 2443787, *7 (N.D. Ga. Aug. 22, 2006) (noting prejudice as the first factor when determining whether spoliation has occurred); Concord Boat Corp. v. Brunswick Corp., 1997 WL 33352759, *7 (E.D. Ark. 1997) (non-destroying party must demonstrate that he has suffered prejudice from the destruction); Smith v. Howard Johnson Co., 67 Ohio St. 3d 28, 1993 Ohio 229, 615 N.E.2d 1037, 1038 (1993) (plaintiff must show "damages proximately caused by the defendant's acts").

Requiring too strict a standard of demonstrated prejudice can be quite unfair to the injured party, however, because that party has been denied access to the evidence through the opponent's destruction. See discussion below.

130. United States v. Henriquez, 731 F.2d 131, 137-38 (2d Cir. 1984), *quoting from* United States v. Paoli, 603 F.2d 1029, 1036 (2d Cir. 1979), *cert. denied*, 444 U.S. 926 (1979) (government destroyed Jencks Act statements that it attempted to justify under a "departmental policy" or "established practice").

diced by the alteration or destruction of the evidence."[131] Of course, regardless of demonstrated prejudice, a logical inference arises about the unfavorable nature of the evidence because the spoliator perceived a need to suppress or destroy it.[132]

Prejudice is a factor in the spoliation equation in two ways. First, there is no spoliation if the evidence destroyed was not relevant to the issues being litigated. There must be some showing that there is a nexus between the proposed inference and the information contained in the lost evidence. This can be relatively easy when there has been testimony about what the deleted materials contained. In *Crescendo Investments, Inc. v. Brice*,[133] for example, two individuals testified that the one who had destroyed the e-mails had e-mailed reports on a weekly basis concerning significant events in the company. Also, when the nature of the data and its relevance to the litigation are apparent from the item lost or destroyed, the burden of demonstrating prejudice is light. For example, in *Williams v. CSX Transportation Inc.*,[134] an outboard computer was lost or destroyed, thereby hindering the plaintiffs from proving the speed of the train at the time of the accident. Similarly, in *Union Pacific Railroad Co. v. Barber*,[135] the railroad could not produce audiotapes and track inspection logs that had been created at the time of the accident.

In *Wm. T. Thompson Co. v. General Nutrition Corp.*,[136] following the destruction of computer inventories of biweekly store inventories, biweekly maximum store inventory levels, and biweekly store order demand data, and the destruction of other computer records from which the destroyed materials might have been re-created, the court was able to identify a litany of issues raised by the complaint that these destroyed materials could have helped to prove. In *Gath v. M/ACOM, Inc.*,[137] the

---

131. Loukinas v. Roto-Rooter Servs. Co., 855 N.E.2d 1272, 1278 (Ohio Ct. App. 2006).

132. Haselmann v. Kelly Servs., Inc., 2006 WL 2465420, *15 (D. N.J. Aug. 22, 2006) (Because it is a less serious sanction, the court approved a jury instruction about the spoliation inference without regard to the prejudice the act created. The court noted four factors: the party's control, actual suppression or destruction, relevance of the evidence, and foreseeable desire for the evidence in later litigation.).

133. 61 S.W.3d 465, 479 (Tex. App. Ct. 2001).

134. 925 F. Supp. 447, 452 (S.D. Miss. 1996).

135. 356 Ark. 268, 149 S.W.3d 325 (2004).

136. 593 F. Supp. 1443, 1450 (C.D. Cal. 1984).

137. 802 N.E.2d 521 (Mass. 2003).

plaintiff was seriously injured by an iron gate swinging in the wind. When the gate was removed after the accident, the defendant claimed that the plaintiff was not prejudiced because whatever evidence an inspection of the gate would have provided was cumulative and unnecessary. M/A-COM did not dispute that the gate had been opened two days before the accident by one of its employees and had remained unsecured; that the gate was unsecured at the time of the accident; or that a MA-COM employee had seen the gate open outward toward the street approximately six years earlier. There were eyewitness accounts, photographs, hospital records, and the report of an investigator hired by M/A-COM's insurer. Prejudice, nevertheless, was found by the trial judge because the destruction "deprived Gath of the opportunity to establish facts such as whether the gate was capable of swinging out onto Chelmsford Street, how far it swung out, and for how long the gate had been swinging freely."[138] The appellate court also noted that "an examination of the gate might have revealed physical evidence (such as rubber or paint from the bicycle) indicating whether the gate had actually struck Gath, which was a question of fact hotly contested at the trial. The evidence therefore also bore on proximate cause."[139] The appellate court went on to note that, "[e]ven though Gath had other evidence available, the actual gate and hinges in their post-accident condition may have been 'far more instructive and persuasive to a jury' than photographs or testimony."[140]

Occasionally, the burden of demonstrating prejudice will be difficult because the discovering party has had no access to the content of the destroyed data, directly or through the testimony of those who previously had access to it.[141] Prejudice may also be difficult to demonstrate when

---

138. *Id.* at 526.

139. *Id.* at 528.

140. *Id.*

141. Wiginton v. Ellis, 2003 WL 22439865 (N.D. Ill. Oct. 27, 2003). Relevant materials were deleted by employees after the duty to preserve arose. These deletions were found to be in bad faith. Nevertheless, the court denied the motion for sanctions because it wasn't known what the content of those documents were and how they related to the plaintiff's claim. The denial, however, was without prejudice to the plaintiff revisiting this issue after the production of documents being re-created from backup tapes. It was thought that this would circumstantially reveal the content of other documents that had been destroyed.

documents similar to the ones destroyed have been produced and no evidence supporting the claim of prejudice has been found.[142] In *Zubulake*, for example, the court repeatedly had to address the problem of destruction of e-mail communications and backup tapes on which such communications were recorded. On the third time around, in *Zubulake III*,[143] 68 e-mails were produced to the Court for in camera examination. The Court concluded that "nowhere [in the 68 e-mails produced to the Court] is there any evidence that Chapin's dislike of Zubulake related to her gender." Subsequently, when the issue had to be addressed again, the Court noted that "those e-mails [produced in *Zubulake III*] were the ones selected by Zubulake as being the most relevant among all those produced in UBS's sample restoration."[144] Because they had produced nothing that was helpful to Zubulake's claim and damaging to the defendant, the Court concluded that "[t]here is no reason to believe that the lost e-mails would be any more likely to support claims."[145]

Courts must be careful, however, not to expect too much of a demonstration from the allegedly injured party; after all, the fact that evidence has been destroyed and is unavailable for examination can a severely limit an aggrieved party's ability to prove its precise significance. As explained by the court in *Shamus v. Ambassador Factors Corp.*,[146] where massive quantities of files were destroyed in violation of a duty to preserve:

---

142. *See, e.g.,* Zubulake v. UBS Warburg, 220 F.R.D. 212, 221 (S.D.N.Y. 2003); Cameron v. Nissan 112 Sales Corp., 2004 WL 2005439, at *1 (N.Y. A.D. Sept. 7, 2004) ("Notably, Nissan's papers failed to include any expert proof, or any proof beyond its counsel's bare assertions, demonstrating that it would be unable to prove its case absent an actual inspection of the now-destroyed minivan. Additionally, there is no evidence that the plaintiffs deliberately destroyed the vehicle. Under these factual circumstances, the Supreme Court erred in granting Nissan's cross-motion [to dismiss the claim against it]".).

143. 216 F.R.D. 280, 284-87 (S.D.N.Y. 2003).

144. 220 F.R.D. at 221.

145. *Id.* The Court went on to note: "Furthermore, the likelihood of obtaining relevant information from the six-plus lost backup tapes at issue here is even lower than for the remainder of the tapes, because the majority of the six-plus tapes cover the time prior to the filing of Zubulake's EEOC charge. . . . Thus, there is no reason to believe that peculiarly unfavorable evidence resides solely on that missing tape. Accordingly, Zubulake has not sufficiently demonstrated that the lost tapes contained relevant information." *Id.*

146. 34 F. Supp. 2d 879, 890 n.7 (S.D.N.Y. 1999).

Shamus notes that Defendants fail to specify what documents of any alleged relevance are missing. However, where, as here, "a party loses the opportunity to identify such a particular document or documents likely to contain critical evidence because the voluminous files that might contain the document[s] have all been destroyed, the situation becomes more complex—but there can be no doubt that some basic principle . . . applies. That is, the prejudiced party may be permitted an inference in his favor so long as he has produced some evidence suggesting his claim would have been included among the destroyed files."

Some courts have been willing to infer relevance from both the general nature of the information contained in the documents and from the apparent bad faith of the spoliator.[147] Where simple negligence triggers

---

147. *See* Residential Funding Corp. v. DeGeorge Fin. Corp., 306 F.3d 99, 109 (2d Cir. 2002); Nation-Wide Check Corp. v. Forest Hill Dist., Inc., 692 F.2d 214, 218-19 (1st Cir. 1982) (The court was willing to draw adverse inference only after being presented with substantial circumstantial evidence supporting facts to be inferred. "[A] party who has notice that a document is relevant to litigation and who proceeds to destroy the document is more likely to have been threatened by the document than is a party in the same position who does not destroy the document."); Stanojev v. Ebasco Serv., Inc., 643 F.2d 914, 923-24 (2d Cir. 1981) (The court would not infer that personnel records contained evidence of discrimination because "it is unlikely that documents containing evaluations relevant to an earlier time and prior positions would support a charge that [plaintiff's] dismissal in 1978 was the result of age discrimination."); Zubulake v. UBS Warburg, 220 F.R.D. 212, 220 (S.D.N.Y. 2003) (When evidence is destroyed in bad faith (i.e., intentionally or willfully), that fact alone is sufficient to demonstrate relevance. By contrast, when the destruction is negligent, relevance must be proven by the party seeking the sanctions. "[B]ecause UBS's spoliation was negligent and possibly reckless, but not willful, Zubulake must demonstrate that a reasonable trier of fact could find that the missing e-mails would support her claims. In order to receive an adverse inference instruction, Zubulake must demonstrate not only that UBS destroyed relevant evidence as that term is ordinarily understood, but also that the destroyed evidence would have been favorable to her. 'This corroboration requirement is even more necessary where the destruction was merely negligent, since in those cases it cannot be inferred from the conduct of the spoliator that the evidence would even have been harmful to him. . . .' It is equally true in cases of gross negligence or recklessness; only in the case of willful spoliation is the spoliator's mental culpability itself evidence of the relevance of the documents destroyed.").

the spoliation sanction, however, courts require proof of relevance. Consequently, corroboration of relevance may be particularly important when the charge of spoliation is premised on negligence.[148] Counterbalancing the need to punish the spoliator and level the playing field for the injured party is the concern that the jury should not be encouraged to base its verdict on what it speculates the absent evidence could have contained,

---

In his treatise, Professor Wigmore warns that requiring too much specificity concerning the probable content of the destroyed documents can be unfair to the injured party. He recommends that the court require only "general marks of identity." 2 WIGMORE ON EVIDENCE § 291, at 228 (Chadbourn, rev. 1979).

Ohio has addressed this problem by shifting the burden to the state to show that evidence was not exculpatory when requested by the defendant and the state fails to respond in good faith, Columbus v. Forest, 36 Ohio App. 3d 169, 173 (1987) ("Where, as here, the state breaches its duty to respond in good faith to a defense request to preserve evidence, we believe the appropriate remedy is to shift to the state the burden of proof as to the exculpatory value of the evidence. . . . We recognize that this burden-shifting remedy may impose upon the state a nearly impossible task in some cases. Just as few criminal defendants are able to prove the apparent exculpatory value of lost or destroyed evidence, so, too, will the state have a similar problem in attempting to prove the evidence was not exculpatory. Despite this concern, we do not believe the remedy is unduly harsh. Even if the prosecution fails, in every case, to carry its burden, the defense still must show that the evidence cannot be obtained via alternate channels. Moreover, we fail to ascertain why the state is unable to simply respond to a defense request to preserve evidence, even if such response merely informs the accused that the evidence will be destroyed in accordance with normal practice."), or when the defendant moves to have evidence preserved and the state destroys it. State v. Benson, 788 N.E.2d 693, 695-96 (Ohio Ct. App. 2003) ("Typically, the defendant bears the burden to prove that the evidence was materially exculpatory. But where the defendant moves to have the evidence preserved and the state destroys the evidence, the burden shifts to the state to show the inculpatory value of the evidence. In this case, it is uncontroverted that the state failed to preserve the evidence despite Benson's specific request; thus, the burden shifted to the state to demonstrate that the tape was not materially exculpatory.").

148.   Turner v. Hudson Transit Lines, Inc., 142 F.R.D. 68, 77 (S.D.N.Y. 1991) ("In order to remedy the evidentiary imbalance created by the destruction of evidence, an adverse inference may be appropriate even in the absence of a showing that the spoliator acted in bad faith. However, where the destruction was negligent rather than willful, special caution must be exercised to ensure that the inference is commensurate with information that was reasonably likely to have been contained in the destroyed evidence. Where, as here, there is no extrinsic evidence whatsoever tending to show that the destroyed evidence would have been unfavorable to the spoliator, no adverse inference is appropriate.").

without some evidence justifying the conclusion.[149] Commenting on the adverse inference sanction, the Court in *Zubulake* noted:

> In practice, an adverse inference instruction often ends litigation—it is too difficult a hurdle for the spoliator to overcome, the *in terrorem* effect of an adverse inference is obvious. When a jury is instructed that it may "infer that the party who destroyed potentially relevant evidence did so 'out of a realization that the [evidence was] unfavorable,'" the party suffering this instruction will be hard-pressed to prevail on the merits. Accordingly, the adverse inference instruction is an extreme sanction and should not be given lightly.[150]

As later explained in *Zubulake V*,[151] "[w]hen evidence is destroyed in bad faith (i.e., intentionally or willfully), that fact alone is sufficient to demonstrate relevance." The court was quick to explain that "only in the

---

149. Felice v. Long Island R.R., 426 F.2d 192, 195 n.2 (2d Cir.), *cert. denied*, 400 U.S. 820 (1970).

150. 220 F.R.D. 212, 219-20 (S.D.N.Y. 2003) (citations omitted). As a consequence, jurisdictions like Florida sanction an adverse inference instruction only when it is shown that the "missing evidence [was] essential to the opposing party's prima facie case." Jordan ex rel. Shealey, 821 So. 2d 342, 347 (Fla. Dist. Ct. App. 2003). The logical inference arising from a party's conduct, however, can be encouraged by counsel in closing arguments. Bambu v. I.E. du Pont de Nemours & Co., 881 So. 2d 565, 581-82 (Fla. Dist. Ct. App. 2004). This is also true in federal courts. *See, e.g.*, United States v. Bolzer, 367 F.3d 1032, 1037 (8th Cir. 2004) (even in a criminal case it is not inappropriate for government to argue permissible inferences that can be drawn from evidence produced).
    As noted in the Zubulake opinion, however, not all courts agree with the assessment of the severity of the adverse inference instruction. In Mosel Vitelic Corp. v. Micron Tech., Inc., 162 F. Supp. 2d 307, 315 (D. Del. 2003), the court commented that "adverse inference instructions are one of the least severe sanctions which the court can impose." When compared to the sanctions of dismissal and default judgment, the conclusion in Zubulake appears to be exaggerated. While the sanction is tough, it needs to be in order to serve the punishment and deterrent functions of the doctrine of spoliation. While it is true that the adverse inference instruction should not be "given lightly," it is equally true that those who have violated their duty to preserve evidence should not be rewarded for actions that may have decreased the likelihood that an injured party can obtain redress.

151. Zubulake v. UBS Warburg, 229 F.R.D. 422, 431 (S.D.N.Y. 2004).

case of willful spoliation does the degree of culpability give rise to a presumption of the relevance of the documents destroyed."[152] The flexibility of the *Zubulake* approach is illusory, however, if courts are reluctant to find bad faith.[153] When a party is shown to have ignored its duty to preserve relevant evidence, particularly after litigation has commenced (and there is no justification for not placing holds on all destruction and pervasively communicating that hold throughout the company), burdens should generally be shifted away from the victim and onto the bad actor. After having proven this breach of duty, it is both unfair to place too great a burden on the discovering party to demonstrate both the relevance and prejudice when the victim, unlike the one that destroyed the communications, has never had a chance to examine that evidence. Nevertheless, with the exception of a few courts, most seem to continue to be overly protective of the proven wrongdoers and require the party moving for sanctions to bear too many burdens. If burdens were shifted, greater care to preserve communications would quickly materialize throughout industry because it is generally understood that whomever gets this burden will not likely be able to meet it. As a consequence, companies will make every attempt to avoid having to face it by complying with their duty of preservation, which, of course, is the purpose of the spoliation doctrine.

When the destroyed evidence has been made substantially available to the discovering party from other sources, prejudice does not exist.[154] In addition, when the portions of the data already received have not been examined and used by the discovering party, courts will be disinclined to find prejudice because the nature of what is not known might be revealed

---

152. Convolve, Inc. v. Compaq Computer Corp., 223 F.R.D. 162, 176 (S.D.N.Y. 2004) ("Where the spoliation occurred as a result of bad faith or gross negligence, it may be presumed that the evidence would have been harmful to the spoliator.").

153. *See* In re Kmart Corp., 371 B.R. 823 (N.D. Ill. 2007).

154. *See* Danis v. USN Commc'ns, Inc., 2000 WL 1694325, at *28 (N.D. Ill. 2000) ("Plaintiffs have failed to establish substantive prejudice from the failure of USN to institute an appropriate document preservation plan in the face of the commencement of this lawsuit. Virtually all of the information that plaintiffs claim they have been deprived of has been produced to them—either by the individual defendants or nonparties."). This may, however, be a risky argument to make because it may cause the court to suspect your preservation and production efforts and prompt the presiding judge to order a more extensive review of those efforts, including a potentially expensive forensic review of computer systems.

from what is known.[155] In *Danis v. USN Communications, Inc.*, for example, the court concluded that the "plaintiffs cannot claim prejudice from the missing months of aged accounts receivable information, when they have not even used the information they have received with their experts."[156]

The second way that prejudice factors into the spoliation equation is in the direct relationship between the degree of harm and the appropriate sanction. "In weighing and determining the appropriateness and severity of sanction, judges should examine the materiality and value of the suppressed evidence upon the ability of a [party] to fully and fairly prepare for trial."[157]

The sanctioning goal is to punish the spoliator and, if possible, to place the injured party in the position he would have been in had the destruction not occurred. If the prejudice is serious (for example, precluding proof of the claim or defense), and the conduct was an intentional effort on the part of the spoliator to influence the outcome of the trial, then the most severe sanction, dismissal or summary judgment, may be appropriate.[158] If the

---

155. *Id.*

156. *Id.*

157. Gates Rubber Co. v. Bando Chem. Indus., Ltd., 167 F.R.D. 90, 104 (D. Colo. 1996).

158. *See* Leon v. IDX Sys. Corp., 464 F.3d 951 (9th Cir. 2006) (Because abuse was willful and in bad faith, the court imposed the sanction of dismissal with prejudice and imposed a monetary sanction in addition.); Flury v. DaimlerChrysler Corp., 427 F.3d 939 (11th Cir. 2005) (The appellate court took the extraordinary step of reversing the trial court's negative instruction sanction and dismissed the plaintiff's case because he had allowed his car to be destroyed after claiming that the air bags failed to deploy. The car was critical evidence. The plaintiff was aware of its importance, knew where it was located, and failed to inform the defendant. Because the evidence was critical to the case, the only reasonable sanction was dismissal. This extreme sanction was imposed even though the failure to inform the defendant was primarily the fault of the attorney.); Samsung Elecs. Co. v. Rambus Inc., 439 F. Supp. 2d 524, 528 (E.D. Va. 2006) (After the court found spoliation of documents by Rambus and pierced its attorney-client privilege through the crime/fraud exception, a bench trial was held in which the extent of their litigation misconduct was explored. After this hearing, the court found unclean hands, barred Rambus from enforcing the four patents-in-suit, and dismissed the action.); Wm. T. Thompson Co. v. Gen. Nutrition Corp., 593 F. Supp. 1443, 1455-56 (C.D. Cal. 1984) (default judgment as punishment for the destruction of documents); Stanley Shenker & Assoc. v. World Wrestling Fed. Entm't, Inc., 48 Conn. Supp. 357, 377, 844 A.2d 964 (Conn. Sup. Ct. 2003) ("It is clear that dismissal of associates' claims with prejudice is warranted. First, Shenker's commission of perjury,

evidence potentially is important but can be partially reconstructed from other sources, the collective sanctions of an award of costs and attorney's fees and a negative inference instruction may be appropriate.[159] If the evidence was destroyed as a result of gross negligence but the injury is slight, because the evidence can be reconstructed from other sources and was

---

and evidence tampering, were undertaken willfully and in bad faith; indeed, Shenker had admitted that he intended to withhold the truth from Federation and its counsel, and that he acted in accordance with this plan. Second, Federation has been severely prejudiced by Shenker's scheme to lie and obstruct, regardless of any extension in discovery or the amount of time left before trial. . . . Finally, . . . to continue to grant Associates and Shenker further opportunities, when they have squandered those previously granted to them, would serve no just purpose here."); Covucci v. Keane Consulting Group, Inc., 2006 Mass. Super. LEXIS 313, *23-24 (Mass. Super. Ct. May 31, 2006) ("Covucci thus concealed the existence of a computer that was the subject of a discovery request until he had eliminated the possibility that any relevant evidence concerning the creation of the document that he relies on and describes as 'crucial' to his case could be retrieved from the hard drive. He made numerous false statements at his deposition and during the evidentiary hearing . . . . I have considered the range of sanctions that are available and determined that dismissal is the only appropriate sanction given Covucci's bad faith and egregious nature of his misconduct. This case does not involve a single hasty act. Covucci lied to his attorneys and caused them to make false representations to defendants. He then engaged in a systematic destruction of material evidence over a period of months. He has deprived the defendants of evidence concerning the creation of the 'crucial' document in the case. He provided false testimony at his deposition and at the hearing on this motion. Whether described as a persistent bad-faith repudiation of discovery obligations, . . . the intentional spoliation of evidence, . . . or a fraud on the court, . . . dismissal is the only appropriate remedy for his misconduct."); Miller v. Weyerhaeuser Co., 3 A.D.3d 627, 771 N.Y.S.2d 200 (Sup. Ct. 2004) (After repeated failures to produce and subsequent loss of a brake chamber, the court struck the defendant's answer.); Alexander v. Jackson Radiology Assoc., 156 S.W.3d 11, 15-16 (Tenn. Ct. App. 2004) (dismissal of claim sanctioned where plaintiff destroyed evidence, lied under oath to cover his transgression, and begrudgingly acknowledged his act after it was proven from a videotape of deposition in which it occurred); County of Sauk v. Douglas, 673 N.W.2d 411, 2003 WL 22799531, ¶ 7 (Wis. Ct. App. 2003) (To impose the sanction of dismissal of a criminal charge for the destruction of evidence, the court must find "bad faith" or "egregious conduct." "'A finding of "bad faith" or egregious conduct in the context of an [evidence] destruction case involves more than negligence; rather, it consists of a conscious attempt to affect the outcome of the litigation or a flagrant, knowing disregard of the judicial process.'").

159. *See* Shaffer v. RWP Group, Inc., 169 F.R.D. 19, 28 (E.D. N.Y. 1996).

only cumulative, then perhaps no sanction should be imposed.[160] Alternatively, the sanction of attorney's fees would suffice.[161] If there is nothing to suggest that the content of the destroyed documents would have been harmful to the spoliator, and the context of the destruction suggests that only negligence was involved, then again, perhaps no sanction needs to be imposed.[162] The court should impose the least severe sanction that will eliminate the advantage the spoliator may have gained through destruction, and this may be influenced by whether the case is being tried by the court or will go to a jury.[163]

It is the context of the act, not the act of destruction itself, that determines the judicial response. Many of the acts of evidence destruction that could constitute spoliation, like destroying documents or equipment, are not acts that are the product of recklessness or evil designs. Enterprises regularly purge files for efficiency's sake.[164] An act of destruction will

---

160. *See* N.Y. State Nat'l Org. for Women v. Cuomo, 1998 WL 395320, at *3 (S.D.N.Y. July 14, 1998); Underwood v. Gale Tschuor Co., Inc., 799 N.E.2d 1122 (Ind. Ct. App. 2003) (The proposition that could have been proven had the evidence not been destroyed was admitted by the defendant. The court, therefore, would not give an inference instruction, but permitted the inference to be argued to the jury.); State v. Hutton, 595 S.E.2d 876, 882 (S.C. Ct. App. 2004) ("While we do not condone the destruction of any statements made by witnesses to the authorities, we consider dismissal of criminal charges a drastic remedy which should rarely be invoked as a sanction for the State's failure to preserve evidence. We still caution the prosecution and law enforcement authorities that the destruction of evidence will be highly scrutinized; however, we cannot find appellant was entitled to a dismissal based on the facts of this case. After considering the lack of evidence of bad faith on the part of the State in the destruction of the evidence, the importance of the missing evidence in light of the availability of evidence of comparable value, and the overwhelming sufficiency of the other evidence produced at the trial to sustain appellant's conviction, we find no error in the trial court's denial of appellant's motion to dismiss.").

161. *See* Mathias v. Jacobs, 197 F.R.D. 29, 39 (S.D.N.Y. 2000).

162. Turner v. Hudson Transit Lines, Inc., 142 F.R.D. 68, 77 (S.D.N.Y. 1991).

163. Kyoei Fire & Marine Ins. Co., Ltd. v. M/V Maritime Antalya, 248 F.R.D. 126 (S.D.N.Y. 2007) (Court found default judgment inappropriate because the sanction was too harsh in light of the fact that the case was being tried to the court and it considered itself well-situated to assess and weigh the appropriate impact of the spoliated evidence in this case.).

164. With the computerization of most records, however, this justification is far less compelling. Once the records exist, the cost of retention is minimal. Therefore, when destruction occurs outside of a regular document management policy, judges view it with a great deal more suspicion.

constitute spoliation, giving rise to an adverse inference or justifying sanctions only when the circumstances surrounding the destruction demonstrate bad faith, recklessness, or negligence.[165] Knowledge is the touchstone of culpability. Once a party knows or has reason to know that information is relevant to pending or reasonably anticipated litigation, documents must be preserved—even if subject to a regularly scheduled purging program. Once the duty to preserve arises, alterations will not be excused solely because they are part of a "bona fide business practice."[166] This is vividly illustrated in *In re Holocaust Victim Assets Litig.,*[167] where Swiss banks systematically destroyed 10-year bank records relevant to pending and anticipated actions by families of Nazi victims. The court explained:

> [H]owever the banks' motives for destruction are described, their motives are wholly irrelevant to the question of whether the banks committed wholesale destruction of documents that would have allowed Nazi victims and their heirs to locate accounts on which they had claims. [Two reports] found that the Swiss banks engaged in 'systematic' destruction of relevant documents once those documents were ten years old. Any spin the defendants choose to put on that fact is irrelevant. The critical fact, and the one that the defendants appear to miss, is that the Swiss banks did not comport with basic notions of equity. For over half a century they destroyed evidence they knew to be relevant to legitimate claims that were being made and that, if substantiated through documentation, would expose the banks to liability. The fact that the destruction may not have violated Swiss law—which was not amended to accommodate the claims of heirs of account holders who the Swiss knew were slaughtered in the Holocaust and who

---

165. *See, e.g.,* Lewy v. Remington Arms Co., 836 F.2d 1104, 1112 (8th Cir. 1988) ("[E]ven if the court finds the policy to be reasonable given the nature of the documents subject to the policy, the court may find that under the particular circumstances certain documents should have been retained notwithstanding the policy."); In re Prudential Ins. Co. of Am. Sales Practice Litig., 169 F.R.D. 598 (D. N.J. 1997) (finding culpability where, after company was notified of importance of documents to pending litigation, company officers negligently failed to inform personnel responsible for regular document destruction).

166. Computer Assoc. Int'l, Inc. v. Am. Fundware, Inc., 133 F.R.D. 166, 169-70 (D. Colo. 1990).

167. 319 F. Supp. 2d 301 (E.D. N.Y. 2004).

could not make a successful claim if records were destroyed—is nothing more than a sad commentary on the manner in which banks were permitted to operate.[168]

Even if prejudice can be demonstrated, the destruction of relevant evidence does not warrant spoliation sanctions when the discovering party was responsible because no reasonable efforts were made to examine or test the materials when they were available. In *Brandt v. Rokeby Realty Co.*,[169] for example, tiles that were the source of a toxic mold were removed from the building and tested after the problem became apparent. During the period when the tiles could have been examined and tested by the plaintiff, no actions were taken. "Any prejudice suffered by Rokeby is self-inflicted. It could have been avoided by prompt action after the tile was removed or by later testing the tile upon its return."[170]

III. IS BAD FAITH REQUIRED?

Bad faith has been characterized as "either intentional or reckless disregard of a party's obligations to comply with a court order."[171] By contrast, "fault" does not "speak to the noncomplying party's disposition at all, but rather only describes the reasonableness of the conduct—or lack thereof—which eventually culminated in the violation."[172] Discovery sanctions for destroying evidence in violation of a court order do not require that the noncompliance was either "willful or deliberate." "[S]anctions may be appropriate in any one of three instances—where the noncomplying party

---

168. *Id.* at 320-21.

169. 2004 WL 2050519 (Del. Super. Ct. Sept. 8, 2004).

170. *Id.* at *13. *See also* Sterbenz v. Attina, 205 F. Supp. 2d 65, 73 (E.D. N.Y. 2002), where the court declined to sanction the defendant for destroying an automobile three months after the defendant notified plaintiff's counsel of its location, informing him that the vehicle was collecting storage charges and should be removed as soon as possible. The lawyer failed to contact the auto body shop and didn't even retain an expert to examine the vehicle for more than four months. The car was subsequently sold and became unavailable. The court explained that "any detriment suffered by plaintiff was thus the product of her counsel's dilatory and unprofessional handling of the case, and not by any tortious conduct on defendants' part."

171. Marrocco v. General Motors Corp., 966 F.2d 220, 224 (7th Cir. 1992).

172. *Id.*

acted either with willfulness, bad faith or fault."[173] Whichever standard is employed, the determination of whether it has been satisfied will be made by the court (or the arbitrators) based on the surrounding circumstances and the credibility of the witnesses offered to explain the loss.[174]

Courts vary in their approach to the element of bad faith when analyzing spoliation claims. Many court impose sanctions for spoliation only on a showing of bad faith.[175] These courts are not satisfied with "mere inad-

---

173. *Id.*

174. Marketing Specialists, Inc. v. Bruni, 129 F.R.D. 35, 53-54 (W.D. N.Y. 1989) (court found testimony of employee who erased materials to be credible and declined to find intentional destruction).

175. *See, e.g.,* Stevenson v. Union Pac. R.R. Co., 354 F.3d 739, 749 (8th Cir. 2004) ("We have never approved of giving an adverse inference instruction on the basis of prelitigation destruction of evidence through a routine document retention policy on the basis of negligence alone. Where a routine document retention policy has been followed in this context, we now clarify that there must be some indication of an intent to destroy the evidence for the purpose of obstructing or suppressing the truth in order to impose the sanction of an adverse inference instruction."); King v. Ill. Central R.R., 337 F.3d 550 (5th Cir. 2003) (To receive an adverse inference instruction, the aggrieved party must show that the opposing party not only destroyed relevant evidence to either the claim or defense, but also that the destruction was intentional and in "bad faith."); Bashir v. Amtrak, 119 F.3d 929, 931 (11th Cir. 1997) ("Mere negligence in losing or destroying the evidence is not enough for an adverse inference as 'it does not sustain an inference of consciousness of a weak case.'"); Aramburu v. Boeing Co., 112 F.3d 1398, 1047 (10th Cir. 1997) ("[B]ad faith destruction of [evidence] relevant to proof of an issue at trial gives rise to an inference that production of the [evidence] would have been unfavorable to the party responsible for its destruction."); Miksis v. Howard, 106 F.3d 754, 763 (7th Cir. 1997); Lewy v. Remington Arms Co., 836 F.2d 1104, 1112 (8th Cir. 1988) ("[T]he court should determine whether the document retention policy was instituted in bad faith."); Gumbs v. Int'l Harvester, Inc., 718 F.2d 88, 96 (3d Cir. 1983) ("Such a presumption or inference arises, however, only when the spoliation or destruction was intentional, and indicates fraud and a desire to suppress the truth, and it does not arise where the destruction was a matter of routine with no fraudulent intent."); Vick v. Texas Employment Comm'n, 514 F.2d 734, 737 (5th Cir. 1975) ("'Moreover, the circumstances of the act must manifest bad faith. Mere negligence is not enough, for it does not sustain an inference of consciousness of a weak case.'"); Eaton Corp. v. Appliance Valves Corp., 790 F.2d 874, 878 (Fed. Cir. 1986) ("[T]he test is whether the court could draw 'from the fact that a party has destroyed evidence that the party did so in bad faith.' . . . If a court finds that both conditions precedent, evidence destruction and bad faith, are met, it may then infer that the evidence would be unfavorable to the destroyed party if introduced in court."); Consol. Aluminum Corp. v. Alcoa, Inc., 244 F.R.D. 335, 2006 WL 2583308, *3

(July 19, 2006); Morgan v. U.S. Xpress, Inc., 2006 WL 1548029, *4 (M.D. Ga. June 2, 2006) ("When a defendant destroys critical evidence, an adverse inference may be drawn from his failure to preserve the evidence if the absence of that evidence is predicated on bad faith." The court noted, however, that "a showing of malice is not required to find bad faith."); Wiginton v. Ellis, 2003 WL 22439865, at *7 (N.D. Ill. Oct. 27, 2003) ("[I]n order to draw an inference that the documents favored Plaintiff, we must first find that the documents were destroyed in 'bad faith.'"); Farr v. Midwest Woodworking, Inc., 2002 WL 31934008, at *4 (D. Kan. Dec. 18, 2002) ("A finding of bad faith is essential to sanctioning the destruction of evidence." The court also noted that "[T]he adverse inference must be predicated on the bad faith of the party destroying the records. . . . Mere negligence in losing or destroying records is not enough because it does support an inference of consciousness of a weak case."); Short v. Anangel Compania Naviera, 2002 WL 31740707, at *2 (E.D. La. Dec. 4, 2002) (finding that "the circumstances of the act must manifest bad faith. Mere negligence is not enough. . . ."); Danis v. USN Commc'ns, Inc., 2000 WL 1694325, at *15 (N.D. Ill. Oct. 23, 2000) (because record did not show that officer embarked on "scheme to willfully destroy documents, or to knowingly turn a blind eye to destruction of documents relevant to this litigation," judge declined to find spoliation; court, however, fined the culpable individual $10,000); United States v. Koch Indus., Inc., 197 F.R.D. 463, 486 (N.D. Okla. 1998) ("Plaintiffs have failed to carry their burden of proof to establish by a preponderance of the evidence that KII destroyed the computer files intentionally or with bad faith. Therefore, no 'adverse inference' jury instruction should arise from KII's destruction of the computer tapes." The court refused to permit party that destroyed tapes to offer any evidence generated from destroyed tapes.); In re Prudential Ins. Co. of Am. Sales Practice Litig., 169 F.R.D. 598 (D. N.J. 1997) (no willful misconduct having been found, the court would impose only a substantial fine); ABC Home Health Servs., Inc. v. I.B.M. Corp., 158 F.R.D. 180, 182-83 (S.D. Ga. 1994) (because defendant's conduct did not constitute deliberate attempt to undermine discovery process, court would not dismiss counterclaim; but because bad faith was apparently involved, court did recognize presumption that destroyed evidence would have been unfavorable to defendant); Computer Assoc. Int'l, Inc. v. Am. Fundware, Inc., 133 F.R.D. 166, 169-70 (D. Colo. 1990) (because destruction was willful and in bad faith, court concluded that only appropriate sanction was adverse judgment); Telectron, Inc. v. Overhead Door Corp., 116 F.R.D. 107, 133 (S.D. Fla. 1987) ("[W]hile it is now impossible to determine precisely what or how many documents were destroyed, the bad-faith destruction of a relevant document, by itself, 'gives rise to a strong inference that production of the document would have been unfavorable to the party responsible for its destruction.'"); Carter v. Cedar Rapids Bowl, Inc., 2002 WL 987934, at *2 (Iowa Ct. App. May 15, 2002) (noting that an inference is "not warranted if the disappearance of the evidence is due to mere negligence, or if the evidence was destroyed during routine procedure"); Grand Casino Biloxi v. Hallmark, 823 So. 2d 1185, 1193 (Miss. 2002) ("[A] presumption or inference

vertence or negligence."[176] In *Aramburu v. Boeing Co.*,[177] for example, an ex-employee claimed that he was discriminated against as a minority when he was not given leaves of absence and was eventually discharged for excessive absenteeism. When Boeing negligently misplaced some of Aramburu's attendance records, he asked for an instruction that would have recognized an adverse inference. The refusal of the instruction was upheld on appeal because all of the records had not been misplaced, a computer record reflecting Aramburu's absences for 1991 was produced, and it supported Boeing's position. The appellate court held that bad faith, a prerequisite for the instruction, had not been shown. It was not clear from the opinion, however, whether the requirement of bad faith was influenced by the additional computer evidence from Boeing, which showed that the lost records would not have been harmful to it.

In criminal cases, for spoliation to be a violation of due process, the government must be shown to have destroyed evidence in bad faith. In addition, the criminal defendant must prove that the destroyed evidence would have been exculpatory.[178]

[that the destroyed evidence was adverse to the spoliating party's case] arises, however, only where the spoliation or destruction was intentional and indicates fraud and a desire to suppress the truth, and it does not arise where the destruction was a matter of routine with no fraudulent intent."); Lykins v. Miami Valley Hosp., 811 N.E.2d 124, 146 (Ohio Ct. App. 2004) (spoliation not established without showing "willful destruction of evidence"); Crescendo Invs., Inc. v. Brice, 61 S.W.3d 465, 479 (Tex. App. 2001) (because e-mails were not destroyed with fraudulent intent, there was no spoliation).

In a criminal case in which the state had destroyed a videotape of the defendant's arrest, a Texas court rejected the defendant's spoliation instruction request because there had been no showing that "the evidence was exculpatory *or* that there was bad faith on the part of the State in connection with its loss." Manor v. State, 2006 WL 2692873, at *5 (Tex. Ct. App. Sept. 21, 2006). The suggestion that either a showing that the destroyed evidence was exculpatory or that the state acted in bad faith justified a spoliation inference instruction appears to have resulted from a misinterpretation of prior case law announced in White v. State, 125 S.W.3d 41, 43-44 (Tex. App. 14th Dist. 2003). In *White*, the court rejected a spoliation instruction because there was no showing that the evidence was exculpatory. Its subsequent discussion of "bad faith" was directed only to the question of when the defendant's due process rights are violated by the state.

176. *See, e.g.*, Ill. Tool Works, Inc. v. Metro Mark Prods., Ltd., 43 F. Supp. 2d 951, 961 (N.D. Ill. 1999)

177. 112 F.3d 1398, 1407 (3d Cir. 1997).

178. Arizona v. Youngblood, 488 U.S. 51, 57-58 (1988) (in order to show a denial of due process when evidence was lost, a defendant must show that the

evidence was (1) material, (2) favorable to the defense, and (3) destroyed in bad faith by the state); Lovitt v. True, 330 F. Supp. 2d 603, 632-33 (E.D. Va. 2004) ("In *Youngblood,* the United States Supreme Court detailed how a court, confronted with the 'failure of the State to preserve evidentiary material of which no more can be said than it would have been subjected to tests, the results of which might have exonerated the defendant,' should analyze due process. . . . Specifically, the court held that 'unless a criminal defendant can show bad faith on the part of the police, failure to preserve potentially useful evidence does not constitute a denial of due process of law.'"); Knowlin v. Benik, 2004 WL 1246070, *at 12 (W.D. Wis. June 3, 2004) ("Knowlin cannot establish a constitutional violation because he has not demonstrated that the police altered the impressions in bad faith."); Guzman v. State, 868 So. 2d 498, 509-10 (Fla. 2003) ("The loss or destruction of evidence that is potentially useful to the defense violates due process only if the defendant can show bad faith on the part of the police or prosecution. . . . [B]ad faith exists only when police intentionally destroy evidence they believe would exonerate a defendant. . . . Evidence that has not been examined or tested by government agents does not have 'apparent exculpatory value' and thus cannot form the basis of a claim of bad faith destruction of evidence."); Felder v. State, 873 So. 2d 1282, 1283 (Fla. Ct. App. 2004) ("The suppression by the prosecution of evidence favorable to the accused violates due process where the evidence is material either to guilt or to punishment, regardless of the good faith or bad faith of the prosecution. Brady v. Maryland, 373 U.S. 83, 87, 83 S. Ct. 1194, 10 L. Ed. 2d 215 (1963). But the loss or destruction of evidence that is only potentially useful to the defense violates due process only if the defendant can show bad faith on the part of the police or prosecution."); Scott v. State, 877 So. 2d 549, 550-51 (Miss. Ct. App. 2004) (The state failed to preserve photographs from which the store clerk identified Scott. The court held that this violated the defendant's right to due process only when (1) the evidence in question possessed an exculpatory value that was apparent before the evidence was destroyed; (2) comparable evidence is not reasonably available; and (3) the prosecution's destruction was in bad faith.); Ohio v. Birkhold, 2002 Ohio 1464, at *4 (Ohio 2002) (finding that "the State's failure to preserve potentially useful evidence violates a defendant's due process rights only when the police or prosecution act in bad faith"); Ohio v. Howell, 2004 WL 1077527, ¶ 19 (Ohio Ct. App. May 14, 2004) ("When evidence is only potentially exculpatory, the destruction of such evidence does not violate due process unless police acted in bad faith."); State v. Greenwood, 2004 WL 1178730, *4 (Ohio Ct. App. May 28, 2004) ("When evidence is only potentially exculpatory, the destruction of such evidence does not violate due process unless police acted in bad faith."); Villarreal v. State, 2004 WL 1801790, at *6 (Tex. App. Aug. 12, 2004) ("This standard of constitutional materiality is met only where the missing evidence possesses an exculpatory value that was apparent before the evidence was destroyed, and is of such a nature that the defendant would be unable to obtain comparable evidence by other reasonably available means. . . . A showing that the evidence might have been favorable

Others courts, however, impose sanctions on the basis of mere negligence.[179] The court in *Shaffer v. RWP Group, Inc.*[180] explained why

does not meet the materiality standard. . . . If evidence was destroyed in good faith and in accord with the normal practice of the police, there is not due process violation."); Wycough v. State, 2004 WL 1126272, *3 (Tex. App. May 20, 2004) ("To show a denial of due process has occurred when evidence was lost, a defendant must show the evidence was: (1) material; (2) favorable to the defense; and (3) destroyed in bad faith by the State. . . . A showing that evidence might have been favorable does not meet the materiality standard.") (unpublished). *But see* State v. Larivee, 656 N.W.2d 226, 230 (Minn. 2003) (Court acknowledged that inadvertent suppression of evidence could result in due process violation. To succeed on a claim of a due process violation due to the destruction of evidence, the court stated that a criminal defendant must show "(1) that the evidence at issue was favorable to him; (2) that evidence was willfully *or inadvertently* suppressed by the state; and (3) that he was thereby prejudiced." (Emphasis added.) (If an act were in bad faith, could it be inadvertent?) and State v. Heath, 685 N.W.2d 48, 55 (Minn. App. 2004) ("When no more can be said of the evidence than it could have been subjected to tests, the results of which might have exonerated the defendant, the defendant must show bad faith on the part of the state to establish a due-process violation.").

179.   Tracinda Corp. v. DaimlerChrysler AG, 502 F.3d 212, 242 (3d Cir. 2007) (Because Rule 16 of the Federal Rules of Civil Procedure permits sanctions to facilitate the "expeditious and sound management of the preparation of cases for trial," and does not require either intent or negligence, the court concluded the trial judge has broad discretion to do what equity demands in its effort to effectively manage the pretrial process. The court imposed expenses for a late disclosure of relevant evidence (a form of spoliation) that proved to be damaging to the demanding party's trial preparation.); Med. Lab. Mgmt. Consultants v. Am. Broadcast Cos., Inc., 306 F.3d 806, 824 (9th Cir. 2002) ("when relevant evidence is lost accidentally or for an innocent reason, an adverse evidentiary inference from the loss may be rejected"); Residential Funding Corp. v. DeGeorge Fin. Corp., 306 F.3d 99, 107 (2d Cir. 2002) ("[A]n adverse instruction based on the destruction of evidence must establish . . . that the records were destroyed 'with a culpable state of mind'. . . ." Interestingly, even though a "culpable state of mind" was held to be necessary, the Second Circuit disagreed with the trial court, and indicated that gross negligence or bad faith was not required—that negligent conduct could satisfy the standard. This was not a typical spoliation case because it involved the late production of e-mail messages, rather than their destruction. Backup tapes, from which the defendant claimed it could not easily retrieve the messages, were rapidly accessed by the plaintiff after their production.); Glover v. BIC Corp., 6 F.3d 1318, 1329 (9th Cir. 1993) ("[A] finding of bad faith is not a prerequisite to this corrective procedure."); Welsh v. United States, 844 F.2d 1239, 1247 (6th Cir. 1988) ("[T]he negligent destruction of evidence foreseeably pertinent to litigation and the consequent failure to perform pathological examination in ac-

cordance with the standards of ordinary medical practice give rise in the circumstances of this case to a rebuttable presumption that the missing specimen would establish that the defendant was negligent in failing to discover the underlying disease process and that this negligence was the proximate cause of the decedent's demise."); Nation-Wide Check Corp., Inc. v. Forest Hills Distribs., Inc., 692 F.2d 214, 218 (1st Cir. 1982) (showing of bad faith not necessary for adverse inference against spoliator); Advantacare Health Partners v. Access IV, 2004 WL 1837997, at *4 (N.D. Cal. Aug. 17, 2004) ("A party's destruction of evidence need not be in 'bad faith' to warrant the imposition of sanction. . . . The Court may impose sanctions against a party that merely had notice that the destroyed evidence was potentially relevant to litigation. . . . However, a party's motive or degree of fault in destroying evidence is relevant to what type of sanction is imposed."); Mosaid Tech. Inc. v. Samsung Elecs. Co., 348 F. Supp. 2d 332, 338 (D. N.J. 2004) ("[N]egligent destruction of relevant evidence can be sufficient to give rise to the spoliation inference. If a party has notice that evidence is relevant to an action, and either proceeds to destroy that evidence or allows it to be destroyed by failing to take reasonable precautions, common sense dictates that the party is more likely to have been threatened by that evidence."); Mastercard Int'l, Inc. v. Moulton, 2004 WL 1393992, at *4 (S.D.N.Y. June 22, 2004) ("As for culpability, we are not persuaded that defendants acted in bad faith, that is, for the express purpose of obstructing the litigation. They appear simply to have persevered in their normal document retention practices, in disregard of their discovery obligations. The absence of bad faith, however, does not protect defendants from appropriate sanctions, since even simply negligence is a sufficiently culpable state of mind to justify a finding of spoliation."); Kelley v. United Airlines, Inc., 176 F.R.D. 422, 428 (D. Mass. 1997) (the negligent destruction of documents was a sufficient basis for adverse inference instruction); Webb v. Dist. of Columbia, 175 F.R.D. 128, 144 (D. D.C. 1997) ("[T]he court does not need to find bad faith destruction in order to impose sanctions."); Shaffer v. RWP Group, Inc., 169 F.R.D. 19, 26 (E.D. N.Y. 1996) ("Of course, a party's destruction of documents not always will fit neatly into categories such as 'negligent' or 'willful.' Instead, culpability runs 'along a continuum of fault—ranging from innocence through the degrees of negligence to intentionality.' . . . In the case at bar, the Court concludes that, while the defendants' conduct may not have risen to the level of bad faith, it nevertheless demonstrated a conscious and reckless disregard for their discovery obligations. . . . [W]hile the Court may be somewhat hesitant to categorize the defendants' activities as willful and taken in bad faith, it nonetheless finds the defendants highly culpable for the destruction of the documents."); Baliotis v. McNeil, 870 F. Supp. 1285, 1291-92 (M.D. Pa. 1994) (despite the lack of evidence of bad faith, the court allowed a spoliation inference); Turner v. Hudson Transit Lines, Inc., 142 F.R.D. 68, 75 (S.D.N.Y. 1991) ("[The adverse inference sanction] should be available even for the negligent destruction of documents if that is necessary to further the remedial purposes of the inference. It makes little difference to the party victimized by the destruction of evidence whether that act was done willfully or negligently."); Barker v. Bledsoe, 85

bad faith cannot be the controlling standard for imposing sanctions on the knowing destruction of relevant documents:

F.R.D. 545 (W.D. Okla. 1979) (negligent destruction of materials by expert warranted an adverse inference instruction); Pfantz v. Kmart Corp., 85 P.3d 564, 568 (Colo. Ct. App. 2003) (approving of spoliation sanctions when the destruction is the result of gross negligence); Public Health Trust v. Valcin, 507 So. 2d 596, 599-601 (Fla. 1987) (spoliation based on negligent loss of evidence shifts burden of proof to spoliator); Kane v. Northwest Special Recreation Ass'n, 108 Ill. Dec. 96, 155 Ill. App. 3d 624, 508 N.E. 257, 261-62 (1987) (adverse inference instruction permitted because plaintiff washed away possible scientific evidence of rape); McCool v. Beauregard Mem'l Hosp., 814 So. 2d 116 (La. Ct. App. 2002) (spoliation can be premised on a breach of duty to preserve, intentionally or negligently); Kippenhan v. Chaulk Servs., Inc., 428 Mass. 124, 127 (1998) (recognizing broad judicial power to sanction parties who negligently or intentionally destroy or alter evidence); Wajda v. Kingbury, 652 N.W.2d 856, 862 (Minn. 2002) ("The law of Minnesota is that spoliation of evidence need not be intentional to warrant sanctions."); Huhta v. Thermo King Corp., 2004 WL 1445540 (Minn. Ct. App. June 29, 2004) ("Spoliation encompasses both intentional and negligent destruction of evidence. . . . Regardless of intent, disposing of evidence constitutes spoliation when a party knows or should know that the evidence should be preserved for pending or future litigation."); Thomas v. Isle of Capri Casino & CDS Systems, 7811 So. 2d 125, 133 (Miss. 2002) ("Requiring an innocent litigant to prove fraudulent intent on the part of the spoliator would result in placing too onerous a burden on the aggrieved party. To hold otherwise would encourage parties with real cases to 'inadvertently' lose particularly damning evidence and then manufacture 'innocent' explanations for the loss. In this way, the spoliator could essentially destroy evidence and then require the innocent party to prove fraudulent intent before the destruction of the evidence could be used against it."); Lipschitz v. Stein, 2004 WL 2039418, at *4 (N.Y. A.D. Sept. 13, 2004) (Party stipulated that it intentionally did not produce a relevant document because a receptionist had altered it (no indication in the opinion of whether the alteration was intentional or negligent). Trial court's refusal to give an instruction on the fraudulent purpose that can be inferred from the destruction was reversible error.); DiDomenico v. C & S Aeromatik Supplies, 252 A.D.2d 41, 53 (N.Y. A.D. 1998) (Spoliation is sanctionable "even if the destruction occurred through negligence rather than willfulness, and even if the evidence was destroyed before the spoliator became a party, provided [the party] . . . was on notice that the evidence might be needed for future litigation."); Travelers Indem. Co. v. C. C. Controlled Combustion Insulation Co., Inc., 2003 WL 22798934, at *3 (N.Y. Civ. Ct. Nov. 19, 2003) ("Spoliation sanctions are appropriate where a litigant, intentionally or negligently, disposes of crucial items of evidence involved in an accident before the adversary has an opportunity to inspect them.").

180. 169 F.R.D. 19, 26 (E.D. N.Y. 1996).

Of course, a party's destruction of documents not always will fit neatly into categories such as "negligent" or "willful." Instead, culpability runs "along a continuum of fault—ranging from innocence through the degrees of negligence to intentionality." . . . In the case at bar, the Court concludes that, while the defendants' conduct may not have risen to the level of bad faith, it nevertheless demonstrated a conscious and reckless disregard for their discovery obligations. RWP has been involved in litigation concerning its Agreement with DSA since 1987, and was in fact served with a document request in the state action in 1989 which encompassed most, if not all, of the documents that ultimately were destroyed. In fact, during defendant Pollack's deposition, he testified that "for the last five years" he had "put documents aside" relating to Mr. Shaffer's claims in the state action. Yet, inexcusably and subsequent to the commencement of the instant federal action, when RWP officials clearly were on notice of the plaintiffs' claims of fraud and willful concealment with respect to commission monies, RWP took a more carefree attitude, ordering numerous and unknown persons to destroy documents relevant to this litigation in order to "make room" for new files. Compounding the defendants' culpability was RWP's utter lack of a coherent system for document retention or disposal.

Although the court was hesitant to categorize the defendants' activities as willful and taken in bad faith, it nonetheless found the defendants "highly culpable for the destruction of the documents."[181]

Similarly, in *United Medical Supply Co., Inc. v. United States*,[182] the bad-faith requirement was rejected as a precondition for spoliation sanctions with a convincing explanation for why it would be unfair:

Requiring a showing of bad faith as a precondition to the imposition of spoliation sanctions means that evidence may be destroyed willfully, or through gross negligence or even reckless disregard, without any true consequences. At least in Hohfeldian terms, in which a duty is the jural correlate of a right, this approach is tantamount to suggesting that the "duty" to preserve evidence is not

---

181. *Id.*
182. 77 Fed. Cl. 257 (Cl. Ct. 2007).

much of a duty at all. Second, imposing sanctions only when a spoliator can be proven to have acted in bad faith defenestrates three of the four purposes underlying such sanctions—to protect the integrity of the fact-finding process, to restore the adversarial balance between the spoliator and the prejudiced party, and to deter future misconduct—and severely frustrates the last, to punish. These objectives are hardly served if the court in effect is constrained to say to the injured party—"sorry about that, but there is nothing I can do, except to let you present your case, such as it remains."

In *United Medical,* the government attorney assigned to the litigation initiated a litigation hold through an e-mail notice, but made no follow-up efforts to verify that the e-mails had been received, read, and followed. As a consequence, numerous documents were destroyed that otherwise would have been retained. The court imposed two sanctions. First the government was prohibited from cross-examining the plaintiff's expert regarding favorable information he had extrapolated to fill gaps in the record. Second, the government was ordered to reimburse the plaintiff for additional costs of discovery plus attorneys' fees relating to both the discovery and the pursuit of the spoliation sanctions.

Still other courts condition the mens rea requirement on the kind of sanctions being sought.[183] "[B]oth negligent and willful destruction can

---

183. For example, a dispositive sanction, like a default judgment, is not appropriate when the destruction is not shown to have been willful or in bad faith—with the intention of destroying relevant evidence. Societe Internationale Pour Participations Industrielles et Commerciales, S.A. v. Rogers, 357 U.S. 197, 208-10 (1958); Goclay v. New Mexico Fed. Sav. & Loan, 968 F.2d 1017, 1020 (10th Cir. 1992); Barsoum v. NYC Hous. Auth., 202 F.R.D. 396, 399-400 (S.D.N.Y. 2001) ("Whether to impose a sanction and the severity of that sanction requires consideration of three factors: first, the obligation of the party against whom sanctions are sought to preserve the evidence at issue; second, the party's intent; and third, the relevance of the evidence to the contested issue, or prejudice. . . . Any sanction 'should be molded to serve the prophylactic, punitive, and remedial rationales underlying the spoliation doctrine.' . . . That is, the sanction should be designed to deter future spoliation of evidence, shift the risk of an erroneous judgment onto the party responsible for the loss of evidence, and remedy the prejudice suffered by the other party. . . . The level of intentionality goes directly to the degree of severity of any sanction that may be warranted. Dismissal requires a showing of 'willfulness, bad faith, or any fault' on the part of the sanctioned party. . . . 'Fault' includes gross

constitute spoliation. . . . [T]he appropriate place to assess the effect of the spoliator's state of mind is in ascertaining an appropriate sanction, not in assessing whether spoliation has occurred."[184] When more severe sanc-

negligence. . . . An adverse inference sanction may also be predicated on a finding 'of bad faith, intentional misconduct, or fault in the form of gross negligence.'"); Gates Rubber Co. v. Bando Chem. Indus., Ltd., 167 F.R.D. 90, 103-04 (D. Colo. 1996); Synanon Found., Inc. v. Bernstein, 503 A.2d 1254 (D.C. Ct. App. 1986) (plaintiff committed fraud during the discovery process through false representations and destroyed relevant evidence; accordingly, the plaintiff's complaint was dismissed).

An adverse inference was rejected in Williams v. CSX Transp., Inc., 925 F. Supp. 447, 452 (S.D. Miss. 1996), because "bad conduct of the defendant" was lacking. When only a fine is being imposed, it may be appropriate even though there is no evidence of bad faith. GTFM, Inc. v. Wal-Mart Stores, Inc., 2000 WL 335558 (S.D.N.Y. Mar. 30, 2000) (misrepresentation about ability to respond to discovery demands resulted in fees and costs being assessed against defendant as sanction); Procter & Gamble Co. v. Haugen, 179 F.R.D. 622, 632 (D. Utah 1998); Marketing Specialists, Inc. v. Bruin, 129 F.R.D. 35, 53 (W.D. N.Y. 1989) (plaintiff awarded counsel's fees incurred in bringing sanctions motion); United States v. Koch Indus., Inc., 197 F.R.D. 463, 486 (N.D. Okla. 1998) (court would not recognize adverse inference without showing of bad faith, but court did preclude party who destroyed tapes from using any evidence produced from tapes). A helpful explanation of this sanction issue was provided in Gates Rubber Co. v. Bando Chem. Indus., Ltd., 167 F.R.D. 90, 103-04 (D. Colo. 1996):

> Where a judge finds no willfulness, bad faith or fault, there exists beneath these states of mind a broad panoply of unintentional conduct: recklessness, gross negligence, negligence, carelessness, inadvertence or accident. The discretion to impose sanctions for reckless or negligent misconduct is as broad as the discretion which is accorded for imposition of sanctions where the misconduct was deliberate and intentional. . . .

The imposition of dispositive sanctions "should be confined to the 'flagrant case' in which it is demonstrated that the failure to produce 'materially affect(s) the substantial rights of the adverse party' and is 'prejudicial to the presentation of his case.'" . . . The proper sanction must be "'no more severe . . . than is necessary to prevent prejudice to the movant.'" . . . The trial judge must consider how the absence of any particular evidence which was not produced would impair a party's ability to establish its case.

It is important to understand, however, that the authority to sanction by default judgment is permissive. The fact that the court can do so does not mean that it must. Jackson v. Harvard Univ., 900 F.2d 464, 468 (1st Cir. 1990).

184. Samsung Elecs. Co., Ltd. v. Rambus Inc., 439 F. Supp. 2d 524, 540 (E.D. Va. 2006) (citing Silvestri v General Motors Corp., 217 F.3d 583, 593-95 (4th Cir. 2001).

tions are sought, like the dismissal of a claim, entering default judgment, or striking pleadings, they require a showing of bad faith.[185] While it is arguable whether bad faith is logically compelled before a negative inference can arise, courts have been split over whether judicially sanctioned remedies are appropriate without a demonstration of intent or bad faith.[186]

185. *See, e.g.,* Arista Records v. Tschirhart, 241 F.R.D. 462 (W.D. Tex. 2006) (The defendant wilfully destroyed critical evidence on her computer after notice of the lawsuit. She used "wiping" software to permanently remove data from her hard drive. Because this was a copyright infringement case, the information on the defendant's hard drive was the best evidence of that violation, and other evidence pieced together from the hard drive was not a sufficient substitute, the court determined that fairness to the plaintiff and deterrence mandated that the blatant disregard of judicial process required that default judgment be entered against the defendant. Iannucci v. Rose, 778 N.Y.S.2d 525, 526 (Sup. Ct. App. Div. 2004) ("Recognizing that striking a pleading is a drastic sanction to impose in the absence of willful or contumacious conduct, courts will consider the prejudice that resulted from the spoliation to determine whether such drastic relief is necessary as a matter of fundamental fairness."); QZO, Inc. v. Moyer, 594 S.E.2d 541, 547 (S.C. Ct. App. 2004) (Appellant failed to produce a computer in a timely manner when ordered and reformatted it prior to actual production, thereby destroying all evidence on hard drive; court struck the appellant's pleadings and entered judgment because bad faith and willfulness were involved.). Generally, in the pretrial process, the sanction of dismissal is an appropriate remedy for discovery abuses only when there is demonstrated prejudice and serious culpability on the part of the producing party. *See* Procter & Gamble Co. v. Haugen, 427 F.3d 727, 738 (10th Cir. 2005).

186. *Compare* Stevenson v. Union Pac. R.R. Co., 354 F.3d 739, 746 (8th Cir. 2004) ("We have never approved of giving an adverse inference instruction on the basis of prelitigation destruction of evidence through a routine document retention policy on the basis of negligence alone. Where a routine document retention policy has been followed in this context, we now clarify that there must be some indication of an intent to destroy the evidence for the purpose of obstructing or suppressing the truth in order to impose the sanction of an adverse inference instruction.") *with* Bashir v. Ambrak, 119 F.3d 929, 931 (11th Cir. 1997) ("In this circuit, an adverse inference is drawn from a party's failure to preserve evidence only when the absence of that evidence is predicated on bad faith.") *and* Coates v. EEOC, 756 F.2d 524 (7th Cir. 1985) (court refused to give adverse inference instruction because bad faith had not been shown) *and* Gates Rubber Co., 167 F.R.D. 90 (D. Colo. 1996) (sanctions not imposed because overwriting of hard drive and resulting destruction of documents were not shown to have been done to destroy evidence prior to inspection); and Phillips v. Covenant Clinic, 625 N.W.2d 714, 719 (Iowa 2001) ("[T]he inference can only be based upon the intentional destruction of evidence. . . . It is not warranted, if the disappearance of the evidence is due to mere negligence . . . .")

with Capellupo v. FMC Corp., 126 F.R.D. 545 (D. Minn. 1989) (imposing monetary sanction only after bad faith demonstrated); and Cortney v. Big O Tires, Inc., 87 P.3d 930, 933 (Idaho 2003) ("For the loss or destruction of evidence to constitute an admission, the circumstances must indicate that the evidence was lost or destroyed because the party responsible for such loss or destruction did not want the evidence available for use by an adverse party in pending or reasonably foreseeable litigation. The merely negligent loss of evidence will not support that inference . . . . There may be circumstances, however, where such inferences could be drawn from the reckless loss or destruction of evidence.") *with* Kelley v. United Airlines, Inc., 176 F.R.D. 422, 428 (D. Mass. 1997) (negligent destruction of documents was sufficient basis for adverse inference instruction); Donato v. Fitzgibbons, 172 F.R.D. 75, 82 (S.D.N.Y. 1997) (adverse inference justified because "bad faith and gross negligence" were shown); In re Prudential Ins. Co. of Am. Sales Practice Litig., 169 F.R.D. 598 (D.N.J. 1997) (company officials negligently failed to inform personnel responsible for regular document destruction that court had ordered no further destruction); Stanton v. Nat'l R.R. Passenger Corp., 849 F. Supp. 1524, 1528 (M.D. Ala. 1994) (because defendants could not explain circumstances surrounding destruction of tape, court found genuine issue fact regarding motivation for conduct; accordingly, for purposes of summary judgment, "this court must give Stanton the benefit of the adverse inference to be drawn from the missing tape, i.e., that the train was traveling in excess of the speed limit."); Stender v. Vincent, 992 P.2d 50, 59 (Haw. 2000) ("This court has never regarded bad faith or intentionality as a talisman in the imposition of discovery sanction; we refuse to do so now. . . . Although nonintentioinal spoliation may not implicate the punitive and deterrent interests in sanctions and may not trigger the inference of consciousness of a weak case, it does create an unfair disadvantage with respect to the lost evidence."); Anderson v. Literg, 694 A.2d 150, 156 (Ct. Spec. App. Md. 1997) ("[A]n adverse presumption may arise against the spoliator even if there is no evidence of fraudulent intent."); Reingold v. Wet'N Wild Nevada, Inc., 113 Nev. 967, 944 P.2d 800, 971 (1997) ("The district court apparently believed that 'willful suppression' requires more than following the company's normal records destruction policy. We disagree. There is no question that the records were 'willfully' or intentionally destroyed. Wet'N Wild claimed that all records are destroyed at the end of each season. This policy means that the accident records are destroyed even before the statute of limitations has run on any potential litigation for that season. It appears that this records destruction policy was deliberately designed to prevent production of records in any subsequent litigation. Deliberate destruction of records before the statute of limitations has run on the incident described in those records amounts to suppression of evidence. If Wet'N Wild chooses such a records destruction policy, it must accept the adverse inferences of the policy."); Wolfe v. Virginia Birth-Related Neurological Injury Compensation Program, 580 S.E.2d 467, 475 (Va. Cir. 2003) ("In Virginia, spoliation 'encompasses [conduct that is either] . . . intentional or negligent.' . . . A spoliation inference may be applied in an existing action if, at the time the evidence was lost or destroyed, 'a reasonable person in the defendant's position should have foreseen that the evidence was material to a potential civil action.'").

Even if the court concludes that an adverse inference jury instruction is not appropriate unless "bad faith" is demonstrated, the court in *United States v. Koch Industries, Inc.*[187] explains that the party whose evidence was destroyed is "not precluded from informing the jury as to which relevant computer tapes were destroyed and the impact that the destruction has had" on his case. In other words, an inference can arise from the evidence of destruction, but the court will not assist the inference with an instruction.

In states that recognize an independent cause of action for spoliation, the same differences exist; some are premised on negligence,[188] and others require willfulness or bad faith.[189]

---

187. 197 F.R.D. 463, 486 (N.D. Okla. 1998).

188. *See, e.g.,* Kammeyer v. City of Sharonville, 311 F. Supp. 2d 653, 663 (S.D. Ohio 2003) ("While Ohio has yet to explicitly recognize such a claim, it has implied that one exists [in Thomas v. Nationwide Mut. Ins. Co., 79 Ohio App. 3d 624, 607 N.E.2d 944]"); Herbin v. Hoeffel, 806 A.2d 186, 191 (D.C. App. 2002); Smith v. Atkinson, 771 So. 2d 429 (Ala. 2000); Boyd v. Travelers Ins. Co. , 166 Ill. 2d 188, 652 N.E.2d 267 (1995) (while generally no duty to preserve evidence, such duty can arise through agreement, contract, statute, or other special circumstances such as assumption of duty by affirmative conduct; if duty can be found, it arises only if a reasonable person in defendant's position should have foreseen evidence was material to potential civil action); Meyn v. Iowa, 594 N.W.2d 31 (Iowa 1999); Williams v. State, 34 Cal. 3d 18, 664 P.2d 137, 192 Cal. Rptr. 233 (1983).

189. *See, e.g.,* Smith v. Superior Court, 198 Cal. Rptr. 829 (Cal. Ct. App. 1984) (first court to recognize the tort of intentional spoliation of evidence); Cox v. State, 849 So. 2d 1257, 1266 (Miss. 2003) ("The intentional spoliation or destruction of evidence raises a presumption or inference that the evidence would have been unfavorable to the case of the spoliator: 'Such a presumption or inference arises, however, only where the spoliation or destruction was intentional and indicates fraud and a desire to suppress the truth, and it does not arise where the destruction was a matter of routine with no fraudulent intent.'"); Coleman v. Eddy Potash, Inc., 905 P.2d 185, 120 N.M. 645 (N.M. 1995); Smith v. Howard Johnson Co., 67 Ohio St. 3d 28, 1993 Ohio 229, 615 N.E.2d 1037, 1038 (1993) (A claim of intentional spoliation of evidence requires: (1) pending or probable litigation involving the plaintiff; (2) knowledge by the defendant of the existing or anticipated litigation; (3) willful destruction of evidence; (4) disruption of the plaintiff's case; and (5) damages caused by the destruction.); Garfoot v. Fireman's Fund Ins. Co., 228 Wis. 2d 707, 599 N.W.2d 411 (1999).

Because spoliation remedies are both remedial and punitive, the presence of bad faith should influence the resulting sanction.[190] When courts are considering a more severe sanction—such as exclusion of evidence, dismissal, or default—they should require some level of willfulness.[191] It is

---

190. Barsoum v. NYC Hous. Auth., 202 F.R.D. 396, 399-400 (S.D.N.Y. 2001) ("Whether to impose a sanction and the severity of that sanction requires consideration of three factors: first, the obligation of the party against whom sanctions are sought to preserve the evidence at issue; second, the party's intent; and third, the relevance of the evidence to the contested issue, or prejudice. . . . Any sanction 'should be molded to serve the prophylactic, punitive, and remedial rationales underlying the spoliation doctrine. . . . That is, the sanction should be designed to deter future spoliation of evidence, shift the risk of an erroneous judgment onto the party responsible for the loss of evidence, and remedy the prejudice suffered by the other party. . . . The level of intentionality goes directly to the degree of severity of any sanction that may be warranted. Dismissal requires a showing of 'willfulness, bad faith, or any fault' on the part of the sanctioned party. . . . 'Fault' includes gross negligence. . . . An adverse inference sanction may also be predicated on a finding 'of bad faith, intentional misconduct, or fault in the form of gross negligence."); Turner v. Hudson Transit Lines, Inc., 142 F.R.D. 68, 74 (S.D.N.Y. 1991) ("The second rationale [for imposing a sanction] is punitive. 'Allowing the trier of fact to draw the inference . . . deters parties from destroying relevant evidence . . . .'"); Vazquez-Corales v. Sea-Land Serv., Inc. 172 F.R.D. 10, 14-15 (D. P.R. 1997) (focusing on whether plaintiff acted in bad faith when determining whether to apply sanctions); Nat'l Ass'n of Radiation Survivors v. Turnage, 115 F.R.D. 543, 547 (N.D. Cal. 1987) (examining factors to bad faith when deciding whether to impose sanctions).

191. *See* Metropolitan Opera Ass'n, Inc., *supra* note 81; Century ML-Cable Corp. v. Conjugal P'ship Composed by Edwin Carillo, 43 F. Supp. 2d 176, 184 (D. P.R. 1998) (because party's destruction of computer records was willful and in bad faith, the court entered a default judgment); Computer Assoc. Int'l, Inc. v. Am. Fundware, Inc., 133 F.R.D. 166, 169-70 (D. Colo. 1990) (because destruction was willful and in bad faith, court concluded that only appropriate sanction was adverse judgment). In both Century and Computer Assoc., the actions were in direct violation of a court order. *See also* Vesta Fire Ins. Corp. v. Milam & Co. Constr., Inc., 2004 WL 1909498, at *9 (Ala. Aug. 27, 2004), where the court explained that although willfulness has been eliminated as a requirement for sanctions under Rule 37, it is still a factor when the most severe sanctions are imposed. "In the context of choice of sanctions to impose when a party refuses to provide discovery owing under Rules 26 through 36, Ala. R. Civ. P., Rule 37 does not require a showing of willfulness. 'Alabama adopted this federal rule [, Rule 37,] subsequent to its 1970 amendment which eliminated the requirement that the failure to respond be "willful."' . . . Nonetheless, '"willfulness' . . . is a key criterion to the imposition of the drastic sanction of dismissal' under Rule 37."

inappropriate, however, to allow parties to recklessly, or even negligently, destroy relevant evidence with impunity. Only through the imposition of sanctions will parties be encouraged to fulfill their responsibility to preserve evidence relevant to a pending or reasonably anticipated litigation.

Courts appropriately employ a balancing test in determining whether spoliation has occurred and what sanctions should be imposed.[192] Generally, they consider such factors as (1) the resulting

192. Schmid v. Milwaukee Elec. Tool Corp., 13 F.3d 76, 78 (3d Cir. 1994) ("We believe the key considerations in determining whether such a sanction is appropriate should be: (1) the degree of fault of the party who altered or destroyed the evidence; (2) the degree of prejudice suffered by the opposing party; and (3) whether there is a lesser sanction that will avoid substantial unfairness to the opposing party and, where the offending party is seriously at fault, will serve to deter such conduct by others in the future."); Bonds v. Dist. of Columbia, 320 U.S. App. D.C. 138, 93 F.3d 801, 808 (D.C. Cir. 1996) ("In determining the appropriate sanction, this court must consider three factors: the prejudice to plaintiff, the prejudice to the judicial system, and the need to deter similar misconduct in the future."); Barsoum v. NYC Hous. Auth., 202 F.R.D. at 399-400 ("Whether to impose a sanction and the severity of that sanction requires consideration of three factors: first, the obligation of the party against whom sanctions are sought to preserve the evidence at issue; second, the party's intent; and third, the relevance of the evidence to the contested issue, or prejudice. . . . Any sanction 'should be molded to serve the prophylactic, punitive, and remedial rationales underlying the spoliation doctrine.' . . . This is, the sanction should be designed to deter future spoliation of evidence, shift the risk of an erroneous judgment onto the party responsible for the loss of evidence, and remedy the prejudice suffered by the other party. . . . The level of intentionality goes directly to the degree of severity of any sanction that may be warranted. Dismissal requires a showing of 'willfulness, bad faith, or any fault' on the part of the sanctioned party. . . . 'Fault' includes gross negligence. . . . An adverse inference sanction may also be predicated on a finding 'of bad faith, intentional misconduct, or fault in the form of gross negligence."); Segura v. K-Mart Corp., 62 P.3d 283, 286 (N.M. Ct. App. 2002) ("We believe the key considerations in determining whether such a sanction is appropriate should be: (1) the degree of fault of the party who altered or destroyed the evidence; (2) the degree of prejudice suffered by the opposing party; and (3) whether there is a lesser sanction that will avoid substantial unfairness to the opposing party and, where the offending party is seriously at fault, will serve to deter such conduct by others in the future."); Felix v. Gonzalez, 87 S.W.3d 574, 580 (Tex. App. 1998) ("Generally, two rules apply to presumptions that derive from the nonproduction of evidence. One, intentional spoliation of evidence raises a presumption that the evidence would have been unfavorable to the spoliator. . . . Two, unintentional spoliation or the failure to produce evidence within a party's control raises a rebuttable presumption that the missing evidence would be unfavorable to the nonproducing party." Since presumptions are, by definition, rebuttable, or else they are rules of law, *see* Chapter Five, *infra*, it appears that the court is referring

harm,[193] (2) the undesirability of the interests furthered by the con-

to permissible inferences.); Henderson v. Tyrrell, 910 P.2d 522, 531 (Wash. Ct. App. 1996) (appropriate remedy is determined by "the relevance or importance of the missing evidence or . . . the culpability of the actor").

193. Roadway Express, Inc. v. Piper, 447 U.S. 752, 764 (1980) ("Before a sanction for destruction of the evidence is appropriate, however, there must also be a finding that the destruction prejudiced the opposing party."); Schmid v. Milwaukee Elec. Tool Corp., 13 F.3d 76, 78 (3d Cir. 1994) ("[T]he expert minimized the impact of his investigation by documenting his findings with photographs. . . . While the expert could have done more—he did not videotape or time the operation of the allegedly defective guard—this omission would not justify severe sanctions absent a showing by the manufacturer that taking these steps would have avoided some substantial prejudice." In addition, plaintiff claimed that all saws of that design were defective; independent testing was possible on other saws of same model.); Simons v. Mercedes-Benz of N. Am., Inc., 1996 WL 103796, at *5 (E.D. Pa. 1996) (In action under Pennsylvania's Lemon Law, defendant was not given opportunity to examine car before it was conveyed to third party; despite this destruction, court would not impose sanctions because defendant had performed all repairs and had preserved voluminous records on vehicle, and Mercedes expert had inspected vehicle before the suit began; "any prejudice suffered by MBNA is questionable in light of the voluminous repair records which purport to show a number of recurring problems with the vehicle . . . ."); Joe Hand Promotions v. Sports Page Cafe, Inc., 940 F. Supp. 102 (D. N.J. 1996) (Even though detective misplaced tape recorder, court would not impose sanctions because detective was still available to testify; through his testimony and opposing party's opportunity to cross-examine, court concluded that truth would come out.); Baliotis v. McNeil, 870 F. Supp. 1285, 1281-93 (M.D. Pa. 1994) (Plaintiffs' fault and defendant's prejudice were limited by particular facts of case; plaintiffs were renters and had no power over preservation or destruction of fire scene; items useful to defendant's investigation were preserved; photographs and videotapes were available; and reports of both plaintiff's investigator and state fire marshal were available to defendants.); Boyd v. Travelers Ins. Co., 652 N.E.2d 267, 271 n.2 (Ill. 1995) (It must be shown that the loss or destruction of evidence denied a reasonable probability of succeeding on the underlying action. "[I]f the plaintiff could not prevail in the underlying action even with the lost or destroyed evidence, then the defendant's conduct is not the cause of the loss of the lawsuit.").

In contrast to Baliotis and Schmid, the defendant in Howell v. Maytag Magic Chef Corp., 168 F.R.D. 502, 506 (M.D. Pa. 1996), suffered greater prejudice due to the destruction of a fire scene: "While Maytag can examine the microwave for the alleged fault which plaintiffs assert gives rise to its liability, as well as the burn patterns in plaintiffs' photographs of the scene, it has been denied the opportunity to examine other possible causes of the fire. This search for alternative causes will be particularly crucial to Maytag's defense, given plaintiffs' stated intention to proceed under a theory of 'circumstantial evidence of malfunction in the absence

duct,[194] (3) the context and circumstances of the conduct,[195] and (4)

of abnormal use and after elimination of reasonably secondary causes.' . . . If plaintiffs intend to argue that a defect in the microwave can be inferred from the lack of alternative causes of the fire, then denying Maytag an opportunity to examine the remainder of the kitchen wiring and appliances leaves Maytag to rely solely on plaintiffs' investigation." *Id.*

194. Any effort (successful or otherwise) to destroy evidence after its relevance has become apparent to a pending or reasonably anticipated action is undesirable and should be deterred. The nature of the act, however, may show less culpability on the part of the actor and, therefore, should be taken into account when assessing the gravity of the sanctions that the actor should suffer.

195. The context and circumstances are intimately tied to the nature of the act. Schmid v. Milwaukee Elec. Tool Corp., 13 F.3d 76, 80 (3d Cir. 1994) (After electric saw injured plaintiff, his lawyer sent it to an expert for examination. When the guard was disassembled to determine the reason for its malfunctioning, debris stored in it fell out, thereby rendering the guard operable. The court concluded that spoliation sanctions were not justified. Expert does not have to delay his examination until all prospective defendants can have their experts examine it at same time. Alteration of condition could not be avoided because disassembly was necessary for expert's examination. The "transient" nature of condition made it necessary for examination to occur before other deterioration naturally occurred. Photographs were taken of saw, before and after disassembly, showing parts removed and debris that fell from it. Sanction of excluding testimony of the eFxamining expert was an abuse of discretion.); Webb v. Dist. of Columbia, 175 F.R.D. 128, 144 (D. D.C. 1997) (Despite obvious relevance of records to cause of action, no procedures were put in place to ensure that relevant employment records were flagged so that they would not be destroyed; judgment of default was entered against defendant.); Dardeen v. Keuhling, 801 N.E.2d 960, 964 (Ill. Ct. App. 2003) (after someone fell because of hole in brick sidewalk, the owner of the property called her insurance company to ask whether she should remove bricks and make repairs to avoid additional injuries. Even though the measures were appropriate in the circumstances, neither homeowner nor insurance company took photographs or videotapes of area before it was altered. The court held that this was sanctionable conduct on the part of the insurance company. "In the instant case, circumstances exist sufficient to impose a duty on State Farm to preserve evidence. State Farm had a contractual relationship with its insured, Alice Kuehling. Kuehling called State Farm the same day the plaintiff fell on the sidewalk and asked whether or not she could remove some bricks so no one else would get hurt. Ronald Couch, a State Farm agent, replied that it would be okay for the plaintiff to remove the bricks. Couch did not recommend that Keuhling take pictures or videotape the sidewalk, nor did he offer to send an investigator to do so prior to the removal of the bricks.").

Once the elements of destruction and knowledge of the relevance of the evidence are established, the context and circumstances may show less culpability on the part of the actor, justifying a lesser sanction. The goal of general deterrence,

the actor's motives.[196] Determining the appropriate spoliation sanctions is a process similar to assessing criminal punishment. Consequently, courts focus on the actor's motive. When bad faith is involved, the other factors tend to take a back seat. When bad faith is not involved, some courts will sanction reckless or negligent conduct only if the opposing party is demonstrably injured. Other courts will not impose sanctions unless intentional acts and bad faith are involved, regardless of whether the acts of spoliation resulted in harm.[197]

Even if attempts to destroy evidence are intentional and in bad faith, they can be unsuccessful because either the destruction does not occur or the evidence is available from another source. Courts are unlikely to impose sanctions in these situations. However, an attempt to destroy evidence shows the actor's belief that it is harmful to his or her case. Consequently, the attempt should be admissible as an admission by conduct, even if the court does not give an instruction about the adverse inference.[198]

<hr />

however, may require a greater sanction if the conduct is widespread (for example, a document destruction policy).

196. Schmid v. Milwaukee Elec. Tool Corp., 13 F.3d 76, 80 (3d Cir. 1994) (When plaintiff gave saw to the expert for examination, neither plaintiff nor expert conducted examination with intention of impairing ability of potential defendant to defend itself; because nature of defect claimed appeared on all saws of same model, it was not unreasonable for plaintiff to conclude that photographing of saw as it was being disassembled was adequate protection for potential defendants.); Computer Assoc. Int'l, Inc. v. Am. Fundware, Inc., 133 F.R.D. 166, 168 (D. Colo. 1990) ("If the abuses are egregious, default judgment is appropriate.").

The actor's motive, of course, is only one factor in assessing how much punishment is needed through the sanction. General deterrence is another equally legitimate goal that may require motives to be given less weight. Computer Assoc. Int'l, Inc. v. Am. Fundware, Inc., 133 F.R.D. 166, 169 (D. Colo. 1990) ("I find and conclude that no alternative sanction short of default judgment would adequately punish [Am. Fundware] and deter future like-minded litigants.").

197. For an excellent article on the breadth of approaches to spoliation, *see* Jeffrey S. Kinsler & Anne Keyes MacIver, *Demystifying Spoliation of Evidence*, 34 Tort & Ins. L. J. 761 (1999).

198. *See, e.g.,* Scott v. IBM Corp., 196 F.R.D. 233, 248 (D. N.J. 2000) (Although sanctions were denied because the destruction was the result of negligence rather than willfulness, the court noted that a negative inference is still appropriate.); Cortney v. Big O Tires, Inc., 87 P.3d 930, 933 (Idaho 2003) ("For the loss or destruction of evidence to constitute an admission, the circumstances must indicate that the evidence was lost or destroyed because the party responsible for such loss or destruction did not want the evidence available for use by an adverse party in pending or

When a spoliation sanction was premised on the untimely production, rather than destruction, of materials that precluded those materials from being used at trial, the court held that the party seeking the sanction must show, among other things, a "culpable state of mind."[199] While this would seem to suggest that something more than negligence is required, the court noted that the standard could be satisfied by "a showing that the evidence was destroyed 'knowingly, even if without intent to [breach a duty to preserve it], or *negligently.*"[200] "The sanction of an adverse inference may be appropriate in some cases involving the negligent destruction of evidence because each party should bear the risk of its own negligence."[201]

---

reasonably foreseeable litigation."); Quintanilla v. State, 2000 WL 34251898, at *3 (Tex. App. March 23, 2000) ("[F]light, rebutted alibis, destruction of evidence and fabrication of evidence are but a few samples of incriminating behavior."); *see generally* text at note 257.

199. Residential Funding Corp. v. DeGeorge Fin. Corp., 306 F.3d 99, 107 (2d Cir. Oct. 8, 2002). However, in Fjelstad v. American Motor Co., Inc., 762 F.2d 1334, 1343 (9th Cir. 1985), the court held that "sanctions may be imposed even for negligent failures to provide discovery." The standard of conduct that courts identify in their opinions as justifying sanctioning is not always clear, and what they say is often tied to the harm done and sanctions the court wishes to impose. Courts have the right, either under the Federal Rules of Civil Procedure or their inherent power, to impose sanctions that are commensurate with the harm caused by the failing party. Rule 37 authorizes sanctions for violating production responsibilities unless the failing party substantially justifies its deficient response. Qualcomm Inc. v. Broadcom Corp., 2008 U.S. Dist. LEXIS 911, *33-35 (S.D. Cal. Jan. 7, 2008). The judge in *Qualcomm* even sanctioned the lawyers because they had signed pleadings and made factual representation to the court without making "'reasonable inquiry' to determine whether discovery responses [were] sufficient and proper." *Id.* at *47. The Qualcomm court, however, did not impose sanctions under a spoliation theory. It focused only on the violation of discovery rules by the party and ethical responsibilities of the attorneys.

200. *Id.*

201. *Id.* at 108. Mosaid Tech. Inc. v. Samsung Elecs. Co., 348 F. Supp. 2d 332, 338 (D. N.J. 2004) ("[N]egligent destruction of relevant evidence can be sufficient to give rise to the spoliation inference. If a party has notice that evidence is relevant to an action, and either proceeds to destroy that evidence or allows it to be destroyed by failing to take reasonable precautions, common sense dictates that the party is more likely to have been threatened by that evidence."); Pace v. Nat'l R.R. Passenger Corp., 291 F. Supp. 2d 93, 98 (D. Conn. 2003) ("[T]he sanction of [an] adverse inference instruction should be available even for the 'negligent destruction of documents, if necessary to further the remedial purpose of the inference,' because it makes little difference to the party victimized by the destruction of evidence whether the act was done willfully or negligently.") (quoting from Turner

Proving bad faith can be a difficult. Direct evidence is rarely available, and the determination depends on the specific circumstances of each case.[202] This is particularly true of spoliation that occurs before an action is filed. After litigation begins, a court may dispense with the factual demonstration, finding bad faith or willfulness implicit in the act. Going a step further, in *E*Trade Securities LLC v. Deutsche Bank AG*,[203] the defendant destroyed hard drives and chose to retain certain documents prior to the destruction *after being made aware* of the *potential for* litigation. The court concluded that because Normura Defendants "were aware of the potential for litigation, the plaintiff need not demonstrate bad faith or willful intent to destroy." The court further noted that "[e]ven though a showing of bad faith is required only for pre-litigation destruction of evidence, the Nomura Defendant's action would satisfy this heightened requirement for pre-litigation destruction. . . . Here, . . . Nomura Canada chose to retain certain documents prior to the destruction of the hard drives. This gives rise to an implication of bad faith on the part of the Nomura Defendants."[204]

IV. CONSEQUENCES OF SPOLIATION

Spoliation has given rise to an independent cause of action in a limited number of state jurisdictions.[205] Federal and state criminal statutes also

v. Hudson Transit Lines, Inc., 142 F.R.D. 68, 75 (S.D.N.Y. 1991)); Wolfe v. Virginia Birth-Related Neurological Injury Compensation Program, 580 S.E.2d 467, 475 (Va. Cir. 2003) ("In Virginia, spoliation 'encompasses [conduct that is either] . . . intentional or negligent.' . . . A spoliation inference may be applied in an existing action if, at the time the evidence was lost or destroyed, 'a reasonable person in the defendant's position should have foreseen that the evidence was material to a potential civil action.'").

202. *See* Morris v. Union Pac. RR. Co., 373 F.3d 896, 901 (8th Cir. 2004) and Stevenson v. Union Pac. R.R. Co., 354 F.3d 739, 748 (8th Cir. 2004).

203. 230 F.R.D. 582 (D. Minn. 2005).

204. *Id.* at 589-90.

205. The District of Columbia and nine states—Alabama, Alaska, Florida, Illinois, Louisiana, Montana, New Jersey, New Mexico, and Ohio—appear to have recognized a cause of action for spoliation. In Florida the essential elements of a spoliation of evidence claim are: (1) the existence of a potential civil action, (2) a legal or contractual duty to preserve evidence which is relevant to the potential civil action, (3) destruction of that evidence, (4) significant impairment in the ability to prove the lawsuit, (5) a causal relationship between the evidence destruction and the inability to prove the lawsuit, and (6) damages. *See* Hagopian v. Publix Supermarkets, Inc., 788 So. 2d 1088, 1091 (Fla Dist. Ct. App. 2001); Miller v.

Allstate Ins. Co., 573 So. 2d 24, 27 (Fla. Dist. Ct. App. 1990); Continental Ins. Co. v. Herman, 576 So. 2d 313, 315 (Fla. Dist. Ct. App. 1990). In Alabama, a cause of action is recognized against a third party who has negligently destroyed material evidence, *see* Smith v. Atkinson, 771 So. 2d 429, 438 (Ala. 2000), but no independent tort is recognized when the spoliator was a party in a pending action. Kaufmann & Assoc., Inc. v. Davis, 908 So. 2d 246, 250 (Ala. Civ. App. May 14, 2004). Florida also appears to have disallowed a claim for spoliation when the alleged spoliator was also the defendant in the underlying cause of action. Martino v. Wal-Mart Store, Inc., 908 So. 2d 342 (Fla. 2005) (Only third-party spoliation actions are recognized. As the court explained: "First-party spoliation claims are claims in which the defendant who allegedly lost, misplaced, or destroyed the evidence was also a spoliator in causing the plaintiff's injuries or damages. These actions are contrasted with third-party spoliation claims, which occur when a person or entity, though not a party to the underlying action causing the plaintiff's injuries or damages, lost, misplaced, or destroyed evidence critical to that action." In rejecting the first-party spoliation action, the court noted that sanction and a presumption of negligence were the appropriate remedies for first-party acts.). Louisiana recognizes a cause of action when the destruction is intentional. Quinn v. Riso Invs., Inc., 869 So. 2d 922 (La. App. 2004) ("A plaintiff asserting a state law tort claim for spoliation of evidence must allege that the defendant intentionally destroyed evidence."). New Jersey recognizes a cause of action under a different theory. Rosenblit v. Zimmerman, 766 A.2d 749 (N.J. 2001) (while not recognizing an independent cause of action for spoliation, the court concluded that the act of spoliation was actionable under a claim of fraudulent concealment). New Mexico recognizes a third-party action for intentional acts of evidence destruction. Coleman v. Eddy Potash, Inc., 905 P.2d 185, 187-89 (N.M. 1995). Arizona, Arkansas, California, Georgia, Idaho, Indiana, Kansas, Kentucky, Maryland, Massachusetts, Michigan, Minnesota, Mississippi, Missouri, New Mexico, New York, Pennsylvania, Texas, and West Virginia have rejected the opportunity to recognize a first-party cause of action for spoliation. *See, e.g.,* Goff v. Harold Ives Trucking Co., 27 S.W.3d 387 (Ark. 2000) (The court refused to recognize an independent tort for first-party spoliation, since the matter should be addressed in the action in which the wrongful conduct occurred. The court appeared to support a third-party cause of action for spoliation.); Temple Comm. Hosp. v. Super. Ct., 976 P.2d 223, 225 (Cal. 1999) ("Many of the considerations that led us in [Cedars Sinai Med. Ctr. v. Superior Court, 954 P.2d 511, 521 (Cal. 1998)] to decline to recognize a tort cause of action for spoliation apply with equal weight when the spoliation is committed by a third party."); Boyd v. Travelers Ins. Co., 652 N.E.2d 267, 270 (Ill. 1995) (recognizing that spoliation is actionable under negligence law); Gribben v. Wal-Mart Stores, Inc., 824 N.E.2d 349, 355 (Ind. 2005) (The court rejected a first-party tort claim for the intentional destruction of evidence because the matter can best be dealt with in the action in which it occurred. The court indicated that a third-party cause of action for spoliation may be needed because existing remedies are inadequate.); Monsanto

exist to address the destruction of evidence and tampering with witnesses.[206] The principles that control the courts authority to impose sanctions for spoliation were summarized by the Minnesota Supreme Court in *Patton v. Newmar Corp.*:[207]

Co. v. Reed, 950 S.W.2d 811, 815 (Ky. 1997) ("We decline the invitation to create a new tort claim. Where the issue of destroyed or missing evidence has arisen, we have chosen to remedy the matter through evidentiary rules and 'missing evidence' instructions."); Fletcher v. Dorchester Mutual Ins. Co., 437 Mass. 544 (2002); Federated Mut. Ins. Co. v. Litchfield Precision Components, Inc., 456 N.W.2d 434, 436 (Minn. 1990) (independent spoliation tort not rejected); Dowdle Butane Gas Co., Inc. v. Moore, 831 So. 2d 1124, 1135 (Miss. 2002) (with extensive discussion of the body of case law exploring the tort of spoliation); Timber Tech Engineered Building Products v. Home Ins. Co., 55 P.3d 952, 954 (Nev. 2002) (quoting, with approval, the California opinion in which first-party causes of action were rejected, Temple Community Hospital, *supra*: "'In sum, we conclude that the benefits of recognizing a tort cause of action, in order to deter third-party spoliation of evidence and compensate victims of such misconduct, are outweighed by the burden of litigants, witnesses, and the judicial system that would be imposed by potentially endless litigation over speculative loss, and by the cost to society of promoting onerous record and evidence retention policies.'"); Trevino v. Ortega, 969 S.W.2d 950, 951 (Tex. 1998) ("Texas does not recognize spoliation as a tort cause of action; spoliation does not give rise to independent damages, and is better remedied within the lawsuit affected by spoliation."); Hannah v. Heeter, 584 S.E.2d 560, 566-69 (W. Va. 2003) (While rejecting a first-party cause of action for spoliation, it did recognize an independent third-party cause of action because existing remedies against litigants is insufficient.). There is no independent tort of spoliation under federal law. For a comprehensive treatment of the tort of spoliation, *see* J. GORELICK, S. MARZEN & L. SOLUM, DESTRUCTION OF EVIDENCE §§ 4:1 through 23 (John Wiley & Sons 1989). *See generally* D. Bell, K. Klesel & T. Turnbull, *Let's Level the Playing Field: A New Proposal for Analysis of Spoliation of Evidence Claims in Pending Litigation*, 29 ARIZ. ST. L. J. 769 (1997); Robert L. Tucker, *The Flexible Doctrine of Spoliation of Evidence: Cause of Action, Defense, Evidentiary Presumption, and Discovery Sanction*, 27 UNIV. OF TOLEDO L. REV. 67 (1995).

206. *See, e.g.,* 18 U.S.C. § 1503 (providing that whoever "obstructs or impedes, or endeavors to influence, obstruct or impede, the due administration of justice" shall be subject to fines or imprisonment) and State v. Braidic, 119 Wash. App. 1075, 2004 WL 52412, at * 2 (Wash. Ct. App. Jan. 13, 2004) (by telephoning the victim and asking her to change her testimony, saying that she had lied to get attention, the defendant committed witness tampering).

207. 538 N.W.2d 116, 118-19 (Minn. 1995).

[C]ourts are vested with considerable inherent judicial authority necessary to their "vital function—the disposition of individual cases to deliver remedies for wrongs and 'injustice freely and without purchase; completely and without denial; promptly and without delay, conformable to the laws.'"

In most jurisdictions, including federal courts, if spoliation occurs after an action has been filed, it could be seen as a form of discovery abuse that can result in (1) dismissing the wrongdoer's claim,[208] (2) entering a default judgment,[209] (3) directing a verdict,[210] (4) imposing mon-

---

208. *Compare* Monsanto Co. v. Ralph, 382 F.3d 1374, 1378 (Fed. Cir. 2004) (infringer's pleadings struck and judgment entered after perjured statements were given, orders were violated, and evidence was destroyed) *with* Computer Assoc. Int'l, Inc., 133 F.R.D. at 166 (default judgment entered against the defendant who intentionally destroyed a computer program that was central to the action) *and* Wm. T. Thompson Co. v. General Nutrition Corp., 593 F. Supp. 1443 (C.D. Cal. 1984) (because of gravity of defendant's conduct and its impact on plaintiff's ability to prove its case, court granted default judgment against defendant and upheld Special Master's monetary sanction) *and* Klupt v. Krongard, 728 A.2d 727, 735-37 (1999) (after suit was filed and evidence was sought through a discovery request, plaintiff willfully destroyed tapes of secretly recorded telephone conversations; trial court dismissed action and sanction was upheld on appeal.) *and* Creazzo v. Medtronic, Inc., 903 A.2d 24 (Pa. Super. Ct. 2006) (Despite notification to the plaintiff that the device in question should be preserved for inspection so as to avoid spoliation claims, it was destroyed. The court dismissed the plaintiff's claim, even though the product was in the possession of a third party at the time of its destruction.) *with* Garfoot v. Fireman's Fund Ins. Co., 599 N.W.2d 411, 415 (Wis. 1999) (Appellate court overturned dismissal of an action because there was insufficient evidence that destruction was willful, deliberate or intentional; court held that sanction of dismissal is appropriate only where it is apparent that party was consciously attempting to affect outcome of litigation or act can be characterized as a "flagrant knowing disregard of the judicial process.").

209. Arista Records v. Tschirhart, 241 F.R.D. 462 (W.D. Tex. 2006) (The defendant willfully destroyed critical evidence on her computer after notice of the lawsuit. She used "wiping" software to permanently remove data from her hard drive. Because this was a copyright infringement case, the information on the defendant's hard drive was the best evidence of that violation, and other evidence pieced together from the hard drive was not a sufficient substitute, the court determined that fairness to the plaintiff and deterrence mandated that the blatant disregard of judicial process required that default judgment be entered against the defendant.)

210. Marrocco v. Goodyear Tire & Rubber Co., 966 F.2d 220, 222 (7th Cir. 1992) (party concealed a violation of court's protective order); Koon To Pau v.

etary sanctions,[211] (5) criminal contempt,[212] or (6) suppressing evidence

---

Yosemite, 928 F.2d 880 (9th Cir. 1991) (summary judgment entered after intentional destruction of evidence relevant to establishing claim); Wm. T. Thompson Co. v. General Nutrition Corp., 593 F. Supp. 1443, at 1455-56 (default judgment entered as punishment for destruction of documents).

211. *See, e.g.,* Google Inc. v. American Blind & Wallpaper Factory, Inc., 2007 WL 1848665 (N.D. Cal. June 27, 2007) (American Blind was required to pay $15,000 to Google. This sum was thought to be sufficient to penalize and deter similar conduct, while reimbursing Google for its expenses in bringing the motion.); Wachtel v. Health Net, Inc., 239 F.R.D. 81 (D. N.J. 2006) (Because of a pattern of successive discovery abuses, including misrepresentations to the court, failure to follow court orders, and failure to preserve and produce documents found to be discoverable by the court, the defendant was ordered to pay costs and attorney fees for the proceedings in which these matters were litigated; privilege claims, if any, were found to be waived; monetary penalties consistent with financial status were imposed; and more severe sanctions of dismissal or the exclusion of evidence were reserved for later assessment in light of future proceedings.); RKI, Inc. v. Grimes, 177 F. Supp. 2d 859 (N.D. Ill. Dec. 2001) (A former employee was accused of misappropriating trade secrets. To avoid detection, he deleted confidential information and software from his home computer and defragmented his computer (reconfigured the alignment of data) three times for the sole purpose of destroying any evidence that confidential communications had been deleted from his hard drive. The defendant was assessed $100,000 in compensatory damages, $150,000 in punitive damages, attorneys' fees, and court costs. It was not clear from the court's opinion whether the assessments were the result of the spoliation, were increased by spoliation, or whether those acts merely formed the basis upon which negative inference was drawn.); In re Prudential Ins. Co. of Am. Sales Practice Litig., 169 F.R.D. 598 (D. N.J. 1997) (court set up procedures to avoid further loss of documents and fined company $1 million); Harkins Amusement Enter., Inc. v. General Cinema Corp., 132 F.R.D. 523, 524 (D. Ariz. 1990) (because other sanctions would affect innocent parties, court awarded attorney's fees and costs); Capellupo v. FMC Corp., 126 F.R.D. 545 (D. Minn. 1989) (court awarded monetary sanction and doubled fees and costs).

212. Kaiser v. Kaiser, 868 So. 2d 1095 (Ala. Ct. Civ. App. 2003). When monetary sanctions are significant, and therefore intended to do more than compensate an opposing party or compel compliance with a court order, they will become criminal in nature. Bradley v. American Household, Inc., 378 F.3d 373, 378-79 (4th Cir. Aug. 6, 2004). This means that the sanctions cannot be imposed without affording the accused party criminal procedure protections. *See* Jake's Ltd. v. City of Coates, 356 F.3d 896, 901 (8th Cir. 2004); Mackler Prod., Inc. v. Cohen, 225 F.3d 136, 142 (2d Cir. 2000); Buffington v. Baltimore Cty., 913 F.2d 113, 133 (4th Cir. 1990). In these instances the district court's fines were meant to vindicate its authority by punishing for past acts.

related to the materials destroyed.[213] Dismissing a claim, of course, is the most drastic remedy, reserved for "those cases where the order for discovery goes to the very foundation of the cause of action . . . or where the refusal to comply is deliberate and contumacious."[214] It is reserved for those instances in which less drastic sanctions have been considered and it is concluded that they will not suffice, either alone or in combination.[215]

---

213. Torres v. Lexington Ins. Co., 237 F.R.D. 533, 533-34 (D. P.R. 2006) (After the opposing party learned that the plaintiff possessed Web pages depicting an active social life and an aspiring singing and modeling career, she deleted the Web sites. This was in direct contradiction of her claim of ongoing mental anguish. The court sanctioned Torres by precluding her from offering any evidence of continuous or ongoing mental anguish on her part.).

214. QZO, Inc. v. Moyer, 594 S.E.2d 541, 547 (S.C. Ct. App. 2004) (appellant failed to timely produce computer when ordered and reformatted it prior to actual production, thereby destroying all evidence on hard drive; sanction was striking pleadings and entering judgment); Lang v. Morgan's Home Equip. Corp., 6 N.J. 333, 339 (1951).

215. Halaco Eng'g Co. v. Costle, 843 F.2d 376, 379-80 (9th Cir. 1988). Three factors control the application of the most severe sanctions: "(1) the degree of fault of the party who altered or destroyed the evidence; (2) the degree of prejudice suffered by the opposing party; and (3) whether there is a lesser sanction that will avoid substantial unfairness to the opposing party and, where the offending party is seriously at fault, will serve to deter such conduct by others in the future." Schmid v. Milwaukee Elec. Tool Corp., 13 F.3d 76, 79 (3d Cir. 1994). In West v. Goodyear Tire and Rubber Co., 167 F.3d 776, 779-80 (2d Cir. 1999), the district judge granted partial summary judgment on punitive damage claims because the instrumentality involved in the death of the plaintiff had been sold without notice to the opposing party. Reversing the sanction, the court remanded with instructions to consider a less severe sanction:

> Although a district court has broad discretion in crafting a proper sanction for spoliation, we have explained that the applicable sanction should be molded to serve the prophylactic, punitive, and remedial rationales underlying the spoliation doctrine. . . . The sanction should be designed to: (1) deter parties from engaging in spoliation; (2) place the risk of an erroneous judgment on the party who wrongfully created the risk; and (3) restore "the prejudiced party to the same position he would have been in absent the wrongful destruction of evidence by the opposing party." . . .
>
> "Outright dismissal of a lawsuit . . . is within the court's discretion. . . . Dismissal is appropriate if there is a showing of willfulness, bad faith, or fault on the part of the sanctioned party. . . . However, because dismissal is a "drastic remedy," it "should be imposed only

in extreme circumstances, usually after consideration of alternative, less drastic sanctions." . . .

We disagree with Judge Owen's conclusion that dismissal constituted the only adequate sanction. It was not necessary to dismiss the complaint in order to vindicate the trifold aims of: (1) deterring future spoliation of evidence; (2) protecting the defendants' interests; and (3) remedying the prejudice defendants suffered as a result of West's actions. . . . Judge Owen could have combined alternative sanctions in a way that would fully protect Goodyear and Budd from prejudice. For example, the trial judge could: (1) instruct the jury to presume that the exemplar tire was overinflated; (2) instruct the jury to presume that the tire mounting machine and air compressor malfunctioned; and (3) preclude Mrs. West from offering evidence on these issues. We have previously endorsed use of these alternative sanctions, and in this case conclude that they will suffice to protect the defendants.

A negative inference was thought to be a more appropriate sanction than default judgment when the case was being tried to the court and the judge felt that he was "well-situated to assess and weigh the appropriate impact of the spoliated evidence" in the case. Kyoei Fire & Marine Ins. Co., Ltd. v. M/V Maritime Antalya, 248 F.R.D. 126, 145 (S.D.N.Y. 2007). *Accord*, Advantacare Health Partners v. Access IV, 2004 WL 1837997, at 5 (N.D. Cal. Aug. 17, 2004) ("Default judgment is a particularly severe sanction . . . and should be entered against a party only if lesser sanctions would be ineffective. . . . A default judgment most often is appropriate where a 'pattern of deception and discovery abuse made it impossible' for the district court to conduct a trial 'with any reasonable assurance that the truth would be available.'"); Mosel Vitelic Corp. v. Micron Tech., Inc., 162 F. Supp. 2d 307, 314 (D. Del. 2000); Vesta Fire Ins. Corp. v. Milam & Co. Constr., Inc., 2004 WL 1909498, at *9 (Ala. Aug. 27, 2004) ("In the context of choice of sanctions to impose when a party refuses to provide discovery owing under Rules 26 through 36, Ala. R. Civ. P., Rule 37 does not require a showing of willfulness. 'Alabama adopted this federal rule [, Rule 37,] subsequent to its 1970 amendment which eliminated the requirement that the failure to respond be "willful."' . . . Nonetheless, '"willfulness' . . . is a key criterion to the imposition of the drastic sanction of dismissal' under Rule 37."); Bridgestone/Firestone North American Tire, LLC v. Campbell, 574 S.E.2d 923 (Ga. Ct. App. 2002) (Even though critical evidence was intentionally destroyed after litigation had commenced, the court refused to dismiss because the remedy of excluding any evidence the offending party had retrieved from the destroyed tires was adequate.). The Texas Supreme Court noted in GTE Communs. Sys. Corp. v. Tanner, 856 S.W.2d 725, 727 (Tex. 1993) that a trial court "was required to consider the availability of lesser sanctions before imposing death penalty sanctions." The court was quick to note, however, that the trial did not have to test the effectiveness of each available lesser sanction by actually imposing them on the party before issuing the death penalty; but the court had to demonstrate that it analyzed the available sanctions and offer a reasonable explanation for imposing the sanction

If the offense has not had serious consequences for the opposing party, and a lesser sanction is warranted, one court has precluded the offending party from cross-examining the expert witness called by the party injured by the destruction.[216] Another court has excluded the testimony of the expert witness of the offending party unless he can re-create, at his expense, the work product that he destroyed.[217] Of course, the use of the negative inference is always available as a sanction regardless of when the destruction occurred, and when the willfulness of the violation is uncertain, even though the violation is in the face of a preservation order, courts may impose only monetary sanctions.[218] Generally, deference is given to a trial

---

employed. *See* Cire v. Cummings, 134 S.W.3d 835, 843 (Tex. 2004) ("[T]he trial court did not abuse its discretion by choosing instead to strike Cummings's pleadings. Sanctions are used to punish those who violate the discovery rules, and this is an exceptional case where the only objective evidence that would have supported or disproved Cummings's claims was deliberately destroyed after the trial court thrice ordered it produced. Such intentionally egregious behavior warrants a harsher sanction." "In a case of such egregious conduct death penalty sanctions will secure compliance with discovery rules, deter other litigants from destruction of dispositive evidence and punish Cummings."). In Copenhagen Reinsurance Co. v. Champion Home Builders Co., Inc., 872 So. 2d 848 (Ala. Civ. App. 2003), rather than dismissing plaintiff's claims, the court limited evidence from which the claim could be proven to that which was acquired from evidence that had been preserved.

216. In re Old Banc One Shareholders Sec. Litig., 2005 WL 3372783 (N.D. Ill. Dec. 8, 2005).

217. Vela v. Wagner & Brown, Ltd., 203 S.W.3d 37, 60 (Tex. App. 2006).

218. Creative Science Sys., Inc. v. Forex Capital Markets, 2006 WL 870973, at *6 (N.D. Cal. April 4, 2006) ("When choosing among possible sanctions, the Court should consider a sanction designed to: (1) penalize those whose conduct may be deemed to warrant such a sanction; (2) deter parties from engaging in the sanctioned conduct; (3) place the risk of an erroneous judgment on the party who wrongfully created the risk; and (4) restore a prejudiced party to the same position he or she would have been in absent wrongful destruction of evidence by the opposing party. . . . Having carefully considered the evidence presented, the Court concludes that there is insufficient evidence to merit imposing the particular nonmonetary sanctions requested by CSS. While it is possible to conclude from the evidence that FXCM's reinstallation of operating systems on certain servers was done in willful disregard of the Preservation Order, it is not clear that this is the only conclusion that could or should be reached. FXCM has provided evidence supporting the alternative explanation that its actions were motivated by need to test and install new middleware.").

judge's sanctions decision because, having direct knowledge of the case, the court is in the best position to fashion appropriate sanctions.[219]

The type of conduct that can justify very severe sanctions was present in *Wachtel v. Health Net, Inc.*[220] In *Wachtel,* the defendant: (1) deliberately failed to search for and produce responsive documents, causing scores of depositions to be taken without adequate preparation; (2) willfully concealed that no effective electronic search had been conducted because it was limited to a database that had been cleansed of messages older than 90 days; (3) employed strategies designed only to delay and increase costs; (4) ignored or distorted adverse rulings to justify their conduct; (5) failed to comply with court orders, (6) made false and misleading statements to the court through perjured affidavits and false statements to its own outside counsel; (7) failed to correct obvious misunderstandings that had been caused by its misleading statements; and (8) concealed damaging documents through partial disclosures.

Alternatively, or if spoliation occurs before an action is filed,[221] the

---

219. Monsanto Co. v. Ralph, 2004 WL 1962085, at *5 (Fed. Cir. Sept. 7, 2004). *But see* Flury v. DaimlerChrysler Corp., 427 F.3d 939 (11th Cir. 2005) (reversing trial court's negative inference instruction sanction and dismissing cause of action).

220. 239 F.R.D. 81, 101-02 (D. N.J. 2006).

221. There is disagreement over whether a court's power to impose discovery sanctions is limited to destruction occurring *after* an action has been filed and production has been ordered. *Compare* Beil v. Lakewood Eng'g & Mfg. Co., 15 F.3d 546, 552 (6th Cir. 1994) (holding that procedural rules, particularly Fed. R. Civ. P. 37, do not apply to actions that occurred prior to initiation of lawsuit) *with* Graves v. Daley, 526 N.E.2d 679, 681 (Ill. App. Ct. 1988) ("'Although it is correct that the plaintiffs did not violate court orders, the fact remains that the furnace was destroyed by plaintiffs at Western State's suggestion. The plaintiffs are not free to destroy crucial evidence simply because a court order was not issued to preserve the evidence. Further, the furnace was destroyed by the plaintiff after their expert had examined it and before the suit was filed, thus, the court could not have issued a preservation order.'"); and Bowmar Instrument Corp. v. Texas Instruments, Inc., 196 U.S.P.Q. 199 (N.D. Ind. 1977) ("The most extreme legal position taken by the defendant is that the court is powerless to punish the wholesale, willful destruction of relevant evidence where the destruction takes place prior to a specific court order for their production. Surely this proposition must be rejected. The plaintiffs are correct that such a rule would mean the demise of the real meaning and intent of the discovery process provided by the Federal Rules of Civil Procedure. . . . It has long been recognized that sanctions may be proper where a party, before a lawsuit is instituted, willfully places himself in such a position that he is unable to comply

court could dismiss a claim under its inherent authority to sanction[222] or impose evidentiary sanctions, such as (1) excluding evidence,[223] (2) giv-

---

with a subsequent discovery order. . . . Although a potential litigant is under no obligation to preserve every document in its possession, whatever its degree of relevance prior to the commencement of a lawsuit . . . some duty must be imposed in circumstances such as these lest the fact-finding process in our courts be reduced to a mockery." The court, however, did not find basis for sanction.). *See generally* I. Johnston, *Federal Courts' Authority to Impose Sanctions for Prelitigation or Pre-Order Spoliation of Evidence*, 156 F.R.D. 313, 319 (1994).

222. Klumpt v. Krongard, 728 A.2d 727, 735 (Md. Ct. Spec. App. 1999) (court dismissed the defendant's counterclaim because he destroyed evidence subject to discovery).

223. Courts have the authority to structure sanctions for spoliation in the pretrial discovery process that are appropriate to the circumstances. For example, in Fischer v. Rheem Mfg. Co., 2004 WL 1088328 (D. Minn. May 13, 2004), the fire scene was destroyed, thereby preventing a party from collecting evidence on causation. In addition to a negative inference instruction, the court precluded the party who destroyed the evidence from relying on evidence that it had obtained from the fire scene, including its experts' opinions and the opinions of the state fire marshal. Similarly, in Thompson v. H.U.D., 219 F.R.D. 93, 100 (D. Md. 2003), the court would permit witness to testify only if the proponent could demonstrate, by a preponderance of the evidence, that each witness had not produced or received e-mail communications that were not produced to the opposing party. In Craftmaster of Brevard, Inc. v. Mean Constr., Inc., 858 So. 2d 1253 (Fla. Dist. Ct. App. 2003), Craftmaster repaired a construction defect that was the subject of a potential lawsuit without informing the contractor who had failed to make the repair and giving interested parties the opportunity to observe and document the repair. This nonemergency repair constituted an intentional destruction of evidence that substantially impaired the opposing party in defending against Craftmaster's claim. The court precluded Craftmaster's witnesses from testifying about any observations made after removal of the slope and any of the work performed while they repaired the foundation. In Hirsch v. General Motors Corp., 628 A.2d 1108, 1122 (N.J. Super. Ct. App. Div. 1993), the plaintiff permitted the equipment that was the subject of the lawsuit to be destroyed, thereby precluding examination by the defendant. As a sanction, the court excluded any evidence that the plaintiff had developed from an examination of the equipment. Similarly, in Newhall Jones, Inc. v. Classic Cedar Constr., Inc., 2000 WL 194658, at *6 (Wash Ct. App. Feb. 14, 2000), the court excluded all testimony and evidence relating to the windows that the plaintiff had destroyed. In Fire Ins. Exch. v. Zenith Radio Corp., 103 Nev. 648, 747 P.2d 911 (1987), the insurance company destroyed the television set after its expert had examined it and concluded that it was the source of the residential fire. The testimony of the plaintiff's expert witness was excluded and summary judgment was granted in favor of the defendant. *See also* Lauren Corp. v. Century Geophysical Corp., 953 P.2d 200 (Colo. Ct. App. 1998). As explained in Donohoe v. Am. Isuzu

Motors, Inc., 155 F.R.D. 515, 520 (M.D. Pa. 1994), evidence of destruction can result in judgment being entered against the spoliator. "[A] party responsible for the spoliation of evidence is not permitted to present that evidence to the jury. If the evidence is critical to that party's case, judgment may be entered against the responsible party. However, even in such cases, the judgment itself is not the sanction; rather, the exclusion of the evidence is the sanction. Judgment only follows because the party cannot otherwise prove its case." *Accord,* Sylla-Sawdon v. Uniroyal Goodrich Tire Co., 47 F.3d 277 (8th Cir. 1995) (knowing that litigation would follow, plaintiff did not retain tires from damaged automobile); Dillon v. Nissan Motor Co., 986 F.2d 263, 267 (8th Cir. 1993) (permitted car to be destroyed after lawyer had been contacted). After an action has commenced, FED. R. CIV. P. 37(b)(2)(B) specifically authorizes a court to "refuse to allow the disobedient party to support or oppose designated claims or defenses, or prohibit[] that party from introducing designated matters in evidence" when a party fails to obey an order to provide or permit discovery.

The level of culpability is also a factor that courts will consider. Blatant and willful spoliation results in the harshest sanctions. *See, e.g.*, Century ML-Cable Corp. v. Conjugal P'ship Composed by Edwin Carillo, 43 F. Supp. 2d 176, 185 (D. P.R. 1998) (After it was demonstrated how defendant's "contumacious bad faith scorched-earth defense tactics" resulted in "a blatant effort to prevent plaintiffs from proving their case, the court levied harshest sanctions possible, default judgment, and award of attorney's fees.). The severity of a default judgment serves as a deterrent to "like-minded litigants" who would engage in willful spoliation of evidence. *See* Cabinetware Inc. v. Sullivan, 1991 WL 327959, at *4, 22 U.S.P.Q.2d 1686 (E.D. Cal. 1991). Other possible sanctions include a presumption imposed on the spoliator which must be overcome at trial. *See* Lauren Corp. v. Century Geophysical Corp., 953 P.2d 200, 201-202 (Colo. Ct. App. 1998) (Court imposed presumption at trial that defendant had engaged in unauthorized use of plaintiff's software after defendant's intentional destruction of computer hardware; court also awarded costs incurred in attempts to gain access to hardware through discovery, as well as attorney's fees.). However, in Mathias v. Jacobs, 197 F.R.D. 29 (S.D.N.Y. 2000), the court concluded that although defendant's erasing of his Palm Pilot's telephone directory was intentional and committed in disregard of a specific discovery order, it was not done in bad faith, and the court therefore declined to grant a motion for default judgment or to allow an adverse inference instruction. The court instead sanctioned the defendant by imposing discovery costs. In Wiginton v. Ellis, 2003 WL 22439865 (N.D. Ill. Oct. 27, 2003), the court denied plaintiff's request for sanctions until the "scope and extent of lost documents" was determined, even after a finding of bad-faith spoliation. Courts also consider prejudice to the suffering party in imposing sanctions. In Danis v. USN Commc'ns, Inc., 2000 WL 1694325 at *34-35, the court commented that "where noncompliance is the result of fault rather than a more culpable mental state . . . prejudice [is used] as a balancing tool or fulcrum upon which the scales may tip in favor of default or against it."

ing an explicit jury instruction that an unfavorable logical inference could appropriately be drawn from proof of evidence destruction,[224] or (3) recognizing a presumption that shifts either the burden of production or the

---

224. Jom, Inc. v. Adell Plastics, Inc., 151 F.3d 15, 18-19 (1st Cir. 1998) (upholding trial court's instruction about adverse inference); Dillon v. Nissan Motor Co., 986 F.2d. 263, 267 (8th Cir. 1993) (jury was instructed that adverse inference could be drawn from the plaintiff's failure to produce the evidence); Akiona v. United States, 938 F.2d 158, 161 (9th Cir. 1991) ("A trier of fact may draw an adverse inference from the destruction of evidence relevant to a case."); Nation-Wide Check Corp., Inc. v. Forest Hills Distrib., Inc., 692 F.2d 214, 217 (1st Cir. 1982) (Breyer, J.) ("[W]hen the contents of a document are relevant to an issue in a case, the trier of fact . . . may receive the fact of the document's . . . destruction as evidence that the party which has prevented production did so out of the well-founded fear that the contents would harm him."); Creative Res. Group of N.J., Inc. v. Creative Res. Group, Inc., 212 F.R.D. 94, 102 (E.D. N.Y. 2002) ("The undersigned will . . .recommend . . . the adverse inference instruction sanction."); Vasquez-Corales v. Sea-Land Serv., Inc., 172 F.R.D. 10, 14-15 (D. P.R. 1997) (adverse inference arose from reckless disregard of duty to preserve evidence); Shaffer v. RWP Group, Inc., 169 F.R.D. 19, 25 (E.D. N.Y. 1996) ("An adverse inference charge serves the dual purposes of remediation and punishment. First, it seeks to put the non-spoliator in a position similar to where it would have been but for the destruction. . . . Second, it carries a punitive effect; 'the law, in hatred of the spoiler, baffles the destroyer, and thwarts his iniquitous purpose, by indulging a presumption which supplies the lost proof, and thus defeats the wrong-doer by the very means he had so confidentially employed to perpetrate the wrong.'"); Faust v. McFarland, 698 N.W.2d 24, 30 (Minn. Ct. App. 2005) (The court approved an inference instruction, even though the spoliation was intentional after considering the prejudice resulting to the opposing party. "Prejudice is determined by considering the nature of the item lost in the context of the claims asserted and the potential for correcting the prejudice." The court imposed the most appropriate sanction to counter the evidentiary advantage gained from the failure to preserve evidence.); McLain v. Taco Bell Corp., 2000 N.C. App. LEXIS 10, at *7 (N.C. Ct. App. Jan. 18, 2000). In contrast, an adverse inference instruction was rejected in Browning v. Minyard Food Store, Inc., 1999 WL 826015, at *4-5 (Tex. App. Oct. 18, 1999), because there was insufficient evidence of either negligence or intentional destruction.

Aside from an instruction to the jury about adverse inferences that can be drawn, it can also be the basis for denying a summary judgment motion. See Morgan v. U.S. Xpress, Inc., 2006 WL 1548029, *5 (M.D. Ga. June 2, 2006) ("These factual disputes give the Plaintiffs the benefit of the adverse inference to be drawn from the missing data for the purpose of summary judgment and render summary judgment inappropriate in this case.").

burden of persuasion to the wrongdoer.[225] The trial judge has broad discretion to determine the appropriate sanction based on the unique circumstances of each case.[226] "Destruction of potentially relevant evidence obviously occurs along a continuum of fault—ranging from innocence through the degrees of negligence to intentionality. The resulting penalties vary correspondingly."[227] The nature of the sanction imposed will turn on four factors: (1) culpability of wrongdoer; (2) the degree of prejudice to the innocent party; (3) fairness; and (4) deterrence.[228] This is illus-

---

225. The clearest example of this was in the inference instruction given in Roberts v. Whitfill, 191 S.W.3d 348 (Tex. App. 2006) (After instructing the jury that it should presume that certain data destroyed by the spoliator would have been unfavorable to his cause, the court noted, "You are further instructed that Dan Roberts bears the burden to disprove these presumptions."). *See* Williams v. CSX Transp., Inc., 925 F. Supp. 447, 452 (S.D. Miss. 1996) (because defendant willfully destroyed evidence in bad faith, court recognized "adverse inference"); ABC Home Health Serv., Inc. v. IBM Corp., 158 F.R.D. 180 (S.D. Ga. 1994) (because defendant's conduct did not constitute deliberate attempt to undermine discovery process, court would not dismiss counterclaim; court, however, recognized presumption that destroyed evidence would have been unfavorable to the defendant because destruction involved bad faith).

226. Unigard Sec. Ins. Co. v. Lakewood Eng'g & Mfg. Corp., 982 F.2d 363, 369 (9th Cir. 1992); Mosaid Tech. Inc. v. Samsung Elecs. Co., 348 F. Supp. 2d 332 (D. N.J. 2004) (court sanctioned with costs and a negative inference instruction when "Samsung waited approximately three years after the beginning of [the] litigation, over a year after the close of fact discovery and approximately seven months after Mosaid filed its sanctions motion before it actually expended any effort to comply with an obligation that existed, at the latest, [over two years previously].").

227. Welsh v. United States, 844 F.2d 1239, 1246 (6th Cir. 1988).

228. *See* Monsanto Co. v. Ralph, 382 F.3d 1374, 1378 (Fed. Cir. 2004) (infringer's pleadings struck and judgment entered after perjured statements were given, judicial orders were violated, and evidence was intentionally destroyed); Mosel Vitelic Corp. v. Micron Tech., Inc., 162 F. Supp. 2d 307 (D. Del. 2000) (client waived attorney-client privilege protection by relying on advice of counsel in patent infringement action; scope of waiver extended to communications within its attorney's files even if they had not been sent to client; accordingly, attorney's destruction of notes and drafts was spoliation, and court approved negative inference instruction and awarded attorney's fees); Menges v. Cliffs Drilling Co., 2000 WL 765082, at *1 (E.D. La. 2000) (delineating the factors of degree of fault, degree of prejudice to injured party, availability of other sanctions, and fairness); Dorsa v. Nat'l Amusements, Inc., 6 A.D.3d 652 (N.Y. A.D. 2d Dept. 2004) (In a slip-and-fall action, the issue was water accumulation due to a negligently maintained water fountain. Under established destruction policy, the defendant disposed of maintenance records

trated in *Fidelity National Title Insurance Co. of New York v. Intercounty National Title Insurance Co.*[229] where an expert witness (Pollard), after having reviewed internal documents of Fidelity, destroyed the documents that did not support his theory. The court sanctioned this spoliation of evidence by excluding Pollard's testimony. Justifying this severe sanction, the court explains:

> Fidelity admits that Pollard was retained by Fidelity to "reconstruct Intercounty's computer records and escrow records, and determine how the multimillion-dollar escrow shortage happened." . . . Pollard conducted his investigation while civil litigation and criminal proceedings were on the forefront. After individuals were interviewed by Pollard, they were indicted and took the Fifth Amendment. The idea that Pollard can admit that he selectively discarded materials while he conducted his research, thus depriving his adversaries of potential evidence in their favor, and now claim that a monetary "slap on the wrist" would be fair is not only ludicrous but it would be a mockery of justice for this court to allow such a result. . . . It is Fidelity that ignores the law that required Pollard to have the work documents available under the rules of discovery for Defendants. It is Fidelity's witness, Pollard, that has destroyed documents. Pollard was not empowered to determine which of his documents would be made available in this case. Fidelity inexplicably stated in its oral argument before the court that Pollard simply destroyed the documents that did not support his theory. However, such an explanation only serves to support this court's decision to bar Pollard's testimony. This court spent considerable time considering all other possible sanctions other than barring Pollard's testimony. However, considering all of the circumstances specifically applying to Pol-

---

that could have proven actual, or at least constructive, notice. The trial court's sanction was to preclude the defendant "from presenting evidence that it lacked notice of the condition that caused plaintiff's accident." This sanction was reversed because it was too severe: "The sanction imposed by the Supreme Court was unnecessarily severe because it shifted the burden of proof as to the issue of notice. Accordingly, we modify the order and grant that branch of the plaintiff's cross-motion only to the extent of precluding the defendant from offering any evidence at trial as to the condition of the water fountain and directing that an adverse inference charge be issued.")

229. 2004 WL 784799 (N.D. Ill. April 12, 2004).

lard, the only just decision was to bar his testimony. We cannot turn the clock back and recover the documents destroyed by Pollard or determine what information those documents contained. The court's decision to bar Fidelity's witness's testimony was due to Fidelity's own witness's misconduct, and Fidelity cannot now claim any unfairness.[230]

In response to Fidelity's attempt to distance itself from the obvious transgressions by its key witness, the court noted: "Fidelity hired Pollard and he was acting on their behalf. There is nothing unfair about holding Fidelity accountable for its own witness's conduct. It would be unfair if Defendants were forced to proceed in this case with Pollard as a witness, and for the court to allow such a witness to testify would be to reward and encourage parties to selectively destroy documents, knowing that they will still be able to proceed at trial."[231] Fidelity attempted to justify Pollard's actions by characterizing them as "inadvertent" and "consistent with his usual practice." The court made two instructive comments. First, "adding limiting adjectives and phrasing Pollard's conduct in a nicer way" was neither convincing nor adequate in light of the evidence before the court. Second, justifying the actions of Pollard by "saying that such conduct . . . was part of the regular business practice [only] raises serious questions as to how the businesses involved conduct their affairs."[232]

Fundamental to the selection of spoliation sanctions is the policy that a party should not be permitted to gain an evidentiary advantage through its failure to preserve evidence after a duty to preserve has arisen. The appropriate sanction is one that puts the injured party in as close a position to where it would have been absent the destruction.[233] Because this is the

---

230. *Id.* at *1.

231. *Id.* at *2

232. *Id.* Management cannot hide behind the acts of people they have employed. Larson v. BankOne Corp., 2005 WL 4652509, *11 (N.D. Ill. Aug. 18, 2005); In re Prudential Ins. Co. of Am. Sales Practices Litig., 169 F.R.D. 598, 615 (D. N.J. 1997).

233. In Jimenez v. Weiner, 779 N.Y.S.2d 23, 24 (Sup. Ct. N.Y. 2004), for example, plaintiff's counsel notified defendant of an intention to inspect a ramp that allegedly caused the accident and noted the defendant's obligation to preserve the ramp. Three and one-half years passed with no inspection by the plaintiff. Defendant's subsequent replacement of the ramp did not warrant the spoliation sanction of striking the defendant's answer because it was not done willfully, contumaciously, or in bad faith. However, the defendant's failure to notify plaintiff's counsel of its

goal, the most important factor to be considered by the court is the resulting prejudice to the opposing party. Other important but subsidiary goals
are punishment and deterrence. These goals become more important as
the gravity of the wrongful act increases.

Generally, the rule on sanctions is that they should be the least stringent
consistent with the punitive and remedial rationales for the spoliation doctrine—general deterrence, placing the risk of an erroneous judgment on the
party who wrongfully created the risk, and restoring the prejudiced party to
the condition that he would have been in absent the wrongful conduct.[234]

A.   Spoliation Is an Implied Admission by Conduct

In addition to prompting specific sanctions, acts of spoliation have independent evidentiary significance insofar as they constitute admissions by
conduct.[235] Spoliation can be interpreted as an implied statement by those

---

intention to remove the ramp did substantially prejudice the plaintiff and require
some relief. Therefore, since plaintiff's expert could formulate an opinion based
on available photographs, the court precluded the defendant from objecting to
the expert's use of such photographs as the basis for an opinion, subject to a
proper foundation having been laid.

234. Kronisch v. United States, 150 F.3d 112, 126 (2d Cir. 1998); Topanian v.
Ehrman, 3 F.3d 931, 937 (5th Cir. 1993); Recinos-Recinos v. Express Forestry,
Inc., 2006 WL 2349459, at *12 (E.D. La. Aug. 11, 2006); Davis v. Speechworks
Int'l, Inc., 2005 WL 1206894, at *3 (W.D. N.Y. May 20, 2005).

235. *See* Scott v. IBM Corp., 196 F.R.D. 233, 248 (D. N.J. 2000) (Although
sanctions were denied because the destruction was the result of negligence rather
than willfulness, the court noted that a negative inference is still appropriate:

> The second inquiry then becomes whether these circumstances of
> spoliation, although not rising to the level of sanctionable conduct,
> should nevertheless give rise to a jury instruction regarding the spo-
> liation inference. Such a jury instruction permits an inference, the
> "spoliation inference," that the destroyed evidence might or would
> have been unfavorable to the position of the offending party. . . .
> When the contents of a document are relevant to an issue in the case,
> the spoliation inference is nothing more than the common sense
> observation that a party who destroys relevant evidence did so out
> of a well-founded fear that the contents would harm him.

Courtney v. Big O Tires, Inc., 87 P.3d 930, 933 (Idaho 2004) ("[W]e recognized
the spoliation doctrine as a form of admission by conduct." The court went on to
emphasize that mere negligence in loss or destruction is not sufficient to invoke
spoliation doctrine. "[I]t does not sustain the inference of consciousness of a
weak case. . . .").

who destroyed the evidence that they believe their position to be so
weak that it cannot succeed without resort to such nefarious measures.[236] Regardless of the specific sanctions imposed by a court for
spoliation, injured parties can argue this logical inference to the jury,

---

236. Dillon, 986 F.2d at 267 (district court allowed defense counsel to repeatedly argue misconduct and spoliation to the jury and gave instruction to
jury about the logical adverse inference that is permissible); Nation-Wide Check
Corp., Inc., 692 F.2d at 218 (1st Cir. 1982) (opinion by now-Justice Breyer)
("The adverse inference is based on two rationales, one evidentiary and one
not. The evidentiary rationale is nothing more than the common sense observation that a party who has notice that a document is relevant to litigation and
who proceeds to destroy the document is more likely to have been threatened
by the document than is a party in the same position who does not destroy the
document. The fact of destruction satisfies the minimum requirement of relevance; it has some tendency, however small, to make the existence of a fact at
issue more probable than it would otherwise be. . . . Precisely how the document
might have aided the party's adversary, and what evidentiary shortfalls its destruction may be taken to redeem, will depend on the particular facts of each
case, but the general evidentiary rationale for the inference is clear. . . . The
other rationale for the inference has to do with its prophylactic and punitive
effects. Allowing the trier of fact to draw the inference presumably deters parties from destroying relevant evidence before it can be introduced at trial. The
inference also serves as a penalty, placing the risk of an erroneous judgment on
the party that wrongfully created the risk. In McCormick's words, 'the real
underpinning of the rule of admissibility [may be] a desire to impose swift
punishment, with a certain poetic justice, rather than concern over niceties of
proof.' McCormick on Evidence § 273, at 661 (1972)."). *Accord,* Akiona v. United
States, 938 F.2d 158, 160-61 (9th Cir. 1991); Welsh v. United States, 844 F.2d
1239, 1246 (6th Cir. 1983); Welsh, 844 F.2d at 1246; Advantacare Health Partners v. Access IV, 2004 WL 1837997, at *7 (N.D. Cal. Aug. 17, 2004) (discussing two rationales); Reingold v. Wet'N Wild Nevada, Inc., 113 Nev. 967, 971,
944 P.2d 800, 802 (1997) ("There are two policy rationales for the adverse
inference. First, the evidentiary rationale springs from the notion that 'a party
with notice of an item's possible relevance to litigation who proceeds nonetheless to destroy it is more likely to have been threatened by the evidence than a
party in the same position who does not destroy it.' . . . 'The second rationale
acts to deter parties from pre-trial spoliation of evidence and serves as a penalty, placing the risk of an erroneous judgment on the party that wrongfully
created the risk.'").

asking its members to draw a negative conclusion about the offending party's claim.[237]

Some scholars have criticized this practice because other logical inferences, consistent with innocence, may also be taken from the act of destruction.[238] There are two fallacies in this argument. The first is that the inference of guilt is tenuous. This is unpersuasive. The apparent motivation for the act of destroying evidence known to be relevant to imminent litigation is anything but tenuous. In fact, of the two conclusions that they argue are possible, either consciousness of guilt or belief in innocence, the former is clearly the most compelling. Second, critics of the inference miss the point. The adverse inference is that the destroyed evidence would

---

237. Mastercard Int'l, Inc. v. Moulton, 2004 WL 1393992, at *4 (S.D.N.Y. June 22, 2004) (Even though acts of spoliation were not considered sufficiently culpable to justify an adverse inference instruction from the court, it was noted that the "plaintiff may prove the facts reflecting the nonretention of the e-mails in question [after informed of his obligation to retain them by defendant's attorney], and may argue to the trier of fact that this destruction of evidence, in addition to other proof offered at trial, warrants the inferences that the public was confused and that the MasterCard marks were diluted and tarnished."). Such conduct would be hearsay under the common law because it is an out-of-court statement through conduct being brought into court to prove the truth of the matter asserted. It, of course, would be admissible under the admissions exception to the hearsay rule. Under Fed. R. Evid. 801(d)(2), admissions have been excluded from the definition of hearsay. Consequently, the evidence of destruction would be admissible as non-hearsay rather than good hearsay under the admissions exception. This same non-hearsay conclusion vis-a-vis the conduct is compelled under Fed. R. Evid. 801(a). Under this rule, if an individual engages in conduct with no intention of conveying a message, the conduct is not be considered a "statement." Consequently, when the definition of hearsay uses the term "statement" it would not encompass such conduct. In all instances, however, the evidence would be admissible.

238. In J. GORELICK, S. MARZEN & L. SOLUM, DESTRUCTION OF EVIDENCE, § 2.3, p.35 (J. Wiley & Sons 1989), the authors argue that "the chain of inference that goes through the spoliator's belief in his guilt would be reversed if the finder of facts were convinced that destruction resulted from the litigant's belief in his innocence. Indeed, a litigant may feel justified in suppressing evidence precisely because he believes that he is innocent. In that case, logic would require that the spoliation of evidence support an inference that the spoliator was innocent of any wrongdoing." They then conclude that the consciousness-of-guilt theory is tenuous. They support a "fair process theory" as a more coherent and persuasive explanation for the spoliation doctrine. *Id.* at 35. Regardless, they conclude that both theories are compatible. *Id.* at 36.

have been harmful to the spoliator's case, regardless of his ultimate guilt or innocence. The spoliator cannot be permitted to undermine the function of the jury by depriving them of relevant evidence merely because he believes in his ultimate innocence.

Critics of the inference theory also appear to confuse the logical inference with judicial instructions about the inference. In every trial, lawyers argue to the jury about the logical inferences that should be drawn from the evidence. The trial judge seldom comments to the jury, either directly or through judicial instructions, about these inferences. But with spoliation, the inference of guilt is so compelling that courts have elected to comment through instructions about the permissible inference.[239]

A fundamental tenet of the principle of admissions is that everyone speaks at his own risk. Whatever one utters, or expresses through conduct, can be offered against him at trial if relevant to the issues being litigated. If an innocent explanation exists for the apparently reprehensible act of destroying evidence known to be relevant to the litigation, as with all other admissions, the actor must give that explanation.

The fact that evidence of document destruction may be prejudicial to the actor is of no consequence. By the nature of the adversarial process, all negative evidence tending to prove the opponent's case is prejudicial to the adversary. The opponent can exclude an admission only by demonstrating that the potential prejudice "substantially outweighs" its probative value.[240]

---

239. Contrary to the conclusion advocated by Gorelick, Marzen & Solum in *Destruction of Evidence,* this spoliation theory can [be] and is justified "on the basis of the consciousness-of-guilt theory." *See* Creative Res. Group of N.J. v. Creative Res. Group, Inc., 212 F.R.D. 94, 102 (E.D. N.Y. 2002) (in addition to awarding attorney fees, magistrate recommended that adverse inference instruction be given at trial).

240. This is the standard delineated in Fed. R. Evid. 403.

> Although relevant, evidence may be excluded if its probative value is substantially outweighed by the danger of unfair prejudice, confusion of the issues, or misleading the jury, or by considerations of undue delay, waste of time, or needless presentation of cumulative evidence.

The same principles were followed under the common law and are currently employed in all states. *See, e.g.,* Thor v. Boska, 38 Cal. App. 3d 558, 566-67, 113 Cal. Rptr. 296, 302 (1974).

B. Logical Inference Instructions

"Where one party wrongfully denies another the evidence necessary to establish a fact in dispute, the court must draw the strongest allowable inferences in favor of the aggrieved party."[241] Judicial instruction on logical inferences is essentially a structured form of judicial comment on the evidence in a specific and limited factual situation. Spoliation instructions are widely employed in both state and federal courts, even in those states that generally prohibit judicial comment.

In jurisdictions that forbid judicial comment by constitution or statute, the instruction may be rationalized as a discovery sanction designed to put the injured party back in the position it would have been in had the spoliation never occurred (and to deter similar actions by others). If judges have the authority to dismiss actions or enter default judgments on the basis of spoliation, surely they have the authority to take lesser measures that only encourage juries to find against offending parties. For the logical inference instructions to be given, generally four factors must be satisfied. First, the evidence in question must have been within the party's control. Second, there must have been an actual suppression or withholding of evidence. Third, the evidence must have been relevant to claims or defenses. Fourth, it must have been reasonably foreseeable that the evidence was discoverable.[242]

C. The Strange Spoliation Presumption

Occasionally, courts refer to spoliation as creating a *presumption* that the substantive content of the materials destroyed were unfavorable to the positions of the litigants that destroyed them.[243] Unlike logical inference instructions, which are permissive, presumption instructions are mandatory.[244] The effect of the spoliation presumption, however,

---

241. Nat'l Ass'n of Radiation Survivors v. Turnage, 115 F.R.D. 543, 557 (N.D. Cal. 1987).

242. Gumbs v. Int'l Harvester, Inc., 718 F.2d 88, 96 (3d Cir. 1983). Veloso v. Western Bedding Supply Co., 281 F. Supp. 2d 743, 746-47 (D. N.J. 2003); Scott v. IBM Corp., 196 F.R.D. 233, 248 (D. N.J. 2000); Brewer v. Quaker State Oil Refining Corp., 72 F.3d 326, 334 (3d Cir. 1983).

243. *See, e.g.,* Mayers v. Black & Decker, Inc. 931 F. Supp. 80 (D. N.H. 1996); Alliance to End Repression v. Rochford, 75 F.R.D. 438 (N.D. Ill. 1976); R.J. Mgmt. Co. v. SRLB Dev. Corp., 282 806 N.E.2d 1074, 1081 (Ill. Ct. App. 2004).

244. Mayers, 931 F. Supp. at 85 (the presumption creates a "mandatory adverse inference").

is not always apparent.[245]

Under Article III of the Federal Rules of Evidence, presumptions only shift the burden of going forward with evidence, compelling an explanation from the party against whom the presumption operates—after which the presumption bubble bursts and nothing is said to the jury.[246] The alternative theory of presumptions, which was rejected by Congress when the Evidence Rules were adopted, shifted the burden of persuasion to the party against whom a presumption is employed. In other words, with the spoliation presumption, the offending party must convince the jury that the presumed fact—that the destroyed evidence would have been harmful to him—is not true.

As presumptions usually work, the judge instructs the jury that if it finds the foundation facts to be true, it *must find* the presumed fact to be true. Judges give this instruction only if the party against whom the presumption operates has failed to come forward with evidence of the nonexistence of the presumed fact.[247] Under the bursting-bubble theory, if evidence of the

---

245. For example, in Alliance to End Repression, 75 F.R.D. at 438, the imposition of sanctions was found to be appropriate when records of informants were mysteriously destroyed. The court ordered that certain paragraphs of the plaintiffs' complaint "be admitted prima facie." The court explained that the "[d]efendants have the burden of rebutting the allegations of these paragraphs to show that they did not [do what was alleged]. . . . [D]efendants have the burden of showing that they have not engaged in the activities there-in described." *Id.* at 441. Because the presumption created only a prima facie case, one could interpret the court as imposing on the spoliator only the burden of producing evidence that disproves the presumed fact—not unlike what a defendant must do at trial after the plaintiff has gotten past the defendant's motion for a directed verdict.

246. *See* Chapter Five, "Presumptions," *infra*. The same theory is followed in states, *see, e.g.*, R.J. Mgmt. Co. v. SRLB Dev. Corp., 282 806 N.E.2d 1074, 1081 (Ill. Ct. App. 2004) ("Under the 'Thayer approach' followed in Illinois, when contrary evidence is produced, the metaphorical bubble bursts and the presumption vanishes entirely."). *See generally* P.R. RICE, EVIDENCE PRINCIPLES & PRACTICES: 150 THINGS YOU WERE NEVER TAUGHT, FORGOT, OR NEVER UNDERSTOOD, Chapter 9 (LEXIS/ NEXIS 2006).

247. Occasionally, however, a court will mistakenly refer to rebutting the presumption by the party against whom it operates presenting evidence of the nonexistence of the foundational facts. *See, e.g.*, Cresthaven Nursing Residence v. Freeman, 134 S.W.3d 214, 227 (Tex. Ct. App. May 19, 2003), where the court noted that intentional destruction was a foundational fact, but later explained that the presumption "may be rebutted with a showing that the evidence was not destroyed

nonexistence of the presumed fact is presented, the presumption has served its purpose. Therefore, the bubble bursts (hence the name of the theory) and the presumption disappears. Consequently, no instruction is given to the jury because the presumption ceases to exist.

Using the term "presumption" in the context of spoliation is awkward. Because the facts upon which the presumption is premised—(1) notice of its potential relevance and (2) destruction—are decided by the judge before the presumption arises, and because the substance of the presumption— that the content of the evidence would have been damaging to the party's case— goes to the heart of the cause of action, opposing parties will always have presented some contrary evidence if they wish to avoid a directed verdict. Consequently, under the classical presumption theory, there would never be anything to mention in the instruction, because the presumption would have disappeared. This, of course, would defeat the very purpose of the presumption as a sanction for the willful destruction of evidence.

Where the presumption instruction continues to be given, it either shifts the burden of persuasion to the party against whom it operates[248] or it serves as an excuse for the judge to comment on the logical inference that could be drawn from the act of destruction.[249] Of the two possibilities, judicial comment on the evidence is the most consistent

---

with a fraudulent intent or purposes." Assuming that "fraudulent intent" is being used synonymously with "intentional destruction," this statement is incorrect.

248. *See, e.g.*, Roberts v. Whitfill, 191 S.W.3d 348, 360 (Tex. App. 2006) (After instructing the jury that it should presume that certain data destroyed by the spoliator would have been unfavorable to his cause, the court noted, "You are further instructed that Dan Roberts bears the burden to disprove these presumptions.").

249. For example, in Shaffer v. RWP Group, Inc., 169 F.R.D. 19 at 28 (E.D. N.Y. 1996), the court, after considering all of the circumstances, instructed the jury that "it *may infer*" that the missing records would have been unfavorable to the defendant (emphasis added). The court also noted that "the defendants remain free at trial to proffer an explanation for the missing documents," but it continued to give the instruction in the face of such evidence. A true presumption would not be permissive, and if the evidence presented negated the presumed fact, a true presumption under Fed. R. Evid. 301 would be destroyed, leaving nothing to instruct about. Similarly, in R.J. Management Co. v. SRLB Dev. Corp., 346 Ill. App. 3d 957, 806 N.E.2d 1074, 1081 (Ill. Ct. App. 2004), the court held that the party that the presumption operated against not only had to come forward with evidence to rebut the presumption, but required that the evidence be "clear and convincing."

with the Federal Rules of Evidence, because (1) Article III of the Evidence Code recognizes only the bursting-bubble theory (shifting only the burden of going forward with the evidence, not the burden of persuasion); (2) Congress has not explicitly recognized a spoliation presumption, particularly one that shifts the burden of persuasion; (3) the common law power of judges to create new presumptions appears to have been abolished by codification of the evidence rules; and (4) judicial comment on the evidence is not prohibited in federal courts.

In *Anderson v. Cryovac*,[250] however, the First Circuit appears to have sanctioned a presumption that shifts the burden of persuasion. The court juxtaposed two situations where the presumption arises from an act of spoliation. The first is when the act of spoliation is shown to have been "knowing or purposeful." In such situations, a presumption arises that the evidence would have been harmful to the destroying party and would have led to the unearthing of further adverse evidence. To rebut this presumption, the party against whom it operates *must* demonstrate "by clear and convincing evidence" that the withheld materials were in fact inconsequential. Precisely what the court was saying is not clear. If the court was envisioning this demonstration being made to the jury with a mandatory instruction regarding what

---

250. 862 F.2d 910 (1st Cir. 1988). *See also* Akiona v. United States, 938 F.2d 158, 160 (9th Cir. 1991), in which the appellate court reversed the trial court's reliance on the logical inference from destruction because it was not justified by the facts. The appellate court's description of what the inference did was interesting. "The district court also facilitated its finding of liability by shifting the burden of proof to the government . . . ." *Id.* This may support the shifting of the burden of persuasion or may mean nothing more than that the presumption shifted the burden of going forward with the evidence. Courts loosely use "burden of proof" to refer to both burdens, and determining a court's meaning often can be difficult. In Sweet v. Sisters of Providence in Wash., 895 P.2d 484, 491 (Alaska 1995), the court shifted the burden of persuasion to the offending party. "Just as the missing records may have impaired the Sweets' ability to prove medical negligence, they would in the same way impair the Sweets' ability to prove a causal connection between any negligence and Jacob's injuries. It is for this very reason that a number of courts in other jurisdictions have created a rebuttable presumption shifting the burden of persuasion to a health care provider who negligently alters or loses medical records relevant to a malpractice claim." A similar result was reached in Easton Sports, Inc. v. Warrior Lacrosse, Inc., 2006 WL 2811261, at *4 (E.D. Mich. Sept. 28, 2006) ("If a threshold showing of spoliation is made, the burden shifts to the possessor of the evidence to prove that the opponent was not prejudiced by the alteration or destruction.").

the jury must find unless the burden is satisfied, the court is shifting the burden of persuasion to the bad actor. Regardless of how equitably justified this result may be, it is legally questionable under the restrictive language of Fed. R. Evid. 301.[251]

D.   *Authority for Penalizing Destruction*

Under the Federal Rules of Civil Procedure, judges have the power to impose discovery sanctions for violating court orders.[252] Judges also have

---

251. A similar result was reached in Welsh v. United States, 844 F.2d 1239, 1248 (6th Cir. 1988) ("When, as here, a plaintiff is unable to prove an essential element of her case due to the negligent loss or destruction of evidence by an opposing party, and the proof would otherwise be sufficient to survive a directed verdict, it is proper for the trial court to create a rebuttable presumption that establishes the missing elements of the plaintiff's case that could only have been proved by the availability of the missing evidence. The burden thus shifts to the defendant-spoliator to rebut the presumption and disprove the inferred element of plaintiff's prima facie case."); *accord,* Public Health Trust v. Valcin, 507 S.2d 596, 600 (Fla. 1987) (drawing parallel to res ipsa doctrine, court shifted burden of persuasion to party who destroyed evidence).

252. Fed. R. Civ. P. 37(b)(2) provides for sanctions on those parties who violate the rules. It delineates seven illustrative sanctions and recognizes that courts can issue any other sanction that is just. These include designating certain facts as established for the purposes of the action and paying reasonable attorney's fees. These attorney's fees may include those related to the seeking of the order to compel, as well as those related to the motion for sanctions. Creative Res. Group of N.J., Inc. v. Creative Res. Group, Inc., 212 F.R.D. 94, 103 (E.D. N.Y. 2002) ("The defendants state . . . that in a Rule 37(b) motion, 'only those reasonable attorneys fees incurred by the moving party as a result of the failure to comply with a Court Order may be recovered.' . . . The defendants also state that attorney fees are calculated using the lodestar method to compute expenses 'incurred in the motion for sanctions, but not expenses incurred in obtaining the Order compelling discovery.' . . . To the extent that the defendants are claiming that fees incurred in a motion to compel are not recoverable under Rule 37, that claim is not simply wrong, but frivolous. Indeed defense counsel's claim that 'the law only provides that attorneys fees be awarded with reference to the work incurred in the motion for sanctions, but no expenses incurred obtaining the Order compelling the discovery,' is so utterly devoid of merit as to approach the threshold of sanctionable behavior in its own right."); Bachmeier v. Wallwork Truck Centers, 507 N.W.2d 527, 532 (1993) ("There are two primary reasons, then, that the order granting summary judgment could not have been invoked under the power of Rule 37. First, there was never a discovery order issued or violated, and the record reflects no failure to respond to a discovery request. Second, any Rule 34 request for Bachmeier to produce the hub for discov-

"inherent discretionary power to make appropriate evidentiary rulings in response to the destruction or spoliation of relevant evidence."[253] They have the inherent authority to protect the integrity of the judicial system, prevent its processes from being abused, and ensure the fair resolution of disputes.[254]

---

ery purposes would have been inapplicable, because Bachmeier never had possession, custody, or control of the hub.").

253. Chambers v. NASCO, Inc., 501 U.S. 32, 43-45 (1991). *See* Roadway Express, Inc. v. Piper, 447 U.S. 752, 764 (1980); Silvestri v. General Motors Corp., 217 F.3d 583, 590 (4th Cir. 2001) ("The policy underlying this inherent power of the courts is the need to preserve the integrity of the judicial process in order to retain confidence that the process works to uncover the truth. '[B]ecause no one has an exclusive insight into the truth, the process depends on the adversarial presentation of evidence, precedent and custom, and argument to reasoned conclusions— all directed with unwavering effort to what, in good faith, it believes to be true and matters material to the disposition.' The courts must protect the integrity of the judicial process because '[a]s soon as the process falters—the people are then justified in abandoning support for the system.'"); Bloemendaal v. Town & Country Sports Center Inc., 659 N.W.2d 684, 686 (Mich. Ct. App. 2002) ("A trial court has the authority, derived from its inherent powers, to sanction a party for failing to preserve evidence that it knows or should know is relevant before litigation is commenced."); West v. Goodyear Tire & Rubber Co., 167 F.3d 776, 779 (2d Cir. 1999) (Courts have "broad discretion in choosing an appropriate sanction for spoliation," and the appropriate sanction "should be molded to serve the prophylactic, punitive, and remedial rationales underlying the spoliation doctrine."); Dillon v. Nissan Motor Co., 986 F.2d 263, 267 (8th Cir. 1993); Glover v. BIC Corp., 6 F.3d 1318, 1331 (9th Cir. 1993); Richardson v. Sport Shindo (Waikiki Corp.), 880 P.2d 169, 182-83 (Haw. 1994) (In addition to Rule 37(b)(2) of the Hawaii Rules of Civil Procedure, the trial court also "has the inherent power . . . to fashion a remedy to cure prejudice suffered by one party as a result of another party's loss or destruction of evidence." Under Rule 37(b)(2), sanctions are only available when a prior discovery order has been violated.); Restaurant Mgmt. Co. v. Kidde-Fenwal, Inc., 986 P.2d 504, 507-08 (N.M. Ct. App. 1999) ("A remedy for the destruction of evidence may be available pursuant to the inherent power of the courts 'to impose sanction on both litigants and attorneys in order to regulate their dockets, promote judicial efficiency, and deter frivolous claims.' . . . The courts' inherent power exists apart from established criminal and civil remedies. . . . The rationale underlying the existence of the inherent power of the courts is that 'a court must be able to command the obedience of litigants and their attorneys if it is to perform its judicial functions.'").

254. Residential Funding Corp. v. DeGeorge Financial Corp., 306 F.3d 99, 107 (2d Cir. 2002) ("Where the nature of the alleged breach of discovery obligation is

A failure to comply with discovery orders[255] or responsibilities under the discovery rules (including the late production of relevant evidence) is a form of spoliation, but courts have the authority to impose sanctions for such violations under Rule 37 of the Federal Rules of Civil Procedure without finding spoliation.[256]

---

the failure to produce evidence, a district court thus has 'broad discretion in fashioning an appropriate sanction, including the discretion to delay the start of a trial . . . , to declare a mistrial if the trial has already commenced, or to proceed with a trial and give an adverse inference instruction.'"); Shepherd v. Am. Broad. Cos., 62 F.3d 1469, 1474, 1475 (D.C. Cir. 1995) ("When rules alone do not provide courts with sufficient authority to protect their integrity and prevent abuses of the judicial process, the inherent power fills the gap." The court went on to note that this power included "drawing [an] adverse evidentiary inference."); Zubulake v. UBS Warburg, 220 F.R.D. 212, 216 (S.D.N.Y. 2003) ("The authority to sanction litigants for spoliation arises jointly under the Federal Rules of Civil Procedure and the court's own inherent power."); Creative Res. Group of N.J., Inc. v. Creative Res. Group, Inc., 212 F.R.D. 94, 102 (E.D. N.Y. 2002) ("Even in the absence of a discovery order, 'a court may impose sanctions on a party for misconduct in discovery under its inherent power to manage its own affairs.'"); Barsoum v. NYC Hous. Auth., 202 F.R.D. 396, 399 (S.D.N.Y. 2001) ("It is well settled that a district court has 'inherent power to regulate litigation, preserve and protect the integrity of the proceedings before it, and sanction parties for abusive practice.' . . . This inherent power includes the authority to impose sanctions for the spoliation of evidence."); Capellupo v. FMC Corp., 126 F.R.D. 545, 551 (D. Minn. 1989) (collecting cases); QZO, Inc. v. Moyer, 594 S.E.2d 541, 547 (S.C. Ct. App. Mar. 15, 2004) (appellant failed to timely produce computer when ordered and reformatted it prior to actual production (thereby destroying all evidence on hard drive); court sanctioned by striking pleading and entering judgment for opposing party). For spoliation problems arising prior to the litigation, courts must rely on their inherent authority to protect the integrity of the judicial process. *See* Schmid v. Milwaukee Elec. Tool Corp., 13 F.3d 76, 78 (3d Cir. 1994); *see generally* I. Johnston, *Federal Courts' Authority to Impose Sanctions for Pre-litigation or Pre-Order Spoliation of Evidence*, 156 F.R.D. 313 (1994).

255. The failure to comply with a discovery order is the equivalent of civil contempt for which trial courts have wide discretion to sanction regardless of whether willfulness or bad faith is demonstrated. Int'l Union, United Mine Workers of Am. v. Bagwell, 512 U.S. 821, 822 (1994); Action Marine, Inc. v. Continental Carbon Co., Inc., 243 F.R.D, 670, 686 (M.D. Ala. 2007). However, the most severe sanctions are not imposed for mere negligence, misunderstanding or inability to comply. Bank Atlantic v. Blythe Eastman PaineWebber, Inc., 12 F.3d 1045, 1049 (11th Cir. 1994).

256. *See, e.g.,* Qualcomm Inc. v. Broadcom Corp., 2008 U.S. Dist. LEXIS 911 (S.D. Cal. Jan. 7, 2008).

There is no uniformity among the states or even within the federal system on how courts should address spoliation sanctions. Even in federal diversity actions, courts disagree over whether spoliation sanctions are substantive or procedural and, therefore, whether state or federal law controls.[257] What the courts do agree on is that the inherent power that courts have to sanction for spoliation should be exercised with restraint and discretion, taking into account needs to (1) penalize those whose conduct deserves sanctioning, (2) deter parties from engaging in such harmful conduct, (3) place the risk of an erroneous judgment on the party who wrongfully created the risk, and (4) restore, as much as possible, the prejudiced party to the same position he would have been in absent wrongful destruction of evidence by the opposing party.[258]

V.   BURDEN OF PERSUASION

Parties claiming spoliation have the burden of convincing the court that their claims are true. While courts sometimes identify the burden of persuasion as a preponderance of the evidence,[259] most courts never address the issue. Consequently, it can be unclear what showing is required. Similar to the courts' treatment of the bad-faith element, courts sometimes allow the burden of persuasion to vary with the severity of the sanction sought. For example, when a lesser sanction such as a fine or exclusion of evidence is sought, it is generally agreed that the burden of persuasion is preponderance of the evidence.[260] When a dispositive sanction like dismissal or default judgment is sought, however, courts have imposed a

---

257. *See* Keller v. United States, 58 F.3d 1194, 1197-98 (7th Cir. 1995) (discussing split over whether state or federal law applied in diversity actions).

258. National Hockey League v. Metro. Hockey Club, Inc., 427 U.S. 639, 643 (1976); West v. Goodyear Tire & Rubber Co., 167 F.3d 776, 779 (2d Cir. 1999); Wyle v. R.J. Reynolds Indus., Inc., 709 F.2d 585, 589 (9th Cir. 1983); Google Inc. v. Am. Blind & Wallpaper Factory, Inc., 2007 WL 1848665, at *3 (N.D. Cal. June 27, 2007).

259. *See, e.g.,* United States v. Koch Indus., Inc., 197 F.R.D. 463, 486 (N.D. Okla. 1998) ("Plaintiff has failed to carry their burden of proof to establish *by a preponderance of the evidence* that KII destroyed the computer files intentionally or with bad faith.").

260. *See* Gates Rubber Co. v. Bando Chem. Indus., Ltd., 167 F.R.D. 90, 108-09 (D. Colo. 1996) (extended discussion of burdens).

higher burden of persuasion—clear and convincing evidence[261]—or required that an evil state of mind be proven, while continuing to impose the preponderance of the evidence burden of persuasion.[262] This fluctuating burden of persuasion has been justified by the fact that the lesser sanctions do not deny parties their right to a trial on the merits.

VI.   CHOICE OF LAW QUESTION

When federal courts hear diversity claims that are controlled by state law under the *Erie* doctrine,[263] what law controls sanctioning for acts of spoliation? *Erie* requires that state law be applied to substantive matters and federal law is applied to procedural matters. Because spoliation involves evidentiary matters, and evidentiary matters are considered procedural, federal law governs spoliation questions.[264]

VII.   PROVING THE CLAIM OF SPOLIATION—YOU'RE NOT BOUND BY THE RULES OF EVIDENCE

When presenting evidence to the trial judge on all preliminary factual questions, the judge is not bound by the rules of evidence. Judges may consider otherwise inadmissible evidence when making preliminary factual determinations under Fed. R. Evid. 104(a). Judges are not limited to hearing evidence admissible under the Federal Rules of Evidence when

---

261.   *See* Anderson v. Cryovac, 862 F.2d 910, 923 (1st Cir. 1988) (court treated claim justifying dismissal like allegation of fraud and required clear and convincing evidence); Gates Rubber Co. v. Bando Chem. Indus., Ltd., 167 F.R.D. 90, 108 (D. Colo. 1996); Synanon Church v. United States, 579 F. Supp. 967, 972 (1984). The court in *Gates* noted that if this higher burden is not satisfied, "the judge may still impose lesser sanctions if a need is shown by a preponderance of the evidence. Where lesser sanctions are imposed, the rights of the parties to a trial on the merits are not completely defeated. Lesser sanctions serve a different purpose than dispositive sanctions." *Id.* at 108-09.

262.   *See* Cabinetware Inc. v. Sullivan, 22 U.S.P.Q.2d 1686 (E.D. Cal. 1991).

263.   Erie R.R. v. Tompkins, 304 U.S. 64, 78 (1938).

264.   Ward v. Texas Steak LTD, 2004 WL 1280776, at *2 (W.D. Va. May 27, 2004) ("Recognizing that it is a court of limited jurisdiction, this court concludes that when spoliation of evidence does not occur in the course of pending federal litigation, a federal court exercising diversity jurisdiction in which the rule of decision is supplied by state law is required to apply those spoliation principles the forum state would apply."); Fakhro v. Mayo Clinic Rochester, 2004 WL 909740, at 2 (D. Minn. Mar. 31, 2004).

ruling on the admissibility of evidence under those rules.[265] This includes spoliation claims. Therefore, when claims are made that evidence has been deleted from a party's hard drive or otherwise destroyed or altered, hearsay statements from computer experts and from current and former employees can be heard by the judge. On the other hand, just because judges *can* accept such evidence does not mean that they *must* do so. As an added guarantee of accuracy, judges may choose to follow the strictures of the evidence rules.

VIII. EVIDENCE OF SPOLIATION—EVIDENCE OF ONE'S CONDUCT TO PROVE THE TRUTH OF ITS IMPLIED MESSAGE—IS IT HEARSAY?

Spoliation evidence was hearsay under the common law. The implied statement read into the spoliator's conduct was that the destroyed evidence was unfavorable to the spoliator, and this statement was being offered into evidence for the truth of the matter asserted. Nevertheless, it was admissible against a party opponent under the admissions exception to the hearsay rule. For two reasons, the analysis has changed under the Federal Rules of Evidence.

First, the term "statement" is defined in Fed. R. Evid. 801(a)(2) as "nonverbal conduct of a person" but only if the conduct was "intended by the person as an assertion." Because spoliation is not an act intended by the spoliator to attract attention and make a statement to anyone about anything, the message read into the spoliator's conduct does not constitute a "statement." This is important, because Fed. R. Evid. 801(c) defines hearsay as "a *statement*, other than one made by the declarant while testifying at the trial or hearing, offered into evidence to prove the truth of the matter asserted." Because the conduct is not a "statement," it also is not hearsay, regardless of the reason it is being offered into evidence.

---

265. FED. R. EVID. 104 provides, in part:

Article I. General Provisions
Rule 104. Preliminary Questions
(a) Question of admissibility generally. Preliminary question concerning the qualification of a person to be a witness, the existence of a privilege, or the admissibility of evidence shall be determined by the court, subject to the provisions of subdivision (b). *In making its determination it is not bound by the rules of evidence except those with respect to privilege.* . . . (emphasis added)

Second, the spoliator's conduct also is not hearsay, because admissions have been excluded from the definition of hearsay by Fed. R. Evid. 801(d)(2), which provides, in part, that "a statement is not hearsay if . . . [t]he statement is offered against a party and is (A) the party's own statement . . . ."[266]

The only practical implication these changes will have for practitioners is that spoliation by third parties that is attributable to a party opponent will now be admissible for truth as non-hearsay if its relevance can be established. Evidence of spoliation will continue to be an implied admission by conduct that is admissible against the party opponent, regardless of its hearsay character.

IX.   SPOLIATION AND THE ATTORNEY-CLIENT PRIVILEGE

Spoliation is an act that is fundamentally inconsistent with the adversarial system—but it may not technically be a crime or a fraud. Therefore, if an attorney is consulted about a document destruction program at a time when there is a duty to preserve existing communications, does the crime/fraud exception to the attorney-client privilege preclude the privilege from applying to those consultations? Developing case law supports the application of the crime/fraud exception.[267]

The District of Columbia Circuit held that the exception was applicable to "misconduct fundamentally inconsistent with the basic premises of the adversary system,"[268] and later applied that reasoning to conduct in furtherance of spoliation.[269] Subsequently, two courts have applied it to overcome the attorney-client privilege when consultations with an attorney were in furtherance of acts of spoliation.[270] Seeking the assistance of an attorney in

---

266. Vermont Elec. Power Co. v. Hartford Steam Boiler Inspection & Ins. Co., 72 F. Supp. 2d 441, 448 (D. Vt. 1999) ("emails are clearly admissions of a party, and therefore admissible as nonhearsay.").

267. The crime/fraud exception to the attorney-client privilege is discussed is detail in Chapter Three, *infra*.

268. In re Sealed Case, 676 F.2d 793, 812 (D.C. Cir. 1982).

269. In re Sealed Case, 754 F.2d 395, 400 (D.C. Cir. 1985).

270. Rambus, Inc. v. Infineo Tech. AG, 220 F.R.D. 264 (E.D. Va. 2004) and Int'l Tel. & Tel. Corp. v. United Tel. Co. of Fla., 60 F.R.D. 177, 180 (M.D. Fla. 1973).

procuring fraudulent corporate documents would be a form of spoliation, and all privileged communications in furtherance of that scheme would lose their privilege protection under the crime/fraud exception.[271]

X. STANDARD OF APPELLATE REVIEW

Both the factual basis for imposing sanctions and the sanctions themselves are reviewed on appeal for abuse of discretion.[272] A district judge's factual findings in support of sanctions will be rejected only if they were clearly erroneous. Questions of law, such as, whether bad faith must be proven, are reviewed de novo.

XI. COMPUTERS AND THE INTERNET EXPAND EVERY POSSIBILITY

Computers and the Internet add interesting wrinkles to spoliation analyses because electronic records not only exist in numerous forms and locations, but are also not easy to destroy. Computer files are stored in a multitude of places. Initially, files are stored in a computer's active directories. Users may remove a file from an active directory by "delet-

---

271. Antidote Int'l Films, Inc. v. Bloomsbury Pub'g, PLC, 242 F.R.D. 248, 250 (S.D.N.Y. 2007) (In an e-mail to the attorney, it was stated that "the minutes of its annual meeting (backdated, if necessary) [must show] that J.T. LeRoy is an authorized signatory for contracts." The court held that through this e-mail the author effectively asked the attorney for assistance in procuring fraudulent corporate documents. The court concluded "the e-mail would provide a prudent person with a reasonable basis for suspecting the attempted perpetration of a fraud, and the email itself is plainly in furtherance of the attempted fraud.").

272. In re Consol. Coal Co., 123 F.3d 126, 131 (3d Cir. 1997); Dillon v. Nissan Motor Co., 986 F.2d 263, 267 (8th Cir. 1993); Sieck v. Russo, 869 F.2d 131, 134 (2d Cir. 1989); Spaise v. Dodd, 2004 WL 1191942 (Minn. Ct. App. June 1, 2004) ("[W]e will not reverse the court's decision [on spoliation sanctions] absent an abuse of . . . discretion."); QZO, Inc. v. Moyer, 594 S.E.2d 541, 547 (S.C. Ct. App. 2004) ("An abuse of discretion may be found where the appellant shows that the conclusion reached by the trial court was without reasonable factual support and resulted in prejudice to the rights of appellant, thereby amounting to an error of law."); Alexander v. Jackson Radiology Assocs., 156 S.W.3d 11, 15 (Tenn. Ct. App. 2004) ("Although 'reasonable judicial minds can differ concerning [its] soundness,' the trial court's determination of the appropriate sanction will be set aside only where the court 'has misconstrued or misapplied the controlling legal principles or has acted inconsistently with the substantial weight of the evidence.'").

ing" the file. When a file has been deleted, however, it remains on the hard drive. The "delete" function merely indicates to the computer that the space where that file information is stored is available for use. In most instances the deleted file is accessible to those willing to go through the time and expense of having the hard drive professionally scanned.[273] Available technology, however, does not necessarily define the scope of permitted or required discovery. The scanning of hard drives creates potential problems of inconvenience, cost, privacy intrusions, and privilege breaches.[274] Consequently, although parties may be capable of retrieving deleted files, in many instances they may not be required to do so by law.

Web pages pose the same problem. They are posted by computers through Internet service providers. Because they are constantly edited, and because past versions may be material to pending litigation, the owner of a Web site may have a responsibility to preserve all prior editions for discovery purposes.[275]

Computer files can easily spread beyond the hard drive of the terminal on which they were created. For example:

(1) Many terminals form part of a larger computer network. Everything stored on the hard drive of each terminal may also exist on the hard drive of the central system.[276]

(2) Anything on the computer can be printed and maintained in hardcopy format.

(3) All information that can be called up on a computer terminal can be downloaded onto diskettes or more capacious memory devices, such as Zip drives and jump drives.[277] These memory de-

---

273. *See generally* Adobe Sys., Inc. v. South Sun Prods., Inc., 187 F.R.D. 636, 642 (S.D. Cal. 1999). The only way that a hard drive can be clean, so that files are destroyed to the point that they cannot be retrieved, is to employ a software program that overwrites all available space on the hard drive so that nothing previously recorded is retrievable.

274. *See* Chapter One, "Discovery," *supra.*

275. Piper Jaffray Cos. v. Nat'l Union Fire Ins. Co., 967 F. Supp. 1148, 1152 n.3 (D. Minn. 1997) ("The Court understands that Piper's website has changed in response to this litigation; the Court fully expects Piper to cause all relevant previous 'editions' to be preserved for discovery.").

276. McGuire v. Acufex Microsurgical, Inc., 175 F.R.D. 149, 152 (D. Mass. 1997) (edited version of document claimed to be lost was later found on office computers of two employees).

vices include the memory cards in digital cameras and MP3 players.

(4) Many computer files are regularly recorded on backup tapes for
security purposes.[278]

(5) Much information is stored on the hard drives of Palm Pilots,
portable computers, and computers in the homes of employees
who can connect to the office computer through telephone lines
and satellite links.[279]

(6) E-mail communications automatically double the possible number of records because they exist on the hard drive of the computer from which they originated and the computer to which they
were sent.[280]

(7) Blind copies of e-mails are often sent to third parties, and the
recipients of each message can forward it to an unlimited number
of additional recipients. As a consequence, the possible sources
from which communications can be retrieved can be many times
what appears on the face of the original message.

This proliferation of records has numerous implications for spoliation. For example, if information is innocently deleted from one source
but still available from another, spoliation may not be found. On the other
hand, because alterations in another location might have evidentiary value,

---

277. Jump drives, or keychain drives, are devices that can be attached to a key
chain and used in most computers' USB ports. These drives are very portable and
have the added advantage of maximum security because large amounts of information can be recorded directly on these drives and never saved on any hard
drives.

278. McGuire, 175 F.R.D. at 150 (to locate missing version of document, defendant attempted to recreate it from backup tapes).

279. *Id.* ("The missing paragraph was 'found' by Anderson on his personal
computer's hard drive, just before his deposition in January of 1997. It was produced at the deposition and seen then for the first time by both parties' counsel.").

280. Actually the use of e-mail multiplies the possibilities by four because the
Internet service providers for both the sender and the receiver have recorded them
on their mail servers. This means that even if deleted from both the sender's and
recipient's computers, a message may still exist on the ISPs' mail servers. Typically, however, such messages are retained by the ISPs for a very short period of
time. As a consequence, it is essential for litigants to notify ISPs of potential
litigation so that such records will not be destroyed in the normal course of
business.

what is available may not be exactly like what was destroyed. If the owner of the records wishes to destroy them for legitimate security purposes, computer technology makes this much more difficult because the records are so widely and easily dispersed. Multiple sources increase production costs because e-records may have to be produced from each source that remains within the possession, custody, or control of the producing party.[281]

The multitude of potential sources also affects the application of other evidentiary rules. If, for example, deleted information on a company's computer was retrieved from the home computer of an employee who had been working by telephone link, problems of authentication will increase, because this information could have been altered while in the control of the employee.[282] Although the records may be admissible as business records under the business records exception to the hearsay rule in Fed. R. Evid. 803(6), the proponent likely will have to address the questions of trustworthiness raised by the source.[283]

A. Do Not Delete Records or Destroy Equipment

If a party controls any of the sources of e-evidence and fails to take measures to preserve them after litigation has commenced, spoliation can be found.[284] Hard copies of potentially relevant documents should not be destroyed, and no potentially relevant file should be deleted from active directories.[285] This is true even if deleted materials are thought to

---

281. *See* FED. R. CIV. P. 34(a).

282. *See* Chapter Six, "Authentication," *infra.*

283. The business records exception to the hearsay rule permits the introduction of regularly maintained business records to prove the truth of what is stated in them, unless the source of information indicates lack of trustworthiness. *See generally* Chapter Seven, "Hearsay," *infra.*

284. Mosaid Tech. Inc. v. Samsung Elecs. Co., 348 F. Supp. 2d 332 (D. N.J. 2004) (Samsung failed to put a "litigation hold" on all technical e-mails relevant to the litigation and was sanctioned with an inference instruction and costs); Procter & Gamble Co. v. Haugen, 179 F.R.D. 622, 632 (D. Utah 1998) (company fined because it did not search and preserve e-mail communications of five individuals who had been identified as having relevant information).

285. After documents have been deleted from a computer system, experts can determine what has been accessed, what has been changed or deleted, and when this occurred. *See, e.g.,* Four Seasons Hotels & Resorts v. Barr, 267 F. Supp. 2d 1268, 1298 (S.D. Fla. 2003) (Expert in forensic computer analysis and electronic evidence generated spreadsheets detailing specific nature of access to computer,

be trade secrets and should not be seen by the other side.[286]

Attempts to delete are unwise for several reasons:

(1) The effort probably will not be successful in defeating the opposing party's discovery because the deleted documents will still exist on the hard drive.

(2) The deletions will only increase the costs of retrieval, and, once that process is completed, the computer will reveal when the deletions occurred. Consequently, the deleting party will likely have to pay any additional costs of retrieval.[287]

(3) Even a failed attempt to destroy evidence is considered spoliation, and guilty parties will suffer the negative inferences from their attempt.

At the beginning of litigation, it is imperative that a general litigation hold be placed on the destruction of all potentially relevant evidence. This should explicitly encompass not only computer files and e-mails, but also backup tapes of each, tapes of telephone conversations, hard drives of computers being replaced or enhanced, jump drives or keychain drives onto which evidence has been downloaded, and particularly ongoing destruction policies relating to any source of potentially relevant evidence. This is particularly important for e-mail communications that are set to be automatically deleted after a designated period of time.[288]

---

files accessed on particular drives, dates of modifications, files that were created, files that were moved from one location to another, and files deleted on designated drives.).

286. Symantec Corp. v. McAffee Assoc., Inc., 1998 WL 740798, at *2 (N.D. Cal. June 9, 1998).

287. In RKI, Inc. v. Grimes, 177 F. Supp. 2d 859 (N.D. Ill. 2001), a former employee was accused of misappropriating trade secrets. In an effort to avoid detection, the defendant deleted confidential information and software from his home computer. Then, to preclude detection of this spoliation, the defendant defragmented his computer (*i.e.*, reconfigured the alignment of data) three times for the sole purpose of destroying any evidence that confidential communications had been deleted from his hard drive. These acts resulted in the defendant being assessed $100,000 in compensatory damages, $150,000 in punitive damages, attorneys' fees, and court costs. The relationship of the acts of spoliation to the assessments was not discussed in detail by the presiding judge.

288. *See* E*Trade Securities LLC v. Deutsche Bank AG, 230 F.R.D. 582 (D. Minn. 2005), for an example of where this was not properly done.

B.   Save the Hard Drives

After a client is on notice of potential litigation, it should preserve hard drives and similar equipment that are replaced while upgrading a preexisting system. When data from old computers is transferred to a new system, only active files are transferred. E-evidence embedded on a discarded hard drive remains with the hard drive. The failure to preserve old hard drives effectively destroys previous versions of any document that was not transferred. Sophisticated technological analysis can reveal whether and when a hard drive has been manipulated. Therefore, parties should preserve old hard drives in their original state.

Outside a potential litigation context, it may be cost-effective to simply discard old hard drives. The possibility of later retrieving helpful documents is seldom worth the cost. Discarding, however, does create security risks, since information can be retrieved from the drives by third parties. However, programs are available that erase the hard drive by overwriting the shadows of deleted data so completely that nothing coherent can be retrieved. Parties generally have the right to destroy records in their possession, as long as it is not done after a duty to preserve evidence has arisen.[289] Therefore, nothing nefarious should be read into the use of a data destruction program.

C.   Don't Forget Personal Digital Assistants and Jump Drives

Just as old hard drives must be preserved like hard copies of written correspondence, a company will be negligent if, when the duty to preserve arises, it does not preserve the handheld computers, such as personal digital assistants (PDAs), used by its employees. Substantively, there is little difference between an employee's desk terminal, portable computer, or PDA. If a PDA is connected to a network, it may have access to all of the information on that network.

The same is true of jump drives (often referred to as keychain or thumb drives), which permit individuals to download massive amounts of materials recorded on a company's mainframe through the USB port on any computer connected to the system. These devices facilitate the trans-

---

289. Anderson v. Crossroads Capital Partners, 2004 WL 256512 (D. Minn. Feb. 10, 2004) (After duty to preserve arose, plaintiff intentionally destroyed evidence on hard drive by running CyberScrub—a program that renders information on computer completely unretrievable.).

portation of large quantities of materials from office to home and to meetings with third parties. They also can provide enhanced security for employees, because sensitive materials do not have to be saved on either their computers' hard drives or the company's mainframe. However, more often than not, companies have found them to be nightmares; most jump drives are unauthorized, they can introduce viruses, and they increase security risks by allowing the secret movement of sensitive information in a relatively undetectable pocket-size form.

Once a company is notified of potential litigation, steps to fulfill evidence preservation responsibilities should include interviews with employees to determine potential sources of relevant evidence, such as jump drives and PDAs. For example:

- Have you used devices of this nature while employed by the company?
- Have you accessed your company e-mail server on your PDA?
- Have any accessed messages been recorded in any other format?
- Have you downloaded any information related to the [specifically identified] issues in the anticipated litigation?
- Has downloaded information been taken home or transferred to other computers?
- Do you have any other external storage devices (portable or otherwise) to which company information has been transferred?

D. Informal Encouragement to Others to Preserve Data

Even when a party does not control the instrumentality upon which relevant communications may be stored, such as the PDA of an employee or computers of third parties who have had access to data on the party's computer, spoliation can still be found in either of two instances:

(1) when efforts are not made to encourage preservation, particularly with those over whom the company may have influence; or
(2) when affirmative efforts are made to encourage others to destroy that which they control.

In such instances, a party is uniquely aware of e-record sources and should contact them because:

(1) the party's computers are connected to those of the third parties, and

(2) the party previously destroyed or lost relevant materials in good faith and knows that third parties now control the only means of retrieving the destroyed records.

Confidentiality and the Attorney-Client Privilege | 3

I.   The Attorney-Client Privilege and Its Elements   193

A. History of the Confidentiality Requirement   195

B. Evolution of the Confidentiality
    Requirement   198

1. Ever-Expanding Circle   198

2. Ignoring Confidentiality   201

a. Stolen documents   201

b. Judicially compelled disclosures   203

c. The unauthorized agent exception   206

d. Inadvertent disclosures—the "oops"
    rule   207

e. Disclosures under protective orders or
    with reservations   210

3. Confidentiality Must Be Maintained
    and Documented—The Increasing
    Problem of Outside Agents Functioning
    as Employees   215

C. E-mail—An Extension of Existing Services and
   Technology   221

1. From Face-to-Face Communications to
    Letters   221

2. From Letters to Telephones   221

3. From Telephones to Computers   222

D. Employees' Personal Expectation of Confidentiality in
E-mail Communications   224

E. Data Behind Electronic Evidence—Metadata   234

F. Electronic Presentations   236

G   Measures to Preserve Confidentiality?   239

H. Asserting Attorney-Client Privilege for E-mails:
The Practical Details, a Growing Concern   243

   1. Expanding the Role of In-House Counsel—
   Jeopardizing the Applicability of the Privilege   244

   2. Complicating the Distinction Between
   Communications and Information   248

   3. How Is the Document Described in a Privilege
   Log?   252

   4. Are Operating Assumptions About the Purpose of
   Communications Appropriate Based on the
   Individuals to Whom They Have Been
   Disseminated?   258

      a. When business and legal communications can
      be separated   261

      b. When business and legal advice are inextricably
      intertwined   264

I. Spoliation and the Crime/Fraud Exception to the Attorney-
Client Privilege   289

J. Work Product Immunity Vis-à-Vis E-evidence   291

E-evidence Overview: The elements of the attorney-client privilege in a traditional context are unchanged in the context of e-evidence. Nevertheless, applying the elements to e-mail communications greatly complicates any privilege analysis by dramatically increasing the potential pitfalls awaiting attorneys, especially in-house counsel and their clients. E-mail is a common way for members of an organization to communicate among themselves and to the organization's attorneys. The total number of communications implicating privilege concerns has increased. This is because e-mail is an easy and convenient form of communication, and because organizational dynamics have evolved in such a way that attorneys for an organization are included in many more communications that primarily concern business (and not legal) matters. Therefore, a complicated but crucial issue that must be addressed is whether a communication and the string of messages to which it is attached have been made for the primary purpose of seeking legal advice from those attorneys. These problems have been compounded by an increasingly popular practice among corporations of sharing confidential attorney-client communications with outside consultants who work with the corporations as functional employees.

I. THE ATTORNEY-CLIENT PRIVILEGE AND ITS ELEMENTS

The attorney-client privilege protects from disclosure those communications from clients to their attorneys that were part of the clients' efforts to obtain legal advice or assistance. The communication must be confidential for the privilege to apply. A communication is confidential when (1) the client subjectively believes the communication is confidential, and (2) that belief is objectively reasonable.[1] The privilege also provides a derivative protection to responsive communications from the

---

1. *See generally* PAUL R. RICE, ATTORNEY-CLIENT PRIVILEGE IN THE UNITED STATES, § 6:1, pp. 7-8 (West Group 2d ed. 1999). "The confidentiality requirement has three dimensions. The first is a subjective element. The client must *intend* his communications with his attorney to be confidential. The second is an objective element. The client's subjective intention of confidentiality must be *reasonable* under the circumstances. Third, the confidentiality must have been subsequently *maintained*." (Emphasis in original.)

attorney to the client to the extent that those communications reveal the content of prior confidential communications from the client.

Summary: While the element of confidentiality poses a theoretical problem for e-mail communications between attorneys and clients, the enhanced possibilities of breached confidentiality will not preclude the attorney-client privilege from protecting them.

E-mail communications can pose a confidentiality issue because e-mail is susceptible to breaches of confidentiality by unauthorized third parties. From a communication's inception through its transmission within the Internet service provider (ISP) to its final destination in the receiving organization, many opportunities exist for unauthorized access to it by individuals within various enterprises charged with shepherding the communication. Hackers within the public-at-large might also gain access to the records of the sender, the ISP, or the recipient. Additional confidentiality issues arise if the computer terminal used to send an e-mail message is connected to a local network. Because a central database stores each message sent and received, the number of individuals who could potentially access such e-mails dramatically increases.

On the recipient's end of the electronic communication, identical confidentiality problems exist. Moreover, if the recipient prints the messages, inadequate security of these "hard copies"—including discarding them without first shredding—spawns additional confidentiality problems. Consequently, one of the most frequently asked questions from lawyers regarding use of the Internet has been whether the confidentiality of e-mail communications can be sufficiently protected to preserve the attorney-client privilege.

To transmit e-mail from an author to a recipient, parties usually must rely on ISPs. An ISP stores the sender's message and relays it either to another ISP or to the recipient, depending on whether both use the same ISP. Once the communication enters this ISP conduit, the sender loses control of it. The ISP has the ability to store, read, and disseminate every message.

Under classic attorney-client privilege theory, relinquishing control destroys both the sender's subjective expectation of confidentiality[2] and

---

2. *Cf.* Bower v. Weisman, 669 F. Supp. 602, 605-06 (S.D.N.Y. 1987) ("By leaving a letter spread out on a table in a room in a suite in which [the third party]

the objective reasonableness of whatever expectation of confidentiality the sender may retain. The sender, accordingly, would be found to have waived any privilege protection for the communication.[3] Whether a third party actually exercised control over the communication did not matter.

Despite the fact that transmissions of electronic communications increase the risk that their confidentiality will be compromised, the attorney-client privilege should and likely will continue to protect electronic communications. This conclusion rests on the historical origins of the confidentiality requirement, its evolution over the past century, and the fact that it has never been a logical imperative.[4]

A.   *History of the Confidentiality Requirement*

The confidentiality requirement, which was a creation of commentators, lacks a strong basis in logic, and judicial decisions have gradually eroded its significance.[5] Thus, while the risk is heightened that a confidentiality breach will occur when communicating electronically, the effect of a breach should not, and likely will not, carry dispositive weight. A brief review of the history and evolution of the confidentiality requirement clarifies this and provides principles on which an attorney may draw when asserting the privilege in the face of a confidentiality breach.

The attorney-client privilege is rooted in 17th-century English common law, which did not require communications between attorney and client to be secret for the privilege to apply. The concept of confidentiality related to the *nature* of the attorney-client relationship rather than

---

was directed to wait fails to reach the level of taking 'all possible precautions to ensure confidentiality.' . . . While not quite as careless as communicating in an elevator, leaving a document out on a table (as opposed to putting it in a briefcase or in a drawer) in a public room in a suite in which another person is staying is insufficient to demonstrate Weisman's objective interest in its confidentiality.").

3. *Cf.* United States v. Betinsky, U.S. v. Betinsky 1988 WL 97673, *3 (E.D. Pa. Sept. 20, 1988) (E.D. Pa. Sept. 20, 1988) (privilege was destroyed, regardless of whether client intended to waive privilege, because he left confidential letters in boxes stored in a neighbor's basement). For a discussion of waiver by voluntary disclosure, *see* PAUL R. RICE, ATTORNEY-CLIENT PRIVILEGE IN THE UNITED STATES, §§ 9:19 and 9:27 (West Group 2d ed. 1999).

4. *See generally* PAUL R. RICE, ATTORNEY-CLIENT PRIVILEGE IN THE UNITED STATES, §§ 6:3-6:4 (West Group 2d ed. 1999).

5. *See generally id.* at § 6:3 (West Group 2d ed. 1999)

the *context* in which the communications took place. Indeed, though an attorney could not be called as a witness to testify against a former client, third parties who had been present during those conversations could properly testify. Their presence when the communication took place did not affect the existence of the privilege vís-a-vìs the attorney.[6] If the client desired secrecy, he could communicate with his lawyer outside the presence of those individuals, but the law was unconcerned about this aspect of confidentiality.

Not until the late 19th century, in the final edition of *Greenleaf on Evidence*, did anyone suggest that confidentiality/secrecy was an element of the attorney-client privilege.[7] In the transition from this last edition of *Greenleaf* (which was edited by Professor Wigmore) to the second edition of Wigmore's own treatise, *Wigmore on Evidence*, Wigmore transformed what first was only a suggestion into an absolute prerequisite, not only for the attorney-client privilege, but for all privileges.[8]

When Professor Wigmore invented the confidentiality requirement, he did not cite a single judicial decision supporting his assertion. Since the birth of the requirement, neither Wigmore nor the legions of judges who continue to follow his lead have justified secrecy as a logical imperative. Even though disputes over this element comprise the overwhelming majority of attorney-client privilege issues brought before courts for

---

6. *See, e.g.*, Gainsford v. Grammar, 2 Camp. 7, 170 Eng. Rep. 1063 (N.P. 1809) (attorney was asked to testify as to what his client instructed him to propose to plaintiff; conversation between attorney and client was privileged, but plaintiff was allowed to call someone who had been present during discussion between the attorney and plaintiff); *see also* Rex v. Withers, 2 Camp. 578, 170 Eng. Rep. 1258 (N.P. 1811) (applying privilege to communication made in presence of third party).

7. GREENLEAF, A TREATISE ON THE LAW OF EVIDENCE § 245 (16th ed. 1899). In illustrations of communications that were not protected by the attorney-client privilege, an additional one was added: "The presence of a third person will usually be treated as indicating that the communication was not confidential; moreover, a third person who overhears the communication is not within the confidence and may disclose what he hears."

8. 4 JOHN HENRY WIGMORE, EVIDENCE § 2311, at 3234-35 (1905). He asserts that confidentiality is one of four "fundamental conditions . . . necessary to the establishment of a privilege against the disclosure of communications." He proceeds to state that confidentiality "must be essential to the full and satisfactory maintenance of the relationship between the parties" before any privilege should be recognized. *Id.* at § 2311, at 599.

resolution, no one has ever convincingly explained why secrecy is necessary.

If the privilege seeks to encourage candid communications between clients and their attorneys, suppressing the use of such communications accomplishes this purpose. There is no apparent reason for insisting that the communication take place in secret, and that such secrecy subsequently be maintained. Although it may be awkward for a court to bar the admission of the contents of communications that are widely known within a community, such a practice is quite common in our Fourth Amendment jurisprudence in the context of unreasonable searches and seizures. Just as suppressing illegally seized evidence serves to discourage police from violating the privacy rights of citizens, suppressing clients' communications with their attorney encourages candor. The confidentiality requirement, however, does nothing to further candor between clients and their attorneys. Indeed, to the extent that the confidentiality requirement creates uncertainty as to whether a particular communication will be protected, the requirement has a chilling effect on attorney-client communications.

If clients wish to keep their communications secret, they can communicate in an environment that ensures secrecy. As long as clients maintain that secrecy, they can be assured that their lawyers are obligated to preserve client confidences under the ethical rules of the profession.[9] Through accepting Wigmore's *ipse dixit* and imposing

---

9. *See* MODEL RULES OF PROF'L CONDUCT 2001.

RULE 1.6 CONFIDENTIALITY OF INFORMATION

(a) A lawyer shall not reveal information relating to representation of a client unless the client consents after consultation, except for disclosures that are impliedly authorized in order to carry out the representation, and except as stated in paragraph (b).

(b) A lawyer may reveal such information to the extent the lawyer reasonably believes necessary:

(1) to prevent the client from committing a criminal act that the lawyer believes is likely to result in imminent death or substantial bodily harm; or

(2) to establish a claim or defense on behalf of the lawyer in a controversy between the lawyer and the client, to establish a defense to a criminal charge or civil claim against the lawyer based upon conduct in which the client was involved, or to respond to allegations in any proceeding concerning the lawyer's representation of the client.

confidentiality as an element, courts have unnecessarily burdened themselves with costly and time-consuming attorney-client privilege disputes over this element.

B. Evolution of the Confidentiality Requirement

Confidentiality has devolved into little more than a condition precedent to the creation of the privilege but not a necessary condition to its continuation. Dissatisfied with the concept, courts have constantly expanded the circle of confidentiality and have now begun to ignore its absence after the inception of the privilege protection.

After adopting the element of confidentiality, judges quickly began to question its necessity. This is clearly demonstrated in judicial decisions that (1) expand the circle of confidentiality beyond the attorney and client and (2) recognize the privilege protection long after the secrecy has been destroyed.[10]

1. Ever-Expanding Circle

The tight circle of confidentiality that initially defined the privilege was immediately enlarged to include *necessary* agents of both the attorney and client. The earliest example of such an enlargement of the circle was the inclusion of interpreters. The circle continued to expand to encompass agents who assisted in either obtaining or rendering legal assistance. This category of persons included secretaries, paralegals, and a host of agents of corporate clients.

Over time, the necessity standard was abandoned. The agents only needed to assist the client or attorney in obtaining or rendering advice sought by the client.[11] During this same period, courts often permitted

---

10. For a discussion of the bankrupt nature of the concept of confidentiality and its evolution as a concept, *see* Paul R. Rice, *Attorney-Client Privilege: The Eroding Concept of Confidentiality Should be Abolished*, 47 Duke L. J. 853 (1998). For a debate about the proposals in the Duke article, *see* M. Leslie, *The Costs of Confidentiality and the Purpose of Privilege*, 2000 Wis. L. Rev. 31 (2000) and Paul R. Rice, *A Bad Idea Dying Hard: A Reply to Professor Leslie's Defense of the Indefensible*, 2001 Wis. L. Rev. 187 (2001).

11. Proposed Fed. R. Evid. 503, which was not enacted but still serves as the standard by which the common law principles are interpreted, provides in subsection (a)(3) that a representative of the lawyer is "one employed to *assist* the lawyer in the rendition of professional legal services." (Emphasis added.) This relaxation has been reflected in the case law. *See generally* Paul R. Rice, Attorney-Client Privilege in the United States, §§ 3:3-4 (West Group 2d ed. 1999) and cases cited therein.

joint clients to communicate with a common attorney in the presence of one another. Soon the circle expanded to include separate clients with separate attorneys joining forces in a *joint defense*.[12] This premise served as the basis for allowing separate clients with separate attorneys, having a *community of interests*, to join forces for the purpose of achieving efficiencies in the rendering of legal services.[13]

The circle of confidentiality was further enlarged when corporations were recognized as clients,[14] a development that created many additional confidentiality concerns. Separate corporate clients often had overlapping members of boards of directors who had access to the confidential attorney-client communications of each corporation.[15]

With lower-level employees, because each lapse in confidentiality was not approved by the corporate clients, the courts concluded that there was not a legitimate waiver of the privilege protection. While this may have been true, the reality in each situation was that the underlying premise for the privilege—confidentiality—was missing and the courts were unconcerned.

Within the lower ranks of the corporate entities, employees with knowledge of the content of confidential communications (if not copies of the actual communications themselves) moved from one corporation to another, and in each instance the breaches of confidentiality were excused by courts that continued to recognize the privilege protection.

---

12. *See generally* PAUL R. RICE, ATTORNEY-CLIENT PRIVILEGE IN THE UNITED STATES, §§ 4:30-38 (West Group 2d ed. 1999).

13. *Id.* at § 4:36.

14. *See* United States v. Louisville & Nashville R.R. Co., 236 U.S. 318, 334 (1915), where the corporation's right to assert the privilege was assumed, and Upjohn Co. v. United States, 449 U.S. 383, 390 (1981), where this assumption was elevated to a rule of law without any meaningful analysis. *See also* Radiant Burners, Inc. v. Am. Gas Assoc., 320 F.2d 314, 323-24 (7th Cir. 1963), where the trial court was summarily reversed when it held that the privilege did not apply to corporations because the element of confidentiality had little meaning in the corporate context.

15. For an interesting case study of the element of confidentiality in the corporate context, and how courts refused to acknowledge problems inherent in that context, consider the following. In Judge Campbell's enlightened opinion in Radiant Burners, Inc. v. Am. Gas Ass'n, 207 F. Supp. 771 (N.D. Ill. 1962), he denied the privilege protection to corporations. This decision was immediately reversed by the Seventh Circuit Court of Appeals, *see* 320 F.2d 314 (7th Cir. 1963), without addressing the breadth of grounds upon which Judge Campbell relied.

Within the corporate entity, the circle of confidentiality has been ever-expanding. While it was initially limited to those who could be privy to confidential attorney-client communications without waiving it to members of the corporation's control group,[16] the circle was expanded to include anyone within the corporate structure who had a need to know the content of the communications within the scope of his or her corporate responsibilities.[17] Over time this greatly enlarged circle has been expanded still further to outside consultants who (1) serve as agents of either the client or the attorney in either the obtaining or providing of complete legal assistance,[18] or (2) have been considered what has been

---

16. City of Philadelphia v. Westinghouse Elec. Corp., 210 F. Supp. 483, 485 (E.D. Pa. 1962), *mandamus and prohibition denied*, 312 F.2d 742 (3d Cir. 1962).

17. Harper Row Publishers, Inc. v. Decker, 423 F.2d 487 (7th Cir. 1970), *aff'd*, 400 U.S. 348 (1971).

18. *See* In re Grand Jury Proceedings Under Seal v. United States, 947 F.2d 1188, 1191 (4th Cir. 1991) (After an accountant provided business and tax assistance, he assisted the client in retaining an attorney and in communicating with the attorney in confidence for legal advice. All communications were protected as part of the attorney-client consultation.); In re Bieter Co., 16 F.3d 929 (8th Cir. 1994) (After providing contractor services, the contractor was accepted as part of the circle of confidentiality for litigation preparation purposes.); Kuehne v. United States, 2006 WL 3350735, *2-3 (D. Or. Oct. 12, 2006) ("Communications between an accountant and a client may be protected by the attorney-client privilege when the accountant's role is 'to facilitate an accurate and complete consultation between the client and the attorney.' . . . However, '[w]hat is vital to the privilege is that the communication be made . . . for the purpose of obtaining legal advice from the lawyer. If what is sought is not legal advice but only accounting service, . . . or if the advice sought is the accountant's rather than the lawyer's, no privilege exists.'" While the petition claimed that legal services were being sought through the accountant, the court concluded that the evidence showed otherwise. "[I]t is the services [the accountant] actually provided that determine whether privilege attaches. . . . It is undisputed that [the accountant] prepared amended tax returns for petitioners . . . and as such any related documents and communications fall outside the scope of the attorney/accountant-client privilege."). *But see* Advanced Tech. Assoc., Inc. v. Herley Indus., Inc., 1996 WL 711018 (E.D. Pa. 1996) (a third party's participation in the confidential attorney-client relationship must be "necessary" to the fulfillment of the purpose of the attorney-client relationship); Liggett Group, Inc. v. Brown & Williamson Tobacco Corp., 116 F.R.D. 205 (M.D. N.C. 1986) (Liggett's representative spoke with legal counsel in the presence of representatives of the company who designed their cigarette packaging. Even though the purpose of the consultation was ostensibly to obtain legal advice on the design of the packaging, the court held that the design company had only a 'working relationship' that was insufficient to create an agency relationship for the purposes of the attorney-client privilege.).

referred to as "functional employees"[19] because they performed services for the company equivalent to that performed by employees[20] regardless of whether their assistance was needed by either the client or the attorney to obtain or render legal advice.

As confidentiality evolved through the expansion of the circle of those who could be privy to privileged communications, courts also demonstrated a willingness to ignore the absence of confidentiality altogether, deviating in practice from traditional privilege theory. Attorneys have every reason to anticipate that courts will view e-mail communications, along with the greatly increased number of recipients and concomitantly greater risk that confidentiality will be broken, as merely the next step in the expansion of the circle of confidentiality.

2. Ignoring Confidentiality

a. Stolen documents

Historically, when documents were stolen, the privilege was destroyed. Responsibility for the theft was irrelevant. In the early part of the 20th century, courts moderated this stance. For example, in the context of purloined communications, courts held that if the client had no responsibility for the theft, the privilege protection survived, and litigants who

---

19. In re Currency Conversion Fee Antitrust Litig., 2003 WL 22389169, at *3 (S.D.N.Y. Oct. 21, 2003).

20. In re Bieter Co., 16 F.3d 929 (8th Cir. 1994); Memry Corp. v. Kentucky Oil Tech., N.V., 2007 WL 39373, *9 (N.D. Cal. Jan. 4, 2007); DE Techs., Inc. v. Dell, Inc., 2006 WL 254823, at *2 (W.D. Va. 2006); Residential Constructors, LLC v. Ace Prop. & Cas. Ins. Co., 2006 WL 3149362, at *15 (D. Nev. 2006); Neighborhood Dev. Collaborative v. Murphy, 233 F.R.D. 436, 2005 WL 3272711, at *5 (D. Md. 2005); Feeport McMoran Sulphur, LLC v. Mick Mullen Energy Equip. Resource, Inc., 2004 WL 1237450 (E.D. La. June 2, 2004); Export-Import Bank of the U.S. v. Asia Pulp & Paper Co., Ltd., 232 F.R.D. 103, 113 (S.D.N.Y. Nov. 8, 2005); In re Currency Conversion Fee Antitrust Litig., 2003 WL 22389169, at *3 (S.D.N.Y. Oct. 21, 2003); In re Bristol-Myers Squibb Securities Litig., 2003 U.S. Dist. LEXIS 26985 (D. N.J. June 25, 2003) (not available on Westlaw); In re Copper Market Antitrust Litig., 200 F.R.D. 213, 218 (S.D.N.Y. 2001); Calvin Klein Trademark Trust v. Wachner, 198 F.R.D. 53, 55 (S.D.N.Y. 2000). *See generally* P.R. RICE, ATTORNEY-CLIENT PRIVILEGE IN THE UNITED STATES, § 4:2, *Agents of Client* (2d ed. 1999) and cases discussed therein.

came into possession of such a stolen document could not use it.[21] Rather than focusing on the absence of confidentiality, courts continued to recognize the privilege protection by focusing on the reason for its ab-

---

21. *See* United States v. Cable News Network, 865 F. Supp. 1549 (S.D. Fla. 1994). A prison tape-recorded all telephone conversations between Manuel Noriega, a criminal defendant, and his defense team. CNN obtained those tapes and broadcast them over the airwaves in violation of a court order. In defense of the contempt citation, CNN claimed the conversations were never privileged because Noriega and his attorneys knew they were being recorded. The court rejected this argument. *See also* State v. Today's Bookstores, Inc., 621 N.E.2d 1283 (Ohio Ct. App. 1993):

> We also disagree with Nichols' argument that the attorney-client privilege was waived and that the document lost its privilege when it was somehow disclosed to the news media. . . . If disclosure was by some person who was not entitled to have the memorandum or who did not have authority to waive the privilege, the document is still privileged. . . . The trial court referred to a 'leak' of the July 9 memorandum, indicating that the trial court had concluded that the disclosure was not voluntary. The trial court erred when it held that the attorney-client privilege had been waived where there is no evidence that the City of Dayton had voluntarily relinquished the memorandum; . . . .

Accord, Blackmon v. State, 653 P.2d 669, 671 (Alaska Ct. App. 1982).

Conversation between defendant and his counsel during a trial recess was confidential for purposes of applying lawyer-client privilege where the measures taken by attorney and client evidenced reasonable care on their part to maintain confidentiality; thus, witness who overheard part of the conversation should not have been allowed to disclose to jury what he had heard, and his testimony in that regard constituted prejudicial error. Early decisions reveal a reluctance to extend the lawyer-client privilege's full protection to situations involving passers-by or eavesdroppers who overheard lawyer-client conversations. . . . However, there has been support in modern cases for extending the privilege where the client and his lawyer intended their communications to be confidential and where precautions to preserve confidentiality were reasonable under the circumstances.

See also Concrete Block & Prods. Co. v. Kurtz, 190 N.W.2d 725, 726 (Mich. Ct. App. 1971) (noting, in case involving communications secretly tape-recorded, that "[t]he attorney's claim of the attorney-client privilege was also properly upheld by the trial court as the record does not support defendant's claim that the privilege was ever waived."); Lanza v. N.Y. State Joint Legislative Comm., 3 N.Y.2d 92, 98, 164 N.Y.S.2d 9, 12, 13, 143 N.E. 772 (1957) (holding the attorney-client privilege was not destroyed when an attorney-client communication was surreptitiously recorded during the client's incarceration).

sence. Courts will likely continue to focus on the reasons underlying any confidentiality breach in the e-evidence and e-mail context. If, for example, hackers steal an e-mail or other electronic document, it is highly unlikely that courts will deviate from the long line of analogous cases concerning stolen documents.[22]

b.   Judicially compelled disclosures

Even if not actually stolen, documents containing a client's communications can be "taken" by judicial decision. This usually occurs when documents sought during pretrial discovery proceedings are withheld by a party on privilege grounds, but the privilege claim is not upheld, and the court orders their production.

These privilege claims reach a judicial officer through one of two avenues. The first is when the privilege proponent—the one who is asked to produce the documents—asks for a protective order. The second, and more common, avenue is for the demanding party—the one who is being denied discovery on privilege grounds—to file a motion to compel the production of the documents.

Under either motion the client will be required to file a privilege log or index delineating each privilege claim for documents that are other-

---

22. *See, e.g.*, Crabb v. KFC Nat'l Mgmt. Co., 952 F.2d 403 (6th Cir. 1992) (unpublished) (ex-employee's possession of privileged documents was excused, even though the breach of confidentiality was unexplained, because efforts to preserve confidentiality were perceived to have been adequate); Sackman v. Liggett Group, Inc., 173 F.R.D. 358 (E.D. N.Y. 1997) ("[T]he assertion of privilege by 'BW' is not waived through public disclosure of a stolen privileged document."); Resolution Trust Corp. v. Dean, 813 F. Supp. 1426, 1429 (D. Ariz. 1993) ("The RTC has come forward and presented testimony . . . affirmatively demonstrating that they took precautions to secure the confidentiality of the ATS memo and that the memo's leak remains inexplicable. . . . The Court finds that the RTC did not voluntarily waive any attorney-client privilege it would have possessed, but for the disclosure."); Suburban Sew 'N Sweep, Inc. v. Swiss-Bernina, Inc., 91 F.R.D. 254, 260 (N.D. Ill. 1981) ("[R]eview of the cases, and particularly of the evolving rule with respect to eavesdroppers, reveals that the privilege is not simply inapplicable any time that confidentiality is breached, as plaintiffs claim, and that the relevant consideration is the intent of the defendants to maintain the confidentiality of the documents as manifested in the precautions they took.").

wise discoverable.[23] The court will then accept supporting affidavits[24] or hold an evidentiary hearing during which testimony is taken. If, at the end of this hearing process, the privilege proponent fails to convince the presiding judge that the communications are protected by the privilege, the judge will deny the claims and order the documents produced.

Under early common law, when the confidentiality requirement was strictly enforced, if the client believed the judge's decision was erroneous, the client had to refuse to produce the documents, stand in contempt of court, and appeal the judge's contempt citation.[25] In the absence of judicial cooperation, the client might seek the extraordinary writ of

---

23. For a thorough discussion of how a privilege index or log is prepared, what should be included in it, why each item is necessary to the privilege resolution process, and a sample index, *see* PAUL R. RICE, ATTORNEY-CLIENT PRIVILEGE IN THE UNITED STATES, § 11:7 (2d ed. 1999). If an objection is made to a discovery request on the ground of scope, the court must resolve that claim first so that it is clear that the documents are otherwise discoverable. If the objection is not upheld, thereby making the document responsive to the discovery demand, the privilege proponent is then required to file an index of claims. *See* United States v. Philip Morris Inc., 347 F.3d 951, 954 (D.C. Cir. 2003) *and* FED. R. CIV. P. 26(b)(5).

24. For an explanation of the evidentiary support that must be filed and a sample affidavit, *see* PAUL R. RICE, ATTORNEY-CLIENT PRIVILEGE IN THE UNITED STATES, §§ 11:10 - 11:12 (2d ed. 1999).

25. Only final judgments are appealable, 28 U.S.C. § 1291. Therefore, even after being held in contempt, the citation, unless the citation were for criminal contempt, was not immediately appealable. Absent exceptional circumstances (justifying writs of mandamus or prohibition), appellate review could only be sought after the action had been tried and final judgment entered. Cobbledick v. United States, 309 U.S. 323 (1940). *See generally* PAUL R. RICE, ATTORNEY-CLIENT PRIVILEGE IN THE UNITED STATES, §§ 11:26-27 (2d ed. 1999). Alternatively, if certain exceptional conditions were present, the party might convince the judge to stay the execution of his order and certify the question for appellate review. Immediate appeals of interlocutory orders in civil cases is provided for in 28 U.S.C. § 1292(b). The district court must certify, within 10 days after entry of the order, that: (1) the order involves "a controlling question of law"; (2) there is a "substantial difference of opinion" on the question of law; and (3) "an immediate appeal from the order may materially advance the ultimate termination of the litigation." This certification can be either at the request of a party or by the court on its own motion. The certification procedure is entirely discretionary. *See* Quantum Corp. v. Tandon Corp., 940 F.2d 642 (Fed. Cir. 1991) (denial of bifurcation of infringement and damage issues at trial); Isaacson v. Keck, Mahin & Cate, 875 F. Supp. 478, 480-81 (N.D. Ill. 1994) ("In the instant case, the court decided the issue based upon the materials before it. In declining to certify the question, the court reasoned that the case was currently two years of age and not even close to being ready for trial. The

prohibition to stop the process from going forward and preserve the confidentiality that the judge's order would otherwise destroy. This process was necessary in order to keep the privilege claims from becoming moot and, therefore, not subject to appellate review, even if the judge's order was erroneous.[26]

Parties were increasingly unwilling to stand in contempt of court, fearing that it would offend the judge who would be presiding over their subsequent trial. Judicial practices were left unchecked without appellate review as the early common law practice of standing in contempt waned, because the attorney-client privilege became a concern subordinate to the parties' desire to remain in judicial good graces.

Two practices emerged from this development. First, appellate courts ignored the loss of confidentiality and reviewed the orders if a judgment was appealed.[27] The second practice was more attenuated and less ob-

---

court found certification would only prolong the life of the litigation. The court further reasoned that the law was not unclear on the question.").

26. *See generally* PAUL R. RICE, ATTORNEY-CLIENT PRIVILEGE IN THE UNITED STATES, §§ 11:31-33 (2d ed. 1999).

27. Ignoring the loss of confidentiality, the courts looked at the problem as a waiver question. They concluded that compliance with a judicial order cannot fairly be construed as a waiver of the attorney-client privilege protection. *See, e.g.*, Gov't Guarantee Fund of Republic of Finland v. Hyatt Corp., 182 F.R.D. 182 (D. V.I. 1998) ("This Court agrees with Hyatt that the compelled production does not constitute a waiver for other lawsuits. The attorney-client privilege is not destroyed by disclosure of protected information to an outside party which is done only under the compulsion of a court order. . . . Similarly, production of privileged materials in one action pursuant to a court order does not constitute a waiver of the privilege for other lawsuits."); Nobelpharma AB v. Implant Innovations, 930 F. Supp. 1241, 1259-60 (N.D. Ill. 1996) ("3i argues that 'this entire issue has been waived since [NP] offered the subject of these very same communications.'. . . This Court rejects 3i's argument because NP offered the testimony after the fact, after Green's testimony. NP could not waive the issue retroactively."); Laxalt v. McClatchy, 116 F.R.D. 438, 455 (D. Nev. 1987) ("[B]y complying with the order of this Court that she refresh her recollection with such privileged documents as necessary, the deponent will not waive the work product or attorney-client privileges."); Studiengesellschaft Kohle mbH v. Hovamont Corp., No. 77 Civ. 4722 (RWS) (S.D.N.Y. Nov. 17, 1980) (LEXIS, Genfed library, Dist. file) ("The record reveals that [the] documents were produced in a good faith effort to comply with prior rulings of the Magistrate regarding the boundaries of the attorney-client privilege. Such good faith compliance with a judicial order is not the same as voluntary partial disclosure, which can constitute a general waiver of related communications. . . . Attempts to comply with court orders ought not to be penalized by subsequent judicial transformation into voluntary waivers.").

viously related to the privilege resolution process. In subsequent litigation involving the client who had been ordered to produce the privileged documents at the first trial, that client was permitted to raise the same privilege claim for the same documents when those documents were sought in a second discovery process.[28]

Although the concept of res judicata would not preclude the subsequent assertion of these claims because discovery orders in the pretrial process are not final decisions and different parties are involved in the subsequent action, collateral estoppel could have been adjusted to preclude these reassertions when the claims had been fairly heard, decided under the same substantive principles, and definitively resolved. Aside from such doctrinal preclusions, however, the client's compliance with the former disclosure orders should have destroyed the confidentiality upon which the subsequent privilege claims must be premised. The courts' apparent lack of concern with confidentiality should carry over to the enhanced possibilities that confidentiality can be breached with the use of e-mail without losing the protection of the privilege.

c.   The unauthorized agent exception

A common example of a court-imposed exception to the confidentiality requirement for corporate clients involves an employee who makes unauthorized disclosures of confidential corporate attorney-client communications to third parties. Because the corporation did not authorize the employee to make these disclosures, courts, over time, ignored the loss of confidentiality, reasoning that it would be unfair to hold the corporation responsible for the unauthorized disclosures of its employees.[29]

---

28. *See* Rattner v. Netburn, 1989 WL 223059, at *9 (S.D.N.Y. June 20, 1989) ("If a party withholds a document from disclosure on the basis of privilege and, on motion of its adversary, the Court holds that the document is not privileged, the resulting disclosure of the document will not be deemed a waiver of the privilege for purposes of other lawsuits.").

29. *See, e.g.*, Crabb v. KFC Nat'l Mgmt. Co., 952 F.2d 403, 1992 WL 1321, at *2 (6th Cir. 1992) (because adequate effort to preserve confidentiality were made, the possession of a privileged document by an ex-employee was excused); Bus. Integration Servs., Inc. v. AT&T Corp., 2007 U.S. Dist. LEXIS 96142, *4-5 (S.D.N.Y. Feb. 4, 2008) (Magistrate found a waiver because a corporate official had voluntarily disclosed the content of attorney communications. Decision was reversed and remanded because the magistrate had not determined that the official had theauthority to waive the defendant's attorney-client privilege.); United States ex rel. Mayman v. Martin Marietta Corp., 886 F. Supp. 1243 (D. Md. 1995)

The logic these courts employed is curious, for two reasons. First and most obvious, it ignores an ostensibly essential element of the privilege—that is, confidentiality. Second, it flies in the face of the doctrine of respondeat superior. Because the corporation (1) voluntarily hired the individuals, (2) knowingly assigned them responsibilities that necessitated access to the privileged communications, (3) benefited from this delegation and access, and (4) could reasonably have anticipated this occurrence, it is not clear why the same factors that prompt those courts to hold corporations responsible for the consequences of an employee's negligence do not also compel the same assumption of responsibility vis-a-vis privileged communications.[30] Regardless, this precedent should result in the continued protection of e-mail communications that are forwarded by employees to third parties outside the appropriate corporate circles of confidentiality.

d.   *Inadvertent disclosures—the "oops" rule*

Burgeoning court dockets, expanded discovery, and judicial efforts to manage the pretrial process by shortening discovery periods with so-called "rocket dockets" have prompted further erosion of the confidentiality requirement. Mistakes are inevitable in these truncated discovery proceedings, particularly when massive numbers of communications have to be screened and produced, or withheld on grounds such as

---

(trusted employee stole document upon departure after certifying that he had returned all company property); Resolution Trust Corp. v. Dean, 813 F. Supp. 1426, 1429 (D. Ariz. 1993) (despite efforts to preserve confidentiality, present or past employees leaked memorandum); Apex Mun. Fund v. N-Group Secs., 841 F. Supp. 1423 (S.D. Tex. 1993); Allen v. Burns Fry, Ltd., 1987 WL 12199, at *2 (N.D. Ill. June 4, 1987) (without authorization the ex-employee left with a privileged document); In re Grand Jury Proceeding Involving Berkley & Co., 466 F. Supp. 863, 868 (D. Minn. 1979) (former employee stole document and disclosed it); O'Leary v. Purcell, 108 F.R.D. 641 (M.D. N.C. 1985) (ex-employee left with privileged document that employer did not attempt to retrieve); Southwire Co. v. Essex Group, Inc., 570 F. Supp. 643 (N.D. Ill. 1983) ; Levin v. C.O.M.B. Co., 469 N.W.2d 512, 516 n.4 (Minn. Ct. App. 1991) ("[T]he company's delay in objecting to use of the letter did not waive the privilege given the former employee's surreptitious actions [in taking the communication and sending it to an employee of the opposing side].").

30. *See generally* PAUL R. RICE, ATTORNEY-CLIENT PRIVILEGE IN THE UNITED STATES, §§ 4:25 et seq. (2d ed. 1999).

privilege, and lengthy privilege logs with supporting affidavits have to be prepared. The risks of inadvertently disclosing e-mail or other electronic communications increased due to the broader distribution of e-mail and the ease with which it can be forwarded to new recipients. Courts have developed varied approaches to inadvertent disclosures concerning non-electronic communications, which likely will be expanded to the e-evidence context.[31] A review of these approaches follows.[32]

Three distinct approaches to the question of whether an inadvertent disclosure waives the attorney-client privilege have emerged from judicial decisions. Under the minority "strict confidentiality" view, any disclosure, including an inadvertent disclosure, is deemed a waiver of the attorney-client privilege.[33] A second approach, also a minority view,

---

31. In United States v. Rigas, 281 F. Supp. 2d 733 (S.D.N.Y. 2003), for example, the government had obtained copies of computer hard drives used by corporate employees. To make this information available to the entire staff, the assistant U.S. attorney directed technology personnel to install hard drives in government computers that gave access to users, but prevented additions or deletions from the drives. In this process a government paralegal's files containing confidential information and communications had inadvertently been copied onto one of the hard drives. When copies of these hard drives were produced to the defendant, these confidential communications were disclosed. This disclosure was excused because efforts had been taken to make the system secure by giving access only to authorized personnel with security clearance and storing everything in private, password-protected accounts on the network.

32. Fed. R. Civ. P. 26 (a)(5)(B) recognize a "clawback" provision that permits inadvertently disclosed communications to be retrieved by a producing party, but that rule does not control whether the disclosure itself waives attorney-client privilege protections. That determination is made pursuant to Rule 501 of the Federal Rules of Evidence, a provision that leaves privilege questions to common law principles interpreted in light of reason and fairness.

33. See, e.g., Sealed Case, 877 F.2d 976, 980 (D.C. Cir. 1989) ("Even assuming Company's disclosure was due to 'bureaucratic error,' which we take to be a euphemism that necessarily implies human error, that unfortunate lapse simply reveals that someone in the company and thereby Company itself (since it can only act through its employees) was careless with the confidentiality of its privileged communications. Normally the amount of care taken to ensure confidentiality reflects the importance of that confidentiality to the holder of the privilege. To hold, as we do, that an inadvertent disclosure will waive the privilege imposes a self-governing restraint on the freedom with which organizations such as corporations, unions, and the like label documents related to communications with counsel as privileged. To readily do so creates a greater risk of 'inadvertent' disclosure by someone

employs an "intent" test.[34] Under this approach, the attorney-client privilege may be waived only if the disclosing party had the specific intent to waive the privilege. Absent some degree of intent, waiver is not possible.[35] The last approach, the majority view, employs the "case-specific" test. This approach focuses on the totality of the circumstances. The client is permitted to raise, belatedly, the privilege claim and have the document returned, provided the client can establish that (1) reasonable efforts had been taken to avoid such mistakes, (2) the errors had been timely discovered, (3) expeditious efforts had been taken to correct them, and (4) the opposing party would not be unfairly preju-

---

and thereby the danger that the 'waiver' will extend to all related matters, perhaps causing grave injury to the organization. But that is as it should be. Otherwise, there is a temptation to seek artificially to expand the content of privileged matter. In other words, if a client wishes to preserve the privilege, it must treat the confidentiality of attorney-client communications like jewels—if not crown jewels. Short of court-compelled disclosure . . . or other equally extraordinary circumstances [*e.g.*, communications acquired by third parties despite all possible precautions] we will not distinguish between various degrees of 'voluntariness' in waivers of the attorney-client privilege."); Carter v. Gibbs, 909 F.2d 1450, 1451 (Fed. Cir. 1990); Wichita Land Cattle Co. v. Am. Fed. Bank, F.S.B., 148 F.R.D. 456, 457 (D. D.C. 1992); FDIC v. Singh, 140 F.R.D. 252, 253 (D. Me. 1992).

34. *See, e.g.*, Alldread v. Grenada, 988 F.2d 1425, 1434 (5th Cir. 1993) ("In our view, an analysis which permits the court to consider the circumstances surrounding a disclosure on a case-by-case basis is preferable to a per se rule of waiver. This analysis serves the purpose of the attorney-client privilege, the protection of communications which the client fully intended would remain confidential, yet at the same time will not relieve those claiming the privilege of the consequences of their carelessness if the circumstances surrounding the disclosure do not clearly demonstrate that continued protection is warranted."); Berg Elecs. v. Molex, Inc., 875 F. Supp. 261, 34 U.S.P.Q.2d 1315 (D. Del. 1995) ("The court finds the rule of law . . . that look[s] to intent best serves the interests of the attorney-client privilege, as it protects the client from the apprehension that consultations with their legal advisors will be inadvertently disclosed and applies the privilege in a way that is predictable and certain."); Georgetown Manor, Inc. v. Ethan Allen, Inc., 753 F. Supp. 936, 938 (S.D. Fla. 1991); Monarch Cement Co. v. Lone Star Indus. Inc., 132 F.R.D. 558, 559 (D. Kan. 1990) ("Waiver imports an intentional relinquishment or abandonment of a known right, and to hold that waiver could occur through inadvertence would be the antithesis of this concept.").

35. Under this approach, if waiver is not possible without an intent to waive, the concept of inadvertence is made irrelevant. Intent has been required for waiver in a number of states. *See generally* PAUL R. RICE, ATTORNEY-CLIENT PRIVILEGE: STATE LAW, § 9:19 (Rice Publ'g 2004).

diced by the belated suppression.[36] The majority approach has been termed the inadvertence exception to the rule of waiver by voluntary disclosure. Unlike stolen documents and documents disclosed by employees in bad faith, these disclosures were voluntary, albeit unknowing. Nevertheless, courts have demonstrated very little reluctance in giving parties a pass on the confidentiality requirement when they make an honest mistake. Even though the attorney-client privilege has not been codified in the Federal Rules of Evidence, a rule recognizing the exception to waiver from inadvertent disclosures has been approved and will likely become law on Dec. 1, 2008.[37]

e.   *Disclosures under protective orders or with reservations*

Beyond merely ignoring the confidentiality requirement, courts have affirmatively promoted the loss of confidentiality by using protective

---

36. *See, e.g.*, Lois Sportwear, U.S.A., Inc. v. Levi Strauss & Co., 104 F.R.D. 103, 105 (S.D.N.Y. 1985):

> The elements which go into [the determination of whether the release of documents is a waiver or an excusable mistake] include the *reasonableness of the precautions to prevent* inadvertent disclosure, the *time taken to rectify the error,* the *scope of the discovery* and the *extent of the disclosure.* There is, of course, an overreaching issue of fairness and the protection of an appropriate privilege which, of course, must be judged against the care or negligence with which the privilege is guarded . . . .

See generally PAUL R. RICE, ATTORNEY-CLIENT PRIVILEGE IN THE UNITED STATES, §§ 9:70-77 (2d ed. 1999).

37. Proposed New Rule 502 provides in part:
Rule 502. Attorney-Client Privilege and Work Product; Limitations on Waiver
The following provisions apply, in the circumstances set out, to disclosure of a communication or information covered by the attorney-client privilege or work product protection.
. . . .
(B) Inadvertent disclosure. – When made in a federal proceeding or to a federal office or agency, the disclosure does not operate as a waiver in a federal or state proceeding if:
(1) the disclosure in inadvertent;
(2) the holder of the privilege or protection took reasonable steps to prevent disclosure; and
(3) the holder promptly took reasonable steps to rectify the error, including (if applicable) following FED. R. CIV. P. 26(b)(5)(B).

orders.[38] Protective orders facilitate the rapid production of massive num-

---

38. Navajo Nation v. Peabody Coal Co., 2001 WL 312117, at *2 (Fed. Cir. Mar. 29, 2001) ("The court then issued an order on November 7, 1996 (the 'Order') referring to the agreement reached between the parties during the November 6 hearing. The Order indicated that Peabody would release all documents presently in dispute, one of which was the Sullivan memorandum. The Order stated that Peabody could stamp the documents as 'confidential' and could 'assert claims of privilege with regard to certain documents.' The Order specifically indicated that 'production of documents for purposes of the present case shall not constitute a waiver of any right of Peabody to raise a claim of privilege as to these documents in any other present or future litigation.'"). The protective order is a mechanism through which the presiding judge anticipates problems and assures parties in advance that negative consequences can be avoided in the event of their occurrence, if certain conditions are met. Such orders are provided for in FED. R. CIV. P. 26(c).

> (c) Protective Orders. Upon motion by a party or by the person from whom discovery is sought, and for good cause shown, the court in which the action is pending or alternatively, on matters relating to a deposition, the court in the district where the deposition is to be taken may make any order which justice requires to protect a party or person from annoyance, embarrassment, oppression, or undue burden or expense, including one or more of the following: (1) that the discovery not be had; (2) that the discovery may be had only on specified terms and conditions, including a designation of the time or place; (3) that the discovery may be had only by a method of discovery other than that selected by the party seeking discovery; (4) that certain matters not be inquired into, or that the scope of the discovery be limited to certain matters; (5) that discovery be conducted with no one present except persons designated by the court; (6) that a deposition after being sealed be opened only by order of the court; (7) that a trade secret or other confidential research, development, or commercial information not be disclosed or be disclosed only in a designated way; (8) that the parties simultaneously file specified documents or information enclosed in sealed envelopes to be opened as directed by the court.

See, e.g., Bayer AG v. Barr Lab., 1994 WL 705331, at *1, 33 U.S.P.Q.2d 1655 (S.D.N.Y. 1994) ("The Protective Order contemplated two distinct and consecutive phases of document production: (1) the production of documents for inspection by opposing counsel, and (2) the formal production of documents requested by the inspecting party. The order also contains a clause providing that 'production of documents and things for purpose of inspection and copying shall not constitute waiver of confidentiality, privilege or immunity.'"); United States v. Derr, 1993 WL 313132, at *2 (N.D. Cal. Aug. 6, 1993) (after documents were inadvertently disclosed, client sought return of documents and protective order prohibiting their use in litigation); James Julian, Inc. v. Raytheon Co., 93 F.R.D. 138, 140 n.1 (D. Del.

bers of documents by assuring parties that privileges will not be waived if privileged communications are mistakenly produced, as long as a prompt privilege claim is made as soon as the inadvertent production is discovered. Sometimes protective orders have even sanctioned the disclosure of privileged communications without waiving the privilege claim if the documents are marked "Attorney-Client Privileged" before being produced. These types of orders amount to a judicially approved equivalent of the "oops" rule before the mistake is made.[39]

Parties have attempted to informally do what protective orders formally promote, i.e., disclosing communications without the traditional consequences of disclosure. For example, many parties have disclosed privileged materials when government agencies sought them in exchange for regulatory concessions.[40] To preserve the privileged status of docu-

---

1982) ("Protected Documents and the information contained therein or derived therefrom may be used at any hearing in this case, subject to any further Protective Order which this Court might, for good cause, then enter, and provided that any use or filing of Protected Documents shall not constitute a waiver by the using or filing party of any attorney-client privilege, work product privilege, confidentiality or other applicable privilege. By making available any such protected documents, or information contained therein or derived therefrom, the parties will not have waived, and do not waive, the right to assert any such privilege or to object to the admissibility of any such Protected Documents into evidence in any other hearing or proceeding in this litigation."); In re Westinghouse Elec. Corp. Uranium Contracts Litig., 76 F.R.D. 47, app. A, at 59-62 (W.D. Pa. 1977); United States v. Am. Tel. & Tel. Co., reproduced and discussed in BRAZIL, HAZARD & RICE, MANAGING COMPLEX LITIGATION: A PRACTICAL GUIDE TO THE USE OF SPECIAL MASTERS, pp. 94-97, app. 9, at 180-83 (Am. Bar. Found. 1983).

39. *See* Cardiac Pacemakers, Inc. v. St. Jude Med., Inc., 2001 WL 699850, at *1 (S.D. Ind. May 29, 2001) ("23. Inadvertent Production. The inadvertent production of any document or information during discovery in the Litigation shall be without prejudice to any claim that such material is privileged under the attorney-client or other privilege, or protected from discovery as work product. No party or entity shall be held to have waived any rights by such inadvertent production so long as the Recipient Party is notified within 30 days of the discovery of such inadvertent production. Upon written request by the inadvertently producing party, the Recipient Party shall (even if the Recipient Party disagrees that the document is privileged) return all copies of the document and not use the information in the document for any purpose until further order of the Court.").

40. *See, e.g.,* Westinghouse Elec. Corp. v. Republic of Philippines, 951 F.2d 1414, 1427 (3d Cir. 1991) (voluntary disclosure waived attorney-client privilege protection even though third party agreed not to disclose the communication to anyone else); Griffith v. Davis, 161 F.R.D. 687, 698 (C.D. Cal. 1995) (After finding that voluntary disclosure waived attorney-client privilege protection, court noted:

ments being disclosed so that broader disclosures, either to the agency or to third parties in future litigation, would not be required, the party making disclosures would do so with the express reservation that no privilege claim was waived by disclosure.

A majority of courts have rejected such informal arrangements.[41] They would not permit parties to accomplish, independently, through reservations, what the court has the authority to sanction with protective orders. Courts saw these reservations as a form of limited waiver that was overwhelmingly rejected when directly addressed,[42] but indirectly sanctioned when protective orders were employed. They saw reservations as an example of a client making intentional disclosures for tactical advantages in order to avoid the consequences—wanting to "have his cake and eat it too." Clients were not permitted to say one thing and do another, even though that is precisely what the courts themselves were doing with the concept of confidentiality in many other contexts.

"This is true despite any agreement defendants may have had with the IRS regarding the 'restricted' nature of the memorandum."); Fox v. Cal.Sierra Fin. Servs., 120 F.R.D. 520, 527 (N.D. Cal. 1988) ("I find that where, as here, information has been voluntarily and selectively disclosed to the SEC without steps to protect the privileged nature of such information, fairness requires a finding that the attorney-client privilege has been waived as to the disclosed information and all information on the same subject."); Teachers Ins. & Annuity Ass'n v. Shamrock Broad. Co., 521 F. Supp. 638, 644-45 (S.D.N.Y. 1981) ("I am of the opinion that disclosure to the SEC should be deemed to be a complete waiver of the attorney-client privilege unless the right to assert the privilege in subsequent proceedings is specifically reserved at the time the disclosure is made.").

41. *Compare* United States v. Miller, 600 F.2d 498, 500-01 (5th Cir. 1979) (seeming to honor client's reservation of right to assert privilege at trial but finding waiver when client raised "good faith" defense) *and* Miller v. Haulmark Transp. Sys., 104 F.R.D. 442, 445 (E.D. Pa. 1984) (court denied that privilege was waived by production of confidential documents at deposition because "[a]n objection was made to the discovery of the document at the time it was produced and marked as an exhibit to the deposition.") *with* Malco Mfg. Co. v. Elco Corp., 307 F. Supp. 1177, 1179 (E.D. Pa. 1969) (The court held that "[a] statement purporting to reserve a claim of privilege cannot be given effect when it is followed by statements or conduct which, in fact and law, constitute a waiver of such privilege.") *and* W.R. Grace & Co. v. Pullman, Inc., 446 F. Supp. 771, 775 (W.D. Okla. 1976) (refused to give any effect to reservation that accompanied production of documents because it "unnecessarily complicates what is designed to be a simplified discovery procedure.").

42. *See, e.g.*, Permian Corp. v. United States, 665 F.2d 1214, 1220 (D.C. Cir. 1981).

Courts are not likely to alter their view of reservations, even with the dramatic increase in electronic evidence and e-mail communications. Instead, the increased volume and complexity of e-mail communications will operate to create greater pressures on courts to employ protective orders in an effort to expedite the discovery process.

In sum, courts have long ignored the confidentiality of communications, and the days of Wigmore's strict confidentiality requirement are gone. The requirement of confidentiality survives predominantly as only a condition precedent to the privilege's creation.[43] Therefore, as long as secrecy was subjectively intended when the communication occurred and "reasonable" efforts were made to preserve that confidentiality, it is unlikely that courts will hold that the expectation of confidentiality is objectively unreasonable, even though the communication occurred over the Internet. Although the attorney-client privilege has not been codified in the Federal Rules of Evidence, a rule recognizing the limited value of agreements among parties while approving of the broader use of protective orders will become law on Dec. 1, 2008, unless objected to by Congress.[44]

---

43. Universally, state and federal courts define the privilege with the element of confidentiality, but quickly disregard it in practice when it is perceived as not serving the interests of fairness or furthering the ends of the privilege.

44. Proposed New Rule 502 provides in part:

Rule 502. Attorney-Client Privilege and Work Product; Limitations on Waiver

The following provisions apply, in the circumstances set out, to disclosure of a communication or information covered by the attorney-client privilege or work product protection.

. . . .

(d) Controlling effect of a court order.—A federal court may order that the privilege or protection is not waived by disclosure connected with the litigation pending before the court – in which event the disclosure is also not a waiver in any other federal or state proceeding.

(e) Controlling effect of a party agreement.—An agreement on the effect of disclosure in a federal proceeding is binding only on the parties to the agreement, unless it is incorporated into a court order.

3. Confidentiality Must Be Maintained and Documented— The Increasing Problem of Outside Agents Functioning as Employees

As explained above, the common law concept of confidentiality (equated with secrecy) has been ignored, if not abandoned, in many contexts. Even though the requirement of secrecy is still often espoused by courts, it is honored more in its violation. As previously discussed, this is reflected in 1) inadvertent disclosures that do not waive privilege, 2) disclosures pursuant to protected orders that do not waive privilege, 3) theft of corporate documents by former corporate employees that courts ignore for waiver purpose, and 4) courts permitting privilege to be claimed for documents that were produced in previous litigation pursuant to court order. The circulation of privileged communications within corporate organizations after the privilege's inception may also become another example of courts ignoring the loss of confidentiality. This is evidenced by the spotty manner in which courts enforce the confidentiality requirement by not insisting that the corporate responsibilities of each recipient of a privileged document be identified and that those responsibilities be tied to the content of each communication on which privilege is claimed.[45] It is also demonstrated by courts ignoring the frequent absence of any verification that secondary distribution by original recipients was limited to those with a need to know within the scope of their corporate responsibilities.[46] However, until the confidentiality requirement has been formally abolished, attorneys must be aware of the requirement and establish company policies that are disseminated, discussed, and enforced, and attend to the requirement when claims are asserted in judicial proceedings by providing necessary explanations through affidavits of knowledgeable individuals.[47]

---

45. Under the most popular subject matter test for deciding who personifies the corporate client for attorney-client privilege purposes, only those employees who need to see the confidential communication in the scope of the employment responsibilities may be privy to it. P.R. RICE, ATTORNEY-CLIENT PRIVILEGE IN THE UNITED STATES §§ 4:11-14, *To Whose Communications Does the Privilege Extend – Who Personifies the Corporate Client?* (2d ed. 1999).

46. This would have to be accomplished either through established company policies or affidavits from each recipient verifying that no further distribution has been made.

47. PAUL R. RICE, ATTORNEY-CLIENT PRIVILEGE IN THE UNITED STATES, § 11:10, *Providing Evidentiary Support for Factual Foundations* (2d ed. 1999).

Both primary and secondary distribution,[48] however, are not limited to corporate employees. For a variety of reasons, corporations increasingly outsource functions to third-party consultants. They are turning to these consultants to perform not only specialty services requiring particular expertise not possessed in-house, but also services that once were performed in-house by corporate employees. These agents have been referred to as "functional employees.[49] As a result, courts increasingly find outside public relations firms and advertising agencies being listed as copyees on the face of confidential attorney-client communications, or (more difficult to detect) receiving those communications as secondary distributees of the original recipients. In the consolidated *Microsoft* cases,[50] public relations firms assisted lawyers in putting a public face on developments in pending litigation. In the consolidated *Vioxx* cases,[51] public relations firms and advertising agencies were assisting Merck in marketing Vioxx before Merck was sued and had voluntarily withdrawn Vioxx from the market.

Many corporations have attempted to expand the circle of confidentiality to outside consultants. Through e-mails, confidential internal communications have been circulated to outside consultants in either of two ways. The first, and more common, form is e-mails between corporate employees and corporate lawyers (both in-house and outside counsel), to which outside consultants have been added as either addressees or copyees. The second form of communication is direct e-mail exchanges between corporate in-house lawyers and employees of the consulting firms.

Under earlier common law principles, the first form of communication would have waived the privilege protection. Because of the strict application of the confidentiality requirement and the limited definition

---

48. Primary distributees are those listed in the header of an e-mail as receiving copies of the communication. Secondary distributees are those to whom the e-mail has subsequently circulated.

49. In re Currency Conversion Fee, 2003 WL 22389169, at *2 (S.D.N.Y. 2003). These outside consultants are performing functions essential to the daily operations of the corporation. They are not consultants who have been hired by either the corporation or its attorneys because their assistance is necessary in either the seeking or rendering of legal advice.

50. In re Microsoft Antitrust Litig., MDL No. 1332 (D. Md.).

51. In re Vioxx Products Liability Litig., MDL No. 1657 (E.D. La.).

of who personified the corporate client, advice would first have to have been sought from legal counsel, and then other corporate employees would have to have transmitted to those outsiders whatever limitations the company's control group agreed to adopt (based on the advice of counsel). The third parties could not be copied on the attorney-client communications, and the content of the attorney's advice could not have been directly disclosed in the subsequent communications (although the general tenor of the advice may have been obvious from the content of the corporate decisions communicated).

The second type of communication would not have been protected unless the outside consultants were viewed as agents of either the attorney or the client, assisting in either the obtaining or rendering of legal advice, and that acceptance would have been based on the demonstrated need for the outside assistance. In the absence of such an agency relationship, in-house corporate counsel's correspondence with third parties would have been seen as the equivalent of any other corporate employee communicating with a third party regarding limitations the corporation wished to impose on the services being sought.

Historically, courts have, in theory, espoused a necessity standard for disseminating confidential attorney-client communications to agents.[52] The practice of distributing confidential communications outside the corporate family, however, is different in kind and often different in purpose as well.

It is *different in kind* because, even though outside consultants function like employees, they are not employees; they do not have the same ties to the corporation and are not as familiar with or committed to the conventions followed by the corporation to preserve confidentiality. Circulation to outside consultants is *different in purpose* in that the circulation is often for the purpose of *advising the consultants* rather than assisting the corporate client in communicating to the lawyers in order to obtain the most informed advice, or assisting the lawyer in rendering the advice sought.

Most troublesome about the circulation to outside consultants for the purpose of advising them as they work with corporate employees is that there is no apparent limitation on the ability of corporations to share their confidential communications with third parties, other than the facts

---

52. *See* Paul R. Rice, Attorney-Client Privilege in the United States, §§ 3:4 and 4:2 (2d ed. 1999).

that (1) the content of the communications must relate to the services they are providing, and (2) the services must be part of some undefined cooperative effort with corporate personnel. Permitting such an expansion of the concept of confidentiality makes the concept less meaningful and less predictable. While it may already have been rendered relatively meaningless through other practices previously discussed, until it has been abolished, circulation to outside consultants must be limited.

Communicating directly with outside consultants may be more efficient, and perhaps even more effective, but convenience and efficiency have never been a sufficient justification for creating or extending privilege protections. Communications with outside consultants should receive the protection of the attorney-client privilege only when those communications are shown to have been essential to the informed advice sought from corporate counsel and would not otherwise have occurred without the protection.

Corporate lawyers are not the lawyers of the consultants. They are the lawyers of the corporate entity, and the consultants are not part of that entity. Usually consultants are part of a separate entity. Consultants seldom have been given the authority to speak or act for the corporation without its express written consent. Generally, every action consultants take must be proposed to the corporation, vetted within the organization (which would include screening by its lawyers), and approved in writing. A corporation's decision to give consent to consultants' proposed courses of action is usually based on its communications with its legal counsel. These communications, however, are not informing consultants on decisions to be made by them. Consequently, there is no need for them to be injected into the confidential relationship. If consultants need to be informed of restrictions on their services that are recommended by legal counsel, those restrictions can be conveyed to them by other corporate personnel after corporate officers and directors have decided to follow the advice.

If legal counsel contacts outside consultants for information before rendering advice because they may possess important information, there is no reason to believe that those consultants would be less candid if their communications were not protected by the corporation's attorney-client privilege. This is particularly true when continued use of the consultants' services depends on both their candor and their compliance with corporate directives and legal norms. If we believe the most fundamental principle of all privilege law—that privileges should not be created or expanded unless their protection is necessary to achieve a desired social end that otherwise would not be possible[53]—there is no justification under that rationale for extending the privilege to outside consultants, particularly those who are only being advised rather than assisting in the obtaining or giving of that advice.

It is questionable whether even the existence of the corporate privilege can be justified under this standard.[54] Therefore, the fact that parallels can be identified between the positions of outside consultants and full-time employees is hardly a justification for expanding the suppression of relevant evidence through the privilege. If anything, the facial inapplicability of the privilege's rationale to outside consultants strongly suggests that the original extension of the privilege to corporations was illogical.

Apparently, however, that conclusion has escaped many courts. Perhaps it is not as obvious as one might think. Throughout the federal judiciary a number of cases have considered, and many have accepted,

---

53. United States v. Nixon, 418 U.S. 683, 710 (1974) ("Exceptions to the demand for every man's evidence are not lightly created nor expansively construed, for they are in derogation of the search for truth."); In re Horowitz, 482 F.2d 72, 81 (2d Cir. 1973) ("[A]s 'an obstacle to the investigation of the truth . . . [the attorney-client privilege] ought to be strictly confined within the narrowest possible limits consistent with the logic of its principles.'" (quoting 8 WIGMORE, EVIDENCE § 2291 at 554) (rev. ed. 1961)).

54. The logical problem with extending the privilege to corporate entities has been that the privilege protection is given to a fictitious legal entity that cannot talk, and the individuals who personify that entity (its officers and employees) are given no direct protection by the privilege. As a consequence, they do not control either its assertion or waiver. Therefore, it is questionable whether the goal of more candid communications is achieved through the corporate privilege protection. PAUL R. RICE, ATTORNEY-CLIENT PRIVILEGE IN THE UNITED STATES, § 4:10, *Should the Attorney-Client Privilege Be Available to Corporations?* (2d ed. 1999). The applicability of the privilege to corporations has been questioned by one court. In Radiant Burners, Inc. v. American Gas Ass'n, 207 F. Supp. 771, 774 (N.D. Ill. 1962), Judge Clark held that the privilege was not applicable to corporations because members of their boards of directors served on other corporate boards. In this opinion, this overlap in board membership destroyed the confidentiality of communications in each corporation. Therefore, he refused to recognize the corporate attorney-client privilege. This decision was immediately reversed by the Seventh Circuit, Radiant Burners, Inc. v. American Gas Ass'n, 320 F.2d 314 (7th Cir. 1963), without directly addressing Judge Clark's confidentiality concerns.

the relaxation of the confidentiality requirement by sanctioning the application of the attorney-client privilege to communications disseminated to outside consultants.[55] None of these decisions, however, has explained why the expansion is necessary to the limited purpose of the privilege. If courts insist on continuing on this tack, they should at least impose a restriction through a standard, like the necessity standard, that theoretically limits circulation to all agents.

Aside from the apparently acceptable expansion of the circle of confidentiality, privilege proponents must be conscious of the second dimension of confidentiality when asserting privilege for documents circulated beyond the corporate entity. This is the problem of its preservation by those third parties. As the privilege holder must document that established confidentiality was preserved within the corporation by limiting secondary distribution to those with a need to know in the scope of

---

55. *See* In re Bieter Co., 16 F.3d 929 (8th Cir. 1994); DE Techs., Inc. v. Dell, Inc., 2006 WL 2548203, at *2 (W.D. Va. 2006); Residential Constructors, LLC v. Ace Prop. & Cas. Ins. Co., 2006 WL 3149362, at *15 (D. Nev. 2006); Neighborhood Dev. Collaborative v. Murphy, 233 F.R.D. 436, 2005 WL 3272711, at *5 (D. Md. 2005); Export-Import Bank of the U.S. v. Asia Pulp & Paper Co., Ltd., 232 F.R.D. 103, 113 (S.D.N.Y. 2005); Freeport McMoran Sulphur, LLC v. Mick Mullen Energy Equip. Resource, Inc., 2004 WL 1237450 (E.D. La. June 2, 2004); In re Bristol-Myers Squibb Securities Litig., 2003 U.S. Dist. LEXIS 26985, *12-15 (D. N.J. June 25, 2003); In re Currency Conversion Fee, 2003 WL 22389169, at *2 (S.D.N.Y. 2003); and In re Copper Market Antitrust Litig., 200 F.R.D. 213, 218 (S.D.N.Y. 2001). Outside the wisdom of expanding the circle of confidentiality to encompass consultants, the central issue with the expansion is whether it will be permitted only when the services of the consultant are shown to be something beyond the normal services for which one would contract. *See* Calvin Klein Trademark Trust v. Wachner, 198 F.R.D. 53, 55 (S.D.N.Y. 2000), where the court refused to broaden the privilege through this functional employee label to encompass employees of a public relations firm. The court based its decision on the fact that the firm had not "been performing functions materially different from those that any ordinary public relations firm would have performed . . . ." Similarly, in SR Int'l Bus. Ins. Co. v. World Trade Ctr. Properties, LLC, 2002 WL 1334821, at *2-3 (S.D.N.Y. June 19, 2002), the court refused to apply the "functional employee" exception to communications between an insurance broker and attorneys for the insured. Other courts, however, have extended the label to third parties because they performed the same functions as in-house employees. *See, e.g.*, Residential Constructors, LLC v. Ace Property & Cas. Ins. Co., 2006 WL 3149362 (D. Nev. Nov. 1, 2006), where the label was applied to an outside insurance adjuster. In a word, the case law is in conflict, and no inherently logical solution is apparent.

their corporate responsibilities, it has the same responsibility for those to whom it distributed its privileged documents. Outside agents could destroy the confidentiality as easily as inside agents and may be less conscious of the need to preserve. Therefore, if this issue is unaddressed by privilege proponents, all privilege claims circulated to outside consultants could be denied.

C. E-mail—An Extension of Existing Services and Technology

E-commerce and e-mail are extensions of telephone services and computer technologies that have been used and judicially approved for decades. All technologies pose threats to the confidentiality of communications. Their use, however, will not jeopardize privilege protections premised on the existence of that confidentiality.

Using computer terminals to transmit communications between attorney and client is only the latest development in a long line of communications technologies that have posed practical challenges to confidentiality. Courts have universally accepted all prior technological developments and have found that the use of such technologies does not jeopardize the attorney-client privilege.

1. From Face-to-Face Communications to Letters

Communications by sealed letters were readily accepted by the courts as sufficiently confidential to preserve privileges that originally attached to those communications. Although these letters passed through many hands, were in the exclusive control of many people, and could have been unsealed, read and resealed, courts readily accepted this risk without question. Not a single case has been found where relinquishing control of a communication to the postal service destroyed confidentiality.

2. From Letters to Telephones

With the advent of telephone services, operators posed a constant threat to the confidentiality of telephone conversations between attorneys and clients. Because operators were connected to the call and had to transfer them physically, operators could, and often did, eavesdrop on telephone conversations. The potential for breach of confidentiality was also present for residential users on party lines.[56] The same problem exists within businesses or homes where there are multiple extensions, and on an even larger scale with mobile phones. Yet in none of these contexts have courts expressed concern for potential breaches of confidentiality.

Reasonable efforts to ensure the secrecy of communications were expected in less high-tech contexts. For example, speaking in the presence of others, leaving documents unattended in the presence of third parties, and speaking with the knowledge that third parties could be listening might serve to diminish a party's subjective expectation of confidentiality. But when the possibility of breaching confidentiality is less apparent, precautionary measures have not been considered imperative.

3.   From Telephones to Computers

Telephones permitted long-distance oral communications between attorneys and clients. Although this gave rise to the confidentiality problems previously discussed (multiplied by the number of operators through whom each call passed), courts have accepted and ignored the loss of confidentiality that may result. Computers connected to the Internet use the same modes of communication as telephones (telephone lines, fiber-optic cables, radio waves, etc.). Accordingly, the Internet represents an extension of the problems posed by telephone communications. Even though operators are no longer directly involved, the Internet poses increased concerns because, unlike the telephone, breaches of confidentiality need not be contemporaneous with Internet communications. All Internet service providers (ISPs) record each communication for retransmission, and both the sender and the recipient have records of each communication on their systems. As a result, not only outside hackers but employees of the ISPs, and of senders and recipients, possess the ability to open or break into computer systems and retrieve past communications. The potential for breach is similar to the threat posed

---

56. The party line was a service provided to a number of customers who used the same line. Calls to individual customers were indicated by a designated number of rings. When the first customer was called, the telephone would ring once and pause; the second customer was called with two rings and a pause, and so on. While all customers heard the ringing of each call, only the appropriate customer was expected to answer. Any customer, however, could inappropriately listen in on calls on the party line. Again, no reported decision expressed any concern with regard to attorney-client communications transmitted over such lines.

by burglars who steal hard-copy communications, except that no physical breaking and entering takes place, and clients may not even be aware that their confidentiality has been breached. But interceptions of e-mail through fraudulent means or for fraudulent purposes has no effect on the privileged character of an e-mail transmission because such interceptions are illegal under the Electronic Communication Privacy Act of 1986.[57]

Moreover, the potential for breach has not prompted courts to conclude that clients' subjective expectations of confidentiality are objectively unreasonable.[58] Most businesses and law firms maintain their records on computer systems. Internet linkage to clients and research facilities has become a necessary part of modern business. Even the courts are beginning to rely extensively on electronic communications to conduct their business. A number of jurisdictions permit electronic filing of pleadings and motions. The Ninth Circuit approved service of process by e-mail in certain circumstances.[59] Given the extent to which electronic communications have become an integral part of day-to-day business, it is unlikely that the expectation of confidentiality on the Internet will be found unreasonable. This will continue to be the case even when parties do not use security technologies such as encryption.

E-mail presents distinct challenges. For example, many e-mail users send e-mail to predefined address groups instead of selecting individual recipients for an address list. This increases the potential for inadvertent disclosure because some members of a predefined group may not be included in the attorney-client relationship. Given that most jurisdictions employ the "case-specific" test to determine whether the privilege

---

57. 18 U.S.C. § 2511 (West 1998).

58. *See* McCook Metals L.L.C. v. Alcoa, Inc., 192 F.R.D. 242, 255 (N.D. Ill. 2000) (noting that e-mail communications should be analogized to and treated the same as other more traditional means of communication); Playboy Enters. v. Welles, 60 F. Supp. 2d, 1050, 1054 (S.D. Cal. 1999) ("Defendant's privacy and attorney-client privilege will be protected pursuant to the protocol outlined below, and Defendant's counsel will have an opportunity to control and review all of the recovered e-mails, and produce to Plaintiff only those documents that are relevant, responsive, and non-privileged."); Ill. St. Bar Ass'n, Op. 9610 (1997) (finding that, for purposes of lawyer's ethical duty to keep clients' confidences, e-mail provides expectation of privacy as reasonable as that provided by telephones).

59. *See* Rio Prop. Inc. v. Rio Int'l Interlink, No. CV-99-01653-PMP (9th Cir. 2002).

has been waived by disclosure, it is unlikely that inadvertent disclosures by e-mail will be any more likely to result in waiver than any other form of communication.[60]

E-mail communications also present confidentiality problems when the client communicates from the workplace with attorneys who represent the client individually. It is not clear, for example, whether employees who communicate with their lawyers through an e-mail account at work, on a network server that is owned and operated by the employer, can reasonably expect that the communication is confidential. As discussed in the following section, although courts have uniformly found that employers may not surreptitiously monitor their employees' personal communications, surveillance is permitted when it serves a business-related purpose.[61]

D.   Employees' Personal Expectation of Confidentiality in E-Mail Communications

The convenience of communicating over an employer's e-mail server has given rise to the difficult question of whether personal communications between an employee and the employee's attorney can be protected by the employee's attorney-client privilege. The key question is whether the client/employee can have a reasonable subjective expectation of confidentiality.

This question is equivalent to the issue of whether an employee can have an expectation of privacy in personal communications on a company's computer or Internet files. If he can, it would stand to reason that courts would also permit the attorney-client privilege to attach to an employee's communications with an attorney for the purpose of obtaining legal assistance when a subjective expectation of confidentiality is held by the employee.

The issue of the reasonableness of expectations of privacy was addressed by the Supreme Court in the context of the Fourth Amendment protection against unreasonable searches in *O'Connor v. Ortega*.[62] In that case, a doctor's private office was searched by representatives of a state hospital, and items were seized that were subsequently used in

---

60. *See* text at note 31, *supra*.

61. *See* Tiberino v. Spokane County, 13 P.3d 1104, 1108-09 (Wash. Ct. App. 2000) (while number of public employee's personal e-mails were discoverable, content of personal e-mails was not subject to disclosure).

62. 480 U.S. 709, 107 S. Ct. 1492, 94 L. Ed. 2d 714 (1987).

disciplinary proceedings. While acknowledging an employer's need and right to search workplace-related property (areas and items that are related to work and are generally within the employer's control), it noted the significant interests of employees in the personal items that they bring to the workplace and the need to balance those interests against the employer's needs.

Not everything that passes through the confines of the business address can be considered part of the workplace context, however. An employee may bring closed luggage to the office prior to leaving on a trip, or a handbag or briefcase each workday. While whatever expectations of privacy the employee has in the existence and the outward appearance of the luggage is affected by its presence in the workplace, the employee's expectation of privacy in the *contents* of the luggage is not affected in the same way. The appropriate standard for a workplace search does not necessarily apply to a piece of closed personal luggage, a handbag, or a briefcase that happens to be within the employer's business address.[63]

The Court went on to note that the expectation of privacy in one's workplace, like the expectation of privacy in one's home, is "based upon societal expectations that have deep roots in the history of the [Fourth] Amendment."[64] The Court acknowledged, however, that "operational realities of the workplace . . . may make *some* employees' expectations of privacy unreasonable when an intrusion is by a supervisor rather than a law enforcement official." The Court also noted that "[p]ublic employees' expectations of privacy in their offices, desks, and file cabinets, like similar expectations of employees in the private sec-

---

63. 480 U.S. at 716. Previously, the court had recognized the reasonableness of such an employee expectation of privacy in Mancusi v. DeForte, 392 U.S. 364 (1968). A reasonable expectation of privacy was also found in a diskette left on a former employer's premises which contained personal and confidential communications. TSE v. UBS Fin. Servs., Inc., 2005 WL 1473815, *2 (S.D.N.Y. June 21, 2005). The diskette was not marked as personal or confidential and contained one business-related memorandum, but a quick perusal of the label clearly indicated that it contained personal documents and confidential communications. While the plaintiff had not sought the return of the diskette after being discharged, this was excused because the company's discharge letter indicated that it would "arrange to have any personal items that [plaintiff had] remaining in [her] office shipped to [her] at [their] expense." No waiver, therefore, resulted, and the defendant was ordered to return any copies of the diskette or communications that were on it.

64. 480 U.S. at 716.

tor, may be reduced by virtue of actual office practices and procedures, or by legitimate regulation."[65] Because the hospital had not established a reasonable regulation or policy discouraging employees from storing personal papers and effects in their desks or file cabinets, the Court concluded that the reasonableness of an employee's expectation of privacy had not been diminished.

While the *Ortega* decision was in the context of the Fourth Amendment protection against unreasonable searches and seizures by government employees, its "reasonableness" language could roughly define the parameters of a private employer's right to monitor the e-mail communications of employees and their use of the Internet. The employer's right to invade the employee's subjective expectation of privacy is controlled by the objective reasonableness of the employer's identified needs for supervision, control, and the efficient operation of the workplace. If these needs can be established, the legitimacy of the employer's privacy invasion turns on the existence, clarity, and communication of policies announcing the nature and degree of employees' lost privacy expectations.

The problem today is not so much whether, but how and the degree to which employers can diminish employees' reasonable expectations of confidentiality or privacy in their personal e-mail communications or Internet transactions on employers' computers. As employees have a reasonable expectation of privacy in the things they bring to the workplace, they also may have such an expectation in the personal things they create at the workplace. But as with all other rights, this expectation must be balanced against employers' invasions of privacy that are needed for the effective supervision and control of employees, complying with governmental regulations, and guarding against liability for tortious acts of employees, as well as maintaining the efficient operation of the workplace.

In that vein, it has become common for employers to require employees to agree to policies that explicitly forbid *any* expectation of privacy in company-owned equipment. Employers often do this to diminish lost time on personal telephone calls, e-mail communications, and perusing of pornographic Web sites. As explained in *TBG Insurance Services Corp. v. Superior Court*,[66] companies often engage in

---

65. *Id.* at 717.
66. 96 Cal. App. 4th 443, 451, 117 Cal. Rptr. 2d 155, 162 (Cal. Ct. App. 2002).

these practices for several reasons:

> including legal compliance (in regulated industries, such as telemarketing, to show compliance, and in other industries to satisfy "due diligence" requirements), legal liability (because employees unwittingly exposed to offensive material on a colleague's computer may sue the employer for allowing a hostile workplace environment), performance review, productivity measures, and security concerns (protection of trade secrets and other confidential information).[67]

In *TBG Insurance,* the signed policy statement eliminated any privacy expectations that the employee had in the use of company computers at the office and in the employee's home.[68]

Can an employer diminish an individual employee's expectation of privacy or confidentiality by unilaterally initiating a policy that elec-

---

67. "First, employers can diminish an individual employee's expectation of privacy by clearly stating in the policy that electronic communications are to be used solely for company business, and that the company reserves the right to monitor or access all employee Internet or e-mail usage. The policy should further emphasize that the company will keep copies of Internet or e-mail passwords, and that the existence of such passwords is not an assurance of the confidentiality of the communications. . . . An electronic communications policy should include a statement prohibiting the transmission of any discriminatory, offensive or unprofessional messages. Employers should also inform employees that access to any Internet [sites] that are discriminatory or offensive is not allowed, and no employee should be permitted to post personal opinions on the Internet using the company's access, particularly if the opinion is of a political or discriminatory nature." Fernandez, *Workplace Claims: Guiding Employers and Employees Safely In and Out of the Revolving Door* (1999), 614 PLI, Litig. and Admin. Prac. Course Handbook Series, Litigation 725, 798-99. *See* Gantt, *An Affront to Human Dignity: Electronic Mail Monitoring in the Private Sector Workplace*, 8 Harv. J.L. & Tech. 345, 404-05 (1995).

68. The court also noted that to the extent that personal or otherwise confidential communications are on the computer, the scope of the employer's search and seizure could be limited by a protective order. "Appropriate protective orders can define the scope of TBG's inspection and copying of information on the computer to that which is directly relevant to this litigation, and can prohibit the unnecessary copying and dissemination of Zieminski's financial and other information that has no rational bearing on this case." 96 Cal. App. 4th 443, 454, 117 Cal. Rptr. 2d 155, 164 (Cal. Ct. App. 2002).

tronic communications are to be used solely for company business, and that the company reserves the right to monitor or access all employee Internet or e-mail usage, regardless of the use of passwords and other security devices? Courts have consistently said yes.[69] Most of these cases, however, have not involved communications that were protected by the attorney-client privilege. Is it unreasonable for employees to expect to be able to be contacted by their attorneys on urgent legal matters while they are at work and expect the confidentiality of the communications to be respected by their employer? In the fast-paced society in which we now live, employees are often involved in divorces, stock transactions, the sale or purchase of real estate, and other legal matters that require constant access to attorneys. Is this not something that employers should have to recognize and accommodate when reasonably made apparent to them and not inconsistent with their needs?

In the small number of cases found where the attorney-client privilege was involved,[70] the courts appeared to make efforts to find that the

---

69. *See* United States v. Angevine, 281 F.3d 1130 (10th Cir. 2002); United States v. Etkin, 2008 U.S. Dist. LEXIS 12834 (S.D.N.Y. Feb. 20, 2008); United States v. Bailey, 272 F. Supp. 2d 822 (D. Neb. 2003). In these three cases the employer notified the employees of its policies through a flash-screen warning that came up each time the user logged onto the computer. Before proceeding, the user had to indicate that the policy was acceptable. *See also* Muick v. Glenoyre Elecs., 280 F.3d 741, 743 (7th Cir. 2002); United States v. Simons, 206 F.3d 392, 398 (4th Cir. 2000) ("[I]n order to prove a legitimate expectation of privacy, Simons must show that his subjective expectation of privacy is one that society is prepared to accept as objectively reasonable. . . . However, office practices, procedures, or regulations may reduce legitimate privacy expectations. . . . Simon did not have a legitimate expectation of privacy with regard to the record or fruits of his Internet use in light of the FBIS Internet policy. The policy clearly stated that FBIS would 'audit, inspect, and/or monitor' employees' use of the Internet, including all file transfers, all websites visited, and all e-mail messages, 'as deemed appropriate.' This policy placed employees on notice that they could not reasonably expect that their Internet activity would be private. Therefore, regardless of whether Simons subjectively believed that the files he transferred from the Internet were private, such a belief was not objectively reasonable after FBIS notified him that it would be overseeing his Internet use.").

70. Sims v. Lakeside School, 2007 WL 2745367, at *1-2 (W.D. Wash. Sept. 20, 2007); Curto v. Med. World Commc'ns, Inc., 2006 WL 1318387 (E.D. N.Y. May 15, 2006); In re Asia Global Crossing, Ltd., 322 B.R. 247 (S.D.N.Y. 2005); Nat'l Econ. Research Assoc. v. Evans, 21 Mass. L. Rep. 337, 2006 Mass. Super. LEXIS 371 (Sup. Ct. Aug. 3, 2006); and People v. Jiang, 131 Cal. App. 4th 1027 (Cal. Ct. App. 2005).

expectation of confidentiality was not overridden by a rather broad-sweeping company policy. The court in *Global Crossing* surveyed judicial decisions that had discussed the reasonableness of employees' expectations of privacy in office computer and Internet files,[71] and laid

---

71. *Compare* United States v. Simons, 206 F.3d 392, 398 n.8 (4th Cir. 2000) (no reasonable expectation of privacy in office computer and downloaded Internet files where employer had a policy of auditing employee's use of the Internet, and the employee did not assert that he was unaware of or had not consented to the policy); Muick v. Glenayre Elec., 280 F.3d 741, 743 (7th Cir. 2002) (no reasonable expectation of privacy in workplace computer files where employer had announced that he could inspect the computer); Thygeson v. U.S. Bancorp, No. CV-03-467, 2004 WL 2066746, at *20 (D. Or. Sept. 15, 2004) (no reasonable expectation of privacy in computer files and e-mail where employee handbook explicitly warned of employer's right to monitor files and e-mail); Kelleher v. City of Reading, No. Civ. A. 01-3386, 2002 WL 1067442, at *8 (E.D. Pa. May 29, 2002) (no reasonable expectation of privacy in workplace e-mail where employer's guidelines "explicitly informed employees that there was no such expectation of privacy"); Garrity v. John Hancock Mut. Life Ins. Co., No. Civ. A. 00-12143, 2002 WL 974676, at *1-2 (D. Mass. May 7, 2002) (no reasonable expectation of privacy where, despite the fact that the employee created a password to limit access, the company periodically reminded employees that the company e-mail policy prohibited certain uses, the e-mail system belonged to the company, and although the company did not intentionally inspect e-mail usage, it might do so where there were business or legal reasons to do so, and the plaintiff assumed her e-mails might be forwarded to others); and Smyth v. Pillsbury Co., 914 F. Supp. 97, 101 (E.D. Pa. 1996) (no reasonable expectation of privacy where employee voluntarily sends an e-mail over the employer's e-mail system) *with* Levethal v. Knapek, 266 F.3d 64, 74 (2d Cir. 2001) (employee had reasonable expectation of privacy in contents of workplace computer where the employee had a private office and exclusive use of his desk, filing cabinets and computers, the employer did not have a general practice of routinely searching office computers, and had not "placed [the plaintiff] on notice that he should have no expectation of privacy in the contents of his office computer"); United States v. Slanina, 283 F.3d 670, 676-77 (5th Cir.) (employee had reasonable expectation of privacy in his computer and files where the computer was maintained in a closed, locked office, the employee had installed passwords to limit access, and the employer "did not disseminate any policy that prevented the storage of personal information on city computers and also did not inform its employees that computer usage and Internet access would be monitored"), *vacated on other grounds*, 537 U.S. 802 (2002); Haynes v. Office of the Attorney General, 298 F. Supp. 2d 1154, 1161-62 (D. Kan. 2003) (employee had reasonable expectation of privacy in private computer files, despite computer screen warning that there shall be no expectation of privacy in using employer's computer system, where employees were allowed to use computers for private communications, were advised that unauthorized access to user's e-mail was prohibited, em-

out four factors that a court should consider in determining whether a reasonable expectation of privacy or confidentiality exists:

1. Does the corporation maintain a policy banning personal or objectionable use?
2. Does the company monitor the use of the employee's computer or e-mail?
3. Do third parties have a right of access to the computer or e-mails? and
4. Did the corporation notify the employee or was the employee aware of the use and monitoring policies?[72]

Based on these criteria, the court reviewed the circumstances in which Asia Global Crossing employees found themselves. First, the company clearly had access to its own servers and other parts of the system where e-mails were stored. Indeed, the court noted that sending a message over the company's e-mail system was "like placing a copy of that message in the company files." Short of encryption, the insider e-mails could be reviewed and read by anyone with lawful access to the system. Second, relative to notice of corporate policies banning certain uses and monitoring, the court found the evidence to be equivocal. Individuals asserted that no policy on use and monitoring was enacted or enforced. A document titled "Corporate E-mail Policy" was produced, however, that stated that all data and information transmitted over the company's system are the property of the company; are not private or secure; must be solely for business purposes; and may be randomly accessed by the company. It was unclear that the policies were those of Global Crossing (a related company) or Asia Global Crossing. Most important to the court's disposition, however, was the fact that individuals within the company insisted that "they did not know of or tell anyone about an Asia Global e-mail policy."[73] Therefore, the court ruled that it was not demonstrated that employees could not communicate with their per-

---

ployees were given passwords to prevent access by others, and no evidence was offered to show that the employer ever monitored private files or employee e-mails); and Scott v. Beth Israel Med. Center Inc., 2007 N.Y. Misc. LEXIS 7114 (Sup. Ct. Oct. 17, 2007).

72. In re Asia Global Crossing, Ltd., 322 B.R. 247, 257 (2005).

73. *Id.* at 260-61.

sonal attorney with a reasonable expectation of privacy and confidentiality.

The court in *Curto v. Medical World Communications, Inc.*[74] found a reasonable privacy expectation for employees in a company's laptop computers that were used at home because they were not connected to the company's server. As a consequence, the employer was not able to actively monitor those computers at any time. Any examination of them necessarily involved notice to employees, because the company either had to go to their homes or had to have employees bring them into the office. With such notice, the employees could delete whatever personal communications they had on the computers. This, coupled with the fact that there was no history of monitoring, convinced the court to conclude that the confidentiality of attorney-client communications could reasonably be preserved, and therefore could reasonably be expected.

In *People v. Jiang,* the company policy signed by employees stated:

I understand that I have no expectation of privacy in the voicemail and electronic mail provided to me by the Company or in any property situated on the Company's premises and/or owned by the Company, including disks and other storage media, filing cabinets or other work areas. I further understand that such property, including voice mail and electronic mail, is subject to inspection by Company personnel at any time.[75]

Despite the breadth of this policy, the court found that "nothing in the . . . agreement barred employees from using their employer-issued computers for personal matters."[76] Therefore, the court concluded "it was objectively reasonable for defendant to expect that attorney-client information in the password-protected documents he placed in a segregated folder marked 'Attorney' on his [company]-issued laptop would remain confidential."[77] Similarly, in *National Economic Research Associates,*[78] company policies forbade personal use of company comput-

---

74. 2006 WL 1318387, at *5-7 (E.D. N.Y. May 15, 2006).

75. 131 Cal. App. 4th 1027, 1045 (6th Dist. 2005).

76. *Id.* at 1054.

77. *Id.*

78. 21 Mass. L. Rep. 337, 2006 Mass. Super. LEXIS 371 (Sup. Ct. Aug. 3, 2006).

ers, but the court found a reasonable expectation of confidentiality in e-mail communications with the employee's personal attorney because (1) he used his personal e-mail account, which reasonably led him to believe that his private messages could not be read by his employer; (2) he did not try to store his messages on his laptop; (3) before returning his computer to the company, he attempted to delete all e-mails that he thought had been stored in it; (4) the company did not adequately inform employees that all e-mails, regardless how they are accessed through the company's computers, are stored in a "screen shot" temporary file; and (5) the company's policies did not expressly reserve the right to retrieve and read the messages (the manual stated only that the company would monitor the Internet *sites* visited, rather than stating that it would monitor the *content* of the Internet communications).

In *Sims v. Lakeside School*,[79] the court acknowledged that company policies generally destroyed any reasonable expectation of privacy for employees in the contents of their company-supplied laptops, but distinguished between e-mails that were locally generated from programs on the user's computer and those that were "web-based generated." If the employee goes to the effort of accessing the Internet and his personal e-mail account, even though through the employer's ISP, the court concluded that he had a reasonable expectation of privacy in all of his e-mails despite company policies applicable to the laptop computer through which the transactions were conducted. The court, however, went even further. It concluded that any communications from the employee to his lawyer or wife, regardless of which e-mail system used, was not subject to review by the employer.

Applying the four factors enunciated in *Global Crossing*, the New York trial court in *Scott v. Beth Israel Medical Center Inc.*[80] found no reasonable expectation of confidentiality by an employee communicating with his attorney over the employer's computer. There were clear company policies about no personal use of the e-mail system, the employee was an administrator and would have been aware of the policies, monitoring by the employer destroyed whatever expectation an employee may have had, and unlike *Jiang*, the employer's e-mail server was used to transmit the messages, rather than a personal server sub-

---

79. 2007 WL 274536, at *1-2 (W.D. Wash. Sept. 20, 2007).
80. 17 Misc. 3d 934, 847 N.Y.S.2d 436 (Sup. Ct. 2007).

scribed to by the employee. In addition, the court noted that the messages were not password-protected or encrypted.

The courts in *Jiang, Global Crossing, National Economic Research Associates,* and *Sims* looked for a way to conclude that circumstances precluded the employers from violating the sanctity of the attorney-client relationship. Rather than searching for such circumstances in the future, courts may simply conclude that the importance of attorney-client communications is sufficiently great to preclude employers from knowingly violating them, regardless of announced policies, when employees have identified the communications as privileged and segregated them from communications relevant to company purposes. This may be part of a larger body of decisional law that will set limits on the types of employee privacy expectations that employers cannot unilaterally make unreasonable because of societal expectations, other rights that are implicated, and the lack of supervisory justification. Coupled with the diminished role of confidentiality in our privilege jurisprudence, one might anticipate greater judicial recognition of employee privacy rights relating to attorney-client communication in the workplace.

When establishing policies designed to diminish employees' privacy expectations in communications over company-owned, -operated and -controlled equipment, companies should:

- Explicitly outline what they intend to monitor and supervise, contents as well as sites accessed.
- Explain why the monitoring will be done (what the company is attempting to guard against), as well as how and when that monitoring will take place. The clearer the policy and its reasons, the greater the compliance and the fewer the challenges.
- Include broad prohibitions of all personal use and disclaimers of all privacy expectations only when the nature of the equipment and the company's use of it is inconsistent with any personal use. Realistic policies are more credible, and therefore more acceptable, to employees. In addition, the broader the elimination of privacy rights, the greater the required justification may be when individual and company needs are balanced against one another. Currently, however, courts have shown little inclination to engage in such balancing.
- Acknowledge employees' needs to engage in certain personal communications with some level of confidentiality (for example,

communications with spouses, children, and lawyers) and delineate the means of communications that are acceptable to the company (for example, by telephone rather than e-mail, because proprietary information can be so easily attached). If personal communications are permitted by e-mail, specify how the company will attempt to respect the privacy of those communications (for example, scanning all communications for key words and reading only those raising reasonable questions relating to workplace needs).

- If personal communications and privacy needs are acknowledged, delineate what the employees are expected to do to alert the employer to the nature of particular communication (for example, informing the company of the e-mail addresses or names and telephone numbers of family members and lawyers).
- Communicate these policies to employees and regularly remind them of their existence.
- Follow the monitoring policy and regularly carry it out so as to establish privacy expectations.

E. Data Behind Electronic Evidence—Metadata

Behind all electronic evidence (e.g., e-mails, spreadsheets, accounting records, and even the most simple letter) is metadata—data about the information appearing on the face of the document. This is information about the history, tracking, or management of an electronic document. One report has defined metadata as "information about a particular data set which describes how, when and by whom it was collected, created, accessed, or modified and how it is formatted (including data demographics such as size, location, storage requirements and media information)."[81]

This information is generally not visible when a document is printed or converted to an image file. This data can be altered and can be extracted from a file and converted to its own document. It can be inaccurate because it can be altered. It can be misleading when a form document is used only as a template, but another person drafted a document on

---

81. The Sedona Guidelines: Best Practice Guidelines & Commentary for Managing Information & Records in the Electronic Age (The Sedona Conference Working Group Series, Sept. 2005 Version, http://www.thesedonaconference.org/content/miscFiles/TSG9_05.pdf.

that form. The metadata will show the original author of the template as the author of the document on the template. While the metadata is usually created automatically by a computer, it can also be supplied by a user. For example, Microsoft Excel spreadsheets and applications such as Word and PowerPoint will contain the following metadata: author name or initials, company or organization name, identification of computer or network server or hard disk where documents is saved, names of previous document authors, document revisions and versions, hidden text or cells, template information, other file properties and summary information, non-visible portion or embedded objects, personalized views, and comments.[82]

The metadata underlying word-processor documents is seldom critical to understanding the substance of the document. Nonetheless, the underlying metadata of a word-processor document can provide critical evidence of its distribution, and thus knowledge or notice of its content by certain individuals, and whether the document's confidentiality has been preserved. By contrast, the metadata underlying spreadsheets or undifferentiated masses of tables of data is often critical to understanding the relationships between the data presented. In the latter instances, it has been held that the producing party must produce the documents in the form in which they are maintained for business purposes.[83]

To avoid the inadvertent disclosures of irrelevant, proprietary, or privileged information not visible on the face of a document, software programs are available that remove the metadata. This "scrubbing" of documents, however, can constitute spoliation if it is done in a litigation context without the consent of the adverse party or permission of the court.[84] To avoid a spoliation sanction, the scrubbing must be done as a matter of course in the daily maintenance of the documents. In the absence of such a routine practice, the producing party must produce the documents as they are maintained in the ordinary course of business (with the metadata)[85] or assert privilege on those portions being withheld. This requires that each identifiable portion of metadata be listed on a privilege log, with a general description of its content documenting

82. Microsoft Office Online: Find and Remove Metadata (Hidden Information) in Your Legal Documents, http://office.microsoft.com/en-us/assistance/HA010776461033.aspx.

83. Williams v. Sprint/United Mgmt. Co., 230 F.R.D. 640 (D. Kan. 2005).

84. *See* Chapter Two, "Spoliation," *supra*.

why it is privileged. Failure to do so can result in the waiver of all privilege claims.[86] Therefore, the subject of metadata is another important issue that parties need to discuss in their initial discovery conference mandated by the recent revisions to Rule 26(f) of the Federal Rules of Civil Procedure.

F.   Electronic Presentations

Presentations by clients to attorneys, or by attorneys to clients, are often made by computer in a Power Point or equivalent program format, with individual frames printed and disseminated to all meeting participants. These printouts facilitate note-taking on the presentations.

Such printouts are frequently produced in a document production process because they fail to indicate that they are either to or from an attorney, or from third parties working as agents of attorneys. If this production was inadvertent, the voluntary disclosure may not constitute a waiver of attorney-client privilege protections if reasonable efforts were made to guard against such disclosures and there were timely efforts to retrieve them once the production was detected.[87] If not inadvertent, the production will waive the privilege protection otherwise

---

85. The producing party has the initial burden to seek a protective order. "The initial burden with regard to the disclosure of the metadata would therefore be placed on the party to whom the request or order to produce is directed. The burden to object to the disclosure of metadata is appropriately placed on the party ordered to produce its electronic documents as they are ordinarily maintained, because that party already has access to the metadata and is in the best position to determine whether producing it is objectionable. Placing the burden on the producing party is further supported by the fact that metadata is an inherent part of an electronic document, and its removal ordinarily requires an affirmative act by the producing party that alters the electronic document." Williams v. Sprint/United Mgmt. Co., 230 F.R.D. 640, 652 (D. Kan. 2005).

86. Williams v. Sprint/United Mgmt. Co., 230 F.R.D. 640, 653-54 (D. Kan. 2005) ("Defendant has not provided the Court with even a general description of the purportedly privileged metadata that was scrubbed from the spreadsheets. As Defendant has failed to provide any privilege log for the electronic documents it claims contain metadata that will reveal privileged communications or attorney work product, the Court holds that Defendant has waived any attorney-client privilege or work product with regard to the spreadsheets' metadata except for the metadata directly corresponding to the adverse impact analyses and social security number information, which the Court has permitted Defendant to remove from the spreadsheets.").

applicable and poses the difficult question of whether the voluntary disclosure waived the privilege protection applicable to other communications on the same subject matter. This issue of the scope of waiver was addressed in *In re OM Group Securities Litigation.*[88]

In *OM Group,* attorneys, assisted by forensic accountants, conducted an investigation of accounting irregularities for the purpose of giving legal advice to the corporation's Audit Committee. At the direction of the Audit Committee, the lawyers and accountants gave a Power Point presentation to OMG's board of directors regarding the findings of the ongoing investigation. In the discovery process, OMG produced the Power Point presentation and two spreadsheets prepared by the accountants but refused to produce the underlying documents related to, referred to, or relied upon in the presentation. The court held that OMG waived the privilege protection not only for the Power Point presentation and spreadsheets, but also for the underlying communications referred to and relied upon. The court explained:

> These documents were not brief or cryptic summaries; nor did they merely acknowledge the existence of an investigation. These documents contained significant disclosures. The Power Point presentation, although containing preliminary findings, was a substantial presentation of the investigation up to that time, was more than 30 pages in length, listed detailed conclusions, and cited specific findings, interviews and documents in support. By way of example, it described the reason for the origination of the Audit Committee's inventory review, directly quoted concerns and observations about the inventory set forth in e-mails by identified individuals, summarized the content of specific e-mails, identified more than ten persons interviewed in connection with the investigation, discussed the scope of the document review and difficulties encountered in obtaining appropriate documentation, set forth a number of points as to whether there was a basis for top-side adjustments to work in progress at a particular facility, discussed the results of interviews with plant personnel and conclusions resulting therefrom, and set forth in-

---

87. *See* text at note 36, *supra. See generally* PAUL R. RICE, ATTORNEY-CLIENT PRIVILEGE IN THE UNITED STATES §§ 9:71-78 (2d ed. 1999).

88. 226 F.R.D. 579 (N.D. Ohio 2005).

vestigative results. Moreover, the entire presentation included inventory analysis and spreadsheets prepared by Ten Eyck. The spreadsheets correspond to the presentation by quantifying OMG's unsupported inventory balances by year, facility and inventory type. . . . This disclosure is far more than a cursory summary, a brief press release or a mere acknowledgment that an investigation exists.[89]

Because this disclosure was substantial, intentional, and deliberate, and formed the basis for OMG's public announcement that it anticipated a restatement of earnings, the court concluded that OMG should not be permitted to withhold information that would allow the plaintiff to assess the totality of the picture voluntary disclosed.

Relative to electronic presentations, it is important to remember several things. First, the fact that a lawyer or a lawyer's agent made the presentation does not necessarily mean that legal advice was being given. Particularly in a corporate context, lawyers often have broad responsibilities that involve services beyond the rendering of legal assistance. And even if legal assistance is part of what is being provided, that legal assistance must be the primary purpose for the presentation.[90] Second, even if legal advice is being given and is the primary purpose of the presentation, under the derivative theory for responsive attorney communications, the presentation is only privileged if it discloses the content of prior confidential client communications.[91] General presentations on legal topics of importance to the client do not satisfy this standard. Third, even if a lawyer or his agent made the presentation and it satisfies the derivative rule, the presentation is still not protected by the privilege if confidentiality was not preserved. During corporate presentations, third parties are often present and making presentations of their own. Fourth, if a non-lawyer made the presentation, the mere fact that a law-

---

89. *Id.* at 591-92.

90. *See generally* PAUL R. RICE, ATTORNEY-CLIENT PRIVILEGE IN THE UNITED STATES, § 7:2 (2d ed. 1999).

91. Under the common law, which still controls the application of the attorney-client privilege in federal courts, the privilege was designed to encourage candor by the client. Therefore, responsive communications from the attorney were only protected to the extent that they revealed the content of prior confidential communications from the client. *See generally* PAUL R. RICE, 1 ATTORNEY-CLIENT PRIVILEGE IN THE UNITED STATES, § 5:2 (2d ed. 1999).

yer was among those to whom the presentation was made does not make the attorney-client privilege applicable. If there were both business and legal purposes behind the presentation, the intermingling of the two would render the privilege inapplicable because the "primary purpose" test is not satisfied.[92]

G. *Measures to Preserve Confidentiality?*

Summary: Special efforts to guard against breaches of confidentiality, like encryption, will not be necessary in order to preserve the attorney-client privilege. Aside from privilege concerns, however, clients may communicate highly sensitive, proprietary information and may desire more protection than is required to maintain the attorney-client privilege. Lawyers should be prepared to provide the extra security of encryption and public key technologies.

Security measures for computer systems and Internet communications vary widely. The level of security they provide also varies significantly. Other than encryption technologies (which involve a measure of inconvenience, as well as additional costs to the sender and recipient), virtually any security measures can be overridden by sophisticated hackers.

For purposes of the attorney-client privilege or ethical responsibilities under the Code of Professional Conduct, neither courts nor bar associations have required the use of security measures like encryption. Nevertheless, encryption or similar measures should be employed if guarantees of secrecy are important to the client.

Besides protecting their computer files against hackers, clients must take reasonable measures to ensure against disclosures to employees within the company who do not have a need to know within the scope of their employment responsibilities. Despite the waning importance of the confidentiality requirement, courts still insist that the *appearance* of confidentiality exists, is expected, and has been preserved. Consequently, all efforts that historically have been taken to protect the secrecy of confidential communications within the direct control of the client should continue. Records of e-mail communications, therefore, should be maintained with the same care as internal memoranda, letters, and reports.

---

92. *Id.*

Recommended Security Measures

- **Segregation of privileged communications.** Confidential e-mail messages should be saved in specially denoted electronic files. If e-mail messages are printed, the hard copies must either be segregated, like all other attorney-client communications, or clearly labeled with a notation such as "Confidential" or "Attorney-Client." Preferably, organizations will employ both procedures.

- **Use of intranet firewalls.** An intranet is a self-contained network accessible only by an organization's employees or others with authorization. Intranet firewalls are technological gates that must be unlocked, and that reduce the probability that electronic communications between members of an organization will be obtained by unauthorized third parties (hackers). If a firewall is used, remember that no technological obstruction, regardless of how complex and expensive, can guarantee complete security.

- **Written policies.** To ensure that employees who do not have a need to know the contents of privileged communications do not read them, written company policies about attorney-client communications should be circulated to all employees. These policies should:

  1. define and explain the nature and purpose of the attorney-client privilege;

  2. emphasize the need for confidentiality;

  3. explain how confidentiality is to be protected by (a) conspicuously marking them "Attorney-Client," so as to notify others, and (b) segregating them in storage;

  4. stress the employee's responsibility to protect the confidentiality of those flagged documents by reading them only when necessary in the scope of their employment responsibilities;

  5. admonish employees not to distribute documents to others unless ordered by a superior to do so, or unless deemed necessary to fulfill their employment responsibilities;

  6. establish a procedure that employees must follow for accessing stored e-mail messages, restricting who can

access messages and under what conditions messages may be read; and

7. include periodic training sessions to ensure that employees have read, understood, and complied with the policies.

- **Limited electronic access.** Access to e-mail files should be restricted by passwords. If e-mail messages are printed or electronically maintained, there is no need for employee access to them other than through the technology staff that assists in file retrievals when the printed copy has been lost. If employee access is needed, the company policies discussed above should include explicit directives about who should access the materials and when they should be read.

- **Secondary distributees.** If attorney-client communications are distributed to third parties because they are: (1) *joint clients* collectively seeking legal assistance from a single attorney, (2) separately represented but *sharing a community of interests* in collectively seeking legal assistance, or (3) participating in a *joint defense* effort in the midst of litigation, it would be wise to inquire about the efforts those third parties have taken to secure the confidentiality of communications within their organization. Although no court has held that disclosure by a third party (other than the attorney) waives the client's privilege protection, the lawyer's responsibility under the Code of Professional Responsibility to protect the client's confidences suggests that lawyers make such inquiries. Before privileged documents are shared with outside consultants, question whether it is necessary. If you conclude that it is necessary, advise the consultants in writing of the confidential nature of the communications and the limitations on any secondary distribution. If the outside consultants have written guidelines, obtain a copy of them. If there are no guidelines, identify the individual(s) who can verify that there has been no secondary distribution within the third party's firm beyond those who had a need to know in the scope of consulting responsibilities.

- **Protect against typographical errors.** Develop a personal address book, indexed by client, that automatically inserts addresses, to avoid typographical errors that could result in unintended individuals receiving the communication.

- **Mark as confidential.** Conspicuously mark confidential or attorney-client-privileged e-mail messages by indicating such status in the reference line. Do not include sensitive information in the reference line. The reference line may be accessed by Internet service providers and the client's in-house technical staff. Also, e-mail messages may be received by clients while in the presence of third parties, who might discern the content of the message from an overly descriptive reference line.

- **Consult with the client.** Consult with the client regarding the security of electronic communications before engaging in regular e-mail correspondence. For example, attorneys should inform their clients that electronically transmitted messages are not secure because third parties may have access to them. If a firm does not encrypt its e-mail messages, the client should be informed. Clients should also be informed that the diminished confidentiality of electronic communications could affect their privileged status.

- **Send a test transmission to the client.** Send an e-mail to the client requesting that they call or e-mail back to confirm receipt of your message. This will provide assurance that you have the correct address before transmitting any sensitive information. It also will alert the recipient that measures may need to be taken to secure the communication from the recipient's end.

- **Include boilerplate assertion of privilege.** Attach to every e-mail a boilerplate assertion of privilege. For example: "This electronic communication, including any authorized attachments, contains information from the law firm of X,Y,Z that may be legally privileged, protected, confidential, and/or exempt from disclosure or certain types of use under applicable law. This information is for the sole use of the intended recipient(s). If you are not the intended recipient(s) or the employee or agent responsible for delivery of this message to the intended recipient(s), you are hereby notified that any review, use, disclosure, copying, distribution, or the taking of any action in reliance on the contents of this e-mail or any attachments is strictly prohibited. You are further advised that review by an individual other than the intended recipient shall not constitute a waiver of any attorney-client privilege that may apply to this communication. If you have received this communication in error, please notify the sender immediately by return e-mail, permanently delete this e-mail and any attachments from all computers on which they may be stored, and destroy any printouts of this message or its attachments. In addition, if you are not currently a client of the firm, this communication is not to be construed as establishing an attorney-client relationship."

H.   Asserting Attorney-Client Privilege for E-mails: The Practical Details, a Growing Concern

Attorney-client privilege claims for e-mail messages present practical problems different from those encountered with other forms of written communications. After identifying these problems, each will be discussed in turn.

1.   The ease with which in-house lawyers can be incorporated into business discussions has expanded the number of communications in which the attorney is involved and has brought the attorneys into corporate discussions at a much earlier stage. Consequently, attorneys tend to be more intimately involved in the business decisions of their client companies. This jeopardizes the privilege protection afforded to all communications with in-house counsel because it increases questions as to the primary purpose of each.

2.   The use of e-mail complicates the distinction between communications and information because it can collapse the two into a single electronic transmission that serves both business and legal purposes. This jeopardizes the applicability of the attorney-client privilege because it cannot be established that the primary purpose of the communication to both business and legal personnel was to obtain legal assistance.

3. E-mail use raises the question of what "document" is being claimed as privileged when a series, thread, or string of e-mail messages is being withheld from production based on the attorney-client privilege. Is each individual communication in the thread a "document" that must be separately listed and described in the privilege log, or is a collective description sufficient?

4. Corporate clients often include lawyers among the addressees of e-mail communications, even though legal advice was not the primary purpose of the communication, solely to get the protection of the attorney-client privilege for business communications. As a result, assumptions about the purpose of e-mail messages are not appropriate when they are based solely on the manner in which the communications have been disseminated.

5. E-mail technology significantly increases the judicial burden of assessing the validity of each claim. The privilege proponent should be conscious of why and how these burdens have increased and should take proactive measures to accommodate them.

1. Expanding the Role of In-House Counsel—Jeopardizing the Applicability of the Privilege

E-mail is well accepted among both state and federal courts as a form of communication to which the attorney-client privilege readily applies despite the threat of breach of confidentiality.[93] A subtle problem is cre-

---

93. *See* Am. Nat'l Bank & Trust Co. v. AXA Client Solutions, 2002 WL 1058776, at *3-5 (N.D. Ill. Mar. 22, 2002) (without particular concerns for increased confidentiality problems, court upheld privilege for e-mails because they involved client's efforts to obtain, or attorney's attempt to render, legal assistance); Mold-Masters Ltd. v. Husky Injection Molding Sys., 2001 WL 1558303 (N.D. Ill. Dec. 6, 2001); Yurick ex rel. Yurick v. Liberty Mut. Ins. Co., 201 F.R.D. 465 (D. Ariz. 2001); United States v. Chevron Texaco Corp., 241 F. Supp. 2d 1065, 1074-75, 1077-79 (N.D. Cal. 2001) (privilege upheld for all e-mails except those conveyed to third parties, which lost their confidentiality); United States v. Geriatric Psychological Servs., Inc., 2001 WL 286838, at *2 (D. Md. Mar. 22, 2001) ("Bers's telephone call with the client on June 8, 1998, and Stodghill's review of an e-mail message from the client on January 5, 2001, fall under the attorney-client privilege."); United States v. Motorola, Inc., 1999 WL 552553, at *3, 6 (D. D.C. May 28, 1999) (e-mail from executive to other company employees held privileged because it contained confidential information and was requesting advice; fax denied

ated, particularly in the corporate context, when many individuals, including both in-house and outside legal counsel, are linked to active, ongoing exchanges concerning business matters. Often part of an active electronic "conversation" and exchange of ideas before any legal issues have been identified, in-house lawyers are regularly drawn into broad-ranging, business-oriented discussions in a manner, depth, and frequency that may jeopardize the applicability of privilege protections. Establishing that the primary purpose of the communication was to obtain legal advice or assistance is becoming increasingly difficult.[94]

---

privilege because it was only cover sheet and contained no confidential communications); Int'l Marine Carriers, Inc. v. United States, 1997 WL 160371 (S.D.N.Y. April 4, 1997); Nat'l Employee Serv. Corp. v. Liberty Mut. Ins. Co., 1994 WL 878920, at *2-3 (Mass. Sup. Ct. Dec. 12, 1994); City of Reno v. Reno Police Protective Ass'n., 59 P.3d 1212, 1218 (Nev. 2002) ("Contrary to the EMRB's [Employee-Management Relations Board] decision, documents transmitted by e-mail are protected by attorney-client privilege; courts have generally looked to content and recipients of e-mail to determine if e-mail is protected.").

94. St. Joe Co. v. Liberty Mut. Ins. Co., 2007 WL 141282, *3 (M.D. Fla. Jan. 16, 2007) ("[T]he descriptions in Defendant's Affidavit and Second Amended Privilege Log fall short of providing Plaintiff and this Court with an objective factual or evidentiary support demonstrating the withheld documents contain or refer to communications in which an attorney rendered legal advice, as opposed to business advice. Because insurance adjusters commonly perform such tasks as examining and evaluating insurance claims and because attorneys are often retained in-house or hired outside to perform such tasks for an insurance company, it is often difficult to discern whether an attorney is acting in the capacity of an attorney or as that of an adjuster/process supervisor. . . . Defendant has again failed to offer a sufficient basis for this Court to determine that the attorneys referred to in the affidavit and privilege log were acting as legal advisers, rather than as claims adjusters or process supervisors. . . . To invoke the attorney-client privilege, Defendant must do more than merely state that the communication related to information by an attorney or in-house counsel for the purpose of securing legal advice."); In re Rivastigmine Patent Litig., 237 F.R.D. 69, 80 (S.D.N.Y. 2006), aff'd, 2006 WL 3376767 (S.D.N.Y. 2006) ("[I]n analyzing communications created at the direction of in-house counsel, courts must be wary that the involvement of the attorney is not being used simply to shield corporate communications from disclosure."); Lugosch v. Congel, 2006 WL 931687, at *14 (N.D. N.Y. Mar. 7, 2006) ("But making statements to an in-house attorney, in and of itself, does not render the communication or the advice privileged. The curious character of an in-house is that they generally have multiple roles and frequently give to their client business, management and other advice. . . . And these dual functions are very likely to become mixed, in some degree obfuscating the true nature of the function performed. . . . Therefore, the request for legal advice must be distinctly clear and void of nuances of business

For example, if the e-mail comments of legal counsel are sandwiched between comments of corporate personnel about product pricing and distribution, prior dealings with customers, and potential technical problems in a product or proposed deal, these comments appear to be, and in fact often are, far more business than legal in nature. This perception is buttressed when the free-form nature of an e-mail string is compared to traditional legal memoranda that addressed limited legal issues in the context of specific business decisions.

Counsel are contacted far more frequently, and through those contacts are encouraged to participate in regular business matters more often than was the case in the past because of the ease with which e-mail technology allows in-house counsel to be brought into discussions.[95] This increased involvement in business matters by in-house counsel will give rise to questions about the primary purpose of many communications that may have been accepted without question in the past as protected by the attorney-client privilege. Consequently, e-mail users

---

consultation or instruction, if it is to be privileged."); SmithKline Beecham Corp. v. Apotex Corp., 232 F.R.D. 467, 478 (E.D. Pa. 2005) ("In general, attorney-client 'privilege does not shield documents merely because they were transferred to or routed through an attorney.' . . . 'What would otherwise be routine, non-privileged communications between corporate officers or employees transacting the general business of the company do not attain privileged status solely because in-house or outside counsel is "copied in" on the correspondence or memoranda.'"); MSF Holdings, Ltd. v. Fiduciary Trust Co. Int'l, 2005 WL 3338510, at *1 (S.D.N.Y. Dec. 7, 2005) ("In-house counsel often fulfill the dual role of legal advisor and business consultant. . . . Accordingly, to determine whether counsel's advice is privileged, 'we look to whether the attorney's performance depends principally on [her] knowledge of or application of legal requirements or principles, rather than [her] expertise in matters of commercial practice.' . . . In this case, the analysis is complicated slightly by the fact that the business decision of whether to honor the letter of credit necessarily occurs against the background of any legal obligation to do so. . . . Nevertheless, the e-mails at issue here reflect the exercise of a predominantly commercial function. Susan Garcia, the author of the communications and FTCI's Senior Vice President and Deputy Corporate Counsel, never alluded to a legal principle in the documents nor engaged in legal analysis. Instead, she collected facts just as any business executive would do in determining whether to pay an obligation. In doing so, she evidently relied on her knowledge of commercial practice rather than her expertise in the law. The documents are therefore not privileged.").

95. If this increased involvement is more apparent than real, then e-mail technology has documented what previously was not apparent.

must bear the burden of dispelling those suspicions.[96]

96. When businesses regularly use their in-house attorneys to perform non-legal functions, many courts have held that parties asserting the attorney-client privilege must satisfy an enhanced burden of demonstrating that legal advice, rather than business assistance, was rendered in a given instance. *See* Lugosch v. Congel, 2006 WL 931687, at *14 (N.D. N.Y. Mar. 7, 2006) ("But making statements to an in-house attorney, in and of itself, does not render the communication or the advice privileged. The curious character of an in-house is that they generally have multiple roles and frequently give to their client business, management and other advice. . . . And these dual functions are very likely to become mixed, in some degree obfuscating the true nature of the function performed. . . . Therefore, the request for legal advice must be distinctly clear and void of nuances of business consultation or instruction, if it is to be privileged."); United States v. Chevron Texaco Corp., 241 F. Supp. 2d 1065, 1076 (N.D. Cal. 2002) ("Because in-house counsel may operate in a purely or primarily business capacity in connection with many corporate endeavors, the presumption that attaches to communications with outside counsel does not extend to communications with in-house counsel. . . . With respect to internal communications involving in-house counsel, Chevron must make a 'clear showing' that the 'speaker' made the communications for the purpose of obtaining or providing legal advice."); B.F.G. of Illinois, Inc. v. Ameritech Corp., 2001 WL 1414468, at *6 (N.D. Ill. Nov. 13, 2001) ("[W]hen a corporation directs an in-house attorney to work with a business team . . . there is a particular burden on that corporation to demonstrate why communications deserve protection and are not merely business documents."); Amway Corp. v. Procter & Gamble Co., 2001 WL 1818698, at *5 (W.D. Mich. April 3, 2001) ("Thus, for the privilege to be applicable, the proponent must demonstrate that the lawyer has acted in a legal capacity rather than in any of the other functions that legally trained individuals perform in our society. The mere fact that a certain function is performed by an individual with a law degree will not render the communications made to the individual privileged. . . . Where, as here, in-house counsel appears as one of many recipients of an otherwise business-related memo, the federal courts place a heavy burden on the proponent to make a clear showing that counsel is acting in a professional legal capacity and that the document reflects legal, as opposed to business, advice."); L.D. Lowery, Inc. v. Int'l Rectifier, Inc., 2000 WL 1521588, at *1 (E.D. Pa. Oct. 5, 2000) ("The attorney-client privilege protects against disclosure of matters occurring in the attorney-client relationship, namely, matters occurring in the seeking and giving of legal advice. In the corporate setting, this does not mean that communications of fact other than in the seeking or delivering of legal advice can properly be withheld. There is room for suspicion that the defendant is attempting to assert a blanket privilege concerning any and all communications to or from any member of the in-house legal staff."); Neuder v. Battelle Pac. Nw. Nat'l Lab., 194 F.R.D. 289, 295 (D. D.C. 2000) ("In cases that involve in-house counsel, it is necessary to apply the privilege cautiously and narrowly 'lest the mere participation of an attorney be used to seal off disclosure.'"). *See generally* Paul R. Rice, Attorney-Client Privilege in the United States, § 7:2 (2d ed. 1999).

2.   Complicating the Distinction Between Communications and Information

The attorney-client privilege protects communications, not information. Whatever is confidentially communicated to an attorney by the client in an effort to obtain legal assistance is protected by the privilege. The privilege protects what is stated in or incorporated into the communication, regardless of its character. If the information was not in itself privileged, it can be discovered from any source other than the communication to the attorney.

To understand how e-mail technology has complicated the distinction between communications and information, it is first necessary to understand the distinction. It can best be explained in the context of traditional communications by memorandum or letter.

The attorney-client privilege protects (1) the content of what was communicated to legal counsel by the client and (2) the substance of the advice rendered by the lawyer in response.[97] The attorney-client privilege does not protect corporate agents' business correspondence that has been sent to legal counsel for examination, comment, or approval. The Supreme Court held in *United States v. Fisher*[98] that the mere act of conveying non-privileged, preexisting communications to an attorney does not convert them into privileged communications simply because they were subsequently used as a vehicle through which legal advice was sought.

The *Fisher* decision has been commonly misunderstood.[99] Many

---

97.   The early common law protected only responsive communications of the attorney that revealed prior confidences of the client. The responsive communications of legal counsel only received a derivative protection. Today, an increasing number of jurisdictions directly protect legal counsel's *advice*. Some even extend the protection of the privilege to *all communications* from legal counsel to the client in the course of his representation. This view has been criticized. *See* PAUL R. RICE, ATTORNEY-CLIENT PRIVILEGE IN THE UNITED STATES, § 5:2 (2d ed. 1999).

98.   425 U.S. 391 (1976).

99.   *See* In re Parmalat Sec. Litig., 2005 WL 1529035, at *2 (S.D.N.Y. June 28, 2005) (while acknowledging that it has been held that "'preexisting documents which could have been obtained by court process . . . may also be obtained from the attorney by similar process following transfer by the client'"); O'Connor v. Boeing N. Am., 185 F.R.D. 272, 280 (C.D. Cal. 1999), for example, the court ordered the defendant to list separately all attachments to documents claimed to be privileged. "As to documents subject to the attorney-client privilege . . . , the plaintiffs are

have construed it to mean that when the client sends non-privileged documents to an attorney as part of an effort to obtain legal assistance, those documents can be discovered *from the attorney* because they are not made privileged by the client's conveyance.[100] In fact, what *Fisher* decided was that the document itself was not thereby made privileged. The Court did *not* hold that what the client did with that document—communicate it in confidence to an attorney in an effort

---

correct in contending that not all attachments to, or enclosures with, such documents are necessarily protected by the privilege. . . . Rather, to claim the attorney-client privilege . . . for an attachment to, or enclosure with, another privileged document, the attachment or enclosure must be listed as a separate document on the privilege log; otherwise, such attachment or enclosure must be disclosed."); McDonald v. St. Joseph's Hosp. of Atlanta, Inc., Civ. A. No. C80-1295A (N.D. Ga. Sept. 20, 1982) (LEXIS, Genfed library, Dist. file) ("These two documents constitute reports of statements made by nonparties to a party which were then relayed in 'memoranda' letters from this party to its counsel. Such statements would clearly have been unprivileged had their declarants communicated directly with St. Joseph's Hospital counsel, since the attorney-client privilege cannot be asserted by either party as to statements made by nonparties. . . . That these statements were instead embodied in letters written by a party to its counsel should not and does not affect the applicability of the attorney-client privilege to either of the documents in question."); Community Sav. & Loan Ass'n v. Fed. Home Loan Bank Bd., 68 F.R.D. 378, 382 (E.D. Wis. 1975) ("The attorney-client privilege does not extend to correspondence from an attorney to a client when that correspondence contains advice based upon *public information* rather than confidential information provided by the client. . . . In this case, it appears that the information which was sent to the office of the General Counsel consisted almost entirely of material which was in the public record. Therefore, the General Counsel's opinion is not protected from discovery by the attorney-client privilege."). Each of these decisions is erroneous because they confuse the information communicated by the client with the communication into which that information was incorporated. The communication is protected, and the information incorporated into it is irrelevant to the application of the privilege. For an extensive discussion of the distinction between communications and information, as well as the cases that have misinterpreted it, *see* PAUL R. RICE, ATTORNEY-CLIENT PRIVILEGE IN THE UNITED STATES, § 5:19 (2d ed. 1999).

100. *See, e.g.*, In re Grand Jury Subpoenas Dated Oct. 22, 1991, and Nov. 1, 1991, 959 F.2d 1158, 1166 (2d Cir. 1992) ("The November subpoena calls for documents created by the telephone company. Those documents, though transmitted to [the law firm], are not the client's confidential communications, are not within the privilege, and did not become exempt from discovery by the transmission.").

to obtain legal advice—was unprivileged. Indeed, this is what the distinction between communications and information means: in the hands of the client, the document communicated to the attorney is not made privileged by the fact that it was sent to the attorney. However, the fact that it was part of a "communication" to the attorney *is privileged.*[101] This is why courts should not permit discovery from the attorney. The court would be compelling the attorney to reveal the substance of what the client previously "communicated" to him by compelling the attorney to reveal the documents he has in his possession.[102] The non-privileged business communication was, and remains, discoverable *from the client.*[103] This distinction between information and communication becomes critically important in the corporate context, particularly when e-mail technology is employed.

Normally, a corporation seeking legal advice sends a written communication to legal counsel with copies to all corporate employees who,

101. *See, e.g.*, Robinson v. Texas Auto. Dealers Ass'n., 214 F.R.D. 432, 447 (E.D. Tex. 2003) ("PRIV 10-13 is a copy of a pre-existing document authored by a third party regarding analysis of a statute. Jim Popp, a lawyer with Popp & Ikard, who provides legal advice and services to TADA, made handwritten notations on the document with his additional analytical points and sent it to Karen Coffey to give her legal advice about the analysis of the statute. Defendants assert the attorney-client privilege for this document. Popp's handwritten comments are obviously privileged because they constitute pure legal advice from Popp to Coffey. The copy of the document itself is also privileged, despite the fact that it was written by a third party. Although the original document was not a communication between attorney and client, Popp's act of sending the pre-existing document to Coffey as the means of providing legal advice constitutes a privileged communication. The document cannot be disclosed without revealing the substance of his legal advice to her, and therefore, the entire document is privileged.").

102. When copies of business communications are sent to legal counsel for review, those copies should always be "blind copies." By indicating on the face of the original business communication that a copy was sent to legal counsel, the client is revealing what he communicated to counsel for the purpose of obtaining legal advice. This is the sum and substance of what the attorney-client privilege is designed to protect.

103. If the client conveys the original of a communication to the attorney and therefore no longer possesses the document, it is still discoverable through the client because in the hands of the attorney, the document remains within the client's "possession, custody or control" and must be retrieved and produced by the client pursuant to FED. R. CIV. P. 26 and 34. In other words, conveying the original or only copy to an attorney cannot be used as a ploy for avoiding production when direct discovery cannot be sought from the attorney.

in the scope of their employment, need to know the legal advice that is being sought and received by the corporation. These communications are often accompanied by copies of prior business communications that give the attorney a factual background of the matter. Unlike the preexisting business documents attached, the direct communications to the attorney that are created for the primary purpose of obtaining legal assistance are protected by the attorney-client privilege and are not discoverable from the author, the attorney, or any individual originally copied on the communication. The fact that the "communication" contains non-privileged facts is irrelevant. The communication cannot be discovered in order to get to those non-privileged facts. While the facts still remain discoverable, they must be discovered through some discovery device other than one that requires the disclosure of what was communicated to the attorney. For example, such information is discoverable through document requests directed to the client, or deposing the client, and inquiring about his knowledge of certain facts.

The advent of e-mail has vastly complicated the distinction between the two types of communications—namely, those created for business purposes and copied to the attorney, and those created for legal assistance purposes and copied to other corporate personnel. Such complications arise because e-mail communications are simultaneously sent to everyone, and because the headers on the messages that indicate primary and secondary recipients often do not accurately reflect the primary purpose of the communication.[104]

This communication/information distinction is further complicated because both corporate businesspeople and corporate legal counsel are simultaneously made privy to e-mail threads on many more corporate matters *as they develop*. While this may be far more efficient and helpful to the client, an inherent side effect is that legal counsel are brought into written business discussions far earlier and more frequently than they were in the past, and are encouraged to participate on a much broader level. Moreover, once a lawyer has been improperly listed as a primary recipient simply to obtain the protection of the privilege and not actually to obtain legal assistance, others in the e-mail thread tend to

---

104. Those listed in the "To:" line of an e-mail message are considered primary recipients. Those listed in the "cc:" line are secondary recipients. It is not uncommon for corporate counsel to advise corporate personnel to list an attorney on the "To:" line of memoranda in order to take advantage of the attorney-client privilege. This topic is discussed in greater detail below.

innocently perpetuate the deceptive header in their responses by using the reply button.[105]

To avoid this and remain loyal to the conditions precedent to invocation of the privilege, different procedures should be considered. The following three steps are recommended:

1. Keep business communications to employees separate from communications that seek legal assistance. If necessary, attach business communications to an e-mail to legal counsel.

2. When communicating with an attorney for the primary purpose of obtaining legal assistance, always make the attorney the sole addressee. All others who receive the message, because the scope of their business responsibilities requires them to remain informed about the advice that is being sought and the information upon which that advice will be given, should be listed as copyees.

3. If copies of business communications are sent to an attorney for information purposes (i.e., screening, in the event that legal problems are unknowingly being created), send only blind copies so that when the documents are discovered in the future, they will not reveal that the material within them was communicated to legal counsel for legal advice purposes.

3.   How Is the Document Described in a Privilege Log?

E-mail communications are like a series of electronic memoranda that are tied together in a thread. Each e-mail communication can

---

105. The deceptive practice of making a communication appear to be for the purpose of legal advice when its true purpose was to communicate business matters to those who were copied on the document is not unique to e-mail communications. Unscrupulous individuals have long addressed business memoranda to legal counsel, with copies to the business personnel who were the individuals for whom the content was actually intended. This practice has been dubbed "funneling." It is fraudulent, but exceptionally difficult to detect. When suspected, the most successful means of proving funneling is to compel the privilege proponent to identify the business correspondence that has been produced on the same subject matter. If the substance of the communications being withheld is important to business that is being transacted, and no such business communications exist, the "legal" documents were actually "business" documents and funneling has occurred, or, at best, the documents had a mixed purpose, and the privilege must still be denied because the primary-purpose test has not been satisfied. *See generally* PAUL R. RICE, ATTORNEY-CLIENT PRIVILEGE IN THE UNITED STATES, § 7:2 (2d ed. 1999).

originate with different e-mail addresses and be sent to different e-mail addresses. The fact that e-mail communications are electronically tied together because they were sequentially created does not change their fundamental character. Each e-mail is a separate communication (like separate letters and memoranda) and should be described separately in the privilege log. Because the separate messages are usually tied together by common subjects, recipients, and purposes, affidavits and other supporting materials for one privilege claim can support the other claims as well.

An e-mail message can be a single communication to which there are no replies or responses. More often, e-mail messages form a string or thread of messages from and to a number of individuals who have been tied into the electronic conversation by any one of the participants in the thread.

When the attorney-client privilege is asserted for a string of messages, the question is how the string should be listed and described in the privilege log that must be served on the party demanding discovery.[106] Privilege proponents want to see the string as a single "document."[107] Under such a definition, however, how would it be described

---

106. *See* FED. R. CIV. P. 26(b)(5); *see generally* PAUL R. RICE, ATTORNEY-CLIENT PRIVILEGE IN THE UNITED STATES, §§ 11:6–11:8 (2d ed. 1999), for a discussion of privilege indices or logs and what information should be included within them.

107. In re Universal Service Fund Telephone Billing Practices Litig., 232 F.R.D. 669, 672-74 (D. Kan. 2005). The court explained why a separate listing of each e-mail message was critical to the privilege resolution process, but acknowledged the difficulties this creates:

> [R]equiring each e-mail within a strand to be listed separately on a privilege log is a laborious, time-intensive task for counsel. And, of course, that task adds considerable expense for the clients involved; even for very well-financed corporate defendants such as those in the case at bar, this is a very significant drawback to modern commercial litigation. But the court finds that adherence to such a procedure is essential to ensuring that privilege is asserted only where necessary to achieve its purpose, *e.g.*, in the case of the attorney-client privilege, protecting disclosures made to obtain legal advice which might not have been made absent the existence of the privilege. In any event, the court strongly encourages counsel, in the preparation of future privilege logs, to list each e-mail within a strand as a separate entry. Otherwise, the client may suffer a waiver of the attorney-client privilege or work product protection (and the lawyer may later draw a claim from the client).

in a way that conveys the differences between each individual message in the string? How is one to characterize the author, addressees, and copyees when each may be different on each individual message?

The *Microsoft* Litigation Experience

In the consolidated *Microsoft* cases,[108] Microsoft listed each e-mail string as a single document, describing the last chronological message in the string being withheld as privileged. Its privilege log identified the author of that message, listed all other people authoring messages in the string under the heading "email thread," listed as "recipients" those to whom the last message was addressed, and collectively revealed as copyees everyone else who was a secondary recipient of any of the messages in the string. While this proved to be adequate for the judicial officers reviewing in camera the documents described in the privilege log, it was an inadequate description for the opposing parties. In reality, there was no privilege log for the vast majority of messages for which privilege was claimed, because the privilege log described only the last message upon which privilege was being asserted. Parties in many actions have begun to gravitate to this collective description format primarily because it is easier, and because the discovering parties who acquiesce apparently do not appreciate the quantity of information they are entitled to receive but are not getting. Of course, it remains just as plausible that because each side is being asked to produce the same type of materials, each wants to enjoy the same convenience.

Often, the last message chronologically is not the most important or relevant message in the e-mail thread. Consequently, what was described in Microsoft's privilege logs was quite different from what was actually produced for judicial examination. The opposing parties, therefore, were given inadequate notice of what was being examined. In fact, this indexing scheme did not reveal how many communications were in the e-mail thread, much less the identity of each author, addressee, and

---

108. In re Microsoft Corp. Antitrust Litig., MDL Docket No. 1332 (before Judge J. Frederick Motz) (hereafter Microsoft) and California Class Action, J.C.C.P. No. 4106 (before Judge Paul H. Alvarado). The privilege resolution processes for both the state and federal cases were merged and Judge Renfrew was appointed Special Master to resolve those claims. Because the size of the undertaking proved to be overwhelming, Mr. John Cooper of Farella, Braun & Martell and I were appointed special counsel to assist Judge Renfrew in examining and ruling on each claim.

secondary recipient. This resulted in the opposing parties never seeing or arguing many substantive issues, and the briefs that were filed in opposition to individual claims were often far afield from the actual concerns raised by the documents in question. To an extent, of course, this problem is inherent in a privilege process in which the opposing party cannot know the substance of what is being debated. Necessity demands that the opposition base its objections on a level of speculation. That necessity, however, need not be exacerbated by the absence of any description (author, primary recipients, secondary recipients, and general content) of the messages under consideration. In the final analysis, these "last message" descriptions proved to be both inadequate and wasteful from an adversarial perspective.

For the adversarial system to function properly, each message needs to be identified and described in a manner that fairly permits the opposing side to assess whether the claim of privilege is valid. It is not sufficient for the privilege proponent to cut and paste the subject line of each e-mail message into a privilege log as a description of each message.[109] Subject lines on e-mail communications are often inadequate, incomplete, and created with too little thought to be the standard for providing adequate notice in an adversarial system. Only with a more informative description can opposing counsel reasonably accept a claim without objection, or conclude that it is invalid and oppose it with appropriate arguments.

For example, many communications did not involve lawyers as either authors or addressees, or listed a lawyer as only one of many recipients. Objections were often raised to these claims on the ground that the primary purpose of the communications was to discuss business matters rather than to obtain legal assistance. The observation was often inaccurate. The privilege log never disclosed that the unidentified messages in the e-mail thread, upon which the claim of privilege was based, were only partially being withheld for those portions that repeated legal advice previously obtained from legal counsel, or that directed someone to contact a lawyer on a particular matter. Had this been made clear

---

109. Muro v. Target Corp., 2006 U.S. Dist. LEXIS 86030, *9-10 (N.D. Ill. Oct. 28, 2006) ("[I]n describing each document on its privilege log, Target merely copied the information contained in the subject line of the underlying e-mail document. Target's method of cutting and pasting does not satisfy its obligation to describe the nature of the document adequately.").

in the original Microsoft privilege logs, it is likely that many objections would never have been filed and briefed.

There is also a more subtle consequence to a privilege log that is obviously incomplete but not objected to by the opposing party. Fairness compels a judicial officer to be more skeptical of the representations of the privilege proponent in order to compensate for the absence of adversarial confrontation. Assumptions about confidentiality and its maintenance or about the primary purpose of a communication appear to be less fair, and therefore are less likely to be followed.

This problem was exacerbated in *Microsoft* because it was agreed among the parties that Microsoft would not file supporting materials that substantiated the elements of each privilege claim until after special counsel (Mr. Cooper and myself) had completed an in camera review. If that review revealed that the privilege claims were facially sound, the claims were granted. If that review revealed a deficiency in the assertion of the privilege, claims were denied in a Tentative Ruling that could be challenged by supplemental filings in the form of affidavits, proffers, and attached exhibits.

In *Muro v. Target Corp.*,[110] the court rejected the idea that individual e-mail messages should be separately listed on a privilege log. The rejection, however, appears to be based on a narrow generality about how the e-mail system is used and messages are linked together in a thread. The central reason for the *Muro* court's rejection was the concern that by listing individual messages, the privilege proponent will be revealing the content of communications with the attorney. This certainly could happen where the attached messages are not privileged (and therefore were independently produced) but are subsequently made part of a larger communication from the client to the attorney in which the entire e-mail thread forms the basis upon which the advice from the attorney is sought. As explained in *Muro*:

> A party can therefore legitimately withhold an entire e-mail *forwarding* prior materials to counsel, while also disclosing those prior materials themselves. It would well be confusing to require a party to list documents in its privilege log that it has already furnished to opposing counsel. More troublingly, the disclosure of this information could very well be a breach of

110. 2007 U.S. Dist. LEXIS 81776 (N.D. Ill. Nov. 2, 2007).

attorney-client privilege. If the opposing party can gather enough materials from the log and already produced material to discover the topic or contents of material forwarded to counsel, then a privileged communication has been revealed to that party. Rule 26(b)(5)(A) requires only that a party provide sufficient information for an opposing party to evaluate the applicability of privilege, "without revealing information itself privileged." Thus, Judge Brown erred by reading this rule to require a method of itemization that will, in some cases, force parties to disclose privileged information.

The forwarding of previous messages certainly can make a string of non-privileged e-mail messages part of a privileged e-mail "communication," and a description of the attached messages can indirectly reveal to the opposing party the content of that "communication" by simply examining the attachments previously produced. In my experience, however, this is not reflective of most e-mail messages, particularly when in-house attorneys are tied into internal corporate communications.

As explained in the discussion of the privilege resolution process of the consolidated *Vioxx* cases,[111] the purpose of many communications is mixed. And the reason legal counsel is tied into the string of discussions is also frequently mixed. While it is true, as the *Muro* court noted, that everything in a communication with legal counsel needs to be legal for it to be protected by the attorney-client privilege, many in-house counsel have business as well as legal responsibilities within the company, and even when they have no business responsibilities, they are often drawn into business discussions from a business, rather than a legal, perspective. As a consequence, each e-mail must be separately assessed because each message is either not privileged or only selected portions of it may be privileged, and separate listing requires the privilege proponent to more carefully examine each in whole and in part. The mere fact that technology permits parties to electronically tie communications together should not change the parties' obligation to separately identify the tied communications when those tied communications would have been separately listed on a privilege log and separately justified under the privilege rule before the adoption of the new technology. When the situation the *Muro* court was concerned about actually arises,

---

111. *See infra* at 266.

it can be dealt with on a thread-by-thread basis in the privilege log, with general assertions that the court can confirm in its in camera inspection of the e-mails.

E-mail technology has exponentially increased the number of communications in which lawyers are casually included for both business and legal purposes, and on which corporate clients attempt to claim privilege. While asserting privilege has created incredible burdens for corporations during the discovery process, they are burdens of their own making. To meet the burdens, corporate clients and their attorneys have become a bit lazy in their efforts to identify and justify each claim. Courts should not be willing facilitators in this expansion and relaxation.

4. Are Operating Assumptions About the Purpose of Communications Appropriate Based on the Individuals to Whom They Have Been Disseminated?

When a client communicates with outside counsel, courts have concluded that it is logical for judges to assume that the purpose of the communications to and from legal counsel was primarily for the purpose of obtaining or providing legal assistance.[112] If the content or other

---

112. *See, e.g.,* United States v. Chen, 99 F.3d 1495, 1501 (9th Cir. 1996) ("If a person hires a lawyer for advice, there is a rebuttable presumption that the lawyer is hired 'as such' to give 'legal advice,' whether the subject of the advice is criminal or civil, business, tort, domestic relations, or anything else. But the presumption is rebutted when the facts show that the lawyer was 'employed without reference to his knowledge and discretion in the law.'"); Diversified Indus., Inc. v. Meredith, 572 F.2d 596, 610 (8th Cir. 1977) ("Here, the matter [an investigation of internal corrupt practices] was committed to Wilmer, Cutler & Pickering, a professional legal adviser. Thus, it was prima facie committed for the sake of legal advice and was, therefore, within the privilege absent a clear showing to the contrary."); Borase v. M/A COM, Inc., 171 F.R.D. 10, 14, (D. Mass. 1997) ("Accordingly, if an in-house counsel has other nonlegal responsibilities, the party invoking the privilege has the burden of producing evidence in support of its contention that in-house counsel was engaged in giving legal advice and not in some other capacity at the time of the disputed conversations. . . . Thus, in the instant case, in order to prevail, M/A COM must prove that Mr. Birchfield was acting as an attorney during the course of these disputed conversations. Merely saying that he was so acting in a memorandum of law is patently insufficient to meet the burden. Neither can it be assumed. . . . M/A COM would have the Court presume [that legal advice was being sought] from the circumstances, arguing that obviously Mr. Birchfield was acting in the

circumstances of the communication do not suggest otherwise, it is reasonable for the judge to conclude that that element of the attorney-client privilege has been satisfied. For several reasons, the same assumption may not be appropriate for internal e-mail communications that have been sent to in-house counsel.[113]

---

same capacity as the attorneys from [the outside law firm of] Edwards & Angell. While such an assumption might be able to be made if M/A COM had retained outside counsel for the particular purpose of representing it in its dealings with Mr. Borase and his attorneys, the assumption cannot be made in the case of an in-house counsel who has other additional responsibilities over and above the rendering of legal advice. On the record before me, it is not possible to find that Mr. Birchfield was giving legal as opposed to business advice."); Weeks v. Samsung Heavy Indus., Ltd., 1996 WL 288511 (N.D. Ill. Mar. 30, 1996) (presumption applied to attorney billing statement); Hartman v. Banks, 1995 WL 453737, at *1 (E.D. Pa. July 26, 1995) ("Although it is not possible to determine from the description given by Nationwide of the purposes of these letters [from Nationwide's outside counsel], it can be assumed in this context that they were written with the purpose of providing legal assistance."); In re Federated Dept. Stores, Inc. v. United States, 170 B.R. 331, 354-55 (S.D. Ohio 1994) (presumption not overcome by opposing party); Coleman v. Am. Broadcasting Cos., 106 F.R.D. 201, 206 (D. D.C. 1985) (after prima facie showing of privilege by proponent, opponent must prove the contrary); Cedrone v. Unity Sav. Ass'n, 103 F.R.D. 423, 427 (E.D. Pa. 1984) ("[A]ll communications from a client to his/her attorney in a professional context are presumptively protected . . . ."); Conn. Mut. Life Ins. Co. v. Shields, 18 F.R.D. 448, 450 (S.D.N.Y. 1955) ("Certainly matters committed to legal advisers are prima facie so committed for purposes to which the privilege attaches."). *But see* Air-Shield, Inc. v. Air Reduction Co., 46 F.R.D. 96, 97 (M.D. Fla. 1968) ("The plaintiff's claim of privilege rests on the fact that outside counsel was present at each of the meetings of the patent committee. To allow this fact to immunize the minutes of a corporate committee meeting . . . would be to give too broad a scope to the attorney-client privilege. It would enable corporations to protect against the possible future production of any committee minutes simply by having outside counsel in attendance."). For a complete discussion of presumptions and assumptions, *see* PAUL R. RICE, ATTORNEY-CLIENT PRIVILEGE IN THE UNITED STATES, §§ 7:28-30 (2d ed. 1999).

113. United States v. Chevron Texaco Corp., 241 F. Supp. 2d 1065, 1076 (N.D. Cal. 2002) ("Because in-house counsel may operate in a purely or primarily business capacity in connection with many corporate endeavors, the presumption that attaches to communication with outside counsel does not extend to communications with in-house counsel. . . . With respect to internal communications involving in-house counsel, Chevron must make a 'clear showing' that the 'speaker' made the communications for the purpose of obtaining or providing legal advice.").

First, as previously discussed, e-mail technology can draw legal counsel into business discussions at any given point and in a way that previously did not occur unless lawyers had been part of oral discussions. Consequently, counsel's role in the company can be far broader than the official job description might suggest.

Second, corporate personnel often hold a broad view of what constitutes legal assistance. For example, it is commonly believed that when a lawyer engages in contract negotiations with prospective customers, this constitutes legal, as opposed to business, assistance because the contract is a legal instrument and the lawyer is applying her special expertise to the terminology that each side seeks to have adopted. While this may appear to be a reasonable argument, if it were accepted by the courts, it would establish a dangerous precedent. Within a corporation, a broad range of activities (public relations, accounting, advertising, etc.) have legal implications. If employing a lawyer to perform them resulted in the application of privilege to the lawyer's communications, then a significant amount of information about internal corporate activities that is currently discoverable would be suppressed. Nothing of importance within the daily affairs of the corporation would be immune from this ploy.

Whether a function is legal or business in nature must ultimately turn on the character of what is being done rather than the status of the person doing it or the legal consequences that could follow. If the function does not require a law degree or legal expertise, and if a non-lawyer performing the service would not be considered practicing law without a license, the service should be considered business rather than legal in nature. Because this may not generally be understood in the corporate community, representations about legal counsel only serving in a legal capacity are not sufficiently credible to be relied upon by judicial officers.

Third, it is a common misunderstanding in the corporate world that placing the name of a lawyer in the "to:" line of an e-mail message or placing the label "Confidential—Attorney-Client Privilege" at the top of the message will make the attorney-client privilege applicable. While sending a communication to a lawyer is essential for the privilege to apply, it is not, by itself, a sufficient basis for legally presuming or even logically assuming a primary legal purpose. The content of the message must request legal assistance, and the information conveyed must be reasonably related to the assistance sought. Therefore, the value of the pattern of distribution does not inherently indicate a legal purpose.

Fourth, when factual communications are exchanged among corporate business personnel and also shared with legal counsel, the primary purpose of the communication cannot be for legal advice if these communications are the only means by which necessary business information is circulated within the company. At best, the purpose of the communication is mixed. Therefore, the entire message cannot be privileged, because the privilege is only applicable when the proponent demonstrates that its primary purpose was to obtain legal assistance. When a lawyer is copied on a business communication, a rational assumption could be that the privilege does not protect the entire e-mail string.[114] Portions of the e-mail string, however, can be protected by the privilege when they are segregable and relate only to communications to, and advice from, the attorney.

a. *When business and legal communications can be separated*

When communications serve both business and legal advice purposes, they may be withheld from discovery on the ground of attorney-client privilege if the portions that address legal matters can be separated from the remainder of the document. For example, in the middle of a business discussion into which in-house counsel had been tied, the author stated, "Charlie [the lawyer], would you look into the antitrust implications of this and get back to us by Friday?" While the communication as a whole is not protected by the privilege because its primary purpose is not to obtain legal assistance, the sentence addressed to the lawyer is. It can appropriately be excised before production.

Merely because legal counsel is included in the discussion of a business deal that has legal implications does not convert the business discussion into a communication protected by the privilege. Otherwise, every business communication within a company could be made privileged by including a lawyer. For example, a business deal may be in the

---

114. *See* In re Vioxx Products Liab. Litig., 501 F. Supp. 2d 789, 809 (E.D. La. 2007). The fact that the lawyer is only a copyee or secondary recipient can be misleading. Occasionally, headers will be cut and pasted from previous messages without serious thought being given to how someone is listed. This may be apparent from the content of the communication. For example, when the content of the document is addressed to the lawyer by name, and the content is clearly legal in nature, obviously the claim of privilege would be warranted.

offing, and in-house counsel is brought into the e-mail string so that potential antitrust problems can be identified and avoided. Even though the entirety of all of the messages may be important to both the business and legal questions explored, the communication is not protected by the privilege. Only the segregable portions primarily concerned with legal assistance receive that benefit.

Prior to e-mail technology, these examples would have involved hard copies of business memoranda being sent to legal counsel for examination. As previously discussed, the fact that the copies were communicated to legal counsel is privileged, but the memoranda themselves remain non-privileged and discoverable.[115] These communications should be sent via blind copy to preserve the confidentiality that the privilege was designed to protect.[116]

When the fact that the copy was sent to counsel is noted on the face of the document, the basis of the privilege protection is destroyed; this should theoretically destroy the privilege protection for responsive communications from the attorney as well.[117] First, many courts extended

---

115. *See* text at note 103, *supra.*

116. The BCC function of e-mail programs, however, may inadequately accomplish this because the hard-copy printout from the author's computer will remain discoverable and will indicate that a blind copy was sent to the attorney. Also the metadata underlying the document will reveal that a copy was sent to the attorney. To completely conceal the act of communicating e-mail messages to a lawyer, the author needs to send a separate communication to the attorney by copying the original into the body of an e-mail message addressed only to the lawyer. In the second transmission to the attorney, the recipients of the original message can safely be disclosed to the attorney.

117. Theoretically, the fact that the client announces on the face of the document that its content was communicated to legal counsel should prevent the application of the privilege to the responsive communications of counsel. The attorney-client privilege *only* encourages the client to be more open and candid with the attorney. The theory behind the privilege has been that the client, by being assured that what he says to an attorney cannot harm him, will be open and candid in his communications with counsel. If the client is candid with counsel, then counsel will be better informed and better able to render the most effective assistance to the client. The privilege was not designed to protect the communications of legal counsel. Responsive communications of legal counsel, however, have been granted a derivative protection.

To the extent that counsel's responsive communications revealed the content of the client's prior confidential communications, they were given the protection of the privilege. The privilege did not protect attorney communication that

the protection of the privilege to the advice of counsel without regard to whether it explicitly revealed prior confidences of the client. These courts assumed that such advice would always reveal such confidences. Second, in certain jurisdictions the privilege began to be defined as protecting communications "between" the attorney and the client without restricting it to either advice or communications that revealed prior client confidences. For example, in jurisdictions such as the Ninth Circuit and the state of California, the derivative nature of the rule for responsive communications has been explicitly abandoned. Consequently, in the corporate context, responsive attorney communications are protected regardless of whether the prior communications of the client to legal counsel have been revealed. Because the law of attorney-client privilege in most states and federal jurisdictions has not evolved in this way from its classical origins, a very different outcome could result in those jurisdictions. Acknowledging that the communication was copied to in-house counsel does not change its primary purpose, does not convert it from business to legal, and does not justify the application of the privilege. This, however, is what many parties attempt to do by openly acknowledging in e-mails and other correspondence that lawyers have been copied, and then privilege is asserted to justify withholding these communications from discovery.

The most that can reasonably be claimed by sending copies of business communications to lawyers is that their purpose is mixed. The only communication in a mixed-purpose e-mail thread that will be protected by the privilege are: (1) the copy sent to the lawyer; (2) communications among businesspeople in preparation for immediate consultations with legal counsel; (3) communications of businesspeople that are responding to requests for information from the lawyer so that informed advice can be given; (4) the responsive communications of legal counsel in which legal advice is given that reveals prior confidential communications of the client; and (4) the repetition by businesspeople of the legal advice previously received. These can appropriately be redacted from the mixed-purpose e-mail thread before it is produced during discov-

did not reveal client confidences. If there were no client confidences, because the content of what the client communicated to legal counsel had already been disclosed (as occurs with corporate communications revealing that copies were sent to an attorney), there would be no reason, under a strict application of the privilege rule, to protect the attorney's responsive advice. Courts have never enforced this restriction against corporations.

ery. Redaction can result in whole messages being deleted or the deletion of paragraphs, sentences, or just clauses.

b. When business and legal advice are inextricably intertwined

In the responsive communications from an attorney, it is often necessary that the attorney give both business and legal advice because they are inextricably intertwined. This concept of "inextricably intertwined" applies only to communications from the lawyer. It should not be applied to communications to the lawyer from the client, because it leads to sharp practices in an effort to conceal discoverable information and communications.

When a lawyer performs a business function, such as negotiating a contract, the lawyer's e-mail communications with other corporate personnel could be privileged to the extent that legal advice is being given about the service he has performed and is reporting upon. However, the lawyer's reports about the actions he has taken for the company during contract negotiations (e.g., the positions the parties have taken, strategies pursued, and the relative strength of various positions) are not privileged. These reports are part of the contract services that are more business than legal in nature. In contrast, comments about how certain proposed actions might create product liability issues or violate antitrust laws would be privileged. There are two reasons why reports for the attorney on the positions taken by the opposing side during negotiations would not be privileged. The first is that the information was not acquired in the course of rendering legal advice or assistance. Second, recounting things said by third parties would not be privileged because it does not reveal the content of any prior confidential communication of the lawyer's client, the corporation.[118]

To the extent that legal advice is incorporated into the lawyer's report, that advice would be privileged, but only if it can be severed from the report itself. The burden is on the privilege proponent to differentiate the legal from the nonlegal. If this is not accomplished, the privilege should fail, because the proponent has failed to demonstrate that the primary purpose of the communication was to render legal assistance.

When lawyers are consulted for the purpose of rendering a particular legal service (unlike the lawyer conducting business negotiations

---

118. *See* PAUL R. RICE, ATTORNEY-CLIENT PRIVILEGE IN THE UNITED STATES, § 5:2, p. 55 (2d ed. 1999).

for the client), the responsive communications of the attorney often involve a mixture of legal and business advice. Complete and meaningful advice can involve business direction that complements the legal service because legal problems arise from the business environment. Courts have accepted that the two are inextricably intertwined and have extended the privilege protection to the entire body of advice.[119] When the

119. In re OM Group Sec. Litig., 226 F.R.D. 579, 590 (N.D. Ohio 2005) (Advice given to Audit Committee by attorneys occasionally was business in nature. Court held privilege applicable because the legal and business concerns were inextricably intertwined.); Coleman v. Am. Broadcasting Co., 106 F.R.D. 201, 206 (D. D.C. 1985); Hercules Inc. v. Exxon Corp., 434 F. Supp. 136, 147 (D. Del. 1977) ("The problem remains, however, of separating business from legal advice. An important responsibility of most patent attorneys, especially those employed by corporate patent departments, is to assess the business implications of the company's patent position. Many of the communications between the patent attorney and nonlegal personnel of the corporation would therefore predominantly reflect business concerns, such as the competitive position of the company, marketing strategy, licensing policy, etc. The Court recognizes that business and legal advice may often be inextricably interwoven. A single proposed course of conduct such as patenting and licensing of an invention will have both legal and business ramifications, and the lawyer may advise as to both in a single communication. As was pointed out in Jack Winter, Inc. v. Koratron Inc. [54 F.R.D. 44 (N.D. Cal. 1971)], it is necessary to separate the two, in the interest of preserving the integrity of the privilege itself: 'As is not infrequently the case in patent matters, the problem of classification here was particularly troublesome as the attorneys for Koratron performed virtually every task incident to filing for and obtaining a patent or trademark registration. They were so closely associated with the activities of Koratron that picking out from the mass of documents presented to the court those which involved nonlegal transactions not soliciting or offering legal advice, and the separating of these from documents which did involve the exercise of the attorney's art, became at times an arduous and complex exercise. Yet we have sought to not lose sight of the importance of the distinction, for it is important that the attorney-client privilege not be downgraded in the interests of expedient results.' 54 F.R.D. at 47. . . . If the primary purpose of a communication is to solicit or render advice on nonlegal matters, the communication is not within the scope of the attorney-client privilege. Only if the attorney is 'acting as a lawyer'—giving advice with respect to the legal implications of a proposed course of conduct—may the privilege be properly invoked. In addition, if a communication is made primarily for the purpose of soliciting legal advice, an incidental request for business advice does not vitiate the attorney-client privilege."); Chore-Time Equip., Inc. v. Big Dutchman, Inc., 255 F. Supp. 1020, 1023 (W.D. Mich. 1966) ("Where a lawyer possesses multifarious talents, his clients should not be deprived of the attorney-client privilege, where applicable, simply because their correspondence is also concerned with highly technical mat-

lawyer is *not* employed primarily for legal assistance, however, he assumes the role of a business consultant, and the extension of the privilege protection under the "inextricably intertwined" concept is unjustified, inappropriate, and dangerous.

Extension of the privilege protection to legal and business advice that is inextricably intertwined was a practical necessity for effective legal services. The application of this concept should be strictly limited to the context in which it originally was recognized. It should not be expanded to include (1) communications from the client to legal counsel in which business and legal matters are intertwined or (2) communications from legal counsel that are a byproduct of nonlegal services. Unlike when an attorney provides legal assistance, the mixture of legal and nonlegal communications noted above is the product of client choice rather than the inherent nature of the service sought.

When a corporation sends an e-mail communication involving business matters to both business and legal personnel, seeking both types of assistance in the same communication, the mixing of the two so that they cannot be separated is a voluntary decision by the client that is not compelled by the legal services being sought. The client could have sent a separate transmission of the e-mail message to the attorney, thereby separating the legal from the nonlegal. Expanding the privilege protection to business communications would permit the client to engage in a form of funneling—sending everything through the attorney, even though business was the primary purpose, solely to obtain the protection of the attorney-client privilege.[120] Having voluntarily chosen this means

---

ters. Patent lawyers should not be banished to the status of quasi-lawyers by reason of the fact that besides being skilled in the law, they are also competent in scientific and technical areas.").

120. Schwab v. Philip Morris USA, Inc., 2006 U.S. Dist. LEXIS 73208, *42 (E.D. N.Y. Sept. 25, 2006) (Outside counsel wrote to the head of research regarding a collection of scientific evidence related to a plaintiff's disease. In an effort to create an attorney-client privilege, he wrote: "Because correspondence on the subject of Buerger's disease exchanged between you and your colleagues in other companies might not be privileged, it is important that the contact between scientists should be routed through the lawyers."); Fru-Con Constr. Corp. v. Sacramento Mun. Utility Dist., 2006 WL 2255538, *4 (E.D. Cal. Aug. 7, 2006) ("If there ever were a manipulated creation of attorney-client privilege, these documents show it. The author of the e-mail underlying the e-mail at issue, a management non-lawyer concerning potential disputes with Fu-Con. The author states that he 'thought it best to offer my thoughts in writing and do so under the privilege.' The writer believes that all he

of transmission, the client should bear the loss of the privilege protection. Otherwise, the opposing party would lose the discovery of non-privileged business information. It is not sufficient that the business and legal parts of the communications are inextricably intertwined, because the client has voluntary chosen to mix them. This is quite unlike the context in which the "inextricably intertwined" logic arose, i.e., responsive advice being given by an attorney, and the mixing of legal and nonlegal matters being necessary because of the nature of the client, the context in which the problem arose, and the type of services being rendered.

Similarly, when the client uses in-house counsel to perform nonlegal services, such as public relations work or contract negotiations, and the lawyer subsequently finds it necessary to mix his factual reporting with his legal advice, this is a situation that the client created by assigning a lawyer to this task, not one that is driven exclusively by the necessities of the advice being given. Consequently, the client should not be rewarded by broadening the privilege protection. Otherwise, corporations will be encouraged to employ lawyers to perform many critical functions that the corporation would like to keep secret.

The requirement that communications between the attorney and client be primarily for the purpose of obtaining legal advice or assistance proved to be a central issue in the consolidated *Vioxx* cases in the Eastern District of Louisiana where, as in the consolidated *Microsoft* cases, massive numbers of privilege claims had been raised for e-mail communications that had been widely disseminated within the company for both business and legal purposes.

The *Vioxx* Litigation Experience

In *In re Vioxx Products Liability* the defendant, Merck & Co., asserted privilege claims on tens of thousands of documents. The volume of withheld documents required a novel judicial resolution process that will be discussed later. Within this mass of withheld communications, the "legal advice or assistance" requirement became a central issue in

---

has to do to automatically imbue the document as privileged is to 'cc' the attorney because nowhere in the document does he indicate that he is seeking any advice whatsoever from the attorney. This ordinary business document was written for an ordinary business reason; clearly the dominant impetus for the document was not the seeking of legal advice.").

several ways. First, because it is a drug company and pervasively regulated by the Food and Drug Administration, Merck made exceptionally broad claims, arguing that virtually every contact with in-house counsel was primarily for legal assistance. Second, usually the communications with in-house counsel for legal assistance were simultaneously sent to non-lawyers within the company for business purposes, thereby giving them a mixed purpose. Third, responsive communications from in-house attorneys were often electronically attached to the client's mixed-purpose communications that were not protected by the attorney-client privilege. Fourth, because in-house counsel had virtual veto power over the dissemination of large numbers of communications generated within the company, Merck claimed that non-privileged mixed-purpose communications should not be discoverable because subsequent changes necessary to the removal of the legal department's "hold" on the communications could be discerned by comparing the initial version with the final published version (a process Merck dubbed "reverse engineering").

Pervasive Regulation Theory. In support of its claim that, because of the pervasive regulation by the Federal Drug Administration (FDA), virtually everything a drug company does involves potential legal problems, Merck submitted an array of articles, manuals, and depositions describing the extensive nature of governmental regulation. While the court was convinced that the government's regulation of things like advertising of drugs could convert what might not appear to be legal assistance to something that could be protected by the attorney-client privilege, Merck still had to address whether a lawyer's comments on any given matter were primarily legal in nature or a mixture of both legal and non-legal assessments that had to be redacted. While the Special Master often found excision to be appropriate, he concluded that the benefits were far outweighed by the costs involved in either the Special Master making those redactions or Merck taking weeks of additional time to make them, after which the Special Master would have to review each document again. This was particularly true since the materials that could be discovered were relatively insignificant in light of the claims being pursued, and equivalent evidence was available from other sources. Therefore, when a lawyer's comments were focused on a regulatory concern, the Special Master overlooked many comments on proposed promotional material because they were sufficiently intertwined with the legal assistance being rendered.

Under its pervasive regulation argument, Merck next claimed that e-mails of draft reports, proposals, letters, and articles addressed to multiple legal and non-legal people within the company were protected by the attorney-client privilege even though the distribution patterns circumstantially indicated that the communications served both legal and non-legal purposes, and therefore were not *primarily* for legal advice or assistance. Its argument was that distribution to every department of the company was part of a "collaborative effort to accomplish a legally sufficient draft." Therefore, Merck claimed that through the responsive commentary of every other department within the company, Merck's in-house attorneys were using the other departments as their necessary agents in their attempt to give the most effective legal assistance. They claimed that dissemination of the proposed materials to departments specializing in such diverse things as science, technology, public relations, or marketing were all primarily for legal advice or assistance. While ingenious, the argument was rejected for two reasons.

First, in every company, all departments are part of a "collaborative effort." If a product were not scientifically or medically valid, it would not be marketable. If a good product did not obtain necessary government approval, it could not be placed on the market. If the public relations department did not effectively increase the company's name recognition and good will, professionals would not recommend the product, or customers would gravitate to competing names. To say that wide dissemination to non-lawyers within a company for their technical input is still primarily legal makes no more sense than saying that communicating with in-house counsel is primarily scientific because scientific validity is at the heart of FDA regulations and, as a consequence, of what lawyers must be concerned about in public statements, advertisements, and labels.

Second, this "collaborative effort" argument, if successful, would effectively immunize all internal communications of the drug industry, thereby defeating the broad discovery authorized in the Federal Rules of Civil Procedure. It would preclude plaintiffs from discovering communications that might be valid to claims of knowledge, failure to timely warn, and intentional misrepresentation. To permit the attorney-client privilege to have such an impact on the discovery process would be allowing the tail to wag the dog.

The court's rejection of the expansive claims under "pervasive regulation" arguments often resulted in a privilege protection being recognized for only the lawyers' responsive comments on widely disseminated materials. The client communications upon which those lawyers' comments were often placed were frequently denied because of the second manner in which legal assistance came to be a central issue in the case—communications circulated within the company for both legal and non-legal purposes.

The Manner in Which Communications Were Circulated Within the Company. The manner in which Merck circulated documents within the company had consequences that Merck had to live with when privilege was asserted. For the vast majority of communications upon which privilege was claimed, Merck simultaneously sent communications to both lawyers and non-lawyers within the company. As a consequence, Merck could not claim that their primary purpose was for legal advice, because the communication served both business and legal purposes.[121]

To make matters worse, when Merck simultaneously circulated communications through e-mails, the authors always listed Merck's attorneys in the headers as recipients with the non-lawyers. Because the copies of the communications being sent to the non-lawyers were not primarily for legal assistance and thus were discoverable, the production of those communications revealed the content of the single message that was sent to the Merck attorneys for legal assistance. Consequently, not even that single message could be protected by the attorney-client privilege, as its confidentiality had been breached. To guard against such disclosures, all copies to lawyers should have been by blind copy. While I regularly advise corporations to employ blind copies, too often their lawyers advise otherwise, because some judges are misled into believing that if even one copy goes to a lawyer, every

---

121. United States v. Chevron Corp., 1996 WL 444597 (N.D. Cal. 1996) ("When a document is prepared for simultaneous review by non-legal as well as legal personnel, it is not considered to have been prepared primarily to seek legal advice and the attorney-client privilege does not apply."); United States v. Int'l Bus. Machines Corp., 66 F.R.D. 206, 213 (S.D.N.Y. 1974) ("If the document was prepared for purposes of simultaneous review by legal and non-legal personnel, it cannot be said that the primary purpose of the document is to secure legal advice.").

circulated copy is also privileged. While this is clearly not true, too often the gamble apparently has been worth the risk.

The consequences for Merck, however, could have been much greater than they actually were. Under the classical definition of the attorney-client privilege, responsive communications from the attorney are only *derivatively* protected.[122] This means that the advice that is given by the attorney is not protected unless it discloses the content of prior confidential communications from the client. Since Merck had disclosed the bulk of its previous communications to its attorneys, thereby destroying their confidentiality, none of the responses should have been privileged because there were no client confidences to protect. The Special Master chose not to impose such severe consequences on Merck because the derivative theory, while still acknowledged as controlling in most jurisdictions,[123] including the Fifth Circuit,[124] is honored more in theory than in practice. Many courts extend the privilege protection to the lawyers' advice as well as their communications that reveal the prior confidential communications of the client.[125]

---

122. See discussion of the derivative rule for responsive attorney communications to the client. *See* PAUL R. RICE, 1 ATTORNEY-CLIENT PRIVILEGE IN THE UNITED STATES, § 5:2 (2d ed. 1999).

123. *See* PAUL R. RICE, *supra* note 122.

124. *See* Garner v. Wolfinbarger, 430 F.2d 1093 (5th Cir. 1970).

125. *See, e.g.,* United States v. Frederick, 182 F.3d 496, 501 (7th Cir. 1999) (In a discussion of how the privilege would operate to protect numerical information communicated to the attorney by the client, the court asserted that a lawyer's estimate of a client's damages would be privileged because it would reflect "the lawyer's professional assessment." The court did not mention whether the assessment had to reveal the confidential communications of the client, but this may have been assumed, since the assessment was premised on the truth of what the client had said.); In re Grand Jury Proceeding (Barton), 68 F.3d 193, 196-97 (7th Cir. 1995) (An attorney was asked questions about his communications to the client and third parties. The court held that "if the questions do not entail legal advice, the attorney-client privilege does not come into play—irrespective of whether the attorney is or is not also the records custodian. *The privilege is limited to legal advice.*") (emphasis added); United States v. Amerada Hess Corp., 619 F.2d 980, 986 (3d Cir. 1980) ("Legal advice or opinion from an attorney to his client, individual or corporate, has consistently been held by the federal courts to be within the protection of the attorney-client privilege. . . . Two reasons have been advanced in support of the two-way application of the privilege. The first is the necessity of preventing the use of an attorney's advice to support inferences as to the content of confidential communications by the client to the attorney. . . . The

Electronic Line Edits on Otherwise Non-privileged Documents. Modern technology has made it possible for lawyers to respond to requests for legal assistance on the electronically transmitted documents in which the advice was sought. Merck's in-house attorneys often provided comments on letters, drafts, and proposals through electronic line edits on

---

second is that, independent of the content of any client communication, legal advice given to the client should remain confidential. . . . To the extent that the trial court predicated its ruling on the general inapplicability of the privilege to communications from the attorney to the client, we disapprove of it."); In re Fischel, 557 F.2d 209, 211 (9th Cir. 1977) ("Ordinarily the compelled disclosure of an attorney's communications or advice to the client will effectively reveal the substance of the client's confidential communication to the attorney. To prevent this result, the privilege normally extends both to the substance of the communication as well as to the attorney's advice in response thereto."); In re Sealed Case, 737 F.2d 94, 99 (D.C. Cir. 1984) ("In practice, however, advice does not spring from lawyers' heads as Athena did from the brow of Zeus. Inevitably, attorneys' opinions reflect an accumulation of education and experience in the law and the large society law serves. In a given case, advice prompted by the client's disclosures may be further and inseparably informed by other knowledge and encounters. We have therefore stated that the privilege cloaks a communication from attorney to client "'based, *in part at least*, upon a confidential communication [to the lawyer] from [the client].'"); Zenith Elecs. Corp. v. WH-V Broadcasting Corp., 2003 U.S. Dist. LEXIS 13816, *9-10 (N.D. Ill. Aug. 7, 2003) (Draft agreements containing notes from the attorney were protected because they were rendering legal advice.) (not available on Westlaw); United States v. Ohio Edison Co., 2003 U.S. Dist. LEXIS 25029, *9-10 (S.D. Ohio Jan. 6, 2003) ("Despite the existence of some authority for a narrow interpretation of the attorney-client privilege as it relates to attorney-initiated communications, the greater and more persuasive weight of authority holds that exactly the type of generalized legal communications which, plaintiffs argue, are not covered by the attorney-client privilege, are privileged. This Court agrees with the general proposition that 'the [attorney-client] privilege . . . extends to communications from counsel to client for the purpose of giving legal advice.'"); Henry v. Champlain Enters., Inc., 212 F.R.D. 73, 90 (N.D. N.Y. 2003) ("Those communications [protected by the privilege] include the information provided by the client and the legal advice given. . . ."); Muncy v. City of Dallas, 2001 WL 1795591, at *1 (N.D. Tex. Nov. 13, 2001) ("An attorney's communications to a client may also be protected by the privilege, to the extent that they are based on or contain confidential information provided by the client, or legal advice or opinions of the attorney."); McCook Metals v. Alcoa Inc., 192 F.R.D. 242, (N.D. Ill. 2000) (granting the privilege protection, throughout the opinion, whenever a communication involved legal advice from counsel).

the face of communications on which privilege claims had been denied because of mixed purposes—not primarily for legal assistance. Merck claimed that documents that were otherwise not privileged, and therefore discoverable, became non-discoverable because of the manner in which its lawyers *chose* to reveal their advice. This argument was rejected because a party cannot be permitted to deprive adversaries of discovery by voluntarily choosing to electronically superimpose that legal advice on discoverable communications. Merck was permitted to delete the electronic line edits, but the otherwise discoverable documents remained discoverable.

While Merck was permitted to withhold the responsive advice provided by its in-house counsel, whether in separate communications or inserted electronically in the client's initial requests, some of the broad array of comments made by Merck's in-house attorneys were not protected. While many were legal advice on their face (for example, proposed changes to draft legal instruments like contracts), many others appeared to be of more of an editorial nature, where sections were deleted, new paragraphs were added, and references to different drugs were inserted. Often comments were offered by attorneys that were technological, scientific, public relations or marketing in nature. These appeared to be comments about matters that would not have been privileged if they had been made by employees of departments primarily responsible for those topics. When lawyers make the same comments as non-lawyers, their comments should not be classified differently, unless the privilege proponent demonstrates on a document-by-document, paragraph-by-paragraph, or even line-by-line basis how the comments primarily related to legal assistance. When that was not provided, claims were denied. Merck could not reasonably expect judicial officers to make that assessment for it, and the Special Master was not willing to presume that everything in-house counsel commented upon was primarily legal in nature.

The Elevated Powers of In-House Counsel. One of the more unique arguments made by Merck for withholding documents that were not primarily circulated for the purpose of obtaining legal assistance (because they served mixed legal and business purposes) was the "reverse engineering" theory. Merck argued that the studies, articles, abstracts, and proposals that were not privileged should still not be discoverable, because adversaries could discern the legal advice that was provided to

Merck by comparing the initial mixed-purpose drafts with the final study or article that was approved by in-house counsel for publication. The differences would be the changes that the lawyers insisted be made.

While there may have been some truth to the "reverse engineering" argument, it was not compelling for a number of reasons. First, the fact that lawyers in the legal department recommend that certain actions be taken by their corporation does not mean that the corporation must follow that advice. Therefore, changes will not necessarily reflect what the lawyer recommended. Second, revisions can be made in the absence of recommendations from lawyers. Third, if the legal department were given control over public dissemination of communications (by being given the authority to place holds on documents until its recommendations are incorporated or its concerns are otherwise satisfied, which was apparently the case with Merck), the role of legal counsel would appear to change from legal advisor to corporate decision-maker. This is a role that a corporation does not have the right to delegate to attorneys and then insist that the decisions they make are immune from discovery.[126]

Certainly when corporate executives make decisions after consulting with an attorney, their decision is not privileged, regardless of whether it is based on that advice or even mirrors it.[127] This cannot be gotten around by the simple expedient of putting a lawyer in the shoes of the executive or, as Merck did, giving the legal department the power of the corporate executive.[128]

---

126. The tobacco industry attempted to do this with departments engaged in scientific research on the effects of nicotine on smokers and was unsuccessful.

127. United States v. Freeman, 619 F.2d 1112, 1119-20 (5th Cir. 1980) ("An attorney's involvement in, or recommendation of, a transaction does not place a cloak of secrecy around all the incidents of such a transaction."). *See* PAUL R. RICE, 1 ATTORNEY-CLIENT PRIVILEGE IN THE UNITED STATES, § 5:15, p. 113 (2d ed. 1999) ("The privilege does not extend to decisions made by the client based on the legal advice the client received. Since the actions taken by the client do not have to be consistent with the advice given, an extension of the privilege to client decisions would be unwarranted. Revealing client actions or decisions would disclose neither the substance of the recommendation nor the content of the client's privileged communications upon which the decisions/actions were based. Disclosure of the client's action, therefore, would not discourage the conduct that the privilege was designed to encourage.").

128. *See* Schwab v. Philip Morris USA, Inc., 2006 U.S. Dist. LEXIS 73196, *32-33 (E.D. N.Y. Sept. 25, 2006); United States v. Philip Morris USA, Inc., 449 F. Supp. 2d 1 (D. D.C. 2006) (cases discussed therein).

Increased Judicial Burden. The judicial burden of assessing the validity of attorney-client privilege claims for e-mail messages within business entities has become increasingly complicated for several reasons. First, corporate businesspeople and corporate lawyers are privy to most corporate matters as they develop. Therefore, unlike the past, when most documents were completely privileged or not, many e-mails have to be evaluated on a paragraph-by-paragraph if not sentence-by-sentence basis, because communications for business and legal purposes have become commingled.

Second, because e-mail technology has made communication so easy, convenient, and rapid, the volume of communications potentially subject to discovery has expanded exponentially. In *Microsoft,* the attorney-client privilege was claimed on more than 10,000 documents. This figure vastly understated the volume of messages that had to be read, evaluated, and ruled upon, because the e-mail thread in a single document designation often involved numerous messages—frequently more than six. The privilege claims in the *Microsoft* litigation may have been closer to 100,000 communications.

The third factor involves a reprehensible practice. Too often, corporations assert privilege for copies of all documents within distribution lists simply because one of them was addressed to an attorney. This is often a misuse of the principle that communications solely for the purpose of obtaining legal assistance can be circulated to all corporate personnel who have a need to know within the scope of their corporate responsibilities. When the content of a communication has both business and legal purposes, the copies sent to corporate personnel for those business purposes are not protected by the attorney-client privilege, even though there may be a legal purpose as to the single copy sent to an attorney. But only that single communication received by the attorney is privileged, assuming the confidentiality of the communications was maintained.

The pattern of distribution cannot be controlling, not only because it can be misleading, but also because it can be manipulated. Indeed, in the hundreds of thousands of corporate privilege claims I have reviewed, I have found many instances where corporations have addressed communications to lawyers solely to make it appear that the privilege attached, when in fact the communications usually had mixed business and legal purposes, and occasionally were for no legal purpose at all. In some instances, each paragraph within the communications was addressed by first name to every other recipient of the communications to the lawyer/addressee. Consequently, addressing the communication to the attorney could be seen as a ruse solely to make it appear to be something it is not. But the problem is much worse. Many corporations withhold documents from discovery on attorney-client privilege grounds simply because a lawyer's name appears in the header as either an addressee or copyee.[129] This is perhaps the most pervasive current abuse of the privilege process and should be sanctioned as such. At the very least, it is a dilatory tactic that makes the process less efficient and more costly. At worst, it is a fraud on both the adversaries and the court that constitutes a form of spoliation.[130] "No fraud is more odious than an attempt to subvert the administration of justice."[131]

E-mail headers normally indicate the author, primary recipients, secondary recipients (or copyees), subject matter, and various routing details. Because distribution patterns reflected in the headers of e-mail messages cannot be relied upon as trustworthy indicators of the author's primary purpose for creating each communication, judicial assessments of purpose necessarily must be based upon: (1) the content of each e-mail communication, (2) the content of messages that preceded and followed the message, (3) the apparent relationship of the communications in the e-mail string to one another, (4) information acquired from collective examination of the documents being withheld, and (5) the material filed in support of privilege claims (for example, affidavits). As a result, the resolution process during *Microsoft* was prolonged and intensified,[132] and the associated costs skyrocketed. Within the bounds of

---

129. It is not uncommon for lawyers to instruct the paralegals and associates screening documents for privilege purposes to withhold and claim privilege on any communication that has the name of a lawyer in the header.

130. The First Circuit has defined fraud on the court as "where it can be demonstrated, clearly and convincingly, that a party has sentiently set in motion some unconscionable scheme calculated to interfere with the judicial system's ability impartially to adjudicate a matter by improperly influencing the trier or unfairly hampering the presentation of the opposing party's claim or defense." Aoude v. Mobil Oil Corp., 892 F.2d 1115, 1118 (1st Cir. 1989). There is no reason why this same logic would not justify sanctioning a party who interferes with another's right to discover relevant, non-privileged materials.

131. Hazel-Atlas Glass Co. v. Hartford-Empire Co., 322 U.S. 238, 251 (1944).

132. In the consolidated Microsoft cases from both the state of California and federal courts, the resolution process was delegated to a single Discovery Master. This cooperation among jurisdictions was to achieve consistency and efficiency.

fairness, every measure that can be taken to streamline the process and make it more efficient should be pursued.

Judicial officers can look to objective signs within mixed business and legal communications that signal when a portion is intended for the business or legal recipients.

1. Paragraphs occasionally address separate individuals by name (either the businesspeople or the attorneys), followed by specific questions or instructions intended for them alone. These directed portions suggest that the remainder of the communication was not primarily for those named individuals.

2. The lawyer/primary recipient may not have participated in the message thread. This suggests that the purpose of the messages addressed to the lawyer was not primarily for the lawyer's assistance. This, however, may be misleading if the lawyer was unavailable at the time of the initial message and neither the author nor the other recipients were aware of this.

3. The named lawyer is not a primary recipient, but only one of numerous secondary recipients or copyees of a message. This strongly suggests that the primary purpose of the communication was not to obtain legal assistance, unless the content of the message is specifically directed to the lawyer by name.

4. A lawyer is one of a limited number of primary recipients (two or less), and there are also a limited number of nonlegal secondary recipients/copyees. In this circumstance the document appears to be for purposes of legal advice. The claim is probably valid if the content of the document and the positions of the nonlegal recipients are such that they would need to know the content of the legal advice being sought to properly carry out their business responsibilities. If, however, the content of the message is fact-laden, more than would be expected for the legal advice allegedly being sought, then the purpose behind the message begins to resemble the scenario described below.

The undertaking proved to be overwhelming for the Master. As a consequence, the privilege resolution process was further delegated to two Special Masters counsel chosen by the parties. This process took approximately a year and a half and involved a staff of three additional lawyers and a number of associates and paralegals.

5. A lawyer is the primary recipient (perhaps with others), and the communication has been copied to a large number of nonlegal individuals. If the content of the communication includes extensive factual information that would be important to the corporate responsibilities of the many recipients, and there is no evidence that this information has otherwise been communicated to those individuals for business purposes,[133] the purpose behind this message is clearly mixed and the privilege claim should be denied.

It is important to emphasize that these signs are not necessarily dispositive. Judicial officers normally must rely on the substance of the message, the names and responsibilities of those to whom the message was sent, and the message's general sense of purpose. The purpose may be revealed by (1) reading all of the messages in the e-mail thread (including those upon which privilege is not being claimed) and (2) observing patterns of practice by major players within the corporate entity. For example, if a corporate executive advises his colleagues to always place a lawyer's name in the "to:" line in their e-mail messages to take advantage of the attorney-client privilege, and experience shows that person uses this deceptive ploy, all doubts should be resolved against that individual's communications.

If the judicial officer's review of documents reveals that the distribution patterns accurately reflect the purpose of the authors, those patterns are an additional piece of reliable circumstantial evidence. Unfortunately, experience has proven that over time, in a broad enough sampling of communications within a large corporate entity, headers are used by some solely for the purpose of garnering the protection of the attorney-client privilege. Indeed, it is not uncommon for corporate personnel to be instructed to place a lawyer's name in the "to:" line, and to promi-

---

133. When evidence is provided that the information contained in a document claimed to be privileged was communicated by other means to businesspeople within the company, and those other communications were produced in the discovery process, it strongly suggests that the document under review was intended solely for the purpose of obtaining legal assistance. It strongly implies that the businesspeople were simply being informed of the advice that was being sought and given. It negates any suggestion of "funneling" because it would serve no apparent purpose in this circumstance.

nently place a label like "Confidential—Attorney-Client Privilege Protected" at the top of the document in order to take advantage of the privilege protection, regardless of whether it is appropriate. This distortion of the privilege results in both the distribution patterns and the label becoming less meaningful guides to the nature of the communication, and ultimately works against the corporation's interests.

This judicial undertaking is complicated further because e-mail messages are often written in shorthand and industry code, with often indecipherable abbreviations and acronyms. When the judicial officer is unfamiliar with the industry jargon and its shorthand conventions, the review process can be slowed significantly. Things can grind to a snail's pace when the communications are made completely incomprehensible through the use of technical jargon.

To combat these problems and facilitate judicial review, privilege proponents should accompany each privilege claim with affidavits from knowledgeable persons who can explain the context and content of each message, translate the verbiage, and, when multiple persons are listed as either primary or secondary recipients, allay suspicions that the document served both business and legal purposes simultaneously. Of course, if the translations in accompanying affidavits will reveal confidential information within the messages, those supporting materials can, with permission from the court, be filed ex parte (without copies being provided to the opposing side). Typically, each affidavit addresses multiple documents about which the affiant has personal knowledge.

The privilege proponent must demonstrate that communications with legal counsel were intended to be confidential (and thus were disclosed within the corporate structure only to those needing to know their content because of job responsibilities—commonly known as the "control group" test for determining who personifies the corporate client) and that the original confidentiality was subsequently maintained. For reasons that have been explored elsewhere,[134] the requirement of confidentiality may have become a relatively meaningless concept vis-à-vis the attorney-client privilege, but it is still an element that ostensibly is enforced in all courts, at least as a condition precedent to the creation of the privilege.

---

134. *See generally* Paul R. Rice, *Attorney-Client Privilege: The Eroding Concept of Confidentiality Should Be Abolished,* 47 Duke L.J. 101 (1998).

Several evidentiary offerings can satisfy the judicial officer that confidentiality was present and has been maintained for all documents, absent proof to the contrary. This should relieve the privilege proponent of the burden of having to address the requirement with each document.

First, the names of everyone appearing in the headers, or otherwise indicated as recipients, of all messages under review should be identified, their positions within the company over the time span of the discovery demands should be delineated, and the responsibilities of each position identified, and all this should be set forth in an alphabetical compilation by person and by position. These are often available in company directories. These compilations can also be supplemented with affidavits from individuals who are knowledgeable about each position. These affidavits should also address why the individuals in those positions needed to be privy to the communications under review.

Second, company policies on the confidentiality of communications with legal counsel and the procedures that are followed to preserve that confidentiality should be produced.

Lastly, give assurances to the judicial officer that those policies are distributed to, known, and followed by employees. This can be provided by employees familiar with company manuals and their distribution, as well as company practices.

If written company policies are not in place (an inexcusable oversight), the assurance that confidentiality is understood by company personnel and preserved in practice can be provided by evidence of the company's customary practices. This evidence must be empirically established by the testimony of individuals with years of experience and observations within the company.[135]

Consistent with the above principles, Guidelines for the Resolution of Electronic Privilege Claims (reproduced below) were promulgated by the Special Master in the consolidated *Vioxx* cases to be used with a

---

135.   FED. R. EVID. 406 provides:

Rule 406. Habit; Routine Practice

Evidence of the habit of a person or of the routine practice of an organization, whether corroborated or not and regardless of the presence of eyewitnesses, is relevant to prove that the conduct of the person or organization on a particular occasion was in conformity with the habit or routine practice.

new sampling process that was established by the Fifth Circuit Court of Appeals and Judge Eldon Fallon to accommodate the resolution of more than 60,000 privilege claims.[136] While managing the privilege processes in both the *Microsoft* and *Vioxx* cases required the appointment of Special Masters, through the use of the sampling process and Guidelines, the privilege resolution process in the *Vioxx* cases took four months, rather than a year and a half, with a cost that was considerably less than half that of the *Microsoft* experience.

The explosion of privilege claims has presented courts with the increasingly difficult problem of resolving those claims efficiently, economically, and consistently. When the volume becomes overwhelming, courts have resorted to appointing Special Masters to perform the task and have charged the costs to the parties. This, however, has been only a partial solution. Special Masters can resolve privilege claims more efficiently, but the costs can be high. While those costs generally have been shared equally by all parties in the litigation, thereby reducing their impact on each party, this cost distribution is unfair to discovering parties when the producing party has made unjustified privilege claims.

In addition, the efficiency achieved by delegating the initial resolution of privilege claims to Special Masters is often diminished by the fact that those decisions or recommendations to the district court judge are frequently contested by the producing party, thereby requiring district judges to engage in a streamlined version of the review already conducted by the Special Masters. The solutions appear to lie in education (substantive guidelines), sanctioning abuse, requiring timely documentation of claims, and establishing procedures that facilitate the speedy resolution of all claims—procedures similar to the sampling process employed in *Vioxx*.

In the consolidated *Vioxx* cases, the defendant, Merck & Co., initially asserted 30,000 privilege claims that had been awaiting resolution for more than one year. During that time, Merck had withheld an additional 30,000 documents on privilege grounds but had not notified the court. In that period, Merck had neither prepared nor filed a single affidavit in support of any of the 60,000 claims because the court had not required it to do so. As a consequence, when Judge Fallon began by

---

136. When the individual messages in the e-mail threads are separately counted as individual claims, the number of claims in both the *Vioxx* and *Microsoft* cases were probably similar.

himself to review in camera the initial 30,000 claims, most were denied because factual foundations had not been established. Merck had not borne its burden of persuasion relative to the primary purpose of the communications having been for legal advice.

On a writ of mandamus to the Fifth Circuit, the court refused to grant the writ, but, inexplicably, remanded the case to the district court with the instruction to conduct another examination of a representative sample of the massive number of documents being withheld, while giving Merck an opportunity to supplement the record with supporting materials to satisfy expressed judicial concerns with each privilege assertion.[137] Merck, in substance, was given a second bite at the privilege apple, with directions from the court on where, when, and how to bite.

What the Fifth Circuit opinion did not address was the interplay between the sample rulings and the remaining 58,000 claims. Was Merck supposed to give up its claims on the remaining documents when a similar claim was denied in the sample? Similarly, were the plaintiffs supposed to give up their demands for documents simply because similar claims had been granted? How the sample was to be employed in the privilege process was left to the discretion of Judge Fallon. To give the process a purpose apart from guidance for Merck on what was necessary to document its privilege claims, Judge Fallon directed that Merck produce or withhold documents in the remaining universe of claims according to the guidelines set out by the Special Master in his opinion and recommendations that the court adopted.[138]

Through an expedited process,[139] the sample documents were chosen by both the plaintiffs and the defendant, tentative decisions were issued by the Special Master, and Merck was given an opportunity to file supporting materials to satisfy the factual concerns that led to the denial of specific claims. Thereafter, a final recommendation was made to Judge Fallon, with guidelines for the resolution of all remaining privi-

---

137. In re Vioxx Products Liab. Litig. Steering Committee v. Merck & Co. Inc., 2006 WL 1726675 (5th Cir. May 26, 2006).

138. In re Vioxx Products Liability Litig., 501 F. Supp. 2d 789 (E.D. La. 2007).

139. This process was outlined in the Special Master's Report at 3-4, reproduced in In re Vioxx Products Liab. Litig., 501 F. Supp. 2d 789, 792-94 (E.D. La. 2007).

lege claims,[140] and the parties were given an opportunity to comment on both the guidelines and recommendations.[141]

To ensure that the guidelines were accurately being followed by Merck, Judge Fallon instructed the Special Master to check a sample of the documents that Merck continued to withhold. Had discrepancies been found, the court indicated that the Special Master would have been instructed to rule on all remaining documents being withheld, and the cost of that process would have been assessed to Merck. Perhaps because Merck had invited this sampling process in its petition for a writ of mandamus following Judge Fallon's initial denial of most of its claims in the original 30,000 withheld documents, Merck accepted the standards of the guidelines and production proceeded without further expense or delay in the resolution process. Once established, this process significantly expedited the return of thousands of cases to jurisdictions throughout the country from which they had been consolidated before Judge Fallon. It also expedited the pretrial process in the tens of thousands of state cases that were awaiting the resolution of privilege issues in the consolidated federal cases.

It is not clear how valuable this process would have been had large numbers of privilege claims not been substantially similar. This, however, is seldom the case when massive numbers of claims are raised by a single corporate client. Wide dissemination in corporations ensures large numbers of identical and nearly identical claims. Equally unclear is how valuable the process would be if Merck had contested the majority of sample decisions. Presumably this would be less of a problem than under normal procedures because a smaller volume of documents would have to be reviewed by the trial judge (if initially resolved by a Special Master) and appellate judges.

With experimentation and refinement, sampling may prove to be an answer for courts having to deal with massive numbers of privilege claims. Indeed, had sampling been in place at the beginning of the Vioxx

---

140. These guidelines were distributed to the parties well in advance of the Special Master's final recommendations to Judge Fallon in order to facilitate the parties' understanding of each recommended ruling.

141. While Judge Fallon adopted the Special Master's Opinion and Recommendations, In re Vioxx Products Liability Litig., 501 F. Supp. 2d 789 (E.D. La. 2007), he reversed a few specific recommendations based on different assessments of the documents in question.

privilege resolution process, and had Merck's documentation of claims been filed before Judge Fallon's first rulings on those claims, months of time would have been saved and probably millions of dollars of expenses could have been avoided. If the sampling process were coupled with other prediscovery directives, like eliminating the assertion of privilege claims simply because lawyers' names appear in headers of e-mail messages, the savings could be even greater.

The Special Master's Substantive Guidelines employed with the Vioxx sampling process appear below.

Special Master's Substantive Guidelines

1. If a memorandum was written to an attorney with apparently limited circulation, and an identifiable legal question was raised by the author (whether or not it was answered by the attorney), it was found to be a classic example of when the attorney-client privilege is applicable.

2. If a memorandum was written to an attorney within the corporation's legal department, with an attachment for examination, review, comment, and approval, we found that the communication and attachment were *sent* primarily for the purpose of obtaining legal advice and, therefore, were protected by the attorney-client privilege. Even when these communications to the legal department were compelled by company policy, we concluded that since the company was the client and legal assistance was necessary, we would not try to discern what was in the minds of the employee-authors of those communications.

   The lawyer's response (often appearing electronically on the attachment) was accepted as legal advice, along with minor grammatical and editorial comments, unless the response had extensive changes and commentary or relates purely to technical, scientific, promotional, management, or marketing matters that did not appear to be related to legal assistance. In the latter instances, we denied the claims and insisted that Merck satisfy its burden of proving that the primary purpose of the responses was providing legal assistance. If the memorandum and attachment related to identifiable legal instruments like a proposed contract, these

---

generally would be found to be privileged, even with extensive editorial and grammatical revisions, because they are the types of instruments that one reasonably expects more extensive input and guidance on from reviewing attorneys.

Often, however, the e-mail covers to which the proposed contract was attached originated in e-mail messages to which no lawyers were copied and legal advice was not the primary purpose of the communications. As a consequence, they would not independently be protected by the attorney-client privilege. However, those messages and attachments could appropriately be part of a confidential communication to an attorney for legal assistance. Therefore, when they were attached to communications sent to an attorney primarily for the purpose of obtaining legal assistance, they were found to be privileged on the assumption that the original messages and attachments were produced from the files of the original authors and recipients. If, however, the integration of an attorney in the e-mail thread was through a communication that was sent to many for review and comment, including an attorney, the primary purpose of that communication was found not to be for legal assistance, and the attachment was found not to be protected by the privilege.

3. At the end of the messages described above, we occasionally encountered e-mail threads that were sent to others after the initial interaction with the lawyer ended. This additional dissemination of the e-mail thread was found not to be privileged when the conveyance was by a non-lawyer recipient, unless it was clear that legal advice previously obtained was being circulated to those within the corporate structure who had a need to know in the scope of their corporate responsibilities. When the conveyance was by the lawyer and it appeared that it was for the purpose of acquiring more information upon which more informed legal advice or assistance could be rendered, the additional conveyance and response were also found to be privileged.

4. When an e-mail was addressed to both lawyers and non-lawyers for review, comment, and perhaps approval, we concluded that the primary purpose of that communication was

not to obtain legal assistance. Neither the message nor the attachment was found to be protected by the attorney-client privilege. As previously noted, while the disclosure of such e-mail communications and attachments reveal that the lawyer was sent a copy, thereby revealing the content of a potentially privileged communication to the attorney, this is a price that companies must pay when they communicate with their attorneys through the same communications being sent to non-attorneys for a non-legal purpose. By noting in the headers of those communications that they were sent to the attorney, the communications are consciously revealing on the face of discoverable communications information that otherwise could have been confidential and protected by the attorney-client privilege. The corporation's choice of means and format in their communications cannot limit their adversaries' right to discover what otherwise is non-privileged and discoverable.

We accepted the possibility that addressing communications to both lawyers and non-lawyers could reflect the seeking of legal advice from the lawyer and the non-lawyers simply being notified about the nature of the legal services sought. Facially, however, it appeared far more probable that the non-lawyers were being sent the communications for separate business reasons. Therefore, Merck had the burden of overcoming the logical inference created by the pattern of distribution.

5. E-mails addressed to an attorney with many being *copied* to non-lawyers throughout the company raised a question as to whether the primary purpose of the communications was for legal advice or assistance. This issue may be no different from when the communications were *addressed* to both lawyers and non-lawyers, except that in the instance of copies to non-lawyers, the possibility was greater that they were being sent copies simply to inform them of the nature of the legal advice being sought, and not for review and comment in the normal course of business. This, however, appeared to be unlikely when the communications were part of a mandatory process of companywide review, comment, and ap-

proval. Accordingly, we denied such claims. because the primary purpose was not demonstrated as being to obtain legal advice or assistance. We found this result to be necessary in light of other corporate documents the Special Master had screened in production processes in other cases where corporations have used lawyers as a front for sending communications for non-legal purposes so that the corporations can facially claim that they are shielded from discovery by the attorney-client privilege. It is important to note, however, that we found no evidence of Merck funneling communications through the legal department to take advantage of the attorney-client privilege. In the absence of any supporting documentation, however, we thought it necessary to put Merck to its proof.

The only thing that we found questionable about communications sent to the legal department was the nature of the services ultimately provided—often appearing to be more technical, scientific, editorial, and promotional than legal in nature. As noted above, however, we were receptive to evidence subsequently being provided that demonstrated that in the highly regulated drug industry, these comments and edits were part of the rendering of legal assistance. In this regard, we insisted that Merck provide us with more than general assertions about the nature of the drug industry. We required specific assertions about each document from individuals with personal knowledge about their nature and purpose.

6. E-mails that were either to or from an attorney but did not reveal the substance of either what the client was communicating (for example, attaching a study, report, article, etc.) or the attorney was advising (because the comments appeared on the attachment) were denied privilege, regardless of what the disposition was on the attachments. While the e-mails may have been the means for obtaining legal advice or assistance, the e-mails themselves did not reveal confidential information about the attorney-client relationship that was protected by the privilege.

7. E-mail threads (a series of e-mail messages) in which attorneys were ultimately involved were usually inappropriately listed on the privilege log as one message. When this occurred, it was noted in our decision. Some of these threads involved 10 to 14 messages that preceded the direct or limited exchanges with the attorneys. Earlier in the process, Merck might have been required to correct its privilege log to disclose these messages and further explain other ambiguous descriptions that were employed. However, at this late stage of the pretrial process, and in the limited role that we were asked to play in the sampling process sanctioned by the Fifth Circuit Court of Appeals, we asked Merck only to inform us and the plaintiffs whether those portions of the e-mail threads previously unacknowledged in the logs had been produced with their attachments. This did not appear to be the case, since privilege had been claimed on the "entire document," which, of course, included the earlier messages. A subsequent report did not assure us that all non-privileged threads had been produced. Therefore, it was necessary that we note this overassertion of privilege on a document-by-document basis in our report.

8. The doctrine of work product was created by the Supreme Court in *Hickman v. Taylor,* 329 U.S. 495 (1943), to preserve the adversarial nature of the trial process. It gives a qualified immunity to communications that are created in preparation for litigation. Therefore, the application of the immunity requires (1) that the litigation anticipated be identified, and (2) that it be proven that the communication in question was in preparation for that litigation. When litigation was identified, but the communications related only to things like news releases, work-product claims were denied. Many of those communications, however, were still protected by the attorney-client privilege.[142]

---

142. In re Vioxx Products Liability Litig., 501 F. Supp. 2d 789 , 813 (E.D. La. 2007).

I.   Spoliation and the Crime/Fraud Exception to the Attorney-Client Privilege

The privilege afforded clients who communicate with attorneys for the purpose of obtaining legal advice or assistance is limited to those communications that are part of the client's efforts to comply with the requirements of the law. When the client abuses the attorney-client relationship by using the advice of counsel to perpetrate a crime or fraud, the protection does not attach to his communications.[143] "When that evidence [of improper purpose] is supplied, the seal of secrecy is broken."[144]

The types of conduct that preclude the application of the attorney-client privilege are not clearly defined. While a "crime" is self-apparent, "fraud" is not necessarily limited to criminal fraud. In fact, the term "fraud" may be a misnomer.[145] The exception has been applied when the wrongful conduct for which legal advice was sought was neither a

---

143. Clark v. United States, 289 U.S. 1, 15 (1933) ("A client who consults an attorney for advice that will serve him in the commission of a fraud will have no help from the law."); United States v. Hodge and Zweig, 548 F.2d 1347, 1355 (9th Cir. 1977) ("In our legal system the client should make full disclosure to the attorney so that the advice given is sound, so that the attorney can give all appropriate protection to the client's interest, and so that proper defenses are raised if litigation results. The attorney-client privilege promotes such disclosure by promising that communications revealed for these legitimate purposes will be held in strict confidence. The privilege encourages persons to seek advice as to future conduct. But so important is full disclosure that the law recognizes the privilege even if the advice is sought by one who has already committed a bad act. Thus, the attorney-client privilege is central to the legal system and the adversary process. For these reasons, the privilege may deserve unique protection in the courts. . . . But a quid pro quo is exacted for the attorney-client confidence: the client must not abuse the confidential relationship by using it to further a fraudulent or criminal scheme, and as a condition to continued representation, the lawyer is required to advise the client to cease any unlawful activities that the lawyer perceives are occurring. Law and society consent to the attorney-client privilege on these preconditions. By insisting on their observance, we safeguard the privilege itself and protect the integrity of the professional relation.").

144. *Id.*

145. Blanchard v. Edgemark Fin. Corp., 192 F.R.D. 233, 241 (N.D. Ill. 2000) (the term crime/fraud exception is "a bit of a misnomer.").

crime nor a fraud.[146] It has been loosely applied to any situations where the courts have concluded that the client has abused the attorney-client relationship.

> [I]t is difficult to see how any moral line can properly be drawn at [the] crude boundary [of the definition of crime or fraud], or how the law can protect a deliberate plan to defy the law and oust another person of his rights, whatever the precise nature of those rights may be.[147]

Spoliation has been recognized as conduct justifying the application of this exception. In *Rambus, Inc. v. Infineon Techs. AG*,[148] for example, the court held that the exception extends to materials or communications created for planning, or in furtherance of, spoliation if

---

146. *See, e.g.*, In re Sealed Case, 737 F.2d 94, 98-99 (D.C. Cir. 1984) (Exception applies to communications made in furtherance of "crime, fraud, or other type of misconduct fundamentally inconsistent with the basic premises of the adversary system."); In re Sealed Case, 676 F.2d 793, 812 (D.C. Cir. 1982) ("Attorney-client privilege is not available to protect communications made in furtherance of a crime, fraud, 'or other type of misconduct fundamentally inconsistent with the basic premises of the adversary system' . . . Whether or not it arises to the level of a crime (or conceivably a fraud upon some other court), this court is satisfied that employment of the services of counsel by public officials to assist in litigation designed to facilitate unconstitutional racial or ethnic discrimination is such misconduct."); Madanes v. Madanes, 199 F.R.D. 135, 149 (S.D.N.Y. 2001) ("At a minimum, then, the attorney-client privilege does not protect communications in furtherance of an intentional tort that undermines the adversary system itself. That is what is alleged here. Dr. Pomiro and Monica are charged with conspiring to violate Dr. Pomiro's duty to maintain confidences communicated to him by his former clients, the Madanes Brothers. If true, this would be sufficient to trigger the crime-fraud exception and remove the attorney-client privilege from communications between Dr. Pomiro and Monica in furtherance of that purpose."); Cleveland Hair Clinic, Inc. v. Puig, 968 F. Supp. 1227, 1237 (N.D. Ill. 1996) (bad-faith litigation justified application of crime-fraud exception); Milroy v. Hanson, 902 F. Supp. 1029, 1033 (D. Neb. 1995) ("I find and conclude that the 'fraud' exception to the attorney-client privilege . . . requires a showing of 'intentional misrepresentation' for the purpose of gain."); In re St. Johnsbury Trucking Co. v. Bankers Trust Co., 184 B.R. 446, 456 (Bankr. D. Vt. 1995) (holding that crime/fraud exception applies when consultation is "in furtherance of some sufficiently malignant purpose"). *See generally* PAUL R. RICE, ATTORNEY-CLIENT PRIVILEGE IN THE UNITED STATES § 8:11 (2d ed. 1999).

147. 8 WIGMORE, EVIDENCE § 2298 at 577 (rev. ed. 1961).

148. 220 F.R.D. 264, 279 (E.D. Va. 2004).

it can be shown (1) that the offending party "was engaged in or planning a scheme of spoliation when it sought the advice of counsel or the input of the lawyers' work product to further the scheme," and (2) that the documents containing the communications . . . "bear a close relationship" to the offending party's scheme to engage in spoliation. Subsequently, the *Rambus* court further explained:

> Communications between [the] lawyer and [the] client respecting spoliation of evidence . . . [are] fundamentally inconsistent with the asserted principles behind the recognition of the attorney-client privilege, namely, "observance of law" and the "administration of justice." . . . Indeed, by intentionally removing relevant evidence from litigation, spoliation directly undermines the administration of justice. . . . Moreover, an attorney who counsels a client about spoliation of evidence is not advancing the observance of the law, but rather counseling misconduct. Thus, there is no logical reason to extend the protection of the attorney-client privilege to communications undertaken in order to further spoliation.[149]

When a client is advised by its attorney to always put a lawyer's name in headers of e-mails to take advantage of the attorney-client privilege, the lawyer is committing an unethical act by encouraging the client to engage in a fraud—a fraud on both third parties and courts—by attempting to make communications appear to be what they are not. As the client participates in the fraud, the client is initiating an act of spoliation—preparing to suppress evidence that may be relevant to future litigation. When the discovery of the documents is demanded in future litigation, the act of spoliation is completed by the client engaging in sham litigation over the privileged status of the bogus claims.

J. Work Product Immunity Vis-à-Vis E-evidence

The work-product immunity protects the work product of the attorney in preparation for litigation. Consequently, the enhanced possibilities of

---

149. Rambus, Inc. v. Infineo Techs. AG, 222 F.R.D. 280, 289 (E.D. Va. 2004). The D.C. Circuit also has held that the crime/fraud exception is applicable to communications in furtherance of spoliation. *See* In re Sealed Case, 754 F.2d 395, 400 (D.C. Cir. 1985).

breach of confidentiality with electronic communications should not affect the application of the protection.

The work-product immunity is fundamentally different from the attorney-client privilege. The immunity is designed to facilitate the adversarial process in which competing interests separately prepare for litigation and present their evidence to an independent finder of facts. All materials developed in anticipation of litigation are protected from disclosure to the adversary, other than those for which good cause can be demonstrated.

As Justice Jackson explained in *Hickman v. Taylor*,[150] the immunity ensures that lawyers preparing for litigation will not do so with "wits borrowed from their adversaries." The attorney-client privilege, by contrast, is designed to encourage open communications between the attorney and client by making those communications absolutely protected from discovery by third parties.

While confidentiality is important to work-product immunity, it is not important in the same way that it is to the attorney-client privilege. Historically, the attorney-client privilege has required that the communications between attorney and client be held in confidence by the attorney, the client, and their authorized agents in order to maintain the privilege protection. By contrast, the work-product immunity has been only marginally concerned with confidentiality. The information developed by the attorney and the client in preparation for litigation had to be withheld only from the adversary to maintain its immunity status. It could be shared with anyone else without effecting a waiver of the protection. For this reason, the increased possibilities of disclosure of electronic evidence should not affect the applicability of the protection.

Like the attorney-client privilege, the work-product immunity can be waived by acts of spoliation. As explained in *Rambus, Inc. v. Infineo Tech. AG*,[151] the reasons for waiving the attorney-client privilege when consultations with an attorney are for the purpose of successfully destroying evidence[152] compel the waiver of the work-product immunity as well.

> [A]ttorney work product materials that relate to the spoliation of evidence neither "work for the advancement of justice" nor fur-

---

150. 329 U.S. 495 (1943).
151. 222 F.R.D. 280, 289 (E.D. Va. 2004).
152. See text at note 141, *supra*.

ther the "rightful interests" of an attorney's client. . . . Declining to afford such materials protection would not have a "demoralizing" effect on the profession nor would it fail to accord attorneys, as officers of courts, their rightful sphere of protection. . . . To the contrary, by removing the ability of lawyers and clients to hide such materials behind the work product privilege, the courts will assure that the work of lawyers is confined to the rightful interests of client, rather than interests—such as the destruction of evidence—that frustrate the administration of justice and cast the legal system (as well as the legal profession) in an unsavory light.[153]

Privilege Checklist

Dissemination Policies. Establish written company policies for the distribution of both internal and external communications to attorneys.

- **Primary and Secondary Dissemination.** The policy should encompass the primary and secondary dissemination of all communications, particularly e-mail communications, because the tendency in the daily affairs of a company is to distribute e-mails widely. Dissemination should be restricted to those with a need to know in the scope of their employment responsibilities.

- **Headers Correctly Reflecting Purpose.** When communications are being written to an attorney *primarily for the purpose of obtaining legal assistance*, list the attorney as the sole addressee and all others as copyees on the "cc:" line.

- **Copies to Attorneys for Review**.
  1. Blind Copies. When *business communications* are being copied to in-house counsel for screening for potential legal problems, don't list the attorney as either an addressee or copyee. The copy to the attorney should be blind. When those business communications are later discovered in litigation, they will not reveal the content of what was previously communicated to legal counsel.

---

153. *Id.* at *9.

2. Attorney Responses. All responsive e-mail communications from legal counsel to business e-mail communications that counsel screens should be through new communications rather than the reply function on an e-mail server. The reply function will reveal the attorney's communications in the e-mail thread, which will require excision in any future discovery process and will reveal that counsel was sent a blind copy.

- **Mixed Purpose Communications.** The attorney-client privilege applies only to those portions of communications that are *primarily for the purpose of obtaining legal assistance.* Therefore, to the extent possible, communications with mixed business and legal purposes should be avoided. When mixed-purpose communications are unavoidable, the topics should be addressed under separate headings to the extent possible. If this is not possible because the two purposes are so intertwined, such communications can be withheld from future discovery only to the extent that the separate purposes can be separated and redacted.

- **Dissemination to Outside Consultants.** Avoid dissemination to outside consultants. Consultants should receive copies of confidential attorney-client communications only when they are assisting in the obtaining or rendering of legal assistance and their responsibilities necessitate that they receive certain specific communications.

- **Label Documents.** Every e-mail communication to an attorney that is primarily for the purpose of obtaining legal assistance should be conspicuously labeled CONFIDENTIAL — ATTORNEY-CLIENT PRIVILEGE. Employees should be cautioned about overusing the label in an attempt to acquire the protection of the privilege when it is not justified. When misuse is detected, courts will ignore the party's self-serving labels.

- **Education Programs.** All policies relating to attorney-client communications should be written and given to each employee who may be part of those communications or given access to them.. Regular educational programs sponsored by the company should inform all employees of the importance of attorney-client communications, the complexities of the privilege protection, and the unique problems created by the use of e-mail.

- **Claiming Privilege.** When privilege is asserted for e-mail communications, they must be listed on a privilege log along with all other types of communications withheld.
- **Each Message Is a Separate Communication.** Privilege must be claimed for each e-mail message rather than multiple messages within a thread. Each message differs in origin and can differ in scope, content, purpose, and privilege protection.
- **Details of Each Claim.** Enough information must be supplied about each communication listed on the privilege log to give the opposing party a fair opportunity to challenge whether legal advice was the primary purpose of the communication as well as whether confidentiality was intended and properly maintained.[154]

---

154. For details on the appropriate content of a privilege log, *see* PAUL R. RICE, ATTORNEY-CLIENT PRIVILEGE IN THE UNITED STATES, ch. 11 (2d ed. 1999).

Best Evidence/ Original Writing Rule

4

I. The Basics 298

II. E-evidence and the Original Writing Rule 303

III. The Added Complexity of Summaries of Voluminous Materials 307

    A. The Hearsay Dimensions of Summaries 308

        1. Non-hearsay Argument 309

        2. Residual Exception Solution 310

    C. Insurmountable Hearsay Problems Created by Summaries of Voluminous Materials from the Internet 311

    D. The Evidentiary Status of Summaries under the Voluminous Writings Exception to the Original Writing Rule 312

E-evidence Overview: For practical purposes, best evidence objections have been eliminated in federal courts because mechanically produced copies of documents, denoted "duplicates," are as admissible as originals unless a genuine question of accuracy is raised by the opponent. Because virtually everything produced in the electronic world is produced mechanically, once a document has been properly authenticated, the best evidence or original writing rule should pose no problems.

I.   THE BASICS

Our jurisprudence places great importance on writings. The Statute of Frauds requires that certain contracts be witnessed by a writing in order to be enforceable. Under the Parol Evidence Rule, if two parties reduce an enforceable oral contract to an integrated writing, the writing supersedes the oral agreement, and testimony about the oral agreement's terms is inadmissible, unless the explicit terms within the written instrument are ambiguous.

Just as the importance of writings affected the development of contract law, so too did it affect the common law evolution of evidence law. Under the common law best evidence rule, if a proponent proves the terms of a contract (not necessarily the truth of those terms, which would create a separate hearsay problem), the proponent must produce the original writing, unless he demonstrates that the original is unavailable through no serious fault of the proponent. Article X of the Federal Rules of Evidence codified the common law best evidence rule, terming it instead the original writing rule.[1]

---

1. Article X of the Federal Rules of Evidence provides:

Rule 1002. Requirement of Original

To prove the content of a writing, recording, or photograph, the original writing, recording, or photograph is required, except as otherwise provided in these rules or by Act of Congress.

[Jones v. Arkansas, 2006 WL 2556379, at *2 (Ark. Ct. App. Sept. 6, 2006) (not proving the content of a writing when a tape recording is being *played*); State v. Allen, 930 So. 2d 1122, 1131 (La. Ct. App. 2d Cir. 2006) (Audiotape of confession was the best evidence. State had to show it was ɔt available due to no serious fault of the State before an authenticated ʿcript could be admitted.); Coddington v. State, 142 P.3d 437, 459

This rule was designed to address fears of fraud or inaccuracy. Unfortunately, because litigants used the rule as a strategic device when no legitimate concerns about fraud or inaccuracy existed, the best evidence rule failed to serve its intended function. This problem is addressed in Federal Rules of Evidence (Fed. R. Evid.) 1001(4) and 1003.

Under the common law, the term "duplicate" referred to multiple originals—that is, duplicate originals. What constituted duplicate originals turned

---

(Okla. Crim. App. 2006) (the best evidence of a videotaped confession was the videotape, rather than the transcript). In contrast, Massachusetts had held that videotapes are not subject to the best evidence rule. Commonwealth v. Leneski, 846 N.E.2d 1195, 1198-99 (Mass. App. Ct. 2006) ("Videotapes, like photographs, are not subject to the best evidence rule. 'The best evidence rule is applicable to only those situations where the contents of a writing are sought to be proved.' . . . The best evidence rule would not apply to a videotape recorded by a store's security system, and a properly authenticated copy would be admissible if otherwise relevant. . . . For similar reasons, we hold that digital images placed and stored in a computer hard drive and transferred to a compact disc are subject to the same rules of evidence as videotapes. . . . In other contexts our courts have deemed that digital images on a hard drive are appropriate evidence even though not specifically provided by statute. . . . As with videotapes, we think that digital image evidence is not subject to the best evidence rule, as such images are not writings." Court admitted a compared copy on CD-rom that witness verified was an accurate reproduction.)]

Rule 1004. Admissibility of Other Evidence of Contents

The original is not required, and other evidence of the contents of a writing, recording, or photograph is admissible if—

(1) **Originals lost or destroyed.** All originals are lost or have been destroyed, unless the proponent lost or destroyed them in bad faith; or

[Ohio v. Patterson, 2006 Ohio 4439, P10-11 2006 Ohio App. LEXIS 4365, *8 (Ohio Ct. App. Aug. 11, 2006) (Video recording was not destroyed in bad faith. It was negligently destroyed. Therefore, it was not error for the court to permit testimony about its content.)]

(2) **Original not obtainable.** No original can be obtained by any available judicial process or procedure; or

(3) **Original in possession of opponent.** At a time when an original was under the control of the party against whom offered, that party was put on notice, by the pleadings or otherwise, that the contents would be a subject of proof at the hearing, and that party does not produce the original at the hearing; or

(4) **Collateral matters.** The writing, recording, or photograph is not closely related to a controlling issue.

on the parties' intentions. Regardless of whether the "originals" appeared to be the same, if their content was the same and the parties intended each to be treated as an original, the law treated both as originals. Before secondary evidence (such as copies or testimony) of the content of those "duplicate originals" could be offered into evidence, the proponent had to establish the unavailability of all duplicate originals.

Although the concept of duplicate originals persists under the Federal Rules of Evidence, the term "multiple originals" is now used to refer to such evidence. Under Fed. R. Evid. 1001(3), an "original" of a writing is defined as "the writing or recording itself or any counterpart intended to have the same effect by a person executing or issuing it."

The term "duplicate" has been restricted to describing a particular type of copy—one that resembles the original because it was *mechanically produced* from the original. Under Rule 1001(4), a duplicate is "a counterpart produced by the same impression as the original, or from the same matrix, or by means of photography, including enlargements and miniatures, or by mechanical or electronic re-recording, or by chemical reproduction, or by other equivalent techniques which accurately reproduces the original." In Rule 1003, these types of copies are admissible *as if they were the original* unless an opponent offers concrete evidence that the duplicate was not produced from a genuine original, or unless it would be unfair to admit the duplicate in lieu of the original.[2]

As a practical matter, Fed. R. Evid. 1003 has eliminated best evidence objections. Copies from the pages of books, treatises, and other papers are

---

2. Fed. R. Evid. 1003 provides:

> A duplicate is admissible to the same extent as an original unless (1) a genuine question is raised as to the authenticity of the original or (2) in the circumstances it would be unfair to admit the duplicate in lieu of the original.

> [State v. Huntsman, 1999 WL 4137, at *8 (Ohio Ct. App. Dec. 7, 1998) ("Regarding the best evidence rule, Evid. R. 1003 permits a duplicate of the original unless there is a genuine question regarding the authenticity of the original, or, if, given the circumstances it would unfair to admit a duplicate. . . . This case is complicated by the fact the original material shown to this victim was necessarily a temporary image on a computer screen. The original images were impossible to present. We find the trial court did not err in insuring the photos shown to the jury were printouts of the exact images the State alleged appellant had used to commit the crime charged [disseminating materials harmful to a juvenile].").]

now introduced in place of the entire volume because photocopies of originals are now admissible as if they were the original.[3]

---

3. When documents are copied from the public record—for example, pages from technical or scientific journals in the Library of Congress, or copies of recorded deeds in the county land record—the certification of the copy by the public official with custody of those documents serves to authenticate the original on the public record and the copy as a duplicate of the original. Fed. R. Evid. Rule 902(4) codifies this principle:

> Extrinsic evidence of authenticity as a condition precedent to admissibility is not required with respect to the following:
>
> ....
>
> (4) Certified copies of public records. A copy of an official record or report or entry therein, or of a document authorized by law to be recorded or filed and actually recorded or filed in a public office, including data compilations in any form, certified as correct by the custodian or other person authorized to make the certification, by certificate complying with paragraph (1), (2), or (3) of this rule or complying with any Act of Congress or rule prescribed by the Supreme Court pursuant to statutory authority.
>
> [State v. Skimmerhorn, 835 N.E.2d 52, 57, 59 (Ohio Ct. App. 2005) (Only a person who saw the original on public record can compare the copy and authenticate it at trial under Evid. R. 902. The "duplicate" rule in Evid. R. 1003 is inapplicable to public records. "[Rule 1003 imposes a] lesser standard than that of Evid.R. 1005, with a presumption of authenticity. Allowing copies of public documents to be admitted under Evid.R. 1003 would render Evid.R. 1005 largely irrelevant.").

For documents not of public record, duplicates are usually offered through a certificate of acknowledgment, such as a notarized affidavit from the custodian under Fed. R. Evid. 902(8), which provides:

> Extrinsic evidence of authenticity as a condition precedent to admissibility is not required with respect to the following:
>
> ....
>
> (8) Acknowledged document. Documents accompanied by a certificate of acknowledgment executed in the manner provided by law by a notary public or other officer authorized by law to take acknowledgments.

Under Fed. R. Evid. 901(b)(1) a person familiar with an original's content also can authenticate the duplicate. As a witness, that person must not only demonstrate familiarity with the content of the original but also certify that the copy is an accurate reproduction of that original. Rule 901(b)(1) codifies authentication through witnesses with personal knowledge.

Rule 901. Requirement of Authentication or Identification

(a) General provision. The requirement of authentication or identification as a condition precedent to admissibility is satisfied by evidence sufficient to support a finding that the matter in question is what its proponent claims.

(b) Illustrations. By way of illustration only, and not by way of limitation, the following are examples of authentication or identification conforming with the requirements of this rule:

(1) Testimony of witness with knowledge. Testimony that a matter is what it is claimed to be.

[Washington v. Kynaston, 134 Wash. App. 1005 2006 WL 2025016, at *1 (Wash. Ct. App. July 20, 2006) (the caller on a 911 tape was permitted to authenticate her own voice on the tape); Ohio v. Skimmerhorn, 835 N.E.2d 52, 57-58 (Ohio Ct. App. 2005) (When offering a copy of a public document that is not certified, it must be authenticated by a witness with personal knowledge. "The relevant document in this case was the calibration-solution certificate maintained at ODH. It is the content of that document, allegedly showing that the solution was approved by ODH, that is at issue. The trial court had to determine whether the copy offered as evidence was an accurate copy of the original held at ODH. That was a fact to which ODH could have attested, but not Officer Edwards, who had never seen the original. For this reason, ODH was the only entity able to certify a copy of the original. Officer Edwards's personal statement that the copy he offered to the court was equivalent to the ODH certified copy he had on file was of no significance. This document is not admissible under Evid.R. 902. . . . The photocopied seal and ODH signature on the photocopy offered to the court were not relevant to this evidentiary determination. The requirement of a seal is not a trivial one and should not be compromised by permitting a photocopy to suffice. A seal is, in effect, a multidimensional signature. Thus, the likelihood of a forgery under seal is minimal and is less than when dealing with merely hand-signed public documents. It is because of this added reliability that documents with an original seal, such as a certified copy, can be allowed into evidence without any other extrinsic evidence of admissibility. Allowing a photocopy of a seal to represent a seal would conflict with a policy interest behind allowing self-authentication. A photocopy of a seal does not provide the greater reliability that justifies special treatment under the Evidence Rules."); Johnson-Woolridge v. Wooldridge, 2001 WL 838986, at *4 (Ohio Ct. App. July 26, 2001) (printouts from Internet Web site of the North Carolina State Board of Education were sufficiently authenticated by testimony or affidavit of party recounting how they were retrieved); State v. Huntsman, 1999 WL 4137, at *7-8 (Ohio Ct. App. Dec. 7, 1999) (minor identified pictures taken from the Internet that the defendant had previously shown to him).]

The pretrial discovery process addresses many of the fraud and inaccuracy concerns because parties exchange copies of exhibits they intend to offer at trial. Moreover, because genuine concerns of fraud or inaccuracy are rarely found, Rule 1003's shifting of the burden from the proponent to the opponent has nearly eliminated best evidence/original writing objections.

II. E-EVIDENCE AND THE ORIGINAL WRITING RULE

Internet transactions are conducted through computers and are visually confirmed by display on the computer monitor. Under the best evidence/original writing rule, what is the original or the Internet transaction?

To answer this question, one must understand that parties on either side of an Internet- or e-mail-based transaction do not view the same image. Each party sees only those images on his computer screen. While the two images usually look identical or at least have the same information, they are still technically two distinct images. Each party views and agrees to the image it assumes the other party sees. Accordingly, for best evidence purposes, no single original exists. Instead, no less than two originals co-exist, as the number of originals corresponds to the number of images to which each contracting party, via computer terminal, views and agrees.

If each respective computer terminal is the source of at least two originals, how can a party satisfy the original writing requirement? The image on the computer monitor reflects only that which the computer has accessed, and the image on the monitor disappears after the monitor is turned off. As long as nothing is tampered with, an item will be the same each time a party retrieves it from the computer's hard drive. Unfortunately, tampering is precisely what the best evidence rule was designed to guard against, but mutual observation of each contracting party's hard drive is not possible.

Because multiple originals exist when contracts are created using computers as the vehicles through which terms are agreed upon, the Federal Rules of Evidence appear to have made everything generated from each computer an original. Fed. R. Evid. 1001(3) provides that "[i]f data are stored in a computer or similar device, any printout readable by sight, shown to reflect the data accurately, is an 'original.'" According to this definition, the hard drive or Web server would be the original, and it can be brought into court and the images it stored called up on a computer terminal in the courtroom. Because doing this would be cumbersome, an alternative is a hard-copy printout from the computer screen in the party's home or place of business that can be presented as the original. In a similar fashion, if a contract is entered into through an instant-messaging program provided by many ISPs, the messages leading to the contract could be copied into a word-processor program and printed in hard copy for subsequent use in court. That printout would also be an "original" under the original writing rule.[4] Additionally, because Fed. R. Evid.1001(4) classifies mechanically produced copies as duplicates, and because Fed. R. Evid. 1003 treats duplicates like originals, an image on a computer monitor in the party's home or office would be an original, and a photograph of the computer monitor would be admissible as an original because it is a duplicate.

Because an opposing party will also have to use an approach like those described in disputes over the terms of a contract, applying the best evidence rule to the Internet is confusing and perhaps meaningless. Fed. R. Evid. 1001(3)'s broad definition of "originals," coupled with Rule 1003's treatment of duplicates as originals, acknowledges this gap between the theory of the best evidence rule and the reality of technological evolution. The Best Evidence Rule is premised on common visual observations of a writing on paper and, as a result, has become a relic in the Internet age. Parties must guard against fraud in other ways.

For contracting parties to ensure they are both on the "same page," they must either engage in repetitive exchanges and acknowledgments of a com-

---

4. Such instant messages will usually be authenticated by individuals who were participants in the conversations. Hammontree v. State, 642 S.E.2d 412, 415 (Ga. Ct. App. 2007) (The defendant challenged the admission of a printed transcript of an instant message between himself and the victim. "Electronic computer messages are held to the same standards of authentication as other similar evidence. . . . The admission of transcripts of Internet chat sessions are akin to the admission of videotapes, which are 'admissible where the operator of the machine which produces it, or one who personally witnessed the events recorded, testifies that the videotape accurately portrayed what the witness saw take place at the time the events occurred.'"); Laughner v. State, 769 N.E.2d 1147, 1159 (Ind. Ct. App. 2002) (Under a comparable Indiana Rule 1001(3), a state trooper, posing as a child, engaged in instant message chats with the defendant and subsequently cut and pasted those chats into a word-processing program. Even though they were susceptible to being edited, the court admitted the hard-copy printouts from the word-processor program after the officer testified that he had personal knowledge of the conversations and that the printed documents accurately reflected the contents of the original chats. Under Rule 1001(3), these printouts were found to be the "best evidence" of the conversation with the defendant, even though other "originals" could have been created by using the logging feature provided by the AOL.).

mon iteration of the contract or use an independent broker to confirm and store the final iteration that would be the original for best evidence purposes.

In the absence of such devices, contractual disputes can be quite complicated. Claim resolution either would have to turn on the contracting parties' credibility (a situation the common law rightly concluded was intolerable both because contracts are vital to free commerce and because human recollection is fallible) or would cause the litigation to become hypertechnical, laden with expert testimony about "shadow" evidence located on individual hard drives that shows that the "original" iteration of the contract was manipulated.

Just as the best evidence rule has become meaningless in the Internet age of e-commerce, so too has the parol evidence rule. The only apparent solution is for both doctrines, and the Statute of Frauds, to be revised to reflect these unique circumstances. The nature of these necessary revisions is beyond the scope of this chapter.

Computers are now also being used to produce and enhance photographs.[5] As with all computer-created documents, this process does not create best evidence problems, because the pictures printed through the digital technology would be originals, along with the images recorded on the camera's hard drive or photo card and those images that are called up on a computer monitor from what has been downloaded from a camera. Assuming that the digital pictures are properly authenticated, all should be equally admissible.

Digital enhancement of ordinary photographs also creates no best evidence problem, but for entirely different reasons. A digital image is made from the photograph and the picture is enhanced by manipulating the pixels in the picture to provide greater clarity. The digitally enhanced image that results creates no best evidence problem because Rule 1003[6] treats duplicates as original unless a genuine question is raised as to the authenticity of the original photograph, or it otherwise would be unfair to admit the duplicate as the original. Again, if a proper foundation is laid for the enhancement process (the process is properly authenticated), best evidence concerns will be satisfied.[7]

---

5. *See* text at note 47, *infra.*

6. FED. R. EVID. 1003.

7. United States v. Seifert, 351 F. Supp. 2d 926, 928 (D. Minn. 2005) ("Here, the evidence showed that the technician adjusted the digital image's brightness and contrast, but maintained the relationships between the light and dark areas of the

The best evidence rule has proven to be a problem with machines used to measure blood-alcohol content. These machines often produce both digital printouts and digital images displayed on the monitor of the machine. Is a best evidence problem created when an officer is permitted to testify to what was displayed on the monitor (which must be erased to continue using it) if the printout is still available for use in the courtroom? While the answer should clearly be yes, in *State v. Gentry* the court ruled that it was not:[8]

> The CMI Intoxilyzer Model 4011 AS provides two separate readings—a digital printout and a digital display. The digital printout, a written document, gave a reading of .11. Officer Fowler, over objection, testified that the digital display read .119. Gentry argues that best evidence in this case was the printout and, based upon K.S.A. 1987 Supp. 60-467(a), the trial court should not have allowed Officer Fowler to testify about the digital reading. The rule is simply inapplicable in this case. The state was eliciting testimony of the officer's observations of the digital display, not attempting to prove the content of the digital printout. A witness may always testify on relevant matters about which he or she has personal knowledge. It was not error for the trial court to admit this testimony.

The error in the *Gentry* ruling stems from two facts that the court did not recognize. First, the image displayed on the machine's monitor was a writing. Second, the machine had produced multiple originals; they were just in different forms. Under the best evidence or original writing rule, secondary evidence of what the machine wrote (the officer's testimony about the content of what he observed) is only admissible after all of the originals created by the machine have been shown to be unavailable due to no serious fault of the proponent of the secondary evidence.[9] Hearsay and the problems of

---

image. . . . The technician testified that he simply 'moved' the brightness relationship on the scale, increasing the light's intensity while maintaining the image's integrity. . . . As a result, the Court finds that the enhanced tape accurately presents a true and accurate replica of the image recorded by the Co-Operative's security camera. It does so in a fashion which maintains the image while assisting the jury in perceiving and understanding the recorded event. . . . Accordingly, the Court finds the enhanced videotape is a duplicate admissible under the best evidence rule. Fed. R. Evid. 1001(4), 1002, and 1003.").

8. State v. Gentry, 1988 Kan. App. LEXIS 187, *4-5 (Kan. Ct. App. Mar. 3, 1988).

9. The officer's testimony did not create a hearsay problem when it repeated what the machine "said" to prove the truth of what it "said," because under the hearsay rule,

perception, memory, sincerity, and ambiguity are no longer a problem when the machine is properly authenticated.

III. THE ADDED COMPLEXITY OF SUMMARIES OF VOLUMINOUS MATERIALS

Because of the use of computers, e-mail, and the Internet, the volume of written materials subject to pretrial discovery and use at trial has greatly increased. Data is regularly recorded and used by computer programs to produce reports that would have previously been impossible. Often, either these reports or the database from which they were created contain information that is relevant to issues being litigated. When this data is extracted from either the reports or the underlying database, the volume of materials being summarized can be voluminous.

Under the best evidence rule, when proving the content of a document, the original of that document must be used in court or the proponent of evidence must demonstrate that the original is not available because of no serious fault of the proponent. While the database and the summarized reports are available, they may number in the tens of thousands of hard-copy pages. Does the trial need to be encumbered with this voluminous material? Under the Federal Rules of Evidence, the answer is no.

Summaries of voluminous records may be used in lieu of the originals if certain conditions are met in Fed. R. Evid.1006.[10] This rule requires the following: (1) a finding by the judge that the records are too voluminous to use conveniently in the courtroom (note that this is *not* a necessity standard); and (2) making available the originals, or duplicates of those records, for examination or copying by the opposing party at a reasonable time and

---

only individuals can utter statements. Kan. Stat. Ann. § 60-459 (2005) defined a statement as "not only an oral or written expression but also nonverbal conduct of a person intended by him or her as a substitute for words in expressing the matter stated.". This also true under the Rule 801(a) of the Federal Rules of Evidence. Fed. R. Evid. 801(a) defines a statement as "(1) an oral or written assertion or (2) nonverbal conduct of a person, if it is intended by the person as an assertion."

10. Fed. R. Evid. 1006 provides:

Rule 1006. Summaries

The contents of voluminous writings, recordings, or photographs which cannot conveniently be examined in court may be presented in the form of a chart, summary, or calculation. The originals, or duplicates, shall be made available for the examination or copying, or both, by other parties at a reasonable time and place. The court may order that they be produced in court.

place. For this second condition to have any meaning, the proponent of the summary should provide pretrial notice to the opposing party of the intended use of the summary and of the availability of the originals for examination at a specific time and place.[11]

Two additional conditions for the admissibility of the summaries are implicit: (1) that the underlying documents being summarized are admissible, and (2) that the summary is properly authenticated—i.e., shown to be relevant and accurate. If the summary was created manually, the individual who performed that task will need to testify. If the information was extracted from a computer database by a special computer program, proper authentication will require the proponent to establish how the program works through the testimony of a qualified witness familiar with the logic of the computer program. This will guarantee that the summary is relevant and accurate, because the appropriate materials were surveyed and the necessary information was extracted and properly summarized.

Rule 1006 requires only that the voluminous underlying documents be made available to the opposing party for examination. It does not mention the summary itself. The Rule, therefore, could be interpreted as not requiring the summary's disclosure. Failure to disclose the summary, however, may jeopardize the admissibility of the summary as substantive evidence because of the hearsay issue it creates and the unavailability of a hearsay exception other than the residual exception in Fed. R. Evid. 807 that requires notice, disclosure, and specific assurances of trustworthiness.[12] While hearsay is generally addressed in Chapter 5, it is briefly explored here because of its close, and often misunderstood or overlooked, relationship to the summary exception to the best evidence rule.

A.   The Hearsay Dimensions of Summaries

When a summary of voluminous materials is offered by the proponent for the truth of the contents, a hearsay problem is created. This evidence often involves two different types of summaries.

The first are summaries created in the regular course of business and relied upon in the business enterprise. They commonly include such reports as income statements, balance sheets, cost of goods sold statements, cash

---

11. One court, however, has rejected this pretrial notification requirement. *See* Duke v. Pfizer, Inc., 668 F. Supp. 1031, 1038-39 (E.D. Mich. 1987)—but that result makes little practical sense.

12. *See* text at note 17, *infra.*

flow statements, and product-line summaries. These first types of summaries are part of the company's regular business records. Consequently, the hearsay issue they pose is resolved through the business records exception, codified in Fed. R. Evid. 803(6).

The second type of summary is one created for use in litigation. It often summarizes many of the first types of summaries that are so voluminous they cannot conveniently be used in the courtroom. This second level of summary creates a second level of hearsay when offered to prove the truth of the content of the first-level summaries.[13] This second level of hearsay is often overlooked by courts.[14] Even though the underlying documents that have been summarized are business records, the Rule 1006 summary does not come within the business records exception because it was made in anticipation of litigation and not in the regular course of business.[15] This second level of hearsay is best addressed in either of two ways.

1.   Non-hearsay Argument

A first way of dealing with the summary is to argue that it is not hearsay at all—because it is not a "statement" as defined in Fed. R. Evid. 801(a). Even though the proponent is offering the summary to prove the truth of the summary's content, if the summary was created by a computer program, and that program has been authenticated, the hearsay "statement" that is being offered would be the "statement" of a machine, not an individual. Under Fed. R. Evid. 801(b), a "declarant" is defined as "a person who makes a statement." Under Fed. R. Evid. 801(a), a "statement" is defined as either an oral or written assertion, "if it is *intended* by the *person* as an assertion." (Emphasis added.) If the summary is eliminated from the definitions of both "statement" and "declarant," it would also be eliminated from the definition of "hearsay" in subsection (c), which employs those terms.

---

13. *See* Indianapolis Minority Contractors Ass'n., Inc. v. Wiley, 1998 WL 1988826, at *7 (S.D. Ind. May 13, 2003) (computer data extracted from business records and used to prepare report for pending litigation; court noted that "the reports are not admissible as business records under Fed. R. Evid. 803(6). . . . Further, as a condition precedent to admissibility of computer records, the proponent must establish that the process or system used produces an accurate result, Fed. R. Evid. 901(b)(9), and that foundation has not been established. In light of the above, the veracity and reliability of these reports are questionable and thus . . . are not admissible and will be stricken.").

14. *See, e.g.*, Ford Motor Co. v. Auto Supply Co., 661 F.2d 1171 (8th Cir. 1981).

15. Palmer v. Hoffman, 318 U.S. 109 (1943).

The same argument can be made under the common law in those juris-dictions like New York where an evidence code, similar to the Federal Rules of Evidence, has not been adopted. Because the hearsay rule addresses the problems of human perception, memory, sincerity, and ambiguity, none of which are present with the use of machines that are authenticated, it can reasonably be argued that the hearsay rule's rationale is not applicable.[16] Of course, under either the common law or the Federal Rules of Evidence, if the summary is created manually, this argument will fail because all potenial hearsay problems will be present.

2.   Residual Exception Solution

Second, on the assumption that the litigation-specific summary is hearsay, the proponent in a federal proceeding might argue that it should be admitted under the residual exception in Fed. R. Evid. 807.[17] If the underlying docu-

---

16. The application of the hearsay rule traditionally has been limited to human assertions—giving rise to what could fairly be characterized as a "Dogs and Nuns Rule." Even though animals communicate with us and we can correctly interpret what they say, their communications are not considered hearsay, because animals are believed to act out of instinct and will not present a sincerity problem. By contrast, nuns who witness an accident and who give the same statements about what they saw is hearsay, even though it is highly probable that they will not fabricate stories, because they possess the potential for ambiguity, insincerity, and inaccuracy in per-ception and memory. On a continuum, machines are on the other side of dogs. Once machines are properly authenticated, there is little need to apply the hearsay rule, because the hearsay problems of perception, memory, sincerity, and ambiguity have either been addressed or eliminated. *But see* Bellsouth Corp. v. Internet Classifieds of Ohio, 1997 WL 33107251, at *15 (N.D. Ga. Nov. 12, 1997), where the court rejected as hearsay the results of Internet searches that revealed the use of "REAL" and "YEL-LOW PAGES" in domain names.

17. Fed. R. Evid. 807 provides:

Rule 807. Residual Exception.
A statement not specifically covered by Rule 803 or 804 but having equiva-lent circumstantial guarantees of trustworthiness is not excluded by the hearsay rule if the court determines that (A) the statement is offered as evidence of a material fact; (B) the statement is more probative on the point for which it is offered than any other evidence which the proponent can procure through reasonable efforts; and (C) the general purposes of these rules and the interests of justice will best be served by admission of the statement into evidence. However, a statement may not be admitted under this exception unless the proponent of it makes known to the adverse party, sufficiently in advance of the trial or hearing to provide the adverse party

ments are properly authenticated, and the proponent of the summary meets all of the requirements of Fed. R. Evid. 1006, reliability is reasonably assured.

The only remaining problems are the explicit requirements in Fed. R. Evid. 807 that do not appear in Rule 1006. Rule 807 requires notice to the opposing party. The proponent should also make the summary available to the opposing party. Although not explicitly required by Rule 807, the rule does require that a fair opportunity be given to the opponent to meet the evidence by disclosing "the proponent's intention to offer the statement and *the particulars of it.*" Regardless of whether it is required, disclosure should be made as a matter of course. It will eliminate any questions about the summary's reliability if the opposing party cannot identify specific problems after having had a chance to examine and test it. Consequently, the court will have little reason to refuse to admit it under Rule 807.

C.   *Insurmountable Hearsay Problems Created by Summaries of Voluminous Materials from the Internet*

Anything can be posted on the Internet. Web pages are established and revised and deleted daily. Nothing about the Internet ensures that materials posted on any Web page are accurate, or that they continue to exist in the form that they were seen in the past. Consequently, authentication of Web page content often poses a difficult hurdle. Calling up a Web page in a courtroom demonstration can authenticate its existence in a particular form on a particular day, but this is not possible for voluminous numbers of Web pages. Therefore, when a summary of such pages is offered, copies of each summarized Web page must be available on a date-stamped printout. This will authenticate its appearance on a date relevant to the cause of action, but it will not establish that the facts stated on the Web page and extracted in the summary were accurate.

Proving facts from statements made in each Web page will create hearsay problems. Even if the Web pages were created by business enterprises, the Web pages likely would not constitute business records of the company, because they are not internally relied upon by the company. A custodian or other qualified person from each business would have to authenticate each Web page even if it could be a business record.

---

with a fair opportunity to prepare to meet it, the proponent's intention to offer the statement and the particulars of it, including the name and address of the declarant.

This would be virtually impossible for voluminous numbers of such pages. The hearsay exception for market reports and commercial publications, codified in Fed. R. Evid. 803(17),[18] is likely inapplicable, because that exception is limited to commercial publications that are "generally used and relied upon by the public or by persons in particular occupations," like the *NADA Blue Book* values for used cars. If all the Web pages were posted by the same party and are offered against that party, they are admissible as non-hearsay under the "admission" provisions codified in Fed. R. Evid. 801(d)(2) that have excluded them from the operation of the hearsay rule.

D. The Evidentiary Status of Summaries under the Voluminous Writings Exception to the Original Writing Rule

When the summary exception to the best evidence rule is employed, logic dictates that those summaries be treated like the originals that they replace. They should be treated as evidence that the jury is permitted to examine during deliberations.[19] Otherwise, the summaries would not be an exception to the rule. Nevertheless, most courts do not treat the summaries as substantive evidence. They require that the originals be admitted into evidence and limit the summaries to a de-

---

18. FED. R. EVID. 803(17) provides:

Rule 803. Hearsay Exceptions: Availability of Declarant Immaterial

The following are not excluded by the hearsay rule, even though the declarant is available as a witness:

. . . .

(17) Market reports, commercial publications.— Market quotations, tabulations, lists, directories, or other published compilations, generally used and relied upon by the public or by persons in particular occupations.

This rule has been used to admit interest rates posted on the Webpage of the Federal Reserve Board in Elliott Assocs. v. Banco de la Nacion, 194 F.R.D. 116 (S.D.N.Y.2000) and Blue Book prices for a used car in State v. Erickstad, 620 N.W.2d 136, 145 (N.D. 2000) ("We recognize that, in this case, the police officer checked the value of the pickup on the *Kelley Blue Book* Internet website, not in the print edition. The defendants have offered no cogent reason why evidence derived from the website, rather than the print edition, should be excluded under [Rule] 803(17).")

19. United States v. Pinto, 850 F.2d 927, 935 (2d Cir. 1988).

monstrative role.[20] This means that the summaries are not admitted into evidence and are not available to jurors during their deliberations.[21]

This practice needlessly restricts the use of summaries. Considering all of the conditions that Fed. R. Evid. 1006 has placed on their use (i.e., notice to and examination by the opposing party prior to trial), there is little justification for treating them as mere learning aids. Changing this practice may be difficult, however, because Rule 1006 explicitly permits the court to order that the underlying documents be produced in court. This restrictive interpretation and use of Rule 1006 eliminates much of its value, rendering it little more than a specific application of the power of the presiding judge to permit the use of demonstrative evidence under Fed. R. Evid. 611.[22]

---

20. *See, e.g.,* United States v. Smyth, 556 F.2d 1179, 1183 (5th Cir. 1977), in which the court characterized the admission of the summary without the underlying documents as the "liberal school" interpretation of Rule 1006. The court followed the "restrictive view" and refused to consider the summaries as substantive evidence.

21. *See* United States v. DeBoer, 966 F.2d 1066, 1069 (6th Cir. 1992); Harris Mkt. Research v. Marshall Mktg. & Commc'ns, Inc. 948 F.2d 1518, 1525 (10th Cir. 1992).

22. Fed. R. Evid. 611 provides in part:

Rule 611. Mode and Order of Interrogation and Presentation.
(a) Control by court.—The court shall exercise reasonable control over the mode and order of interrogating witnesses and presenting evidence so as to (1) make the interrogation and presentation effective for the ascertainment of the truth, (2) avoid needless consumption of time, and (3) protect witnesses from harassment or undue embarrassment.

Presumptions 5

I.   The Basics 317

II. Common Law Presumptions That Can Be
     Relevant to Authenticating E-commerce and
     E-mail 323

     A. Receipt of Mailed Letters 323

     B. Authority to Transact Business 325

     C. Authority to Use an Instrumentality 325

     D. Responsibility for Damage or Loss 326

III. Authentication of E-commerce—Problems
     with Presumptions Under the Federal Rules
     of Evidence 326

E-evidence Overview: Presumptions could be an important tool for authenticating electronic communications. Common law presumptions could provide meaningful guidance on when and how presumptions might be used for authentication purposes in the digital age. Unfortunately, the Federal Rules of Evidence do not recognize a single presumption, and so there may be doubt about whether any common law presumptions have survived codification. If they have survived, which is likely, there is confusion as to whether judges have the power to revise them or create new ones to accommodate the computer age.

All messages sent over the Internet have numbers associated with them that identify (1) the Internet service provider (ISP) facilitating the communication and (2) the computer from which the message was sent. The information about the computer is recorded with the ISP when the contract for service is created. If the computer is owned by an individual or assigned to an individual by a business, is this enough information to create a presumption that the individual who either owned or controlled the computer was the author of the communication?

The answer is yes. Logically, the individual who controls a computer is probably responsible for messages sent from it. Others may be given access or use it without permission, but the individual with control has the best access to evidence that could disprove his or her responsibility. While Congress, state legislatures, and the courts have not recognized such a presumption, there is as much reason to do so as there is to presume that the owner of a registered automobile was responsible for its operation.[1]

In the area of electronic evidence, one of the most difficult problems is authentication: proving that a communication was from the individuals identified in the header. Because headers in e-mail messages can be spoofed, the recipient of a message may have difficulty proving authorship.[2] The most direct solution to this problem is for courts to presume authorship, based on probabilities created by evidence of that message's origin. The origin, however, should have to be proven through evidence other than the name appearing in the header.

The answer, however, may not be so straightforward. In federal courts, for example, it is unclear whether judges continue to have the power to

---

1. *See* note 16, *infra.*
2. *See* Chapter 6, "Authentication," *supra.*

create *new* presumptions because the codification of the Rules of Evidence may well have taken that power from them. Would recognition of the presumption be a new presumption if the presumption already exists about operation of an automobile by the registered owner? Is this new application of an established presumption a "new" presumption?

While a presumption could be a critical tool in the authentication of electronic evidence, the presumption is a deceptively complex principle in both theory and application that is fraught with ambiguities and uncertainties that are not generally understood. Compounding the confusion about presumptions is the fact that they are frequently confused with the logical inferences upon which they are usually premised. Therefore, this chapter will briefly explore the basics of presumptions, clarifying ambiguities where possible; identify common law presumptions that could be expanded to accommodate the authentication of electronic evidence; and explore some of the problems created by Article III of the Federal Rules of Evidence that may prevent presumptions from being judicially recognized.

I.   THE BASICS

Presumptions are a shortcut to proof. The presumption is a mechanism employed during trial to shift burdens to the opposing side based on evidence that has been produced. If evidence is offered at trial establishing certain foundational facts, for example (A) that a letter was written, (B) properly addressed, (C) stamped, and (D) posted, courts have presumed (E) that the letter was received by the addressee. This presumption is premised on the regularity of our mail service and the high probability of delivery.

The presumption shifts burdens relative to the inferred fact. The question that has been the subject of historical debate is, what burden? There are two burdens that could shift: (1) the burden of going forward with evidence, or (2) the burden of persuasion. In the example of the mailed letter, if the presumptions shifted only (1), the burden of going forward with evidence to disprove the presumed fact, the party against whom it operated would only need to come forward with some evidence that he did not receive the letter. He could take the witness stand claiming that it was not received, and this would satisfied the burden. The opposing party would still have to convince the jury that the addressee actually received it. If the presumption shifted (2), the burden of persuasion, the alleged recipient of the mailed letter would have to convince the jury that he did not receive it. Each theory and its implications are discussed below.

Like the presumptions about mailed letters, most presumptions are premised on the high *probability* that the presumed fact is true after the primary or foundational facts have been proven.[3] Other policies can be important as well. For example, when a party has greater access to evidence, the law has presumed the existence of facts that, if not true, can be easily refuted by the party with the better access.[4] Other presumptions are based on social policy.[5] If society disfavors a particular conclusion, like a child's illegitimacy, it can presume the opposite to be true, thereby shifting to the party advocating the disfavored position the burden of coming forward with evidence to the contrary. More often than not, presumptions, both statutory and common law, have been prompted by a combination of probability, access to proof, and social policy.[6]

Presumptions are mandatory instructions to the jury that if it finds the foundational facts to be true, it must find the presumed fact to be true, absent evidence to the contrary. For instance, with the properly mailed

---

3. *See, e.g.*, the following common law presumptions: (1) Receipt of letters properly addressed and mailed and (2) authority of company employee to transact business by telephone. Examples of statutory presumptions based on probability are (1) black spots on a coal miner's lungs are black lung disease, and (2) disparate treatment of women is sex-based. Each of these presumptions is discussed in the text below.

4. *See, e.g.*, presumption of authority to use an instrumentality. For a discussion of this presumption, *see* text at note 16, *infra*.

5. In order to protect the child, it is presumed that the husband of the woman giving birth to the child is the child's biological father.

6. For example (1), the death of a person who has not been heard from over a specified period of time. If a person has disappeared for a period of over seven years despite diligent efforts to find him, it is presumed that he died at some time during his absence. This is based on the probability that an individual would not fail to contact his family over such a lengthy period of time if he were alive, and concern for the individual's heirs who need to collect on insurance policies and settle the estate. (2) Damage to goods placed in the custody of a commercial bailee is presumed to have been caused by the last bailee. This is based on probability and the superior access to proof by the commercial bailees who were present when the goods were transferred from the possession of one to the other. Had the goods been damaged before transfer, that damage should have been noted or the transfer of possession should have been refused.

letter presumptions, the law presumes that the letter was received by the addressee, and the jury is instructed to find this fact to be true absent evidence that it was not received.[7] The presumption forces the opposing side to *come forward with evidence* to disprove the presumed fact.

Jury instructions about presumptions can create confusion, however. This confusion has arisen because the instructions differ based on two factors: first, whether the proponent of the presumption has offered evidence that only attacks the foundation facts or has offered evidence that challenges the presumed facts; second, the purpose assigned to the presumption, *i.e.*, whether it operates to shift only the burden of going forward with evidence or shifts the burden of persuasion as well.

When the opposing party presents evidence that *disproves only the foundation facts* (properly mailed letter) *and not the presumed fact* (receipt of the letter or e-mail), the presumption remains intact. When this occurs, the presiding judge instructs the jury at the end of the trial the same way it would have had no evidence been offered by the opposing party: "If you find that the letter or e-mail was written, properly addressed to the opposing party, stamped and placed in an appropriate mail receptacle or, in the case of an e-mail, was properly sent through the e-mail

---

7. Originally approved by the U.S. Supreme Court in Rosenthal v. Walker, 111 U.S. 185, 193 (1884), its continued vitality was reaffirmed in Busquets-Ivars v. Ashcroft, 333 F.3d 1008 (9th Cir. 2003) ("The rule is well settled that 'if a letter properly directed is proved to have been either put into the post-office or delivered to the postman, it is presumed, from the known course of business in the post-office department, that it reached its destination at the regular time, and was received by the person to whom it was addressed.'"). The court in Busquets-Ivars ruled that the presumption was not operative, however, because the government failed to put the correct Zip code on the envelope, even though the proper street address and city were on the envelope. The court concluded that "[a] Zip code was an operative part of a properly directed piece of mail," citing 39 C.F.R. § 111.1 (2003). Consequently, the court concluded that the burden of establishing that the letter was properly directed was not satisfied. "E-mail is a computer-to-computer version of the postal service that enables users to send and receive messages and in some instances graphics or voice messages, either to individual recipients or in broadcast form to larger groups. In order to establish proof that electronic messages have been sent, courts may look, for example, to proof of electronic mail return-receipt or to the confirmation of downloading or printing. As new technologies continue to develop, the sort of proofs required to demonstrate proof of mailing and receipt will likewise change." SSI Med. Servs., Inc. v. Dep't of Human Servs., 685 A.2d 1, 6 (N.J. 1996).

service provider with no indication that it was not deliverable, you *must find* that the addressee received it."[8]

If the opposing side comes forward with evidence to *disprove the presumed fact* (receipt of the letter or e-mail), the differing theories about the purpose of presumptions come into play. Under the most popular common law theory, and the theory adopted in Fed. R. Evid. 301, presumptions are designed only to force the opposing party to come forward with evidence to disprove the presumed fact. Once the opposing party has done so, the presumption disappears because its sole purpose has been fulfilled. This theory was dubbed the "bursting-bubble" theory. Consequently, the jury must decide the case based on the logical inferences

---

8. A modification of this presumption of receipt-after-mailing rule has developed around tax returns. Because Internal Revenue Code § 7502 addresses how timely mailing is treated as timely filing and paying, it has been argued that the congressional enactment preempts the common law "mailbox" rule. This argument has been accepted in Deutsch v. Comm'r, 599 F.2d 44, 46 (2d Cir. 1979) and Miller v. United States, 784 F.2d 728 (6th Cir. 1986) because it is "an easily applied, objective standard." It has been rejected, however, in Sorrentino v. IRS, 383 F.3d 1187 (10th Cir. 2004); Davis v. United States, 230 F.3d 1383 (Fed. Cir. 2000); Anderson v. United States, 966 F.2d 487 (9th Cir. 1992); and Estate of Wood v. Comm'r, 909 F.2d 1155 (8th Cir. 1990). As explained in Sorrentino, "I am not prepared, based upon § 7502's plain language, to hold a taxpayer may *never* prove delivery to the IRS of the 'undelivered return' in the absence of a registered, certified, or electronic mail receipt. In other words, given the uncertainty as to what extent, if any, Congress intended to supplant the mailbox rule in enacting § 7502, I decline to hold the production of a registered, certified, or electronic mail receipt are the only means by which a taxpayer may establish timely delivery. . . . Section 7502's silence, however, is insufficient to entirely supplant the mailbox rule because '[i]t is a well-established principle of statutory construction that the common law ought not to be deemed to be repealed, unless the language of the statute be clear and specific for this purpose.'"

While the Sorrentino court permitted the use of the presumption to satisfy the taxpayer's burden of proving receipt by the IRS, it imposed an increased burden on the proof of the primary facts establishing mailing. The court deemed it unwise to endorse a mailbox rule based solely upon a taxpayer's uncorroborated, self-serving testimony of mailing, especially where the taxpayer has a history of filing untimely returns. Therefore, like the Eighth Circuit in Wood, the court required more than "mere proof of mailing, such as direct proof of postmark which is 'verifiable beyond any self-serving testimony of a taxpayer who claims that a document was timely mailed.'" It is not clear that his type of restriction is necessary. As the court was skeptical of misuse by delinquent taxpayers, jurors would also be skeptical when this type of proof is offered by them.

that can be drawn from the evidence of mailing, independent of the presumption. No presumption instruction is appropriate because the presumption ceases to exist—disappearing like a pricked bubble.[9]

A popular alternative to the "bursting-bubble" theory[10] assigns to presumptions the far greater effect of *shifting the burden of persuasion* to the party against whom the presumption operates. Unlike the "bursting bubble" theory, which requires the opposing party to come forward with *some evidence* of the nonexistence of the presumed fact, the alternative theory *requires the party against whom it operates to convince the jury that he didn't receive it.*[11]

In the case of the presumption about properly mailed letters or e-mail messages, the alternative theory would require the court to instruct the jury that if it finds the foundational facts to be true (written, addressed,

---

9. When a mandatory instruction is inappropriate, an instruction about the logical inferences that *could* be drawn from proof of the foundational facts might be appropriate in jurisdictions that permit judges to comment on the evidence.

10. When the FEDERAL RULES OF EVIDENCE were originally promulgated and approved by the Supreme Court, the theory of presumptions that had been adopted was one that shifted the burden of persuasion to the opposing party. This was dubbed the Morgan-McCormick theory, because these were the leading scholars who advocated it. *See* Fed. R. Evid. 301, Advisory Committee's Note, 56 F.R.D. 183, 208 (1972). The Senate, however, rejected the Morgan-McCormick theory, adopting instead current Rule 301. This was a questionable alteration that should be reexamined by the Advisory Committee on the Federal Rules of Evidence.

11. Although Article III of the Federal Rules of Evidence has adopted the "bursting-bubble" theory of presumptions, this discussion is not an academic exercise for two reasons. First, if Congress enacts presumptions, they can be designed to shift the burden of persuasion regardless of the position that has been taken in the Federal Rules of Evidence. More important, despite the clear language of the rules, courts have shown a willingness to disregard their explicit language when the logic and policy underlying them convince courts that a different interpretation and application would best serve the interests of justice.

The best example of this was the judicial reaction to Rule 407, Subsequent Remedial Measures. The rule originally excluded evidence of subsequent remedial measures only in cases in which "negligence or culpable conduct" was being proven. As written, the rule did not apply to product liability cases where neither negligence nor culpability was at issue. Despite this limitation, courts disregarded the language and applied Rule 407 in product liability cases. Only after the language of the rule had been unanimously disregarded did the Advisory Committee amend it to include product liability cases.

and properly mailed), the jury *must* find that the addressee received the message *unless the addressee convinces them otherwise*. The court gives this instruction regardless of the evidence the alleged recipient has presented. In other words, if the foundational facts have been proven but the jury is still in doubt, the party sending the message wins. By contrast, under the "bursting bubble" theory adopted in Fed. R. Evid. 301, which does not shift the burden of persuasion from the sender to the addressee, if the jury is in doubt, the party sending the message loses. To advocates of this alternative approach, the bursting-bubble theory gives too little value to presumptions.

The factors that determine the initial allocation of the burden of persuasion—probability, fairness, access to proof, and social policy—are the same factors that control the creation of presumptions. Consequently, proponents of the alternative theory argue that the presumption should control the burden of persuasion by reassigning it on the basis of evidence that has been presented at trial. They argue that presumptions should do something more significant based on the demonstrated equities and needs of each case.[12]

Judges often indirectly convert the codified "bursting bubble" presumption into presumptions that shift burdens of persuasion by continuing to instruct juries about the presumption after the "bubble" has been burst. For example, even if the alleged recipient of a letter testifies that he didn't receive it, thereby bursting the presumption bubble and leaving nothing to instruct about, some judges have continued to give an instruction that if the jury finds that the letter was properly addressed, stamped, and mailed, the jury *may* find that it was received. Judges also have referred to presumptions as "evidence" of the presumed facts that the jury should weigh. In each of these instances, the judges have changed the

---

12. Because of dissatisfaction with the minimal purpose given to presumptions under FED. R. EVID. 301, Congress often creates presumptions in legislative enactments that shift the burden of persuasion. For example, under the Black Lung legislation, if a claimant is proven to have been a coal miner for a particular period of time and black spots are found on his lungs (the foundational facts), then the black spots are presumed to be Black Lung disease caused by his employment in the mines. This presumption shifts to the coal company the burden of proving that the claimant does not have Black Lung disease. This presumption is based on a combination of probability and social policy (i.e., wanting to provide proper treatment and compensation to anyone who may have the disease). Such legislation, of course, overrides FED. R. EVID. 301.

nature of the presumption by changing its effect. In a sense, they have used the presumptions as an excuse to comment on the evidence and the logical inferences that may be drawn from the foundational facts.[13] Whether this reflects judicial dissatisfaction with the bursting-bubble theory, confusion about the difference between presumptions and logical inferences, or both, is unclear.

II. COMMON LAW PRESUMPTIONS THAT CAN BE RELEVANT TO AUTHENTICATING E-COMMERCE AND E-MAIL

The following common law presumptions can have direct applicability to electronic evidence if either the courts or Congress recognize and extend them. Through these established common law presumptions, litigants could prove that notice was received by recipients, authenticate responses as having been authored by specific individuals, authenticate the authority of individuals to speak for others, and establish responsibility for the use of a computer or injury (such as the introduction of viruses and worms) that originated from a specific computer terminal.

A. *Receipt of Mailed Letters*

As noted, the common law recognized a presumption about the receipt by the addressee of a properly mailed letter. If the plaintiff offers evidence that he (1) wrote a letter, (2) properly addressed it to the defendant, (3) put the proper amount of postage on it, and (4) placed it in a mail receptacle, the law presumed that the addressee received the letter and had notice of its content. This presumption was based on the regularity of the mail service and the probability that the letter was properly delivered in the due course of that mail service.

---

13. *See, e.g.*, R.J. Mgmt. Co. v. SRLB Dev. Corp., 282, 806 N.E.2d 1074, 1081 (Ill. Ct. App. 2004) where the court held that the party against which the presumption operated not only had to come forward with evidence to rebut the presumption that destroyed evidence was unfavorable to the offending party, but also required that the evidence be "clear and convincing" because a fiduciary relationship was involved, making it a "strong" social policy presumption. For an examination of the misuse of presumptions in judicial opinions in antitrust law, *see* Paul R. Rice & Slade S. Cutter, *Problems With Presumptions: A Case Study of the "Structural Presumption" of Anticompetitiveness*, Antitrust Bull., p. 557, Winter 2002.

Once evidence is presented that an e-mail message was written, properly addressed to a particular party, and sent via the Internet, the same presumption could operate with e-commerce. As it is presumed that the addressee of a letter received it at the designated address within days after it was posted, a reasonable presumption could be that the addressee received the message on his computer within minutes, if not seconds, of its transmission, because of the reliability of the Internet and the e-mail server that the sender employed.

In *SSI Medical Services, Inc. v. Department of Human Services,*[14] the court explained the transference of the presumption from letters to e-mail:

> One of the fastest-growing methods of communication is electronic mail or e-mail. E-mail is a computer-to-computer version of the postal service that enables users to send and receive messages and in some instances graphics or voice messages, either to individual recipients or in broadcast form to larger groups. In order to establish proof that electronic messages have been sent, courts may look, for example, to proof of electronic mail return-receipt or to confirmation of downloading or printing. As new technologies continue to develop, the sort of proofs required to demonstrate proof of mailing and receipt will likewise change.

SSI Medical includes an extended discussion of using business custom to prove that the e-mail was sent. This is often the case for larger enterprises where the employees will not remember a particular mailing. The court held that the existence of the custom "alone is insufficient to trigger the presumption of mailing and receipt." The reason for this conclusion was the fact that the custom and habit rule in New Jersey required corroboration that the custom was followed in a particular instance. This limitation existed at common law. The common law requirement of corroboration has been eliminated in Fed. R. Evid. 406.[15] Proof of the mail-

---

14. 685 A.2d 1, n.1 (N.J. 1996).
15. **Rule 406. Habit: Routine Practice**.
    Evidence of the habit of a person or of the routine practice of an organization, whether corroborated or not and regardless of the presence of eyewitnesses, is relevant to prove that the conduct of the person or organization on a particular occasion was in conformity with the habit or routine practice.

ing could be either by testimony of someone with firsthand knowledge or of someone who is familiar with the business custom.

B. Authority to Transact Business

A similar presumption operates with regard to telephone calls to businesses. If an individual proves (1) that he dialed the telephone number of a business establishment and (2) spoke with someone about a particular matter (3) that is normally dealt with over the telephone, the law presumes (A) that the receiver of the call was the person who identified himself and (B) that he had the authority to speak for the business enterprise on that matter. This presumption is based on probability and fairness because of the company's superior access to proof as well as the social policy of holding a business responsible for telephone contacts that it has encouraged by listing its number in the telephone directory.

With electronic communications, the same presumption would be appropriate. If a message is shown to have been sent via the Internet and a message is received in reply, it could be presumed that the person was authorized to send that reply message if the original recipient was a business establishment. A similar presumption might be reasonable concerning the identity of an individual who was sent a message and replied to it. When a computer terminal is registered to an individual and is within his control (which can be determined through the identification number that the ISP assigns and attaches to each message originating from the licensed terminal), probabilities are that he authored responses originating on that computer. If the individual to whom the computer was registered did not send the reply, because he had given others access to the terminal on the date in question and had not take proper precautions to guard against its inappropriate use (with password protection, for example), that individual would be in the best position to refute the claim of authorship.

C. Authority to Use an Instrumentality

If one is injured by another's negligent operation of an automobile, an agency relationship between the driver and the owner will be presumed when ownership by a third party is established.[16] This presumption is

---

16. *See, e.g.*, CONN. GEN. STAT. ANN. § 52-182 (2003); N.C. GEN. STAT. § 20-71.1(a) (2003); TENN. CODE ANN. § 55-10-311(a) (2003).

based primarily on fairness because of the owner's superior access to proof and the social policy of encouraging individuals to be responsible for the use of the vehicles they own. This presumption is directly transferable to computers. Those who make commitments on another's computer terminal could be presumed to have had the authority to do so on behalf of the person with whom the terminal is associated because of the social policy of encouraging e-commerce and the computer owner's superior access to proof.

D.   *Responsibility for Damage or Loss*

When undamaged goods are given to a common carrier and later delivered in damaged condition, it is presumed that the damage was due to the negligence of the carrier/bailee.[17] If there are a series of bailees, it is presumed that the damage was caused by the last bailee. This is based on probability and fairness. Only the bailee had both control of the goods and superior access to proof of who else may have caused the damage. By analogy, the owner of a computer has control of it. The computer can easily be disabled to prevent others from using it. This ability to control computer access could justify a presumption that the owner is responsible for things that are done from the terminal. The control the owner exercises is no different than the control a bailee has over goods given to him for delivery. Consequently, viruses that are introduced to the Internet through a particular computer (causing damage to the computers of others) could be presumed to have been introduced by the owner of the computer unless he convinces the finder of facts that he did not introduce the virus.

These are just a few of the common law and statutory presumptions that could be relevant to e-evidence. However, there is a lingering question as to whether these, or any other presumptions, have survived the codification of the rules of evidence.

III.   AUTHENTICATION OF E-COMMERCE—PROBLEMS WITH PRESUMPTIONS UNDER THE FEDERAL RULES OF EVIDENCE

While many judges find it convenient and fair to employ presumptions to compel what logic will permit, federal judges will encounter signifi-

---

17. *See, e.g.,* Minn. Stat. § 540.17 Subd. 2 (2000); Miss. Code Ann. § 13-1-121 (2003); Ohio Rev. Code Ann. § 4907.57 (West 1994-2003).

cant problems under Article III of the Federal Rules of Evidence.[18] That Article has adopted the most restrictive and least useful theory about the effect of presumptions—the "bursting-bubble" theory. This, coupled with the fact that it fails to recognize a single presumption and provides no guidance on the status of previously existing common law presumptions, creates a significant question about whether any common law presumptions have survived codification. Given the inherent complexities of presumptions, previously discussed, Article III has helped to make this evidentiary principle one of the most confusing, misunderstood, and ignored areas of evidence law.[19]

---

18. Acts like the Uniform Computer Information Transactions Act (UCITA) and the Uniform Electronic Transactions Act (UETA) address and resolve questions about how e-commerce should comply with requirements that transactions shall be in writing and signed by participating parties. These Acts do not address the means by which electronic communications and the signatures attached to them are authenticated or the evidentiary presumptions that apply. *See, e.g.*, Uniform Electronic Transactions Act, § 9 (Attribution and Effect of Electronic Record and Electronic Signature), which provides:

> (a) An electronic record or electronic signature is attributable to a person if it was the act of the person. The act of the person may be shown in any manner, including a showing of the efficacy of any security procedure applied to determine the person to which the electronic record or electronic signature was attributable.
> (b) The effect of an electronic record or electronic signature attributed to a person under subsection (a) is determined from the context and surrounding circumstances at the time of its creation, execution, or adoption, including the parties' agreement, if any, and otherwise as provided by law.

In the accompanying Draft Comments, the National Conference of Commissioners on Uniform State Laws explains: "[L]aw other than this Act would ascribe both the signature and the action to the person if done in a paper medium. Subsection (a) expressly provides that the same result will occur when an electronic medium is used."

19. *See* Paul R. Rice, *The Evidence Project: Proposed Revisions to the Federal Rules of Evidence with Supporting Commentary*, 171 F.R.D. 330 (1997); and Paul R. Rice & Neal W. Delker, *Federal Rules of Evidence Advisory Committee: A Short History of Too Little Consequence*, 191 F.R.D. 187 (2000).

The two rules within Article III provide:

Article III. Presumptions in Civil Actions and Proceedings
Rule 301. Presumptions in General in Civil Actions and Proceedings

In all civil actions and proceedings not otherwise provided for by Act of Congress or by these rules, a presumption imposes on the party against whom it is directed the burden of going forward with evidence to rebut or meet the presumption, but does not shift to such party the burden of proof in the sense of the risk of nonpersuasion, which remains throughout the trial upon the party on whom it was originally cast.

Rule 302. Applicability of State Law in Civil Actions and Proceedings

In civil actions and proceedings, the effect of a presumption respecting a fact which is an element of a claim or defense as to which State law supplies the rule of decision is determined in accordance with State law.

These rules address only the *effect* of presumptions in civil actions. Rule 301 provides that "a presumption imposes on the party against whom it is directed the *burden of going forward with evidence* to rebut or meet the presumption . . . ." (Emphasis added.) Unlike the Evidence Code of California,[20] for example, not a single presumption is delineated in Article III. This raises the question, what has survived codification?

There is no clear answer to this question because courts have not addressed the issue, and it is only the first of a series of unresolved issues. If common law presumptions have survived, can courts still modify them for use in the Internet age, as they would have under the common law? Can courts create new presumptions without going through the cumbersome congressional legislative or quasi-legislative Advisory Committee processes?

---

20. *See* Cal. Evid. Code §§ 600 et seq.

Fed. R. Evid. 102 provides that the "rules shall be construed to secure fairness in administration, elimination of unjustifiable expense and delay, and promotion of growth and development of the law of evidence to the end that the truth may be ascertained and proceedings justly determined." This rule does not perpetuate common law evidentiary rules unless they are essential to, and thus implicit in, the rules that have been codified.[21] On what rules, if any, would the recognition and creation of presumptions be based?

To interpret Article III as abolishing all common law presumptions would be significant, but it would not be irrational or render the provisions of Article III meaningless. It would merely leave the codified provisions in control of fewer statutory presumptions that do not expressly reject the bursting-bubble approach. Rule 301 would still have a purpose. Elsewhere in the Evidence Code, when Congress intended common law rules to be perpetuated, for instance, in Article V, Privileges, the perpetuation was *explicit*.[22] Therefore, nei-

---

21. For example, the Supreme Court has held that the common law restrictions on the admissibility of co-conspirator admissions were not perpetuated by silence when Rule 801(d)(2)(D) was enacted. This rule codified a skeletal version of the common law's co-conspirator admission rule. The language of the rule did not explicitly mention the common law restrictions that had modified co-conspirator admissions for decades. Under the common law restrictions, a co-conspirator admission was not admissible against a criminal defendant until the government had proven with evidence independent of the statement in question (1) that the conspiracy existed and (2) that the defendant was a participant. In United States v. Bourjaily, the Supreme Court concluded that the common law restrictions had been silently abandoned, based on the plain language of Rule 801(d)(2)(D).

Conversely, the Supreme Court held that prior consistent statements were not admissible to bolster the credibility of a witness unless they had been made before the motive to fabricate had arisen, even though that restriction was not incorporated in the Federal Rules of Evidence. The limitation was read into the rule because the Court concluded that a consistent statement was not relevant to bolstering credibility unless the statement was made before the witness possessed the reason to utter the alleged fabrication.

22. FED. R. EVID. 501 provides:

Except as otherwise required by the Constitution of the United States or provided by Act of Congress or in rules prescribed by the Supreme Court pursuant to statutory authority, the privilege of a witness, person, government, State, or political subdivision thereof *shall be governed by the principles of the common law as they may be interpreted by the courts of the United States in light of reason and experience.* However, in civil actions and proceedings, with respect to an element of a claim or defense

ther logic nor legislative intent demands an interpretation of the Evidence Code that preserves all common law presumptions.

The most compelling justification for judicial recognition of presumptions may be the inherent power of judges to comment on the evidence. If courts are empowered to suggest to the jury logical inferences and conclusions that can be drawn from the evidence that has been heard,[23] it would not be too great a stretch to conclude that they can convert such comments into a presumption that compels the conclusion. The reply doctrine provides a helpful example. If an e-mail message is shown to have been in response to a prior e-mail message and it incorporates a reference to the prior message (or with e-mail, it attaches to the prior message), the strong logical inference is that the response was from the person to whom the initial message was sent. This inference likely would carry the day unless refuted by the opposing party, especially if federal trial judges chose

---

as to which State law supplies the rule of decision, the privilege of a witness, person, government, State or political subdivision thereof shall be determined in accordance with State law. (Emphasis added.)

23. A judge's power to comment on the evidence descended from English common law. "In the courts of the United States, as in those of England, from which our practice was derived, the judge, in submitting a case to the jury, may, at his discretion, whenever he thinks it necessary to assist them in arriving at a just conclusion, comment upon the evidence, call their attention to parts of it which he thinks important, and express his opinion upon the facts; and the expression of such an opinion, when no rule of law is incorrectly stated, and all matters of fact are ultimately submitted to the determination of the jury, cannot be reviewed on writ of error." Vicksburg & M.R. Co. v. Putnam, 118 U.S. 545, 553 (1886). At least one scholar suggests that the devices of presumptions and judicial comments on the evidence act as "functional equivalents." "When a judge instructs a jury that it may presume the existence of certain unproved incriminating facts from the proof at trial of other less incriminating facts, or suggests by comment that the jury may draw various reasonable inferences, the effect is to increase the weight of the evidence presented by the prosecution." Ronald J. Allen, *Structuring Jury Decisionmaking in Criminal Cases: A Unified Constitutional Approach to Evidentiary Devices*, 94 HARV. L. REV. 321-22, 330 (1980) (following an "unbroken line of cases" in which the Supreme Court has upheld authority of trial judges to comment on evidence); *see also* Charles R. Nesson, *Rationality, Presumptions, and Judicial Comment: A Response to Professor Allen*, 94 HARV. L. REV. 1574, 1588-89 (1980).

to exercise their power to encourage it.[24] A presumption would compel what otherwise may be inevitable.

Article III is in dire need of attention. One simple fix would be for Congress or the Advisory Committee on the Federal Rules of Evidence to adopt the language of Rule 501 governing privileges. If, like privileges, presumptions were "governed by the principles of the common law as they may be interpreted by the courts in light of reason and experience," the problems of (1) whether common law presumptions have survived codification and (2) whether new presumptions, or amendments to old presumptions, can be created by the courts, would be resolved. Both Congress and the Judicial Conference could leave the resolution of these matters to those who are most familiar with them—that is, the trial judges. This also would leave to trial judges the more controversial question about the nature of the presumption: whether it is simply a procedural device that shifts to the opposing party only the burden of coming forward with evidence (current practice), or one that shifts to the opposing party the burden of persuasion (the alternative that gives the presumption greater force and effect). If neither Congress nor the Advisory Committee is willing to address the problems,[25] a second solution would be for judges to reassume the authority and responsibility for maintaining the Rules of Evidence through their obligation to conduct trials in a manner that ensures that fairness and justice are achieved.

---

24. If a judge decides to comment on the evidence, the court must always remind jurors that the responsibility for making factual determinations is theirs and theirs alone, and that nothing the judge says about permissible factual inferences is binding on them. Many states, either in their constitutions or through statutory enactments, forbid judicial comment on the evidence.

25. Congress delegated to the Federal Judicial Conference the task of maintaining the FEDERAL RULES OF EVIDENCE because it had neither the time nor the expertise necessary to perform this task. The Federal Judicial Conference has shown no inclination to address these problems in the 30 years that the Evidence Code has existed.

Authentication 6

I. The Basics   335

II. Methods of Authentication   339

   A. Self-identification   348

      1. Self-identification by the *Sender*: Establishing That a Letter Was Actually Written by the Person Named as Author   348

      2. Self-identification by the *Recipient*: Establishing That a Message Was Received by the Fact That It Was Sent to That Individual's Address and He Responded to It   350

   B. Content   352

   C. Extrinsic Circumstances   354

III. Authenticating Digital Photographs   357

   A. The Key Is the Chain of Custody   360

   B. Desirable Enhancement Versus Unacceptable Manipulation   362

   C. Authenticate the Computer Program Too   367

   D. The Internet Complication   367

   E. A Spoliation Problem   368

IV. Authentication of Web Page Postings from the Internet   369

   A. Relaxation of Authentication Requirements   374

   B. Self-authentication and the Internet   376

      1. Public Document under Seal   381

      2. Business Solicitations and Postings   382

      3. Government Postings   384

      4. Newspapers and Periodicals   385

      5. Limits of Self-authentication   385

   C. Authenticating with Technology   386

      1. Data Trails   386

      2. Electronic Signatures   387

      3. Public Key Infrastructure   390

      4. Biometric Authentication   391

V. Authentication of Computer Animations, Models, and Simulations   391

VI. Authentication of Authenticating Technology   393

VI. Other Issues Relating to Authentication of E-evidence   395

   A. Chain of Custody   395

   B. Expanded Pretrial Discovery May Justify a Lesser Foundation   399

   C. Admissibility and Weight: Two Bites at the Same Apple   400

   D. A Reality Check   400

E-evidence Overview: All evidence submitted to a court must be authenticated—proven to be what the proponent claims it is. Authentication is the most challenging evidentiary problem facing litigators in the Internet/information age. The inherent mutability of electronic data has prompted many to question the continuing validity of traditional authentication methods. The growing use of electronic communications to effect legally binding relationships has amplified this uncertainty. While circumstantial methods of authentication remain exceptionally broad under both the common law and Federal Rules of Evidence, the unique potential for fraud with electronic evidence has diminished the value of each established method.

The basic concerns of authentication are the same, whether dealing with electronic or paper documents. First, the proponent should be able to show that the content of a document is complete and unaltered. Second, the proponent should be able to show that a document originated from the named source. And finally, in the case of documents that purportedly create legally binding relationships, the proponent should be able to show that the identified originator intended to be bound by the substance of the communication.

As with paper documents, challenges to the authenticity of electronic documents typically implicate one or more of these basic concerns. While the advent of digital technology has expanded the ways in which documents can be corrupted or forged, it has also expanded the ways in which they can be authenticated.

I.   THE BASICS

Before discussing authentication specific to e-evidence, it is necessary to clarify the process of authentication and the different standards that apply to the questions of authenticity and relevance. All evidence must be shown to be logically relevant to the proposition it is intended to prove.[1] The proponent of the evidence has this burden. If the evidence is too inflammatory, or presenting the evidence would be too time-consuming, misleading, or confusing to the jury, relevant evidence can be excluded.

---

1. FED. R. EVID. 402.

Relevant evidence may be excluded if its potential prejudice "substantially outweighs" its probative value.[2] The party seeking to exclude relevant evidence because of its unfair prejudice has the burden of persuasion.

Personal Knowledge. All electronic evidence must be properly authenticated, whether the evidence is offered in the form of *electronically produced* documents or in the form of live testimony that is based on *electronically acquired* information. Part of this foundation is demonstrating that both the author of an electronic writing and a testifying witness must be shown to possess personal knowledge of the facts about which they wrote or propose to speak. Every witness or thing must be proven to be what the proponent claims the witness or things to be. Authentication is a form of qualification, and both are forms of logical relevance.

Witnesses, generally, must testify on the basis of personal knowledge. Without personal knowledge, witnesses are either speculating about those facts (which is not particularly helpful to the finders of fact) or are relating what someone else has communicated to them. The latter, of course, is hearsay and excluded, because the value of the testimony depends on the untested perception, memory, and sincerity of the out-of-court declarant (the source of the information), as well as the unexplored ambiguity of the manner in which the declarant described those facts. For example, when a statement is offered into evidence that was translated from Spanish to English by an interpreter, and that statement was written in English and read back to the speaker in Spanish by the translator, the written English statement must be authenticated by the translator who possesses personal knowledge of each translation.[3]

The limits of the personal knowledge requirement are being tested by modern technology. For example, if one security guard, in real time, watched a crime being committed on a surveillance camera, and another subsequently watched the videotape of the incident made simultaneously with the first guard's observations, and both were able to identify the defendants, should the testimony of either guard be excluded because the guards lacked personal knowledge? If the videotape was no longer available for viewing by the jury, thereby precluding the jurors from acquiring

---

2. FED. R. EVID. 403. *See, e.g.,* Ruth v. Superior Consultant Holdings Corp., 2000 WL 1769576, at *6 (E.D. Mich. Oct. 6, 2000) (e-mail message contained term "Monkey-boy" and the defendant claimed it was a term of endearment intended to be humorous; court refused to exclude e-mail on Rule 403 grounds, finding its use "not more prejudicial than probative").

3. State v. Cooke, 874 A.2d 805, 816-17 (Conn. App. 2005).

the same information possessed by the two guards, should that change the admissibility decision?

As explained in *Frazier v. El-Amin*,[4] only the guard who saw the crime on the videotape would lack personal knowledge. If the videotape were still available, the testimony of the guard who subsequently acquired knowledge of the facts by watching the tape would not be admissible in lieu of the videotape. The tape would be the best evidence of the event that it recorded. Under Rule 1002,[5] when the content of a writing or recording is being proven (which it would be, since the tape was the source of the subsequent guard's knowledge), the original recording must be shown to the jury.[6]

The same is not true of the first security guard who obtained his knowledge watching the event in real time as the videotape was being made. The first guard did *not* acquire his knowledge from the videotape. What he observed was recorded on the videotape. The requirement of personal knowledge should not preclude the first guard from testifying about the information he acquired through the use of the video camera.

Simply because someone uses technology to observe an event in real time does not change the nature or source of his knowledge. Otherwise, a witness would not be permitted to testify to what he saw through binoculars using infra-red technology—or even through a camera using natural light. This would be absurd.

If technology employed by a witness is proven to be trustworthy and properly used, the information acquired by that witness through real-time observations employing that technology should be considered personal

---

4. 2004 WL 1964504 (Minn. App. Sept. 7, 2004).

5. FED. R. EVID. 1002.

6. Under FED. R. EVID. 1004, this requirement is excused when the original is lost or destroyed due to no serious fault of the proponent. Therefore, after it is demonstrated that the tape was reused after the event due to no fault of the state, the second guard's testimony would not be excluded by the best evidence rule. *But see* People v. Jimenez, 796 N.Y.S.2d 232, 234 (N.Y. Sup. Ct. 2005), where the court refused to let the witness, who acquired his knowledge through an unavailable videotape, testify, claiming that it violated the best evidence rule. "[W]hile an expert might well be able to recount or recite substantially and with reasonable accuracy all of the pertinent contents of one such photograph, the same cannot be said of the innumerable details of the literally thousands of images that constitute videotape footage. Inevitably, the witness' testimony would be no more than a summary of his interpretation of what he had seen on the tape and not a reliable and accurate portrayal of the original."

knowledge. Therefore, events witnessed through video cameras, video cell phones and video-linked Internet communications should not be excluded because the basis of the witness's testimony was not personally observed. Similar to *Frazier*, the court in *United States v. Perez*[7] permitted agents to testify about events observed while monitoring a video surveillance system. The defense argued that the agents should not have been permitted to describe the events they observed on the video system monitor because the videotape that was simultaneously being made was the best evidence. This was rejected because "the use of an electronic or mechanical aid does not make one any less an eyewitness. The existence of a videotape recording of what the witness saw is of significant value to the court in verifying the accuracy of the witness' perceptions and memories, but we are unaware of any rule of evidence that would exclude the witness' eyewitness testimony." By rejecting the best evidence objection, because the agents were eyewitnesses, the court was implicitly, if not explicitly, holding that they possessed personal knowledge of the facts they were relating.

Conditional Relevance Questions. Questions of admissibility are decided by the presiding judge under a preponderance standard, unless the question is one of conditional relevance.[8] An issue of conditional relevance arises when the relevance of a piece of evidence is premised on proof of other facts. For example, a letter containing an admission of liability would not be relevant to the issue of negligence until the proponent had established that the defendant or the defendant's authorized agent had authored the letter. Conditionally relevant evidence is initially screened by the presiding judge under a prima facie standard. The judge, putting aside all issues of credibility, must be convinced that a *reasonable jury could find*, from other evidence presented, that the disputed evidence is what the proponent claims.[9] Having passed this prima facie test, the evidence is admitted and the jury is given the responsibility of determining

---

7. 36 M.J. 583, 584-85 (A.F.C.M.R. 1992).

8. FED. R. EVID. 104(b).

9. United States v. Tank, 200 F.3d 627, 630 (9th Cir. 2000) ("The foundational 'requirement of authentication or identification as a condition precedent to admissibility is satisfied by evidence sufficient to support a finding that the matter in question is what its proponent claims.'" Chat room logs were properly authenticated: "[i]n testimony at the evidentiary hearing and at trial, Riva explained how he created the logs with his computer and stated that the printouts . . . appeared to be an accurate representation of the chat room conversations among members of the Orchid Club.").

whether the facts upon which the relevance of the evidence is conditioned have been proven by a preponderance of the evidence. If the first stage of this two-stage process is not satisfied (i.e., the judge determines that a reasonable jury could not find the conditioning facts to be true), the evidence is excluded, and the jury never gets the chance to decide the question. Authenticity is a classic issue of conditional relevance.

II. METHODS OF AUTHENTICATION

E-evidence presents a number of novel authentication challenges, and Article IX of the Federal Rules of Evidence provides sufficient flexibility to respond to most of these challenges. The means by which a proponent may seek to establish authenticity are limited only by the demands of logical relevance. Existing methods of authentication can usually be modified in their application to accommodate the unique difficulties posed by e-evidence.

All methods of authentication employed under the common law may be used under the Federal Rules of Evidence. The possibilities are virtually unlimited. Anything tending to establish authenticity is admissible as long as its potential prejudice does not substantially outweigh its probative value.[10]

For example, Fed. R. Evid. 901 lists a number of authentication methods. The specific wording of these provisions is not exclusive. Each provision merely describes one acceptable method, which can be redefined as needed by the presiding judge.

Article IX. Authentication and Identification
Rule 901. Requirement of Authentication or Identification
(a) **General provision.** The requirement of authentication or identification as a condition precedent to admissibility is satisfied by evidence sufficient to support a finding that the matter in question is what its proponent claims.

---

10. "Electronic mail communications can normally be authenticated by affidavit of a recipient, comparison of the communications content with other evidence or statements, or other statements from the purported author acknowledging the e-mail communication." Whatley v. S.C. Dep't of Pub. Safety, 2007 U.S. Dist. LEXIS 2391, *40-41 (D. S.C. Jan. 10, 2007). *See* United States v. Siddiqui, 235 F.3d 1318, 1322-23 (11th Cir. 2000); Fenje v. Feld, 301 F. Supp. 2d 781, 809 (N.D. Ill. 2003).

[United States v. Jackson, 208 F.3d 633, 638 (7th Cir. 2000) (evidence taken from Internet not authenticated because proponent unable to show information had been posted by the organization to which it was attributed); Wady v. Provident Life & Accident Ins. Co. of Am., 216 S. Supp. 2d 1060, 1064-65 (C.D. Cal. 2002) (Internet postings taken from Unum Provident's Web site not properly authenticated because person offering postings could not establish who maintained Web site, who authored documents, or accuracy of their contents); St. Clair v. Johnny's Oyster & Shrimp, Inc., 76 F. Supp. 2d 773, 775 (S.D. Tex. 1999) (private Web site on Internet not authenticated because hackers can adulterate the content on any site at any time).]

(b) Illustrations. By way of illustration only, and not by way of limitation, the following are examples of authentication or identification conforming with the requirements of this rule:

(1) Testimony of witness with knowledge. Testimony that a matter is what it is claimed to be.

[*See* Hardison v. Balboa Ins. Co., 4 Fed. Appx. 663, 669 (10th Cir. 2001) (individual with personal knowledge of company's business records identified computer-generated documents as records produced and maintained in regular course of company's business activities); St. Luke's Cataract & Laser Institute, P.A. v. Sanderson, 2006 WL 1320242, at *2 (M.D. Fla. May 12, 2006) (When evidence is obtained from a Web site, the site must be authenticated. "To authenticate printouts from a website, the party proferring the evidence must produce 'some statement or affidavit from someone with knowledge [of the website] . . . for example [a] web master or someone else with personal knowledge would be sufficient.'"); Securities & Exch. Comm'n v. Berger, 244 F. Supp. 2d 180, 192 (S.D. N.Y. 2001) (witness who retrieved documents from company's computers affirmed in affidavit that documents attached to another individual's affidavit were same documents she had retrieved); United States v. Scott-Emuakpor, 2000 WL 288443, at *14 (W.D. Mich. Jan. 25, 2000) (witness who observed procedure by which documents were obtained from defendant's computers sufficiently authenticated them as defendant's); Page v. State, 125 S.W.3d 640, 647 (Tex. Ct. App. 2003) (videotape of store robbery was sufficiently authenticated by employee who had no personal knowledge of robbery but who described digital recording system, how it automatically records images on a computer hard drive, how he accessed the hard drive shortly after robbery, reviewed recording with police, and then made a copy on videotape and gave it to officers); Stafford v. Stafford, 641 A.2d 348, 349 (Vt. 1993) (individual testified that source of document was file on family computer; testimony was circumstantial evidence that defendant who owned computer generated document.). *But see* In re Vinhnee, 336 B.R. 437, 448-49 (9th Cir. 2005) (Trial court held that the written declaration was an insufficient foundation for admitting electronic records because the proponent needed to show the accuracy of the computer in the retention and retrieval of the information at issue. "The declaration merely identified the makes and models of the equipment, named the software, noted that some of the software was customized, and asserted that the hardware and software are standard for the industry, regarded as reliable, and periodically updated. There is no information regarding American Express' computer policy and system control procedures, including control of access to the pertinent databases, control of access to the pertinent programs, recording and logging of changes to the data, backup practices, and audit procedures utilized to assure the continuing integrity of the records. All of these matters are pertinent to the accuracy of the computer in the retention and retrieval of the information at issue.").]

(2) Nonexpert opinion on handwriting. Nonexpert opinion as to the genuineness of handwriting, based upon familiarity not acquired for purposes of the litigation.

(3) Comparison by trier or expert witness. Comparison by the trier of fact or by expert witnesses with specimens which have been authenticated.

(4) Distinctive characteristics and the like. Appearance, contents, substance, internal patterns, or other distinctive characteristics, taken in conjunction with circumstances.

[*See* Sinotes-Cruz v. Gonzales, 468 F.3d 1190, 1196-97 (9th Cir. 2006) (Court accepted as authentic an electronically transmitted record because of the stamps that were on it. "Here, the two INS stamps at the end of the records clearly indicate that the documents were received by an INS official on the dates specified, and the records on their face give every indication of being official Arizona court records. Further, the dates given in the upside-down FAX notations on the bottom of the pages indicate that the documents were FAXed on the same day they were stamped as received by the INS, and the term "LEGALRECORDS" in the same notations strongly suggest that the records were FAXed from an Arizona legal records depository."); United States v. Siddiqui, 235 F.3d 1318 (11th Cir. 2000), *cert. denied*, 533 U.S. 940, 150 L. Ed. 2d 737, 121 S. Ct. 2573 (2001) (e-mail authenticated because it bore the appellant's e-mail address; the reply automatically dialed the appellant's e-mail address as the sender; the factual details of the message were known to the appellant; they bore his nickname; and they were followed up by phone conversations involving the same subject matter); United States v. Tank, 200 F.3d 627 (9th Cir. 2000) (chat room log printouts authenticated by appellant's admission that he used the screen name "Cessna" when participating in one of the conversations recorded; several co-conspirators testified appellant used the name; and when a meeting was arranged with the person who used the screen name "Cessna," the appellant showed up); United States v. Simpson, 152 F.3d 1241, 1249-50 (10th Cir. 1998) (chat room discussions authenticated through e-mail address registered to defendant and printouts found near defendant's computer with the name, street address, e-mail address, and telephone number of detective who gave it to him in the chat room); Wapnick v. Comm'r IRS, 83 T.C.M. (CCH) 1245, 2002 WL 215993, at *4-5 (Tax. Ct. Feb. 13, 2002) (Even though individuals had personal knowledge of how, when, and why business records were created and maintained (as required under Rule 803(6)), the court approved their introduction because their accuracy as evidence of interest income had been circumstantially verified. Two special agents had testified that they had compared petitioner's copies of clients' tax returns with the information in the computer records, compared the names of clients in the computer records to client names petitioner wrote on the bank deposit slips, obtained copies of clients' canceled checks and compared them to the computer records, and contacted the clients and compared their records to the computer records.); Hammontree v. State, 642 S.E.2d 412, 415 (Ga. Ct. App. 2007) (An instant message was proven to have been sent to a particular computer terminal, testimony established that the defendant had access to the computer, the sender identified himself by the defendant's first name, and the individual in whose name the Internet account was registered (the son of the defendant) testified that he was not the sender of the messages and had not participated in the conversations.); CCP Ltd. P'ship v. First Source Fin., Inc., 856 N.E.2d 492, 499 (Ill. App. Ct. 2006) (E-mail message was retrieved from regularly maintained business records, but no one was called to testify or other methods of authentication presented that would limit the time of the creation of the message or possible authors. The court noted that there was "no evidence of an ongoing correspondence that might provide circumstantial evidence of the authorship of the message." Therefore, the court was compelled to ignore the papers purporting to represent e-mails received from Dart.); In re F.P., 878 A.2d 91, 95-96 (Pa. Super. Ct. 2005) ("The argument is that e-mails or text messages are inherently unreliable because of their relative anonymity and the fact that while an electronic message can be traced to a particular computer, it can rarely be connected to a specific author with any certainty. Unless the purported author is actually witnessed sending the e-mail, there is always the possibility it is not from whom it claims. As appellant correctly points out, anybody with the right password can gain access to another's e-mail account and send a message ostensibly from that person. However, the same uncertainties exist with traditional written documents. A signature can be forged; a letter can be typed on another's typewriter; distinct letterhead stationary can be copied or stolen. We believe that e-mail messages and similar forms of electronic communication can be properly authenticated within the existing framework of Pa. R.E. 901 and Pennsylvania case law. . . . We see no justification for constructing unique rules for admissibility of electronic communications such as instant messages; they are to be evaluated on a case-by-case basis as any other document to determine whether or not there has been an adequate foundation showing of their relevance and authenticity."); Massimo v. State, 144 S.W.3d 210 (Tex. App. 2004) (e-mails admissible because

victim recognized the appellant's e-mail address; the e-mails discussed things only the victim, the appellant, and a few other people
knew about; they were written in the way in which the appellant
would communicate; and a third party had witnessed the appellant sending a similar threatening e-mail to the victim previously);
Robinson v. State, 2000 WL 622945, at *4 (Tex. Crim. App. 2000)
(content of message known only by few people and individual's
computer user name appeared on message); Swanton v. Brigeois-
Ashton, 134 Wash. App. 1067, 2006 WL 2664497, at *2 (Wash.
Ct. App. Sept. 18, 2006) (E-mails received were authenticated by
testimony of recipient and uncontroverted corroborating evidence
documenting payments referred to in the e-mail.]

(5) Voice identification. Identification of a voice, whether heard
firsthand or through mechanical or electronic transmission or recording, by opinion based upon hearing the voice at any time
under circumstances connecting it with the alleged speaker.

(6) Telephone conversations. Telephone conversations, by evidence that a call was made to the number assigned at the time by
the telephone company to a particular person or business, if (A)
in the case of a person, circumstances, including self-identification,
show the person answering to be the one called, or (B) in the case
of a business, the call was made to a place of business and the
conversation related to business reasonably transacted over the
telephone.

(7) Public records or reports. Evidence that a writing authorized
by law to be recorded or filed and in fact recorded or filed in a
public office, or a purported public record, report, statement, or
data compilation, in any form, is from the public office where
items of this nature are kept.

(8) Ancient documents or data compilation. Evidence that a document or data compilation, in any form, (A) is in such condition as
to create no suspicion concerning its authenticity, (B) was in a
place where it, if authentic, would likely be, and (C) has been in
existence 20 years or more at the time it is offered.

(9) Process or system. Evidence describing a process or system
used to produce a result and showing that the process or system
produces an accurate result.

[*See* In re Vinhnee, 336 B.R. 437, 448-49 (9th Cir. 2005) (Trial court held that the written declaration was an insufficient foundation for admitting electronic records because the proponent needed to show the accuracy of the computer in the retention and retrieval of the information at issue. "The declaration merely identified the makes and models of the equipment, named the software, noted that some of the software was customized, and asserted that the hardware and software are standard for the industry, regarded as reliable, and periodically updated. There is no information regarding American Express' computer policy and system control procedures, including control of access to the pertinent databases, control of access to the pertinent programs, recording and logging of changes to the data, backup practices, and audit procedures utilized to assure the continuing integrity of the records. All of these matters are pertinent to the accuracy of the computer in the retention and retrieval of the information at issue."); Indianapolis Minority Contractors Ass'n., Inc. v. Wiley, 1998 WL 1988826, at *7 (S.D. Ind. May 13, 2003) (computer data was extracted from business records and used to prepare report for pending litigation; court noted that "the reports are not admissible as business records under Fed. R. Evid. 803(6). . . . Further, as a condition precedent to admissibility of computer records, the proponent must establish that the process or system used produces an accurate result, Fed. R. Evid. 901(b)(9), and that foundation has not been established. In light of the above, the veracity and reliability of these reports are questionable and thus . . . are not admissible and will be stricken."); In re Welfare of L.J.L., 2006 Minn. App. Unpub. LEXIS 1365, *15-16 (Minn. Ct. App. Dec. 19, 2006) (videotape could be authenticated through testimony of video technician, who explains how the video is made, stating that it produces an accurate result, and producing other evidence of chain of custody).]

(10) Methods provided by statute or rule. Any method of authentication or identification provided by Act of Congress or by other rules prescribed by the Supreme Court pursuant to statutory authority.

When the authenticity of an e-mail message or instant-message conversation is at issue, the proponent must authenticate the communication by establishing authorship.[11] The fact that e-mail communications received by a company are maintained in the normal course of business does not establish their authenticity.[12] A witness testifying about his receipt of a message only establishes that it was received. Such testimony does not authenticate the message as having been authored by the indicated sender.[13] Other methods of authentication must be employed. These other methods may include the context of the message in light of other evidence at trial. For example, for instant messages, such authentication might involve the fact that a message was proven to have come from a particular computer terminal, that testimony established that the defendant had access to the computer, that the sender identified himself by the defendant's first name, and that the individual in whose name the Internet account was registered (the son of the defendant) testified that he was not the sender of the messages and had not participated in the conversations.[14]

---

11. *See* Amicus Commc'ns v. Hewlett Packard Co., 1999 WL 495921, at *16 n. 226 (W.D. Tex. June 11, 1999) (e-mails had not been authenticated by their authors); Hasbro Inc. v. Clue Computing Inc., 66 F. Supp. 2d 117, 124 (D. Mass. 1999) (noting that without verifying source of an e-mail, it is "of limited value as evidence").

12. In CCP Ltd. Partnership v. First Source Financial, Inc., 856 N.E.2d 492, 496 (Ill. App. Ct. 1st Dist. 2006), for example, e-mails were attached to a summary judgment motion and accompanied by an affidavit in which it was sworn that the papers "have been maintained in the ordinary course of business in [FSFP's] computer system." The court held that this did not adequately authenticate the e-mail communications.

At most, the evidence could show that FSFP kept copies of the documents in the regular course of its business. FSFP did not present any direct evidence of authentication, as it had no affidavit or deposition of the putative author of the alleged e-mail. . . . Palmer's affidavit includes no evidence that Palmer had any personal knowledge regarding FSFP's receipt of the e-mail. He knew only that at some time before he helped retrieve the message, someone somewhere entered into FSFP's computers a message that listed an officer of Dart on the line of the sender. No evidence limits the time of the creation of the message. Nor does the evidence limit the possible authors. Palmer's affidavit includes no evidence of an ongoing correspondence that might provide circumstantial evidence of the authorship of the message. . . . In the absence of proper authentication, this court must ignore the papers purporting to represent e-mails FSFP received from Dart. . . .

13. Morgenstern v. EntPro, Inc., 2007 Cal. App. Unpub. LEXIS 1219, *13 (2d Dist. Feb. 15, 2007); Claudio v. Regents of Univ. of Cal., 134 Cal. App. 4th 224, 244 (2d Dist. 2005).

14. Hammontree v. State, 642 S.E.2d 412, 415 (Ga. Ct. App. 2007).

Among the methods set forth above, some will be particularly helpful in e-commerce litigation; others may be more problematic. The "cold," or unanticipated, nature of many e-mail contacts, the susceptibility to manipulation of e-mail headers, and the possibility of hackers manipulating Web postings will often create the need for additional methods of proof.[15] Litigants are not limited to one method of authentication for each piece of evidence, and all available sources of identification should be employed. Each can complement and reinforce the other so that deficiencies with one method can be overcome with another.

Because information can be falsified and manipulated so easily through Internet fraud, litigants may find courts skeptical of the reliability of information obtained from it. For example, in *St. Clair v. Johnny's Oyster & Shrimp, Inc.*,[16] the judge commented:

> Plaintiff's electronic "evidence" is totally insufficient to withstand Defendant's Motion to Dismiss. While some look to the Internet as an innovative vehicle for communication, the Court continues to warily and wearily view it largely as one large catalyst for rumor, innuendo, and misinformation. So as to not mince words, the Court reiterates that this so-called Web provides no way of verifying the authenticity of the alleged contentions that Plaintiff wishes to rely upon in his Response to defendant's Motion. There is no way Plaintiff can overcome the presumption that the information he discovered on the Internet is inherently untrustworthy. Anyone can put anything on the Internet. No web-site is monitored for accuracy and nothing contained therein is under oath or even subject to independent verification absent underlying documentation. Moreover, the Court holds no illusion that hackers can adulterate the content on any web-site from any location at any time. For these reasons, any evidence procured off the Internet is

---

15. *See* United States v. Jackson, 208 F.3d 633 (7th Cir. 2000) (finding Web postings proclaiming that crimes were committed by organizations on whose Web sites postings appeared were properly excluded from evidence for lack of authentication; defendant failed to show that Web postings were posted by those organizations, as opposed to being slipped onto their Web sites by defendant herself, who was skilled computer user).

16. 76 F. Supp. 2d 773, 774-75 (S.D. Tex. 1999).

adequate for almost nothing, even under the most liberal interpretation of the hearsay exception rules found in FED. R. EVID. 807.

Instead of relying on the voodoo information taken from the Internet, Plaintiff must hunt for hard copy back-up documentation in admissible form from the United States Coast Guard or discover alternative information verifying what Plaintiff alleges. Accordingly, Plaintiff has until February 1, 2000 to garner legitimate documents showing that Defendant owns the CAPT. LE'BRANDO.[17]

Selected methods of authentication are discussed below.

A. *Self-identification*

1. Self-identification by the *Sender*: Establishing That a Letter Was Actually Written by the Person Named as Author

When the recipient of an e-mail attempts to prove that the message was authored by a particular individual whose name appears in the header, such self-identification by designated sender is insufficient to establish authorship.[18] Self-identification, however, complements other authenticating factors, such as content, circumstances, internal patterns, and extrinsic evidence.[19] These factors, along with self-identification, can establish authorship.

Unsolicited letters cannot be authenticated by the name stated in the letter under the common law. The same has been true of unsolicited tele-

---

17. *See* United States v. Jackson, 208 F.3d 633, 638 (7th Cir. 2000) (evidence taken from Internet not authenticated because proponent unable to show information had been posted by the organization to which it was attributed); Wady v. Provident Life & Accident Ins. Co. of Am., 216 S. Supp. 2d 1060, 1064-65 (C.D. Cal. 2002) (Internet postings taken from UnumProvident's Web site not properly authenticated because person offering postings could not establish who maintained Web site, who authored documents, or accuracy of their contents).

18. Morgenstern, *supra* note 13 (The fact that the recipient testifies that he received e-mails with the defendant's name on them does not authenticate the e-mails as having been authored by the named individual.).

19. *See* Robinson v. State, 2000 WL 622945, at *4 (Tex. Crim. App. May 12, 2000) (content of message with information known only by few people and individual's computer user name on message sufficient authentication).

phone calls.[20] When someone initiates a communication, identification is exclusively within his control. Self-identification in the context of cold calls or other unsolicited communications has been and should remain inadequate. Therefore, self-identification in an unsolicited e-mail header supports authenticity but should not, by itself, be considered sufficient proof. The opportunities for fraud are simply too great.[21]

Other characteristics of e-mail communications further complicate authentication through self-identification. Unlike letters, e-mail communications bear no postmark indicating place of origin. Although an e-mail may contain an identification code assigned by the ISP, through which the origin of the message can eventually be discovered, no third-party mark directly identifies origin on the e-mail's face. Also, e-mails contain no preprinted letterhead, and e-mail messages can be "spoofed."[22] Spoofing occurs when senders of e-mail messages use another's name and make messages appear to originate from different locations. Additionally, the same spoofing possibilities exist after an e-mail has been sent. Anyone with access to an e-mail server can alter stored e-mail messages with little fear of detection. This is why the facial inadequacy of self-identification applies with particular force to e-mail communications. Therefore, the apparent source must be supplemented with other evidence like the content of the message and other surrounding circumstances.

With telephone calls, caller ID is commonly available to supplement self-identification. Comparable supplementation is not currently available with e-mail communications. As noted above, e-mail communications will contain identification numbers through which the ISP and the com-

---

20. *See* United States v. Puerta Restrepo, 814 F.2d 1236, 1239 (7th Cir.1987); United States v. Pool 660 F.2d 547, 560 (5th Cir. 1981); United States v. Zane, 495 F.2d 683, 696-97 (2d Cir.), *cert. denied,* 419 U.S. 895 (1974) ("[S]elf-identification by a person *who makes a call,* alone, is insufficient for authentication purposes.") (emphasis in original).

21. Hood-O'Hara v. Wills, 873 A.2d 757, 760 (Pa. Super. Ct. 2005) ("[T]here were authentication problems with regard to the e-mails. Although testimony revealed that the e-mail address did in fact belong to O'Hara's mother, Mrs. Hood, it was denied by Mrs. Hood that she was the author of the e-mails. . . . We find that the e-mails were properly excluded.").

22. The PC Webopedia, at http://www.pcwebopedia.com/TERM/s/spoof.html, defines "spoof" in the following manner: "To fool. In networking, the term is used to describe a variety of ways in which hardware and software can be fooled. IP spoofing, for example, involves trickery that makes a message appear as if it came from an authorized IP address."

puter from which the message originated can be identified. However, this still does not identify the individual using the terminal. Presumption may be the most reasonable, and perhaps the only successful, method of accomplishing identification of authorship.[23]

2. Self-identification by the *Recipient*: Establishing That a Message Was Received by the Fact That It Was Sent to That Individual's Address and He Responded to It

Under the common law, when a call was placed to a particular number and the recipient of the call answered by identifying himself, such self-identification by *recipients* was generally considered a reliable method of authentication. With e-mail, this method may prove less effective because there is no spontaneous identification when the e-mail is received. Practitioners seeking to authenticate an e-mail message using this method should present corroborating evidence, such as the content of the response which reveals knowledge that only the alleged recipient of the e-mail message knows.

In contrast to self-identification by the initiator of a message, self-identification by the recipient of a message has additional guarantees of reliability. The probability of fraud by the recipient in identifying himself is significantly diminished because the sender made the initial contact. This is why the common law held that if an individual telephones a business using a number listed in the telephone directory and testifies to this, a prima facie case of authenticity is established when a person answers and identifies the establishment as the business that was called. Such testimony is admissible and can be heard by the jury. When considered in conjunction with other evidence of authenticity, the jury may accept the call as authentic. Central to the success of this method of authentication is the credibility of the person claiming to have made the telephone call.

The same method of authenticating telephone conversations was recognized for contacts between private individuals. In this context, however, courts often insisted on additional evidence of authenticity. For example, courts often required that recipients identify themselves upon answering the telephone, without being prompted by the caller. Thus, if the recipient did not automatically volunteer something like "Hello, Rice's residence. Paul Rice speaking," a prima facie case of authenticity was not

---

23. *See* Chapter Five, "Presumptions," *supra*.

established. As households became less formal in answering the telephone, this rule was correspondingly relaxed. This rule also has been relaxed because courts have increasingly recognized that conversations following the initial greetings often provide additional means of authentication.[24]

E-mail is transmitted in large part by means that parallel the transmission of telephone signals—both often use the same telephone line. Interception of e-mail is more likely than interception of telephone calls, however, because e-mail is written and stored on recipients' computers. Anyone with access to recipients' computer terminals can intercept the messages and, they can do this for a much longer time period than with telephone conversations. Even mailed letters present less risk of fraud, because fewer people have immediate access to the communication. Self-identification by the recipient of an e-mail message, therefore, is far less persuasive than self-identification by the recipient of a phone call or mailed letter. Nevertheless, this does not mean that self-identification should not be used. It only means that there is a greater need to combine it with other methods of authentication.

Many consumers contact businesses through Web pages. Those Web page addresses are available in directories, similar to telephone books. Therefore, when this contact is made, the testimony of the person making that contact should establish a prima facie case of authenticity guaranteeing admissibility under Fed. R. Evid. 901(b)(6).[25] This is particularly true if the person making the computer contact prints a hard copy of the trans-

---

24. *See* subsection B, below.

25. In Apple Computer Inc. v. Micro Team, 2000 WL 1897354, at *8 (N.D. Cal. Dec. 21, 2000), the court concluded that a telephone conversation had not been properly authenticated because the telephone number that the witness claimed he had obtained from a Web site was not shown to be "the number assigned at the time by the telephone company," as required by Fed. R. Evid. 901(b)(6). Such a literal interpretation of the delineated methods under Rule 901(b) is inappropriate, since they are only listed as "Illustrations." Subsection (a) states that authentication can be satisfied by "evidence sufficient to support a finding that the matter in question is what its proponent claims." In subsection (b) the drafters were careful to note that the delineated methods that followed were "by way of illustration only, and not by way of limitation." Therefore, testimony of the witness in Apple Computer should have been sufficient to reach the jury. Whether it is adequate in the eyes of the finder of facts is a question of credibility reserved exclusively for the finder of facts. Certainly, if a telephone directory indicated that the number claimed to have been dialed had been assigned to the defendant, that would bolster the plaintiff's claim, but unlike the common law, the absence of such evidence should not be controlling.

action with the date indicated—a habit everyone who transacts business via the Internet should develop. Even in the absence of a hard copy, the authentication of the contacts can rely on the content of the Web page, the manner in which inquiries were answered, and the information supplied through e-mail contacts from the Web page. As under the common law regarding authentication of telephone conversations, without the e-mail or Web page printout, successful authentication can turn exclusively on the jury's willingness to believe the person claiming to have made the contact. When absolutely necessary, both telephone and Internet contacts can be verified from the records of the telephone company and Internet service providers of both the sender and the recipient. These records, however, only confirm the contact, not the content of the correspondence.

B.   Content

Absent an admission by the opposing party, the content of a written instrument (i.e., any confidential information revealed and patterns of misspellings, punctuation, and expression) is often the most probative evidence of authorship. This method of authentication remains useful for e-evidence.

Messages often contain information that supports the claimed identity of the sender. For example, the message may disclose information known only by the identified individual, such as a particular name, like a father's middle name or mother's maiden name; credit card number; account number; password; or the content of a previous confidential message. This unique information may be the most common circumstantial method of authentication. Using content to establish authenticity is codified in Fed. R. Evid. 901(4).

In addition to the substantive information within the communication, the content, form, and structure of the communication may help with identification. For example, punctuation, spelling or other unique characteristics may circumstantially point to a particular source. In fact, form may reveal the identity of the author as much as voice or fingerprint evidence. The individual may employ unique spelling, like "explodesives" for "explosives" or "figuar" for "figure," or the author may use no capitalization or punctuation. The author's writing style and word usage may be unique. He may abbreviate proper names, with or without a period. Although psycholinguistics has not been recognized as a legitimate science, because there are no objective standards for measuring the importance of various factors, the evidence upon which psycholinguistics would rely is probative of authorship. Therefore, the evidence is admissible, although it must stand on its own, without an expert witness's spin.[26]

Authentication is most often achieved by a combination of methods. While no single oddity normally controls, a collection of such idiosyncrasies may establish authorship. This is illustrated in *United States v. Siddiqui*.[27]

In this case a number factors support the authenticity of the e-mail. The e-mail sent to Yamada and von Gunten each bore Siddiqui's e-mail address, misiddiqui@jajuarl.usouthal.edu, at the University of South Alabama. This address was the same as the e-mail sent to Siddiqui from Yamada, as introduced by Siddiqui's counsel in his deposition cross-examination of Yamada. Von Gunten testified that when he replied to the e-mail apparently sent by Siddiqui, the "reply-function" on von Gunten's e-mail system automatically dialed Siddiqui's e-mail address as the sender. . . . The context of the e-mail sent to Yamada and von Gunten shows the author of the e-mail to have been someone who would have known the very details of Siddiqui's conduct with respect to the Waterman Award and the NSF's subsequent investigation. In addition, in one e-mail sent to von Gunten, the author makes apologies for cutting short his visit to EAWAG, the Swiss Federal Institute for Environmental Science and Technology. In his deposition, von Gunten testified that in 1994 Siddiqui had gone to Switzerland to begin a collaboration with EAWAG for three or four months, but had left after only three weeks to take a teaching job. . . . Moreover, the e-mail sent to Yamada and von Gunten referred to the author as "Mo." Both Yamada and von Gunten recognized this as Siddiqui's nickname. Finally, both Yamada and von Gunten testified that they spoke by phone with Siddiqui soon after the receipt of the e-mail, and that Siddiqui made the same requests that had been made in the e-mail. Considering these circumstances, the district court did not abuse its discretion in ruling that the documents were adequately authenticated.

Given the skepticism with which some judges view e-evidence, authentication by multiple methods is always advisable.[28]

---

26. United States v. Clifford, 704 F.2d 86, 90 (3d Cir. 1983).

27. 215 F.3d 1318, 1322-23 (11th Cir. 2000).

28. *See* Robinson v. State, 2000 WL 622945, at *4 (Tex. Crim. App. May 12, 2000) (state authenticated a computer message as having been written by M.T. using (i) content of message that contained information uniquely known by M.T. and few others and (ii) appearance of his user name on message).

C. Extrinsic Circumstances

The context of a writing can establish its authenticity. If, for example, a writing follows a promise to communicate or is in response to a previous contact by the current recipient, the logical inference is that the person acted consistently with his stated intentions or with established business patterns and practices. As long as an e-mail communication is supported by evidence that the sender had an Internet service provider account, used it properly, and did not receive an "undeliverable" message in response to his initial communication, this method of authentication should be effective in establishing prima facie authenticity.

As noted, the content of e-mail, taken in conjunction with circumstances, can be highly probative of authenticity. Indeed, this is the basis of the common law reply doctrine. That doctrine holds that if a letter states that it is from X, or X's authorized agent, is in response to a previous letter that the recipient sent to X, and the alleged response is received without undue delay, a logical inference arises that the letter actually is from X or X's agent. This establishes prima facie authenticity, and the matter is then given to the jury to be decided by a preponderance of the evidence.

Although the Federal Rules of Evidence do not explicitly mention the reply doctrine in Artile IX, this is inconsequential because the methods outlined in Fed. R. Evid. 901(b) are only illustrative. Moreover, subsection (b)(4), quoted above, is broad enough to encompass the reply doctrine when it mentions "content . . . taken in conjunction with circumstances."

If an e-mail message is properly addressed and sent to an individual or company and a response is received, particularly if it is via the "reply" function, courts should hold that a prima facie case of authenticity has been established. Like a properly addressed, stamped, and posted letter, which is presumed to have been received by the addressee,[29] the e-mail equivalent should be established through testimony that an Internet service provider was providing contracted e-mail service, the service was properly used, and no subsequent message was received from the ISP that the message was undeliverable. This should give rise to a presumption of receipt by the addressee. This presumption, coupled with the addressee's prompt reply, could be the "context and circumstance" that establishes prima facie authenticity of the reply.

---

29. *See* Chapter Five, "Presumptions," *supra*.

As previously discussed, the content of the message and corroborating circumstances may be used to identify the author or sender. Similarly, extrinsic circumstances can verify the genuineness of the e-mail message. For example, the recipient can contact the alleged sender through an address that is acquired independent of the communication in question.[30] If independent contact produces a response that confirms the first message, the reply doctrine could assist in the authentication of the original message.

Circumstances often arise in which the alleged author acknowledges a particular message or confirms its content at a later time. When offered against the person who gave the confirmation, the message would constitute an admission of authorship (assuming, of course, that the jury believes the witness who claims to have received confirmation).

Admissions of authenticity regularly occur during pretrial discovery. When the party produces a document in response to a discovery request, the act of production authenticates the document because it is an implied representation that the document is what the demanding party has sought.[31] Litigants, therefore, should be conscious of evidentiary needs when they draft discovery demands. The evidentiary significance of the response will be linked to the language of the demand. Rather than asking for all e-mail messages on a particular topic, for example, one might ask for e-mail messages to and from specific individuals on specific topics.[32]

If the alleged author indicated beforehand that he was planning to send the e-mail message, his then-existing state of mind would be circumstantial evidence that he later did what he had planned to do. When offered against the person who made the statement, the statement would constitute an admission. If, however, the statement was offered against someone other than the person who made it, it would not be an admission

---

30. Use of the reply function will not suffice because that merely returns the recipient to the individual whose identity is in question.

31. *See, e.g.,* Superhighway Consulting, Inc. v. Techwave, Inc., 1999 U.S. Dist. LEXIS 17910, *5 (N.D. Ill. Nov. 16, 1999) ("[T]he production of documents during discovery from the parties' own files is sufficient to justify a finding of authentication."

32. This method of authentication can be problematic, however, because discovery responses often contain prefatory qualifiers which, in essence, say, "These documents appear to be responsive to your discovery demands, but we have not confirmed and do not concede their authenticity."

and would constitute hearsay. However, the statement would still be admissible under the hearsay exception for present state of mind.[33] The statement would be circumstantial evidence that the planned conduct was carried out[34] and, therefore, that the e-mail in question is the message the declarant planned to send.

The authentication of computer-generated evidence also involves proving that the contents of documents have not been altered. When the absence of alteration cannot be established through a chain of custody, this can be a problem. For example, when spreadsheet values and data are produced by a third party, how do you establish that the figures have not been tampered with, either before or after production? In the electronic age, this can be done with "hash marks." This is a process in which the party originally possessing the document runs the data through a mathematical process to generate a short symbolic reference to the original file, called a "hash mark." This hash mark will be unique to that particular file. This is a sort of "digital fingerprint" similar to the seal on a software package that shows whether the content of the electronic document was altered. If the document has been altered after transmission, this will change the hash mark, and this can be detected by running the creator's hash mark algorithm. If the resulting hash mark in the second run is not the

---

33. Whenever a statement is offered against the person who made it, the proponent should always offer it as an admission because admissions have no restrictions. Unlike a declaration against interest, codified in Fed. R. Evid. 804(b)(3), an admission does not have to be against the interests of the declarant when the statement was made, and the declarant does not have to be unavailable.

34. Fed. R. Evid. 803(3) codifies the present state of mind exception:

Rule 803. Hearsay Exception; Availability of Declarant Immaterial

The following are not excluded by the hearsay rule, even though the declarant is available as a witness:

. . . .

(3) Then existing mental, emotional, or physical condition. A statement of the declarant's then existing state of mind, emotion, sensation, or physical condition (such as intent, plan, motive, design, mental feeling, pain, or bodily health), but not including a statement of memory or belief to prove the fact remembered or believed unless it relates to the execution, revocation, identification, or terms of declarant's will.

Hearsay in the context of e-evidence is discussed in detail in Chapter Seven, "Hearsay," *infra*.

same as the first, the document has been altered.[35] "This method allows a large amount of data to be self-authenticating."[36]

III. AUTHENTICATING DIGITAL PHOTOGRAPHS

Digital cameras work on the same basic principles as their predecessors. They are essentially a series of lenses that focus light. The key difference is that conventional cameras focus that light onto a piece of film, creating a negative, which is then developed into the familiar prints we know. The cameras use mechanical shutters to expose film, and later chemicals are used to develop the picture. A digital camera focuses the light onto a semiconductor device that records the information as a series of ones and zeros (binary code), which can be read and interpreted by a computer. From this binary code, the computer or display creates pixels, tiny colored dots that make up the larger image.[37] It is the ability to manipulate these minuscule portions of the image that facilitates easy alterations of the larger picture. This ease is what makes digital image editing such a boon to photographers and such a potential hazard for proponents of digital image evidence.[38]

Typically, the images are stored on a memory card, sometimes called a memory stick, which is essentially a very small computer disc. Alternatively, the images may be stored directly on the camera, which may include a hard drive, much like those found in computers. If the camera

---

35. Dean M. Harts, *Reel to Real: Should You Believe What You See?*, 66 DEF. COUNS. J. 514, 522 (1999) ("Keeping the good and eliminating the bad of computer-generated evidence will be accomplished through methods of self-authentication and vigilance.").

36. Williams v. Sprint/United Mgmt. Co., 230 F.R.D. 640, 655 (D. Kan. 2005).

37. "[A] pixel is the smallest discrete element of an image. . . . It is a set of bits that represents a graphic image, with each bit or group of bits corresponding to a pixel in the image. The greater the number of pixels per inch, the greater the resolution. A rough analogy to painted art is that a pixel is the same as each colored dab of a pointillist painting." United States v. Grimes, 244 F.3d 375, 378 n.4 (5th Cir. 2001). *See* State v. Grimes, 268 Conn. 781, 800, 847 A.2d 921, 935-36 (Conn. 2004).

38. "[D]igital images are easier to manipulate than traditional photographs and digital manipulation is more difficult to detect." F. Witkowski, *Can Juries Really Believe What They See? New Foundation Requirements for Authentication of Digital Images*, 10 WASH. U. J.L. & POL'Y 267, 271 (2002).

uses a memory card, the card may be removed and used to transport images from the camera to a computer or other device for viewing or alteration. In a sense, these cards act as rolls of conventional film, storing the captured images until they are either altered, using a computer, or printed. The memory cards may be used to store pictures as well, much like other magnetic media, such as CD-ROMs or computer diskettes.

There is concern about the use of digital photographs in court because they can be so easily altered and manipulated. Individuals can be either deleted from or added to them. Professional photographers have found this helpful when family photographs are taken and one or more family members are absent The photographer can transport a face from one photograph to another (often referred to as "morphing"), or add an entirely new person to the shot. Of course, more subtle and sinister alterations could be made. For example, shadows could be added to adjacent buildings to make the time of the photograph and the ambient light appear to be different from that which existed when the accident or crime happened; a drawn gun could be placed in the hands of a police officer; an identifying badge could be added to a hat.

While these alterations generally could not be detected by the naked eye, technology used to be able to detect changes in the pixels around the edges of the inserted figures and the original photograph. Usually, the pixels in the two images would be different sizes. Now, however, technology has advanced to the point where the pixel sizes in the insert can be altered to conform to those in the original photographs. As a consequence, fraud can be perpetrated with no way to detect it.[39]

What does this mean for the admissibility of such evidence? Does it require the exclusion of digital photographs because of the possibility of undetectable fraud? No. Even though the possibility of fraud cannot be eliminated, it can be significantly diminished through proper foundations in the authentication of such evidence. Even though the technological problems posed by digital photographs are novel, the evidentiary problems they pose are not. Established evidentiary principles, if properly understood and applied, will provide sufficient guarantees of authenticity to admit the evidence. Once admitted, lingering problems of manipulation can be considered by the jury on the question of how much weight, if any, should be given to such evidence.

39. *See* M. Cherry, *Reasons to Challenge Digital Evidence and Electronic Photography*, 27 CHAMPION 42-43 (2003).

In resolving such authentication problems, it is first essential to understand what must be established to justify admissibility. Authentication of the most sophisticated technical evidence is still an issue of conditional relevance under Fed. R. Evid. 104(b). The proponent need only present sufficient evidence from which a reasonable person "could find" that the item in question is what its proponent claims. The law refers to this as a prima facie case of authenticity. Whether the evidence is, in fact, accurate and reliable is ultimately a determination made by the jury by a preponderance of the evidence standard (the standard usually employed by the judge in making admissibility determinations under Rule 104(a)).[40]

Under both the common law and Federal Rules of Evidence, authentication of a photograph (digital or otherwise) would be through a sponsoring witness. From personal knowledge, this witness would testify that the photograph accurately reproduces facts that the witness remembers having existed at the time of the dispute being litigated.

Alternatively , if an eyewitness of relevant facts is not available—for example, if an infrared photograph were taken of images in the dark, or the print were from a surveillance camera—the photograph's proponent could authenticate the print with testimony of the individual who either took the took the photograph or set up the equipment that automatically took the photograph. This foundation would establish that the camera was functioning properly, that its operator knew how to operate it correctly (or, in the case of the surveillance camera, how it is set to automatically record under certain circumstances), the camera's settings, and how the print accurately reproduces the images recorded by the camera.

This is the point at which the technology of digital photography requires additional foundation testimony. Prior to digital photography, once the film was exposed and the negative was created, limited manipulation was possible when the negative was printed and developed, and most of

---

40. No new authentication rules are likely to be enacted by the Advisory Committee on the Federal Rules of Evidence and the Judicial Conference of the United States because every Task Force and Commission that has studied this problem in both the United States and England has concluded that established principles of authentication are currently sufficient to guard against the possibilities of fraud that have not materialized. Procedures and technologies that could be employed to eliminate possibilities of fraud would be expensive and time-consuming, they might result in the exclusion of too much reliable evidence, and the magnitude of the heretofore-undetected problem has not been shown be worth the costs.

that was apparent to the naked eye. With digital photography, printing is where the flower of fraud can bloom.

Still, if there are eyewitnesses who can testify that the photograph accurately depicts relevant facts as they existed at the time the cause of actions arose, this establishes a prima facie case of authenticity, and the photograph should be admissible. Suggestions of manipulation in the face of this assurance of accuracy should be issues decided by the jury on the question of weight.

A similar problem exists in prosecutions for broadcasting pornographic images of children on the Internet. When these images are photographed, the prosecution is confronted with authentication requirements for both the photograph and the images on the computer monitor. Computer-imaging technology has advanced to the stage where pornographic images of children may be produced without using real children. How is the reality of the image authenticated? Must the prosecution offer more than a photograph that appears to depict real children? In *People v. Normand*,[41] the Illinois Supreme Court concluded that because such technology is not widely available, the prosecution need not rebut the possibility of alteration in every case. "We conclude that a trier of fact is capable of determining whether real children were used in pornographic images simply by viewing the images themselves."[42] What this means when the technology becomes more common, as it inevitably will, is unclear. For digital photographs taken by automated traffic enforcement systems, legislation in the District of Columbia has ignored the problem of alteration, perhaps because of context, and made the images admissible without authentication—in substance, making the photographs self-authenticating.[43]

A.   The Key Is the Chain of Custody[44]

Problems of digital manipulation come to the fore when there are no eyewitness assurances of accuracy. When the sponsoring witness is not testifying on the basis of personal knowledge, assurances that there have been

---

41. 831 N.E.2d 587, 595 (2005).

42. *Id.* at 596.

43. Agomo v. Fenty, 916 A.2d 181, 185 (D.C. 2007), discussing D.C. CODE § 50-2209.01, which states that "(b) Recorded images taken by an automated traffic enforcement system are prima facie evidence of an infraction and may be submitted without authentication."

44. *See generally* § VI.A, Chain of Custody, *infra*.

no digital manipulation can be provided only through chains of custody for (1) the *digital card* that was used in the digital camera, and (2) the *computer* onto which the images on the digital card were downloaded.

Scenario One: Camera and Digital Card Within Exclusive Custody of Witness. If the camera and the digital card from it have been in the exclusive custody of a single individual, that person's testimony that he has not tampered with the image on the card should be sufficient authentication of the card. If the digital photograph on that card is either printed in the courtroom with a portable printer or displayed on a monitor in the courtroom, it should be admissible.

Scenario Two: Digital Images Downloaded to a Personal Computer Outside the Courtroom. If a print of the image from the digital camera is made outside the courtroom, and that print is offered into evidence through a sponsoring witness who *does not possess personal knowledge of the condition or event depicted* (and therefore cannot give assurances of its accuracy by comparing it to what was remembered), the potential for fraudulent manipulation is at its highest.

After the photograph was taken, it could have been downloaded to a computer, altered, and recorded again on the card before the photograph was printed. Even if the image on the digital card was not altered, when the image was downloaded to a computer for printing, anyone with access to that computer, a program through which manipulation could occur, and the downloaded image itself could be a potential manipulator. Therefore, a *chain of custody* will have to be established, identifying everyone who has had access to both the digital image and the computer on which it was stored. Each person in the chain of custody should testify that he or she did not access or change the images.[45] If there were changes, each would have to be described, and the presiding judge would have to decide whether it constituted acceptable enhancement or unacceptable manipulation.

---

45. Digital images could be stored on an archiveable, unalterable storage medium (*e.g.*, unalterable CD-ROM). This would provide a guarantee that the image has not been altered *on that CD-ROM*. It would not guarantee that the image was not downloaded to another medium (*e.g.*, a personal computer), altered, and recorded on another unalterable storage medium. Consequently, the use of this medium still requires the proponent to establish a chain of custody of the original unalterable medium.

B.   Desirable Enhancement Versus Unacceptable Manipulation

One of the advantages of digital photography is that poor photographs can be improved after the event has occurred. Conventional photography can also manipulate a print from a negative, but the possibilities are minuscule compared to the enhancement options available through digital technology. Conventional printing can change appearance by increasing or decreasing contrast, focus, or size. But computer alteration of digital photographs can range from enhancement (clarifying images, contrasting figures, and improving visibility)[46] to fraudulent manipulation (changing the content of the story originally told by the recorded images).

This problem of whether a change is enhancement or manipulation also arises with videotapes[47] and audiotapes.[48] In each of these situations the concern is the same: were the changes equivalent to adjusting a television picture so as to improve the contrast for better definition, or did they alter the basic story told by the pictures? Did the changes add something new, or change what was already present?[49] The authentication process

---

46. State v. Swinton, 847 A.2d 921 (Conn. 2004) (enhanced digital photographs of bite marks); State v. Hayden, 950 P.2d 1024, 1028 (Wash. Ct. App. 1998) ("The digital photographs are enhanced using software that improves sharpness and image contrast. In addition, pattern and color isolation filters remove interfering colors and background patterns. This is a subtractive process in which elements are removed or reduced; nothing is added. At trial, Berg testified that the software he used prevented him from adding to, changing, or destroying the original image. In contrast with 'image restoration,' a process in which things that are not there are added based on preconceived ideas about what the end result should look like, 'image enhancement' merely makes what is there more usable."). *See* 2 P. GIANNELLI & E. IMWINKELRIED, SCIENTIFIC EVIDENCE § 25-6.11, pp. 92-93 (3d ed. 1999) ("Image enhancement technology was developed during the late 1960s and early 1970s for the [National Aeronautics and Space Administration (NASA)] space program. . . . Due to the weight and power limitation of spacecraft, it was impractical for NASA to use state-of-the-art camera systems on unmanned craft. The cameras used produced somewhat degraded photographs. Image enhancement reverses the degradation . . . and thereby improves the sharpness and image contrast of the photograph . . . [by] eliminating background patters and colors.").

47. Nonner v. State, 907 S.W.2d 677 (Ark. 1995); Dolan v. State, 743 So. 2d 544 (Fla. Ct. App. 1999).

48. United States v. Calderin-Rodrigues, 244 F.3d 977 (8th Cir. 2001).

49. *See* United States v. Seifert, 351 F. Supp. 2d 926, 928 (D. Minn. 2005).

[T]he court finds that adjustments to brightness or contrast, or enlarge-

described in *Nooner v. State*[50]—where the trial court had admitted digital photographs that had been copied from a videotape—helps explain this distinction.

> We emphasize that there is nothing before us that indicates that the still photographs of the suspect ultimately introduced into evidence were changed to include a face, features, or physique of someone not present in the original videotape. Indeed, the jury and the circuit court watched a slowed version of the original videotape and then saw the "enhanced" still photographs. Thus, the viewers of the tape had the opportunity to identify distortion in the photographs of the depicted suspect.
>
> In the pretrial hearing regarding whether the photographs should be suppressed, the state witnesses, including representatives of the private firms, meticulously described their role in the enhancement process. Rupert Robertson, a video specialist for Arkansas Power and Light Company, testified that he slowed the original videotape down by making an exact duplicate of it in the

---

ment of the image, while arguably a manipulation, are in fact no more manipulative than the recording process itself. The image is black and white; the world is not. In the non-digital world, a camera's lens, its aperture, shutter speed, length of exposure, film grain, and development process—all affect the image. Each of these is entirely unremarkable so long as the 'image' remains an accurate recording of that which occurred before the camera. If a photographic negative were magnified by lens, and an enlarged image resulted, no one would question the larger picture. Similarly, in the event of a tape recording, no one would comment if the volume were increased to make a recorded conversation more easily heard—again, so long as the volume-increased words were accurately recorded by the recording medium. ... Here, the evidence showed that the technician adjusted the digital image's brightness and contrast, but maintained the relationships between the light and dark areas of the image. As an example, if the moving figure's clothing were a certain percentage lighter or darker than the wall behind it, that light/dark relationship was maintained. The technician testified that he simply 'moved' the brightness relationship on the scale, increasing the light's intensity while maintaining the image's integrity. .... As a result, the Court finds that the enhanced tape accurately presents a true and accurate replica of the image recorded by the Co-Operative's security camera. It does so in a fashion which maintains the image while assisting the jury in perceiving and understanding the recorded event.

50. 907 S.W.2d 677, 686 (Ark. 1995).

Betacam format and then freezing each frame for several seconds. Tom Burney of Jones Productions testified that he took a still frame from the duplicate videotape, transferred it to his computer, and softened the pixels on the suspect's face to remove the graininess. He did not add or subtract features from the original, except to "mosaic out" the victim. Carl Tillery of Color Masters testified that he took the computer disk prepared by Tom Burney and made still photographs. He multiplied the pixels per square inch to improve the contrast and adjusted the brightness in one of the still photographs. He also testified that he in no way altered the features in the photographs. Jeff Bishop from Camera Mart testified that he made still photographs from the original videotape. He only adjusted the brightness in the photographs.

As explained in *Dolan v. State*,[51] "[w]here there is testimony as to the nature of the store's video security system, the placement of the film in the camera, how the camera worked, the circumstances of removal of the tape and chain of possession of the tape, such testimony is sufficient authentication of the tape. Once authenticated and the forensic analyst explains the computer enhancement process and establishes that the images were not altered or edited, then the computer enhancements become admissible as a fair and accurate replicate of what is on the tape, provided the original tape is in evidence for comparison."

Generally, the standard of authentication for digitally enhanced evidence can be satisfied by evidence that (1) the computer equipment is accepted in the field as standard and competent and was in good working order, (2) qualified computer operators were employed, (3) proper procedures were followed in connection with the input and output of information, (4) a reliable software program was utilized, (5) the equipment was programmed and operated correctly, and (6) the exhibit is properly identified as the output in question.[52]

---

51. 743 So. 2d 544, 546 (Fla. Ct. App. 1999).

52. State v. Swinton, 847 A.2d 921, 943-44 (Conn. 2004). The court applied these standards to enhanced digital photographs that had been made of bite marks.

First, Palmbach testified that the computer equipment is accepted as standard equipment in the field. He testified that the Lucis program was relied upon by experts in the field of pattern analysis in a forensic setting. He further testified that the program had been used in "fingerprint pattern identification, blood stain patterns identification, footwear and tire impression identification, and in bite mark identification." Second, it was established that a qualified computer operator produced the enhancement. Palmbach's testimony clearly demonstrated that he was well versed in the Lucis program. He was a well trained and highly experienced forensic analyst, and he testified to his qualification as an expert in the analysis of pattern evidence and the enhancement of that evidence. . . . Additionally, Karazulas, an odontological expert, was with Palmbach throughout the process and was able to aid him in determining when the image was appropriately enhanced for forensic comparison. . . . Third, the state presented evidence that proper procedures were followed in the connection with the input and output of information. During direct examination, Palmbach testified accurately, clearly, and consistently regarding the process of the digitization of the image—wherein the photograph is transformed into pixels . . . —and how Pambach then had used the Lucis software to select comparable points of contrast and array them into layers. He also testified as to how the Lucis program then diminished certain layers in order to heighten the visual appearance of the bite mark. During voir dire and cross-examination, Palmbach further explained and clarified this process. In fact, he even demonstrated the enhancement process to the jury using a laptop demonstration. Importantly, Pambach compared the enhanced photographs with the unenhanced photographs in front of the jury. When asked whether there was anything in the enhanced image that was not present in the original image, Palbach testified: "NO . . . there's not. One of the features of Lucis is that it does not remove any pixels. It is only selecting to show you the range that you've asked for. Every one of those pictures and every bit of that contrast is still present in the enhanced portion. . . . It's just that we're diminishing some and bringing others forward . . . just for viewing purposes. But every bit of that information is still present. We have not deleted some of these pixels or any of the pixels." . . . Fourth, the state adequately demonstrated that Lucis is a reliable software program. Palmbach testified that, in a forensic setting, the "Primary concern is accuracy. . . . We can't choose a program in which it will delete, alter, or change that material in any form or fashion. If it does, it's not suitable for this type of analysis." He further testified that the Lucis program, unlike other computer programs such as Adobe Photoshop, does not even have image editing features and was not designed to edit the images it enhances. . . . "Although Palmbach testified that he was not aware of the error rates regarding the Lucis program, he stated that he was aware of Lucis' marketing papers and an article that had been written concerning Lucis, both of which claimed that the program was artifact free, which would contribute greatly to a low error rate. Additionally, Palmbach personally tested Lucis' accuracy by making a known exemplar using a bite mark made by Karazulas on his own arm and then subjecting it to enhancement.

In both *Nooner* and *Dolan*, the original videotapes from which the photographs were made were in evidence so that the sources and the products could be compared. This would have been required by the best evidence or original writing rule. It is not clear, however, that the availability of the original tape is essential to authentication and admissibility of the photographs if the videotapes had been lost due to no fault of the proponent of the photographs.[53] This is an exception to the of the original writing rule. A proper foundation for the photographs through the process described in *Dolan* should be sufficient to ensure admissibility.[54]

Alterations must be judged on a case-by-case basis. Their acceptability should turn on whether they change the relevant substance of what is depicted. For example, changing the degree of lighting or adding a contrasting color to make something more visible without altering what is seen should be welcomed. If, however, the level of light is being used to demonstrate how poorly witnesses would have been able to see, this enhancement changes the relevant substance of what is depicted and becomes unacceptable.[55]

Even when the substance of what is depicted has been changed, this should not affect the admissibility of the photograph if that substance is unrelated to the reason for using the photograph at trial. For example, an unavailable family member's head may have been morphed into the pho-

---

53. *See* State v. Allen, 930 So. 2d 1122, 1131 (La. Ct. App. 2006) ("At a hearing conducted outside the presence of the jury, the trial court allowed a copy of the transcript of the taped conversation to be admitted into the record, ruling that the state had shown that the tape had been lost through no fault of its own, and there was no bad faith on the part of the state."). Massachusetts does not even recognize a best evidence problem with videotapes. "Videotapes, like photographs, are not subject to the best evidence rule. 'The best evidence rule is applicable to only those situations where the contents of a writing are sought to be proved.' . . . The best evidence rule would note apply to a videotape recorded by a store's security system, and a properly authenticated copy would be admissible if otherwise relevant." Commonwealth v. Leneski, 846 N.E.2d 1195, 1198 (Mass. App. Ct. 2006).

54. Authentication of digitally enhanced audiotape requires a similar foundation. *See* United States v. Calderin-Rodriguez, 244 F.3d 977, 986-87 (8th Cir. 2001).

55. Some aspects of photography remain the same, whether digital or otherwise. For example, the lens used on the camera can distort the apparent distance and relationship of things to one another. The accuracy of the photograph's depiction of these relationships must be attested to by the sponsoring witness.

tograph. This clearly changes the substance of what was depicted. If, however, the photograph was offered to show the appearance of another family member who was present when the photograph was taken, the alteration should not affect the admissibility decision.

C.   *Authenticate the Computer Program Too*

While it often is uncontroversial, one nevertheless should not forget to authenticate the computer program through which the digital photograph was printed. Again, this is an issue only when there are no eyewitnesses sponsoring the photographic print. If identified by an eyewitness as an accurate depiction of the event or condition that he witnessed, the process by which the print was created is of little or no concern.

When made necessary by the absence of eyewitnesses, Fed. R. Evid. 901(b)(9) has simplified this task. The proponent need only put on a sponsoring witness testimony "describing the process or system used to produce a result and showing that the process or system produces an accurate result." In business enterprises, this is accomplished through the testimony of a corporate official who describes what the computer program and system is designed to do, why it does it, and how the enterprise uses and relies upon the product. When a commercial program like PhotoPro, Photoshop, Paint Shop Pro, or Imagemagick has been employed, a court may take judicial notice of its reliability under Fed. R. Evid. 201(b)(2) as a fact "capable of accurate and ready determination by resort to sources whose accuracy cannot reasonably be questioned."

D.   *The Internet Complication*

When the computer onto which a digital photograph is downloaded for printing has been connected to the Internet, the risk of manipulation by hackers increases greatly. Theoretically, every computer connected to the Internet can be hacked into and everything on it manipulated. Reality, however, may be different. There is no evidence that hacking, while possible, poses a sufficient risk to justify the exclusion of digital photographs absent assurances that hacking has not occurred.[56]

---

56. This absence of evidence, however, may be due to the fact that when hacking has occurred, the most sophisticated hackers can cover their trail completely. They can destroy any evidence that there has been a breach of security and of which files were accessed, and how, if at all, they were altered.

The likelihood of Internet hacker manipulation depends on the nature of the controversy and the importance of the evidence stored on the computer. A chain of custody requirement, however, has never required an air-tight assurance that there has been no tampering. Therefore, it may be unreasonable to expect the proponent of digital evidence generated by an Internet-linked computer to prove such a negative. Digital evidence generated by computers has been admitted in court since the invention of the Internet. All of the written communications on a computer are digitally created and are subject to the same manipulation as digital photographs. Nevertheless, courts have shown no concern for this possibility. Because a picture speaks a thousand words, should our concern for manipulation begin with photographs?

The answer is probably no, for a number of reasons. First, there is extensive discovery in all litigation, particularly civil. Second, because of the scope of this discovery, both sides can employ the services of forensic experts to examine both the photographic evidence and the computers of the photograph's proponent to determine whether there has been hacking and manipulation. Third, fact witnesses can be called to contest the accuracy of whatever the photograph depicts. And finally, an expert witness can be called by the opposing side to explain to the jury the myriad possibilities of fraudulent manipulation.

Because of these possibilities, proponents of digital photographs are compelled to present the most convincing available evidence of authenticity. Therefore, there is little reason for judges to take a more intrusive role in the outcome of the trial by imposing restrictive admissibility standards. The engine of truth, the adversarial process, will provide adequate assurances of reliability.

E.   A Spoliation Problem

As discussed in Chapter Two, spoliation is the intentional or reckless destruction of evidence that may be relevant to pending or reasonably anticipated litigation. Digital photographs pose a potential spoliation problem because of the nature of the technology. Unlike negatives in conventional photography that cannot be reused, the digital cards and hard drives on the digital camera are designed to be recorded over, thereby destroying the original image. After being downloaded to the photographer's computer for printing, the digital card or hard drive are emptied for reuse. This is one of the convenience and cost-saving aspects of digital photography.

Film is no longer needed, and there is nothing to be developed before a print can be made. But this advantage may prove to be a disadvantage.

The manipulation of digital photographs usually follows their downloading to the photographer's computer system. Through imaging editing programs, photographs are manipulated to satisfy the desires of the operator. Absent programs that reveal all alterations to a photograph, the most convincing evidence of the absence of alterations would be the original image on the digital card that was used in the digital camera. If the digital card is reused after the possibility of litigation has become apparent, the photographer may be guilty of spoliation, which could result in the exclusion of the photographic evidence or worse, if credible evidence of alteration were produced. If the digital camera uses a non-portable hard drive rather than a digital card, it may be unreasonable to expect the photographer to abandon use of the camera.

IV. AUTHENTICATION OF WEB PAGE POSTINGS FROM THE INTERNET

When printouts from Web pages are offered into evidence, authentication will likely be a difficult problem.[57] At least three levels of authentication

---

57. For example, in Novak v. Tucows, Inc., 2007 WL 922306, at *5 (E.D. N.Y. Mar. 26, 2007), the plaintiff wanted to offer printouts he had obtained through a Web site called Internet Archive, a site that allowed users, through a service called the "Wayback Machine," to obtain archived Web pages as they appeared at a particular moment in time as well as other postings. The court rejected the documents because the sponsoring witness lacked personal knowledge necessary to give needed assurances that the documents obtained from third-party Web sites were what he claimed them to be.

This problem is even more acute in the case of documents procured through the Wayback Machine. Plaintiff states that the Web pages archived within the Wayback Machine are based upon "data from third parties who compile the data by using software programs known as crawlers," who then "donate" such data to the Internet Archive, which "preserves and provides access to it." . . . Based upon Novak's assertions, it is clear that the information posted on the Wayback Machine is only as valid as the third party donating the page decides to make it. The authorized owners and managers of the archived Web sites play no role in ensuring that the materials posed in the Wayback Machine accurately represent what was posted on their official Web sites at the relevant time.

Similar comments have been made in United States v. Jackson, 208 F.3d 633, 638 (7th Cir. 2000) (declining to admit Web posting because the offering party was unable to establish that the postings were authentic.); Costa v. Keppel Singmarine Dockyard PTE, Ltd., 2003 WL 24242419, at *7 n.74 (C.D. Cal. Apr. 24, 2003). *See*

must be addressed.[58]

The first, and least troublesome, level of authentication is the printout. It must be shown to accurately reflect the content of the Web page from the image that appeared on the computer monitor and from which the print was made. The common law would permit a witness to authenticate the printout by testifying that the Web page was compared to the printed copy and the two were the same. This was called a "compared copy."

---

generally St. Clair v. Johnny's Oyster & Shrimp, Inc., 76 F. Supp. 2d 773, 775 (S.D. Tex. 1999) (where the court noted that "any evidence procured off the Internet is adequate for almost nothing, even under the most liberal interpretations of the hearsay exception rules." "Anyone can put anything on the Internet. No web-site is monitored for accuracy and nothing contained therein is under oath or even subject to independent verification absent underlying documents.").

58. For a similar discussion of the multiple levels of authentication involved in the use of a simple computer printout, *see* United States v. Duncan, 30 M.J. 1284, 1288 (Navy-Marine Ct. 1990). "When a shopkeeper entered a transaction in his shopbook, at or near the time of the transaction and in the regular course of business, the shopkeeper was the declarant, and the shopbook was a business record in both the literal and the hearsay rule senses. It has, of course, scarcely been thought necessary to demonstrate through testimonial or other proof that a pencil is a reliable implement which accurately traces the movement of the declarant's hand. Similarly, it is unnecessary to demonstrate that a typewriter accurately prints the letters and numbers that the typist (declarant) types. But when a declarant enters data into a computer, which processes them and prints them out in a different format, it may well be necessary to authenticate the print-outs specially as an accurate representation of the input data, pursuant to [Rule] 901(b)(9), in addition to authenticating the print-out generally as the genuine print-out that it purports to be, pursuant to [Rule] 901(a). Such double authentication will then be sufficient for admissibility if, and only if, the purpose for which the print-out is offered is *merely to show which keys the operator pressed.* But if the proponent's purpose is to establish the underlying business transaction, such double authentication still does not ensure admissibility, because the operator, being human, may have deliberately or inadvertently inserted false or erroneous data. Consequently, to introduce such evidence for the truth of the matters stated therein, it may be necessary to do three things: (1) *authenticate the exhibit* as the print-out it purports to be; (2) authenticate the process by which it was prepared to show that it produces print-outs which accurately reflect the input data; and (3) lay a foundation for admissibility of the exhibit as a record of regularly conducted activity. Such data maintained in computerized form are sometimes referred to as 'computer-stored' data. Print-outs of them are hearsay because they are generated by a human declarant. It is of the greatest importance to note that the keystrokes of the declarant who enters the data into the computer are not themselves the business transaction being recorded; the keystrokes are the declarant's statement of the transaction; hence, they may either truly or falsely, or correctly or incorrectly, record the underlying transaction."

Under the Federal Rules of Evidence, the printout would not even be considered a copy. Under Fed. R. Evid. 1001(3), an original of data stored in a computer or similar device includes "any printout or other output readable by sight, shown to reflect the data accurately." In addition, Fed. R Evid. 1001(4) recognizes a "duplicate" that Fed. R. Evid. 1003 makes admissible as if it were the original unless a "genuine question is raised as to the authenticity of the original" or in the circumstances "it would be unfair to admit the duplicate in lieu of the original."[59] These provisions should eliminate most debates about the printout itself.

The second level of authentication is what is displayed on the Web page shown on the monitor of the computer that called it up. It must be established that the Web page that was examined and copied was the same unchanged Web page that was posted by the owner of the Web site. The concern here is with hackers breaking into the Web page and changing its content. This is part of what led one judge to refer to materials taken from the Internet as "voodoo information."[60]

Courts have two options here. First, if the court has a serious concern about authenticity, proponents could be required to obtain certifications of the accuracy of the content of the copied Web pages from the Web pages' owners. This would be much like the common law process of obtaining a certified copy of a public record. Requiring this would have the effect of relegating computer Internet searches and printouts to research tools that cannot directly produce evidence that is usable in the courtroom. But, due to the susceptibility of the Internet and the Web pages posted on it to alteration by hackers, it would not be irrational for judges to conclude that the Internet format should not be used at trial without added assurances that there has been no tampering. Just because something can be discovered through a computer connected to the Internet does not mean that the research product must be admissible in a court of law. Trials do not occur suddenly. Litigants usually have ample time to obtain copies of those materials from the individuals or entities responsible for the posting they have found.

Second, courts could assume that most Web pages appear the same as they did when posted by the owner because Web page manipulation is the exception rather than the rule. This option might be palatable if judges

---

59. *See* Chapter 4, *supra.*

60. St. Clair v. Johnny's Oyster & Shrimp, Inc., 76 F. Supp. 2d 773, 774-75 (S.D. Tex. 1999).

require the proponents to provide the opposing side with sufficient advance notice of intended use, so that reliability can be verified when suspicions exist. Under this approach, courts would be treating Web pages
the same as copies classified as duplicates by assuming reliability unless a
genuine question is raised by the opposing party.

The third level of authentication arises when the proponent offers the
content of the Web page to prove the truth of something stated in it. This
creates a hearsay problem. To admit the evidence from a Web page, the
proponent must establish, or authenticate, that the Web page is admissible
under an exception to the hearsay rule. When the Web page is offered
only to establish that something was stated on a Web page, only content is
being proven and not the truth of that content. Consequently, this third
level of authentication would be inapplicable. If, however, substantive
truth is important to the relevance of the content, the owner of the Web
page will have to establish the factual foundation for admissibility under
one of the delineated hearsay exceptions. For example, if a business posted
its records on the Internet and someone wanted to prove facts stated in
those records, the proponent of the Web page printout would have to
establish that the postings were part of the business records of the Web
page owner under Fed. R. Evid. 803(6). This can only be accomplished
through someone with knowledge of how and why those records were
maintained.

The foundation for business records has commonly been established
through the testimony of a custodian or other qualified person testifying
that the records were regularly made and maintained, at or near the time
of the transactions or occurrences,[61] by persons with both personal knowl-

---

61. While the issue of timeliness does not arise often relative to the entry of test
results into a computer database, the court had to address it in Glatman v. Valverda,
2006 Cal. App. Unpub. LEXIS 11148, *5-12 (4th Dist. Dec. 12, 2006). The report in
question was dated Aug. 1, a week after the event in question, and nothing supported
the claim that the analysts promptly entered the test results into the computer at an
earlier time. No procedures were in place requiring timely recording, and the evidence circumstantially suggested that the entries were made on the date on the face of
the document. The court noted that had this involved only the transference of written
data from another written instrument, the delay may not have been important. Here,
however, the data was based on the memory of the individuals making the entry. The
court concluded that this presented too great a danger of "inaccuracy by lapse of
memory" and therefore did not meet the "at or near" requirement for the business
records exception to the hearsay rule.

edge of the events being recorded and a duty to make that recording. Alternatively, the foundation for the business records exception can now be laid by a certification under Fed. R. Evid. 902(11) requiring the same information in writing. This latter method of authentication is classified as self-authentication. Methods of self-authentication are discussed below.

Occasionally a court short-circuits the multilevel authentication process by jumping from the first level of authentication to the third without even acknowledging the intervening issues. In *Johnson-Woolridge v. Woolridge*,[62] for example, records of the Board of Education taken from the Internet were found to be admissible because the person who took them from the board's Web page could testify to what he did to retrieve them. From the conclusion that the printout was authentic, the court jumped to the conclusion that the materials from which the information was retrieved were admissible for their truth under the public records exception to the hearsay rule in Fed. R. Evid. 803(8). Similarly, in *Daimler-Benz Aktiengesellschaft v. Olson*,[63] an affidavit was filed with the court that had a number of attachments. One of them was a printout from Web sites. To authenticate this, the affiant stated that "within his personal knowledge, the attachments are accurate copies of the original documents." This was accepted as adequate under Rule 901(b)(1) (testimony of a witness with knowledge) without indicating what was authenticated, other than the fact that the printouts accurately reflected what the affiant had retrieved from Web sites that he had called-up. If the contents of those Web sites were relied upon by the affiant for their truth, levels of authentication were ignored.[64]

Theoretically, there is a fourth level of authentication: the computer processes and systems of both the proponent of the printout and the owner of the system producing the Web page. This level of authentication is often

---

62. 2001 WL 838986, at *4-5 (Ohio Ct. App. 2001).

63. 21 S.W.3d 707, 717 (Tex. App. 2000).

64. This should be contrasted with Villas at Hidden Lakes Condominiums Ass'n v. Guepel Constr. Co., Inc., 847 P.2d 117 (Ariz. Ct. App. 1993), where an affidavit was submitted to the court by the president of a company with computer-generated exhibits attached. While the affiant's conclusions were said to be based on his personal knowledge, no information was provided explaining how the exhibits were prepared. The court held that before conclusions based on the truth of the exhibits could be admissible, they first had to be shown to be admissible under the business records exception to the hearsay rule. When such exhibits are taken from Internet Web pages, as they were in *Daimler-Benz*, the same problem exists, except that there is another level of computer technology added.

ignored because it is so easily satisfied. Under Fed. R. Evid. 901(9), a process or system is authenticated by "[e]vidence describing a process or system used to produce a result and showing that the process or system produces an accurate result." Because computer systems and use of the Internet are popular and generally reliable, requiring evidence on the subject can easily be seen as little more than a procedural technicality. Therefore, unless genuine questions are identified, this phase in the authentication process is usually ignored. As the court in *People v. Huehn*[65] acknowledged, "courts have generally declined to require testimony regarding the functioning and accuracy of the computer process where, as here, the records at issue are bank records reflecting data entered automatically rather than manually."

A.   *Relaxation of Authentication Requirements*

As reflected in the often-forgotten fourth level of authentication just discussed, the recent trend has been to reduce or ignore the authentication of computer systems because it has little practical value. Virtually everyone relies on computers to maintain their records, and there are seldom controversies about that method of record maintenance. Little attention, therefore, may be justified This reflects a tendency by judges to accept things as authentic if they seem authentic, and if no questions are raised by the opponent, who has had advance notice and an opportunity to check. When minor or theoretical problems are raised, judges will often admit the evidence and relegate the identified concerns to the jurors' assessment of the weight to be given to the evidence.[66] The bottom line is that "[f]ew jurisdictions have attempted to enunciate a formula or fixed set of guidelines to govern the establishment of a foundation for computer-generated evidence . . . ."[67]

---

65.   553 P.3d 733, 737 (Colo Ct. App. 2002).

66.   United States v. Meienberg, 263 F.3d 1177, 1181 (10th Cir. 2001) ("'Any questions as to accuracy of the printouts, whether resulting from incorrect data entry or the operation of the computer program, as with inaccuracies in any other type of business records, would have affected only the weight of the printouts, not their admissibility.'").

67.   Bray v. Bi-State Dev. Corp, 949 S.W.2d 93, 99 (Mo. Ct. App. 1997). Oregon has addressed the authentication issue for computer-generated evidence from public records and their certification through a new hearsay exception in OEC 803(25) and self-authentication provision in OEC 902(1). These provisions permit data to be taken from a computer and presented in court without the intermediate step of creating a document that would qualify as a public record and then preparing a certified copy of that docu-

Whether this assumption of authenticity is appropriate and will continue to expand to Web pages that businesses upload to the Internet, so that those records are accepted as business records and admitted for the truth of their contents without additional foundational evidence, will likely turn on a number of factors: (1) the confidence of judges that such Web postings would be authentic because the Web page site and name are leased and operated exclusively by the business; (2) the confidence of judges that such records would satisfy the elements of the "business records" exception; (3) the judges' belief that such records generally have not been tampered with by hackers. Judges' willingness to adopt this belief may be influenced by the fact that authentication issues for admissibility purposes need only be established by a prima facie standard—sufficient proof upon which a reasonable person could find that the evidence is what it purports to be; (4) the notice given to the opposing side of the intention to use the Internet posting; and (5) the willingness of judges to relieve the proponent of the foundation burden and impose the reverse burden on the opponent, simply because the value of requiring the foundation is slight, coupled with a corresponding burden on the opponent that is not onerous. This shifted burden may be slight if the incidence of actual manipulation is, in fact, small, and the ability to satisfy the burden is easily complied with after adequate notification. In substance, this is what has been done with the best evidence rule under Fed. R. Evid. 1003, and it appears to have eliminated meaningless best evidence objections with no apparent adverse consequences.

Hutchens v. Hutchens-Collins[68] illustrates how courts are approaching the issue of authentication of documents downloaded from the Web sites on the Internet. The plaintiff, Hutchins, objected to various documents submitted by the defendant, Hutchens-Collins, in support of a motion for summary judgment. These documents initially had been found by the defendant's attorney, Purcell, on the Internet Web site while conducting a Google search for the name of Hutchens. Later, a lawyer named Purcell obtained two CD-ROM disks containing these documents from Sean Barry, a senior consultant in the forensics e-discovery group at New

---

ment. Oregon v. Barber, 149 P.3d 260, 264 (Ore. Ct. App. 2006). In the past, the authentication of public records was accomplished by signed, hard-paper copies that were provided upon request and manually filed. Today, unsigned certifications of authenticity may be provided by computers for data they have retrieved from their databases.

68. 2006 WL 3490999 (D. Ore. Nov. 30, 2006).

Technologies, Inc. (NTI), a company specializing in the preservation, identification, extraction, and documentation of computer evidence.

A declaration from the senior consultant verified the accuracy of the
CD-ROM disks. His declaration also verified that (1) he made the CD-
ROMs on a particular date by downloading all the files associated with the
Internet address given to him by lawyer Purcell, (2) the Internet address
was not password-protected, and therefore freely available to anyone with
a computer and access to the Internet, and (3) the domain name for the
Web site was registered to a company associated with Hutchens, as found
through a service called WHOIS. Those to whom a Web site is registered
are given both the practical and legal ability to control all materials up-
loaded to the site.

The fact that the CD-ROMs were "write-only" made it impossible to
alter or modify the files they contained and then resave them on the disks.
This authenticated the content of the CD-ROM disks as being unchanged.
The content of the CD-ROM disks were printed by lawyer Purcell. His
declaration certified that he had not altered the electronic data that produced the hard copies or manipulated the results before they were printed.

While the defendant, Hutchens-Collins, presented no information about
the company to which the Web site had been registered, the plaintiff,
Hutchens, had submitted a certified copy of that company's business account signature card, which linked the plaintiff to the company, and the
address of the company coincided with the plaintiff's personal address.

Based on the totality of these facts and circumstances, the court concluded that sufficient evidence had been presented to authenticate the
documents under Fed. R. Evid. 901(b)(4), which permits evidence to be
authenticated by "[a]ppearance, contents, substance, internal patterns,"
taken in conjunction with circumstances.[69]

B.   Self-authentication and the Internet

Under the common law, certain types of evidence were considered authentic without extrinsic evidence. The concept of self-authentication included official publications, certified copies, and acknowledged
documents. The concept was expanded in Fed. R. Evid. 902:

---

69. *Id.* at *2-3.

Article IX. Authentication and Identification
Rule 902. Self-Authentication

Extrinsic evidence of authenticity as a condition precedent to admissibility is not required with respect to the following:

(1) Domestic public documents under seal. A document bearing a seal purporting to be that of the United States, or of any State, district, Commonwealth, territory, or insular possession thereof, or the Panama Canal Zone, or the Trust Territory of the Pacific Islands, or of a political subdivision, department, officer, or agency thereof, and a signature purporting to be an attestation or execution.

[United States v. Hampton, 464 F.3d 687, 689 (7th Cir. 2006) ("This [rule] means that the document is admissible in evidence without any need for a witness to testify that it is authentic, that is, that it is what it purports to be (an official document stating what it states). . . . But seals are used to attest the authenticity of the document on which the seal is stamped, and no seal was stamped on the copies. The copies were copies of sealed documents rather than sealed document themselves. The rationale of Rule 902(1) . . . is that a seal is difficult to forge. . . . But that is not true of a copy of a seal—or at least the government has made no effort to show that the authenticity of the seal can be inferred with confidence from its copy.")]

(2) Domestic public documents not under seal. A document purporting to bear the signature in the official capacity of an officer or employee of any entity included in paragraph (1) hereof, having no seal, if a public officer having a seal and having official duties in the district or political subdivision of the officer or employee certifies under seal that the signer has the official capacity and that the signature is genuine.

(3) Foreign public documents. A document purporting to be executed or attested in an official capacity by a person authorized by the laws of a foreign country to make the execution or attestation, and accompanied by a final certification as to the genuineness of the signature and official position (A) of the executing or attesting person, or (B) of any foreign official whose certificate of genuineness of signature and official position relates to the execution or

attestation or is in a chain of certificates of genuineness of signature and official position relating to the execution or attestation. A final certification may be made by a secretary of an embassy or legation, consul general, consul, vice consul, or consular agent of the United States, or a diplomatic or consular official of the foreign country assigned or accredited to the United States. If reasonable opportunity has been given to all parties to investigate the authenticity and accuracy of official documents, the court may, for good cause shown, order that they be treated as presumptively authentic without final certification or permit them to be evidenced by an attested summary with or without final certification.

(4) Certified copies of public records. A copy of an official record or report or entry therein, or of a document authorized by law to be recorded or filed and actually recorded or filed in a public office, including data compilations in any form, certified as correct by the custodian or other person authorized to make the certification, by certificate complying with paragraph (1), (2), or (3) of this rule or complying with any Act of Congress or rule prescribed by the Supreme Court pursuant to statutory authority.

(5) Official publications. Books, pamphlets, or other publications purporting to be issued by public authority.

[*See* Hispanic Broadcasting Corp. v. Educational Media Foundation, 69 U.S.P.Q. 2d 1524, 2003 WL 22867633, at *5 (C.D. Cal. 2003) ("exhibits which consist of records from government websites, such as the FCC website, are self-authenticating"); Sannes v. Jeff Wyler Chevrolet, Inc., 1999 WL 33313134, at *2 n.3 (S.D. Ohio Mar. 31, 1999).]

(6) Newspapers and periodicals. Printed materials purporting to be newspapers or periodicals.

[United States v. Premera Blue Cross, 2006 WL 2841998, *4 (W.D. Wash. Sept. 29, 2006) (online version of newspaper rejected as self-authenticating under this rule because the historical indicia of authenticity, like distinctive headlines and unique typesetting techniques that made purported copies of the original text difficult to forge, are missing); United States v. Handal, 63 N.J. 610, 611 (A.F. Ct. Crim. App. May 30, 2006) (online version of a newspaper article held to have failed to meet self-authentication requirements because they do not bear the indicia of reliability demanded for self-authenticating documents).]

(7) Trade inscriptions and the like. Inscriptions, signs, tags, or labels purporting to have been affixed in the course of business and indicating ownership, control, or origin.

[*See* Elliott Assoc. v. Banco de la Nacion, 194 F.R.D. 116, 121 (S.D. N.Y. 2000) (affidavit based on interest rates that had been taken from Federal Reserve Board Web page admitted under Rule 803(17) because "if the Defendants genuinely disputed the rates and the default dates from which Finnerty performed his calculations, they certainly had the resources, and were given the time by this Court, to discover such information and present contrasting rates on default dates"); State v. Erickstand, 620 N.W.2d 136 (N.D. 2000) (court admitted evidence of value of stolen truck proven from information listed on the *Kelley Blue Book* Web site); Superhighway Consulting, Inc. v. Techwave, Inc., 1999 WL 1044870, at *2 (N.D. Ill. Nov. 16, 1999) (e-mails and facsimiles are considered self-authenticating under 902(17) unless opposing side produces evidence proving they are not authentic).]

(8) Acknowledged documents. Documents accompanied by a certificate of acknowledgment executed in the manner provided by law by a notary public or other officer authorized by law to make acknowledgments.

[*See* Matthews v. Commonwealth, 163 S.W.3d 11, 26 (Ky. 2005) (with an extensive discussion of the two rules, court concludes that an acknowledgment under Rule 902(8) cannot be used in lieu of a certification under 902(11)).]

(9) Commercial paper and related documents. Commercial paper, signatures thereon, and documents relating thereto to the extent provided by general commercial law.

(10) Presumptions under Acts of Congress. Any signature, document, or other matter declared by Act of Congress to be presumptively or prima facie genuine or authentic.

(11) Certified domestic records of regularly conducted activity. The original or a duplicate of a domestic record of regularly conducted activity that would be admissible under Rule 803(6) if accompanied by a written declaration of its custodian or other

qualified person, in a manner complying with any Act of Congress or rule prescribed by the Supreme Court pursuant to statutory authority, certifying that the record—

(A) was made at or near the time of the occurrence of the matters set forth by, or from information transmitted by, a person with knowledge of those matters;

(B) was kept in the course of the regularly conducted activity; and

(C) was made by the regularly conducted activity as a regular practice.

A party intending to offer a record into evidence under this paragraph must provide written notice of that intention to all adverse parties, and must make the record and declaration available for inspection sufficiently in advance of offer into evidence to provide an adverse party with a fair opportunity to challenge them.

[*See* In re Vinhnee, 336 B.R. 437, 448-49 (9th Cir. 2005) (Trial court held that the written declaration was an insufficient foundation for admitting electronic records because the proponent needed to show the accuracy of the computer in the retention and retrieval of the information at issue. "The declaration merely identified the makes and models of the equipment, named the software, noted that some of the software was customized, and asserted that the hardware and software are standard for the industry, regarded as reliable, and periodically updated. There is no information regarding American Express' computer policy and system control procedures, including control of access to the pertinent databases, control of access to the pertinent programs, recording and logging of changes to the data, backup practices, and audit procedures utilized to assure the continuing integrity of the records. All of these matters are pertinent to the accuracy of the computer in the retention and retrieval of the information at issue." This enhanced foundation appears to be in conflict with Rule 902(11). Should the factors identified by the court in *Vinhnee* go to weight rather than admissibility?); United States v. Wittig, 2005 WL 1227790, at *2 (D. Kan. May 23, 2005) (concluding that use of this certification against a criminal defendant violated his right to confrontation); Stang v. Comm'r Internal Revenue, 89 T.C.M. (CCH) 1490, 2005 WL 1503682, at *7 (T.C. June 27, 2005) (providing the declaration and evidence to the opposing side a "couple of weeks" before trial was adequate notice); Matthews v. Commonwealth, 163 S.W.3d 11, 26 (Ky. 2005) (acknowledgment under Rule 902(8) cannot be used in lieu of a certification under 902(11).]

(12) Certified foreign records of regularly conducted activity. In a civil case, the original or a duplicate of a foreign record of regularly conducted activity, which would be admissible under Rule 803(6), if accompanied by a written declaration by the custodian or another qualified person certifying that the record—

(A) was made at or near the time of the occurrence of the matters set forth by, or from information transmitted by, a person with knowledge of those matters;

(B) was kept in the course of the regularly conducted activity; and

(C) was made by the regularly conducted activity as a regular practice.

The declaration must be signed in a manner that, if falsely made, would subject the maker to criminal penalty under the laws of the country where the declaration is signed. A party intending to offer a record into evidence under this paragraph must provide written notice of that intention to all adverse parties, and must make the record and declaration available for inspection sufficiently in advance of their offer into evidence to provide an adverse party with a fair opportunity to challenge them.

While self-authentication practices can be used in the Internet age, some adjustments will be necessary because the context is slightly different.

1. Public Document Under Seal

The reason that public documents under seal can be self-authenticating is that it is difficult to forge a public seal. Therefore, a seal on a document is convincing evidence—or at least prima facie evidence (the standard for admissibility)—that the document to which it is attached is what it purports to be. The same cannot be said for copies of sealed documents to which a second seal has not been attached. Without a seal on the copy, there are no objective assurances that the content of the original sealed document has not been altered in the copy.[70] The solution, of course, is to present other evidence of the copy's authenticity. This might best be accomplished through testimony from those who have compared the content of the copy in question with the original that is on the public record.[71]

2. Business Solicitations and Postings

The application of the doctrine of self-authentication to Internet communications has been mixed in the few cases that discuss the issue.[72] Under Fed. R. Evid. 902(6), "printed materials purporting to be newspapers or periodicals" are accepted as prima facie evidence of what they appear to be. In Fed. R. Evid. 902(7), "inscriptions, signs, tags, or labels" are presumed to have been produced by and to have originated with the institution whose marks they bear. The continued use of these rules with Internet communications turns on how broadly courts are willing to define such terms as "periodicals," "printed material," and "signs, tags, or labels."

Material typed into a computer or placed on a Web page, for example, may be construed as "printed material " under the Federal Rules. Self-authentication of printed materials was premised on the assumption that if someone has gone to the trouble of printing a document, it is likely to be authentic. A document attached to an e-mail message, however, is hardly the equivalent of "printed material" to which this assumption has attached. E-mail communications are little more than typed letters to which files can be attached with the click of a mouse. E-mails should therefore not be equated with "printed materials" merely because they are typewritten and printed. Additional evidence of authenticity should be required before such evidence is admitted. Courts may be persuaded to adopt the broader definition of "printed material" when dealing with a printout of a Web page, given that the opposing party may own the Web page and, therefore, have superior access to the original posting, thereby easily exposing altered or inaccurate printouts.

Is a Web page a "periodical" because it is periodically updated? Probably not, but that is not certain, because there is no case law on the subject. The individual or business controlling the Web page must purchase the name, lease the space, design the Web page, and pay the expenses of uploading information to it and periodically changing the content. As

---

70. *See* cases cited under Rule 902(1), above.
71. This means of authentication is provided for in FED. R. EVID. 901(b)(1).
72. *See* cases cited under Rule 902(6), above.

with a newspaper or periodical, it is highly unlikely that the Web page will be fabricated. However, unlike a traditional periodical, there is only one copy of this publication, absent backups or printouts from it. Consequently, unlike a newspaper or magazine, it may be significantly harder to verify its accuracy.

The most difficult problem with authenticating Web pages will be authenticating their content *at a particular time*. Most Web pages change regularly. As a result, *dated printouts* of the computer screen on which the Web page is viewed are particularly important. Without dated printouts, proof will depend on the possibly biased or imperfect recollections of witnesses. A printout of the Web page on a particular occasion may also be discoverable from the owner of the Web page if past versions are re-tained. The more frequently the Web page changes, the less likely it is that the owner will retain printouts of all prior iterations.

"Inscriptions, signs, tags, or labels" recognized in Rule 902(7) are less likely to be accurate indicators of "ownership, control, or origin" for Web pages because a company's mark can be copied or forged, attached to limitless numbers of communications, and widely disseminated with ease. At its inception, Rule 902(7) envisioned labels on cans identifying the manu-facturer of the product. E-commerce does not possess the same tangibility that provides this added assurance of authenticity in normal commerce.

Nevertheless, such trade inscriptions on e-mail messages have been held to be self-authenticating, although the application of the doctrine of self-identification in an e-commerce context seems unfounded because unsolicited self-identification is otherwise inadequate.[73] Nevertheless, judges will probably continue to construe Rule 902(7) broadly for several reasons. First, the probability of fraud is quite low when solicitations are made for the benefit of the identified company. Second, as between the recipient of the solicitation and the alleged sender benefiting from it, the recipient usually has the least access to information to prove or disprove

---

73. Superhighway Consulting, Inc. v. Techwave, Inc., 1999 WL 1044870, at *2 (N.D. Ill. Nov. 16, 1999) ("It appears from reviewing the e-mails and facsimiles in question, however, that they are self-authenticating. Furthermore, other courts in this district have held that the production of documents during discovery from the parties' own files is sufficient to justify a finding of authentication. . . . The court will make this final determination at trial unless Superhighway produces evidence that these e-mails and facsimiles either are not self-authenticating under Federal Rule of Evidence 902(7) or that they were not provided by Superhighway to Techwave during discovery.").

authenticity. Third, and perhaps most important, a broad interpretation serves to encourage, rather than discourage, e-commerce. Fourth, a judicial determination that evidence is facially authentic does not guarantee that the jury will accept it as such. Other evidence of authenticity will often be necessary to remove suspicions of fraud. Finally, courts may insist upon additional circumstantial evidence of authenticity if the nature of the writing is suspicious.

3.   Government Postings

Government agencies publish a broad range of materials on the Internet. Courts are struggling to decide if printouts from government Web sites are admissible under Fed. R. Evid. 902(5) as "books, pamphlets, or other publications purporting to be issued by public authority." One federal court has admitted Federal Trade Commission press releases[74] under this exception. A state court has excluded population statistics from state Web sites on the belief that "[a]n unauthenticated printout obtained from the Internet does not meet the public records exception to the hearsay rule . . . [n]or does it qualify as a self-authenticating document under [the state's equivalent of Fed. R. Evid. 902(5)]." The court reasoned that this was so because it was not certified by the officer having custody of the record being copied.[75] Another court excluded records of the Bureau of Motor

---

74. *See* Sannes v. Jeff Wyler Chevrolet, Inc., 1999 WL 33313134, at *3 n.3 (S.D. Ohio Mar. 31, 1999) (finding that the Federal Trade Commission's (FTC) press releases, printed from FTC's government Web site, were self-authenticating official publications under Rule 902(5) even though they were not attached to authenticating affidavit).

75. *See* State v. Davis, 10 P.3d 977, 1010 (Wash. 2000); *see also* Dumes v. State, 718 N.E.2d 1171, 1178 (Ind. Ct. App. 1999) ("At trial the state introduced into evidence Dumes' driving record. The BMV records were obtained via the Internet and certified by a paralegal employed by the prosecutor's office. . . . The Indiana Supreme Court has stated that public records cannot be placed into evidence merely upon a party's offering a copy and claiming it to be accurate copy of the original. . . . We realize that it is convenient for the prosecutor's office to obtain driving records via the Internet and certify the records internally, effectively bypassing the administrative process of the BMV. The prosecutor's office not only saves time, but also resources which would otherwise be spent on obtaining certified records from the BMV. However, convenience does not defeat the purposes served by the self-authentication requirements imposed by the Trial Rules, the Rules of Evidence, or Indiana statute.").

Vehicles taken from the Web by the prosecutor because the records had not been certified.[76]

4. Newspapers and Periodicals

While newspapers and periodicals have been considered self-authenticating for decades because the possibility of forgery was slight—in part because of unique headlines and distinctive typesetting—such indicators are missing when newspaper articles and periodical excerpts are taken from an online posting. This has prompted some courts to reject such evidence as not being properly authenticated without other circumstantial assurances of genuineness to compensate for what is lost in the new format.[77] Such evidence might be testimony from the individual who retrieved the publication from the Internet, documenting the site visited, the procedures followed to find and retrieve the evidence, and assurances that the content of the document has not been altered since its retrieval.[78]

5. Limits of Self-authentication

Self-authentication has its limits. Extrinsic evidence of authenticity may be dispensed with under Fed. R. Evid. 902, but it is only for the *preliminary judicial determination* of admissibility under Fed. R. Evid.104(a). As discussed, authenticity is an issue of conditional relevance. Consequently, evidence that falls within one of the 13 delineated categories under Rule 902 only ensures *admissibility* by satisfying the prima facie standard. This initial presumption of authenticity does not guarantee that the jury will agree. Where the opposing party has challenged the authenticity presumption, the proponent of such evidence should present additional evidence of authenticity to satisfy the preponderance standard that the jury will be instructed to use in evaluating the document.

Despite the presumption of authenticity, the burden of persuasion (the need to convince the jury) remains with the proponent of the evidence. Like presumptions under Article III of the Federal Rules of Evidence,[79]

---

76. Berry v. State v. 725 N.E.2d 939, 942-43 (Ind. 2000).

77. *See* cases cited under Rule 902(6), *supra*.

78. In United States v. Premera Blue Cross, 2006 WL 2841998, at *4 (W.D. Wash. Sept. 29, 2006), where the online version of a newspaper was rejected as self-authenticating, the court noted that the defense attorney had no personal knowledge regarding where the documents were found, and his assistant who obtained them was not called as a witness.

79. *See* Chapter Five, "Presumptions," *supra*.

self-authentication shifts to the opposing party only the burden of going forward with evidence on that issue. It does not shift the burden of persuasion, which remains with the proponent of the evidence. Consequently, getting evidence admitted, and therefore heard, is not the same as persuading the finder of fact. To the extent that courts construe the authentication provisions broadly, it is not advisable for litigants to rely solely on the doctrine of self-authentication because it only opens the door to admissibility.

C. Authenticating with Technology

At present, the use of technology to authenticate e-mail messages is limited to identification of the computer terminal from which the message was sent. Without a legislatively created evidentiary presumption,[80] proof of authorship of the e-mail by a particular individual must be established through the other means that have been discussed.

1. Data Trails

Many tools are becoming available to assist in identification and authentication. Tracking so-called "data trails" provides information on the source and time of a given electronic transmission or entry. Telephone caller ID is a familiar example of this technology. The origin of an e-mail message can also be identified by tracing a message back to the network account from which the transmission originated. This information is available through codes printed on the messages by the Internet service providers. Unlike caller identification, however, the account number on the message does not directly reveal the point of origin. The code must be translated by the ISP.

In both instances, however, the technology only identifies the instrument used (the telephone, account, or computer terminal). One may draw a logical inference that the owner or account holder used his own equipment at the time in question. That inference, however, may only be strong enough to satisfy the judge's prima facie screen in situations where others have access to that equipment.

This problem could be addressed adequately through a presumption shifting the burden of persuasion to the owner of the computer terminal to prove that he was not responsible for the communication. No such pre-

---

80. *Id.*

sumption exists under common law, the Federal Rules of Evidence, or other congressional enactments, and it is unclear whether judges have the power to create such a presumption.[81]

It will often be necessary to use technology in conjunction with other forms of authentication. With telephone caller identification, for example, the recipient of the call may recognize the sound of the caller's voice. The content of e-mails may possess unique characteristics that will help identify a particular individual. Low-tech authentication is always an excellent supplement.

2.   Electronic Signatures

An individual can make his mark in any way. Theoretically, making a mark with a pen in hand is the same as making a mark with a keyboard or a rubber stamp. If a person's mark is proven, and is found on a written instrument, the mark is circumstantial evidence that the individual signed the instrument.[82]

Individuals can digitally apply cursive signatures to a message using an electronic signature pad. These are currently used with credit card purchases in many retail establishments. The mark and its manner of placement, however, is not legally restricted. An individual's mark need not appear as a handwritten, cursive signature; an "X" suffices. Of course, it is necessary to prove that the particular individual placed the "X" on the instrument and intended it to serve as his mark. That same "X" could be placed on a computer screen.

Marks other than cursive signatures, however, present a number of problems. First, proponents must establish that the mark is employed as the personal signature of the individual in question. Second, that individual must have placed the mark on the instrument under consideration. This problem is amplified when the mark is such that it can be placed on instruments by other individuals, as in the case of an electronic image.

---

81. *Id.*

82. Haywood Securities, Inc. v. Ehrlich, 149 P.3d 738, 740 (Ariz. 2007) ("The court of appeals apparently assumed that 'signed' means only a manual signature. In fact, the ordinary understanding of 'signed' is not so limited. For example, under the statute of frauds, a document is valid 'if it is signed by the person to be charged by any of the known modes of impressing a name on paper, namely by writing, printing, lithographing, or other such mode, provided the same is done with the intention of signing.'").

Electronic instruments are often "signed" using codes that employ a set of characters common to all users. Typed passwords and PIN numbers are examples of these codes. Any user with knowledge of such a code can flawlessly replicate it.

The final link in authentication by signature is proving that the individual intended to use the mark as his signature at the time in question. Logical inferences will play a significant role in this process. If a mark belongs to an individual, for example, its presence on an instrument gives rise to a strong inference that he put it there if, like a cursive signature, it is difficult for others to forge. Conversely, a generic "X" would give rise to a weak inference, and would need to be accompanied by other evidence that the defendant used an "X" rather than a cursive signature.

If an actual signature appears on the computer message, this can be authenticated through the same methods that have been used for centuries—non-expert opinions by those familiar with the signature, expert witness comparison with exemplars, and jury comparisons with exemplars.[83]

A digitally applied cursive signature on a document gives rise to a strong inference of authenticity. A difference exists, however, between direct cursive signatures and digitally applied cursive signatures. Unlike a physically forged signature, once a signature pad has stored a signature, that signature can be reapplied to many other instruments by many other people who have access to the stored file. Electronic signatures can become little more than a signature stamp that can be used by unauthorized people. Therefore, an electronic signature may create a strong inference of authenticity, but not as strong as a direct cursive signature. The value of the inference will turn on whether evidence of fraud is presented at trial.

Signature stamps and electronic signature pads are signature devices. Users must be required to accept responsibility for a more heightened level of security when employing a signature device. If the device was misused, users should have to convince the jury of that fact. In light of the compelling nature of the logical inference of authorized use that would arise from the presence of an electronic signature on an instrument, per-

---

83. *See* Colson Corp. v. NLRB, 347 F.2d 128, 134 (8th Cir.1965), *cert. denied,* 382 U.S. 904, 86 (1965) (noting that signature may be authenticated by testimony of witness to execution thereof by its subscriber as well as by comparison of signature with known specimen of handwriting of person claimed to have subscribed it). These methods are delineated in FED. R. EVID. 901(b)(2) and (3).

haps a formal evidentiary presumption (which does not currently exist) will eventually be recognized, shifting the burden of persuasion to the party claiming that the mark is not authentic.[84]

A court could conclude that a mark placed on an instrument by a computer was the mark of the machine rather than the signature of the individual using the machine. This would be absurd. It would be equivalent to claiming that a signature is the mark of the pen, rather than the person using the pen. This position has been anticipated and rejected in model acts, like the Uniform Electronic Transactions Act (1999),[85] which have been adopted throughout the country. This act makes electronic marks the marks of the individual using the computer. The Uniform Computer Information Transaction Act (2000) (UTICA) uses similar language.[86]

---

84. *See* Chapter Five, "Presumptions," *supra.*

85. The Uniform Electronic Transactions Act provides in part:

Section 9. Attribution and Effect of Electronic Recording and Electronic Signature.

(a) An electronic record or electronic signature is attributable to a person if it was the act of the person. The act of the person may be shown in any manner, including a showing of the efficacy of any security procedure applied to determine the person to which the electronic record or electronic signature was attributable.

(b) The effect of an electronic record or electronic signature attributed to a person under subsection (a) is determined from the context and surrounding circumstances at the time of its creation, execution, or adoption, including the parties' agreement, if any, and otherwise as provided by law.

Section 11. Notarization and Acknowledgment.

If a law requires a signature or record to be notarized, acknowledged, verified, or made under oath, the requirement is satisfied if the electronic signature of the person authorized to perform those acts, together with all other information required to be included by other applicable law, is attached to or logically associated with the signature or record.

86. The Uniform Computer Information Transaction Act provides in part:

Section 212. Efficacy and Commercial Reasonableness of Attribution Procedure.

The efficacy, including the commercial reasonableness, of an attribution procedure is determined by the court. In making this determination, the following rules apply:

(1) An attribution procedure established by law is effective for transactions within the coverage of the statute or rule.

3. Public Key Infrastructure

Public Key Infrastructure (PKI) technology offers a means of ensuring the authenticity of an electronic document. It is more sophisticated, and presumably more reliable, than digitally applied signatures. Instead of merely requiring users to place their mark electronically, PKI technology provides each participant in a transaction with their own "key pair," consisting of a secret "private key" and a publicly available "public key." These keys are strings of alphanumeric characters that are linked to each other in such a way that they are complementary "toggle switches."

The use of Certification Authorities (CAs) in conjunction with PKI technology offers further assurances that a given electronic document is what its proponent claims.[87]

---

(2) Except as otherwise provided in paragraph (1), commercial reasonableness and effectiveness is determined in light of the purposes of the procedure and the commercial circumstances at the time the parties agreed to or adopted the procedure.

(3) An attribution procedure may use a security device or method that is commercially reasonable under the circumstances.

Section 213. Determining Attribution.

(a) An electronic authentication, display, message, record, or performance is attributed to a person if it was the act of the person or his electronic agent, or if the person is bound by it under agency or other law. The party relying on attribution of an electronic authentication, display, message, record, or performance to another person has the burden of establishing attribution.

(b) The act of a person may be shown in any manner, including a showing of the efficacy of an attribution procedure that was agreed to or adopted by the parties or established by law.

(c) The effect of an electronic act attributed to a person under subsection (a) is determined from the context at the time of its creation, execution, or adoption, including the parties' agreement, if any, or otherwise as provided by law.

(d) If an attribution procedure exists to detect errors or changes in an electronic authentication, display message, record, or performance, and was agreed to or adopted by the parties or established by law, and one party conformed to the procedure but the other party did not, and the nonconforming party would have detected the change or error had that party also conformed, the effect of noncompliance is determined by the agreement but, in the absence of agreement, the conforming party may avoid the effect of the error or change.

87. Walter A. Effross, *Notes on PKI and Digital Negotiability: Would the Cybercourier Carry Luggage?*, 38 JURIMETRICS J. 385, 395 (Spring 1998).

4. Biometric Authentication

Biometric authentication involves the use of an optical scanner or voice-recognition device to detect individual physical characteristics, like fingerprints, retinal blood-vessel patterns, or speech patterns. When used in conjunction with PKI technology, these techniques can help authenticate e-documents by demonstrating that access to a given PKI "private key" was restricted to a certain individual or group of individuals.

Biometric technology is not a panacea for electronic authentication problems. Although most biometric technology is quite effective at detecting fraudulent identifiers, like recordings of voices or reproduction of fingerprints, the output data of a biometric reader is vulnerable to capture as it is transmitted for verification. Once captured, biometric data can easily be used to "spoof" a source or point of origin.

V. AUTHENTICATION OF COMPUTER ANIMATIONS, MODELS, AND SIMULATIONS

A computer animation is usually authenticated by a testifying expert who has observed the animation and verifies that it accurately demonstrates a particular principle that the expert has concluded is involved in the case. For example, if an animation is designed to show the means of injury to a child allegedly hurt by violent shaking, an expert witness would have to testify that (1) he believes that the child victim in question was injured by violent shaking (this establishes the relevance of a subsequent demonstration), (2) the animation showing an adult's arms shaking a doll for eight seconds is an accurate depiction of the amount of force typically needed to cause the severe brain injuries diagnosed, and (3) the animation accurately reflects what could have occurred in the incident in question based on all the available evidence.[88] The trial judge would then have to give to the jury a cautionary instruction on the limited purpose for the demonstrations and the fact that it is not demonstrating how the defendant injured the victim in the case.[89]

---

88. Commonwealth v. Hardy, 2007 Pa. Super. 48, 918 A.2d 766 (2007); State v. Sayles, 662 N.W.2d 1 (Iowa 2003).

89. State v. Sayles, 662 N.W.2d 1 (Iowa 2003). These instructions can save an otherwise questionable animation. In re Air Crash Disaster, 86 F.3d 498 (6th Cir. 1996) (Demonstration could easily have been seen by the jury as reflecting what the airline assistants did in the case at hand (disengage a circuit breaker), but the jury was told what the limited purpose was, and what it should not be taken as doing—simulating what happened in the case.).

If the animation is established as accurately demonstrating a point, the court should ignore the technology employed in making the demonstration, because it is unnecessary to the admissibility of the evidence in light of the expert's assurances. The process is much like authenticating a photograph: If the sponsoring witness testifies that the photograph accurately depicts something, there is no need to establish the details of the camera, film speed, exposure readings, and qualifications of the operator. However, if the program employed to create an animation was designed for one type of accident and the accident in question was another type, the fact that the scientific community has not recognized it as a reliable program for predicting the movement of bodies in the immediate context requires its exclusion.[90]

When an animation is only offered for demonstrative purposes and not as substantive evidence, a number of courts have held that the standard for admitting scientific evidence (in most state courts it is still general acceptance in the relevant scientific community—the *Frye* test rejected in the Supreme Court's *Daubert* decision)[91] does not have to be complied with.[92] All that is necessary is that the witness be qualified to give the testimony being elicited from him, and he then provides assurances that the animation accurately portrays the facts as he understands them and the substance of the opinions he has offered.

If the animation is illustrating testimony about how a crime unfolded, the relevant facts critical to the animation must be established, and the sponsoring witness must verify that those facts are accurately reflected in the animation and that the animation accurately demonstrates the testimony he has given.[93] In *People v. Kelly,* measurements were made of the crime scene, facts were taken from the reports of the pathologist who performed the autopsy and the ballistics and gunshot residue expert, and these facts were incorporated into the computer animation. The court noted that simple animations could be authenticated as if they had been done by hand, rather than by a computer. Animations not created by computer

---

90. State v. Sipin, 106 P.3d 277 (Wash. Ct. App. 2005) (program was not accepted in the community for proving multiple occupant movement in a single-vehicle accident).

91. For a discussion of both the Frye and Daubert tests for screening scientific evidence, see Chapter 8, "Science and Technology," *infra.*

92. *See, e.g.,* Pierce v. State, 718 So. 2d 806 (Fla. Ct. App. 1997); People v. McHugh, 124 Misc. 2d 559, 476 N.Y.S.2d 721, 722 (Sup. Ct. 1984).

93. People v. Kelly, 17 Cal. 3d 24, 130 Cal. Rptr. 144, 549 P.2d 1240 (1976).

programs would not have to establish that the underlying animation program was generally accepted as accurate and reliable in the relevant scientific community and was operated correctly by a qualified person.[94]

As in any demonstration, the closer the animation gets to illustrating how the event in question occurred, the more the proponent must be concerned with duplicating all operative circumstances.[95] In *Commonwealth v. Serge,* an animation of how the prosecution theorized the murder was committed was properly authenticated by witnesses testifying to the physical evidence and measurements at the crime scene and the animator testifying that the forensic evidence was faithfully reproduced and that the program produced an accurate graphic presentation of the expert's opinion. If the animation contains erroneous facts, its product, of course, may be rejected.[96]

To the extent that the animation alters, or is in variance with, any of the facts involved in the case, the trial judge will have to assess how each variance affects the probative value of the evidence and whether it creates unfair prejudice under Federal Rules of Evidence 403 that substantially outweighs its probative value. Such variances can be adding too much information in the animation with no factual support in the record.[97] In making this determination, the judge usually should view the animation outside the presence of the jury.[98]

VI. AUTHENTICATION OF AUTHENTICATING TECHNOLOGY

As previously discussed, evidence often must be authenticated on several levels. Science and technology add another level. If, for example, a technology (telephone caller ID, for example) was used in authenticating other

---

94. People v. McHugh, 124 Misc. 2d 559, 476 N.Y.S.2d 721 (Sup. Ct. 1984).

95. Commonwealth v. Serge, 586 Pa. 671, 896 A.2d 1170 (2006), *cert. denied,* 127 S. Ct. 275, 166 L. Ed. 2d 211 (2006).

96. Smith v. Kansas City Southern Ry. Co., 846 So. 2d 980 (La. Ct. App. 2003) (The animation attempted to produce what the motorist allegedly saw as she approached the railroad crossing, but did so with inaccurate facts.).

97. *See* State v. Stewart, 643 N.W.2d 281 (Minn. 2002) (An animation included facial expressions of the victim when he was shot, which was not important to the autopsy findings. Consequently, the animation was unfairly prejudicial, but the error was found to be harmless.).

98. Hinkle v. City of Clarksburg, 81 F.3d 416 (4th Cir. 1996).

evidence, the proponent of the technology also must authenticate the technology itself. The proponent must show that the technology does what he claims it has done, and does so accurately. Computer systems are usually authenticated through the testimony of someone who has used them. Such a witness typically describes the process or system and the results it produces, and attests to the accuracy of those results.

To simplify the process through which systems and processes are authenticated, Fed. R. Evid. 901(9) requires nothing more than evidence describing the system or process and verifying the accuracy of its product.

Article IX. Authentication and Identification
Rule 901. Requirement of Authentication or Identification

(b) Illustrations. By way of illustration only, and not by way of limitation, the following are examples of authentication or identification conforming with the requirements of this rule:

. . . .

(9) Process or system. Evidence describing a process or system used to produce a result and showing that the process or system produces an accurate result.

This method of authentication was designed to accommodate authentication of computer systems used by a business to store its data and produce its reports and records upon which the enterprise relied. Similarly, this method may be used to authenticate the computer program through which information was retrieved from other systems. In *United States v. Whitaker*,[99] for example, the government had retrieved financial information from the defendant's computer records. The court held that the testimony of the FBI agent who installed the program and was present during its use was sufficient authentication:

> The government laid the foundation for the computer records and provided their authentication through the testimony of [an] FBI special agent . . . . [He] testified that the records were retrieved from Frost's computer, which was seized during the execution of a federal search warrant of Frost's home. . . . The records were retrieved from the computer using the Microsoft Money program. [The agent] was present when that program was installed on the

---

99. 127 F.3d 595, 601 (7th Cir. 1997).

computer and when the records were retrieved. [He] testified concerning his personal knowledge and his personal participation in obtaining the printouts. . . . [H]is testimony was sufficient to establish the authenticity of the computer records of the drug business . . . .

This method encompasses the technical details of systems that are within the exclusive control of an enterprise. Fed. R. Evid. 901(b)(9) is, however, broad enough to authenticate technologies that are not within the exclusive control of an enterprise. For example, the technologies underlying e-mail service provided by an Internet service provider could be authenticated through the testimony of someone with knowledge of and experience with the system.[100]

E-mail service has become as common as telephone service. Its reliability is well established. Consequently, courts would be justified in taking judicial notice of the reliability of the sciences and technologies underlying e-mail services.[101]

VII. OTHER ISSUES RELATING TO AUTHENTICATION OF E-EVIDENCE

A. *Chain of Custody*

Authentication of evidence occasionally requires verification that the evidence has not been altered from the time it became relevant to the time of the trial in which it is being used.[102] This requires the establishment of a chain of custody. Each sequential custodian of the evidence must establish that he has not altered the evidence and has protected it from alteration by others. Although a chain of custody requirement may not generally be imposed for admissibility of computer-generated documents, proponents can establish chain of custody by demonstrating established com-

---

100. FED. R. EVID. 901(b)(9) has been used to authenticate a broad variety of technologies—*e.g.*, the technology used to produce Internal Revenue Service tax records. *See, e.g.*, In re Clark, 138 B.R. 579, 581 (1991).

101. For a complete discussion of the concept of judicial notice, *see* Chapter Nine, "Judicial Notice," *infra*.

102. When authenticating a digital photograph, however, establishing a chain of custody for both the digital card used in the camera and the images that were downloaded to a computer may be critical to establishing that the images were not altered from the time they initially were recorded with the camera. *See* § III, Authenticating Digital Photographs, *supra*.

pany policies regarding electronic storage and restricted access, the use of devices that limit access through passwords and encoding, and entry logs indicating when and by whom documents have been accessed or changed.

The chain of custody requirement is imposed most frequently in criminal cases where latent evidence, like fingerprints, blood samples, and narcotics residue, is retrieved from tangible evidence. Chain of custody questions could arise, of course, when forensic officers make copies of the hard drives of a defendant's computers and make hard copies of documents on the duplicate hard drives.[103] Without specific evidence of alteration or deletions, courts will be inclined to conclude that the materials have been sufficiently authenticated and leave questions about alterations to the jury when it decides what weight to give the evidence. Without specific evidence of alteration, for example, the testimony of the officer who seized items, tagged them, placed them in storage for safekeeping, and retrieved them for trial will be sufficient to get the communications admitted into evidence at trial.

The chain of custody requirement, of course, is not limited to criminal cases. In tort actions where an instrumentality like a bicycle, appliance, or brake system on an automobile is alleged to have been negligently maintained, the party offering expert testimony about the instrumentality's condition must prove that the condition was unchanged from the time the cause of action arose to the time when the expert examined and tested it. If a witness cannot testify to this fact from personal observation, a chain of custody may need to be established circumstantially so the court can be assured that the evidence has not been altered.

Contrary to popular belief, a chain of custody does not require the proponent to establish an airtight guarantee against all possibilities of alteration. The level of assurance that the proponent will be required to provide will vary according to the nature of the item, the item's importance to the litigation, and the probabilities of alteration.[104] For example,

---

103. *See, e.g.,* Kupper v. State, 2004 WL 60768, at *2-3 (Ct. App. Tex. Jan. 14, 2004) (unpublished).

104. The authentication of tape recordings is, in many respects, much like that applicable to other forms of electronic evidence. For example, in United States v. Eberhart, 467 F.3d 659, 667 (7th Cir. Nov. 1, 2006), the court was addressing the authentication of a tape recording, the content of which had only been partially heard by the sponsoring witness. "Though Agent Foley did not listen to Eberhart's half of the conversations as they occurred, his testimony sufficiently established the tapes' authenticity by clear and convincing evidence. Just as a court may admit a

in *United States v. Whitaker,*[105] financial information was seized from the defendant's computer during a search. Although the government could not prove, through a chain of custody, that agents did not manipulate information on either the computer or the seized disks, this was not fatal to the admissibility of the computer-generated evidence. The judge would not base his admissibility decision on nothing more than "wild-eyed speculation" about alteration for which there was no evidence.

In contrast, if the disputed evidence is a small amount of white powder seized from a defendant and taken to the laboratory for testing, the officer who seized it must identify the package bearing his mark that contains the white powder. The proponent would also have to call the other individuals who had control of the evidence after its seizure because the contents of the identified container can be so easily altered, and the officer would be unable to detect this from his visual observations. Each would be required to testify that he had not tampered with the contents and had maintained the evidence in a manner that protected against tampering by others while it was in their possession. If, as is true in most civil litigation, both sides offer expert testimony based on tests each side has conducted on an instrumentality, each will have to establish that he did not alter it from the time he took control of it.

---

tape recording despite a gap in the chain of custody, . . . a court may admit a recording where a witness testifies that he only heard half of the recorded conversation. What the witness did not hear goes to the evidentiary weight of the recording, not to its admissibility." The court also noted that "'[m]erely raising the possibility (however hypothetical) of tampering is not sufficient to render evidence inadmissible.'" Even if the recording being offered into evidence "is not of the best quality and does have gaps and unintelligible portions," the recording may be "sufficiently trustworthy for submission to the jury." United States v. Robinson, 763 F.2d 778, 781 (6th Cir. 1985).

105. 127 F.3d 595, 602 (7th Cir. 1997). *See* United States v. Howard-Arias, 679 F.2d 363 (4th Cir. 1982), where the items being offered into evidence were bales of marijuana thrown overboard when the Coast Guard stopped a suspicious vessel. The government was not required to establish a complete chain of custody (*e.g.*, from the individuals who retrieved the bales from the water to the individuals who transported them from the Coast Guard boat to a truck waiting at the dock, to the driver of the truck who transported them to a warehouse, to the individuals who maintained them at the warehouse, to those who retrieved them from the warehouse for ultimate transport to the courtroom). An identifying tag placed on the bales by one of the officers who collected them from the water, his in-court identification of his mark on the tag attached to a bale, and the testimony of the individuals who secured them at the warehouse were sufficient to ensure the admissibility of the evidence.

Computer-generated and -stored communications often can be altered as easily as a plastic bag containing white powder, and also with little possibility of detection. Consequently, some judges might be far more strict than the judge in *Whitaker*[106] and will require that a chain of custody be established for stored and seized communications. Consistent with *Whitaker*, this likely will be limited to situations where there is reason to believe that data has been altered because of the difficulty for the proponent in proving a negative. When found to be necessary, the proponent will be required to provide adequate assurance that a particular communication stored on the computer system has remained unaltered. This can be accomplished through a paper trail—printouts both before and after the access was given. Care must be taken, by both the courts and the proponent of such evidence, because the potential for fabrication remains.

Assurance can also be obtained through (1) proof of established company policies about storage and restricted access, (2) the use of technological devices that limit access, or (3) use passwords and encoding, and entry logs that indicate when and by whom a document has been accessed and whether it has been changed.

While skilled hackers can thwart all of these precautions, the proponent is only required to demonstrate to the judge by a prima facie standard, and then to the jury by a preponderance of the evidence, that the proffered evidence is what he claims it is and, therefore, that it is logically relevant. Like relevance guaranteed through a chain of custody, airtight assurances are seldom necessary. Both parties usually can testify to the content of a communication and any changes made because they were involved in the communication's creation. This alone means that electronically created, computer-stored instruments might not be akin to any of the types of evidence for which a chain of custody has been required. Moreover, unlike the common law situations where the chain was very important, the proponent of a computer-generated document is not retrieving or creating additional evidence from the content of the evidence being presented (like fingerprint, DNA, or ballistics evidence). Consequently, it is unclear that such assurances against possibilities of tampering are even appropriate when only admissibility is being decided by the presiding judge. The presence or absence of such assurances generally should be factors that go only to the question of weight, and not to the admissibility of the evidence.

---

106. 127 F.3d 595, 602 (7th Cir. 1997).

B. Expanded Pretrial Discovery May Justify a Lesser Foundation

Pretrial discovery increasingly focuses on the computer hard drives and backup tapes of adversaries because they often contain documents and information not available from other sources due to their accidental or intentional destruction.[107] As it becomes common for courts to require parties to make hard drives available in some form to the opposing side, significant evidence will be made available to adversaries to prove alteration.[108] With shadows of various iterations of documents available to the

---

107. Spoliation is often the concern giving rise to requests for such discovery. *See, e.g.*, Crown Life Ins. Co. v. Craig, 995 F.2d 1376, 1382-83 (7th Cir. 1993); Wachtel v. Guardian Life Ins. Co., 2006 WL 1320031 (D. N.J. May 12, 2006); E*Trade Securities LLC v. Deutsche Bank AG, 230 F.R.D. 582 (D. Minn. 2005); Zubulake v. UBS Warburg, 220 F.R.D. 212, 218 (S.D. N.Y. 2003); Wiginton v. Ellis, 2003 WL 22439865 (N.D. Ill. Oct. 27, 2003); Zubulake v. UBS Warburg LLC, 217 F.R.D. 309, 318 (S.D. N.Y. 2003); Playboy Enters., Inc. v. Welles, 60 F. Supp. 2d 1050 (S.D. Cal. 1999); United States v. Koch Indus., Inc., 197 F.R.D. 463, 486 (N.D. Okla. 1998); Synanon Church v. United States, 579 F. Supp. 967 (D. D.C. 1984); Taylor v. State, 93 S.W.3d 487, 502-03 (Tex. Crim. App. 2002); and Covucci v. Keane Consulting Group, Inc., 2006 Mass. Super. LEXIS 313, *23-24 (Mass. Super. May 31, 2006). *See generally* Chapter One, "Discovery of Electronic Evidence," and Chapter Two, "Spoliation," *supra.*

108. Most courts have refused to compel litigants to make their hard drives available to adversaries in the absence of proof that relevant evidence has been deleted from active directories. *See, e.g.*, Williams v. Mass. Mut. Life Ins. Co., 226 F.R.D. 144, 146 (D. Mass. 2005) ("Before permitting such an intrusion into an opposing party's information system—particularly where, as here, that party has undertaken its own search and forensic analysis and has sworn to its accuracy—the inquiring party must present at least some reliable information that the opposing party's representations are misleading or substantively inaccurate.") (citations omitted); Scotts Co. v. Liberty Mutual Ins. Co., No. 2:06-CV-899, 2007 U.S. Dist. LEXIS 43005 (S.D. Ohio, June 12, 2007) (court refused to allow extensive forensic search of defendant's sources of ESI based on "mere suspicion" that information was withheld, stating, "Plaintiff is no more entitled to access to defendant's electronic information storage systems than to defendant's warehouses storing paper documents."). *See generally* Chapter One, "Discovery of Electronic Evidence," *supra.* Such a disclosure is usually limited to situations where the requesting party "could present evidence to demonstrate the likelihood of retrieving purged information, and if the trial court finds that there is no other less intrusive manner to obtain the information, then the computer search might be appropriate. In such an event, the order must define parameters of time and scope, and must place sufficient access restrictions to prevent compromising patient confidentiality and to prevent the harm to defendant's computer and data bases." Strasser v. Yalamanchi, 669

opponent, courts may have a greater expectation that *opponents* will raise and prove particularized claims of tampering, alteration, or deletion rather than requiring the proponent to establish the negative. This would be similar to what has been done with documents under the best evidence rule.

C.   Admissibility and Weight: Two Bites at the Same Apple

As has been mentioned a number of times throughout this chapter, it is important to remember that all of the methods of authentication discussed are used only to satisfy a prima facie standard for admissibility. On cross-examination of the sponsoring witness, it may be established that the evidence being authenticated was assumed to be accurate without independent verification. If this occurs, the judge may either exclude the evidence or allow it to be heard by the jury. If the evidence is admitted, the lack of any independent verification of reliability will be considered by the jury when determining the weight of the evidence.

Admissibility is only the first bite at the apple. The same arguments that did not convince the presiding judge to exclude the evidence can be presented to jurors to convince them to ignore it.

D.   A Reality Check

Authentication is rarely litigated. Forgery cases or instances were alteration is suspected are exceptions to this rule. Procedural tools, like requests for admission under Fed. R. Civ. P. 36, which can result in the cost of authentication being shifted to the party that refuses to admit authenticity, and judicial dislike for time-consuming authenticity battles create strong pressure to resolve authenticity issues through stipulations. How this practice will translate to digital information that can be altered so easily, and information from the Internet that can be laden with garbage, is hard to predict.

So. 2d 1142, 1145 (Fla. Ct. App. 1996). Courts have rejected undirected and undefined "fishing expeditions" into an adversary's hard drives. The potential benefits are slight, and there are clear risks posed to the confidentiality of communications. There is also the risk that files will be corrupted, infected with viruses, or deleted.

Hearsay

I. The Basics 403

   A. Two Truths of Hearsay 404

II. Hearsay Admissible Through Exceptions 409

   A. Multiple Levels of Hearsay 410

   B. Writings Are Like Another Person Speaking, Repeating the Out-of-Court Declarations of the Author 412

III. Why Is It Relevant? 414

IV. Mechanically Produced Statements Are Not Hearsay 415

V. Evidence from the Internet 417

   A. Nonhearsay from the Internet 417

   B. Hearsay from the Internet 421

   C. Admissible Hearsay under Applicable Exceptions 422

VI. A Reality Check on Hearsay 430

   A. The Internet as Part of Business or Government Records 430

B. Web Pages Are Not Business Records of the Internet Service Provider (ISP) 433

C. Government Records and Reports 433

VII. Constitutional Dimensions of Hearsay 435

A. The Accused's Right of Confrontation 436

1. Two-Prong *Ohio v. Roberts* Test 438

2. The "Testimonial" Standard of *Crawford v. Washington* 439

3. Why "Testimonial"? 441

4. Does the "Testimonial" Label Give an Absolute Right? 443

B. Due Process 446

1. Due Process Before *Crawford* 446

a. Excluding hearsay offered by an accused 446

b. Excluding hearsay offered by the government 447

2. Due Process After *Crawford* 448

C. Constitutional Wild Card 449

E-evidence Overview: The application of the hearsay rule to electronic evidence does not differ from its application to all other forms of evidence. Whether evidence is hearsay or not turns on why it is relevant. If it is relevant because of the truth of the content of a message rather than its mere existence, it is hearsay.

The application of the hearsay concept is complicated by the fact that some evidence can involve multiple levels of hearsay. Again, the rules about the application of the hearsay concept to multiple levels of hearsay are not different for e-evidence, but are made more difficult to apply because of the new context. This chapter is offered as a refresher to former students of evidence law. It will take this familiar evidence rule and its many exceptions and apply them to e-evidence.

I.   THE BASICS

Hearsay is an out-of-court statement offered in court to prove the truth of the matter asserted by the out-of-court declarant. It is offered into evidence through the testimony of a witness to that statement or through a written account by the declarant. The hearsay rule excludes such evidence because the potential dangers of perception, memory, sincerity, and ambiguity in the original statement cannot be tested through oath and cross-examination. Hearsay is unreliable because it is tied to the untested credibility of a witness, the declarant, who was not before the finder of facts, under oath, and subject to cross-examination when the statement was made.[1]

---

1. Although hearsay is excluded from evidence unless it falls within a recognized exception to the hearsay rule, a major exception to the rule of exclusion arises when a judge rules on evidentiary matters under FED. R EVID. 104(a). When ruling on the admissibility of evidence in that context, a judge is not bound by the rules of evidence. When ruling on a summary judgment motion, unlike a Rule 104(a) ruling, the judge remains bound by the evidence rules. Under FED. R. CIV. P. 56(e), the presiding judge can only consider admissible evidence in an affidavit that is based on the affiant's personal knowledge. *See, e.g.,* Sea-Land Serv., Inc. v. Atlantic Pac. Int'l, Inc., 61 F. Supp. 2d 1102, 1110 (D. Haw. 1999) ("The information regarding Matson was apparently taken from Matson's Web site. Although incorporated into API's counsel's affidavit, counsel does not purport to have any personal knowledge of the underlying facts. Moreover, this evidence would be inadmissible as hearsay.").

A.   Two Truths of Hearsay

There are always two truths with every hearsay statement. The first is the truth that the out-of-court declarant *uttered* certain words. The second is the truth of the substance of the information provided by those words. Testimony is hearsay only if its relevance turns on the finder of facts believing that what the declarant said was true—the second truth. Both truths give rise to perception, memory, sincerity, and ambiguity concerns, but the first truth—that certain words were uttered—can be tested because the witness who heard them is on the witness stand, under oath, and subject to cross-examination. It is the second truth—whether the content of the out-of-court statement was true—that creates hearsay because the substance of the story told by the out-of-court declarant cannot be tested, as he or she was not on the witness stand before the jury.

As an illustration, assume Defendant orders commodity X on the Internet. Witness #1 hears D acknowledge that he placed the order and subsequently states to Witness #2: "D said he ordered commodity X from Company's Web site yesterday." When D does not pay and the matter goes to trial, Witness #2 is asked to testify to what Witness #1 said Defendant admitted. In this hypothetical, there are two out-of-court declarants, Witness #1 and D. This is illustrated in Diagram 1.

Diagram 1

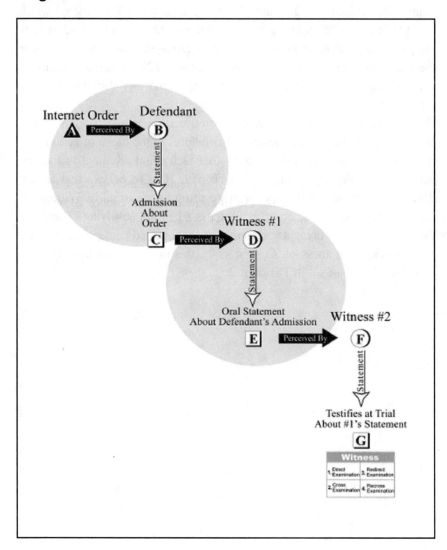

The hearsay analysis begins where the testimony of Witness #2 is being given (G on the Diagram). To prove that Witness #1 uttered words (E), you must go through the mind of Witness #2 (F). Witness #2 is testifying in court, under oath, and subject to cross-examination; this link in the Diagram does not involve hearsay. Witness #2's perception, memory, and sincerity can be tested in the presence of the jury through cross-examination.

The mere fact that Witness #1 uttered certain words (E) is not why Witness #2's testimony is relevant.[2] It is helpful to the cause of action only if we believe what Witness #1 said—that Defendant admitted that he ordered Item X on Best Company's Web page (C). To believe that Defendant uttered those words, you must go through the mind of Witness #1 (D). Unlike Witness #2, however, Witness #1 is not testifying. Therefore, the finder of facts is being asked to rely on the untested perception, memory, and sincerity of Witness #1. Consequently, this link creates a hearsay problem. This is illustrated in Diagram 2.

---

2. The utterance of a statement is often relevant where the testimony of the witness is being offered to establish, for example, that a warning was given or that someone had been put on notice of a condition. In those instances, all the jury is being asked to believe is that the words were uttered and not the accuracy of what those words describe.

Diagram 2

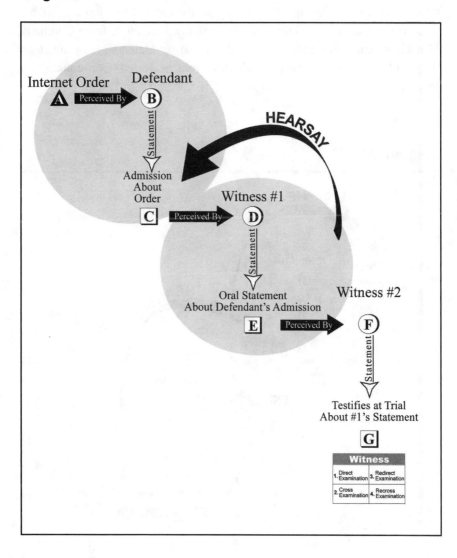

The mere fact that Defendant uttered words (C) is not why Witness #2's testimony is relevant. It is helpful to the cause of action only if we believe what Defendant said—that he actually ordered X from Company (A). Here again, to believe the act described by Defendant, we must go through Defendant's mind (B), which cannot be tested. Consequently, a second level of hearsay is created. This is illustrated in Diagram 3.

Diagram 3

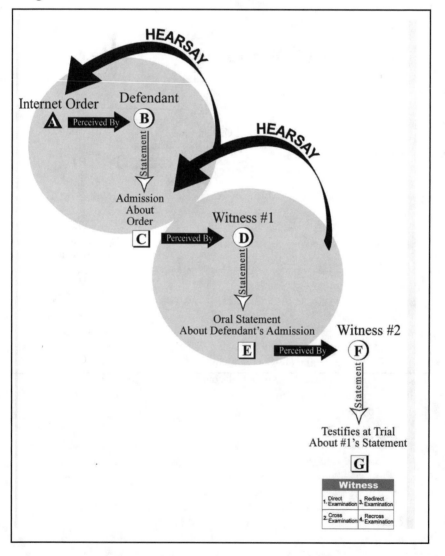

II.   HEARSAY ADMISSIBLE THROUGH EXCEPTIONS

As a general rule, hearsay exceptions are premised on the perceived reliability of statements made in particular circumstances. These range from dying declarations to excited utterances to business records. In Fed. R. Evid. 803, 804, and 807, 30 classes of exceptions are recognized. These exceptions for the most part codify the common law.

There is one major exception to the reliability basis for most exceptions to the hearsay rule: the admissions exception, which is, instead, premised on the adversarial nature of our justice system. When you make a statement and it is later used against you, you cannot object to its admissibility on the ground that it is untrustworthy. The statement is admissible against you, and you have the burden of explaining to the finder of facts why it should not be relied upon. This difference in theory underlying the admissions exception prompted the drafters of the Fed. R. Evid. 801(d)(2) to exclude admissions from the definition of hearsay rather than admit them under an admissions exception to the hearsay rule.[3]

A new exception in Fed. R. Evid. 804(b)(6), forfeiture by wrongdoing, is another example of an exception not premised on reliability. This exception makes all prior statements of a witness admissible if he has intentionally been made unavailable by the party against whom those statements are offered. This exception is a penalty premised on culpability, which may be applicable regardless of the inherent reliability of the missing witness's previous statements. This difference in treatment, however, has no substantive consequence. Under either the common law approach or the Federal Rules of Evidence approach, the statement is admissible for the truth of the matter asserted.

---

3. This distinction is unfortunate for two reasons. First, it is inconsistent with the definition of hearsay and therefore confusing. While admissions look like ducks and quack like ducks because they are out-of-court statements being offered to prove the truth of the matters they assert, they have been eliminated from the definition of a duck. Second, the Advisory Committee has used the classification inconsistently. There are other hearsay exceptions that, like admissions, are not premised on the inherent reliability of the statements at issue, but are still classified as hearsay that is admissible under an exception.

Ancient documents are one example. Documents that have been in existence for over 20 years are admitted because memories probably have faded, and other evidence of their contents probably does not exist. This exception is premised on necessity, not reliability, and it is still recognized in FED. R. EVID. 803(16).

A. Multiple Levels of Hearsay

Whether under the common law or the Federal Rules of Evidence, each hearsay link that is identified must comply with the elements of an established hearsay exception. Testimony that is relevant only through multiple levels of hearsay, like the hypothetical above, is admissible only if hearsay exceptions can be found to form a complete chain of links from the facts being proven (Diagram at A) to the point in the witness's testimony where hearsay begins (Diagram at E). An exception must apply to each instance of hearsay. If any link in the chain is broken, the testimony of Witness #2 is inadmissible hearsay.

In the above hypothetical, the top hearsay link would be admissible under the admissions exception to the hearsay rule (shown by the downward arrow from A to C in Diagram 4, below). As previously noted, there is *technically* no hearsay problem at this link under the Federal Rules of Evidence, because Rule 801 (d)(2) no longer defines admissions as hearsay. For the second hearsay link (from C to E), there is no apparent hearsay exception. Consequently, the hearsay chain from A to E is broken, and Witness #2's testimony is rendered inadmissible hearsay. Diagram #4 illustrates:

Diagram 4

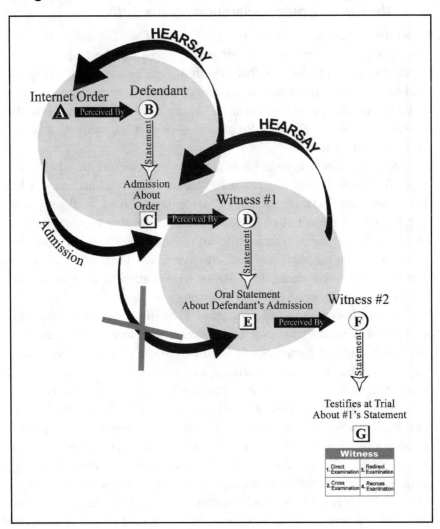

B. *Writings Are Like Another Person Speaking, Repeating the Out-of-Court Declarations of the Author*

A written statement offered to prove the truth of what it says is hearsay. The writing functions like another person repeating the author's statement. The only difference is that the writing itself has perfect perception and memory, and there are no sincerity problems regarding what was written. But, like an oral statement, a writing can be hearsay, because the out-of-court declarant's—i.e., the writer's—perception, memory, and sincerity cannot be tested.

When a writing is authenticated, the proponent must identify the author. The writing, however, can only recount (with total accuracy) what the out-of-court declarant, the author, wrote down. Like a third party who overhears what the out-of-court declarant said, a writing provides no way to confront and cross-examine the individual upon whose knowledge and recollection the statement's accuracy depends. There is no assurance that the out-of-court declarant spoke or wrote sincerely, because he was not under oath when he created the writing.

As an illustration, assume the same facts illustrated in Diagram #1, except that Witness #1 writes a letter to Witness #2 in which he states that "D said he ordered commodity X from a Web site on the Internet yesterday." If Witness #1's letter is offered into evidence to prove the truth of what Witness #1 wrote, instead of offering Witness #2's testimony (testifying either to what Witness #1 spoke or wrote in the letter), the hearsay problem with Witness #1 would remain the same. In both instances, the reliability of what Witness #1 claims to have heard and remembered cannot be tested. The fact that Witness #1 reduced the statement to writing eliminates the perception, memory, and sincerity problems caused when Witness #2 repeated Witness #1's statement in the first illustration. Once the writing is authenticated as Witness #1's written statement, it poses no sincerity problems and enjoys perfect perception and memory. Diagram #5 illustrates this point. As in the first hypothetical, the letter will not be admissible because of an unresolved hearsay problem.

Diagram 5

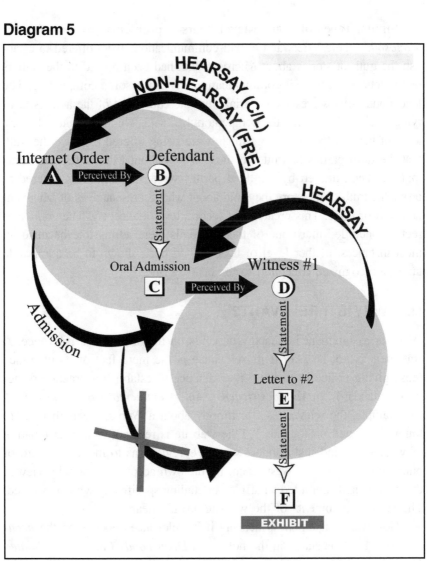

Similar types of double-level hearsay problems arose in *State v. Microsoft*,[4] where letters and e-mail communications were offered to establish the truth of stories about Microsoft that had been related to the authors of the letters and e-mail communications by Microsoft's competitors. The letters and e-mails presented at trial were the equivalent of the authors testifying in absentia to what the competitors had said. This constituted the first level of hearsay, because the e-mails were being offered to prove the truth that the third parties had uttered those words about Microsoft. The words that had been uttered by the third parties were, in turn, being offered to prove the truth of the story they told about what representatives of Microsoft had said or done. This created the second level of hearsay. The court correctly concluded that none of these e-mails were admissible because, in most instances, neither level of hearsay had been shown to be admissible under a recognized exception to the hearsay rule.[5]

III.   WHY IS IT RELEVANT?

Whether a statement is hearsay depends on the statement's relevance. A statement is not hearsay if its relevance is the mere fact of its utterance (e.g., giving notice or proving its existence to establish a practice or accepted standard). In *Van Westrienen v. Americontinental Collection Corp.*,[6] for example, the relevance of testimony about a Web site was that something was stated on the site. "[T]he website is relevant to a determination of whether defendants' conduct was so egregious as to merit an award of punitive damages. . . . Westrienen, by his own account, personally viewed the website and submitted an affidavit detailing specifically what he viewed. Therefore, the contents of the website are not hearsay."

However a statement *is* hearsay if its relevance depends on the *accuracy* of what was stated in the notice. In *Dean Foods Co. v. Consolidated Freightways*,[7] for example, an administrative assistant took the cost of a laser coding machine off the Internet, but the court would not admit her affidavit into evidence because it was reporting on hearsay. The truth of the cost appearing on the screen depended on the credibility of someone other than the testifying witness.[8]

---

4. 2002 WL 649951 (D. D.C. April 12, 2002).
5. *Id.* at *3.
6. 94 F. Supp. 2d 1087, 1109 (D. Ore. 2000).
7. 29 F. Supp. 2d 495, 496 (N.D. Ill. 1998).
8. *Id.* at 496.

Evidence obtained from e-mail messages will be written.[9] As previously discussed, this does not answer the question of whether the evidence's use will create a hearsay problem. If the e-mail message is relevant because of the truth of what the author observed and recorded, then use of the evidence will create a hearsay problem. If, however, the evidence is relevant simply because the statement was uttered, no hearsay problem arises. Examples of this are a warning that gave notice, or that contained legally operative language (such as an offer or acceptance that was an element of a legal contract). In the latter instances, the proponent must prove only that the statement was made, the first truth of hearsay, and that the witness testifying about the statement has personal knowledge of the statement's utterance.

IV. MECHANICALLY PRODUCED STATEMENTS ARE NOT HEARSAY

The problems of hearsay (perception, memory, sincerity, and ambiguity) arise only when there is direct human influence over the recorded statement's existence. When statements are produced mechanically, through any type of recording device or computerized data translation and manipulation, admissibility turns on the proper authentication of the technology and on the logic of the computer program that directed the work of the computing device.

Hearsay is an exclusionary rule premised not only on the untested perception, memory, and sincerity of the out-of-court declarant, but also any ambiguity that his statement may contain. But there are no sincerity problems when statements are recorded mechanically. Perception and memory concerns are addressed if the proponent of the statement: (1) demonstrates that the recording device makes accurate recordings; (2) establishes that the device functioned correctly at the time the evidence was created; and (3) (if an individual was involved in the operation of the device) shows that the person was properly trained and correctly used the device at the time the evidence was recorded. For this reason, Fed. R. Evid. 801(a) excludes communications by machines from the hearsay rule.[10] Hearsay statements are

_____

9. Subject, of course, to attachments that can transmit images and sounds.

10. Iowa v. Reynolds, 730 N.W. 2d 210, 2007 WL 601185, at *3 (Iowa Ct. App. Feb. 28, 2007) ("It is questionable whether the computerized recording Harmon heard could be considered hearsay because it was not made by a human declarant."); Ly v. State, 908 S.W.2d 598, 600 (Tex. App. 1995) (Applying a rule patterned after FED. R. EVID. 801, the

limited to words or conduct "of a person." The definition of "declarant" in Fed. R. Evid. 801(b) is also limited to "a person."

While the definition of "hearsay" is the same as it was under the common law, the definition of the term "statement" in Rule 801(a) has changed.

Article VIII. Hearsay
Rule 801. Definitions

The following definitions apply under this article:

(a) Statement. A "statement" is (1) an oral or written assertion or (2) nonverbal conduct of a person, if it is intended by the person as an assertion.

[United States v. Brock, 667 F.2d 1311, 1315 n.2 (9th Cir. 1982) ("Such testimony concerned 'nonverbal conduct' and, consequently, is a 'statement' within the hearsay rules only 'if it (was) intended by him as an assertion.'"); Florida Conf. Assoc. of Seventh-Day Adventists v. Kyriakides, 151 F. Supp. 2d 1223, 1225-26 (C.D. Cal. 2001) ("Only nonverbal conduct which is intended as an assertion is hearsay.")]

(b) Declarant. A "declarant" is a person who makes a statement.

(c) Hearsay. "Hearsay" is a statement, other than one made by the declarant while testifying at the trial or hearing, offered in evidence to prove the truth of the matter asserted.

[McNeal-Tunstall v. Marsh USA, 307 F. Supp. 2d 955, 970 (W.D. Tenn. 2004) (e-mails complaining about plaintiff's performance were hearsay to prove dissatisfaction with performance); Rombom v. Weberman, 2002 WL 1461890, at *7 (N.Y. Sup. June 13, 2002) (under comparable New York definition of hearsay, e-mails introduced to establish effect upon plaintiff, as opposed to truth of

---

court concluded: "A computer self-generated printout that does not represent the output of statements placed into the computer by out of court declarants is not hearsay. . . . [T]he electronic recording device was activated automatically; it was not the result of the observations or reproduction of statements entered into the device by a declarant. . . . Because there is no reliance upon human input, the determination that such computer self-generated data is not hearsay is in accord with Rule 801.").

content, did not constitute hearsay); State v. Simmons, 2002 WL 31370463, at *8 (Tenn. Crim. App. Oct. 21, 2002) (under comparable Tennessee definition of hearsay, list of checks taken from computer hard drive listing dates, amounts, and payees hearsay because offered to prove truth of matter asserted).]

Under subsection (a), a "person" must produce the "oral or written assertion" or the "nonverbal conduct." Under subsection (c), hearsay is defined as a "statement" made by "the declarant" who, in subsection (b), is limited to "a person" who makes a statement.[11]

Although mechanical devices, such as computers, can record hearsay statements from other sources, such as business records and third-party statements, such devices do not create an additional hearsay link.

V.   EVIDENCE FROM THE INTERNET

Authenticated evidence taken from the Internet[12] does not create hearsay problems when its relevance turns on its mere existence. The following are examples of such non-hearsay statements.

A.   *Nonhearsay from the Internet*

- *Web Page Upload*. The act of transferring data from one location to another is a mechanical process. This process does not create a hearsay problem because a "statement" is defined in Rule 801(a) as "an oral or written assertion" or nonverbal conduct of "a person." Once the download process has been authenticated, the four hearsay dangers of perception, memory, sincerity, and ambiguity are not present.
- *Consumer Confusion or Understanding*. In a trademark action in which a party claims consumer confusion resulting from Internet postings and e-mails, offering those postings creates no hearsay

---

11. The term "person" includes corporate entities because the entity only functions through individuals who personify it. The term "person" includes corporate entities because the entity only functions through individuals who personify it.

12. *See* Chapter Six, "Authentication," *supra.*

problem because they are relevant on their face.[13] The evidence is relevant without believing the truth of what its writer described. Whether trademark protection is deserved depends on how the mark is perceived and understood. The content of Internet sites is not considered hearsay when offered for this purpose.[14] These cases might be criticized, however, because, like in *Dodart*, where e-mail messages had been received from customers inquiring about products sold by another firm, the e-mails were offered to prove customer confusion. Because the e-mails were circumstantial evidence of the senders' state of mind, the court concluded that they were not hearsay. Therefore, it did not need to decide whether they were admissible under the state of mind or residual exception. Whether something is directly or indirectly stated, however, is irrelevant to the hearsay character of the statement. Just because the customers did not say "I'm confused" does not alter the hearsay dangers present when their inquiries about products are offered to indirectly prove the same thing—that they are confused.[15]

---

13. *See* Microware Sys. Corp. v. Apple Computer, Inc., 126 F. Supp. 2d 1207, 1211 n.2 (S.D. Iowa 2000) (noting that "to the extent any of these stray comments bear on the issue of confusion, they come in for that purpose"); Mid City Bowling Lanes & Sports Palace, Inc. v. Don Carter's All-Star Lanes-Sunrise Ltd., 1998 WL 118103, at *2 (E.D. La. Mar. 12, 1998) ("One of the main issues to be tried in this action, whether a term is entitled to trademark status, is dependent on how the mark is understood and perceived by the purchasing public. Proper evidence of purchaser understanding may be derived from the direct testimony of consumers, consumer surveys, trade journals, dictionary listings, newspapers, and other publications.").

14. Dodart v. Young Again Products Inc., 2006 U.S. Dist. LEXIS 72122, *77 (D. Utah Sept. 29, 2006); Mid City Bowling Lanes & Sports Palace, Inc. v. Don Carter's All-Star Lanes-Sunrise Ltd., 1998 WL 118103, at *2 (E.D. La. Mar. 12, 1998).

15. P.R. Rice & R. Katriel, *Circumstantial Evidence Trap,* § 4.01[A][5] in EVIDENCE: COMMON LAW AND THE FEDERAL RULES OF EVIDENCE 304 (LEXIS/NEXIS 5th ed. 2005). The only justification for calling such e-mails non-hearsay under the Federal Rules of Evidence might be the distinction between intended and unintended assertions in the definition of a "statement" under Rule 801(a). The more reasoned interpretation of that assertive/nonassertive distinction, however, only applies it to instances where conduct is being used to infer an unintended message, never to the use of words. *Id.* at § 4.02[B][2], pp. 320-26.

- *Comparison Purposes.* Web pages are able to present visual images through the use of a universal "html" code. The manner in which the programmers use this code determines the Web site's appearance. If a party claims that one Web site copied html codes from another Web site, the site's similarity will be evidence of the alleged infringement, evidence that may succeed when coupled with evidence that the allegedly infringing party visited the allegedly copied site numerous times. Although the pictures appearing on each Web site are the product of the html codes, presenting copies of the visual images on each Web site for comparison purposes creates no hearsay problem. Each site is relevant because of its appearance. No message needs to be taken from the Web site or the codes that produced its visual images. Each site functions as a separate photograph being presented for visual examination and for the conclusions that can be drawn from the similarities, or lack thereof, that are found.[16]

- *Operative Fact of a Contract.* Under the parol evidence rule and the statute of frauds, when an oral contract is reduced to a writing, the writing controls.[17] Under the objective theory of contract law, once a written agreement is authenticated, the writing is an operative fact of the parties' contract because of its existence. Once authenticated as the written evidence of the parties' agreement, it stands on its own as evidence of the agreement and the terms. When the writing is presented at trial, no hearsay problem is created, because nothing must be believed beyond the fact that it exists with the terms it contains. No out-of-court declarant's credibility, perception, memory, or sincerity is important to the value

---

16. *See* ACTONet, Ltd. v. Allou Health & Beauty Care, 219 F.3d 836, 848 (8th Cir. 2000). Interestingly, this opinion erroneously applied the hearsay concept to a magazine article discussing the Web site that was the subject of the lawsuit. The article critiqued the Web site, drawing favorable conclusions. The court said the article's use was not hearsay because it was offered to impeach the expert testimony offered on the unsatisfactory nature of the site. Such a ruling is erroneous because the article can only impeach if you believe the truth of its content. Had one of the opposing party's expert witnesses written the favorable review, its use would not have been hearsay because the article would have constituted a prior inconsistent statement of that witness. Only in this situation would the court's conclusion have been correct.

17. *See generally* Chapter Ten, "Statute of Frauds & Parol Evidence Rule," *infra.*

of the evidence.[18] Therefore, when an e-mail message or Web page through which a contract was entered is printed,[19] the only evidentiary problem is authentication.[20]

- *Admissions.* If the opposing party's statements are offered against that party, those statements are not classified as hearsay under the Federal Rules of Evidence, even when offered to prove the truth of what was said. Fed. R. Evid. 801(d)(2) excludes admissions from the hearsay definition. Once a communication (letter, e-mail, Web page) is authenticated as having been created by the opposing party, it is admissible for any purpose as non-hearsay.[21] Un-

---

18. Mueller v. Abdnor, 972 F.2d 931, 937 (8th. Cir. 1992) ("The hearsay rule excludes out-of-court assertions used to prove the truth of the facts asserted in them. Verbal acts, however, are not hearsay because they are not assertions and not adduced to prove the truth of the matter. . . . The Federal Rules of Evidence 'excludes from hearsay the entire category of "verbal acts" and "verbal parts of an act," in which the statement itself affects the legal rights of the parties or is a circumstance bearing on conduct affecting their rights.' . . . A contract, for example, is a form of verbal act to which the law attaches duties and liabilities and therefore is not hearsay. . . . In particular, evidence of lost profits based on a contract is not subject to the hearsay rule because such evidence concerns the existence of the contractual terms rather than an assertion of their 'truth.' . . . In addition, various communications—e.g., conversations, letters, and telegrams—relevant to the making of the contract are also not hearsay . . . The contracts and the letters from Jordan's attorney were therefore not hearsay when they are offered to show the making of the contract and the potential loss of benefit to SBA."); United States v. Tann, 425 F. Supp. 2d 26, 31 (D. D.C. 2006) ("the hearsay rule does not exclude relevant evidence as to what the contracting parties said or wrote with respect to the making or terms of an agreement.").

19. Under the best evidence rule codified in FED. R. EVID. 1001 and 1002, "any printout readable by sight, shown to reflect the data accurately, is an 'original.'"

20. *See* Chapter Six, "Authentication," *supra.*

21. Metro-Goldwyn-Mayer Studios, Inc. v. Grokster, Ltd., 454 F. Supp. 2d 966, 974-75 (C.D. Cal. 2006) (E-mails from corporate officers and independent contractors were considered non-hearsay vicarious admissions as long as they related to the responsibilities of those corporate agents. Relative to the independent contractor, a graphic designer, the court stated: "Regardless of her precise contractual status, Schaffer's responsibilities were comparable to that of an in-house graphic designer." Schaffer was considered a StreamCast agent and her statements were admissions under Rule 801(d)(2)(D).); Vermont Elec. Power Co. v. Hartford Steam Boiler Inspection & Ins. Co., 72 F. Supp. 2d 441, 449 (D. Vt. 1999) ("The e-mails are intracompany correspondence which analyzes VELCO's expert reports on how the damage to the transformers occurred. In particular, they assert that the expert reports are not conclusive regarding the

der the common law it also would be admissible, but under the admissions exception to the hearsay rule.

B. *Hearsay from the Internet*

As previously discussed, the mechanical recording of data on a Web page on the Internet does not create hearsay. Hearsay is an issue only if what was mechanically recorded incorporated information the value of which could be affected by the human problems of perception, memory, sincerity, and ambiguity. For example, when unidentified authors post on the Internet favorable reviews of a product that are offered into evidence to establish the reviewer's positive experience, such documents would constitute hearsay.[22] By contrast, no hearsay problem exists if the printouts from third-party Web sites are offered only to establish that certain images and text are on the sites.[23]

Often, data taken from the Internet involves multiple levels of hearsay. Consider the owner of a Web page who reports a story given to him by a third party. If the online report is offered in court to prove the truth of what the story related to the reporter, two levels of hearsay are created—the mind of third party and the mind of the reporter making the entry on

---

timing of the damage. [In response to VELCO's claim that the evidence was inadmissible because it was hearsay and unqualified expert statements, the court stated:] First, the e-mails are clearly admissions of a party, and therefore admissible as non-hearsay. Second, they do not implicate the Federal Rules addressing admission of expert testimony, because they are not offered as expert testimony. Nothing in the Federal Rules of Evidence prohibits a party from serving as an expert witness . . . ."); Dassouf v. White, 2000 WL 235770, at *4 (Ohio Ct. App. Mar. 2, 2000) (without requiring more authentication, court permitted affidavit to be filed in support of summary judgment motion premised on pricing information taken from opposing side's Web page; without explicit acknowledgment, court appears to have accepted basis for truth through admissions theory).

22. *See, e.g.,* Sony Computer Entm't Inc. v. Connectix Corp., 48 F. Supp. 2d 1212, 1222-23 (N.D. Cal. 1999) (acknowledging that Connectix's evidence, which consisted of various anonymous Internet postings offering commentary on Sony videogame system, were hearsay, and were of limited relevance to the trademark issues central to the case).

23. Perfect 10, Inc. v. Cybernet Ventures, Inc., 213 F. Supp. 2d 1146, 1155 (C.D. Cal. 2002) ("Cybernet objects to the printouts from third-party Web sites as a violation of the rule against hearsay. . . . To the extent these images and text are being introduced to show the images and text found on the Web sites, they are not statements at all—and thus fall outside the ambit of the hearsay rule.").

the Web page. If the third-party report relayed factual accounts learned from still others, at least three levels of hearsay would exist. As explained below, each level of hearsay must be admissible under a hearsay exception to admit the Internet report.

C. Admissible Hearsay under Applicable Exceptions

Hearsay evidence is inadmissible unless the statement was made under circumstances indicating reliability sufficient to overcome the absence of an oath, confrontation, and cross-examination. The common law and the Federal Rules or Evidence recognize numerous hearsay exceptions that correspond to various circumstances believed to indicate trustworthiness or a sufficient need to override the dangers of hearsay.[24] For statements to be admissible under these exceptions, the proponent must make a factual showing that the elements of an exception have been satisfied. When there are multiple levels of hearsay, multiple exceptions or multiple applications of one exception must be shown.

For apparently arbitrary reasons,[25] these exceptions were divided into two categories under both the common law and Federal Rules of Evidence. The first category consists of those statements admitted because of their perceived reliability, regardless of whether the declarant is available. These exceptions are codified in Fed. R. Evid. 803, which specifies in its title that the "availability of [the] declarant [is] immaterial." The second category, codified in Fed. R. Evid. 804, requires the proponent to demonstrate that the declarant is unavailable. In effect, as to this second category, the proponent must demonstrate need before certain types of hearsay statements can be used.

Under the Federal Rules of Evidence, the equivalent of a third category of hearsay exceptions unofficially exist that require the availability of the out-of-court declarant. Rule 801(d)(1) excludes certain statements from the definition of hearsay when the declarant is *in court and testifying*. The effect of this rule is that these out-of-court statements are admitted for their truth. These statements include: (1) prior inconsistent statements

---

24. This would include such exceptions as ancient documents (under both the common law and FED. R. EVID. 803(16)), admissions (under the common law), and forfeiture by wrongdoing (FED. R. EVID. 804(b)(6)). As explained above, admissions do not constitute hearsay at all under the FEDERAL RULES OF EVIDENCE.

25. *See* PAUL R. RICE & R. KATRIEL, EVIDENCE: COMMON LAW AND FEDERAL RULES OF EVIDENCE § 5.01 (LEXIS/NEXIS 5th ed. 2005).

made under oath in a previous trial, hearing, or other proceeding, subsection (d)(1)(A); (2) prior consistent statements offered to rebut a charge of recent fabrication or improper influence or motive, subsection (d)(1)(B); and (3) prior identifications, subsection (d)(1)(C).[26]

The accompanying footnote is a compilation of cases in which the exceptions codified under Rules 803 and 804 have been applied to e-evidence issues.[27]

Some hearsay statements do not fall within the scope of a delineated exception, but nevertheless appear sufficiently reliable to be considered

---

26.　FED. R. EVID. 801(d)(1) provides:

Rule 801. Definitions.

The following definitions apply under this article:

. . . .

(d) Statements which are not hearsay. A statement is not hearsay if—
(1) Prior statement by witness. The declarant testifies at the trial or hearing and is subject to cross-examination concerning the statement, and the statement is (A) inconsistent with the declarant's testimony, and was given under oath subject to the penalty of perjury at a trial, hearing, or other proceeding, or in a deposition, or (B) consistent with the declarant's testimony and is offered to rebut an express or implied charge against the declarant of recent fabrication or improper influence or motive, or (C) one of identification of a person made after perceiving the person; .

. . .

27.　The following is a compilation of cases applying the hearsay exceptions and exclusions from the definition of hearsay to e-evidence.

Article VIII. Hearsay
Rule 801. Definitions

. . . .

(d) Statements which are not hearsay. A statement is not hearsay if—

. . . .

(2) Admission by party opponent.
(A) the party's own statement:

See, e.g., United States v. Siddiqui, 235 F.3d 1318, 1323 (11th Cir. 2000) (noting that, despite fact that Siddiqui had not preserved hearsay objections to introduction of e-mails sent by him to third parties, had he done so, such e-mails would be admissible as admissions by party opponent); United States v. Sprick, 233 F.3d 845, 852 (5th Cir. 2000) (holding that unsent e-mail messages are admissions); Ermolaou v. Flipside, Inc., 2004 WL 503758, at *6 (S.D. N.Y. Mar. 15, 2004) (e-mail notification announcing winning number held not an admission because judge apparently accepted proffered testimony that it was product of a computer glitch); Means v. Cullen, 297 F. Supp. 2d 1148, 1151-52 (W.D. Wis. 2003) (e-mail from psychologist not admission because used against state rather than psychologist); Van Westrienen v. Americontinental Collection Corp., 94 F. Supp. 2d 1087, 1109 (D. Ore. 2000) (representations made on Web page of opposing party may be offered as admissions even though statements from that same Web page are inadmissible hearsay when offered by that party); Vermont Elec. Power Co. v. Hartford Steam Boiler Inspection & Ins. Co., 72 F. Supp. 2d 441, 448 (D. Vt. 1999) (holding that insured's intracompany e-mails indicating that expert reports were not conclusive on an issue in dispute with insurer were admissions by party opponent and not hearsay).

(B) statements of which the party has manifested an adoption or belief in its truth:

See, e.g., Sea-Land Serv., Inc. v. Lozen Int'l, LLC, 285 F.3d 808, 821 (9th. Cir. 2002) (e-mail sent by one employee to another who incorporated its content into another e-mail to another recipient; court noted that because first recipient incorporated and adopted contents of original message and, through her comments, manifested an adoption or belief in truth of information contained in original e-mail, it was made admissible under Rule 801(d)(2)(B) as adoptive admission).

(C) a statement by a person authorized by the party to make a statement concerning the subject:

Because subsection (D) permits statements of employees to come in if they are within the scope of their employment responsibilities, it subsumes statements that would fall within subsection (C). As a consequence, this subsection is employed far less than it was under the earlier common law.

(D) a statement by the party's agent or servant concerning a matter within the scope of the agency or employment:

See, e.g., Sea-Land Serv., Inc. v. Lozen Int'l, LLC, 285 F.3d 808, 821 (9th. Cir. 2002) (court held that employee's agency could be established by content of communication in question, taken in conjunction with fact that another letter written by same employee had been admitted, and both related to same subject matter); Metro-Goldwyn-Mayer Studios, Inc. v. Grokster, Ltd., 454 F. Supp. 2d 966, 974-75 (C.D. Cal. 2006) (E-mails from corporate officers and independent contractors were considered non-hearsay vicarious admissions as long as they related to the responsibilities of those corporate agents. Relative to the independent contractor, a graphic designer, the court stated: "Regardless of her precise contractual status, Schaffer's responsibilities were comparable to that of an in-house graphic designer." Schaffer was considered a StreamCast agent and her statements were admissions under Rule 801(d)(2)(D).).

Rule 803. Hearsay Exceptions; Availability of Declarant Immaterial
(1)   Present sense impression.
   See, e.g., United States v. Ferber, 966 F. Supp. 90, 98-99 (D. Mass. 1997) (admitting e-mail message describing previous telephone conversation).

(3)   Then existing mental, emotional, or physical condition.
   See, e.g., Mota v. Univ. of Texas Houston Health Ctr., 261 F.3d 512, 527 (5th Cir. 2001) (holding that e-mail sent by university president correctly admitted by district court because, inter alia, it demonstrated his state of mind); Sara Lee Corp. v. Aris Indus., Inc., 2001 WL 607005, at *4 (S.D. N.Y. Jan. 4, 2001) (e-mail messages offered to show customer confusion were excluded as inadmissible hearsay); Microware Sys. Corp. v. Apple Computer, Inc., 126 F. Supp. 2d 1207, 1211 n.2 (S.D. Iowa 2000) (holding that, to extent stray comments contained in e-mails bear on issue of confusion, they come in for that purpose, and alternatively, under Rule 803(3), such comments may come in for "whatever truth they hold"); People v. Lee, 1999 WL 595455 (Cal. Ct. App. Nov. 10, 1999) (holding e-mail established author's state of mind and was, therefore, not hearsay).

(5)   Recorded recollection.
   See, e.g., De Bolt v. Outboard Marine Corp., 2001 WL 311300, at *2 (W.D. Mich. Jan. 16, 2001) (holding the past recollection recorded exception is not "a mechanical trap to exclude evidence," and admitting computer files containing transcribed, handwritten notes previously taken by witness where circumstances indicated the original notes were made when witness's memory was fresh and accurately reflected witness's knowledge).

(6)   Records of regularly conducted activity.
   See, e.g., Haag v. United States, 485 F.3d 1, 3 (1st Cir. 2007) ("The IRS computerized records would be admissible at trial and are a conventional method of proving correspondence under the business records exception to the hearsay doctrine. . . . A government deponent described the operation of the computer-generated system of sending letters; and an affiant described the location in an IRS computer of copies of the letters sent to the Haags with certified mail numbers matching the numbers on the receipts signed by Robert Haag."); United States v. Kassimu, 188 Fed. Appx. 264, 265 (5th Cir. 2006) ("There is no requirement, as Kassium contends, that the witness laying the foundation for the admissibility of computer records 'be the one who entered the data into the computer or be able to attest personally to its accuracy.' . . . Postal Inspector Brandon Tullier's testimony satisfied the authentication requirement because he explained his familiarity with the procedure by which the records were generated and established the requirements of Fed. R. Evid. 803(6)."); Shelton v. Consumer Prods. Safety Comm'n, 277 F.3d 998, 1010 (8th. Cir.

2001) (Computer-maintained laboratory reports shown to have met elements of business records exception will only be excluded if opponent can demonstrate that "the source of information or the method or circumstances of preparation indicate lack of trustworthiness."); United States v. Salgado, 250 F.3d 438, 451-54 (6th Cir. 2001) (affirming district court's decision to admit computer-generated printouts of telephone records); United States v. Reyes, 157 F.3d 949, 951-53 (affirming district court's decision to admit computerized prisoner's logbook); United States v. Cestnik, 36 F.3d 904, 907-09 (10th Cir. 1994) (holding computer-generated money transfer orders admissible, even when offered by customer and not business); United States v. Catabran, 836 F.2d 453, 456-57 (9th Cir. 1988) (articulating general rule that inaccuracies in computerized business records go to weight and not admissibility). *But see, e.g.*, United States v. Jackson, 208 F.3d 633, 637-39 (7th. Cir. 2000) (noting that Internet service providers are merely conduits for those parties that post messages using space rented from the providers, and the fact that ISPs may be able to access information posted by customers or e-mailed by its customers fails to transform material into business records of ISP); Monotype Corp. PLC v. Int'l Typeface Corp., 43 F.3d 443, 450 (9th Cir. 1994) (internal e-mail messages of third party are not business records because they are not routinely made pursuant to business duty, are not necessarily based on personal knowledge, and are not routinely relied upon by company); In re Vinhnee, 336 B.R. 437, 448-49 (9th. Cir. 2005) (Trial court held that the written declaration was an insufficient foundation for admitting electronic records because the proponent needed to show the accuracy of the computer in the retention and retrieval of the information at issue. "The declaration merely identified the makes and models of the equipment, named the software, noted that some of the software was customized, and asserted that the hardware and software are standard for the industry, regarded as reliable, and periodically updated. There is no information regarding American Express' computer policy and system control procedures, including control of access to the pertinent databases, control of access to the pertinent programs, recording and logging of changes to the data, backup practices, and audit procedures utilized to assure the continuing integrity of the records. All of these matters are pertinent to the accuracy of the computer in the retention and retrieval of the information at issue."); Westfed Holdings, Inc. v. United States, 55 Fed. Cl. 544, 566 (2003) (e-mails not admissible business records because casually created and lack of obligation regularly to record meeting impressions or conversations); New York v. Microsoft, 2002 WL 649951, at *2 (D. D.C. April 12, 2002) (fact that e-mails were used as a regular form of communication did not alone make them business records); Wapnick v. Comm'r IRS, 83 T.C.M. (CCH) 1245, 2002 WL 215993, at *4-5 (Tax. Ct. Feb. 13, 2002) (Even though individuals with personal knowledge of how, when, and why business records were created and maintained (as required under Rule 803(6)) were not available, the court approved their introduction because their accuracy as evidence of interest income had been circumstantially verified. Two special agents had testified that they had compared petitioner's copies of clients' tax returns with the information in the computer records, compared the names of clients in the computer records to client names petitioner wrote on the bank deposit slips, obtained copies of clients' canceled checks and compared them to the computer records, and contacted the clients and compared their records to the computer records.); United States v. Ferber, 966 F. Supp. 90, 98-99 (D. Mass. 1997) (e-mail not considered business record because there was no business duty to make and maintain such communications, and there was no evidence that Merrill Lynch followed any routine practice).

(8) Public records and reports.

See, e.g., United States v. Griffin, 191 F.3d 453, 453-54 (6th Cir. 1999) (holding official IRS documents, including printouts generated by computer, admissible as public records); United States v. Koontz, 143 F.3d 408, 412 (8th. Cir. 1998) (computer-generated booking report admitted); United States v. Thomas, 87 F.3d 1325 (9th Cir. 1996) (computer-generated certificates of assessment from IRS were admitted after being authenticated by custodian of records); United States v. Stallins, 993 F.2d 344, 347 (3d Cir. 1993) (holding computerized police records may be admitted under public records exception, but that statements made by 911 caller contained within such records requires independent hearsay exception); United States v. Smith, 973 F.2d 603, 605 (8th Cir. 1992) (holding district court did not abuse its discretion by admitting computerized records of other crimes, not committed by defendant, that occurred in area near bank that defendant robbed); Chapman v. San Francisco Newspaper Agency, 2002 WL 31119944, at *3 (N.D. Cal. Sept. 20, 2002) (court admitted a printout from the U.S. Postal Service Web site, confirming the date that a right-to-sue letter from EEOC was delivered to employee); Johnson-Woolridge v. Woolridge, 2001 WL 838986, at *4 (Ohio App. 2001) (records of Board of Education taken from Internet were considered authentic simply because person who took them from Web page could have authenticated them, but wasn't permitted; having authenticated only copy of page, court conclude that what was copied from Web page was admissible under public records exception to hearsay rule. Presumably the court considered the public records self-authenticating because they were posed on the Web); Tiberino v. Spokane County, 13 P.3d 1104, 1107-08 (Wash. Ct. App. 2000) (noting e-mail messages made by former employee of county prosecutor's office were public records within scope of public records act). *But see, e.g.*, Moore U.S.A., Inc. v. Standard Register Co., 139 F. Supp. 2d 348, 363 (W.D. N.Y., 2001) (holding that pages from Web site are not public records for purposes of Rule 12(b)(6) motion); State ex rel. Simmons v. Lake

by the finder of fact. To accommodate these statements, the Federal Rules of Evidence codified the inherent common-law power of judges to create new exceptions when the circumstances surrounding the statement justify doing so. In Rule 807, hearsay statements can be admitted when "circum-

County Sheriff's Dep't, 693 N.E.2d 789, 792 (Ohio 1998) (indicating e-mails generated by Sheriff's Department were not considered public records); State v. Davis, 141 Wash. 2d 798, 854 (Wash. 2000) (holding an unauthenticated printout of population statistics obtained from Internet was not admissible under public records exception to hearsay rule).

(10) Absence of public record or entry.
See, e.g., United States v. Spine, 945 F.2d 143, 148-49 (6th. Cir. 1991) (holding computer-generated data compilations created by IRS about taxpayers and testimony concerning such documents admissible under exception to hearsay rule for evidence as to absence of public records or entries that would be regularly made and preserved).

(17) Market reports, commercial publications.
See, e.g., Elliott Assocs., L.P. v. Banco de la Nacion, 194 F.R.D. 116, 121 (S.D. N.Y. 2000) (prime rates taken from Web site of Federal Reserve Board admitted into evidence). *Compare* State v. Erickstand, 620 N.W.2d 136, 145 (N.D. 2000) (admitting evidence as to value of stolen truck proven from information listed on *Kelley Blue Book* Web site), *and* Irby-Greene v. M.O.R., Inc., 79 F. Supp. 2d 630, 636 n.22 (E.D. Va. 2000) (basing the court's valuation, in part, on information he took from the Kelley Web site), *with* Sain v. State, 2001 WL 518322, at *3 (Ark. Ct. App. May 16, 2001) (sustaining objections to testimony concerning results of Internet search to determine automobile's value).

(18) Learned treatises.
See, e.g., Baker v. Barnhart, 457 F.3d 882, 891 (8th. Cir. 2006) (A five-page article posted on the Internet that had never been subject to peer review, and was little more than an advertising brochure written by biased company employees was not an authoritative treatise that the court could judicially notice and rely upon); Charles E. Hill & Assocs., Inc. v. Compuserve Inc., 2000 WL 1473875, at *13 (S.D. Ind. Aug. 24, 2000) (holding Microsoft manual purporting to instruct users about Internet Explorer was not considered "learned treatise" for purposes of hearsay exception).

Rule 804. Hearsay Exceptions; Declarant Unavailable
(a) Definition of unavailability.
See, e.g., Attorney Grievance Comm'n of Md. v. Johnson, 770 A.2d 130, 140-41 (Md. 2001) (noting evidence of attempted contact via e-mail constitutes "good faith" effort to procure unavailable witness).

stantial guarantees of trustworthiness" exist equal to the codified excep-tions,[28] and the proponent of the evidence has given advance notice to the opposing party of his "intention to offer the statement and the particulars of it, including the name and address of the declarant."[29]

---

28. There is a vast range of reliability in the delineated exceptions. Excited utterances, for example, may be sincere, but can possess significant problems of perception and ambiguity when a statement is made while the declarants' reflective thought processes are overwhelmed. By contrast, prior testimony was given under oath in a prior trial, hearing, or other proceeding and cross-examined. Consequently, it has a significant level of reliability because the party against whom it is being offered, or his predecessor in interest, had an opportunity to confront the declarant and question him about his perception, memory, and sincerity, and explore any ambiguity in the words uttered. Because the range of reliability is so great within the delineated exceptions, courts tend to require that hearsay not otherwise falling within a delineated exception must be shown to possess significant reliability.

29. FED. R. EVID. 807 provides:

Rule 807. Residual Exception.

A statement not specifically covered by Rules 803 or 804 but having equivalent circumstantial guarantees of trustworthiness, is not excluded by the hearsay rule, if the court determines that (A) the statement is offered as evidence of a material fact; (B) the statement is more proba-tive on the point for which it is offered than any other evidence which the proponent can procure through reasonable efforts; and (C) the gen-eral purposes of these rules and the interests of justice will best be served by admission of the statement into evidence. However, a statement may not be admitted under this exception unless the proponent of it makes known to the adverse party sufficiently in advance of the trial or hearing to provide the adverse party a fair opportunity to prepare to meet it, the proponent's intention to offer the statement and the particulars of it, including the name and address of the declarant.

See, e.g., United States v. Guerena, 142 F.3d 446, 449 (9th Cir. 1998) (holding it was not error for district court to admit computerized records of cellular phone bills pursuant to residual exception); United States v. Blackburn, 992 F.2d 666, 670-71 (7th Cir. 1993) (The court held com-puter printouts of lensometer readings for eyeglasses left in a stolen get-away car were admissible under residual hearsay exception. This should never have been classified as hearsay because the "statement" was the product of a machine.); Symantec Corp. v. Computer Assoc. Int'l, Inc., 2006 WL 3950278, at *8-9 (E.D. Mich. Aug. 31, 2006) (A hearsay state-ment of Richardson was offered to establish that the PKSFANSI program was posted on the Internet and thus publicly available. "Richardson's hearsay statement was made contemporaneously with his purported up-loading of the PKSFANSI program on the Internet, and was obviously

VI.   A REALITY CHECK ON HEARSAY

While hearsay is a relatively straightforward concept, its application is often complex and difficult. Problems are exacerbated by the added complexities of the intentional/unintentional assertion distinction incorporated into the definition of hearsay in Fed. R. Evid. 801(a).[30] This complexity is compounded by esoteric exceptions like Rule 803(3) for statements addressing the present state of mind of the out-of-court declarant—probably the most widely misunderstood and misapplied exception.

Many lawyers and judges do not understand or apply the panoply of issues under the hearsay concept as well as they should. What is certain, however, is that through their varied experiences with hearsay, they have developed little tolerance for the minutiae that a correct analysis may entail. As a consequence, trial judges, being the pragmatists that their positions compel, often approach hearsay with an eye to efficiency and common sense. As a result, they often summarily resolve the myriad questions before them by assuming that a statement is hearsay and then admitting it under the residual exception in Rule 807. These judges believe that the circumstantial guarantees of trustworthiness make the evidence as reliable as other hearsay evidence being admitted. Thus, an increasing number of jurists are demonstrating that fussing over details is not worth the effort.

Litigators, however, cannot rely on this growing judicial laxity. They must be prepared to accommodate judges that have a penchant for evidentiary details. However, in any argument over the admissibility of hearsay, the proponent of the evidence should allude to the judge's authority under Rule 807 to short-circuit the entire debate.

A.   The Internet as Part of Business or Government Records

For at least three decades, computers have been an established means by which business records are maintained. Now that businesses regularly use their computers to access the Internet as part of their efforts to communi-

---

made on personal knowledge. It is a simple statement of a recent past act, and thus does not bear the risk of faulty perception, memory, or narration, and Richardson repeated the statement in a subsequent posting. Further, nothing in Richardson's posting, nor any other evidence, suggests that Richardson would have had any motive to fabricate his claim to have posted the program on the Internet.").

30.   *See* § IV, Mechanically Produced Statements Are Not Hearsay, *supra.*

cate with customers, can hearsay from a company's Web page or e-mail correspondence with customers be offered *by the company* under the business records exception to the hearsay rule in Fed. R. Evid. 803(6)?[31]

Although such records theoretically could be business records, as a general rule, Rule 803(6) records are generally thought of as those that a company maintains for its own use and, therefore, depends upon for the records' accuracy.[32] The business's reliance upon the records provides an assurance of their trustworthiness.[33] If the records are not maintained for internal use, other assurances of reliability must be present, such as systematic maintenance and checking, or a proven habit of precision on the part of the keeper.[34]

Internet postings might be regularly maintained by employees with personal knowledge and a business duty to make the record, but interactive Web pages may be precluded from admission as business records under Rule 803(6). Of course, when offered against the business that maintains the Web page, its contents could be introduced under the common law admissions exception that has been codified in Rule 801(d)(2) as non-hearsay. Also, when entries are made on an interactive Web page, even if the Web page were considered a business record, the entries of third parties would not be admissible under that exception, because the third parties would not have made their entries pursuant to a business duty.

Two factors may be significant in determining whether a Web page posting is an admissible business record. First, even though information

---

31. If such records were being offered against the company, they would be admissible as non-hearsay admissions under Rule 801(d)(2).

32. *See* Monotype Corp. PLC v. Int'l Typeface Corp., 43 F.3d 443, 450 (9th Cir. 1999) (holding that internal e-mail messages were not company's business records for purposes of Rule 803(6) hearsay exception).

33. "The business records exception is based on a presumption of accuracy, accorded because the information is part of a regularly conducted activity, kept by those trained in the habits of precision, and customarily checked for correctness, and because of the accuracy demanded in the conduct of the nation's business." United States v. Snyder, 787 F.2d 1429, 1433-34 (10th. Cir. 1986), *citing* United States v. Baker, 693 F.2d 183, 188 (D.C. Cir. 1982). "Interests of business may be such that there exists sufficient self-interest in accuracy of the document that contents are trustworthy." United States v. McIntyre, 997 F.2d 687, 700 (10th. Cir. 1993).

34. WEINSTEIN & BERGER, WEINSTEIN'S EVIDENCE, § 803.08[6][a] at 803-66.

on those Web pages may be relied upon by the company, the possibility that hackers could manipulate the Web page diminishes its reliability. This possibility prompted the court in *United States v. Jackson*[35] to exclude Web postings taken from a white supremacists' Web page. The court explained, "Jackson needed to show that the web postings in which the white supremacist groups took responsibility for the racist mailings actually were posted by the groups, as opposed to being slipped into the groups' Websites by Jackson herself, who was a skilled computer user." The court thus held that the content of the page was not properly authenticated as a business record of the supremacy groups.

Second, the purpose of most Web pages is to inform prospective customers, not preserve data for subsequent internal use. While some pages may be reliable if they are regularly updated by knowledgeable people acting pursuant to a business duty, many are not. Web pages that are not actively maintained increasingly become out of date and unreliable, and they should not be considered business records. Even if Web pages are initially classified as business records, courts can exclude them from evidence if, in the language of Rule 803(6), "the circumstances of preparation indicate lack of trustworthiness."

Parties may use any applicable exception to justify the admission of materials acquired from both an intranet or the Internet. For instance, an employee's e-mail to his superior may be admitted under the present-sense impression exception of Rule 803(1)[36] if it "described or explained an event or condition made while the declarant was perceiving the event or condition, or immediately thereafter." Government Internet records also have been admitted under the hearsay exception for market reports and other commercial publications in Rule 803(17).[37]

---

35. 208 F.3d 633, 637-38 (7th. Cir. 2000).

36. Fed. R. Evid. 803(1) provides:
     Rule 803. Hearsay Exceptions; Availability of Declarant Immaterial
     The following are not excluded by the hearsay rule, even though the declarant is available as a witness:

     . . . .

     (1) Present sense impression. A statement describing or explaining an event or condition made while the declarant was perceiving the event or condition, or immediately thereafter.

37. *See, e.g.*, Elliott Assoc., L.P. v. Banco de la Nacion, 194 F.R.D. 116, 121 (S.D. N.Y. 2000) (admitting prime rates taken from Web site of Federal Reserve Board). *Compare* Irby-Greene v. M.O.R., Inc., 79 F. Supp. 2d 630, 636 n.22 (E.D. Va. 2000)

B.   Web Pages Are Not Business Records of the Internet Service Provider (ISP)

Although the ISP is in the business of hosting the Web pages of its sub-scribers, those Web pages are not the business records of the ISP.[38] The ISP does not create the pages, does not check their accuracy, does not have personal knowledge of the pages' content, and does not rely upon the pages' accuracy. However, internal records of the ISP regarding a customer's account that include information about the time that customer spent online, or about which exact times different customers were online, could be admitted as business records of the ISP as long as someone within the ISP organization properly qualifies the records as required by the business records exception.[39]

C.   Government Records and Reports

Government records on the Web may be treated differently from private business records. Although Rule 803(8) records are often referred to as the public equivalent of private business records, public records are

---

(basing the court's valuation, in part, on information obtained from Kelley Web site) *and* State v. Erickstand, 620 N.W. 2d 136 (N.D. 2000) (admitting evidence as to value of stolen truck proven from infirmation listed on *Kelley Blue Book* Web site) *with* Sain v. State, 2001 WL 518322, at *3 (Ark. Ct. App. May 16, 2001) (sustaining objections to testimony concerning results of Internet search to determine automo-bile's value).

38. *See* United States v. Jackson, 208 F.3d, 633, 637 (7th Cir. 2000) ("The web postings were not statements made by declarants testifying at trial, and they were being offered to prove the truth of the matter asserted. That means they were hearsay. Fed. R. Evid. 801. Jackson tries to fit the web postings in as a hearsay exception under Fed. R. Evid. 803(6) as business records of the supremacy group's Internet service providers. Internet service providers, however, are merely conduits. The Internet ser-vice providers did not themselves post what was on [the particular] Web sites. Jack-son presented no evidence that the Internet service providers even monitored the contents of those Web sites. The fact that the Internet service provider may be able to retrieve information that its customers posted or e-mail that its customers sent does not turn that material into a business record of the Internet service provider. 'Any evidence procured off the Internet is adequate for almost nothing, even under the most liberal interpretations of the hearsay exception rules.' St. Clair v. Johnny's Oys-ter & Shrimp, Inc., 76 F. Supp. 2d 773, 775 (S.D. Tex. 1999).").

39. *See* Bower v. Bower, 758 So. 2d 405, 414-15 (Miss. 2000) (holding records were inadmissible as business records of America On Line when customer and not custodian or other qualified person attempted to qualify them).

different. Because the government agency does the public's work, and is required to make certain disclosures, more and more government records, reports, and data compilations are likely to be posted on the Web. Theoretically, Rule 803(8) could be used to admit government records from those Web pages far more than Rule 803(6) could be used to admit private records from privately owned and operated Web pages. Such a result may be unlikely, however, because concerns about data manipulation affect both types of Web pages.

For both government records and business records, it is important to distinguish between the underlying materials being posted on the Web page and the Web page itself. All entities, both business and government, will create records that are admissible under Rules 803(6) and (8). The issue with Internet postings is the means by which these records are being made available to the public. The question that judges will have for litigants is: What assurances are there that the copy you present from the Web page posting accurately reflects the content of the admissible underlying records? Under the common law in the pre-electronic period, this same concern for copies or records was addressed through the requirement for a certified copy. What is the equivalent in the electronic world of the Internet? If an actual certification of the copy is required, it may defeat the purpose of making the information available on the Internet. A check on authenticity and accuracy comparable to a certified copy might be the continued availability of the materials on a Web page that the judge can access on a computer.[40]

The most significant problem for government printouts from the Internet will likely be authentication. As discussed in Chapter Six, such printouts may not be considered self-authenticating because they are not accompanied by a certification from a public official.[41] The self-authentication provision in Rule 902(4) requires that the copy from a public office be "certified as correct."[42] As a practical matter, such authentication concerns

---

40. For example, in United States v. Douglas, 215 Fed. Appx. 907, 910 (11th Cir. 2007), the court held that "a judgment of conviction recorded in a district court's electronic filing system is a presumptively reliable indication of a defendant's prior conviction in absence of evidence to the contrary."

41. State v. Davis, 10 P.3d 977, 1010 (2000).

42. In the state of Oregon, statutes have addressed the admissibility of public records generated from databases of public agencies through a hearsay exception and a self-authentication rule for documents complying with the new hearsay exception. *See*

will often be resolved by stipulation, or a party can seek an admission of authenticity under Fed. R. Civ. P. 36. If the party receiving requests declines to provide the admission, the expenses incurred in establishing authenticity can be imposed under Rule 37(a)(4) on the recalcitrant party. Of course, individuals who are familiar with the Internet postings—for example, those who logged onto the site and reviewed its content—can compare the copy to the postings and testify to its accuracy.[43]

VII. CONSTITUTIONAL DIMENSIONS OF HEARSAY[44]

Electronic communications are part of virtually every enterprise. When these communications are offered for the truth of their content in the criminal prosecution of corporate officers and directors, they may be admissible under the business records exception to the hearsay rule, but the Bill of Rights imposes additional restrictions that must be addressed.

The U.S. Constitution restricts the admissibility of hearsay through several of its Amendments. The Confrontation Clause of the Sixth Amendment provides that "the accused [in all criminal prosecutions] shall enjoy the right . . . to be confronted with the witnesses against him . . . ." Under the Due Process Clause of the Fifth Amendment, "[n]o person shall be . . . deprived of life, liberty, or property, without due process of law." The Fourteenth Amendment prevents any state from making or enforcing any law that "deprive[s] any person of life, liberty, or property, without due process of law," and through that guarantee the Bill of Rights has been made applicable to state prosecutions. The Due Process Clauses can both restrict the use of hearsay otherwise admissible under the rules of evidence and compel the admission of hearsay otherwise excluded by the same evidence rules.

The following sections explore the confused history of these constitutional restrictions on the use of hearsay. Understanding this confusion is critical to understanding current case law and indispensable to appreciat-

---

generally Oregon v. Barber, 149 P.3d 260 (Ore. Ct. App. 2006). These provisions no longer require a signed, hard-copy certification.

43. Fed. R. Evid. 901(b)(1) recognizes the sufficiency of testimony of a witness with knowledge that a matter is what it is claimed to be. This is the "compared copy" method of authentication recognized under the common law.

44. I acknowledge the helpful comments of my colleagues, Jamin Raskin, Herman Schwartz, and Steve Wermeil, in the preparation of this section of this hearsay chapter.

ing why constitutional standards governing e-evidence are, and likely will remain, checkered and uncertain.

A.   The Accused's Right of Confrontation

The relationship between the right of confrontation and the admissibility of hearsay evidence has never been satisfactorily explained by the Supreme Court. While the Court has noted that the Confrontation Clause does not "constitutionalize" the hearsay rule—meaning that it does not automatically require the exclusion of such evidence against criminal defendants—the court has never resolved the question of what specific restrictions the Confrontation Clause places on the government's use of hearsay evidence. While acknowledging that the hearsay rule and the confrontation right stemmed from the same roots and protected similar values, the Supreme Court has never equated the two.[45] Unfortunately, it also has failed to define the difference between the two. Offering no formula for the application of the confrontation right to all hearsay exceptions, the Court has resolved each confrontation issue on the particular facts of each case before it. Factors that are significant to these determinations are:

- the gravity, or probative value, of the evidence in question;
- the possibility of the jury's misuse of the evidence;
- the statement's inherent reliability as reflected in the circumstances under which it was made;
- whether the evidence involved perception and memory problems that could be exposed through cross-examination; and
- the availability of other evidence demonstrating the guilt of the accused.[46]

In *Dutton v. Evans,*[47] the Supreme Court accepted the government's use of hearsay in lieu of an available witness, because the utility of trial confrontation would have been remote. *Dutton* involved a murder prosecution in which the defendant was convicted primarily on the basis of testimony of one of his co-conspirators. This testimony was corroborated by a hearsay statement of another co-conspirator who, in response to the

---

45. *See* Dutton v. Evans, 400 U.S. 74, 86, 27 L. Ed. 2d 213, 218, 91 S. Ct. 210 (1970); California v. Green, 399 U.S. 149, 174-75, 26 L. Ed. 2d 489, 90 S. Ct. 1930, 1943-44 (1970).

46. Dutton v. Evans, 400 U.S. 74, 85-89 (1970).

47. *Id.* at 87.

question "How did you make out in court?" (he had been arraigned on the murder charge), uttered the statement, "If it hadn't been for that dirty son-of-a-bitch Alex Evans, we wouldn't be in this now."[48]

The Court's conclusion about the remote utility of trial confrontation was based on a number of factors: (1) the hearsay statement was not an expression about a past fact; (2) the declarant was obviously in a position to have known whether Evans was involved in the murder; (3) there was little chance of faulty recollection; (4) the circumstances under which the statement was made indicated no reason for Evans' involvement in the crime to be misrepresented; (5) the primary evidence against Evans came from the testimony of another co-conspirator; (6) the possibility that cross-examination of the declarant would have enlightened the jury on the accuracy of the statement was highly unlikely; and (7) the witness who heard the statement uttered was fully cross-examined.[49]

This decision provided little guidance to prosecutors on when it would be safe for them to rely on hearsay statements without attempting to obtain the presence of the hearsay declarant at trial. The analysis in *Dutton* was completely fact-dependent. Consequently, the prosecutor rolled the dice in concluding that no efforts were needed to obtain the testimony of the witnesses at trial. Rather than always making that effort, prosecutors generally have sought the attendance of hearsay declarants only when explicitly required to do so by the elements of the particular hearsay exceptions applicable to the statements. If offered under a Rule 804 exception or its common law equivalent, which required a showing that the declarant was unavailable before the statement was admissible, they made a good faith-effort to obtain the presence of the declarant at trial. When offered under a Rule 803 exception or its common law equivalent, which made availability immaterial, few, if any, efforts were made to obtain the hearsay declarant's presence at trial.

The *Dutton* test, premised on a case-by-case analysis of the need for confrontation in a particular case, proved to be unworkable. Therefore, in 1980 the Supreme Court announced a new interpretation of the confrontation right in *Ohio v. Roberts*.[50] In this decision, for the first time, the Court gave a concrete definition of the right guaranteed by the Confrontation Clause.

---

48. *Id.* at 77.
49. *Id.* at 88-89.
50. 448 U.S. 56, 65 L. Ed. 2d 597, 100 S. Ct. 2531 (1980).

1. Two-Prong *Ohio v. Roberts* Test

Roberts involved testimony given at a preliminary hearing by a defense witness. The testimony proved to be unfavorable to the defense, and the government introduced the witness's statements at the subsequent trial through the preliminary hearing transcript. The Court held that this use of hearsay satisfied the requirements of the Confrontation Clause because it complied with a new two-prong test. First, the declarant was shown to be unavailable after a good faith-effort had been made to locate and subpoena her. Second, the hearsay used in lieu of the witness's live testimony possessed indicia of reliability. "[A]n unavailable witness's out-of-court statement may be admitted so long as it has adequate indicia of reliability—i.e., falls within a 'firmly rooted hearsay exception' or bears 'particularized guarantees of trustworthiness.'"[51]

In subsequent decisions, the Court never applied the demonstration of unavailability requirement to any hearsay that did not require such a demonstration because of where it was classified—i.e., hearsay exceptions under Rule 804 (prior testimony, dying declarations, declarations against interest, and statements of personal or family history). In substance, therefore, the right of confrontation became defined by the arbitrary classification of exceptions under Rule 804 and the common law counterparts of those exceptions that made unavailability material to the admissibility of the statements.[52]

The second prong of the *Roberts* decision—the indicia of reliability requirement—is the substantive equivalent of the due process component of the *Roberts* confrontation formula. If the physical right to confront an accuser was satisfied or excused (either because the exception under which the statement was being offered did not require a demonstration of unavailability or unavailability was, in fact, demonstrated), the hearsay used in lieu of the witness had to be a reliable substitute.

---

51. Ohio v. Roberts, 448 U.S. 56, 65-66, 65 L. Ed. 2d 597, 100 S. Ct. 2531, 2535 (1980).

52. "Because the categorization of hearsay exceptions is at times both illogical and inconsistent, one could conclude that the pattern of categorization is little more than the product of historical accident. After first recognizing the exceptions in the factual contexts of particular cases, court thereafter rigidly defined the exceptions by the contexts in which they initially were created." PAUL R. RICE, EVIDENCE: COMMON LAW AND FEDERAL RULES OF EVIDENCE § 5:01, p. 370 (LEXIS 4th ed. 2000).

This was an easily met requirement, because hearsay offered under a "deeply rooted"common law or codified hearsay exception (which was generally translated to mean a recognized exception) automatically carried with it the requisite indicia of reliability.[53] Through these decisions, the Supreme Court effectively allowed Congress to define our right to confrontation and due process of law, because those rights are given definition by the hearsay exceptions Congress chose to adopt and where Congress elected to classify them in the Federal Rules of Evidence.

The *Roberts* test eventually led a majority of the Court to conclude that unacceptable results were being reached because of erroneously perceived indicia of reliability. As a result, the Court redefined the right of confrontation for a third time in the last half century in *Crawford v. Washington*.[54] This time the right of confrontation was held to be applicable only to hearsay that is "testimonial" in nature. While overruling *Roberts*'s confrontation analysis, the decision has left unresolved the question of whether the due process component of that confrontation analysis remains a viable constitutional screen.[55] This is unresolved because the Court never acknowledged in *Roberts* or subsequent opinions that the second prong of the *Roberts* test was a right guaranteed by the Due Process Clause rather than the Confrontation Clause.

2. The "Testimonial" Standard of *Crawford v. Washington*

Crawford involved a declaration against interest[56] by a wife that was used against her husband. The Court held that the use of this statement against the husband violated the husband's right to confront his accuser. From the 16th- and 17th-century context in which the right of confrontation evolved, the Court extrapolated that the right was meant to apply only to hearsay that was of a "testimonial" nature. What "testimonial" means was not defined by the Court, but alternative definitions were discussed:

Various formulations of this core class of "testimonial" statements exist:

---

53. Ohio v. Roberts, 448 U.S. 56, 66, 65 L. Ed.2d 597, 100 S. Ct. 2531, 2539 (1980).

54. 541 U.S. 36, 124 S. Ct. 1354, 158 L. Ed. 2d 177 (2004).

55. *See* § VII B, Due Process, *infra*.

56. FED. R. EVID. 804(b)(3).

ex parte in-court testimony or its functional equivalent—that is, material such as affidavits, custodial examinations, prior testimony that the defendant was unable to cross-examine, or similar pretrial statements that declarants would reasonably expect to be used prosecutorially," . . . ; "extrajudicial statements . . . contained in formalized testimonial materials, such as affidavits, depositions, prior testimony, or confessions," . . . ; "statements that were made under circumstances which would lead an objective witness reasonably to believe that the statement would be available for use at a later trial, ..."[57]

In its discussion of hearsay that is testimonial in nature, the Court appeared to exclude business records from that category:

Most of the hearsay exceptions covered statements that by their nature were not testimonial—for example, business records or statements in furtherance of a conspiracy.[58]

This suggests that a confrontation issue would not arise in a prosecution in which electronic business records were used against corporate executives. However, it would be unwise for prosecutors to draw such a broad conclusion from the opinion.

Many jurisdictions require emergency room physicians to conduct an examination and to fill out medical reports whenever a patient complains of sexual assault, spousal abuse, child abuse, or other enumerated offenses. These statutes typically require the hospital to inform law enforcement authorities (either child protective services, police, or another enforcement agency) and to turn over a copy of that report to law enforcement so that the government may take appropriate action.[59]

---

57. 541 U.S. at 51-52, 124 S. Ct. at 1364, 158 L. Ed. 2d at 193.

58. 541 U.S. at 56, 124 S. Ct. at 1367, 158 L. Ed. 2d at 195-96.

59. *See, e.g.*, ALA. CODE § 26-14-1 (West 2000) ("All physicians and other practitioners of the healing arts or any caregiver having reasonable cause to believe that any protected person has been subjected to physical abuse, neglect, exploitation, sexual abuse, or emotional abuse shall report . . . [to law enforcement]."); CAL. PENAL CODE § 11165.9 (West 2004) ("Reports of suspected child abuse or neglect shall be made by mandated reporters to any police department or sheriff's department, not including a school district police or security department, county probation department, if designated by the county to receive mandated reports, or the county welfare department.");

In a prosecution for child abuse or sexual assault, statements of the treating physician in a statutorily compelled business record would be "testimonial" under any of the definitions delineated by the Court. After the hospital staff and physician completed the form and submitted it to authorities, they would have an objectively reasonable belief that their statements and conclusions could be used at a future prosecution of the alleged offender.

3. Why "Testimonial"?

The right of confrontation was created to counter the abuses of the Star Chamber prosecutions in the 16th and 17th centuries in England. In those proceedings, enemies of the state were prosecuted with fabricated hearsay, and no meaningful opportunity was afforded defendants to expose those fabrications. Through these hearsay statements, the English state pursued two goals through the Star Chambers: the conviction of each defendant and the ultimate sanction of execution. To achieve both goals, it was necessary for the state to employ the most convincing evidence it could "produce." The most convincing evidence at that time was a sworn statement because of the value of an oath in past centuries.[60] Consequently,

---

COLO. REV. STAT. ANN. § 19-3-307(3), 308(5.5) (West 2004); KY. REV. STAT. ANN. § 209.030 (Michie 2003) ("Any person, including, but not limited to, physician, law enforcement officer, nurse, social worker, cabinet personnel, coroner, medical examiner, alternate care facility employee, or caretaker, having reasonable cause to suspect that an adult has suffered abuse, neglect, or exploitation, shall report or cause reports to be made in accordance with the provisions of this chapter.").

California also requires the welfare department to file child abuse reports with the district attorney. CAL. PENAL CODE § 11166(g) (West 2004). Further, the California Code provides that "county counsel or district attorney shall, at the request of the juvenile court judge, appear and participate in the hearing to represent the petitioner." CAL. WELF. & INST. CODE § 318.5 (West 2004).

60. Chief Justice Rehnquist notes in his concurring opinion, "In the 18th century, unsworn hearsay was simply held to be of much lesser value than were sworn affidavits or depositions." Crawford, 541 U.S. at 71 n.1, 124 S. Ct. at 1375 n.1, 158 L. Ed. 2d at 204 n.1.

> Hearsay is no Evidence . . . though a Person Testify what he hath heard upon Oath, yet the Person who spake it was not upon Oath; and if a Man had been in Court and said the same Thing and had not sworn it, he had not been believed in a Court of Justice; for all Credit being derived from Attestation and Evidence, it can rise no higher than the Fountain from whence it flows, and if the first Speech was without Oath, an Oath that there

sworn statements were the most commonly used hearsay to justify the extreme sanctions sought.

Defining the confrontation right solely by the testimonial nature of the hearsay used in these ancient proceedings is limiting the right of confrontation to a snapshot of prosecutorial abuses at a distant point in time. While this is understandable as a matter of historical analysis, it is highly questionable for the Court to limit the confrontation right to the *means* by which prosecutorial abuses took place. The specific type of hearsay that was predominantly used was only the symptom. The disease being treated by the right of confrontation was the abuse of using unreliable, if not fraudulently produced, evidence with no meaningful way for the defendant to test and challenge it. The "testimonial" definition of the right of confrontation intolerably focuses on the form of the evil rather than its substance. As a consequence, there is little reason to believe that *Crawford* will be the last word on the definition of this right.

A criminal defendant's need to confront the individuals who speak against him is unchanged regardless of the hearsay exception used. When personal liberty is at stake, the use of any form of hearsay creates a compelling need to physically confront accusing witnesses, regardless of whether the charges are fabricated, as they often were in the Star Chamber, or mistaken, as some inevitably are today.

Societal attitudes about the value of an oath explain the reason for the predominance of "testimonial"-type hearsay in the Court's snapshot of the ancient past. The limitation of the confrontation right to this type of hearsay is curious in our contemporary society, where beliefs about the sanctity of an oath have significantly diminished. The Court also ignores that there were few recognized exceptions to the hearsay rule during the Star Chamber prosecutions. Therefore, the focus on testimonial hearsay statements in those proceedings may reflect nothing more than the limited number of exceptions that were then available and the extreme results they were seeking through them.

The Court justifies its new "testimonial" analysis by claiming that the new test is rooted in the history of the Confrontation Clause and its antecedent common law jurisprudence. The Court argues that after the adop-

---

was such a Speech makes it no more than a bar speaking, and so of no Value in a Court of Justice, where all Things were determined under the Solemnities of an Oath . . . .

1 G. GILBERT, EVIDENCE 216 (C. Lofft ed. 1791).

tion of the confrontation right, the types of hearsay to which it was applied were statements of a testimonial nature. Yet in the Court's historical discussion, it concedes that dying declarations were routinely admitted as evidence, even when the declarations at issue were indisputably "testimonial" in nature.[61] The Court suggests that the practice of admitting dying declarations in criminal prosecutions ought to be viewed as a "deviation" and, without furnishing any analysis, suggested that, in any event, the admissibility of such "testimonial" dying declarations ought to be viewed as "sui generis." Future justices may find this ipse dixit unconvincing, because the fact that dying declarations were routinely admitted in prosecutions after the creation of the confrontation right, despite their testimonial character, clearly refutes, rather than supports, the Court's thesis.

4.   Does the "Testimonial" Label Give an Absolute Right?

Crawford appears to make the right of confrontation *absolute* for "testimonial" hearsay statements. If the declarant is unavailable, is the testimonial hearsay automatically excluded by the Confrontation Clause because there has not been and will not be an opportunity to cross-examine? Under the *Roberts* standard, the government's burden was satisfied when unsuccessful, but good-faith, efforts to produce the declarant were demonstrated. If the Court concludes that the right is absolute when the hearsay statement is "testimonial" in nature, future opinions will likely turn on a circumscribed definition of "testimonial." One instance where this may occur is where business records are authenticated through the use of certifications under Fed. R. Evid. 902(11), which permits the proponent of such records to employ a pre-certification by the sponsoring witness in lieu of calling that witness at trial. When this certification is of business records that are being used against a criminal defendant, the certification is clearly a statement made to prosecution authorities for the purpose of being used in a judicial proceeding, thereby making it testimonial under the most likely definition

---

61. "The one deviation we have found involves dying declarations. The existence of that exception as a general rule of criminal hearsay law cannot be disputed. . . . Although many dying declarations may not be testimonial, there is authority for admitting even those that clearly are. . . . We need not decide in this case whether the Sixth Amendment incorporates an exception for testimonial dying declarations. If this exception must be accepted on historical grounds, it is *sui generis*." *See* Crawford, 541 U.S. at 56 n.6, 124 S. Ct. at 1367 n.6, 158 L. Ed. 2d at 196 n.6.

of that term. In *United States v. Wittig*,[62] the court concluded that this use of such a certification violated the defendant's right to confrontation.

The statements within a certification contemplated by Rule 902(11) are testimonial statements because they contain "solemn declarations or affirmations made for the purpose of establishing or proving some fact," namely that the proper foundation for the admission of the business record exists. They are the functional equivalent of ex parte in-court testimony that defendants cannot cross-examine. Indeed, the Rule 902(11) procedure itself takes the place of live, sworn testimony of a witness. Moreover, the Rule 902(11) declarants know that they are providing foundational testimony for business records to the government, and thus, must reasonably expect that their certifications will be used prosecutorially. Therefore, the Court concludes that the Rule 902(11) procedure violates defendants' right to confrontation.

To avoid such a result, the Court could make an exception for testimonial statements that are more procedural than substantive in nature, or statements that are provided to the defendant beforehand and about which the defendant cannot identify a need for confrontation, or statements that are not incriminating on their face.

Justice Scalia wrote the majority opinion in *Crawford*. The last time he wrote a Confrontation Clause decision that was absolute was *Coy v. Iowa*.[63] In *Coy*, the Court held that the state could not screen a juvenile witness from the defendant during his testimony. Two terms later, in *Maryland v. Craig*,[64] the Court backed away from the absolute *Coy* mandate and sanctioned the giving of testimony on closed-circuit television. One can only guess whether that will occur here too.

---

62. 2005 WL 1227790, at *2 (D. Kan. May 23, 2005).
63. 487 U.S. 1012, 108 S. Ct. 2798, 101 L. Ed. 2d 857 (1988).
64. 497 U.S. 836, 110 S. Ct. 3157 (1990)

Evolving Confrontation		
Dutton v. Evans	*Ohio v. Roberts*	*Crawford v. Washington*

The right to physically confront witnesses was based on assessed need, made on a case-by-case basis.	Confrontation right imposed two burdens on government:
	
	1. To use good-faith efforts to produce the hearsay declarant (no clear indication of the types of hearsay to which burden applied);
	2. The hearsay used in lieu of the declarant testifying had to possess indicia of reliability (presumed when "firmly rooted" exception employed).
		1. Confrontation right applies only to "testimonial" hearsay: statements that appear to be premised on the mind-set of the declarant when the hearsay was uttered.
		2. Judicial assessments of need for confrontation (*Dutton*) and indicia of reliability (*Roberts*) have been abandoned.
		3. "Testimonial" label carries two consequences:
		  • The right to confront the hearsay declarant is absolute. The evidence is excluded if confrontation is not afforded when the hearsay was first uttered (e.g., prior testimony) or when hearsay is subsequently used (declarant testifying).
		  • Good-faith efforts by the prosecution to produce the declarant are irrelevant.

B.   Due Process

Under the second prong of the *Ohio v. Roberts* test, hearsay used in lieu of the declarant's testimony had to possess "indicia of reliability." As previously noted, "indicia of reliability" was probably the due process dimension of hearsay after confrontation rights had been satisfied. Does the *Crawford* decision abandon the due process concern because the right to physical confrontation now has a different focus? May the government now use non-testimonial hearsay against criminal defendants without constitutional restriction? The answer to this question first requires an exploration of how the Due Process Clause has been employed by the Court to control the use of hearsay. While this examination might suggest that Supreme Court supervision under the Due Process Clause will be significantly less than it has been under the Confrontation Clause, consequences of the *Crawford* decision may prompt a different result.

1.   Due Process Before *Crawford*

The Due Process Clause of the Fourteenth Amendment is the wild card played by the Supreme Court when actions of state courts cross the line of fundamental fairness and other provisions of the Bill of Rights do not address the conduct. While the Court possesses the same power over lower federal courts under the Fifth Amendment's Due Process Clause, resort to that source is unnecessary because the Supreme Court has supervisory powers over all federal courts. This is particularly true with regard to their interpretation and application of the Rules of Evidence.

Due process, or fundamental fairness, has prompted the Court to compel states to admit hearsay that was not admissible under any well-established and universally recognized exception.[65] Under this clause, the Court has also excluded hearsay that was otherwise admissible under the state's interpretation of one of its hearsay exceptions.[66] Both decisions were in the context of criminal prosecutions. While the Court theoretically possesses the same power over the use of hearsay in civil proceedings, it has never done so.

a.   Excluding hearsay offered by an accused

Chambers v. Mississippi involved a defendant who had been shot errone-

---

65. Chambers v. Mississippi, 410 U.S. 284, 285, 93 S. Ct. 1038 (1973).
66. Idaho v. Wright, 497 U.S. 805, 110 S. Ct. 3139, 111 L. Ed. 2d 638 (1990).

ously by the police during an altercation, and later was charged with armed assault on the police who shot him. While the police had custody of the individual who actually committed the assault on the officer and confessed to it, they released him because he retracted his confession. Apparently the police pursued Chambers because they feared that acknowledging the responsibility of another person for the assault would have enhanced the prospects of a successful civil rights action against them by Chambers.

At his trial, Chambers attempted to offer testimony from a number of individuals to whom the real culprit, McDonald, had confessed. These were offered as declarations against interest that exonerated Chambers. The trial court excluded the testimony for two reasons. First, McDonald was available. Second, the statements were against McDonald's penal interests, rather than his pecuniary or proprietary interests, and the hearsay exception in Mississippi did not encompass declarations against penal interests. These limitations on the declaration against interest exception were consistent with federal law and the common law of virtually every other state. Nevertheless, the Supreme Court concluded that the exclusion of the testimony was a violation of Chambers's right to due process of law. The Court's conclusion was premised on the inherent reliability of the evidence, and that conclusion was explicitly influenced by the fact that McDonald's utterances were against his penal interests and he was available for cross-examination—the very factors that made the exception inapplicable!

While *Chambers* involved extremely compelling facts, the decision underscores the Court's unpredictable use of its due process review powers. *Chambers* also admonishes state judges not to apply their evidence rules "mechanistically" in criminal cases. Accordingly, the due process limitations on the use of e-evidence in criminal cases can be assessed only in the context of each hearsay declaration's creation and use.

b. Excluding hearsay offered by the government

Idaho v. Wright involved the state's use of hearsay statements that the child victim of sexual abuse made to third parties. The state admitted the statements under the residual exception to the hearsay rule, the state's equivalent of Fed. R. Evid. 807. The Supreme Court concluded that the admission of the evidence at trial violated the due process prong of the right of confrontation because the context in which the statements were made provided no assurances, or indicia, of reliability.

Curiously, the majority did not dispute that other evidence offered at the trial corroborated the reliability of the victim's statements. This evidence included the presence of physical evidence of abuse, the opportunity of the defendant to commit the offense, and the older daughter's corroboration through similar experiences with the defendant. Nevertheless, the Court reversed the conviction, insisting that hearsay statements must possess stand-alone indicia of reliability—i.e., indicia consisting only of factors surrounding the making of the statement. The state court in *Wright* probably produced a fair result, but the conviction was reversed.

Fundamental fairness has traditionally been the standard against which a state's application of its evidence rules were evaluated under the Due Process Clause. If the actions of the state produced a fair result, it was customarily thought to be inappropriate for the U.S. Supreme Court to intervene and impose its preferred interpretation of a particular state rule, even if that rule was identical to the federal rule over which the Court has supervisory power. Historically, states have had the right to follow rules and procedures of their choice, as long as individuals were not deprived of fundamental fairness. The *Wright* decision would not have been unusual if the prosecution had been in federal court and the Supreme Court was interpreting how Rule 807 should be applied. In the context of a state prosecution, however, *Wright* represents a significant expansion of the Court's willingness to intrude into prosecutions previously left to state prerogative.[67]

2. Due Process After *Crawford*

As previously noted, the Supreme Court has not acknowledged that it merged due process and confrontation rights in its *Ohio v. Roberts* two-prong test. Therefore, its supervision of state courts' admission and exclusion of hearsay may remain limited to extreme factual circumstances where convictions have resulted in a clear travesty. This will not be true if the Supreme Court wishes to preserve the results, if not the theory, of its previous confrontation decisions.

In *Lilly v. Virginia*,[68] the Court held that its previous decision in

---

67. This willingness to intrude upon state prerogatives was also demonstrated in Lilly v. Virginia, 527 U.S. 116, 119 S. Ct. 1887, 144 L. Ed. 2d 117 (1999), where the Court extended its interpretation of a federal evidence rule to the states under the Confrontation Clause. Lilly is discussed below.

68. 527 U.S. 116, 119 S. Ct. 1887, 144 L. Ed. 2d 117 (1999).

Williamson v. United States,[69] where it held that Fed. R. Evid. 804(b)(3), declarations against interest, did not encompass collateral portions of inculpatory statements (i.e., portions that inculpated third parties as well as the declarant), was applicable to comparable state hearsay exceptions through the Confrontation Clause. Declarations against interest can be made in any context, not just to police with an expectation that they will be used as evidence in a subsequent prosecution. Many of these declarations will not be "testimonial" under *Crawford*. Consequently, they will not be subject to the new confrontation right. Therefore, the Court can preserve the *Lilly* exclusion of collateral portions of declarations against interest only through the Due Process Clause of the Fourteenth Amendment.

If the Court acknowledges the due process aspects of its previous confrontation decision under *Roberts*, there will be another significant consequence. Decisions about state evidence rules will be applicable to both civil and criminal proceedings. The Confrontation Clause only binds states in their use of hearsay against a criminal accused, because the Fifth Amendment is applicable only in "criminal prosecutions" and affords protections only to the "accused."[70] In contrast, the Fourteenth Amendment prevents a state from depriving "any person" of life, liberty, or property without due process of law.

C.   Constitutional Wild Card

Where the Supreme Court will go with its confrontation and due process theories cannot be predicted. The Court may restrict future oversight of state evidentiary decisions through its restrictive *Crawford* analysis, increase the scope of its constitutional mandates through a new employment of due process theories, or completely change the playing field again with a fourth definition of confrontation.

---

69. 512 U.S. 594, 114 S. Ct. 2431, 129 L. Ed. 2d 476 (1994).

70. Therefore, after the Lilly decision, Virginia may still employ its old interpretation of the declarations against interest exception in civil cases.

A CASE STUDY
FACTS

Internet service provider (ISP) is suing Spammer[71] for illegally using its server to send unsolicited advertisements to Internet service subscribers (Users). ISP was made aware of Spammer's practices through complaints that Users sent to ISP with the unsolicited advertisements attached. ISP regularly stores the complaints it receives in a computer file. In preparation for trial, Employee scans the hundreds of thousands of complaints in this file and separates those relating to Spammer. Based on his examination of attachments, Employee separates these complaints into three distinct types and develops statistics about each. This information is summarized in a report, and the report is offered as evidence at trial to prove the volume, subject, length, and time of the unsolicited advertisements.

ANALYSIS

Multiple-Level Hearsay. The problem creates three potential levels of hearsay that must be addressed.

First-Level Hearsay. The ISP lacks personal knowledge of the unsolicited advertisements received by Users. The ISP knows about the unsolicited advertisements only because Users voiced complaints like "I got the attached obscene advertisement, which I neither requested nor wanted to receive." User complaints, therefore, are hearsay when offered into evidence to prove the truth of what was stated in them.

This first level of hearsay may be admissible under the state of mind exception to the hearsay rule, codified in Fed. R. Evid.

---

71. Spamming is the practice of sending copies of an electronic message to many different newsgroups with no regard to whether the subject is appropriate or sending the same message by e-mail to large numbers of people indiscriminately. Sometimes spams are advertisements. The spammer is the sender of such messages. *See* Computer User.com, *High-Tech Dictionary, at* definition.html?lookup= 4750 (last visited May 25, 2004).

803(3).[72] The Users are expressing their present state of mind about an advertisement received by them. Each is stating that the advertisement is unwanted and similar solicitations should be stopped. Because each complaint appears to have been made under conditions of apparent sincerity, it is likely that this hearsay issue can be overcome.

Second-Level Hearsay. Communications from machines are not considered hearsay. Unless recorded mechanistically, a second-level hearsay problem arises when reports of unsolicited advertisements are recorded in a complaint file. If a proper foundation is laid for the admission of such evidence, the hearsay dangers of perception, memory, sincerity, and ambiguity are adequately addressed.

If the sorting is done manually, the employees who receive the complaints and who transfer them from the e-mail server to a regularly maintained computer file are asserting that these complaints were received by the ISP on the indicated days at the indicated times. The file would constitute hearsay if offered to prove the receipt of those complaints, because the file speaks for every employee who made an entry in it.

The second level of hearsay may be admissible under the business records exception to the hearsay rule, codified in Fed. R. Evid. 803(6).[73] Each employee placed the complaints in the com-

---

72. FED. R. EVID. 803(3) provides:

Rule 803. Hearsay Exception; Availability of Declarant Immaterial
The following are not excluded by the hearsay rule, even though the declarant is available as a witness:

. . . .

(3) Then existing mental, emotional, or physical condition. A statement of the declarant's then existing state of mind, emotion, sensation, or physical condition (such as intent, plan, motive, design, mental feeling, pain, and bodily health), but not including a statement of memory or belief to prove the fact remembered or believed unless it relates to the execution, revocation, identification, or terms of declarant's will.

73. FED. R. EVID. 803(6) provides:
Rule 803. Hearsay Exception; Availability of Declarant Immaterial

The following are not excluded by the hearsay rule, even though the declarant is available as a witness:

plaint file pursuant to a *business duty*. Each placement was based on *personal knowledge* that the complaint had been received with each attachment. Each complaint would be placed in the complaint file immediately upon receipt. Therefore, the business records exception should satisfy the second level of hearsay as long as the record is properly authenticated by the "custodian or other qualified witness." A qualified witness is anyone within ISP who knows how, when, and on what basis each entry is made and how the institution relies on that information. The sponsoring witness does *not* have to possess knowledge of any particular entry, either its substantive content or who made it.

While sponsoring witnesses are usually called to testify in court, thereby giving the opposing party an opportunity to cross-examine them, Fed. R. Evid. 902(11) permits business records to be authenticated by certification. This rule makes such records self-authenticating when accompanied by a certificate from a custodian or other qualified person.[74]

It remains unclear how often this relatively new certification method will be employed. The method creates an adversarial problem—the proponent must "make the record available for inspection sufficiently in advance of its offer into evidence to provide an adverse party with a fair opportunity to challenge it."[75] With limitations on the amount of discovery and shortened pretrial dis-

----

. . . .

(6) Records of regularly conducted activity. A memorandum, report, record, or data compilation, in any form, of acts, events, conditions, opinions, or diagnoses, made at or near the time by, or from information transmitted by, a person with knowledge, if kept in the course of a regularly conducted business activity, and if it was the regular practice of that business activity to make the memorandum, report, record, or data compilation, all as shown by the testimony of the custodian or other qualified witness, unless the source of information or the method or circumstances of preparation indicate lack of trustworthiness. The term "business" as used in this paragraph includes business, institution, association, profession, occupation, and calling of every kind, whether or not conducted for profit.

74. *See* § E, Self-Authentication and the Internet, *supra.*
75. *See id.*

covery periods, many parties will not want to give their adversaries a cost-free opportunity to find problems with their records. Militating in favor of authentication through the testimony of a witness is the fact that most sponsoring witnesses are chosen from employees already scheduled to testify on other matters, minimizing the inconvenience in using a live witness.[76]

The business records exception contains the following qualification: If all of the conditions are satisfied, the business record is admissible "unless the source of the information or the method or circumstances of preparation indicate lack of trustworthiness." E-mail poses problems of untrustworthiness because such messages can be "spoofed."[77] In the header of e-mail messages, the sender can create the appearance that the message came from a different individual and from a different location. Moreover, the volume of complaints does not guarantee authenticity, because thousands of these fraudulent complaints can be sent instantaneously or automatically over a specified period of time. Accordingly, the ISP would be wise to verify by telephone a random selection of the accumulated complaints.

The ISP may be permitted to offer these records of complaints under the business records exception because these files were (1) "kept in the course of a regularly conducted business activity" (pursuant to a business duty), and (2) prepared from information supplied by employees "with knowledge." Specific concerns about trustworthiness, however, would have to be addressed and satisfied..

Instead of offering the content of the files, the ISP offers an employee's summary of the file's contents. When the ISP submits a written summary of these business records, two additional problems are created. First, it creates a third level of hearsay if the summaries are created by an individual as opposed to a computer

---

76. *See* Paul R. Rice, Best Kept Secrets of Evidence Law: 101 Principles, Practices & Pitfalls, No. 56, p. 125 (Anderson 2001).

77. To be "spoofed" is to fall victim to a spoofer program. A spoofer is a program used by a hacker to gain access to a computer system by making himself appear to be an authorized user. *See* ComputerUser.com, *High-Tech Dictionary, at* http://www.computeruser.com/resources/dictionary/definition.html?lookup =4793 (last visited May 25, 2004).

driven by a program. If the summaries were produced mechanically—i.e., without human involvement, other than in the writing of the program that runs the computer—courts will not find a hearsay problem, because the authentication of the program and computer on which it was used adequately addresses hearsay concerns of perception, memory, sincerity, and ambiguity. Assuming the summary was manually created on the computer, the second problem resulting from a summary is one of best evidence. Each problem will be considered in turn.

Third-Level Hearsay. When a piece of paper is offered to prove what the author of the paper knows, the piece of paper is analogous to a second person saying, "The author told me [whatever the paper's content is]." The writing is hearsay because the author is not in court, under oath, or subject to cross-examination. The problems of the author's perception, memory, sincerity, and ambiguity cannot be explored through cross-examination.[78]

This third level of hearsay cannot be satisfied by the business records exception. While the summary is of a business record, the summary itself was not made in the regular course of business. A different exception must be found. One that might be applicable is the past-recollection recorded exception, codified in Fed. R. Evid. 803(5).[79] A second exception that could apply is the present-

---

78. If a computer produces a summary through software that directs it to extract specific information and to conduct particular calculations (usually with financial information), the results are not hearsay. Rule 801(c) defines hearsay as only an out-of-court "statement" offered to prove the truth of the matter asserted. The word "statement" is defined in Rule 801(a) as "(1) an oral or written assertion or (2) nonverbal conduct of a *person*, if it is intended by the *person* as an assertion." Once the computer results are properly authenticated, they are admissible for their truth as nonhearsay.

79. FED. R. EVID. 803(5) provides:

Rule 803. Hearsay Exceptions; Availability of Declarant Immaterial
The following are not excluded by the hearsay rule, even though the declarant is available as a witness:

. . . .

(5) Recorded recollection. A memorandum or record concerning a matter about which a witness once had knowledge but now has insufficient recollection to enable the witness to testify fully and accurately, shown to have been made or adopted by the witness when the matter was fresh in the wit-

sense impression exception, codified in Fed. R. Evid. 803(1).[80] Rule 803(1) is an exception under the Federal Evidence Code that has no common law counterpart.

The past-recollection recorded exception could solve the third level of hearsay only if the person who prepared the summary served as the sponsoring witness and testified that he: (1) had *personal knowledge* of the nature of these complaints and their attached advertisements; (2) made the summary when his *memory was fresh*; and (3) has "*insufficient recollection*" to "testify fully and accurately." Lawyers should avoid this exception because the rule only permits the report to be read into evidence. The report cannot be introduced as a physical exhibit that jurors can take to the deliberation room.

Although the present-sense impression exception is not limited in this way, it could create problems for another reason. Even though the employee's summary (1) "describes" the content of the complaints and (2) was made at the time the employee "perceived" those complaints, thereby making the exception literally applicable, courts could be reluctant to allow parties to circumvent the past-recollection recorded exception so easily.

Unlike Rule 803(5), the present-sense impression exception does not require the declarant to (1) testify, (2) authenticate the writing as having been made from personal knowledge when his memory was fresh, and (3) demonstrate that he has "insufficient recollection to testify fully and accurately." The exception also

---

ness' memory and to reflect that knowledge correctly. If admitted, the memorandum or record may be read into evidence but may not itself be received as an exhibit unless offered by an adverse party.

80. FED. R. EVID. 803(1) provides:
Rule 803. Hearsay Exceptions; Availability of Declarant Immaterial
The following are not excluded by the hearsay rule, even though the declarant is available as a witness:

(1) Present sense impression. A statement describing or explaining an event or condition made while the declarant was perceiving the event or condition, or immediately thereafter.

does not prohibit admitting the written summary into evidence as an exhibit. If circumventing the requirements of Rule 803(5) was permitted through Rule 803(1), everyone would, and the past-recollection recorded exception would become a virtual dead letter. Consequently, courts might (although to date they have not) limit the use of present-sense impression statements to oral statements.

When all else fails, the proponent could resort to the residual exception, codified in Fed. R. Evid. 807,[81] to satisfy the third level of hearsay.

Using the residual exception requires the proponent to establish that the evidence has "equivalent circumstantial guarantees of trustworthiness." Equivalent to what? The rule envisions a level of reliability equivalent to that reflected in the numerous delineated exceptions. This standard is meaningless, however, because the enumerated exceptions vary significantly in reliability. Consequently, courts have adopted a "substantial reliability" standard. Under this standard, the court must be convinced that the evidence has such assurances of reliability that the accuracy of the fact-finding process would be diminished without the evidence.[82]

---

81. FED. R . EVID. 807 provides:

Rule 807. Residual Exceptions

A statement not specifically covered by Rule 803 or 804 but having equivalent circumstantial guarantees of trustworthiness, is not excluded by the hearsay rule, if the court determines that (A) the statement is offered as evidence of a material fact; (B) the statement is more probative on the point for which it is offered than any other evidence which the proponent can procure through reasonable efforts; and (C) the general purposes of these rules and the interests of justice will best be served by admission of the statement into evidence. However, a statement may not be admitted under this exception unless the proponent of it makes known to the adverse party sufficiently in advance of the trial or hearing to provide the adverse party with a fair opportunity to prepare to meet it, the proponent's intention to offer the statement and the particulars of it, including the name and address of the declarant.

82. *See, e.g.*, United States v. Am. Cyanamid Co., 427 F. Supp. 859, 865-67 (S.D. N.Y. 1977) (outlining requirements of residual exception to hearsay rule and discussing exception's scope).

The complaint summaries in our example of the aggrieved ISP would satisfy this "substantial reliability" standard if the person who made them explained how the summaries were made. If the court is convinced that all relevant materials were extracted and assembled in such a way as to assist jurors rather than mislead them, the evidence will be admitted if Rule 807's other conditions are satisfied. These other conditions are threefold and are delineated in subsections (A) through (C) of the rule.

Subsection (A) requires that the statement must be offered as evidence of a "material fact." In effect, this subsection requires little more than that the evidence be logically relevant and worth the time that it will take to hear and consider the evidence.

Subsection (B) directs that the statement must be "more probative on the point for which it is offered than any other evidence which the proponent can procure through reasonable efforts." This subsection appears to create an unavailability requirement, because testimony of the individual who created the statement would usually be more probative of the truth of the matter asserted in the out-of-court statement. Although logical, this is inconsistent with the rule's original codification in Rule 803(24), in which the unavailability of the declarant was immaterial. An identical residual exception initially was codified in Rule 804(b)(5), in which the declarant's unavailability must be demonstrated as a condition precedent to admissibility. Subsequently, the two exceptions were consolidated into Rule 807. If unavailability was the true purpose behind subsection (B), the Advisory Committee likely would not have moved the exception from Rule 804. Because the purpose behind subsection (B) is ambiguous, it has been ignored.[83]

---

83. Because the residual exception appeared in both Rules 803(24) and 804(b)(5), unavailability was not seen as a significant issue. If the hearsay statement under consideration involved a declarant who was not available, and the court was persuaded to admit the statement, it was admitted under Rule 804(b)(5). Conversely, if the statement involved an available declarant, courts would admit it under Rule 803(24). Now that the exception is joined in one rule, the apparent requirement of unavailability may surface.

Subsection (C) serves little purpose. It requires that "the general purpose of these rules and the interests of justice . . . be served by admission of the statement into evidence." This phrase does nothing more than restate the general fairness provision in Fed. R. Evid.102.[84]

Other than requiring trustworthiness, the residual exception requires that proponents give advance notice of the intention to offer the evidence, so that the opponent will have a fair opportunity to challenge it. The rules offer no specific directives on how and when notice should be given, except that it should be given in a manner verifiable at trial if contested. Such notice should give the opposing party (1) the particulars of the statement (or a copy if it is in writing), (2) the name of the declarant, and (3) the declarant's address, if known.

The notice requirement of Rule 807 leads to the final evidentiary problem that the proponent of the summaries must address. Under the best evidence rule, when the content of a writing is being proven, regardless of whether the contents are being offered for their truth, the original of those writings must be offered, unless they are shown to be unavailable or collateral, that is, not material to the litigation. This problem is discussed after Diagram #6, which illustrates the three levels of hearsay and the exceptions to the hearsay rule that should be argued.

---

84. FED. R. EVID. 102 provides:
   Rule 102. Purpose and Construction
   These rules shall be construed to secure fairness in administration, elimination of unjustifiable expense and delay, and promotion of growth and development of the law of evidence to the end that the truth may be ascertained and proceedings justly determined.

Diagram 6

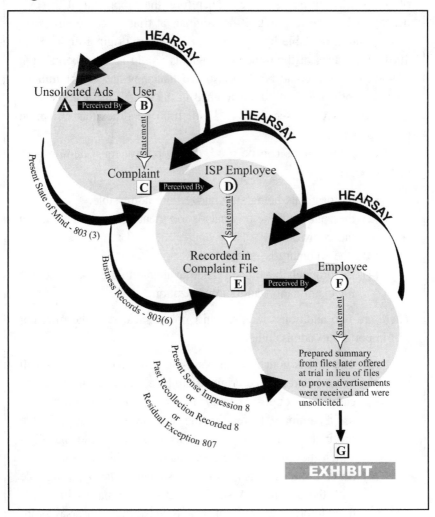

Unsolicited Ads — A — Perceived By — User B

Present State of Mind - 803 (3)

Statement

Complaint — C — Perceived By — ISP Employee D

HEARSAY

Business Records - 803(6)

Statement

Recorded in Complaint File — E — Perceived By — Employee F

HEARSAY

Present Sense Impression 8
or
Past Recollection Recorded 8
or
Residual Exception 807

Statement

Prepared summary from files later offered at trial in lieu of files to prove advertisements were received and were unsolicited.

G

EXHIBIT

Summaries and a Best Evidence Issue. The contents of the thousands of complaints are being proven. Therefore, the proponent of the evidence would have to produce the originals at trial. Because any computer printout readable by sight is considered an original under Rule 1001(3), the tens of thousands of originals would have to be brought to court unless it could be demonstrated that they are so voluminous they "cannot conveniently be examined in the court." In such instances a summary may be used. Fed. R. Evid. 1006[85] codifies this exception to the best evidence rule.

Before summaries can be used, the proponent must demonstrate that:

(1) the originals being summarized are admissible;
(2) the volume of the originals is too great for convenient use in the courtroom;
(3) the summary is reliable; and
(4) the originals have been made available to the opposing side for examination and summarization.

There are two additional requirements not delineated in the rule, but still important to admissibility.

(5) The first is notice to the opposing party that summaries will be used and that the originals are being made available. Logically, if an opposing party does not know that you plan to use a summary, thereby giving him the right to examine the originals, there can be no "reasonable time and place" at which they would have been made available to him.
(6) Second, the summary should be shown to the opposing side with the originals. Assuming that the summary will be offered to prove the truth of what is stated in it, a hearsay problem will be created.

---

85. FED. R. EVID. 1006 provides:
    Rule 1006. Summaries
    The contents of voluminous writings, recordings, or photographs which cannot conveniently be examined in court may be presented in the form of a chart, summary, or calculation. The originals, or duplicates, shall be made available for examination or copying, or both, by other parties at [a] reasonable time and place. The court may order that they be produced in court.

The present-sense impression exception, Rule 803(1), may be applicable, because the writing was made contemporaneously with the witness's examination of the complaint file. Theoretically, a problem could be posed for the successful use of this exception because the hearsay is in a written format, and such writings are specifically addressed in Rule 803(5), past recollection recorded. Because courts have generally rejected the idea that any exception is preclusive—precluding general provisions from applying because more specific provisions may have been ruled applicable—this should pose no problem.

Alternatively, Rule 803(5), past recollection recorded, might be employed. The rules requires that the testifying witness verify the writing's accuracy and has a sufficient loss of memory to be unable to testify fully and accurately about the writing's content.

If necessary, the proponent can resort to the residual exception in Rule 807. This rule permits courts to accept hearsay that does not comply with the elements of any of the delineated exceptions if the hearsay can be shown to possess "equivalent circumstantial guarantees of trustworthiness." The residual exception is applicable only if the proponent makes known to the adverse party, "sufficiently in advance of the trial to provide the adverse party a fair opportunity to prepare to meet it, the proponent's intention to offer the statement and the particulars of it." The proponent increases the likelihood that it will be admitted for its truth under this exception by giving the summary to the opposing side before trial.

Even if the originals are offered into evidence, summaries are still admissible under Fed. R. Evid. 611(a)[86] as pedagogical devices—demonstrative evidence that assists the jury in understanding the content of the originals.

---

86. FED. R. EVID. 611 provides in relevant part:
   Rule 611. Mode and Order of Interrogation and Presentation
   (a) Control by court. The court shall exercise reasonable control over the mode and order of interrogating witnesses and presenting evidence so as to (1) make the interrogation and presentation effective for the ascertainment of the truth, (2) avoid needless consumption of time, and (3) protect witnesses from harassment or undue embarrassment.

Science and Technology 8

I. Judicial Screening Under the Common Law 464

    A. The Advent of the *Frye* "General Acceptance" Test 465

    B. Expanding the Scope of *Frye* 466

II. Judicial Screening Under the Federal Rules of Evidence 467

    A. Out of the *Frye*ing Pan, Into the Fire? 468

    B. The Logic of *Daubert* 468

III. Consequences for E-science and E-technology 472

E-evidence Overview: E-evidence relies upon computer science and Internet technologies, both of which are evolving rapidly. The explosion of Internet technologies presents a challenge to courts seeking to prevent the admission of unreliable evidence. The Supreme Court has exacerbated this judicial challenge by placing responsibility on the judiciary to screen all scientific[1] and technological[2] evidence, and not just evidence that is novel.[3] The screening function sounds more rigorous than the review that was required under the common law, but the Court did not explain the difference. This evolving judicial screening responsibility complicates the task of predicting how the judiciary will deal with the admissibility of e-evidence. It does, however, seem very likely that courts will take judicial notice of the established reliability of computer science and Internet technologies.

I. JUDICIAL SCREENING UNDER THE COMMON LAW

Scientific and technical information became increasingly useful in resolving factual disputes as the twentieth century progressed. This placed an increased burden on judges to determine whether such evidence was reliable enough to be made part of the proceedings. The potentially overwhelming influence that expert opinions could have on lay jurors amplified the importance of the judicial screening function, sometimes called its "gate-keeping" role.

Consistent with their role in determining the admissibility of all evidence, judges initially asked whether scientific evidence made the asserted proposition more or less likely than it would have been without the evidence.[4] Unlike other evidence, however, proponents could not estab-

---

1.   Daubert v. Merrell Dow Pharms., Inc., 509 U.S. 579, 113 S. Ct. 2786, 112 L. Ed. 2d 469 (1993).

2.   Kumho Tire Co. v. Carmichael, 526 U.S. 137, 119 S. Ct. 1167, 143 L. Ed. 2d 238 (1999).

3.   Frye v. United States, 293 F. 1013 (1923).

4.   FED. R. EVID. 401 defines the term "relevant evidence" as follows:

Rule 401. Definition of "Relevant Evidence"

"Relevant evidence" means evidence having any tendency to make the existence of any fact that is of consequence to the determination of the action more probable or less probable than it would be without the evidence.

lish the logical relevance of science and technology by simply identifying underlying premises that intuitively connected a fact to a proposition. Science was often offered to establish propositions for which there was no intuitive link in the common experiences of the judges and jurors.

As a consequence, judges became embroiled in disputes over the *reliability* of novel scientific principles. Even when reliability could be determined by judges themselves (which was rare, because judges are seldom versed in the scientific and technological disciplines), concerns persisted that jurors were incapable of understanding and properly using the evidence. Commentators suggested that the evidence would overwhelm jurors, prompting them to decide arbitrarily between competing experts based on the experts' personalities and appearances rather than on the substance of their testimony.

A.   The Advent of the Frye *"General Acceptance" Test*

Over the late ninete enth and early twentieth centuries, it became clear that judges were ill-equipped to determine the reliability of evidence derived from rapidly advancing areas of science. In order to encourage consistency among the courts, a screening standard was promulgated by the Court of Appeals for the District of Columbia in *Frye v. United States.*[5] Under the *Frye* standard, evidence based on a *novel* scientific principle was not admissible until it had gained "general acceptance" in the relevant scientific field.[6]

This test allowed judges to avoid a determination of reliability. That substantive decision was left to the experts—knowledgeable people in the relevant scientific fields. Judges were only required to define the relevant scientific field. This task, however, often proved pivotal to the ultimate admissibility of evidence. In *Frye,* for example, the novel science at issue was the detection of lying by measuring an individual's systolic

---

5.   293 F. 1013, 1014 (1923). Subsequently, this decision was adopted throughout the United States.

6.   "Just when a scientific principle or discovery crosses the line between the experimental and demonstrable stages is difficult to define. Somewhere in this twilight zone the evidential force of the principle must be recognized, and while courts will go a long way in admitting expert testimony deduced from a well-recognized scientific principle or discovery, the thing from which the deduction is made must be sufficiently established to have gained general acceptance in the particular field in which it belongs." *Id.*

blood pressure, commonly referred to as the lie detector test. The judge defined the relevant scientific field as that of "physiology and psychology." Given this broad definition, it is not surprising that the novel science of lie detection was not considered to have gained general acceptance. If the judge had defined the relevant scientific field as a narrow subset of applied psychology that employed the technology, the probability of finding "general acceptance" would have been far greater.

Under the *Frye* standard, those called as witnesses to represent a "field" were given no instructions regarding the standard of general acceptance because the law did not provide one. Each witness was expected to define the standard and decide whether the principle being assessed had achieved it. If a qualified expert testified that a scientific principle had achieved general acceptance, the evidence passed the minimum reliability standard and was admitted. Disputes about ultimate reliability went to the jury on the question of weight. The judge could still exclude the evidence if the potential prejudice or confusion from admitting the evidence *substantially outweighed* its probative value.[7] Not surprisingly, judges were delighted with *Frye*. They universally followed it because it shifted the responsibility from them to those most qualified to make the assessment.

B.   EXPANDING THE SCOPE OF *FRYE*

After *Frye* was accepted for screening novel scientific principles, courts naturally gravitated to the general acceptance test to screen *novel methodologies*—the methods by which the scientific principles are employed. After novel methodologies, courts confronted *novel applications* of accepted principles and methodologies. This issue often arose in toxic tort litigation, where litigants sought to prove causation. When the general acceptance screen was extended to these novel applications, a growing dissatisfaction with the *Frye* test emerged, because it excluded a dispro-

---

7. This standard has been codified in Fed. R. Evid. 403, which provides:

> **Rule 403. Exclusion of Relevant Evidence on Grounds of Prejudice, Confusion, or Waste of Time**
>
> Although relevant, evidence may be excluded if its probative value is substantially outweighed by the danger of unfair prejudice, confusion of the issues, or misleading the jury, or by considerations of undue delay, waste of time, or needless presentation of cumulative evidence.

portionate amount of evidence involving applications so unusual that no one in the relevant sciences had any familiarity with them. Consequently, injured plaintiffs could not prove their claims because their evidence of causation relied on novel applications, the general acceptance of which could not be established.

To avoid this potential unfairness, courts began experimenting with a "balancing test" that weighed the probative value of the evidence against the potential unfair prejudice from its misuse by jurors. In substance, this was a step backward to the state of the law before the *Frye* general acceptance test.

II. JUDICIAL SCREENING UNDER THE FEDERAL RULES OF EVIDENCE

The Federal Rules of Evidence were enacted in 1973, during the infancy of the "balancing" test modifying *Frye*.[8] Rule 702 provides the only reference to scientific or technological evidence in the Federal Rules of Evidence. It provides, in part, that "[i]f *scientific, technical, or other specialized knowledge* will assist the trier of fact to understand the evidence" and the witness has a requisite level of knowledge, skill or experience, the witness may testify. Neither the Federal Rules of Evidence nor the accompanying Advisory Committee Notes directly address either

---

8. FED. R. EVID. 702 and 703 provide:

Rule 702. Testimony by Experts (before 2000 revisions)
If scientific, technical, or other specialized knowledge will assist the trier of fact to understand the evidence or determine a fact in issue, a witness qualified as an expert by knowledge, skill, experience, training, or education, may testify thereto in the form of an opinion or otherwise.

Rule 703. Basis of Opinion Testimony by Experts (before 2000 revisions)
The facts or data in the particular case upon which an expert bases an opinion or inference may be those perceived by or made known to the expert at or before the hearing. If of a type reasonably relied upon by experts in the particular field in forming opinion or inferences upon the subject, the facts or data need not be admissible in evidence in order for the opinion or inferences to be admitted. If the facts or data are otherwise inadmissible, they shall not be disclosed to the jury by the proponent of the opinion or inferences unless their probative value substantially outweighs their prejudicial effect.

the admissibility of scientific evidence in general or novel scientific principles in particular.[9]

A. Out of the Fryeing Pan, Into the Fire?

Twenty years after adopting the Federal Rules of Evidence, and after an overwhelming majority of federal courts had concluded that *Frye* continued to reign, the Supreme Court addressed the issue of judicial screening of scientific evidence in *Daubert v. Merrell Dow Pharmaceuticals, Inc.*[10] To the surprise of many, the Court announced that the *Frye* general acceptance test had been silently abandoned in the Evidence Code as the *exclusive* test for the admissibility of scientific evidence. Removing the shelter of the scientific community and its general acceptance, the Court tossed judges out of the *Frye*ing pan and back into the heat of the scientific "fire" from which they had retreated.

B. The Logic of Daubert

In *Daubert*, the Court first noted that scientific testimony had to be both relevant and reliable.[11] By "relevant," the Court simply meant that the application of the technical principles at issue had to be shown to produce a result that would assist the jury—that is, make the proposition to which it was directed more or less likely. This was referred to as the "fit" between the issues and the evidence. Part of this assessment requires the presiding judge to determine whether the principles and their application represent "good science" or, as the Court put it, "scientific knowledge."[12]

The Court further stated that "general acceptance" in the relevant science is no longer a prerequisite to admissibility. General acceptance is now only a *factor* in the ultimate determination. Other factors mentioned by the Court included (1) whether the principle has been tested, (2) the results of peer review in professional publications, and (3) the potential rate of error.[13]

---

9. Following the adoption of these rules, virtually all federal trial judges (as well as state trial judges in those jurisdictions where the Federal Rules of Evidence had been adopted) continued their common law screening practices under the Frye general acceptance standard.

10. 509 U.S. 579, 113 S. Ct. 2786, 112 L. Ed. 2d 469 (1993).

11. 509 U.S. at 589.

12. *Id.* at 590.

13. *Id.* at 592-94.

An additional surprise in the *Daubert* opinion was the Court's announcement that the judicial screening role it was outlining was applicable to *all* scientific evidence offered at trial, not just to novel scientific principles.[14] Seven years later, after lower courts had thwarted *Daubert* by construing evidence as technological rather than scientific, thereby giving themselves freedom to look exclusively to the relevant technological community for general acceptance, the Supreme Court stopped this practice. In *Kumho Tire Co. v. Carmichael*,[15] the Court extended the *Daubert* screen to all *technological* evidence as well.[16] Rule 702 was amended in 2000 to codify the *Daubert* and *Kumho Tire* decisions.[17]

By expanding the operation of Rule 702 beyond "novel sciences," the Federal Rules of Evidence appear to have perpetuated the principle, methodology, and application concerns that plagued the *Frye* test. Scientific and technological evidence, like all other forms of evidence, must be authenticated. The proponent needs to authenticate the scientific prin-

---

14. In note 11 of the Daubert decision, the Court stated:

> Although the Frye decision itself focused exclusively on "novel" scientific techniques, we do not read the requirements of Rule 702 to apply specifically or exclusively to unconventional evidence. Of course, well-established propositions are less likely to be challenged than those that are novel, and they are more handily defended. Indeed, theories that are so firmly established as to have attained the status of scientific law, such as the laws of thermodynamics, properly are the subject of judicial notice under Fed. R. Evid. 201.

15. 526 U.S. 137, 119 S. Ct. 1167, 143 L. Ed. 2d 238 (1999).

16. The Daubert and Kumho Tire decisions were interpreting Rule 702, which provides, in part, that "[i]f scientific, technological, or other specialized knowledge will assist the trier of fact," then qualified expert opinions may be admitted. The question left open after Kumho Tire is whether the Court will impose the same screening, or gate-keeping, responsibilities on the presiding judge when opinions involving "other specialized knowledge" are offered. Logic suggests that the Court will.

17. FED. R. EVID. 702 was amended to read:

Rule 702. Testimony by Experts (Revisions have been underlined)
If scientific, technical, or other specialized knowledge will assist the trier of fact to understand the evidence or to determine a fact in issue, a witness qualified as an expert by knowledge, skill, experience, training, or education, may testify thereto in the form of an opinion or otherwise, if (1) the testimony is based upon sufficient facts or data, (2) the testimony is the product of reliable principles and methods, and (3) the witness has applied the principles and methods reliably to the facts of the case.

ciple, the manner in which that principle was employed, and the subject to which it was applied. If, for example, the science and the methodology are undisputed but the value of their product when applied to a particular subject is disputed, a court need only address the application.

When the underlying scientific and technological principles are no longer novel, judges often take judicial notice of their reliability. Such notice, however, is only the first step in determining admissibility. The reliability of methodologies by which the scientific and technological principles were employed must still be shown. After this is established, there is also the question of application. *Daubert* and *Kumho Tire* simply emphasized the range of concerns judges must address when determining admissibility.

The problem outlined above was illustrated in *United States v. Brown*,[18] where neutron activation analysis was used to determine the chemical makeup of hair follicles found at the scene of a crime and to match them to the hair follicles of a particular individual. The science of identifying a substance by its chemical makeup is reliable. Using neutron activation as the means for accomplishing this end is a reliable methodology when the proper technology is employed. However, analyzing the chemical makeup of hair follicles does not help identify the source of the hair. Although neutron activation analysis produces accurate and reliable evidence of the follicles' chemical composition, this is not useful evidence, because the chemical makeup of hair follicles varies with such factors as their location on an individual's head, the food that the individual has eaten, and the emotional swings of that individual during the time the follicle was developing. The common origin of two hair samples cannot be established by comparing their chemical composition.[19] DNA testing, of course, has eliminated the need for such evidence.

Daubert and *Kumho Tire* do not necessarily assign a broader screening role to the judges. These decisions merely interpret Rule 702 as preventing judges from passing the entire screening function off on a scientific or technological community of the judge's choosing. Of course, to the extent that judges were passing on that responsibility, it has broadened their screening role. These decisions may have failed to return the

---

18. 557 F.2d 541 (6th Cir. 1977).
19. *Id.* at 556.

screening function predominantly to judges, however, because of the complex and highly technical nature of that endeavor.[20]

---

20. While some may claim that the Daubert and Kumho Tire decisions returned to trial judges the broad discretion they possessed under the common law in determining the admissibility of scientific and technological evidence, the truth is that there was nothing to return. They have always possessed that discretion. The Supreme Court has simply interpreted Rule 702 as directing judges to stop relying exclusively on experts in fulfilling their gatekeeping function. The factors the scientific experts previously considered in determining reliability are now supposed to be weighed by the judge. As Judge Kozinski observed in his opinion in the Daubert remand, trial judges now have the responsibility to "resolve disputes among respected, well-credentialed scientists ... where there is no scientific consensus." Daubert v. Merrell Dow Pharms., Inc., 43 F.3d 1311, 1316 (9th Cir. 1995).

In theory, this is a major shift. In reality, however, little may have changed. The common law adopted the Frye test because trial judges lacked the expertise to make these assessments. If judges now have no greater scientific and technological expertise than they did under the common law, how is it possible for judges now to make the sophisticated decisions they were incapable of making previously? The very factors delineated by the Court in Daubert require input from the same professional communities that judges looked to for approval of the scientific principles, methodologies or applications under the Frye test. Their necessary input into an intelligent application of the factors delineated by the Court is so great that courts are doing indirectly under Daubert what they did directly under Frye—relying exclusively on the scientific and technological communities.

When contested evidence involves the application of a scientific principle, for example, the Court has directed the trial judge to consider whether the community has *tested* the scientific or technological principles. Here, of course, judges immediately turn to the relevant scientific community that previously was consulted. If such testing has taken place, how does the trial judge determine whether the tests were adequate? Variations in the ways in which the tests were administered can skew the results. How is the judge to know what variations are significant, and what consequences each may have on the results that were achieved? The truth is that few judges have this expertise. After all, many lawyers and judges studied law because they were not successful in the study of the sciences! By necessity, therefore, most judges are compelled to go back to the most relevant scientific community for assistance—likely the very community that the judge previously relied upon under Frye.

In Daubert, the Court acknowledged that *peer review* remains an important source of helpful information. The reliability of scientific evidence that has been developed specifically for the litigation in which it is offered is naturally met with some skepticism. When developed for such a limited purpose, critical documentation is often lacking, and test results are usually not disseminated to the larger community for evaluation. Therefore, the existence of peer review is often critical to an accurate assessment of reliability. Who are the peers that are expected to have reviewed these materi-

III.   CONSEQUENCES FOR E-SCIENCE AND E-TECHNOLOGY

Computer systems are normally authenticated under Fed. R. Evid. 901(b)(9). This provides that "[t]he requirement of authentication or identification as a condition precedent to admissibility is satisfied by evidence sufficient to support a finding that a matter in question is what its proponent claims," including "[e]vidence describing a process or system used to produce a result and showing that the process or system produces an accurate result."

Computer hardware and software are usually authenticated by testimony describing what they are designed to do and how the offering party relies upon their product. At trial, an executive who is present to testify on other substantive matters usually fulfills this function. Witnesses need only familiarize themselves with those reports and records that are regularly maintained and used by the company. They need not have technical knowledge about the computer hardware or the logic of the software that it employs. They also need not have personal knowledge of the substantive information recorded or the identity of the individuals responsible for recording it. The burden is relatively light.

Does the advent of the Internet and e-mail require a change in this practice? While these services add levels of technical complexity to commercial transactions and to the records of those transactions, courts are, nevertheless, unlikely to require proponents to demonstrate the reliability of new computer sciences and technologies. Although little of this techni-

---

als? The answer, of course, is the people of the *same scientific community* identified and relied upon under the Frye test.

Without question, the *rate of error* is also central to a judge's determination of scientific or technological reliability. The Court in Daubert acknowledged this as well. What is an acceptable rate of error? Intuitively, a judge would know that the acceptable rate of error for industrial adhesives is probably greater than for materials used in synthetic body parts, but specific levels are not apparent. How does a judge go about making that determination? Not surprisingly, they consult the very people whose general opinion, according to the Supreme Court, has ceased to be dispositive.

When a judge finally gets around to considering the last factor enumerated by the Court—"general acceptance" in the relevant scientific field—that field, by necessity, will already have influenced all of the other factors that the Court has instructed the judge to consider. Consequently, Daubert may prove to be little more than Frye in drag, and federal decisions on the admissibility of scientific evidence under Frye and Daubert will likely be the same or very similar.

cal complexity is within the control of commercial users, reliability of the service, like the reliability of an individual computer system, is adequately addressed through regular business use and reliance.

Although the Internet depends upon the conduit services of many Internet service providers (ISPs), this service is no different from the worldwide telephone network that also employs analogous conduit services of many local and long-distance operating companies. If evidence derived from telephone services does not require foundational evidence about the sciences involved in telephony, i.e., "that the [telephone] system produces an accurate result" (Rule 901(b)(a)), the same should be true of evidence derived from the Internet.

Indeed, Internet and telephone services are intimately related. The Internet employs the same telephone lines and satellites as the telephone service. In fact, the Internet is capable of providing telephone services as well. Conversely, the telephone companies rely on computers and computer technology. Therefore, if a similar level of use, reliance, and apparent accuracy is demonstrated, courts should draw the same logical inferences about reliability.

We know e-mail technology and the Internet are widely used and relied upon, and we know they are reliable through broad and lengthy experiences. Courts therefore should follow the suggestion of the Supreme Court in footnote 11 of the *Daubert* decision and take judicial notice of the accuracy of the technology involved.[21]

Everyone has had decades of positive experience with telephones and computer-generated messages. Even if judges do not take judicial notice of the reliability of the means by which electronic information is transmitted, a strong logical inference would arise that the means of transmission and its application to written data are sufficiently trustworthy to be heard and considered by the finder of facts. Indeed, the reliability of

---

21. "Although the Frye decision itself focused exclusively on 'novel' scientific techniques, we do not read the requirements of Rule 702 to apply specifically or exclusively to unconventional evidence. Of course, well-established propositions are less likely to be challenged than those that are novel, and they are more handily defended. Indeed, theories that are so firmly established as to have attained the status of scientific law, such as the laws of thermodynamics, properly are subject to judicial notice under Fed. Rule Evid. 201." For a broader examination of the concept of judicial notice, *see* Chapter Nine, "Judicial Notice," *infra*.

such services is so assured, a formal presumption based on that logical inference would be appropriate.[22]

Due to interference of one kind or another, occasional issues may arise concerning the reliability of a particular electronic communication. Such evidence should still be admitted and disputed before the jury on the question of the weight. Of course, if the opponent identifies enough problems in a particular circumstance—if, for instance, the combinations of technologies are unproven—judicial notice may be inappropriate. If, however, the problems identified only relate to outside interference in a particular instance, such matters would best be dealt with on the question of weight.[23]

The technology by which documents are retrieved from "shadows" on a party's hard drive has long been recognized and accepted as a reliable means of data recovery. Will courts treat the programs used to accomplish this like copying machines, and permit the technician who employed them to describe what he did and the results produced by the program and equipment he employed, or must a witness with greater scientific and technological expertise explain the underlying science and technology? While the process can be fully explained and its reliability demonstrated to the court by a computer expert, there is no clear answer as to when this will be required.[24] The proponent of such evidence will

---

22. *See* Chapter Five, "Presumptions," *infra*.

23. If, however, the evidence shows that the identified problems cause the probative value of the evidence to be substantially outweighed by the "danger of unfair prejudice, confusion of the issues, or misleading the jury," then the evidence should be excluded under Rule 403.

24. In Williford v. State, 127 S.W.3d 309 (Tex. Ct. App. 2004), for example, a mirror image of the defendant's hard drive was made by using the software EnCase. The defendant contended that the detective who testified was not qualified to authenticate the scientific technique that was used to reproduce the pornographic pictures taken from the defendant's computer's hard drive. The court disagreed, giving the following explanation: "Detective Owings is the computer expert for the Brownwood Police Department and is knowledgeable about EnCase. He testified that EnCase is generally accepted in the computer forensic investigation community, that EnCase is used worldwide, that he knew how to use EnCase, that he knew how EnCase worked, that he had successfully used EnCase in the past, that EnCase can be tested by anyone because it was commercially available and anyone could purchase it, that EnCase has been tested, that there have been several articles written about EnCase and other computer forensic software programs, that *SC Magazine* gave EnCase an

also have to demonstrate that the technology was properly used by a qualified person on a hard drive that is authenticated as part of a particular party's computer system. This process might fail to retrieve portions of some communications because of successful erasing efforts or extensive use of the computer after things have been deleted. The only evidentiary problems that should arise are those relating to the authentication of the communications and the unfairness in using them because they are incomplete and, therefore, possibly misleading.

After establishing the reliability of the underlying sciences, technologies, methodologies, and applications (by judicial notice, presumptions, logical inferences or evidentiary demonstrations), the normal evidentiary concerns of fraud, manipulation, and error must be addressed. This will be accomplished through compliance with such evidentiary rules as authentication,[25] the original writing rule,[26] hearsay,[27] and spoliation.[28]

---

overall five-star rating out of five stars, that EnCase has a low potential rate of error, that he successfully copied appellant's hard drive by using EnCase, and that EnCase verified that he had successfully copied appellant's hard drive. Detective Owings described in detail for the trial court how EnCase worked. Detective Owings's testimony established EnCase's reliability." *Id.* at 312-13.

25. *See* Chapter Six, "Authentication," *supra.*
26. *See* Chapter Four, "Best Evidence/Original Writing Rule," *supra.*
27. *See* Chapter Seven, "Hearsay," *supra.*
28. *See* Chapter Two, "Spoliation," *infra.*

Judicial Notice 9

I. The Basics 478

II. Judicial Notice Under the Federal Rules of Evidence 479

    A. Things *Not* Addressed in Rule 201 481

    B. Distinguishing Judicial Notice of Adjudicative Facts/Jury Notice of Facts/Judicial Notice of Legislative Facts 481

III. Judicial Notice and E-commerce 483

IV. Evidence From Web Pages: A Practical Assessment 484

E-evidence Overview: It is likely that courts will take judicial notice of the reliability of the sciences and technologies upon which the Internet is built because of the inherent reliability of the Internet and its proven ability to transmit data and images reliably. Consequently, there should be minimal judicial screening for admissibility purposes.

I.   THE BASICS

Like presumptions, judicial notice provides a short-cut to proof. Unlike presumptions, parties need not establish foundational facts at trial to rely on judicial notice. The party requesting judicial notice must convince the judge that the fact to be noticed is sufficiently certain that it would be a waste of time to require proof. After an initial factual hearing,[1] if the court takes judicial notice of a fact, the judge instructs jurors to accept that fact as true with no evidence presented by the parties.[2] After the court has given parties an opportunity to be heard on the propriety of taking judicial notice, the matter is closed.

Judges can take notice of facts that are commonly known everywhere (e.g., the sun rises in the east and New York City is in the state of New York) or in the local community (e.g., the speed limit in the middle of the business district is 15 miles per hour and that Main Street runs in a north/south direction). Judges also can take notice of facts that can be easily verified from unimpeachable sources (e.g., using an almanac to establish

---

1. While FED. R. EVID. 201(e) provides an opportunity to be heard, judicial notice can be taken at any stage of the judicial process without notice being given or an opportunity to be heard before the fact. When this occurs, however, a hearing may be requested after the fact by the adversely affected party.

2. This has been the majority rule in most states, and the position adopted in FED. R. EVID. 201(g). An alternative theory allowed judges to take judicial notice without the facts necessarily being undisputed. What happened when evidence was offered to disprove the noticed fact was unclear. For the most part, this alternative theory treated judicial notice like Thayer/Wigmore presumptions that shifted only the burden of production. *See* Chapter Three, "Presumptions," *infra*. Because this theory resulted in judicial notice and presumptions being indistinguishable, it was roundly rejected. *See generally* Edmund M. Morgan, *Judicial Notice*, 57 HARV. L. REV. 269 (1944); Note, *Judicial Notice: Rule 201 of the Federal Rules of Evidence*, 28 U. FLA. L. REV. 723 (1976).

whether there was a full moon on a particular date or using a map to determine the distance between two locations).

What evidence is later precluded at trial by the taking of judicial notice of a fact depends on the substance of what was noticed. For example, if the court takes judicial notice that a technology was reliable, evidence about the technology's reliability would be precluded. Such judicial notice, however, would not preclude evidence on the unreliable manner in which the technology was employed.

II.   JUDICIAL NOTICE UNDER THE FEDERAL RULES OF EVIDENCE

Judicial notice is addressed in Fed. R. Evid. 201, which provides:

Rule 201. Judicial Notice of Adjudicative Facts

(a) **Scope of rule.** This rule governs only judicial notice of adjudicative facts.

(b) **Kinds of facts.** A judicially noticed fact must be one not subject to reasonable dispute in that it is either (1) generally known within the territorial jurisdiction of the trial court or (2) capable of accurate and ready determination by resort to sources whose accuracy cannot reasonably be questioned.

[United States v. Hilton, 257 F.3d 50, 54-55 (1st Cir. 2001) (To prove the images were transmitted over the Internet, the testimony referred to modems. No evidence was offered on the definition, purpose, and operation of a modem. The court suggested that taking judicial notice of a modem would be inappropriate because it probably was an adjudicative fact, but the error in doing so was harmless because the transcript revealed that the "district court, the attorneys, and the witnesses understood the relationship of a modem to the Internet and telephone lines."); Polley v. Allen, 132 S.W.3d 223, 225-26 (Ky. App. 2004) (under an identical Kentucky rule, the court held it proper to take judicial notice of statistics collected and maintained by federal government on Internet if uniform resource locator (url) of Web site on which they are published is provided so accuracy can be determined); United States *ex rel.* Dingle v. Bioport Corp., 270 F. Supp. 2d 968, 972 (W.D. Mich. 2003) ("Public records and government documents are generally considered 'not to be subject to reasonable dispute.' . . . This includes public records and government documents available from reliable sources on the Internet." Court took judicial notice of six sources of congressional documents and refused to take judicial notice of three private Web sites, finding that these sources were subject to reasonable dispute relative to accuracy or authenticity.); New Trier Mortgage Corp. v. U.S. Dep't of Housing & Urban Dev., 252 F. Supp. 2d 446, 449 (N.D. Ill. 2002) ("HUD established Multifamily Accelerated Processing ('MAP') program. The MAP Guide, a HUD publication, sets forth the procedures and requirements for participation in MAP. A complete copy of the current MAP Guide, which indicates changes since the MAP Guide was first issued on May 17, 2000, is available on the Internet . . . . The Court has taken judicial notice of the MAP Guide under Rule Federal Rules of Evidence 201."); Grimes v. Navigant Consulting, Inc. 185 F. Supp. 2d 906, 913 (N.D. Ill. 2002) (judicial notice of stock prices posted on Web site); Hendrickson v. eBay Inc., 165 F. Supp. 2d 1082, 1084 n.2 (C.D. Cal. 2001) (judicial notice taken of eBay's Web site and the information contained therein).]

(c) **When discretionary.** A court may take judicial notice, whether requested or not.

(d) **When mandatory.** A court shall take judicial notice if requested by a party and supplied with the necessary information.

(e) **Opportunity to be heard.** A party is entitled upon timely request to an opportunity to be heard as to the propriety of taking judicial notice and the tenor of the matter noticed. In the absence of prior notification, the request may be made after judicial notice has been taken.

(f) **Time of taking notice.** Judicial notice may be taken at any stage of the proceeding.

(g) **Instructing jury.** In a civil action or proceeding, the court shall instruct the jury to accept as conclusive any fact judicially noticed. In a criminal case, the court shall instruct the jury that it may, but is not required to, accept as conclusive any fact judicially noticed.

A.   *Things* Not *Addressed in Rule 201*

Rule 201 only addresses judicial notice of *adjudicative facts*—who did what, when, where, why, and how, as to the matter in dispute. Judicial notice of *legislative facts*—facts relevant to judicial interpretations of the law, or *of the law* itself (either foreign or domestic), are not addressed in the evidence code. These concepts are addressed in Fed. R. Civ. P. 44.1[3] and Fed. R. Crim. P. 26.1.[4] Once the law has been established, its interpretation and application are controlled by non-evidentiary facts considered an inappropriate subject for the evidence code.

B.   *Distinguishing Judicial Notice of Adjudicative Facts/Jury Notice of Facts/Judicial Notice of Legislative Facts*

Facts subject to *jury* notice are essentially those that jurors know by virtue of their common sense through universal experiences. Each individual understands commonly used words and simple causal relationships. For example, jurors know from common experience that a car generally has four wheels. They also know that when such a vehicle is traveling 60 miles an hour, it cannot be turned 45 degrees without slowing down. Jurors are aware of the physical differences between males and females. Therefore, litigants do not have to prove the laws of physics that preclude an item traveling at a certain speed from turning on a dime, like cars driven in cartoon films. Litigants also do not need to prove basic realities of biology and physiology.

---

3. FED. R. CIV. P. 44.1 provides:

   Rule 44.1 Determination of Foreign Law
   A party who intends to raise an issue concerning the law of a foreign country shall give notice by pleadings or other reasonable written notice. The court, in determining foreign law, may consider any relevant material or source, including testimony, whether or not submitted by a party or admissible under the Federal Rules of Evidence. The court's determination shall be treated as a ruling on a question of law.

4. FED. R. CRIM. P. 26.1 provides:

   Rule 26.1. Foreign Law Determination
   A party intending to raise an issue of foreign law must provide the court and all parties with reasonable written notice. Issues of foreign law are questions of law, but in deciding such issues a court may consider any relevant material or source—including testimony—without regard to the Federal Rules of Evidence.

Parties have the right to assume that jurors will know these things. This understanding is dubbed *jury notice*.

Jury notice differs from judicial notice in that there are no instructions or other explicit pronouncements to the jury by the presiding judge regarding the knowledge it is assumed they possess. Judges do, however, occasionally comment on the evidence. For example, the court might suggest that a particular conclusion would be reasonable if other facts are found to be true.[5] Judicial comment on the evidence is precluded in many jurisdictions, and, where allowed, it has been sparingly employed.[6] In substance, judicial comment on the evidence is little more than the judge focusing the jurors' common sense.

Legislative facts are the policies, sciences, and purposes underlying legislative enactments or common law rules. Noticing such facts is an essential tool when judges interpret and apply common law or legislative rules. The

---

5. Judicial comment on the evidence could take the form of a suggestion that the evidence establishing Facts A and B is strong, and the jury could reasonably find those facts to be true. If those facts are found to be true, the jury also could reasonably conclude that Fact C is true. This is the equivalent of the instruction that is given on presumptions when they are used in criminal cases against defendants. Because the court cannot direct the jury to find any element of the government's charge (due to the Sixth Amendment right to a trial by jury), any presumption against the criminal defendant is only permissive. Similar to judicial comment on the evidence, the jurors are told that if they find Facts A and B to be true, they *may* find Fact C to be true as well.

6. States originally adopted the English practice of permitting judges to comment on the evidence. Renee Lettow Lerner, *The Transformation of the American Civil Trial: The Silent Judge*, 42 Wm. & Mary L. Rev. 195, 204-13 (October 2000). However, the practice waned, and now 41 states have abolished it completely. Douglas G. Smith, *The Historical and Constitutional Contexts of Jury Reform*, 25 Hofstra L. Rev. 377, 442-43 (Winter 1996). Judges limit comments on the evidence so as not to trespass on the fact-finding province of the jury. *See* United States v. Quercia, 289 U.S. 466, 470 (1933). "[A judge's] privilege of comment in order to give appropriate assistance to the jury is too important to be left without safeguards against abuses. The influence of the trial judge on the jury 'is necessarily and properly of great weight' and 'his lightest word or intimation is received with deference, and may prove controlling.' This court has accordingly emphasized the duty of the trial judge to use great care that an expression of opinion upon the evidence 'should be so given as not to mislead, and especially that it should not be one-sided'; that 'deductions and theories not warranted by the evidence should be studiously avoided." *See also* Billeci v. United States, 184 F.2d 394, 402-03 (D.C. Cir. 1950); United States v. Fuller, 162 F.3d 256, 259 (4th Cir. 1998).

power to notice such facts is within judges' inherent power. Neither evidence nor procedural codes address this aspect of judicial notice.

III.   JUDICIAL NOTICE AND E-COMMERCE

Many levels of science and technology are used when computers access the Internet. The e-mail programs, telephone lines, and satellite links, with the assistance of Internet service providers and the range of equipment they use, are just a few examples. What responsibilities do litigants have to verify the reliability of these sciences and technologies under the Supreme Court's decisions in *Daubert v. Merrell Dow Pharmaceuticals, Inc.*[7] and *Kumho Tire Co., Ltd. v. Carmichael*?[8] As explained in Chapter Eight, the Supreme Court expanded the gate-keeping role of judges to include screening the reliability and admissibility of all scientific and technological evidence. Because evidence generated on the Web involves many layers of science, technology, and the application of both, what type of gate-keeping function will be expected of trial judges? What evidence must litigants prepare? The probable answer is none.

The reliability of the sciences and technologies that permit the transmission of data over telephone lines and through satellite links is well established. Although the science and technology are not understood by most individuals, their reliability can be verified in scientific literature and through the common experience of most people in most communities. The reliability of the science involved and the technology through which that science is used has been so well-established for such an extended period that it cannot reasonably be disputed. Testimony about, or documents reflecting, information conveyed by computer link is as trustworthy and reliable as testimony about information received orally by telephone. Consequently, judges should take judicial notice of the reliability of the service, which would lump science and technology together, without explaining such things as the binary code upon which all computer science and computer technology are built.

If the reliability of the sciences and technologies underlying computer/telephone/Internet service is judicially noticed, what evidence will be eliminated from the trial? Judicial notice of the underlying sciences and tech-

---

7. 509 U.S. 579 (1993).
8. 526 U.S. 137 (1999).

nologies will permit the product of such transmissions to be presented without first establishing their reliability. From the proponent's perspective, however, judicial notice of reliability will not eliminate the normal evidentiary concerns with each piece of evidence—logical relevance, authentication, best evidence, and hearsay.

From the opponent's perspective, noticing the reliability of the science and technology will not preclude evidence challenging the accuracy of a particular transmission due to other factors, such as power outages, incompatible equipment, or other mechanical or human interference (like hackers). Even with telephone communications, evidence can be offered on voice manipulation when relevant.

On the question of the reliability of particular communications, people's favorable experience with Internet communications would give rise to a logical inference that the communication in question is reliable. Eventually, the strength of this experience could justify its formal recognition in a presumption.[9] This presumption would be the equivalent of the presumption that properly mailed letters are received by the addressees.[10]

Regardless of whether presumptions will be involved, litigants must always be conscious of the scope of judicial notice when a hearing is held on the propriety of taking judicial notice. At the hearing required by Rule 201(e), the court will consider both the taking of judicial notice and "the tenor of the matter noticed." Loss on the first issue can be minimized by the limitations on the scope or characterization of the issues that are being eliminated by the judicial notice.

IV. EVIDENCE FROM WEB PAGES: A PRACTICAL ASSESSMENT

In the context of evidence taken from Web pages hosted on the Internet,

---

9. *See* Chapter Five, "Presumptions," *supra.*

10. Currently, the status of all common law presumptions under FED. R. EVID. 301 is unclear. In Rule 301, Congress directed how presumptions are to be employed, but failed to recognize a single presumption. Consequently, Congress has left unaddressed the question of whether all common law presumptions have silently been perpetuated or abolished. If perpetuated, we are left with no answers to two additional questions: (1) Can courts modify the common law presumptions to accommodate contemporary needs? (2) Can judges create new presumptions as new factual circumstances unfold? These questions are addressed in Chapter Five. Without legislative action, the questions cannot be answered with certainty.

judicial notice may have limited value. The science and technology of the Internet and the ability of individuals and organizations to post information on Web pages from their personal computers are widely known and easily verifiable. Consequently, courts should take judicial notice of the feasibility, existence, and accuracy of the technology without requiring evidence to authenticate it. In other words, *Daubert* hearings on these issues should be unnecessary. Courts can also take judicial notice that a Web page exists, the type of information posted there, and that a particular address will give access to it on the Internet,[11] because these matters are easily verifiable from unimpeachable sources.

The fact that a court may take judicial notice of the science and technology underlying the Web and permitting retrieval of evidence from it does not, however, guarantee the admissibility of the evidence retrieved. It is like the use of radar to prove the speed of a vehicle: A court may take judicial notice of the science and technology of such of radar, but the admissibility of the radar's results requires the government to (1) establish the reliability of the equipment in which it was employed, (2) prove the qualifications of the individuals operating the equipment (to ensure that it was operated properly), and (3) identify the results produced from a particular use (for example, authenticating the printout that may have been provided by the equipment).[12] Merely because a science or technology is reliable does not mean that it was *used* reliably.[13]

Judicial notice of the sciences and technologies involved in the Internet only establishes (authenticates) the reliability of those sciences and

---

11. Richards v. Cable News Network, Inc., 15 F. Supp. 2d 683, 691 (E.D. Pa. 1998) (because the opposing party could confirm online address and Web page, court took notice of Internet sites and of what appeared on each site); Gentry v. eBay, Inc., 121 Cal. Rptr. 2d 703, 706 n.1 (Cal. Ct. App. 2002) (lower court took judicial notice of manner in which eBay describes its operations from its Web site.

12. *See* State v. Shelt, 346 N.E.2d 345, 346 (Ohio Ct. App. 1976). *See generally* A. MOENSSENS, J. STARRS, C. HANDERSON, F. INBAU, SCIENTIFIC EVIDENCE IN CIVIL AND CRIMINAL CASES §§ 4:10-11 (Found. Press 4th ed. 1995).

13. An exception to this is where the Web page is an official government site. In these instances, it would be appropriate for courts to take judicial notice of documents designated as having been filed with the office maintaining the Web page. Twentieth Century Fox Film Corp. v. Marvel Enters., Inc., 220 F. Supp. 2d 289, 293 n.4 (S.D. N.Y. 2002). In taking notice of such filings, the court is not assessing the truth of any assertions made in them, only their existence as a public filing.

technologies. It does not address an essential second level of authentication—the reliability of the evidence that was actually posted on and retrieved from a particular Web page.[14] Indeed, Web pages can be, and are being, constantly changed. Therefore, the reliability of the Internet as a means of communication does not speak to the accuracy of (1) anything posted on a Web page or (2) a printout that allegedly reflects the content of a Web page at a particular time in the past. Proponents of such evidence will be required to authenticate it (i.e., prove what it is, who authored it, the basis upon which it was authored, and when) through other means, such as the testimony of individuals who witnessed or did the posting, or through the responses to discovery demands.

If only the content, and not the truth, of a Web page is being proven (perhaps to establish that certain representations were made by the Web page's owner), the person who retrieved the information from the Web

---

14. Fenner v. Suthers, 194 F. Supp. 2d 1146, 1148-49 (D. Colo. 2002) ("I doubt that a Website can be said to provide an 'accurate' reference, at least in normal circumstances where the information can be modified at will by the web master and, perhaps, others." "The third and final obstacle to judicial notice here is that the court has substantial doubt, on this record, that the information constitutes admissible evidence. Although the court has certainly heard of the National Institutes of Health, I am unsure what it is, what it does and what connection, if any, it has to the federal government. Further, defendants and the magistrate judge have wholly omitted to explain whether NIH sponsors, endorses, collects, or simply provides the information on the Websites. Finally, most of the information cited is expert opinion and/or hearsay and it is simply not clear whether there is any foundation for its admission. Because of these evidentiary defects, defendants have wholly failed to establish that the facts are clear and undisputed or that they are entitled to judgment on the claim that they have been deliberately indifferent to plaintiff's serious medical needs."); Hartwell Corp. v. Superior Court, 115 Cal. Rptr. 2d 874, 894, 38 P.3d 1098, 1115 n.12 (2002) ("Plaintiffs request that we take judicial notice of what appear to be Internet articles found on a DHS Website. These articles indicate, as of January 3, 2001, that chromium VI is an unregulated chemical that required monitoring. Plaintiffs seek judicial notice of those articles as proof that their allegations raise no conflict with PUC policy because neither the PUC nor DHS has set water quality standards that govern chromium VI, an 'unregulated chemical.' The regulated utilities and the industrial defendants oppose the motion for judicial notice. We deny plaintiffs' request. As stated by the industrial defendants, the articles contain unauthenticated statements with no indication of author, custodian, date of creation, purpose, reliability, or veracity.").

page could authenticate its content at the time he observed it. The witness would be competent, because testimony would be based on personal experience. There would be no hearsay problem, because the existence of the representation is what is relevant, not the truth of what was said.

If the content of a Web page is offered to prove the truth of what it states, a hearsay problem is created, because the printout is being offered to prove the truth of the out-of-court statement's content. Such evidence is excluded unless the proponent can show that it falls within an exception to the hearsay rule.[15] If the assertion in the Web page purports to be from the owner of the Web page, and the owner is a party in the litigation, those statements would constitute admissions.

If the content of the third-party statement taken from the Web page is

---

15. *See* Chapter Seven, "Hearsay," *supra*; *see also* Stearns v. City of Gig Harbor, 1999 WL 167703, at *4 (Wash. Ct. App. Mar. 26, 1999) (unpublished). Because it is appropriate for a court to take judicial notice of legislative facts—the background information upon which the need for legislation was premised—the court was asked to take judicial notice of comments that had been posted on the Web page of the city council. The court in *Stearns* refused because the proponent was unable to authenticate the comments as being those of the members of the city council as opposed to staff interpretations of the code.

16. The common law had a general prohibition against opinion testimony by lay witnesses. Under the FEDERAL RULES OF EVIDENCE, this general prohibition has been abolished. FED. R. EVID. 701 provides:

> If the witness is not testifying as an expert, the witness' testimony in the form of opinions or inferences is limited to those opinions or inferences which are (a) rationally based on the perception of the witness and (b) helpful to a clear understanding of the witness' testimony or the determination of a fact in issue. [Boone v. State, 811 So. 2d 402, 405 (Miss. Ct. App. 2001) (testimony by deputy that he looked at rape victim's hard drive and did not find a certain item was admissible under Rule 701 because deputy had stated that he was "fairly " computer-literate and had personally examined the hard drive; court rejected claim that he was not a properly qualified expert witness under Rule 702).

As long as the lay witness' testimony is rationally based on that witness' firsthand perceptions, it is now admissible.

Experts have long been permitted to offer opinions to the finders of fact that will assist them in performing their fact-finding role. The common law initially restricted the admissibility of expert testimony to those instances where the jury could not adequately perform its fact-finding role without such assistance.

in the form of an opinion, and a reliable opinion on the subject addressed in the statement requires special expertise, that expertise must be shown to have been possessed by the author.[16] In addition, the proponent must establish that the writer has a reliable basis for the opinion—either personal knowledge or acceptable forms of hearsay.[17]

If an opinion taken from a Web page is being offered as an admission, it will be admitted into evidence even if the basis of the opinion

---

Over time that restriction was relaxed, and this relaxed standard was codified in FED. R. EVID. 702, which provides:

> If scientific, technical, or other specialized knowledge will assist the trier of fact to understand the evidence or to determine a fact in issue, a witness qualified as an expert by knowledge, skill, experience, training, or education, may testify thereto in the form of an opinion or otherwise.

Not only was the standard for admissibility relaxed, but the required level of expertise possessed by the witness was relaxed as well. To qualify as an expert under the common law, the witness must have possessed substantially more knowledge than the average juror. Under FED. R. EVID. 702, the witness need only be "qualified as an expert by knowledge, skill, experience, training, or education . . . ."

17.   Under FED. R. EVID. 602, all witnesses, other than qualified experts, must possess personal knowledge of the matters about which they speak. Rule 602 provides:

> A witness may not testify to a matter unless evidence is introduced sufficient to support a finding that the witness has personal knowledge of the matter. Evidence to prove personal knowledge may, but need not, consist of the witness' own testimony. This rule is subject to the provisions of Rule 703, relating to opinion testimony by expert witnesses.

FED. R. EVID. 703 provides:

> The facts or data in the particular case upon which an expert bases an opinion or inference may be those perceived by or made known to the expert at or before the hearing. If of a type reasonably relied upon by experts in the particular field in forming opinions or inferences upon the subject, the facts or data need not be admissible in evidence.

Rule 703 permits an expert to rely on otherwise inadmissible evidence if it is common practice within the profession to use that type of evidence. The rule presumes that the expert is capable of assessing the reliability of this evidence because they generally make that assessment in their practice.

is not apparent, and the author lacks demonstrable expertise. The admissions rule is premised on the adversarial nature of the judicial process and not on the inherent reliability of the statement, like most recognized exceptions to the hearsay rule.[18] The statement is admissible simply because the party opponent said it. The theory is that everyone speaks at his own risk and has an obligation to explain his own statements when they are later offered against him.

As explained in Chapter Six, the many levels of authentication required for most evidence may pose the most significant evidentiary problem for proponents of evidence taken from the Internet.

---

18. "Admissions by a party-opponent are excluded from the category of hearsay on the theory that their admissibility in evidence is the result of the adversary system rather than satisfaction of the conditions of the hearsay rule." Strahorn, *A Reconsideration of the Hearsay Rule and Admissions,* 85 U. PA. L. REV. 484, 564 (1937); EDMUND M. MORGAN, BASIC PROBLEMS OF EVIDENCE 265 (1962); 4 WIGMORE § 1048. "No guarantee of trustworthiness is required in the case of admission. The freedom which admissions have enjoyed from technical demands of searching for an assurance of trustworthiness in some against-interest circumstances, and from the restrictive influences of the opinion rule and the rule requiring first-hand knowledge, when taken with the apparently prevalent satisfaction with the results, calls for generous treatment of this avenue to admissibility." Advisory Committee's Note, FED. R. EVID. 801(d)(2).

Future's Challenge 10

Fitting the rules of evidence into the Internet age is a bit like pouring old wine into new bottles. Some will fit neatly, while others will require a degree of dexterity and ingenuity, and there will be an occasional miss and mess.

The federal judicial system and most states (following the lead of the Federal Rules of Evidence) have codified evidence rules. These rules, for the most part, reflect the evolved common law. The new evidentiary problems faced in the Internet Age have been directly addressed in few, if any, of these evidence codes. Consequently, trial judges are increasingly called upon to resolve evidentiary concerns in contexts they have not seen before. In doing this, courts fall back on the principles and policies of the common law—the foundation upon which the codified evidence rules were built.

This, of course, is not a new phenomenon. Since the enactment of the Federal Rules of Evidence, judges have had to resolve ambiguities and compensate for inadequacies in the codified language using common law principles, guided by common sense and fairness.[1] After more than 30 years, many ambiguities still exist in the evidence code and will have to be addressed on a case-by-case basis along with the new problems created by the use of e-evidence. Because some of these codified problems have no common law counterpart, they may prove difficult to resolve.[2]

---

1. Take, for examples, FED. R. EVID. 407, Subsequent Remedial Measures, and FED. R. EVID. 803(8)(B), Public Records. Rule 803(8)(B) contains language that was inserted by Congress when the evidence code was enacted and that courts uniformly ignore because it is illogical, unfair, inconsistent with subsection (8)(C), inconsistent with the purpose of the limitation in the rule, and violates principles of due process. *See, e.g.*, United States v. Smith, 521 F.2d 957 (D.C. Cir. 1975).

2. For example, Rule 801 defines hearsay as an out-of-court statement brought into court to prove the truth of the matter asserted. The rule, however, also defines a "statement" as "(1) an oral or written assertion or (2) nonverbal conduct of a person, if it is intended by the person as an assertion." Does the clause "if it is intended by the person as an assertion" modify oral and written utterances in (1), as well as nonverbal conduct in (2)?

The theory behind the modifying clause addressing the intent of the out-of-court speaker (the hearsay declarant) was to eliminate statements that did not involve the danger of insincerity from the definition of hearsay. The theory was that, if an individual unintentionally made a statement, there would be no insincerity in the communication. The Advisory Committee indicated that the other three dangers of hearsay—perception, memory, and ambiguity—were to be considered by the jury on the question of the weight to be given to the statements. Of course, it was

Every existing evidence rule has potential applications to evidence generated in the new computer/Internet format. During the review of this manuscript, one reviewer suggested that the delineation in the text of the hearsay exception for ancient documents and the ancient document method of authentication was unnecessary because some exceptions, like this one, have no application to e-evidence. That claim cannot be made with certainty. For example, the ancient document rules relating to both hearsay and authentication are based on necessity due to the probable unavailability of the author of the statement after 30 years at common law and 20 years under Fed. R. Evid. 803(16), and not on the inherent reliability of the statement. Accordingly, would it be unreasonable for a judge to admit a document taken from a hard drive that was more than 20 years old? Indeed, why would the exception not be applicable to ancient documents that were scanned into the computer two decades ago so that the hard copies could be destroyed? One should never assume that existing rules have no application to the Internet context. The ancient document excep-

---

not clear how this could be done, other than through speculation, because there would be no way for the jury to quantify those concerns when the declarant was not available and subject to cross-examination in their presence.

Ignoring the lack of wisdom in this theory (because the hearsay dangers of perception, memory, and ambiguity are still present in the assertion), the question persists: How can a person intentionally use words to express himself, orally or in writing (under subsection (1)), without creating potential insincerity problems, even though he may not have intended the implied communication being read into his words? Having intended the one communication from which another is inferred, it is unclear how the indirect communication can be any more trustworthy than the direct. This has prompted two states where the assertive/nonassertive distinction has been adopted to reject its application to spoken or written words. Stoddard v. State, 389 Md. 681, 887 A.2d 564 (2005); State v. Dullard, 668 N.W.2d 585 (Iowa 2003) (the implied messages from the use of words can be no more reliable than the direct intended message).

Although few judges have addressed the question, many have opted for the least logical conclusion—that the clause modifies both oral and written statements, as well as conduct. *See, e.g.*, United States v. Zenni, 492 F. Supp. 464 (E.D. Ky. 1980), which subsequently was followed by the D.C. Circuit in *United States v. Long*, 905 F.2d 1572 (D.C. Cir. 1990). For a more fully developed critique or this assertive/nonassertive conduct distinction, *see* Paul R. Rice, *Should Unintended Implications of Speech Be Considered Nonhearsay? The Assertive/ Nonassertive Distinction Under Rule 801(a) of the Federal Rules of Evidence*, 65 TEMPLE L. REV. 529 (1992).

tion to the hearsay rule and means of authentication[3] have as much potential application to computer-generated evidence as the public records hearsay exception[4] and means of authentication[5] have to e-evidence.

The problems of rule interpretation that have arisen in the past will continue to exist until they are addressed by the Federal Judicial Conference.[6] Like those problems, the new problems generated in the Internet Age will simply be added to the responsibilities delegated to trial judges. Judges, therefore, will be required to continue to act as though they are operating under the common law, even though their power to create new rules was theoretically taken from them by Congress through codification.

The shortcomings of the Federal Judicial Conference and its Advisory Committee on the Federal Rules of Evidence offer lawyers an exciting opportunity to be directly involved in the judges' decisions on how to handle the myriad new issues that will arise in this Internet context. This will be done case-by-case, based on the equities confronting courts in specific factual contexts, the logic of the rules, and the ability of lawyers to structure coherent theories and arguments that tie the past to the present. Litigators from the common law tradition should be invigorated.

---

3. FED. R. EVID. 901(b)(8).
4. FED. R. EVID. 804(8).
5. FED. R. EVID. 901(7).
6. 28 U.S. C. §§ 2072-2074.

Index

A

attorney-client privilege 191–295
   business communications 244,
      251–52, 261, 293
      non-privileged 250
   confidentiality. *See also.*
   crime/fraud exception 289–91
   e-mail 243
      business and legal advice,
         intertwined 264–95
      business and legal communi-
         cations, separating 261
      distinction between communi-
         cations and information
         248–52
      document description in
         privilege log 252–58
      Microsoft litigation 254
      purpose of communications
         258
   in-house counsel, elevated
      powers of 244, 273
   manner in which communications
      are circulated 270
   pervasive regulation theory 268
   Vioxx litigation experience 267
   work product immunity 291
authentication 333–400
   admissibility 358
      and weight 400
   basics of 335–39
   biometrics 400
   business solicitations and
      postings 382–86
   chain of custody 360, 395–98

computer animations, models,
   simulations 400
computer programs 367
concerns of 335
conditional relevance questions
   338
data trails 386–95
digital photographs 357–69
   enhancement versus manipu-
      lation 362–67
electronic signatures 400
expanded pretrial discovery 399–
   400
government postings 384–86
identification 339
Internet complications 367–68
judicial notice 485
methods of. *See* methods of
   authentication.
newspapers and periodicals 385
personal knowledge 336
public document under seal 381
public key infrastructure 390
reality check 400
relaxation of requirements 374–
   76
self-authentication and the
   Internet 376–36
self-authentication, limits of 385–
   86
spoliation 368–74
technology 386–91
   authenticating 393
web page postings 369–91

B

backup tapes 50, 107
best evidence rule 297–313
    basics of 298–303
    e-evidence 303–07
    insurmountable hearsay prob-
        lems 311
    summaries 307–13
        admissibility of 308
        complexity of 307–13
        hearsay 308–11
        non-hearsay argument 309
        residual exception solution
            310
        voluminous records 307
    voluminous writings exception
        312
business communications 261

C

computers
    active files 106
    and the Internet 183–90
    animations, models, simulations
        400
    drives 108
    programs 367
confidentiality 198–244
    e-mail 221
        expectation of confidentiality
            224–44
    electronic presentations 236–39
    evolution of the requirement 198–
        221
    expansion of 198–201
        community of interests 199
        joint defense 199
    history of requirement 195–198
    ignoring 201–14
        disclosures under protective
            orders 210–61
        disclosures with reservations
            210–95

        inadvertent disclosures 207–
            210
        stolen documents 201–03
        unauthorized agent exception
            206–07
    maintaining and documenting
        215–21
    measures to preserve 239–43
        recommended security
            measures 240
    metadata 234–44
    outside consultants 200
    stolen documents
        judicially compelled disclo-
            sures 203

C

confrontation, right of 436
    absolute right? 443–46
    Confrontation Clause 437–43
    Crawford v. Washington 439, 442
    Due Process Clause 439
    good faith 437
    Ohio v. Roberts 437
    reliability requirement 438
    remote utility of trial confrontation
        437
    "testimonial" standard 439–46
    United States v. Wittig 444

D

Daubert test 468–75
disclosure 17–20
    accuracy, need for 18
    initial 17–20
discovery 3–77
    accuracy, need for 18
    archiving 34
    as a weapon 36
    backup tapes 50
    Blackberries 67
    burden on discovering parties 28,
        32
    burden on requesting party 36

cost 28, 31–36, 43
  shifting of 34, 43
cost allocation, approaches to
  37–45
  sampling 49
counsel understanding of ESI
  62–77
data not reasonably accessible
  28–29
data storage 5
disaster recovery 29, 34, 50
e-discovery team 64–73
electronic discovery response
  plan 14
electronically stored information
  12–16
  conference of the parties 21–
   23
  early attention, need for 16–
   27
  initial disclosures 17–20
evolution of 3–11
inaccessible data 31
information technology architecture 65
interrogatories 58
legacy format 30
obsolete format 30
Palm Pilots 67
planning conference 23–37
practical side of 62–77
preservation process 67–73
  legal framework of 68
  work product tension 74
privilege 52
production, format of 55–56
response program 63
Rowe test 40
rules of 11–59
  National Conference of
   Commissioners on Uniform
   State Laws 11
sampling 55–56
sanctions 59
Sedona Principles 58

spoliation 59
subpoenas 59–61
testing 55
tiers of discoverable information
  28–49
Treos 67
work product 53
written 55–59
Zubulake test 40

E

e-mail 99
  business and legal advice,
   intertwined 264–95
  business and legal communications, separating 261
  duty to preserve 83, 99, 107, 113
  distinction between communications and information 248–52
  document description in privilege
   log 252–58
  expectation of confidentiality
   224–44
  Microsoft litigation 254
  purpose of communications 258
electronic evidence, future of 491–
  94
electronic evidence, discovery of.
  See discovery.

F

fraud 75, 289–91

H

hearsay 401-461
  analysis of 406
  basics of 403–408
  constitutional dimensions 435–
   61
   accused's right of confronta-
    tion 436–41
   Confrontation Clause of the
    Sixth Amendment 435

Crawford v. Washington 439–46

Ohio v. Roberts test 438–39

"testimonial" standard 439–46

constitutional wild card 449–61

due process 446–49

  after *Crawford* 448

  before *Crawford* 446–48

evolving confrontation 445

exceptions 409–14

  admissions 409–14

  levels of 410

  written statements 412–17

excluding hearsay offered by an accused 446

excluding hearsay offered by the government 447

government records and reports 433–36

Internet, evidence from 417–29

  as hearsay 421

  exceptions 422–30

  nonhearsay 417–21

Internet records 430–32

mechanically produced statements 415–17

perceived reliability of 409

reality check 430–35

relevancy 414–15

two truths of 404

web pages 433

J

judicial notice

  adjudicative facts 479–89

  basics 478–79

  e-commerce 483–84

  Federal Rules of Evidence 479–83

  Internet 485

  jury notice of facts 481–89

  legislative facts 481–89

  presumptions 484

science and technology 485

web pages 484

judicial notice 477-89

M

metadata 6, 114, 234–44

methods of authentication 339–57

  content 352–53

  extrinsic circumstances 354–60

  presumption 350–54

  self-identification 348–52

    by recipient 350–81

    by sender 348

N

National Conference of Commissioners on Uniform State Laws 11

O

Ohio v. Roberts test 438–39

original writing rule. *See* Best Evidence Rule.

P

preservation process

  custodians, instructions for 77

  guidelines for 77

  metadata 6

  preferred vendor networks 77

  retention plans 76–77

  tools, acquiring or licensing 77

presumptions 315–31

  authentication 326

    difficulty of 316

  basics of 317–23

  civil actions 328

  common law 317

  common law theory 320

  common law, types of 323–25

    authority to transact business 325

authority to use an instrumentality 325
receipt of mailed letters 323
responsibility for damage or
loss 326
judicial notice 484
jury instructions about 319
methods of authentication 350–
54
problems under Federal Rules of
Evidence 326
purpose of
"bursting-bubble" theory 321–
23, 327–29
shifting burden of going
forward with evidence 317–
19, 328
shifting burden of persuasion
317–19, 322, 331
reply doctrine 330

spoliation 475
Sedona Principles 58
spoliation 79–190
active computer files 106
attorney-client privilege 182–83
authentication 368–74
back-up tapes 107
bad faith 133–53
basics of 86–133
choice of law 180
computers and the Internet 183–
90
consequences of 153–79
defined 80
destruction, authority for penalizing 176–86
doctrine of spoliation, requirements of 86

R

Rowe test 40

S

science and technology 463–75
admissibility factors 464
authentication 475
data recovery 474
Daubert test 468–75
e-science 472–75
e-technology 472–75
evidentiary demonstrations 475
fraud 475
Frye test 465–68
hearsay 475
Internet service providers 473
judicial notice 475–85
judicial screening 467–71
Kumho Tire Co. v. Carmichael
469
original writing rule 475
presumptions 475
reliability standard 466

duty to preserve 89–101
  administrative proceedings 94
  backup tapes 107
  computer drives 108
  destructive acts of third parties 101
  document destruction 109
  document retention policies 96, 114
  duration of 118–90
  e-mail 113
  employee actions 99
  encouraging others to preserve 189–90
  evidence, types of 111
  legal counsel duties 101–06
  metadata 114
  notified parties, obligations of 97
  prejudice to discovering party 120–21
  privileged materials 116–17
  relevant evidence, defined 106
  retrieval expenses 110
  scrubbing 115
  storage expenses 110
e-mail 83, 99, 107
equipment destruction 186–87
hard drives 107
  saving of 188
hearsay, spoliation as 181–82
implied admission by conduct 168–71
jump drives 188–89
logical inference 172
overview 80–86
personal digital assistants 188–89
persuasion, burden of 179–80

preservation orders 84
  standards for 84
proving the claim 180
record deletion 186–87
relevant evidence, determining 93
sanctions for 82
standard of appellate review 183
strange spoliation presumption 172–76

T

"testimonial" standard 439–46

V

viruses 189

W

work product 53
  immunity 291
  tension 74

Z

Zubulake test 40